MCSE

Exam 70-227

Microsoft® Internet Security and Acceleration Server 2000

Training Kit

Microsoft®

PUBLISHED BY
Microsoft Press
A Division of Microsoft Corporation
One Microsoft Way
Redmond, Washington 98052-6399

Copyright © 2001 by Microsoft Corporation

All rights reserved. No part of the contents of this book may be reproduced or transmitted in any form or by any means without the written permission of the publisher.

Library of Congress Cataloging-in-Publication Data
MCSE Training Kit : Microsoft Internet Security and Acceleration Server 2000 / Microsoft Corporation.
     p. cm.
  Includes index.
  ISBN 0-7356-1347-8
    1. Internet--Security measures.   2. Computer security.

TK5105.875.I57 M384   2001
005.8--dc21   2001022225

Printed and bound in the United States of America.

1 2 3 4 5 6 7 8 9   QWT   6 5 4 3 2 1

Distributed in Canada by Penguin Books Canada Limited.

A CIP catalogue record for this book is available from the British Library.

Microsoft Press books are available through booksellers and distributors worldwide. For further information about international editions, contact your local Microsoft Corporation office or contact Microsoft Press International directly at fax (425) 936-7329. Visit our Web site at mspress.microsoft.com. Send comments to *tkinput@microsoft.com*.

Active Directory, BackOffice, Microsoft, Microsoft Press, Windows, and Windows NT are either registered trademarks or trademarks of Microsoft Corporation in the United States and/or other countries. Other product and company names mentioned herein may be the trademarks of their respective owners.

The example companies, organizations, products, domain names, e-mail addresses, logos, people, places, and events depicted herein are fictitious. No association with any real company, organization, product, domain name, email address, logo, person, place, or event is intended or should be inferred.

Acquisitions Editor: Thomas Pohlmann
Project Editor: Lynn Finnel
Desktop Publisher: Design Laboratory, Inc.
Technical Editor: Ethan Wilansky

Author: J. C. Mackin
Appendix B Author: Jeff L. Fellinge

Body Part No. X08-03799

Contents

About This Book	**xxiii**
Intended Audience	xxiv
Prerequisites	xxiv
Reference Materials	xxiv
About the CD-ROM	xxv
Features of This Book	xxv
Notes	xxvi
Conventions	xxvi
Notational Conventions	xxvi
Keyboard Conventions	xxvii
Chapter and Appendix Overview	xxviii
Finding the Best Starting Point for You	xxx
Where to Find Specific Skills in This Book	xxx
Installing ISA Server	xxx
Configuring and Troubleshooting ISA Server Services	xxxi
Configuring, Managing, and Troubleshooting Policies and Rules	xxxii
Deploying, Configuring, and Troubleshooting the Client Computer	xxxiii
Monitoring, Managing, and Analyzing ISA Server Use	xxxiii
Getting Started	xxxiv
Hardware Requirements	xxxiv
Software Requirements	xxxv
Setup Instructions	xxxv
The Microsoft Certified Professional Program	xxxvii

Microsoft Certification Benefits xxxviii
    Microsoft Certification Benefits for Individuals xxxviii
    Microsoft Certification Benefits for
    Employers and Organizations xxxix
Requirements for Becoming a
Microsoft Certified Professional xl
Technical Training for Computer Professionals xli
    Self-Paced Training xli
    Online Training xli
    Microsoft Certified Technical Education Centers xlii
Technical Support xlii

Chapter 1 Introduction to Microsoft Internet Security and Acceleration Server 2000 1

About This Chapter 1
Before You Begin 2
Lesson 1 Overview of ISA Server 3
    Editions Comparison 3
        ISA Server Enterprise Edition 3
        ISA Server Standard Edition 4
        Key Differences 4
    ISA Server Roles 4
        Internet Firewall 5
        Secure Server Publishing 5
        Forward Web Caching Server 5
        Reverse Web Caching Server 5
        Integrated Firewall and Web Cache Server 5
    Windows 2000 Integration 6
    Scalability 9
    Extensibility 9
    ISA Server Architecture 10
    Practice: ISA Server Overview Presentation 15
    Lesson Summary 16

Lesson 2 Introduction to the ISA Server Firewall 17
   Filtering Methods 17
      IP Packet Filtering 17
      Circuit-Level (Protocol) Filtering 18
      Application Filtering 19
   Bandwidth Rules 22
   Integrated Virtual Private Networking 22
   Integrated Intrusion Detection 24
      Packet Filter Intrusions 24
   Secure Publishing 25
   Lesson Summary 27
Lesson 3 Overview of ISA Server Caching 28
   High-Performance Web Cache 28
   Forward Web Caching Server 28
   Reverse Web Caching Server 30
   Scheduled Content Download 31
   Active Caching 31
   CARP and Cache Server Scalability 32
   Hierarchical Caching 33
   Web Proxy Routing 34
   Lesson Summary 35
Lesson 4 ISA Server's Management Features 37
   Intuitive User Interface 37
   Integrated Administration 38
   Policy-Based Access Control 38
   Tiered Policy 40
      Array Policy 40
      Enterprise Policy 41
   Lesson Summary 41
Review 43

Chapter 2 Installing Microsoft Internet Security and Acceleration Server 2000   45

About This Chapter 45
Before You Begin 46
Lesson 1 Planning for an ISA Server Installation 47
    Capacity Planning 47
        Minimal Requirements 48
        Remote Administration Requirements 48
        Firewall Requirements 48
        Forward Caching Requirements 49
        Publishing and Reverse Caching Requirements 50
    Array Considerations 50
        Array Requirements 51
        Standalone Servers and Single-Server Arrays 51
    ISA Server Mode 52
    Internet Connectivity Considerations 53
        Publishing and Connectivity 54
    ISA Server in the Network 54
        Windows NT 4.0 Domain 54
        ISA Server Configuration Data 54
        Internet Connection Server 55
        Remote Access Server 55
    ISA Server Network Topology Scenarios 55
    Small Office Scenario 55
    Enterprise Scenario 56
        Enterprise Network Configuration 56
    Web Publishing Topologies 58
        Co-Located Web Server 58
        Web Server on Local Network 58
    Exchange Server Publishing Topologies 59
        Co-Located Exchange Server 59
        Exchange Server on Local Network 60
    Perimeter Network (DMZ) Scenarios 60
        Back-to-Back Perimeter Network Configuration 61
        Three-Homed Perimeter Network (DMZ) Configuration 62

Lesson Summary	63
Lesson 2 Performing an ISA Server Installation	64
Before You Install ISA Server	64
Setting Up the Network Adapter	64
TCP/IP Settings	65
Setting Up a Modem or ISDN Adapter	65
Windows 2000 Routing Table	66
Installing ISA Server	66
Initializing the Enterprise	67
Installation Procedure	68
Constructing the Local Address Table	70
Windows 2000 Routing Table	71
Default Settings	71
Troubleshooting ISA Server Installation	72
Practice: Installing ISA Server Enterprise Edition	73
Exercise 1: Initializing the Enterprise	73
Exercise 2: Installing ISA Server Software	74
Lesson Summary	77
Lesson 3 Migrating from Proxy Server 2.0	78
Migrating from Microsoft Proxy Server 2.0	78
Operating System Considerations	78
Proxy Server on Windows 2000	78
Proxy Server on Windows NT 4.0	79
Proxy Server 2.0 Array Considerations	80
Migrating to an Array	81
Migrating Proxy Server 2.0 Configuration	82
Proxy Chains	82
Web Proxy Client Requests	82
Publishing	82
Cache	82
SOCKS	82
Rules and Policies	83
Lesson Summary	83
Review	84

Chapter 3   Configuring Secure Internet Access   85
About This Chapter 85
Before You Begin 86
Lesson 1 Configuring Local Clients for Secure Internet Access 87
   About ISA Server Clients 87
   Assessing Client Requirements 88
   Configuring SecureNAT Clients 90
      Configuring SecureNAT Clients on a Simple Network 91
      Configuring SecureNAT Clients on a Complex Network 91
      Additional SecureNAT Configuration for Dial-up Networks 91
   Resolving Names for SecureNAT Clients 92
      Internet Access Only 92
      Internal Network and Internet Access 92
   Firewall Clients 92
   Firewall Client Application Settings 94
      Advanced Client Configuration 94
      Sample Wspcfg.ini File 95
   Web Proxy Service 97
      Configuring Web Proxy Clients 98
      Direct Access 99
   Practice 1: Establishing Secure Internet Access for
   Web Proxy Clients 99
      Exercise 1: Creating a Protocol Rule 100
      Exercise 2: Configuring Internet Explorer to
      Use the Web Proxy Service 101
   Practice 2: Installing Firewall Client 101
      Exercise: Installing Firewall Client over the
      Local Network 102
   Lesson Summary 102
Lesson 2 Configuring ISA Server Dial-up Connections 103
   Configuring Dial-up Entries 103
   Dial-on-Demand 105
   Configuring Dial-on-Demand 106
      Limiting ISA Server Dial-out to External Sites 107

Closing Dial-up Connections 108
Practice: Configuring a Dial-up Entry 108
    Exercise 1: Testing Internet Connectivity 108
    Exercise 2: Creating a New Dial-up Entry 109
    Exercise 3: Configuring ISA Server to
    Route through the Dial-up Entry 110
    Exercise 4: Restarting the Firewall Service 110
    Exercise 5: Viewing SecureNAT Session Information 111
Lesson Summary 111
Lesson 3 Configuring Automatic Discovery of ISA Server 112
    Automatic Discovery 112
        Configuring WPAD and WSPAD
        on the DNS or DHCP Server 113
        Automatic Discovery for Firewall Clients 115
        Verifying Automatic Discovery for Firewall Clients 115
        Automatic Discovery for Web Proxy Clients 116
        Troubleshooting Automatic Discovery 116
    Practice: Configuring Automatic Discovery 117
        Exercise 1: Publishing Automatic Discovery 117
        Exercise 2: Creating a WPAD Alias (CNAME)
        Record in DNS 118
        Exercise 3: Enabling Automatic Discovery on a
        Firewall Client 118
        Exercise 4: Testing Automatic Discovery 118
    Lesson Summary 119
Lesson 4 Troubleshooting ISA Server Client Connectivity 120
    Troubleshooting Client Connections 120
    Troubleshooting Dial-up Entries 122
    Restarting Services after Configuration Changes 123
    Lesson Summary 126
Review 127

Chapter 4 Configuring Internet Security Using Access Policies   129

About This Chapter 129
Before You Begin 130
Lesson 1 Creating an Access Policy with ISA Server 131
   Controlling Outgoing Requests 131
      Configuring Access Policy 133
   Rules and Authentication 134
      SecureNAT Clients and Authentication 134
      Firewall Clients and Authentication 135
      Web Proxy Clients and Authentication 135
   ISA Server System Security (System Hardening) 136
   Getting Started Wizard 137
   Lesson Summary 139
Lesson 2 Creating Customized Policy Elements 140
   Policy Elements 140
      Array-Level and Enterprise-Level Policy Elements 140
   Configuring Schedules 141
   Configuring Destination Sets 142
   Client Address Sets 144
   Client Users and Groups 145
   Configuring Protocol Definitions 145
      Direction 146
   Configuring Content Groups 147
   Practice: Creating Policy Elements 149
      Exercise 1: Creating a Schedule 149
      Exercise 2: Creating a Destination Set 150
   Lesson Summary 151
Lesson 3 Configuring Protocol Rules 152
   Protocol Rules 152
   Protocol Rule Configuration Scenario 153
   Protocol Availability 154
      Application Filters and Protocol Availability 155
   Processing Order 156
   Array-Level and Enterprise-Level Protocol Rules 156
   Web Protocols 156
   Protocol Definitions that are Installed with ISA Server 157

Practice: Assigning Protocol Rules to User Accounts 160
    Exercise 1: Monitoring Sessions in ISA Management 161
    Exercise 2: Requiring Authentication for Web Sessions 161
    Exercise 3: Assigning a Protocol Rule to a
    Windows 2000 User 162
Lesson Summary 164

Lesson 4 Configuring Site and Content Rules 165
Site and Content Rules 165
    Processing Order 165
    Allow and Deny Actions 166
Destination Sets and Path Processing 166
Array-Level and Enterprise-Level Site and Content Rules 167
    Sample Site and Content Rule 168
Content Groups 168
Practice: Creating New Site and Content Rules 174
    Exercise 1: Denying User1 Access to Audio and Video Content . . 175
    Exercise 2: Testing the Configuration 176
Lesson Summary 177

Lesson 5 Configuring IP Packet Filters 178
When to Use IP Packet Filters 178
Creating IP Packet Filters 179
Configuring Packet Filter Options 183
IP Fragment Filtering 183
IP Options Filtering 184
Logging Packets 184
Practice: Running Internet Services on the
ISA Server Computer 185
    Exercise 1: Creating an IP Packet Filter for
    Incoming (POP3) Mail 185
    Exercise 2: Creating an IP Packet Filter for
    Outgoing (SMTP) Mail 187
    Exercise 3: Creating an IP Packet Filter for NNTP 188
    Exercise 4: Creating an IP Packet Filter to
    Allow Outgoing Web Requests (DNS Queries) 189
    Exercise 5: Creating an IP Packet Filter for
    Web Content (HTTP) 190
Lesson Summary 191

Lesson 6 Configuring ISA Server to Detect
External Attacks and Intrusions 192
    Intrusion Types and Alerts 192
    Port Scan Attack 193
        All Ports Scan Attack 193
        Enumerated Port Scan Attack 193
    IP Half Scan Attack 194
    Land Attack 194
    Ping of Death Attack 194
    UDP Bomb Attack 195
    Windows Out-of-Band Attack (WinNuke) 195
    Configuring Intrusion Detection 195
    Practice: Configuring Intrusion Detection on ISA Server 197
        Exercise: Enabling Intrusion Detection 197
    Lesson Summary 198
Review 199

Chapter 5 Configuring Internet Acceleration through the ISA Server Cache   **201**

About This Chapter 201
Before You Begin 201
Lesson 1 Creating a Basic Cache Policy with Routing Rules 202
    How Caching Works 202
    Processing Caching Rules 202
        Cache Configuration Properties 203
        Routing Rules 203
        When to Cache Content 203
        When to Retrieve Objects from the Cache 204
        Applying Routing Rules to Particular Destinations 204
        Rule Order 208
        Default Routing Rule 208
    Processing Flow for Caching 208
    Cache Filtering 210

Additional Cache Policy 211
Practice: Caching Dynamic Content 211
    Exercise: Creating a Routing Rule Caching Both
    Non-Dynamic and Dynamic Content 211
Lesson Summary 213
Lesson 2 Configuring Cache Properties in ISA Server 214
    Configuring Cache Drives 214
        Cache Requirements and Recommendations 214
        Configuring Size and Location 215
    Cache Content Files 216
    Configuring How ISA Server Caches Objects 217
        Configuring Which Content to Cache 217
        RAM Caching 218
        Response Headers 218
        Request Headers 218
    Configuring Expiration Policy 218
        HTTP Object Caching 219
        FTP Object Caching 220
        Returning Expired Objects 221
    Configuring Active Caching 223
    Configuring Negative Caching 224
    Practice 1: Enabling Active Caching 224
        Exercise: Enabling Active Caching 224
    Practice 2: Adjusting the Amount of
    RAM Used for Caching 225
        Exercise: Adjusting the Percentage of
        Available Memory Used for Caching 225
    Lesson Summary 225
Lesson 3 Scheduling Cache Content Downloads 226
    Scheduled Cache Content Downloads 226
        Updating Cache Content Automatically 226
        Configuring Properties for Existing Download Jobs 227
        Downloading Dynamic Content 229
        Configuring the Schedule for Content Download Jobs 229

Practice: Creating a Scheduled Content Download Job 230
    Exercise: Scheduling a Content Download for
    Microsoft Online Seminars 230
Lesson Summary 231
Review 232

Chapter 6 Secure Server Publishing   233

About This Chapter 233
Before You Begin 233
Lesson 1 Publishing Servers Securely 234
    Publishing Policy Rules 234
    Server Publishing Rules 235
    How Server Publishing Works 235
    Server Publishing Rule Actions 237
        Sample Rule Action 237
    Client Address Sets 238
    Server Publishing Rules and IP Packet Filters 239
        Publishing Servers on a Perimeter Network 239
        Server on the Same Computer as ISA Server 240
    Practice: Publishing an Internal Server 240
        Exercise 1: Creating a Publishing Rule on Server1 241
        Exercise 2: Verifying the FTP Server Connection 242
    Lesson Summary 243
Lesson 2 Publishing Web Servers Securely 244
    Web Publishing Rules 244
    Destination Sets and Client Sets 244
    Web Publishing Rule Actions 246
    SSL and HTTP Bridging 247
    Rule Order 248
        Default Web Publishing Rule 248
    Sample Web Publishing Rule 248
    Publishing a Web Server on the Local Network 249
    Publishing a Web Server Hosted on the ISA Server Computer 250
    Using Packet Filters to Publish a Web Server on the
    ISA Server Computer 250

Practice: Publishing a Web Server on the ISA Server Computer 251
    Exercise 1: Configuring Incoming Web Request Properties 251
    Exercise 2: Creating a Destination Set for the Web Server 252
    Exercise 3: Preparing the Web Site 253
    Exercise 4: Creating a Web Publishing Rule 253
    Exercise 5: Testing the Configuration 254
Lesson Summary 255
Lesson 3 Publishing Mail Servers 256
  Mail Server Security Wizard 256
    Mail Wizard Settings 257
    Content Filtering 257
    Configuring Exchange Server on the Local Network 258
    Exchange Server on the ISA Server Computer 258
  Practice: Publishing the SMTP Service 259
    Exercise 1: Configuring the SMTP Service 259
    Exercise 2: Creating a Mail Wizard Rule 260
    Exercise 3: Configuring Outlook Express 261
    Exercise 4: Testing the Configuration 262
  Lesson Summary 263
Review 264

Chapter 7 Securing Enterprise Networks with ISA Server   265

About This Chapter 265
Before You Begin 265
Lesson 1 Applying Enterprise Policies 266
  Enterprise Policies and Arrays 266
    How Enterprise Policies are Applied 266
    Creating an Enterprise Policy 267
  Configuring the Policy Settings for an Enterprise 268
  Backing Up and Restoring an Enterprise Configuration 271
  Practice: Creating and Applying an Enterprise Policy 272
    Exercise 1: Creating an Enterprise Policy 272
    Exercise 2: Creating a New Array that
    Inherits the Default Enterprise Policy 274
    Exercise 3: Testing the Configuration 275
  Lesson Summary 277

Lesson 2 Configuring ISA Server Arrays 279
   Creating ISA Server Arrays 279
      Array Requirements 280
      Arrays and Standalone Servers 280
   Promoting Standalone Servers 281
   Array Member Settings 283
   Storing an Array Configuration 283
   Controlling Array Membership 284
   Backing Up and Restoring an Array Configuration 285
      Backing Up the Configuration 285
      Backing Up a Standalone Server Configuration 286
   Restoring the Configuration 286
   Using Arrays to Provide Fault Tolerance 287
   Fault Tolerance for Firewall Clients 288
   Fault Tolerance for SecureNAT Clients 288
   Cache Array Routing Protocol 290
      How CARP Works 290
   Configuring CARP 291
      Configuring the Load Factor 292
      CARP and Scheduled Content Download 292
   Lesson Summary 293
Lesson 3 Securing Virtual Private Networks with ISA Server 294
   Integrating Virtual Private Networks with ISA Server 294
   Configuring the Network for VPN Connectivity 295
   Using the ISA Server VPN Configuration Wizards 296
      Local ISA Server VPN Configuration Wizard 296
      Remote ISA Server VPN Configuration Wizard 297
      ISA Virtual Private Network Configuration Wizard 298
   Reconfiguring the VPN 298
   ISA Server and IPSec 299
   Large Network Scenario with VPN and Routing 300
      Large Network VPN Description 300

Contents   xvii

    Meeting Network Requirements 301
        ISA Server Array at the United States Headquarters 301
        ISA Server Array at the Canada Branch Office 301
        ISA Server Array at the United Kingdom Branch Office 301
        Enterprise Policy at Headquarters 302
        ISA Server Policy at the Canada Branch Office 303
        ISA Server Policy at the United Kingdom Branch Office 304
    Lesson Summary 304
  Review 305

Chapter 8   Secure Videoconferencing with H.323 Gatekeeper   307
  About This Chapter 307
  Before You Begin 308
  Lesson 1   Configuring Clients to Use H.323 Gatekeeper 309
    H.323 Protocol 309
    Overview of H.323 Gatekeeper 310
        H.323 Gatekeeper Snap-in 310
    H.323 Gatekeeper Usage Scenarios 310
        Intra-Enterprise Conference Call Scenario 310
        Inter-Enterprise Conference Call Scenario 311
        PSTN Call Scenario 312
    Registering Clients with H.323 Gatekeeper 313
    Endpoint Attributes 314
    Aliases 314
    Client Address Translation 315
        From within Your Company 316
        At the Destination 316
    Installing H.323 Gatekeeper 317
    Practice: Configuring a Client to use H.323 Gatekeeper 318
        Exercise 1: Adding a Gatekeeper 318
        Exercise 2: Configuring NetMeeting to
        Use H.323 Gatekeeper 318
        Exercise 3: Testing the Configuration 320
    Lesson Summary 320

Lesson 2 Routing Conference Calls with H.323 Gatekeeper 322
    Call Routing Rules 322
        Phone Number Rules 323
        Example of a Phone Number Rule 324
    IP Address Rules 326
        IP Address Rule Resolution Example 327
    E-mail Address Rules 327
    Rule Processing and Destinations 330
        None 330
        Registration Database 330
    Gateway/Proxy 331
    Internet Locator Service (ILS) 331
    Gatekeeper 332
    Multicast Gatekeeper 332
    DNS 332
    Active Directory Directory Services 332
    Local Network 332
    Applying Rules to Calls 333
        Inbound Calls 333
        Outbound Calls 334
    Lesson Summary 335
Review 336

Chapter 9 Monitoring and Optimizing ISA Server Performance 337

About This Chapter 337
Before You Begin 338
Lesson 1 Configuring Alerts 339
    Preconfigured Alerts 339
    Alert Conditions 341
    Event Location 342
    Event Thresholds 342
    Alert Action 343
    ISA Server Events 345

Practice: Configuring an Alert to Send an
E-mail Message 348
    Exercise: Configuring the Intrusion Detected Alert to
    Send You an E-mail Message 348
Lesson Summary 349
Lesson 2 Logging ISA Server Activity 350
Managing ISA Server Logs 350
Logging to a File 352
W3C Format 353
ISA Format 354
Log File Names 354
Log File Options 355
Logging to a Database 356
Logging Packets 359
Firewall and Web Proxy Log Fields 360
Packet Filter Log Fields 370
Practice: Reading Web Logs 372
    Exercise: Analyzing a Web Log 372
Lesson Summary 373
Lesson 3 Creating ISA Server Reports 374
Configuring Reports 374
Viewing Reports 375
    Summary Reports 375
    Web Usage Reports 376
    Application Usage Reports 376
    Traffic & Utilization Reports 377
    Security Reports 377
Configuring Report Jobs 377
Report Job Credentials 379
Configuring Report Log Summaries 380
Report Database 381
Practice: Creating and Viewing Reports 382
    Exercise 1: Creating a Report Job 382
    Exercise 2: Viewing Reports 384
Lesson Summary 385

Lesson 4 Controlling Bandwidth 386
    Determining Effective Bandwidth 386
        Effective Bandwidth for Dial-up Connections 386
        Effective Bandwidth for Dedicated Network Connections ... 387
    Configuring Bandwidth Priorities 389
    Configuring Bandwidth Rules 391
    Rule Order 393
    Default Bandwidth Rule 394
    Practice: Creating a Bandwidth Rule 394
        Exercise 1: Creating a New Bandwidth Priority Policy Element .. 394
        Exercise 2: Creating a New Bandwidth Rule 395
    Lesson Summary 396
Lesson 5 Additional Tuning and Monitoring Tools 397
    Tuning ISA Server Performance 397
    Tuning Cache Performance 398
    ISA Server Performance Objects and Counters 399
    ISA Server Performance Monitor 400
        Performance Objects and Counters Included in ISA Server ... 402
    Lesson Summary 421
Review 422

Chapter 10 Troubleshooting ISA Server   423

About This Chapter 423
Before You Begin 423
Lesson 1 Troubleshooting Tools in ISA Server 424
    Troubleshooting Tools 424
        ISA Server Reports 424
        Event Viewer 425
        Performance Monitor 426
        Netstat 426
        Telnet 428
        Network Monitor 429
    The Routing Table 430
        The Route Determination Process 431
        Troubleshooting Routing Tables 431

Practice: Testing Port Status 432
　　　　　　Exercise: Testing ISA Server ports 432
　　　Lesson Summary 435
　Lesson 2　Troubleshooting Strategies in ISA Server 436
　　　Troubleshooting User Access 436
　　　　　　Authentication 436
　　　Troubleshooting Packet-Based Access Problems 438
　　　　　　VPN Network Considerations 439
　　　Additional Troubleshooting Notes 440
　　　Lesson Summary 444
　Review 446

Appendix A　Questions and Answers　　　　　　　　　　　　　　449

Appendix B　Deploying and Administering
ISA Server in a Complex Network　　　　　　　　　　　　　　　479
　　　About This Appendix 479
　　　Before You Begin 479
　Scenario Background 480
　　　Questions 480

Appendix C　Event Messages　　　　　　　　　　　　　　　　　489
　Alert Event Messages 490
　Bandwidth Event Messages 491
　Cache Event Messages 492
　Common Service Event Messages 495
　Dial-up Connection Events 499
　Firewall Service Event Messages 500
　Winsock Error Code Messages 505
　Intrusion Detection Event Messages 538
　Log Event Messages 543
　Control Service Event Messages 547
　Packet Filter Event Messages 549
　Server Event Messages 551
　Web Proxy Service Event Messages 555
　HTTP Messages 558

HTML Messages 561
Gopher Messages 562
FTP Messages 563
Internet Messages 563

Appendix D   Glossary   **567**

Index   **581**

About This Book

Welcome to *MCSE Training Kit: Microsoft Internet Security and Acceleration Server 2000*. This training kit teaches you how to install and configure Microsoft Internet Security and Acceleration Server 2000 (ISA Server), an enterprise-class firewall and Web caching server. The book begins with an overview of the features and benefits of ISA Server and then describes how to plan and perform an ISA Server installation. It then teaches you how to configure the various features of ISA Server, including the firewall, caching, publishing, multilevel policies, and H.323 Gatekeeper features. The book then reviews various methods of monitoring and troubleshooting ISA Server performance.

Note For more information on becoming a Microsoft Certified Systems Engineer, see the section titled "The Microsoft Certified Professional Program" later in this chapter.

Each chapter in this book is divided into lessons. Most lessons include hands-on procedures that allow you to practice or demonstrate a particular concept or skill. Each chapter ends with a short summary of all chapter lessons and a set of review questions to test your knowledge of the chapter material.

The "Getting Started" section of this chapter provides important setup instructions that describe the hardware and software requirements to complete the procedures in this course. It also provides information about the networking configuration necessary to complete some of the hands-on procedures. Read through this section thoroughly before you start the lessons.

Intended Audience

This book was developed for information technology (IT) professionals who need to design, plan, implement and support Internet Security and Acceleration Server 2000 or who plan to take the related Microsoft Certified Professional exam 70-227: Installing, Configuring, and Administering Microsoft Internet Security and Acceleration (ISA) Server, Enterprise Edition.

Prerequisites

This course requires that students meet the following prerequisites:

- At least one year of hands-on experience administering networks, including at least 6 months experience with the Windows 2000 operating system.
- Strong familiarity with implementing TCP/IP features such as DNS, gateways, subnetting, and routing tables.
- Strong familiarity with implementing Windows 2000 features such as Active Directory directory service, Routing and Remote Access, Performance Monitor, Quality of Service (QoS), Microsoft Management Console (MMC).

Reference Materials

You might find the following reference materials useful:

- **The ISA Server official Web site.** Available online at http://www.microsoft.com/isaserver
- **Microsoft TechNet.** Available monthly on CD-ROM and online at http://www.microsoft.com/technet
- **MCP Magazine Online.** Available online at http://www.mcpmag.com
- **Windows 2000 TCP/IP Protocols and Services Technical Reference.** By Thomas Lee and Joseph Davies. Microsoft Press, 2000.

About the CD-ROM

The Supplemental Course Materials compact disc contains a variety of informational aids that may be used throughout this book. Included on this CD-ROM is the evaluation version of Microsoft Internet Security and Acceleration Server 2000, Enterprise Edition software. For more information regarding this software, see the section titled "Getting Started" late in this introduction.

The CD-ROM also contains a fully searchable electronic version of the book. For information about the electronic book, see the section "About the Electronic Book" later in this introduction.

The Supplemental Course Materials CD-ROM also contains files required to perform the hands-on procedures. These files can be used directly from the CD-ROM or copied onto your hard disk. The files include a demonstration of Microsoft ISA Server 2000, and practice files that accompany the book exercises.

Features of This Book

Each chapter opens with a "Before You Begin" section, which prepares you for completing the chapter.

▶ The chapters are then broken in to lessons. Whenever possible, lessons contain practices that give you an opportunity to use the skills being presented or explore the part of the application being described. All practices offer step-by-step procedures that are identified with a bullet symbol like the one to the left of this paragraph.

The "Review" section at the end of the chapter allows you to test what you have learned in the chapter's lessons.

Appendix A, "Questions and Answers" contains all of the book's questions and corresponding answers.

Notes

Several types of Notes appear throughout the lessons.

- Notes marked **Tip** contain explanations of possible results or alternative methods.
- Notes marked **Important** contain information that is essential to completing a task.
- Notes marked **Note** contain supplemental information.
- Notes marked **Caution** or **Warning** contain warnings about possible loss of data.

Conventions

The following conventions are used throughout this book.

Notational Conventions

- Characters or commands that you type appear in **bold** type.
- *Italic* in syntax statements indicates placeholders for variable information. *Italic* is also used for book titles.
- Names of files and folders appear in Title caps, except when you are to type them directly. Unless otherwise indicated, you can use all lowercase letters when you type a file name in a dialog box or at a command prompt.
- File name extensions appear in all lowercase.
- Acronyms appear in all uppercase.
- Monospace type represents code samples, examples of screen text, or entries that you might type at a command prompt or in initialization files.
- Square brackets [ ] are used in syntax statements to enclose optional items. For example, [*filename*] in command syntax indicates that you can choose to type a file name with the command. Type only the information within the brackets, not the brackets themselves.
- Braces { } are used in syntax statements to enclose required items. Type only the information within the braces, not the braces themselves.

- Icons represent specific sections in the book as follows:

Icon	Represents
(CD-ROM)	A file contained on the CD-ROM. Some files are needed to complete a hands-on practice; others contain supplemental information about the topic being discussed. The purpose of the file and its location are described in the accompanying text.
(Notebook)	A hands-on practice. You should perform the practice to give yourself an opportunity to use the skills being presented in the lesson.
(?)	Chapter review questions. These questions at the end of each chapter allow you to test what you have learned in the lessons. You will find the answers to the review questions in the Questions and Answers section at the end of the book.

Keyboard Conventions

- A plus sign (+) between two key names means that you must press those keys at the same time. For example, "Press ALT+TAB" means that you hold down ALT while you press TAB.
- A comma (,) between two or more key names means that you must press each of the keys consecutively, not together. For example, "Press ALT, F, X" means that you press and release each key in sequence. "Press ALT+W, L" means that you first press ALT and W together, and then release them and press L.
- You can choose menu commands with the keyboard. Press the ALT key to activate the menu bar, and then sequentially press the keys that correspond to the highlighted or underlined letter of the menu name and the command name. For some commands, you can also press a key combination listed in the menu.
- You can select or clear check boxes or option buttons in dialog boxes with the keyboard. Press the ALT key, and then press the key that corresponds to the underlined letter of the option name. Or you can press TAB until the option is highlighted, and then press the spacebar to select or clear the check box or option button.
- You can cancel the display of a dialog box by pressing the ESC key.

Chapter and Appendix Overview

This self-paced training course combines notes, hands-on procedures, multimedia presentations, and review questions to teach you how to install, configure, and implement Microsoft Internet Security and Acceleration Server 2000. It is designed to be completed from beginning to end, but you can choose a customized track and complete only the sections that interest you. (See the next section, "Finding the Best Starting Point for You" for more information.) If you choose the customized track option, see the "Before You Begin" section in each chapter. Any hands-on procedures that require preliminary work from preceding chapters refer to the appropriate chapters.

The book is divided into the following chapters:

The "About This Book" section contains a self-paced training overview and introduces the components of this training. Read this section thoroughly to get the greatest educational value from this self-paced training and to plan which lessons you will complete.

Chapter 1, "Introduction to Microsoft Internet Security and Acceleration Server 2000," provides an overview of the features and benefits of ISA Server.

Chapter 2, "Installing Microsoft Internet Security and Acceleration Server 2000," teaches you how to perform an ISA Server installation, including the process of planning for an installation and migrating from Proxy Server 2.0.

Chapter 3, "Configuring Secure Internet Access," teaches you how to establish secure Internet access for ISA Server clients. This includes installing and configuring clients as Firewall clients and SecureNAT clients, configuring automatic discovery, configuring Internet access through a dial-up connection, and troubleshooting Internet connectivity.

Chapter 4, "Configuring Internet Security through Access Policies," explains how to create a customized and secure Internet access policy. This chapter teaches you how to create policy elements such as schedules and destination sets that you may later use in site and content rules or in protocol rules. It also shows you how to create these rules so that you can control network traffic to and from your network. The chapter then includes a lesson describing ISA Server's packet filtering feature and how to configure packet filters suited to your network needs. Finally, the chapter explains how to configure intrusion detection in ISA Server so that you will know when someone has launched an attack against your network.

Chapter 5, "Configuring Internet Acceleration through the ISA Server Cache," teaches you how to use ISA Server as a means to accelerate Internet connectivity for server clients. This includes configuring cache properties, active caching, and scheduled content downloads.

Chapter 6, "Secure Server Publishing," teaches you how to publish servers on the Internet securely behind ISA Server. This includes publishing Web servers, mail servers, and other Internet servers (such as FTP servers).

Chapter 7, "Securing Enterprise Networks with ISA Server," teaches you how to deploy ISA Server in more complex enterprise networks, including those that require the use of virtual private networks and of a centralized, multi-tiered policy.

Chapter 8, "Secure Videoconferencing with H.323 Gatekeeper," teaches you how to deploy videoconferencing in an ISA Server network. This chapter describes how to use ISA Server's H.323 Gatekeeper as a central switch for videoconferencing calls, and how to use rules to route calls to aliases.

Chapter 9, "Monitoring and Optimizing ISA Server Performance," teaches you how to use various tools in ISA Server to monitor and optimize ISA Server behavior. This includes configuring alerts, using ISA Server logs and reports, configuring bandwidth rules, and using ISA Server Performance Monitor counters.

Chapter 10, "Troubleshooting ISA Server," introduces you to the many tools and strategies that you can use to troubleshoot problems in ISA Server behavior.

Appendix A, "Questions and Answers," lists all of the review questions from the book showing the page number where the question appears and the suggested answer.

Appendix B, "Deploying and Administering ISA Server in a Complex Network," walks you through several hypothetical installations of Microsoft Internet Security and Acceleration Server 2000 (ISA Server) Enterprise Edition to test your understanding of and ability to troubleshoot the product. Because the exam is based on both knowledge of the software and real-world experience, we strongly recommend that you study this appendix before taking MCP exam 70-227.

Appendix C, "Event Messages," is a reference used to aid troubleshooting in ISA Server. It presents the full list of Event Messages in ISA Server, along with a description of the probable cause and action necessary to remedy problems, if necessary.

A Glossary of terms related to firewalls and ISA Server is also included as a means to help you become familiar with these topics.

Finding the Best Starting Point for You

Because this book is self-paced, you can skip some lessons and revisit them later. Note, however, that in many cases you must complete exercises in early chapters before completing exercises in the other chapters. Use the following table to find the best starting point for you:

If you	Follow this learning path
Are preparing to take the Microsoft Certified Professional exam 70-227: Installing, Configuring, and Administering Microsoft Internet Security and Acceleration (ISA) Server, Enterprise Edition.	Read the "Getting Started" section. Then work through Chapters 1–3. Work through the remaining chapters in any order.
To review information about specific topics from the exam,	Use the "Where to Find Specific Skills in This Book" section that follows this table.

Where to Find Specific Skills in This Book

The following tables provide a list of the skills measured on certification exam 70-227, Installing, Configuring, and Administering Microsoft Internet Security and Acceleration (ISA) Server, Enterprise Edition. The table provides the skill, and where in this book you will find the lesson relating to that skill.

Note Exam skills are subject to change without prior notice and at the sole discretion of Microsoft.

Installing ISA Server

Skill Being Measured	Location in Book
Preconfigure network interfaces.	Chapter 2, Lesson 2
Verify Internet connectivity before installing ISA Server.	Chapter 2, Lesson 2
Verify DNS name resolution.	Chapter 2, Lesson 2
Install ISA Server. Installation modes include integrated, firewall, and cache.	Chapter 2, Lesson 1; Chapter 2, Lesson 2
Construct and modify the local address table (LAT).	Chapter 2, Lesson 2
Calculate the size of the cache and configure it.	Chapter 2, Lesson 1; Chapter 2, Lesson 2; Chapter 5, Lesson 2

Skill Being Measured	Location in Book
Install an ISA Server computer as a member of an array.	Chapter 2, Lesson 2; Chapter 7, Lesson 2
Upgrade a Microsoft Proxy Server 2.0 computer to ISA Server.	Chapter 2, Lesson 3
Back up the Proxy Server 2.0 configuration.	Chapter 2, Lesson 3
Troubleshoot problems that occur during setup.	Chapter 2, Lesson 2

Configuring and Troubleshooting ISA Server Services

Skill Being Measured	Location in Book
Configure and troubleshoot outbound Internet access.	Chapter 3, Lesson 4
Configure ISA Server hosting roles.	Chapter 6, Lesson 1; Chapter 6, Lesson 2; Chapter 6, Lesson 3
Configure ISA Server for Web publishing.	Chapter 6, Lesson 2
Configure ISA Server for server proxy.	Chapter 3, Lesson 1; Chapter 5, Lesson 1; Chapter 5, Lesson 2
Configure ISA Server for server publishing.	Chapter 6, Lesson 1; Chapter 6, Lesson 3
Configure H.323 Gatekeeper for audio and video conferencing.	Chapter 8, Lesson 1; Chapter 8, Lesson 2
Configure gatekeeper rules. Rules include telephone, e-mail, and Internet Protocol (IP).	Chapter 8, Lesson 2
Configure gatekeeper destinations by using the Add Destination Wizard.	Chapter 8, Lesson 2
Set up and troubleshoot dial-up connections and Routing and Remote Access dial-on-demand connections.	Chapter 3, Lesson 4; Chapter 10, Lesson 2
Set up and verify routing rules for static IP routes in Routing and Remote Access.	Chapter 5, Lesson 1; Chapter 10, Lesson 1
Configure and troubleshoot virtual private network (VPN) access.	Chapter 7, Lesson 3; Chapter 10, Lesson 2
Configure the ISA Server computer as a VPN endpoint without using the VPN Wizard.	Chapter 7, Lesson 3; Chapter 10, Lesson 2

(continues)

Configuring and Troubleshooting ISA Server Services *(continued)*

Skill Being Measured	Location in Book
Configure the ISA Server computer for VPN pass-through.	Chapter 7, Lesson 3; Chapter 10, Lesson 2
Configure multiple ISA Server computers for scalability. Configurations include Network Load Balancing (NLB) and Cache Array Routing Protocol (CARP).	Chapter 7, Lesson 2

Configuring, Managing, and Troubleshooting Policies and Rules

Skill Being Measured	Location in Book
Configure and secure the firewall in accordance with corporate standards.	Chapter 4, Lesson 1
Configure the packet filter rules for different levels of security, including system hardening.	Chapter 4, Lesson 1; Chapter 4, Lesson 5
Create and configure access control and bandwidth policies.	Chapter 9, Lesson 4
Create and configure site and content rules to restrict Internet access.	Chapter 4, Lesson 4
Create and configure protocol rules to manage Internet access.	Chapter 4, Lesson 3
Create and configure routing rules to restrict Internet access.	Chapter 5, Lesson 1
Create and configure bandwidth rules to control bandwidth usage.	Chapter 9, Lesson 4
Troubleshoot access problems.	Chapter 10, Lesson 1; Chapter 10, Lesson 2
Troubleshoot user-based access problems.	Chapter 10, Lesson 2
Troubleshoot packet-based access problems.	Chapter 10, Lesson 2
Create new policy elements. Elements include schedules, bandwidth priorities, destination sets, client address sets, protocol definitions, and content groups.	Chapter 4, Lesson 2
Manage ISA Server arrays in an enterprise.	Chapter 7, Lesson 1; Chapter 7, Lesson 2
Create an array of proxy servers.	Chapter 7, Lesson 2
Assign an enterprise policy to an array.	Chapter 7, Lesson 1

Deploying, Configuring, and Troubleshooting the Client Computer

Skill Being Measured	Location in Book
Plan the deployment of client computers to use ISA Server services. Considerations include client authentication, client operating system, network topology, cost, complexity, and client function.	Chapter 2, Lesson 1
Configure and troubleshoot the client computer for secure network address translation (SecureNAT).	Chapter 3, Lesson 1; Chapter 3, Lesson 4
Install the Firewall Client software. Considerations include the cost and complexity of deployment.	Chapter 3, Lesson 1
Troubleshoot autodetection.	Chapter 3, Lesson 2
Configure the client computer's Web browser to use ISA Server as an HTTP proxy.	Chapter 3, Lesson 1

Monitoring, Managing, and Analyzing ISA Server Use

Skill Being Measured	Location in Book
Monitor security and network usage by using logging and alerting.	Chapter 9, Lesson 1; Chapter 9, Lesson 2
Configure intrusion detection.	Chapter 4, Lesson 6
Configure an alert to send an e-mail message to an administrator.	Chapter 9, Lesson 1
Automate alert configuration.	Chapter 9, Lesson 1
Monitor alert status.	Chapter 9, Lesson 1; Chapter 10, Lesson 1
Troubleshoot problems with security and network usage. Chapter 10, Lesson 2	Chapter 10, Lesson 1;
Detect connections by using Netstat.	Chapter 10, Lesson 1
Test the status of external ports by using Telnet or Network Monitor.	Chapter 10, Lesson 1
Analyze the performance of ISA Server by using reports. Report types include summary, Web usage, application usage, traffic and utilization, and security.	Chapter 9, Lesson 3
Optimize the performance of the ISA Server computer. Considerations include capacity planning, allocation priorities, and trend analysis.	Chapter 2, Lesson 1; Chapter 9, Lesson 5

(continues)

Monitoring, Managing, and Analyzing ISA Server Use *(continued)*

Skill Being Measured	Location in Book
Analyze the performance of the ISA Server computer by using Performance Monitor.	Chapter 9, Lesson 5
Analyze the performance of the ISA Server computer by using reporting and logging.	Chapter 9, Lesson 2; Chapter 9, Lesson 3
Control the total RAM used by ISA Server for caching.	Chapter 9, Lesson 5

Getting Started

This self-paced training course contains hands-on procedures to help you learn about Microsoft Internet Security and Acceleration Server 2000, Enterprise Edition.

To complete some of these procedures, you must have two networked computers. Both computers must be capable of running Windows 2000 Server. Service Pack 1 must be installed on each computer.

Hardware Requirements

Each computer must have the following minimum configuration. All hardware should be on the Microsoft Windows 2000 Server Hardware Compatibility List.

- Computer with 300 MHz or higher Pentium II-compatible CPU running Microsoft Windows 2000 Server or Windows 2000 Advanced Server with Service Pack 1 or later, or Windows 2000 Datacenter Server operating system
- 256 megabytes (MB) of RAM
- Hard drive of at least 2 GB formatted as a single NTFS partition
- 200 MB of available hard-disk space after OS is installed
- Network adapter for communicating with the internal network
- Modem for communicating with the Internet
- CD-ROM drive
- Sound card and audio output
- Microsoft Mouse or compatible pointing device

Software Requirements

The following software is required to complete the procedures in this course. A 120-day evaluation copy of Microsoft Internet Security and Acceleration Server 2000, Enterprise Edition, is included on a CD-ROM in this kit.

- Windows 2000 Server (Service Pack 1 or later)
- Microsoft Internet Security and Acceleration Server 2000, Enterprise Edition

Note The 120-day Evaluation Edition provided with this training is not the full retail product and is provided only for the purposes of training and evaluation. Microsoft Technical Support does not support this evaluation edition. For additional support information regarding this book and the CD-ROM (including answers to commonly asked questions about installation and use), visit the Microsoft Press Technical Support web site at Http://mspress.microsoft.com/support/. You can also email TKINPUT@MICROSOFT.COM, or send a letter to Microsoft Press, Attn: Microsoft Press Technical Support, One Microsoft Way, Redmond, WA 98502-6399.

Setup Instructions

Many of the exercises in this training kit are performed in a two-computer Ethernet network. To perform the exercises properly, you must set the network up according to the following specifications.

The first computer should have an internal network adapter and an external modem connected to a working telephone line. The computer should be named Server1 and configured as a domain controller in the domain domain01.local. Server1 will be assigned an IP address of 192.168.0.1/24 on its internal network adapter. No default gateway should be specified for the internal interface, but a valid external DNS Server on the Internet should be specified as the preferred DNS server and 192.168.0.1 as the alternate DNS server. The following two Windows 2000 components should be installed on Server1 in addition to the defaults: Management and Monitoring Tools, Windows Media Services. Create a dial-up connection to your ISP from Server1. Verify that you can successfully connect to your ISP and access the Internet before beginning the installation of ISA Server in Chapter 2.

After you install Windows 2000 on Server1, install and configure Active Directory from Server1 with the following specifications:

Configure the server as the first domain controller in a new forest of domain trees.

- The new domain name is "domain01.local." This is also the name of the new forest.
- The NetBIOS name of the domain is "DOMAIN01"
- Database location: C:\WINNT\NTDS
- Log file location: C:\WINNT\NTDS
- Sysvol folder location: C:\WINNT\SYSVOL
- The DNS service will be installed and configured on the computer.
- Permissions compatible with pre-Windows 2000 servers will be used with this domain; this will allow anonymous access to domain information.
- Active Directory is installed on this computer for the domain "domain01.local."
- This domain controller is assigned to the site "Default-First-Site-Name." Sites are managed with the Active Directory Sites and Services administrative tool.

Once you have finished configuring Server1, you can install Windows 2000 on the second computer. This computer needs only one network adapter, which is connected to the local area network. The computer should be named Server2 and configured as a member server of the domain Domain01. Server2 should be assigned an IP address of 192.168.0.2/24, with the default gateway specified as 192.168.0.1. Specify a valid external DNS server on the Internet as the preferred DNS server and 192.168.0.1 as the alternate DNS server. The following Windows 2000 components should be installed on Server1 in addition to the defaults: Management and Monitoring Tools, Networking Services, and Windows Media Services.

Note If your computers are part of a larger network, you *must* verify with your network administrator that the computer names, domain name, and other information used in setting up Microsoft Internet Security and Acceleration Server 2000 as described in Chapters 2 and 3 do not conflict with network operations. If they do conflict, ask your network administrator to provide alternative values and use those values throughout all of the exercises in this book.

About the Electronic Book

The CD-ROM also includes an electronic version of the book that you can view on-screen using Microsoft Internet Explorer 5.0 or later.

▶ **To use the electronic version of this book**

1. Insert the Supplemental Course Materials CD-ROM into your CD-ROM drive.

2. Select Run from the Start menu on your desktop, and type **D:\Ebook\Autorun.exe** (where D is the name of your CD-ROM disk drive).

   This will install an icon for the electronic book to your desktop.

3. Click OK to exit the Installation wizard.

Note You must have the Supplemental Course Materials CD-ROM inserted in your CD-ROM drive to run the electronic book.

The Microsoft Certified Professional Program

The Microsoft Certified Professional (MCP) program provides the best method to prove your command of current Microsoft products and technologies. Microsoft, an industry leader in certification, is on the forefront of testing methodology. Our exams and corresponding certifications are developed to validate your mastery of critical competencies as you design and develop, or implement and support, solutions with Microsoft products and technologies. Computer professionals who become Microsoft certified are recognized as experts and are sought after industry-wide.

The Microsoft Certified Professional program offers eight certifications, based on specific areas of technical expertise:

- **Microsoft Certified Professional (MCP).** Demonstrated in-depth knowledge of at least one Microsoft operating system. Candidates may pass additional Microsoft certification exams to further qualify their skills with Microsoft BackOffice products, development tools, or desktop programs.

- **Microsoft Certified Systems Engineer (MCSE).** Qualified to effectively plan, implement, maintain, and support information systems in a wide range of computing environments with Microsoft Windows NT Server and the Microsoft BackOffice integrated family of server software.

- **Microsoft Certified Database Administrator (MCDBA).** Individuals who derive physical database designs, develop logical data models, create physical databases, create data services by using Transact-SQL, manage and maintain databases, configure and manage security, monitor and optimize databases, and install and configure Microsoft SQL Server.

- **Microsoft Certified Solution Developer (MCSD).** Qualified to design and develop custom business solutions with Microsoft development tools, technologies, and platforms, including Microsoft Office and Microsoft BackOffice.
- **Microsoft Certified Trainer (MCT).** Instructionally and technically qualified to deliver Microsoft Official Curriculum through a Microsoft Certified Technical Education Center (CTEC).

Microsoft Certification Benefits

Microsoft certification, one of the most comprehensive certification programs available for assessing and maintaining software-related skills, is a valuable measure of an individual's knowledge and expertise. Microsoft certification is awarded to individuals who have successfully demonstrated their ability to perform specific tasks and implement solutions with Microsoft products. Not only does this provide an objective measure for employers to consider; it also provides guidance for what an individual should know to be proficient. And as with any skills-assessment and benchmarking measure, certification brings a variety of benefits: to the individual, and to employers and organizations.

Microsoft Certification Benefits for Individuals

As a Microsoft Certified Professional, you receive many benefits:

- Industry recognition of your knowledge and proficiency with Microsoft products and technologies.
- A Microsoft Developer Network subscription. MCPs receive rebates or discounts on a one-year subscription to the Microsoft Developer Network (msdn.microsoft.com/subscriptions/) during the first year of certification. (Fulfillment details will vary, depending on your location; please see your Welcome Kit.) The rebate or discount amount is U.S. $50 for MSDN Library.
- Access to technical and product information direct from Microsoft through a secured area of the MCP web site (go to www.microsoft.com/trainingandservices/ then expand the Certification node from the tree directory in the left margin, and then select the "For MCPs Only" link).
- Access to exclusive discounts on products and services from selected companies. Individuals who are currently certified can learn more about exclusive discounts by visiting the MCP secured web site (go to www.microsoft.com/trainingandservices/, then expand the Certification node from the tree directory in the left margin, and then select the "Form MCPs Only" link) and select the "Other Benefits" link.

- MCP logo, certificate, transcript, wallet card, and lapel pin to identify you as a Microsoft Certified Professional (MCP) to colleagues and clients. Electronic files of logos and transcript may be downloaded from the MCP secured web site (go to www.microsoft.com/trainingandservices/, then expand the Certification node from the tree directory in the left margin, and then select the "Form MCPs Only" link) upon certification.

- Invitations to Microsoft conferences, technical training sessions, and special events.

- Free access to *Microsoft Certified Professional Magazine Online*, a career and professional development magazine. Secured content on the *Microsoft Certified Professional Magazine Online* web site includes the current issue (available only to MCPs), additional online-only content and columns, an MCP-only database, and regular chats with Microsoft and other technical experts.

An additional benefit is received by Microsoft Certified System Engineers (MCSEs):

- A 50 percent rebate or discount off the estimated retail price of a one-year subscription to *TechNet* or *TechNet Plus* during the first year of certification. (Fulfillment details will vary, depending on your location. Please see your Welcome Kit.) In addition, about 95 percent of the CD-ROM content is available free online at the *TechNet* web site (www.microsoft.com/technet/).

Microsoft Certification Benefits for Employers and Organizations

Through certification, computer professionals can maximize the return on investment in Microsoft technology. Research shows that Microsoft certification provides organizations with:

- Excellent return on training and certification investments by providing a standard method of determining training needs and measuring results.

- Increased customer satisfaction and decreased support costs through improved service, increased productivity and greater technical self-sufficiency.

- Reliable benchmark for hiring, promoting and career planning.

- Recognition and rewards for productive employees by validating their expertise.

- Retraining options for existing employees so they can work effectively with new technologies.

- Assurance of quality when outsourcing computer services.

To learn more about how certification can help your company, see the backgrounders, white papers and case studies available at www.microsoft.com/trainingandservices/ (expand the Certification node from the tree directory in the left margin, and then select the "Case Studies" link):

- A white paper, MCSE Criterion Validity Study White Paper, Oct. 1998, that evaluates the Microsoft Certified Systems Engineer certification (SysEngrCert.doc 339 KB)
- Compaq Case Study (Compaq.doc 85 KB)
- CrossTier.com Case Study (CrossTier.doc 246 KB)
- Extreme Logic Case Study (Extreme Logic.doc 74 KB)
- Financial Benefits to Supporters of Microsoft Professional Certification, IDC white paper (1998wpidc.doc 948 KB)
- Lyondel Case Study (lyondel.doc 20 KB)
- Prudential Case Study (prudentl.exe 74 KB self-extracting file)
- Stellcom Case Study (stellcom.doc 72KB)
- Unisys Case Study (Unisys.doc 48 KB)

Requirements for Becoming a Microsoft Certified Professional

The certification requirements differ for each certification and are specific to the products and job functions addressed by the certification.

To become a Microsoft Certified Professional, you must pass rigorous certification exams that provide a valid and reliable measure of technical proficiency and expertise. These exams are designed to test your expertise and ability to perform a role or task with a product, and are developed with the input of professionals in the industry. Questions in the exams reflect how Microsoft products are used in actual organizations, giving them "real-world" relevance.

Microsoft Certified Product Specialists are required to pass one operating system exam. Candidate may pass additional Microsoft certification exams to further qualify their skills with Microsoft BackOffice products, development tools, or desktop applications.

Microsoft Certified Systems Engineers are required to pass a series of core Microsoft Windows operating system and networking exams, and BackOffice technology elective exams.

Microsoft Certified Database Administrators are required to pass three core exams and one elective exam that provide a valid and reliable measure of technical proficiency and expertise.

Microsoft Certified Solution Developers are required to pass two core Microsoft Windows operating system technology exams and two BackOffice technology elective exams.

Microsoft Certified Trainers are required to meet instructional and technical requirements specific to each Microsoft Official Curriculum course they are certified to deliver. In the United States and Canada, call Microsoft at (800) 636-7544 for more information on becoming a Microsoft Certified Trainer or visit www.microsoft.com/trainingandservices/ (expand the Certification node from the tree directory in the left margin, and then select the "MCT" link). Outside the United States and Canada, contact your local Microsoft subsidiary.

Technical Training for Computer Professionals

Technical training is available in a variety of ways, with instructor-led classes, online instruction, or self-paced training available at thousands of locations worldwide.

Self-Paced Training

For motivated learners who are ready for the challenge, self-paced instruction is the most flexible, cost-effective way to increase your knowledge and skills.

A full-line of self-paced print and computer-based training materials is available direct from the source—Microsoft Press. Microsoft Official Curriculum courseware kits from Microsoft Press are designed for advanced computer system professionals are available from Microsoft Press and the Microsoft Developer Division. Self-paced training kits from Microsoft Press feature print-based instructional materials, along with CD-ROM based product software, multimedia presentations, lab exercises, and practice files. The Mastering Series provides in-depth, interactive training on CD-ROM for experienced developers. They're both great ways to prepare for Microsoft Certified Professional (MCP) exams.

Online Training

For a more flexible alternative to instructor-led classes, turn to online instruction. It's as near as the Internet and it's ready whenever you are. Learn at your own pace and on your own schedule in a virtual classroom, often with easy access to an online instructor. Without ever leaving your desk, you can gain the expertise you need. Online instruction covers a variety of Microsoft products and technologies. It includes options ranging from Microsoft Official Curriculum to choices available nowhere else. It's training on demand, with access to learning resources 24 hours a day. Online training is available through Microsoft Certified Technical Education Centers.

Microsoft Certified Technical Education Centers

Microsoft Certified Technical Education Centers (CTECs) are the best source for instructor-led training that can help you prepare to become a Microsoft Certified Professional. The Microsoft CTEC program is a worldwide network of qualified technical training organizations that provide authorized delivery of Microsoft Official Curriculum courses by Microsoft Certified Trainers to computer professionals.

For a listing of CTEC locations in the United States and Canada, visit http://www.microsoft.com/CTEC/default.htm.

Technical Support

Every effort has been made to ensure the accuracy of this book and the contents of the companion disc. If you have comments, questions, or ideas regarding this book or the companion disc, please send them to Microsoft Press using either of the following methods:

E-mail:

TKINPUT@MICROSOFT.COM

Postal Mail:

Microsoft Press
Attn: MCSE Training Kit: Microsoft Internet Security and Acceleration Server 2000 Editor
One Microsoft Way
Redmond, WA 98052-6399

Microsoft Press provides corrections for books through the World Wide Web at the following address:

mspress.microsoft.com/support/

To connect directly to the Microsoft Press Knowledge Base and enter a query regarding a question or issue that you may have, go to http://mspress.microsoft.com/support/search.htm.

Please note that product support is not offered through the above mail addresses. For further information regarding Microsoft software support options, please connect to www.microsoft.com/support/ or call Microsoft Support Network Sales at (800) 936-3500.

The Evaluation Edition of Microsoft Internet Security and Acceleration Server 2000 included with this book is unsupported by both Microsoft and Microsoft Press, and should not be used on a primary work computer. For online support information relating to the full version of Microsoft Internet Security and Acceleration Server 2000 that might also apply to the Evaluation Edition, you can connect to http://support.microsoft.com/.

For information about ordering the full version of any Microsoft software, please call Microsoft Sales at (800) 426-9400 or visit www.microsoft.com. Information about any issues relating to the use of this evaluation edition with this training kit is posted to the Support section of the Microsoft Press Web site (http://mspress.microsoft.com/support/).

CHAPTER 1

Introduction to Microsoft Internet Security and Acceleration Server 2000

Lesson 1 Overview of ISA Server 3

Lesson 2 Introduction to the ISA Server Firewall 17

Lesson 3 Overview of ISA Server Caching 28

Lesson 4 ISA Server's Management Features 37

Review 43

About This Chapter

This chapter introduces the features and benefits of Microsoft Internet Security and Acceleration Server (ISA Server). It begins with an overview of ISA Server's basic roles as an Internet firewall and Web caching server that provide increased security and superior performance, manageability, scalability, and extensibility. The chapter also gives a detailed account of ISA Server's configurable firewall protection, its cache server functionality, and its powerful management features.

Before You Begin

To complete this chapter, you must have basic knowledge of the following Microsoft Windows 2000 features:

- Microsoft Active Directory directory services
- Group Policy
- Microsoft Management Console (MMC)

Lesson 1 Overview of ISA Server

This lesson introduces the features and benefits of ISA Server.

After this lesson, you will be able to
- Explain the difference between the two editions of ISA Server
- Describe the types of functionality supported by ISA Server
- Explain how ISA Server draws upon features in Windows 2000 to provide advanced security, performance, and manageability
- Describe the scalability and extensibility features that are built into ISA Server

Estimated lesson time: 45 minutes

ISA Server is an extensible, enterprise-class firewall and Web cache server built on the Windows 2000 operating system. ISA Server's multilayer firewall helps protect network resources from viruses, hackers, and unauthorized access, and its Web cache server enables organizations to provide faster Web access for users by serving objects locally rather than over the Internet. When you install ISA Server in your network, you can configure it as a firewall, a Web cache server, or both.

ISA Server minimizes the difficulty in implementing and administering a robust firewall and cache server by providing intuitive yet powerful management tools, which include a Microsoft Management Console (MMC) snap-in, graphical taskpads, and step-by-step wizards.

Editions Comparison

ISA Server is available in two editions.

ISA Server Enterprise Edition

ISA Server Enterprise Edition was designed to meet the performance, management, and scalability needs of high-volume Internet traffic environments. This edition offers centralized server management, multiple levels of access policy, server clustering through arrays, and fault-tolerant capabilities.

ISA Server Standard Edition

ISA Server Standard Edition provides enterprise-class firewall security and Web caching capabilities for small business, workgroups, and departmental environments. The standard edition provides excellent price/performance for business-critical environments.

Key Differences

The security, caching, management, performance, and extensibility capabilities of ISA Server are the same in both editions. The standard edition, however, can run only as a standalone ISA Server computer with local policy and can support no more than four processors. The enterprise edition supports multiserver arrays with centralized management, enterprise-level and array-level policy, and limitless scalability.

Though this book focuses primarily on configuring and administering ISA Server Enterprise Edition, knowing the differences between the two editions enables you to decide which edition is best suited to your network needs. Table 1.1 lists these differences.

Table 1.1 ISA Server Editions Comparison

	ISA Server Standard Edition	ISA Server Enterprise Edition
Server deployment	Standalone only	Multiserver with centralized management
Policy level support	Local only	Enterprise and array
Hardware scalability limit	4 CPUs only	No limit

ISA Server Roles

ISA Server can provide value to information technology (IT) managers, network administrators, and information-security professionals in organizations of all sizes who are concerned about the security, performance, manageability, or operating costs of their networks. ISA Server can be installed in three different modes: Firewall mode, Cache mode, and Integrated mode, which implements the firewall and Web caching on the same computer. Organizations can deploy ISA Server in numerous networking scenarios, including those described in the following paragraphs.

Internet Firewall

ISA Server can be deployed as a dedicated firewall that acts as the secure gateway to the Internet for internal clients. The ISA Server computer is transparent to the other parties in the communication path. Unless access or security rules are violated, ISA Server cannot be seen by any users or applications passing through the firewall.

As a firewall, ISA Server allows you to implement your business Internet security policy by enabling you to configure a broad set of rules that specify which sites, protocols, and content can be passed through the ISA Server. By monitoring requests and responses between the Internet and internal client computers, ISA Server controls who can access which computers on the corporate network. ISA Server also controls which computers on the Internet your internal clients can access.

Secure Server Publishing

ISA Server allows you to publish services to the Internet without compromising the security of your internal network. This is achieved by allowing the ISA Server computer to handle external client requests on behalf of an internal publishing server.

Forward Web Caching Server

As a forward Web cache server, ISA Server maintains a centralized cache of frequently requested Internet content that can be accessed by any Web browser in your private network. This improves client browser performance, decreases response time, and reduces bandwidth consumption on Internet connections.

Reverse Web Caching Server

ISA Server can act as a Web server by fulfilling incoming client requests for Web content from its cache and forwarding requests to the Web server only when the requests cannot be served from its cache.

Integrated Firewall and Web Cache Server

Organizations can deploy ISA Server as separate firewall and caching components, but some administrators will choose to have a single integrated firewall and Web cache server to provide secure and fast Internet connectivity. No matter how organizations choose to deploy the ISA server, they will benefit from the centralized and integrated policy-based management.

Windows 2000 Integration

ISA Server is built on Windows 2000 technology for advanced security, performance, and management. The following is a list of Windows 2000 technologies that work with ISA Server to provide better security, performance, and management capabilities.

- **Network Address Translation.** ISA Server extends Windows 2000 Network Address Translation (NAT) functionality by enforcing ISA Server policy for SecureNAT clients (see Figure 1.1).

Note NAT refers to a set of standards defined in the Internet Engineering Task Force (IETF) Request for Comments (RFC) 1361. NAT is built into Windows 2000 and provides a gateway that can hide the Internet Protocol (IP) addresses of internal local area network (LAN) clients from external clients. This is achieved by masking the internal addresses with a different set of addresses that is visible to the outside.

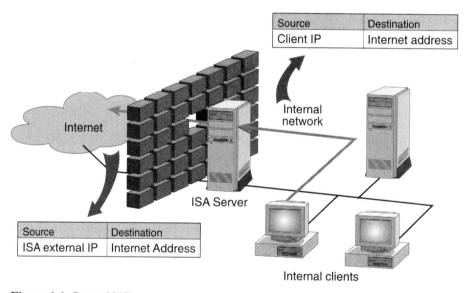

Figure 1.1 SecureNAT

- **Integrated Virtual Private Networking.** ISA Server can be configured as a virtual private networking (VPN) server to support secure, gateway-to-gateway communication or client-to-gateway remote access communication over the Internet. Windows 2000 standards–based VPN supports Point to Point Tunneling Protocol (PPTP) and Layer 2 Tunneling Protocol (L2TP)/Secure Internet Protocol (IPSec) technology.

- **Authentication.** ISA Server supports Windows authentication methods, including Basic, NT LAN Manager (NTLM), Kerberos, and digital certificates.

- **System Hardening.** ISA Server uses the Windows 2000 security templates to lock down the operating system at different levels of security.

- **Active Directory Storage.** When ISA Server Enterprise Edition is configured to use multiserver arrays, configuration and policy information is stored centrally in the Active Directory directory store. In addition, ISA Server can apply access controls to users and groups defined in the Active Directory directory store.

- **Tiered-Policy Management.** ISA Server Enterprise Edition allows you to build on the distributed nature of Active Directory directory services by defining one or more enterprise policies and applying them to arrays in the enterprise. This process supports a tiered and scalable administration model.

- **MMC Administration.** The ISA Server management interface is called ISA Management (see Figure 1.2). ISA Management is an MMC snap-in that provides both a Taskpad view and an Advanced view for navigation. MMC is extensible; it allows third-party products to integrate seamlessly into ISA Server's administration console.

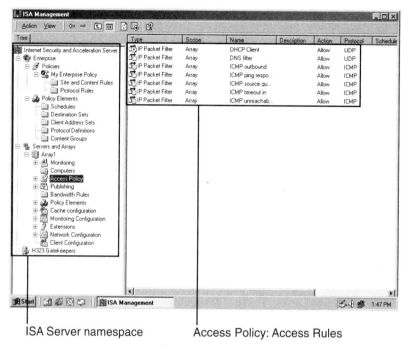

Figure 1.2 The ISA Management interface

- **Quality of Service (QoS).** ISA Server provides bandwidth control management, building on the Windows 2000 QoS technology to prioritize data traffic.

- **Multiprocessor Support.** ISA Server takes advantage of the symmetric multiprocessing (SMP) architecture of Windows 2000 to improve performance.

- **Client-Side Auto-Discovery.** By supporting Web Proxy Autodiscovery Protocol (WPAD), Firewall Client software running on ISA Server clients automatically connect with ISA Server on the network, without requiring you to configure each new client individually.

- **Administration Component Object Model (COM) Object.** ISA Server provides programmatic access to the rules engine and all administrative options.

- **Web Filters.** ISA Server Web filters, which are based on Internet server application programming interface (ISAPI), can inspect or control Hypertext Transfer Protocol (HTTP) and File Transfer Protocol (FTP) traffic coming across the gateway.

- **Alerts.** ISA Server writes alerts to the Windows 2000 Event Log.

Scalability

Computers running ISA Server Enterprise Edition can be grouped together in arrays. In ISA Server, an array is a group of ISA Server computers used to provide fault tolerance, load balancing, and distributed caching. Arrays allow a group of ISA Server computers to be treated and managed as a single, logical entity. An array installation also means increased performance and bandwidth savings. Grouping your ISA Server computers in an array allows your client requests to be distributed among multiple ISA Server computers, thereby improving response time for clients. Because load is distributed across all the servers in the array, you can achieve improved performance even with moderate hardware.

Other features that enhance the scalability of ISA Server include:

- **Symmetric Multiprocessing.** ISA Server takes advantage of Windows 2000 SMP in order to use multiple processors in scaling up performance. ISA Server Standard Edition supports up to four processors on a single computer, and ISA Server Enterprise Edition supports unlimited CPUs through arrays. Unlike other products, ISA Server utilizes the extra processing power to boost performance.

- **Network Load Balancing.** ISA Server uses the Windows Network Load Balancing (NLB) Services of Microsoft Windows 2000 Advanced Server or Windows 2000 Datacenter Server to provide fault tolerance, high availability, efficiency, and improved performance through the clustering of multiple ISA Server machines. NLB is especially useful in the firewall, reverse caching (Web publishing), and server publishing deployment configurations.

Extensibility

A number of third-party vendors offer extensions to ISA Server that include features such as virus detection, content filtering, site categorization, advanced reporting, and advanced administration.

Customers and developers can also create their own extensions to ISA Server. ISA Server includes a comprehensive software development kit (SDK) for developing tools that build on the ISA Server firewall, caching, and management features. In addition, ISA Server includes sample scripts that eliminate the need for administrators to develop scripts from scratch. Instead, you can modify the sample script by specifying the desired protocols, rules, or sites that the script will use for its actions.

ISA Server Architecture

ISA Server works at various communication layers to protect the corporate network. At the packet layer, ISA Server implements packet filtering. When packet filtering is enabled, ISA Server can statically control data on the external interface, evaluating inbound and outbound traffic before it has the chance to reach any resource. Data that is allowed to pass the packet-filtering layer is passed to the Firewall and Web Proxy services, where ISA Server rules are processed to determine whether the request should be serviced.

As illustrated in Figure 1.3, ISA Server protects three types of clients: firewall clients, SecureNAT clients, and Web Proxy clients.

Firewall clients are computers that have Firewall Client software installed and enabled. Requests from firewall clients are directed to the Firewall service on the ISA Server computer to determine whether access is allowed. Subsequently, the firewall client traffic may be inspected by application filters and other add-ins. If the firewall client requests an HTTP object, the HTTP redirector redirects the request to the Web Proxy service. The Web Proxy service may also cache the requested object, or it may serve the object from the ISA Server cache.

SecureNAT clients are computers that do not have Firewall Client installed. Requests from SecureNAT clients are directed first to the NAT driver, which substitutes a global IP address that is valid on the Internet for the internal IP address of the SecureNAT client. The client request is then directed to the Firewall service to determine if access is allowed. Finally, the request may be filtered by application filters and other extensions. If the SecureNAT client requests an HTTP object, the HTTP redirector redirects the request to the Web Proxy service. The Web Proxy service may also cache the requested object or deliver the object from the ISA Server cache.

Web Proxy clients are any CERN-compatible Web applications, such as Microsoft Internet Explorer. Requests from Web Proxy clients are directed to the Web Proxy service on the ISA Server computer to determine if access is allowed. The Web Proxy service may also cache the requested object or serve the object from the ISA Server cache.

Chapter 1 Introduction to Microsoft Internet Security and Acceleration Server 2000

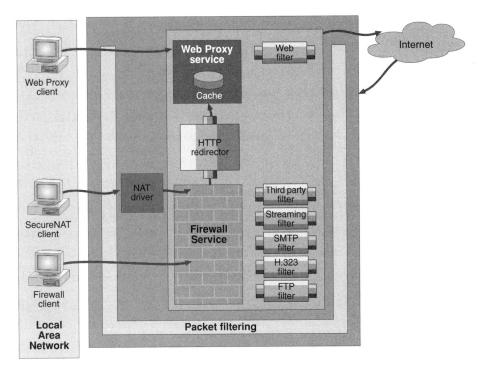

Figure 1.3 Overview of Microsoft ISA Server architecture

Table 1.2 provides an overview of the main features and benefits of ISA Server

Table 1.2 Microsoft ISA Server Features at a Glance

Enterprise Firewall Security	
Feature	**Benefit**
Stateful inspection	ISA Server dynamically and intelligently examines traffic crossing the firewall in the context of its protocol and the state of the connection to ensure integrity of communications and to prevent security breaches.

(continues)

Table 1.2 Microsoft ISA Server Features at a Glance *(continued)*

Enterprise Firewall Security

Feature	Benefit
Smart application filtering	ISA Server goes beyond basic application filtering by controlling application-specific traffic with data-aware filters. Traffic can be accepted, rejected, redirected, and modified based on its contents through intelligent filtering of HTTP, FTP, Simple Mail Transfer Protocol (SMTP) e-mail, H.323 (multimedia) conferencing, streaming media, and Remote Procedure Call (RPC).
Secure server publishing and Web server publishing	Organizations can protect Web servers, e-mail servers and e-commerce applications from external attacks through secure server publishing. ISA Server can impersonate the published server, adding a layer of security. Web publishing rules protect internal Web servers by allowing organizations to specify which computers can be accessed. Server publishing rules protect internal servers from unwarranted access by external users.
Intrusion detection	Integrated intrusion detection based on technology from Internet Security Systems (ISS) can generate an alert and execute an action if it detects a network intrusion attempt such as port scanning, WinNuke, or Ping of Death.
Integrated virtual private networking	Organizations can provide standards-based secure remote access with the integrated virtual private networking services of Windows 2000. ISA Server supports secure VPN access that can connect branch offices or remote users to corporate networks through the Internet.
System hardening	The Security Configuration wizard allows organizations to lock down Windows 2000 by setting the appropriate level of security, depending on how ISA Server functions in their network.
Streaming media splitting	Organizations can save bandwidth by splitting live media streams through ISA Server's streaming media filters. ISA can obtain information from the Internet once, then make it available locally on a Windows Media Technologies Server for access by other clients.
Firewall transparency	SecureNAT provides extensible, transparent firewall protection for all IP clients by substituting a globally valid IP address for an internal IP address, with no client software or Client configuration necessary.

Feature	Benefit
Strong user authentication	Strong user authentication is supported with integrated Windows authentication (NTLM and Kerberos), client certificates, and digest; basic and anonymous Web authentication is also supported.
Dual-hop SSL	For Web servers that require authenticated and encrypted client access, ISA Server can provide end-to-end security and firewall filtering through dual-hop SSL authentication. ISA Server verifies the client certificate from the user, inspects the data, and then presents its own server certificate to the Web server for the second authentication. Unlike most firewalls, ISA Server allows encrypted data to be inspected before it reaches the Web server.

Web Caching Server

Feature	Benefit
High-performance Web caching	Web performance is accelerated for internal clients accessing the Internet and external Internet users accessing a corporate Web server with ISA Server's fast RAM caching and efficient disk operations.
Smart caching	The freshest content can be ensured for each user thanks to ISA Server's proactive caching of popular content. ISA Server automatically determines which Web sites are used most and how frequently their content should be refreshed based on how long an object has been cached or when that the object was last retrieved. ISA Server can proactively preload that Web content into cache during periods of low network use without requiring network manager intervention.
Scheduled caching	Organizations can preload the cache with entire Web sites on a defined schedule. Scheduled downloads ensure fresh cache content for users and mirrored servers.
Distributed and hierarchical caching	With ISA Server Enterprise Edition, organizations can set up distributed content caching among an array of ISA Server computers. ISA Server further extends distributed caching by allowing them to set up a hierarchy of caches, chaining together arrays of ISA Server–based computers so clients can access the cache nearest them.

(continues)

Table 1.2   Microsoft ISA Server Features at a Glance *(continued)*

Unified Management

Feature	Benefit
Policy-based access control	Organizations can control inbound and outbound access by user and group, application, destination, content type, and schedule. Policy wizards can specify which sites and content are accessible and whether a particular protocol is accessible for inbound and outbound communication, and they can allow or block communication between specified IP addresses using the specified protocols and ports.
Multilevel management	ISA Server Enterprise Edition supports multilevel policy management through array-level access policies and enterprise-level policies. This enables administrators at branch and departmental levels to adopt governing enterprise policies and set local access rules based on their specific needs.
Bandwidth management	Organizations can save bandwidth and manage network usage by prioritizing bandwidth allocation for any specific Internet request in terms of group, application, site, or content type. ISA Server takes advantage of the Windows 2000 QoS features.
Active Directory directory services integration	Although integration with Active Directory directory services is not a requirement to deploy ISA Server, all users, rules, and configuration information can be centrally stored and managed by using Active Directory directory services. In ISA Server Enterprise Edition, Active Directory directory services allows organizations to share schema, implement caching arrays, and automatically adopt enterprise settings, access policies, publishing policies, and monitoring configurations.
Graphical taskpads and configuration wizards	Graphical taskpads and wizards simplify navigation and configuration of common tasks. For example, wizards can publish Microsoft Exchange Server–based servers on the network behind the ISA Server computer, configure ISA Server to be a VPN gateway, or create a new site and content rule.
Remote management	ISA Servers can be managed remotely by using MMC or Microsoft Windows 2000 Terminal Services, which is included in Windows 2000 Server. In addition, administrators can use command-line scripts to manage ISA services remotely.

Feature	Benefit
Logging, reporting and alerting	Detailed security and access logs are provided in standard data formats like W3C and ODBC. Organizations can run scheduled built-in reports on Web usage, application usage, network traffic patterns, and security. Event-driven alerts can e-mail administrators, start and stop services, and take automated action based on alert criteria.
User-level management	For ISA Firewall service clients, organizations can restrict access on a per-user basis, not just IP addresses, thereby enabling even more specifically targeted access control for both inbound and outbound access for all protocols.

Extensible Platform

Feature	Benefit
Broad vendor support	ISA Server supports many Internet protocols, including HTTP, FTP, RealAudio and RealVideo, Internet Relay Chat (IRC), H.323, Windows Media streaming, and mail and news protocols.
Broad vendor support	Independent vendors offer products, such as virus detection, management tools, and content filtering and reporting tools that build on and can be integrated with ISA Server. For example, organizations can use third-party filters to prevent the latest viruses, Java scripts, or ActiveX controls from being downloaded into their secured networks.
Extensive SDK	ISA Server includes a comprehensive SDK for developing tools that build on ISA Server's firewall, caching, and management features. Full API documentation and step-by-step samples are provided that can be used to build additional Web filters, application filters, MMC snap-ins, reporting tools, scriptable commands, alert management capabilities, and more.

Practice: ISA Server Overview Presentation

In this practice, you will view a 15-minute multimedia presentation that introduces the features and benefits of ISA Server. Run the program now by double-clicking on the ISA_Demo.exe file found in the \Exercises\Chapter1\ folder of the Supplemental Course Materials CD-ROM accompanying this book.

Lesson Summary

ISA Server offers an enterprise-class Internet connectivity solution that contains both a robust, feature-rich firewall and a scalable Web cache for Internet acceleration. The firewall and Web cache components of ISA Server can be deployed separately or installed together, depending on the organization's network design and requirements.

ISA Server is available in two editions designed to meet your business and networking needs. ISA Server Standard Edition provides enterprise-class firewall security and Web caching capabilities for small business, workgroups, and departmental environments. ISA Server Enterprise Edition, designed for larger organizations, provides a more scalable firewall and Web caching server through its support for multiserver arrays and multi-tiered policies.

ISA Server's advanced security features draw upon the power of the Windows 2000 security database and allow you to configure security rules based on particular traffic types for users, computers, and groups defined in Windows 2000.

ISA Server makes firewall and cache management easy through the use of its console, ISA Management. This tool centralizes and integrates server management by using the MMC and through its extensive use of taskpads and wizards, which greatly simplify the most common management procedures. ISA Server also provides powerful policy-based security management. This enables administrators to apply access and bandwidth control to any policy elements that they configure—such as users, computers, protocols, content types, schedules, and sites. Finally, ISA Server is a highly extensible platform containing its own SDK and sample scripts, which allow you to customize Internet security solutions according to the needs of your business.

Lesson 2 Introduction to the ISA Server Firewall

The Internet provides organizations with new opportunities to connect with customers, partners, and employees. While this presents great opportunities, it also opens new risks and concerns in areas such as security, performance, and manageability. As the use of the Internet continues to expand, so do the security and performance challenges. Many security problems can be addressed with the ISA Server Firewall service, which allows you to control access to and from network resources through rules based on any number of configurable policy elements.

After this lesson, you will be able to

- Describe how ISA Server provides three layers of filtering methods
- Describe ISA Server's built-in application filters
- Describe the types of packet-level or application-level attacks that can be detected by ISA Server

Estimated lesson time: 35 minutes

Filtering Methods

A firewall enhances security by using various filtering methods, including packet filtering, circuit-level (protocol) filtering, and application filtering. Advanced enterprise firewalls, such as ISA Server, combine these methods to provide protection at multiple network layers.

IP Packet Filtering

Packet filters allow you to control the flow of IP packets to and from ISA Server, as shown in Figure 1.4. When Packet Filtering is enabled (this setting can be viewed or modified on the IP Packet Filters Properties dialog box), all packets on the external interface are dropped unless they are explicitly allowed. With IP packet filtering, your system intercepts and evaluates packets before they are passed to higher levels in the firewall engine or to an application filter.

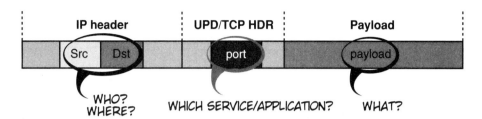

Figure 1.4 IP packet filtering

If you configure IP packet filters to allow only certain specified packets to pass through the ISA Server, you can greatly enhance the security of your network. IP packet filtering also allows you to block packets originating from specific Internet hosts and reject packets associated with many common attacks. With IP packet filtering, you can also block packets destined to any service on your internal network, including the Web Proxy service, Web server, or an SMTP server.

IP packet filters can filter packets based on service type, port number, source computer name, or destination computer name. IP packets filters are static; they apply to specific ports, and they are always either allowed or blocked. *Allow* filters allow the traffic through, unconditionally, at the specified port. *Block* filters always prevent the packets from passing through the ISA Server computer.

Note Even if you do not enable packet filtering, communication between your local network and the Internet is allowed only when you explicitly configure protocol rules that permit access.

Circuit-Level (Protocol) Filtering

You can configure circuit-level or protocol filtering in ISA Server through access policy rules and publishing rules. As shown in Figure 1.5, this feature lets you inspect sessions as opposed to connections or packets. A session can include multiple connections, which provides a number of important benefits for Windows-based clients running Firewall Client software.

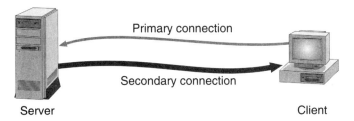

Figure 1.5 Circuit-level or protocol filtering sessions may comprise more than one connection.

Dynamic Filtering

ISA Server supports dynamic filtering through access policy rules and publishing rules. With dynamic filtering, ports open automatically only as required for communications, and ports close when the communication ends. This approach minimizes the number of exposed ports in either direction, and it provides a high level of hassle-free security for your network.

Support for Session-Based Protocols

Circuit-level filtering provides built-in support for protocols with secondary connections, such as FTP and streaming media. It also allows you to define the protocol's primary and secondary connection in the user interface without any programming or third-party tools. You can achieve this by specifying the port number or range, protocol type, Transmission Control Protocol (TCP) or User Datagram Protocol (UDP), and inbound or outbound direction.

Application Filtering

The most sophisticated level of firewall traffic inspection is application-level security. Good application filters allow you to analyze a data stream for a particular application and provide application-specific processing including inspecting, screening or blocking, redirecting, or modifying the data as it passes through the firewall. As illustrated in Figure 1.6, this mechanism is used to protect against hazards such as unsafe SMTP commands or attacks against internal Domain Name System (DNS) servers. Third-party tools for content screening, including those used for virus detection, lexical analysis, and site categorization, all use application and Web filters to enhance the functionality of your firewall.

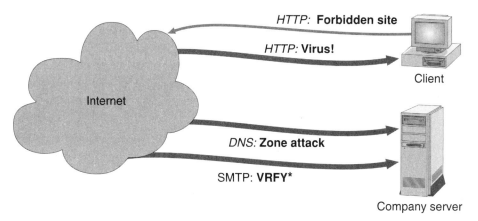

Figure 1.6 Application-level filtering

ISA Server includes the following built-in application filters:

- **HTTP Redirector Filter.** The HTTP redirector filter forwards HTTP requests from the firewall and SecureNAT clients to the Web Proxy service. This creates transparent caching for clients that do not have their browser configured to direct to the Web Proxy service.

- **FTP Access Filter.** The FTP filter intercepts and checks FTP data. A kernel-mode data pump gives you high-performance data transfer for approved traffic.

- **SMTP Filter.** The SMTP filter intercepts and checks your SMTP e-mail traffic, protecting mail servers from attack. The filter recognizes unsafe commands and can screen e-mail messages for content or size, rejecting unapproved e-mail before it ever reaches the mail server.

- **SOCKS Filter.** For clients without Firewall Client software, the SOCKS filter forwards requests from SOCKS 4.3 applications to the ISA Firewall service. The access policy rules determine whether the SOCKS client application communicates with the Internet. Unlike Winsock, SOCKS can support any client platform, including Unix, Macintosh, and non-standard computer devices.

- **RPC Filter.** The RPC filter allows sophisticated filtering of RPC requests based on specific interfaces. You select RPC interfaces to expose.

- **H.323 Filter.** The H.323 filter directs H.323 packets used for multimedia communications and teleconferencing. It provides call control, including the capability to handle incoming calls and to connect to a specific H.323 gatekeeper.

- **Streaming Media Filter.** The streaming media filter supports industry-standard media protocols, including Microsoft Windows Media Technologies and both streaming media protocols from RealNetworks, Progressive Networks Audio (PNA) and Real-Time Streaming Protocol (RTSP). It also allows users to split live Windows Media streams, thus saving bandwidth.

- **POP and DNS Intrusion Detection Filters.** These two filters recognize and block attacks against internal servers, including DNS Host Name Overflow, DNS Zone Transfer, and Post Office Protocol (POP) Buffer Overflow.

H.323 Gatekeeper

H.323 Gatekeeper works together with the H.323 protocol filter to provide full communications capabilities to H.323-registered clients that use applications compliant with H.323 Gatekeeper, such as NetMeeting 3.x. H.323 Gatekeeper provides registered clients with call routing and directory services and enables others to reach them using their well-known alias. Clients registered with H.323 Gatekeeper can use H.323 Gatekeeper to participate in video, audio, and data conferences in local area networks (LANs) and wide area networks (WANs); across multiple firewalls; and over the Internet. As shown in Figure 1.7, H.323 Gatekeeper is configured in ISA Management through the H323 Gatekeepers node.

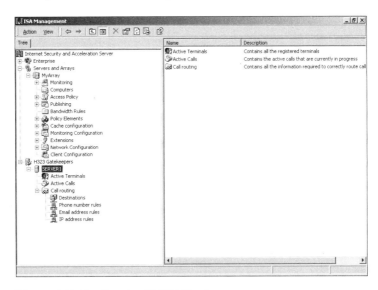

Figure 1.7 Configuring H.323 Gatekeepers

Broad Application Support

ISA Server predefines about 100 application protocols and allows administrators to define additional protocols based on port number, type, TCP or UDP, and direction. Protocols with secondary connections are supported using Firewall Client software or an application filter.

Bandwidth Rules

Bandwidth rules determine which connection gets priority over another. ISA Server bandwidth control does not limit how much bandwidth can be used. Rather, it informs the Windows 2000 QoS packet scheduling service how to prioritize network connections. Any connection that does not have an associated bandwidth rule receives a default scheduling priority. On the other hand, any connection with an associated bandwidth rule will be scheduled ahead of default-scheduled connections.

Integrated Virtual Private Networking

ISA Server helps administrators set up and secure a virtual private network (VPN). As illustrated in Figure 1.8, a VPN is an extension of a private network that encompasses links across shared or public networks like the Internet. A VPN enables you to send data between two computers across a shared or public intranet in a manner that emulates the properties of a point-to-point private link. ISA Server can be configured as a VPN server to support secure, gateway-to-gateway communication or client-to-gateway remote access communication over the Internet.

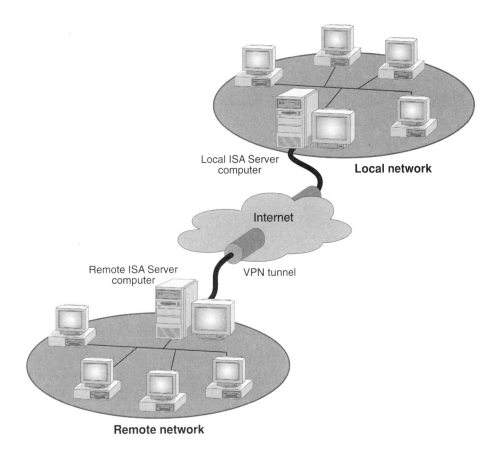

Figure 1.8 VPN integration with ISA Server

The local VPN wizard runs on ISA Server on the local network. The local ISA VPN computer connects to its Internet Service Provider (ISP). The remote VPN wizard runs on the ISA Server on the remote network. The remote ISA Server VPN computer connects to its ISP. When a computer on the local network communicates with a computer on the remote network, data is encapsulated and sent through the VPN tunnel. Windows 2000 standards–based VPN supports PPTP and L2TP/IPSec tunneling technology. A tunneling protocol, such as PPTP or L2TP, is used to manage tunnels and encapsulate private data. Data that is tunneled must also be encrypted to be a VPN connection.

Integrated Intrusion Detection

ISA Server features an integrated intrusion-detection mechanism. This identifies when an attack is attempted against your network. The firewall administrator can set alerts to trigger when an intrusion is detected. You can also specify, with alerts, what action the system should take when the attack is recognized. This may include sending an e-mail message or page to the administrator, stopping the Firewall service, writing to the Windows 2000 Event Log, or running any program or script. ISA Server implements intrusion detection at both the packet filter and the application filter level.

Note ISA Server's intrusion detection feature is based on technology licensed from Internet Security Systems (ISS), Inc., Atlanta, GA, *http://www.iss.net*.

Packet Filter Intrusions

At the packet filter level, ISA Server detects the following attacks:

- **All Ports Scan Attack.** An attempt is made to access more than the preconfigured number of ports.

- **Enumerated Port Scan Attack.** An attempt is made to count the services running on a computer by probing each port for a response.

- **IP Half Scan Attack.** Repeated attempts are made to connect to a destination computer, but no corresponding connection is established. This indicates that an attacker is probing for open ports while evading logging by the system.

- **Land Attack.** A land attack involves a TCP connection that was requested by a spoofed source IP address and port number that match the destination IP address and port number. If the attack is successfully mounted, it can cause some TCP implementations to go into a loop that crashes the computer.

- **Ping of Death Attack.** A large amount of information is appended to an Internet Control Message Protocol (ICMP) echo request/ping packet. If the attack is successfully mounted, a kernel buffer overflows when the computer attempts to respond, and crashes the computer.

- **UDP Bomb Attack.** This is an attempt to send an illegal UDP packet. A UDP packet that is constructed with illegal values in certain fields causes some older operating systems to crash when the packet is received.

- **Windows Out of Band Attack.** This means an out-of-band, denial-of-service attack is attempted against a computer protected by ISA Server. If mounted successfully, this attack causes the computer to crash or causes a loss of network connectivity on vulnerable computers.

POP and DNS Application Filters

ISA Server also includes POP and DNS application filters that analyze all incoming traffic for specific intrusions against the corresponding servers. The DNS intrusion detection filter helps you to intercept and analyze DNS traffic destined for the internal network. The POP intrusion detection filter intercepts and analyzes POP traffic destined for the internal network. The administrator can configure the filters to check for the following intrusion attempts.

- **DNS Hostname Overflow.** A DNS hostname overflow occurs when a DNS response for a host name exceeds a certain fixed length. Applications that do not check the length of the host names may return overflow internal buffers when copying this host name, allowing a remote attacker to execute arbitrary commands on a targeted computer.

- **DNS Length Overflow.** DNS responses for IP addresses contain a length field, which should be four bytes. By formatting a DNS response with a larger value, some applications executing DNS lookups will overflow internal buffers, allowing a remote attacker to execute arbitrary commands on a targeted computer.

- **DNS Zone Transfer from Privileged Ports (1-1024).** A DNS zone transfer from privileged ports (1-1024) occurs when a client system uses a DNS client application to transfer zones from an internal DNS server. The source port number is a privileged port number (between 1 and 1024), indicating a client process.

- **DNS Zone Transfer from High Ports (above 1024).** A DNS zone transfer from high ports (above 1024) occurs when a client system uses a DNS client application to transfer zones from an internal DNS server. The source port number is a high port number (above 1024) that indicates a client process.

- **POP Buffer Overflow.** A POP buffer overflow attack occurs when a remote attacker attempts to gain root access of a POP server by overflowing an internal buffer on the server.

Secure Publishing

ISA Server uses server publishing to process incoming requests to internal servers, such as SMTP servers, FTP servers, database servers, and others. Requests are forwarded downstream to an internal server, which is located behind the ISA Server computer.

Server publishing allows virtually any computer on your internal network to publish to the Internet. Security is not compromised, because all incoming requests and outgoing responses pass through ISA Server. When a server is published by an ISA Server computer, the IP addresses that are published are actually the IP addresses of the ISA Server computer. Users who request objects think that they are communicating with the ISA server—whose name or IP address they specify when requesting the object—while they are actually requesting the information from the publishing server.

For example, when you use Microsoft Exchange Server with ISA Server, you can create server-publishing rules that specifically allow the e-mail server to be published to the Internet. In this scenario, the ISA Server firewall intercepts the Exchange Server's incoming e-mail. This makes ISA Server appear as an e-mail server to clients. With ISA Server, you can filter the traffic and forward it to the Exchange Server according to whatever rules and policies you configure. Your Exchange Server is never exposed directly to external users and sits in its secure environment, maintaining access to other internal network services.

Figure 1.9 illustrates how you can use ISA Server in a similar way to publish securely to Web servers. When a client on the Internet requests an object from a Web server, the request is actually sent to an IP address on the ISA Server. Web publishing rules configured on the ISA Server forward the request as applicable to the internal Web server.

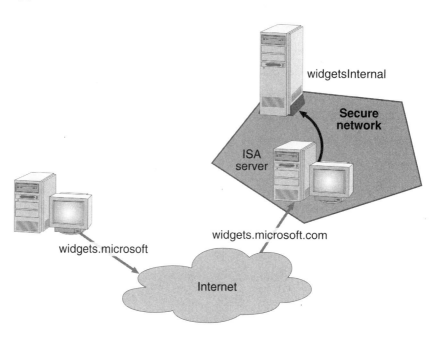

Figure 1.9 ISA Server protects internal publishing servers.

Lesson Summary

The ISA Server firewall provides filtering at three separate levels. First, through IP packet filters, ISA Server either blocks or allows a connection based on service type, port number, source computer name, or destination computer name. IP packets filters are static; they apply to specific ports, and they are always either allowed or blocked. Second, ISA Server provides session-aware circuit filtering in the form of access policy rules and publishing rules. This capability allows for dynamic packet filtering and provides support for protocols with secondary connections. Finally, ISA Server's application filters allow you to analyze a data stream for a particular application and provide application-specific processing including inspecting, screening or blocking, redirecting, or modifying the data as it passes through the firewall.

The sophisticated, multilayer nature of ISA Server's Firewall service allows you to configure powerful and flexible access control policies, intrusion detection, secure server publishing, bandwidth prioritizing, and VPN integration.

Lesson 3 Overview of ISA Server Caching

ISA Server implements a cache of frequently requested objects to improve network performance. You can configure the cache to ensure that it contains the data that is most frequently used by the organization or accessed by your Internet clients.

After this lesson, you will be able to

- Explain the difference between forward and reverse Web caching with ISA Server
- Explain how Cache Array Routing Protocol benefits an ISA Server cache server array configuration
- Describe the benefits of hierarchical caching configuration with ISA Server

Estimated lesson time: 30 minutes

High-Performance Web Cache

The Web Proxy service of ISA Server offers a cache of Web objects that fulfills client requests from the cache. If the request cannot be fulfilled from the cache, a new request on behalf of the client is initiated. Once your remote Web server responds to the ISA Server computer, the ISA Server computer caches the response to the original client request. The client then receives a response.

Fast RAM caching in ISA Server stores most frequently accessed items in RAM. It optimizes response time by retrieving those items from memory rather than from disk. ISA Server gives you an optimized disk cache store that minimizes disk access on both read and write operations. Those techniques improve response time and your overall system performance.

Forward Web Caching Server

ISA Server can be deployed as a forward Web caching server that provides internal clients with access to the Internet. ISA Server maintains a centralized cache of frequently requested Internet objects that can be accessed by any Web browser behind the firewall. Objects served from the disk cache require significantly less processing than objects served from the Internet. This improves client browser performance, decreases user response time, and reduces bandwidth consumption on Internet connections.

Figure 1.10 illustrates how users benefit when ISA Server caches objects. Although the figure focuses on a forward Web caching scenario (internal clients accessing the Internet), the process is identical for reverse Web caching, when Internet users access a corporate Web server. The following steps are illustrated in Figure 1.10.

1. The first user (Client 1) requests a Web object.
2. ISA Server checks if the object is in the cache. Since the object is not in the ISA Server cache, ISA Server requests the object from the server on the Internet.
3. The server on the Internet returns the object to the ISA Server computer.
4. The ISA Server computer retains a copy of the object in its cache and returns the object to Client 1.
5. Client 2 requests the same object.
6. The ISA Server computer returns the object from its cache, rather than obtaining it from the Internet.

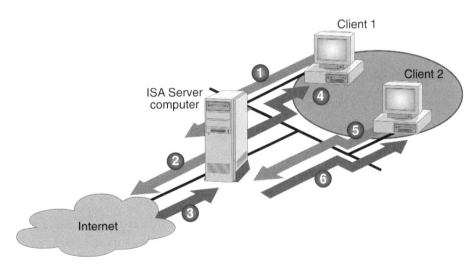

Figure 1.10 Forward caching with ISA Server

Reverse Web Caching Server

ISA Server can be deployed in front of an organization's Web server that is hosting a commercial Web business or providing access to business partners. With incoming Web requests, ISA Server can impersonate a Web server to the outside world, fulfilling client requests for Web content from its cache and forwarding requests to the Web server only when the requests cannot be served from its cache.

As illustrated in Figure 1.11, when an Internet client located in France requests an object on a Web server on the local network in France, the ISA Server computer in France checks the request. If the requested object is in the cache on the ISA Server computer in France, the object is returned to the client. The performance savings here is that the object is served from an ISA Server computer geographically closer to the requesting client.

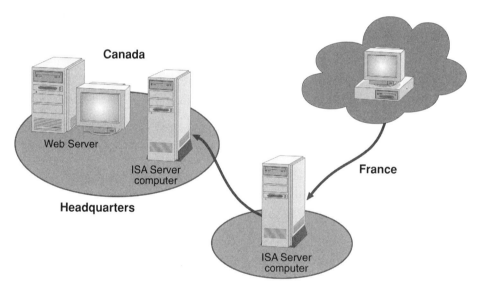

Figure 1.11 Reverse caching with ISA Server

If the requested object is not in the ISA Server computer in France, the request is routed to the ISA Server computer in Canada. If the object is not in the cache on the array in Canada, the ISA Server array in Canada retrieves the object from the Web server.

Scheduled Content Download

ISA Server extends your caching performance with a customizable cache download feature. By using the ISA Server Scheduled Content Download feature, you download the HTTP content directly to the ISA Server cache, either upon request or as scheduled. You then update the ISA Server cache with HTTP content that you anticipate will be requested by clients in your organization. This content is then available for access directly from the ISA Server cache, rather than from the Internet.

You can download a single URL, multiple URLs, or an entire Web site. When you schedule a cache content download job, you can limit which content should be downloaded, for example by limiting the download to a single domain or a certain number of links to be followed. You can also limit the download to text content only. When you schedule content download, you can configure dynamic content to be cached by configuring the ISA Server cache to store the objects, even if the HTTP cache control headers indicate that they are not necessarily cacheable. The download occurs according to a preconfigured and, optionally, recurring schedule.

Scheduled content download jobs are also configurable for outgoing Web requests and for incoming Web requests. For outgoing Web requests, you determine which objects on the Internet users most often request. You then schedule jobs that retrieve the objects from the Internet and load them into the cache. For incoming Web requests, you can schedule content download jobs that will retrieve content from your internal Web servers and maintain the content in the ISA cache.

Active Caching

ISA Server can be configured to automatically update objects in a cache. With active caching enabled, ISA Server analyzes objects that are in the cache to determine which are most frequently accessed. When popular objects in the cache get ready to expire, ISA Server automatically refreshes the content in the cache.

Active caching is a way to keep objects fresh in the cache by verifying them with the origin Web server before the object actually expires and is accessed by a client. The goal is to speed up those client accesses that would normally require a round trip to the origin server to revalidate the data. Because this involves some expense (in both proxy processing and network bandwidth), the goal is to refresh only the objects that are likely to be accessed in the future by a client.

Popularity alone is not a good criterion for determining which objects to refresh because many popular pages never expire due to clients refreshing the pages manually to keep the data updated. In addition, an object may be popular for only a short time. The active caching code tries to identify objects that precisely follow the pattern of accessed content that would be helped by active refreshing: an object that expires and then is requested again by a client.

CARP and Cache Server Scalability

ISA Server Enterprise Edition uses the Cache Array Routing Protocol (CARP) to provide seamless scaling and improved efficiency when using multiple ISA Server computers arrayed as a single logical cache. CARP uses hash-based routing to provide a "request resolution path" through an array. The request resolution path determines either exactly where in the array information requested from a browser or downstream proxy server is cached, or whether ISA Server must make a first Internet hit for delivery and caching of the requested information.

CARP also provides the following benefits:

- Because CARP provides a deterministic request resolution path, there is none of the query messaging between proxy servers that is found with conventional Internet Cache Protocol (ICP) networks, a process that increases congestion as the number of servers increases.

- CARP eliminates the duplication of content that otherwise occurs on an array of proxy servers. With an ICP network, an array of five servers can rapidly evolve into essentially duplicate caches of the most frequently requested URLs. The hash-based routing of CARP keeps this from happening, allowing all five proxy servers to exist as a single logical cache. The result is a faster response to queries and a far more efficient use of server resources.

- CARP has positive scalability. Due to its hash-based routing and, hence, its independence from peer-to-peer pinging, CARP becomes faster and more efficient as more proxy servers are added. This is in marked contrast to ICP arrays, which must conduct queries to determine the location of cached information, an inefficient process that generates extraneous network traffic. ICP arrays have "negative scalability" in that the more servers are added to the array, the more querying is required between servers to determine location.

- CARP automatically adjusts to additions or deletions of servers in the array. The hashed-based routing means that when a server is either taken off line or added, only minimal reassignment of URL cache locations is required.
- CARP ensures that the cache objects are stored with even distribution between all servers in the array, or as specified by the load factor you configure for each server.

Because of CARP's deterministic request resolution path, there is no need to maintain massive location tables for cached information. The browser simply runs the same math function across an object to determine where it is.

Because ISA Server computers in an array may have different hardware—and some computers may be more powerful than others—you may want to divide the cache load differently. For this reason, the CARP functionality is configurable: you can specify the load factor for any given server in the array.

Furthermore, CARP is configurable for both incoming and outgoing Web requests. For example, CARP can be enabled for all outgoing Web requests and disabled for all incoming Web requests.

Hierarchical Caching

With ISA Server Enterprise Edition, you can support chained, or hierarchical, caching. The term *chaining* refers to a hierarchical connection between individual ISA Server computers, or arrays, of ISA Server computers. Your client requests are sent upstream through the chain of cache servers until the requested object is found. When the object is located on an upstream server, it is cached at every server's cache, until the object is returned to the client. Chaining is an effective means of distributing server load and fault tolerance. You can arrange ISA Server computers in a hierarchy for branch office or departmental use.

Figure 1.12 illustrates a client at a branch office requesting an Internet object. The request is sent to the branch office ISA Server computer, then on to the regional or corporate headquarters before being sent to the Internet. After retrieving the object from the Internet, the ISA Server at the main office caches the requested object and returns it to the ISA Server at the branch office. At the branch office, the ISA Server caches the object and then returns it to the client. Hierarchical caching is useful in this scenario as objects are initially routed through the main office to the Internet while subsequent requests for the same object are serviced directly from the branch office ISA Server arrays.

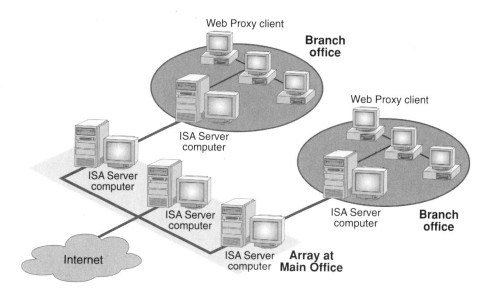

Figure 1.12 Hierarchical caching

Chained caching is significant for your business, because it enables caching to take place closer to users. For example, within an enterprise, caching can move beyond a single, central location at the edge of an organization's network and toward the branch office and workgroup levels. With an ISP, caching can move toward a regional ISP point of presence as opposed to one central ISP point of presence. In addition, chained caching provides fault tolerance, because it provides a backup route when your primary route is not working.

Web Proxy Routing

Web Proxy routing rules take the concept of chaining one step further, by allowing you to route requests conditionally, depending on the destination. For example, an organization with a branch office in the United Kingdom might set up an ISA Server computer at the branch office. The branch office array might be connected to an ISP in the United Kingdom. A routing rule on the ISA Server computer at the branch office could direct requests for Internet hosts in the United Kingdom to the local ISP, with all other requests directed to the ISA Server array at headquarters in the United States. The downstream ISA Server computer, in this example the branch office in the United Kingdom, benefits from the ISA Server cache at headquarters. This also benefits the organization with additional caching of local objects retrieved from the local ISP on the ISA Server in the branch office.

Figure 1.13 illustrates how Web Proxy requests can be routed to different servers, depending on the requested destination. Here, the ISA Server computer in the branch office routes client requests for all domestic sites to the Internet. Client requests for all other sites are routed to the upstream ISA Server computer at U.S.A. headquarters.

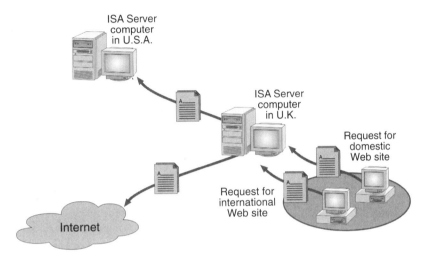

Figure 1.13 Web Proxy routing

Lesson Summary

You can use ISA Server to improve communication between your local network and the Internet. With forward Web caching, ISA Server stores data for internal clients accessing servers on the Internet. With reverse Web caching, ISA Server provides communication for external clients accessing internal publishing servers. Both scenarios can benefit from ISA Server's ability to make information more quickly available to users.

ISA Server caching also includes the following features:

- **Scheduled caching.** You can configure when the ISA Server should fetch commonly requested content from the Internet to its cache.
- **Active caching.** When this feature is enabled, objects that are accessed frequently are updated automatically during periods of low network traffic.

- **Distributed caching.** ISA Server Enterprise Edition uses CARP to enable multiple ISA Server computers to be arrayed as a single logical cache.
- **Hierarchical caching.** You can set up a hierarchy of caches, chaining together arrays of ISA Server Enterprise Edition computers, so that clients can access objects from the cache geographically nearest to them.

Lesson 4 ISA Server's Management Features

Industry research has shown that more security vulnerabilities are caused by poorly configured firewalls than by design flaws in hardware or software. ISA Server helps to avoid such risks, minimizing the difficulty in implementing a robust firewall through the use of its intuitive yet powerful management tools.

After this lesson, you will be able to

- Describe how ISA Server centralizes administration tasks and how this can improve security on your network
- Explain how managers can apply both enterprise policies and array policies to achieve flexible control of Internet access

Estimated lesson time: 20 minutes

Intuitive User Interface

ISA Management is an MMC snap-in that provides a familiar and easy-to-navigate interface for all ISA Server administration tasks. This feature lends simplicity and manageability to ISA Server administration. Graphical taskpads in ISA Management provide one-click access to common tasks, and step-by-step wizards simplify the most common management procedures.

Some of the functions that the ISA Server wizards allow you to perform include the following:

- Getting started
- Configuring local, remote, and client-to-server VPNs
- Defining a protocol rule
- Creating a site and content rule
- Creating a bandwidth rule
- Configuring secure publishing
- Configuring a mail server behind ISA Server, publishing and securing the mail server, and configuring policy for the mail services
- Securing the system with system hardening

Integrated Administration

ISA Server combines firewall and cache functions in a single product. You can integrate these functions in a single server or (with ISA Server Enterprise Edition) in an array of servers. Alternatively, you can deploy each function in a modular fashion, using separate machines for each component but sharing administration through one tool. Unified management addresses the challenge of managing both network security and Web performance. From a single interface, administrators set access policies that are applied to both the firewall and the cache, providing consistent control over Internet access.

- **Unified Policy and Access Control.** Whether deployed as a firewall, Web cache server, or both, ISA Server allows you to manage Internet access consistently by using access control policies. Access restrictions placed on the firewall are also applied to the Web cache server.

- **Unified Management.** There are benefits from using a single management interface for firewall and Web caching. The firewall and Web cache share the same logging, reporting, and alerting services of ISA Server.

The centralized administration can also mean greater security. All the administrative tasks can be performed from one computer and the configuration is applied to all, ensuring that all the servers have the same access policies configured. This is particularly useful in large organizations, where arrays can include many ISA Server computers.

Policy-Based Access Control

ISA Server allows you to define and enforce Internet usage policy for an organization. ISA Server ensures that internal and external users comply with these policies by inspecting all incoming and outgoing requests and applying access rules.

ISA Server rules use predefined, customizable, extensible, and reusable policy elements, including the following:

- **Client address sets.** IP addresses or, with Active Directory directory services, authenticated users and groups
- **Destination sets.** URLs
- **Protocols.**
- **Content groups.** For particular content types found on the Web, such as audio, video, text, or images; or more specific types, such as .wav, .mp3, .mov, or .gif

- **Schedules.**
- **Bandwidth priorities.**

You can define any of these policy elements in ISA Management, as illustrated in Figure 1.14.

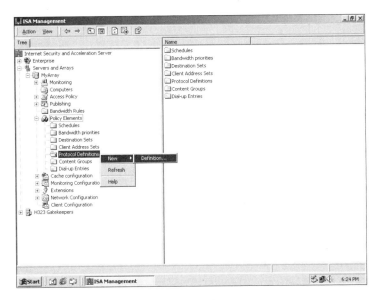

Figure 1.14 Defining a new policy element

Once policy elements are defined, you use them to create an access policy—one that consists of protocol, site, and content rules. Defining protocol rules, as shown in Figure 1.15, allows you to determine which protocols can be used for communication between the local network and the Internet. For example, a protocol rule might allow clients to use the HTTP protocol. Site and content rules define what content on which clients behind the ISA Server computer can access Internet sites. For example, a site and content rule might allow clients to access any destination on the Internet.

Figure 1.15 Configuring Access Policy through rules

In addition to configuring Internet access policy, you can configure a publishing policy for incoming requests. This consists of server publishing and Web publishing rules. Server publishing rules filter all incoming requests and map incoming requests to the appropriate servers behind the ISA Server computer. Web publishing rules map incoming requests to the appropriate Web servers behind the ISA Server computer.

Tiered Policy

ISA Server Enterprise Edition supports two levels of policy: array level and enterprise level.

Note ISA Server Standard Edition supports policy at the standalone server level only.

Array Policy

ISA Server Enterprise Edition can be installed as a standalone server or as an array member. For that array or standalone server, the *array policy* consists of its site and content rules, protocol rules, IP packet filters, Web publishing rules, and server publishing rules. Array members share the same configuration, easing management and administration. When you modify the array configuration, all the ISA Server computers in the array are also modified, including all the access policies and cache policies.

Enterprise Policy

Enterprise policy takes this centralized management one step further, allowing you to configure one or more *enterprise policies* that can be applied to the arrays in your corporate network. The enterprise policy includes site and content rules and protocol rules. The enterprise policy, as shown in Figure 1.16, can be applied to any array and can be augmented by the array's own policy.

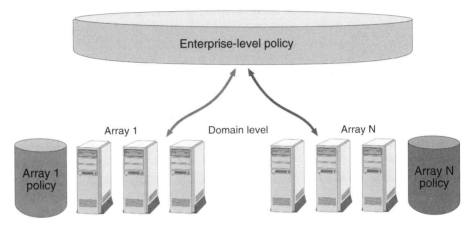

Figure 1.16 Enterprise policies can be applied to multiple arrays.

By allowing both enterprise and array policies, you ensure that a corporate policy is implemented throughout the organization. At the same time, you are able to allow configuration at the department or branch level, enabling ground-level managers to create additional rules as necessary. For example, an enterprise policy might only allow access to HTTP addresses and deny communication using all other protocol definitions. An array that uses this enterprise policy allows you to add a rule that limits who can use the HTTP protocol. The array policy cannot overwrite the enterprise policy and allow communication using other protocols.

Lesson Summary

ISA Server minimizes the difficulty in implementing an Internet firewall and cache server through the use of its intuitive yet powerful management tools. Graphical taskpads in ISA Management provide one-click access to common tasks, and step-by-step wizards simplify the most common management procedures. Centralized administration is also provided through the use of a single interface, which can result in greater security. All administrative tasks can be performed from one computer and the configuration is applied to all, ensuring that all the servers have the same access policies configured.

ISA Server allows you to define and enforce Internet usage policy for an organization through the application of rules to both predefined and customizable policy elements. By configuring both enterprise and array policies in ISA Server Enterprise Edition, you ensure that a corporate policy is implemented throughout the organization. At the same time, you are able to allow configuration at the department or branch level, enabling ground-level managers to create additional rules as necessary.

Review

The following questions are intended to reinforce key information presented in the chapter. If you are unable to answer a question, review the appropriate lesson and then try the question again. The answers for these questions are located in Appendix A, "Questions and Answers."

1. What protocol enables Web browsers to connect automatically to an ISA Server computer?

2. What is the function of the HTTP redirector filter?

3. How and when is Active Directory directory services used in ISA Server configurations?

4. What advantages does CARP provide over ICP?

5. What is the purpose of using a multitier policy approach with ISA Server Enterprise Edition?

6. What feature in Windows 2000 Advanced Server or Windows 2000 Datacenter Server benefits array performance in ISA Server Enterprise Edition?

CHAPTER 2

Installing Microsoft Internet Security and Acceleration Server 2000

Lesson 1 Planning for an ISA Server Installation 47

Lesson 2 Performing an ISA Server Installation 64

Lesson 3 Migrating from Proxy Server 2.0 78

Review 84

About This Chapter

This chapter outlines the steps necessary to complete a successful Microsoft Internet Security and Acceleration Server 2000 (ISA Server) installation. The success of your ISA Server installation depends in large part on your planning and preparedness. This chapter prepares you for an ISA Server installation by helping you assess your network needs and helping you design a network topology that best suits those needs. It also walks you through the procedures of initializing the enterprise, installing ISA Server, and creating a local address table (LAT). This chapter also introduces the key issues that an administrator should consider when planning a migration from Proxy Server 2.0 to ISA Server.

Before You Begin

To complete the lessons in this chapter, you must have

- Completed the setup procedures described in "About This Book"
- Completed all the lessons and review questions in Chapter 1, "Introduction to Microsoft Internet Security and Acceleration Server 2000"

Lesson 1 Planning for an ISA Server Installation

When you install ISA Server, you will be asked to provide information that you should have gathered in advance. You prepare for the installation by assessing your network needs and then designing a suitable network topology if one doesn't already exist.

After this lesson, you will be able to

- Determine whether installing ISA Server as a standalone server or as an array best suits your network needs
- Determine whether installing ISA Server in Firewall mode, Cache mode, or Integrated mode best suits your network needs
- Determine what hardware you need for your ISA Server configuration
- Design a network topology suitable for your ISA Server configuration

Estimated lesson time: 60 minutes

Planning your ISA Server installation requires you to weigh your network needs against the practical limitations of cost and maintenance. Specifically, you will need to decide:

- Whether you will install ISA Server as a standalone server or an array
- Whether you will use the ISA Server as a firewall, cache server, or both
- How you will connect to the Internet
- Whether you intend to include publishing servers behind your ISA Server installation
- How you will configure *or* modify your network topology in order to incorporate ISA Server
- How many computers you will need to set up your chosen configuration

Capacity Planning

You should plan the ISA Server's hardware configuration and Internet connectivity to meet the expected network load. The following sections describe recommended system configurations for various usage scenarios.

Minimal Requirements

ISA Server requires a computer running one of the editions of Microsoft Windows 2000 Server. In addition to the network adapter that Windows 2000 uses to communicate on your internal network, ISA Server needs an external network adapter, modem, or Integrated Services Digital Network (ISDN) adapter to connect to the Internet.

To meet the minimum requirements for ISA Server, you need the following hardware:

- Computer with 300 MHz or higher Pentium II–compatible CPU running Windows 2000 Server or Microsoft Windows 2000 Advanced Server with Service Pack 1 or later, or Microsoft Windows 2000 Datacenter Server operating system
- 256 MB of RAM
- 20 MB of available hard disk space
- Windows 2000–compatible network adapter for communicating with the internal network
- Windows 2000–compatible external network adapter, modem, or ISDN adapter for communicating with the Internet
- One local hard disk partition formatted with the NT file system (NTFS)

To implement array and enterprise policies, you also need Windows 2000 Active Directory directory services on your network.

Remote Administration Requirements

For remote ISA Server administration, you need only to install ISA Management, which runs on Windows 2000 Professional or any edition of Windows 2000 Server. The client computer running ISA Management for remote administration must be a member of a Windows 2000 domain in order to connect to an ISA Server computer.

Alternatively, you can run Microsoft Terminal Server on the ISA Server computer and use Terminal Client to connect remotely to ISA Server.

Firewall Requirements

ISA Server can be installed as a dedicated firewall that acts as the secure gateway to the Internet for internal clients. In this case, you will need to consider how much throughput is required for your internal clients when they access the Internet.

Table 2.1 lists hardware configurations and network connections for expected throughput for firewall clients and SecureNAT clients accessing objects on the Internet.

Table 2.1 CPU and Internet Connection Requirements

Throughput Requirements	ISA Server running on...	Internet Connection
1 to 25 MBits/second	Pentium II, 300 MHz	T1, cable modem, or xDSL
25 to 50 MBits/second	Pentium III, 550 MHz	T3 or better
More than 50 MBits/second	1 Pentium III, 550 MHz, for each 50 MBits/second required	T3 or better

Forward Caching Requirements

ISA Server can be installed as a forward Web and File Transfer Protocol (FTP) caching server that maintains a centralized cache of frequently requested Internet objects. These objects can be accessed by any Web browser client behind the firewall. In this case, you should consider how many Web browser clients will be accessing the Internet. Table 2.2 lists hardware configurations for projected numbers of internal clients accessing objects on the Internet.

Table 2.2 Memory and Disk Requirements

# Users	ISA Server Computer	RAM (MB)	Disk Space Allocated for Caching
Up to 250	Single ISA server with Pentium II, 300 MHz	256	2 to 4 GB
Up to 2,000	Single ISA server with Pentium III, 550 MHz	256	10 GB
More than 2,000	1 ISA server with Pentium III, 550 MHz, for each 2,000 users	256 per 2,000 users	10 GB per 2,000 users
	If necessary, you can use Performance Monitor to identify bottlenecks and determine whether to add servers to the array.		

If you want to use the ISA Server caching feature, you must install ISA Server on a computer that has at least one partition formatted as an NTFS volume. If your current server disk volume uses file allocation table (FAT) partitions, you can convert these partitions to NTFS by using convert.exe, which is included with Windows 2000 Server. Convert does not overwrite the data on the disk. For more information on using Convert, type **convert /?** at a command prompt.

Publishing and Reverse Caching Requirements

ISA Server can be deployed in front of an organization's Web server that is hosting a commercial Web business or providing access to business partners. In this case, you need to consider how often external clients will request objects on the publishing servers.

Table 2.3 lists hardware configurations for projected numbers of requests from Internet (external) users in a reverse caching scenario.

Table 2.3 Hardware Requirements for Various Hit Rates

Hits/Second	ISA Server	RAM (MB)
Less than 500	Single ISA server with Pentium II, 300 MHz	256
500 to 900	Single ISA server with Pentium III, 550 MHz	256
More than 900	1 ISA server with Pentium III, 550 MHz, for each 800 hits/second increment	256 per server
	You can also use Performance Monitor to identify bottlenecks and determine whether to add more servers.	

Array Considerations

If you determine that you will need multiple computers to handle your network load, consider setting up an array of ISA Server computers. Arrays allow a group of ISA Server computers to be treated and managed as a single, logical entity.

All the servers in an array share a common configuration. This saves on management overhead, since the array is configured once and the configuration is applied to all the servers in the array. Furthermore, with ISA Server Enterprise Edition, you can apply an enterprise policy to an array. This allows you to centralize management for all the arrays in your enterprise.

A unique array policy can be applied to each array in the enterprise. This can provide you with a method of dividing your organization into departments. For example, you might want to allow clients protected by one array unlimited access to the Internet and place more restrictions on clients in another array.

An array installation also means improved performance with less hardware. Arrays allow client requests to be distributed among several ISA Server computers, which increases response time for clients. Because load is distributed across all the servers in the array, you can achieve good performance even with moderate hardware.

In order to install ISA Server as an array member, the computer on which you are installing ISA Server must be a member of a Windows 2000 domain. Furthermore, the ISA Server enterprise must be initialized before you can install ISA Server as an array member. (Initializing the enterprise refers to the process of installing the ISA Server schema updates into Active Directory schema.)

If you choose not to install ISA Server as an array member, you can install ISA Server as a standalone server. If you perform a standalone server installation, the computer does not have to belong to a Windows 2000 domain.

Array Requirements

All array members must be in the same domain and in the same site. A site is a set of computers in a well-connected (reliable and fast) Transmission Control Protocol/Internet Protocol (TCP/IP) network. A domain is a collection of computers, defined by the administrator, that share a common directory (Active Directory) store. For more information, see the Windows 2000 Help.

> **Note** While it is not a requirement, using Windows 2000 Advanced Server or Windows 2000 Datacenter Server with array installations is recommended to allow for network load balancing among array components.

Standalone Servers and Single-Server Arrays

Even if you are installing just one ISA Server computer, you should consider installing it as an array member. When ISA Server Enterprise Edition is installed as an array member, enterprise policy can be applied to the array. Furthermore, an array installation means that future expansion is easier—an additional server can be added to the array with ease.

Table 2.4 compares the features of an ISA Server array to those of a standalone server.

Table 2.4 Features Comparison of an Array and Standalone Server

	Array	Standalone server
Scalability	Can have one or more array members.	Limited to one member only.
Active Directory required?	Yes. Can be installed only in Windows 2000 domains with Active Directory directory services installed. The local network can still be a Windows NT 4.0 domain.	No. Can be installed in Windows NT 4.0 domains. Configuration information is stored in the registry.
Enterprise policy	Yes. A single policy can be applied to all arrays in the enterprise.	No.

If you configure arrays, you may choose to set them up at each branch in your organization. Because each branch then has its own array, each branch can define unique usage policies that will be common to all the servers in the array.

ISA Server Mode

As part of the setup process, you select which ISA Server mode to use: Firewall mode, Cache mode, or Integrated mode.

When you use Firewall or Integrated modes, you can secure network communications by configuring rules that control communications between your corporate network and the Internet. In Firewall and Integrated modes, you can also publish internal servers, thereby sharing data on your internal servers with Internet users.

If you use Cache or Integrated modes, you can improve network performance and save bandwidth by storing commonly accessed Internet objects closer to the user. You can also route requests from Internet users to an appropriate internal Web server.

Depending on which mode you select, different features are available. Table 2.5 lists which features are available when you use Firewall and Cache modes. All the features are available in Integrated mode.

Table 2.5 Features Comparison of Firewall and Cache Modes

Feature	Firewall	Cache
Access policy	Yes	Yes, but only for HTTP protocol
Alerts	Yes	Yes
Application filters	Yes	No
Cache configuration	No	Yes
Enterprise policy	Yes	Yes
Packet filtering	Yes	No
Real-time monitoring	Yes	Yes
Reports	Yes	Yes
Server publishing	Yes	No
Web publishing	Yes	Yes

Internet Connectivity Considerations

The first step to providing Internet access is finding an appropriate Internet Service Provider (ISP). The business of providing connectivity to the Internet is quite competitive, and many access methods are now available, including Digital Subscriber Line (DSL), cable modems, satellite, bundled phone lines, and T-1 service. When deciding which of these options is best for you, consider price, data throughput, and reliability.

You can connect ISA Server to the Internet with either a direct link or a dial-up link. If you connect using a direct link or using DSL or cable modem, you must set up an external network adapter. If you connect using a dial-up link, you must use a modem or an ISDN adapter with your server.

If you are using ISA Server to publish Web servers and other servers, and plan to make these readily available to Internet clients, you must reserve static IP addresses with your ISP and register at least one domain name through a registrar accredited by the Internet Corporation for Assigned Names and Numbers (ICANN). (You can find a list of ICANN-accredited registrars at http://www.icann.org/registrars/accredited-list.html. Internet users are likely to access your internal servers by using a fully qualified domain name (FQDN), which is comprised of the computer (host) name, such as "www," plus the domain name that you have registered, such as "microsoft.com."

If you have already registered an Internet domain name, you may decide to have your ISP handle the details of how to administer the listing of your domain name in a Domain Name System (DNS) server for use by others on the Internet.

Publishing and Connectivity

When you publish internal servers, you must obtain IP addresses with which to associate the domain or server name. When external clients access your Web site or domain, the ISP's DNS server will find the IP address associated with the requested Web site name—usually an IP address on your ISA Server computer or on a perimeter network (DMZ). Alternatively, you can use an internal DNS server to resolve requests from external clients.

ISA Server in the Network

ISA Server secures and connects an existing network of services, which may be centralized on a single server or dispersed across many servers. The following sections describe network issues to consider when installing ISA Server.

Windows NT 4.0 Domain

ISA Server can be installed as a standalone server in a Windows NT 4.0 domain. In this case, no special configuration is required.

Arrays can also be used to connect and secure Windows NT 4.0 domain users and clients to the Internet. However, the array of ISA Server computers must be set up on a separate Windows 2000 domain. A trust relationship must then be established between the Windows NT 4.0 domain and the domain to which the ISA Server computer belongs.

ISA Server Configuration Data

If you install ISA Server as a standalone server, all configuration information is saved to the registry.

If you install ISA Server in an array configuration, all its configuration information is saved to the Active Directory store. In other words, ISA Server arrays require that Active Directory be installed on the Windows 2000 domain, of which ISA Server is a member.

Internet Connection Server

Before ISA Server was available, you may have used Internet Connection Sharing (ICS) to access the Internet. ISA Server replaces ICS and provides greater functionality in your organization. ISA Server provides the connectivity enabled by ICS as well as sophisticated security and caching features.

Warning Do not install or enable ICS on a computer running ISA Server. If you previously installed and enabled ICS, remove it before installing ISA Server.

Remote Access Server

Before ISA Server was available, you may have used Windows 2000 Server's remote access server to make network services and computers available to remote clients. ISA Server provides the remote connectivity and improved remote access server features with more extensive and flexible security. ISA Server packet filtering replaces the remote access server's packet filtering. ISA Server also uses the dial-up entries configured for the remote access server and extends their functionality.

ISA Server Network Topology Scenarios

ISA Server can be deployed in various network topologies. This section describes some typical network configurations. While your actual network configuration may differ from those described here, the basic concepts and configuration logic will help you plan your network topology.

Small Office Scenario

In the small office network configuration, the ISA Server computer can be placed between the corporate local area network (LAN)/wide area network (WAN) and the Internet. A small office network might have fewer than 250 clients on a single LAN segment, use the IP network protocol, and demand-dial connectivity to an ISP. A single ISA Server computer can provide Internet connectivity and security for the entire network, as shown in Figure 2.1.

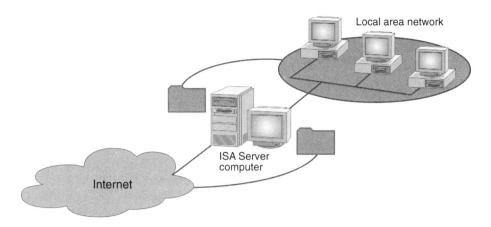

Figure 2.1 Small office scenario

The scenario depicted in Figure 2.1 is that of a small organization whose array contains just one ISA Server computer. To allow for future expansion, the server is set up as an array member.

In a slightly larger organization, you may configure an array of ISA Server computers. Assuming that most of the clients are located on a single site and in a single domain, one ISA Server array can be set up to service the entire organization. This array can contain one or more ISA Server computers, depending on bandwidth and cache requirements.

Enterprise Scenario

The scenario depicted in Figure 2.2 is that of a large corporation that has its headquarters in the United States and two branch offices, one in Canada and one in the United Kingdom. Each of the three locations has an array of one or more ISA Server computers installed. At the central office, an enterprise policy is created that defines one access policy for all clients. The network administrator at Headquarters is responsible for implementing a corporate policy and ensuring that all branch offices follow the guidelines stipulated in that policy. The Headquarters network administrator allows branch administrators to create more restrictive rules.

Enterprise Network Configuration

The branch office in Canada is connected via a router to Headquarters. The branch office in the United Kingdom is connected via a virtual private network (VPN) to Headquarters.

Figure 2.2 illustrates the network configuration for the large corporation described.

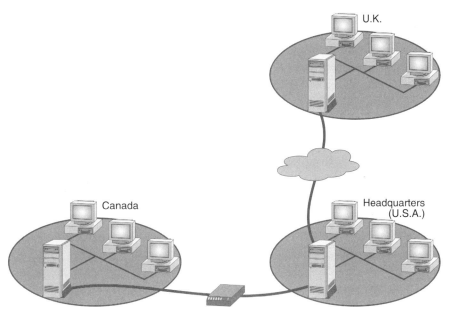

Figure 2.2 Enterprise network configuration

Each ISA Server computer that is a member of the array at Headquarters is configured with two network interfaces: one network adapter to connect to the internal network and one network adapter to connect to the Internet. For this scenario, it is possible to assume direct connectivity to the ISP through a router and a T1/E1 line, with a fallback to a backup dial-up line.

The ISA Server in the Canada office is installed in Cache mode and is chained (hierarchically connected) to the ISA Server at Headquarters. The Canada server has two network adapters, one connected to a local router and the other connected to a router at Headquarters.

The ISA Server array in the United Kingdom is set up in Integrated mode and serves as the branch's firewall and cache server. In addition, the ISA Server computers are configured so that requests for domestic Internet computers can be routed directly to the Internet.

Web Publishing Topologies

The Web publishing functions of ISA Server benefit organizations that want to publish Web content securely from within their protected intranet. For organizations that receive incoming Web requests, ISA Server can protect the Web server that is hosting a commercial Web business or providing access to business partners. The ISA Server impersonates a Web server to the outside world, while the Web server maintains access to internal network services.

The Web server that you are publishing can be located either on the same computer as the ISA Server or on a different computer.

Co-Located Web Server

Figure 2.3 illustrates another common Web publishing scenario, in which the Web server is located on the same computer as the ISA server.

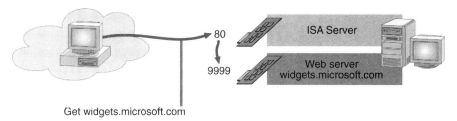

Figure 2.3 Co-located Web server

In this scenario, the ISA Server computer is configured to listen for incoming requests on port 80 of the external interface card.

However, by default, the Web server also listens on port 80 for incoming requests. To avoid the two servers conflicting, the Web server should be configured so that it listens on a port other than 80. The ISA Server Web publishing rule is then modified so that ISA Server forwards the requests to the appropriate port on the Web server.

Alternatively, you can configure the Internet Information Services (IIS) server to listen on a different IP address. You might set the IIS Server to listen on 127.0.0.1, thereby accepting requests only from the ISA Server computer.

Web Server on Local Network

Figure 2.4 illustrates a Web publishing scenario in which the Web servers are located behind the ISA Server computer.

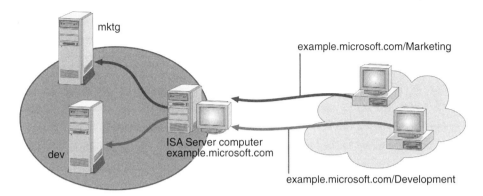

Figure 2.4 Web servers located behind ISA Server

Two Web servers are located on the internal network, which is protected by ISA Server. When an Internet user requests an object on example.microsoft.com/Marketing or example.microsoft.com/Development, the request is sent to the ISA Server computer, which then routes the request to the appropriate Web server.

Notice that when external clients request objects from the Web servers, they actually gain access to the ISA Server computer. This way, ISA Server ensures that the network is never penetrated by external users. Furthermore, the IP addresses of the Web servers are never exposed. Instead, the Internet clients gain access to Web server content from the IP address of the ISA Server computer.

Exchange Server Publishing Topologies

A common ISA Server scenario involves securing the Simple Mail Transfer Protocol (SMTP) communication of mail servers. For example, ISA Server can protect a Microsoft Exchange Server. The Exchange Server that you are publishing can be co-located on the ISA Server computer or it can be located on the local network or on a perimeter network (DMZ).

Co-Located Exchange Server

Figure 2.5 illustrates a scenario in which ISA Server and Exchange Server are on the same computer.

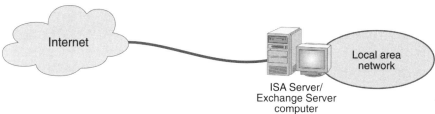

Figure 2.5 Co-located Exchange Server

Exchange Server on Local Network

Figure 2.6 illustrates a scenario in which the Microsoft Exchange Server computer is on the local network and is protected by the ISA Server computer.

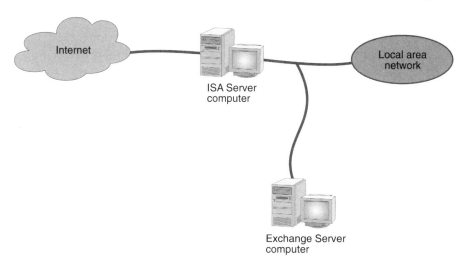

Figure 2.6 Exchange Server on LAN protected by ISA Server

Perimeter Network (DMZ) Scenarios

A *perimeter network,* also known as a DMZ, is a small network that is set up separately from an organization's private network and the Internet. The perimeter network allows external users access to the specific servers located in the perimeter network while preventing access to the internal corporate network. An organization may also allow very limited access from computers in the perimeter networks to computers in the internal network.

A perimeter network, also known as a screened subnet, is commonly used for deploying the e-mail and Web servers for the company. The perimeter network can be set up in one of the following configurations:

- Back-to-back perimeter network configuration, with two ISA Server computers on either side of the perimeter network (Figure 2.7)
- Three-homed ISA Server, with the perimeter network and the local network protected by the same ISA Server (Figure 2.8)

The perimeter network may include the company's Web server, so that Web content can be sent to the Internet. However, the perimeter network does not allow access to any other company data that may be available on computers in the local network. So then even if an external user penetrates the perimeter network security, only the perimeter network servers are compromised.

Back-to-Back Perimeter Network Configuration

In a back-to-back perimeter network configuration, two ISA Server computers are located on either side of the perimeter network. Figure 2.7 illustrates a back-to-back perimeter network configuration.

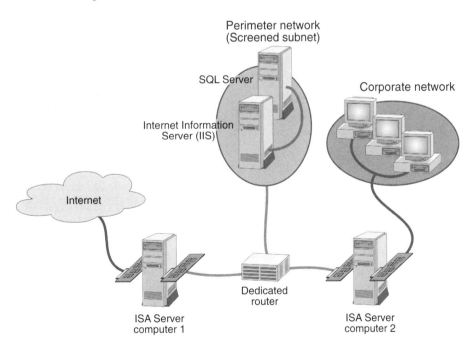

Figure 2.7 Back-to-back perimeter network

In this configuration, two ISA Server computers are hooked up to each other, with one connected to the Internet and the other to the local network. The perimeter network resides between the two servers. Both ISA Servers are set up in Integrated mode or Firewall mode, thereby essentially reducing the risk of compromise, since an attacker would need to break into both systems in order to get to the internal network.

Three-Homed Perimeter Network (DMZ) Configuration

In a three-homed screened perimeter network, a single ISA Server computer (or an array of ISA Server computers) is set up with three network cards. Figure 2.8 illustrates this perimeter network scenario.

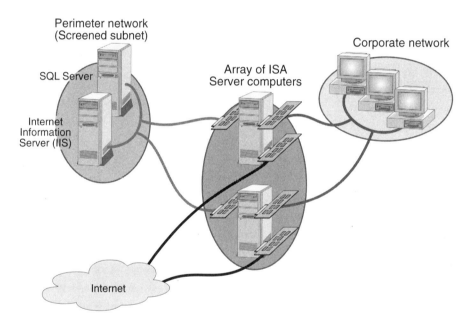

Figure 2.8 Three-homed perimeter network

Lesson Summary

You should prepare for an ISA Server installation by assessing your network needs and then designing a network topology suitable to those needs. When determining your ISA Server installation's hardware requirements, you should plan to meet or exceed the expected network load. For a firewall, you will need to consider how much throughput is required for your internal clients when they access the Internet. For caching, consider how many Web browser clients will be accessing the Internet. For publishing and reverse caching, you need to consider how often external clients will request objects on the publishing servers. After assessing your needs, you should decide whether to install ISA Server in Firewall mode, Cache mode, or Integrated mode. If you determine that you will need multiple computers to handle your network load, you should set up an array of ISA Server computers instead of one standalone server.

ISA Server can be installed in various network topologies. In the small office network configuration, a single ISA Server computer can be placed between the corporate LAN and the Internet. For a larger, distributed enterprise, separate locations may each have an array of one or more ISA Server computers installed.

For secure server publishing behind a firewall, your publishing mail or Web servers can be located either on the same computer as the ISA Server or on a different computer. If you need even higher security, you may decide to place your publishing servers within a perimeter network.

Lesson 2 Performing an ISA Server Installation

To perform a complete ISA Server installation on your server computer, you will first need to set up your network and configure connections based on your chosen network topology. If you will be using array or enterprise policies, you must also initialize the enterprise, which installs array schema information into the Active Directory store. During the actual ISA Server installation process, you will need to construct a local address table (LAT) that lists your internal network address ranges.

After this lesson, you will be able to

- Prepare your server computer for ISA Server installation
- Initialize the enterprise and describe its purpose
- Construct a LAT and describe its function
- Complete an ISA Server installation
- Troubleshoot an ISA Server installation

Estimated lesson time: 50 minutes

Before You Install ISA Server

Before you install ISA Server, you must set up the hardware and configure the software of the computer that will run ISA Server.

Setting Up the Network Adapter

You can choose to connect your network to the Internet through either a direct connection (such as T1, T3, xDSL, or cable modem) or a dial-up connection. If you choose a direct connection, you need to install and configure an external network adapter.

When you set TCP/IP properties for the external network adapter, check with your ISP for the correct settings. Specifically, you need your subnet mask and the IP addresses assigned to your external adapter, your default gateway, and your DNS servers. In some cases, your ISP may be using Dynamic Host Configuration Protocol (DHCP) for dynamic assignment of client addresses.

Typically, ISA Server will have only one IP default gateway. You should only configure the IP address of the default gateway on the external network adapter and not on the internal network adapter. Simply leave the internal card's Default Gateway setting blank.

Refer to Windows 2000 Server Help for instructions on setting up network adapters.

TCP/IP Settings

When setting TCP/IP properties for any network adapter, you should enter a permanently reserved IP address for the ISA Server computer and an appropriate subnet mask for your local network. Since the internal clients on your network will specify the ISA Server computer's address as a default gateway, and since DHCP could reset the address of the ISA Server computer, you should not use DHCP-assigned addressing for your server's internal network adapter. The external NIC's address, however, can be either DHCP-enabled or statically defined, along with the default gateway and DNS settings.

Windows 2000 identifies each adapter added to the system by the adapter's unique MAC address. You can run the ipconfig /all command to get the media access control (MAC) addresses of both network adapters on your ISA Server computer and to make sure you are configuring the correct settings on each card.

After configuring your adapters and IP addresses, you should test your connectivity to other computers by using the Ping utility. If you can successfully ping the clients on your internal network from the ISA Server computer, your internal network adapter is correctly configured. If from the ISA Server computer you can ping your upstream Internet gateway, your ISP's DNS server, or any Internet address, you have correctly configured your external network adapter. After you have verified network connectivity, you can verify name resolution by using the nslookup utility to search for the IP address associated with a Web address. For example, nslookup www.microsoft.com.

Setting Up a Modem or ISDN Adapter

If you choose to connect to the Internet through a dial-up link instead of a direct link by using an external network adapter, you must use a modem or an ISDN adapter with your server.

Depending on the ISDN adapter, you may not be able to view the two ISDN channels in Windows 2000. Typically, the drivers for the ISDN card manage bandwidth-based connectivity for the second channel; you cannot use the Routing and Remote Access console in Windows 2000 to manage the driver. Be sure that the network adapter is set up so that both channels can be configured, and that your ISP supports connecting to both channels.

Refer to Windows 2000 Server Help for instructions on setting up an ISDN adapter or modem.

Windows 2000 Routing Table

Before installing ISA Server, configure the routing table on the ISA Server computer to include all of the IP address ranges in your internal network. You can use the Windows 2000 route utility to view and configure the routing table. You can also use the Windows 2000 Routing and Remote Access console; however, you must first configure and enable Routing and Remote Access Service. Then, during installation, ISA can construct the LAT based on your Windows 2000 routing table. If the above is not done correctly, the LAT can be corrected manually at any time.

A correctly configured LAT ensures that ISA Server knows which network adapter to use in order to access different portions of your internal network. If you fail to set the routing table correctly, the ISA Server LAT may not be built correctly. This can result in a client request for an internal IP address being incorrectly routed to the Internet or being redirected through the Firewall service.

If needed, the LAT should be edited manually to include all other networks, including those across internal routers so that the ISA Server and firewall clients can correctly determine when to use ISA Server and when to go directly to a resource.

Installing ISA Server

Setup is invoked from the ISA Server Setup screen that is displayed when you insert the ISA Server CD-ROM into the drive. The ISA Server Setup screen is illustrated in Figure 2.9.

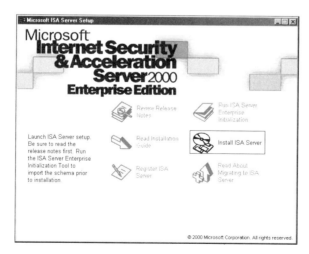

Figure 2.9 ISA Server Setup screen

- If this is the first time you are installing ISA Server as an array member, you must run the ISA Server Enterprise Initialization Tool first.
- If you are installing a standalone server, or if you have previously installed an ISA Server in your enterprise, you can select Install ISA Server.

Initializing the Enterprise

With ISA Server Enterprise Edition, an ISA Server computer can be set up as a member of an array. Before you can set up an ISA Server computer as a member of an array, the ISA Server schema updates must be installed to the Active Directory schema on the domain controller. ISA Server includes an Enterprise Initialization utility that you can use to install the ISA Server schema updates. You can access this utility on the ISA Server Setup screen, as shown in Figure 2.10.

After the ISA Server schema updates are applied, all subsequent ISA Server installations to computers in the domain use the updated Active Directory schema.

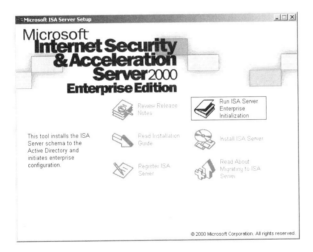

Figure 2.10 Running enterprise initialization

Note In order to install the ISA Server schema updates, you must be a member of the Enterprise Admins group. See Windows 2000 Server Help for specific instructions on user and group permissions.

When the ISA Server Enterprise Initialization Tool completes, the ISA Server schema updates will have been installed to the Active Directory schema. You can now install ISA Server as an array member, creating the array which the ISA Server should join.

Note The array creation process takes place for the first computer in the array. The information added to the Active Directory store may take some time to replicate. It is therefore recommended that you wait before creating another array.

Installation Procedure

When you install ISA Server, you will be requested to supply the following information.

Important Be sure to install Windows 2000 Service Pack 1 or later before you install ISA Server.

1. **CD Key.** This is the 10-digit number located on back of the ISA Server CD-ROM case.

2. **Installation options.** You can perform a Typical installation, Full installation, or Custom installation. Table 2.6 shows which components are installed during a Typical installation. A Full installation installs all options; a Custom installation allows you to select individual components.

Table 2.6 ISA Server Installation Options

Installation Option	Option Components	Typical Installation?	Description
ISA services	None	Yes	Controls access of network services for traffic between networks
Add-in services	Install H.323 Gatekeeper Service	Yes	Allows NetMeeting calls from the Internet or other secure networks to reach users inside your network
	Message Screener	No	Performs content screening on incoming SMTP traffic that arrives on an ISA Server

Installation Option	Option Components	Typical Installation?	Description
Administration tools	Administration Tools	Yes	Enables central management of ISA Server components and other add-on services
	H.323 Gatekeeper Administration Tools	No	Extension for ISA Management that allows you to manage how NetMeeting calls are routed within your organization and between your organization and the Internet

3. **Array selection.** If you previously initialized the enterprise, you can select which array to join. If you did not initialize the enterprise, ISA Server will be installed as a standalone server.

4. **Mode.** You can select to install ISA Server in Firewall mode, Cache mode, or Integrated mode.

5. **Cache configuration.** If you install ISA Server in integrated or Cache mode, you must configure which cache drives to use and the size of the cache.

   Figure 2.11 shows the dialog box on which you can configure cache settings.

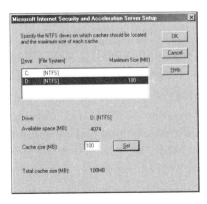

Figure 2.11 Configuring cache drives during setup

6. **Local Address Table configuration.** If you install ISA Server in integrated or Firewall mode, you must configure the address ranges to include in the local address table.

Constructing the Local Address Table

If you install ISA Server in Firewall mode or in Integrated mode, as part of the setup process, you must specify the local address table, or LAT. The LAT is a table of all internal IP address ranges used by the internal network behind the ISA Server computer. ISA Server uses the LAT to control how machines on the internal network communicate with external networks.

Typically, the LAT contains all IP addresses associated with the internal network cards on the ISA Server computer, in addition to the private IP address ranges defined by the Internet Assigned Numbers Authority (IANA). The dialog box on which to configure the LAT during Setup is shown in Figure 2.12.

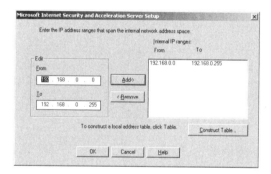

Figure 2.12 The LAT is based on the internal address ranges of your network

ISA Server can construct the LAT by basing it on your Windows 2000 routing table. You can also select the private IP address ranges, as defined by the Internet Assigned Numbers Authority (IANA) in Request for Comments (RFC) 1918. These three blocks of addresses are reserved for private intranets only and are never used on the public Internet.

The default LAT includes addresses known as *private IP addresses*. These addresses are listed in the local routing table. Because of the way ISA Server reads the routing table for Windows 2000 Server, the default LAT may not contain all your organization's addresses. You can add these addresses manually. You can also add addresses that are not part of your network as local addresses.

The LAT is maintained centrally at the ISA Server computer. Firewall clients automatically download and receive LAT updates at preset intervals. When a firewall client requests an object, the client checks the LAT. If an IP address request is in the LAT, the firewall client requests the object directly. If the IP address request is not in the LAT, the client asks the ISA Server computer to request the object on its behalf.

Secure network address translation (SecureNAT) clients do not have a local copy of the LAT. Therefore, when a SecureNAT client requests an object, the request is sent through ISA Server. If the request is to an external IP address, ISA Server makes the request on behalf of the client.

Windows 2000 Routing Table

When ISA Server constructs the LAT, it uses the Windows 2000 routing table to determine which address ranges in your internal network are internal. If you fail to set the routing table correctly, the ISA Server LAT may not be built correctly. This can result in a client request for an internal IP address being routed to the Internet or being redirected through the Firewall service. You can use the Windows 2000 routing utility to configure the routing table accordingly. Then, during installation, you can construct the LAT, based on your Windows 2000 routing table.

Default Settings

After installation, ISA Server uses the default settings that are listed in Table 2.7.

Table 2.7   ISA Server Default Settings

Feature	Default Setting
Local Address Table	This table contains entries specified during the installation process.
Enterprise policy settings	When creating a new array, the array adopts the default enterprise policy settings.
Packet filtering	This setting is enabled in Firewall mode and in Integrated mode and disabled in Cache mode.
Access control	Unless the enterprise policy settings are configured to prohibit array-level "allow" rules, a default site and content rule named "Allow Rule" allows all clients access to all content on all sites always. However, since no protocol rules are defined, no traffic will be allowed to pass.

(continues)

Table 2.7 ISA Server Default Settings *(continued)*

Feature	Default Setting
Publishing	No internal servers are accessible to external clients. A default Web publishing rule discards all requests.
Routing	All Web Proxy client requests are retrieved directly from the Internet.
Caching	The cache size is set to the size that was specified during setup. HTTP and FTP caching are enabled. Active caching is disabled.
Alerts	All alerts except the following are active: All port scan attack, Dropped packets, Protocol violation, and UDP bomb attack.
Client configuration	When installed or configured, Firewall and Web Proxy clients will have automatic discovery enabled. Web browser applications on firewall clients are configured when the firewall client is installed.

Troubleshooting ISA Server Installation

You should not encounter any problems during the actual installation process; however, if trouble does arise, first verify that your system meets the minimal system requirements. If you can rule out hardware problems and are still experiencing installation errors, check your network configuration for errors by viewing the logs in Event Viewer. For example, a faulty DNS configuration may lead to errors in enterprise initialization, and an incorrectly configured LAT may cause a setup error. Also, when initializing the enterprise, verify that you are a member of the Enterprise Admins group: this group has permission to write to the Active Directory schema.

Some problems may be caused during setup if you have been running ICS on your computer. Verify that ICS is disabled and that your computer has rebooted before attempting to install ISA Server.

Finally, if you continue to experience problems and are unable to install ISA Server on any computer, suspect a media error. In this case, contact a Microsoft representative for information about replacing your installation CD-ROM.

Practice: Installing ISA Server Enterprise Edition

In this exercise, you install ISA Server on a single computer. To allow for future scalability, you will first run the ISA Server Enterprise Initialization, which updates the ISA Server schema to Active Directory schema. This permits you to configure an ISA Server array, configure an ISA Server enterprise, and to apply multitiered policy to your firewall and cache server.

Perform both of the following procedures on the Server1 computer. (This computer should have the internal network address 192.168.0.1.)

Note ISA Server requires Windows 2000 Service Pack 1 or later. If you have not already done so, install Service Pack 1 before proceeding with this exercise.

Exercise 1: Initializing the Enterprise

In this exercise, you initialize the enterprise. The enterprise initialization process copies the ISA Server schema updates to the Active Directory schema. This allows you to configure arrays of ISA Server and to apply enterprise-level policies. Note that because Active Directory directory services does not support deletion of schema objects, the enterprise initialization process is irreversible.

▶ **To initialize the enterprise**

1. Log on to Server1 as Administrator.

2. Insert the Microsoft Internet Security and Acceleration Server 2000 Enterprise Edition CD-ROM into your CD-ROM drive.

    If the ISA Server Setup screen does not open automatically, double-click the ISA Server icon in My Computer to open it manually or locate and double-click the ISAAUTORUN.EXE file at the root of the CD-ROM.

3. Select Run ISA Server Enterprise Initialization from the Microsoft ISA Server Setup screen.

    An ISA Enterprise Initialization message box appears, warning you that the ISA Server schema will be installed to the Active Directory and that this action is irreversible.

4. Click Yes to continue.

    The ISA Enterprise Initialization dialog box appears.

5. In the ISA Enterprise Initialization dialog box, select the Use Array Policy Only radio button.

6. Select the Allow Publishing Rules check box.

   If you want to publish internal servers and make those servers accessible to external (Internet) clients, select the Allow Publishing Rules check box. If you don't select this option, no Web publishing or server publishing rules are allowed through the ISA Server.

7. Clear the Force Packet Filtering On The Array check box.

   In general, you can leave the Force Packet Filtering On The Array check box selected if packet filtering should always be enabled for the arrays in the enterprise. If you select this option, packet filtering will always be enabled for the arrays in the enterprise. The array administrator will not be able to disable packet filtering.

8. Click OK.

   An ISA Enterprise Initialization progress message box appears.

   When the initialization is complete, an ISA Enterprise Initialization message box appears, stating that the ISA Server schema has successfully extended the Active Directory schema. ISA Server can now be configured as an array member.

9. Click OK.

Exercise 2: Installing ISA Server Software

In this exercise you observe the various installation options for ISA Server and then perform a full installation of ISA Server onto the Server1 computer.

▶ **To install ISA Server**

1. With the Microsoft Internet Security and Acceleration Server 2000 Enterprise Edition CD-ROM still in your CD-ROM drive, select Install ISA Server from the Microsoft ISA Server Setup screen.

   The Microsoft Internet Security and Acceleration Server Enterprise Edition Setup window appears.

2. In the Microsoft ISA Server (Enterprise Edition) Setup message box, click Continue.

3. For the ISA Server CD key, type the product identification number listed here (**880-4486616**) and on the back of the CD sleeve provided in this book, and then click OK.

   A product ID message box appears, displaying a message about the assigned product ID.

4. Click OK.

   A license agreement message box appears.

5. Read the License Agreement and click I Agree.

   The Microsoft ISA Server (Enterprise Edition) Setup dialog box appears, displaying three installation options: Typical Installation, Full Installation, and Custom Installation.

6. On the Microsoft ISA Server (Enterprise Edition) Setup dialog box, click Full Installation.

   The Microsoft Internet Security And Acceleration Server Setup dialog box appears. This dialog box asks whether you want to install ISA Server as an array member.

7. Click Yes to install the server as an array member.

   The New Array dialog box appears.

8. In the text box of the New Array dialog box, highlight SERVER1 and type **MyArray**.

9. Click OK.

   The Configure Enterprise Policy Settings dialog box appears.

10. Click the Use Custom Enterprise Policy Settings radio button.

11. Click the Use Array Policy Only radio button.

12. Verify that the Allow Publishing Rules check box is selected and the Force Packet Filtering On This Array check box is cleared.

13. Click Continue.

    The Microsoft ISA Server Setup dialog box appears, displaying the three installation modes: Firewall, Cache, and Integrated. The Integrated Mode radio button is selected.

14. Click Continue.

    The Microsoft Internet Security And Acceleration Server Setup message box appears, warning you that the IIS publishing service is being stopped. The IIS publishing service is stopped because its default port is 80, the port standard for HTTP traffic. ISA Server uses this port to allow Web publishing and it listens for Web requests on port 80 and 8080 from both internal and external clients when Web publishing rules are created.

15. Click OK.

    A cache settings dialog box appears, prompting you to select a cache drive. By default, Setup searches for the largest NTFS partition and sets a default cache size of 100 megabytes (MB) if there are at least 150 MB available. When configuring the cache drives, you must, at a minimum, allocate 5 MB for caching. However, it is recommended that you allocate at least 100 MB and add 5 MB for each Web Proxy client, rounded up to the nearest full megabyte.

16. Use the Set button and Cache Size text box to specify a single cache location on the C: drive of 105 MB.

17. Click OK.

    An IP address range dialog box appears, prompting you to enter the IP addresses that span the internal network address space. This information is used to configure a LAT.

18. Click the Construct Table button.

    The Local Address Table dialog box appears.

19. On the Local Address Table dialog box, clear the Add The Following Private Ranges check box.

20. Verify that that the Add Address Ranges Based On The Windows 2000 Routing Table check box is selected.

21. Select the 192.168.0.1 check box appearing in the bottom pane. If any other check boxes appear in the bottom pane, make sure they are not checked.

22. Click OK.

    A Setup Message message box appears, confirming that the LAT was successfully constructed.

23. Click OK to close the message box and click OK again to continue.

    ISA Server stops services and proceeds to install the necessary files onto Server1. This process takes a few minutes. When installation is complete, the Launch ISA Management Tool message box appears.

24. Read the text appearing in the message box.

    The Getting Started wizard helps you through the first steps in the ISA Server configuration process.

25. Click OK.

    The Microsoft ISA Server (Enterprise Edition) Setup message box appears, confirming that setup has been completed successfully.

26. Click OK.

    The ISA Management console appears. Briefly navigate the Getting Started wizard by clicking Next in the details pane and reading the text that appears. Do not change any settings.

Lesson Summary

Performing an ISA Server installation requires that you first set up the hardware and network connectivity of the computer that will run ISA Server. After configuring your adapters and IP addresses, you should test your connectivity to other computers by using the Ping utility.

If you plan to set up an ISA Server computer as a member of an array, you must install the ISA Server schema updates to the Active Directory schema on the domain controller. ISA Server includes an Enterprise Initialization utility that you can use to install the ISA Server schema updates.

When you install ISA Server, you will be requested to supply the CD key, installation options, array selection, mode, cache configuration, and local address table configuration. ISA Server uses the LAT to determine which address ranges in your internal network are internal.

To troubleshoot an ISA Server installation, first verify hardware requirements and hardware functionality. If you can rule out hardware problems, verify that your network settings are properly configured, that you have proper permissions to initialize the enterprise, and that you have not been running ICS on the ISA Server computer.

Lesson 3 Migrating from Proxy Server 2.0

ISA Server introduces many new features and changes over Proxy Server 2.0. These changes affect the server configuration and upgrade scenarios. This lesson outlines the key issues that an administrator should consider as part of the migration process to Microsoft ISA Server.

After this lesson, you will be able to

- Migrate a Proxy Server 2.0 installation to a single ISA Server
- Migrate a Proxy Server 2.0 installation to an ISA Server array

Estimated lesson time: 20 minutes

Migrating from Microsoft Proxy Server 2.0

Compared to Proxy Server, ISA Server offers significantly improved features in Internet security, Web caching, management, and extensibility. In order to assist in the transfer to this advanced platform, ISA Server supports a full migration path for Microsoft Proxy Server 2.0 users. Most Proxy Server rules, network settings, monitoring configuration, and cache configuration will be automatically migrated to ISA Server. In addition, ISA Server will continue to support Winsock proxy client software, together with its own Firewall Client software, in a heterogeneous client base.

Important Make sure to perform a full backup of the current Proxy 2.0 settings prior to upgrade. To back up a Proxy Server configuration, open Internet Services Manager, right-click the server icon of the server you want to back up, and select Backup/Restore Configuration.

Operating System Considerations

ISA must be installed on Windows 2000 Server or Windows 2000 Advanced Server with Service Pack 1 or later, or Microsoft Windows 2000 Datacenter Server operating system.

Proxy Server on Windows 2000

To migrate to ISA Server on a Windows 2000 computer that is already running Proxy Server 2.0, simply perform an ISA Server installation, and the setup program will recognize an older version of ISA Server installed. This dialog box is shown in Figure 2.13. Click OK to replace the previous version.

Chapter 2 Installing Microsoft Internet Security and Acceleration Server 2000

Figure 2.13 Replacing the previous version of ISA Server

Then, when Setup asks whether you want to migrate your Proxy Server 2.0 settings and policy into an ISA Server policy, click Yes. This message box is shown in Figure 2.14.

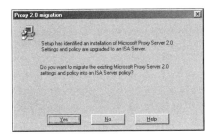

Figure 2.14 Migrating from Proxy Server 2.0

Proxy Server on Windows NT 4.0

If your current version of Microsoft Proxy Server 2.0 is installed on Windows NT 4.0, follow these steps:

1. Stop and disable all Proxy Server services, by typing **net stop** *service_name* at a command line. The services that need to be stopped are listed in Table 2.8.

   Table 2.8 Proxy Server Services

Display Name	Service Name
Microsoft Winsock Proxy Service	Wspsrv
Microsoft Proxy Server Administration	Mspadmin
Proxy Alert Notification Service	Mailalrt
World Wide Web Publishing Service	w3svc

2. Upgrade to Windows 2000 Server or later. You may receive a message indicating that Proxy Server will not work on Windows 2000. This message can be safely ignored.

3. You can now begin ISA Server setup.

   Since the core services required for firewall operation are inactive during setup, it is recommended that the computer being upgraded be disconnected from the Internet for the duration of the installation.

   Note Direct upgrade from Proxy Server 1.0, BackOffice Server 4.0 or Small Business Server 4.0 is not supported.

   ISA Server does not support the IPX protocol.

   Warning There is no automatic option to return to Proxy Server 2.0 once the upgrade to ISA Server has been started.

Proxy Server 2.0 Array Considerations

When you migrate Microsoft Proxy Server 2.0 to ISA Server, you can install the ISA Server computer as an array member or a standalone server.

If you migrate the Proxy Server to a standalone server, most of the rules and other configuration elements previously created for Proxy Server are also migrated. If you migrate to a new array, the ISA Server enterprise policy default settings determine how the Proxy Server rules are migrated.

Before you migrate an array of Proxy Server computers, remove all the members. Each member will retain an identical set of rules, which was replicated to all the servers in the array. Similarly, all the servers will retain identical network configurations (such as dial-on-demand settings) and monitoring configurations (such as alerts).

After you remove the servers from the array, you can migrate each Proxy Server to ISA Server. To retain a similar array configuration, perform the following steps:

1. During setup of the first server migrating from Proxy Server 2.0, create a new array.

2. During setup of each subsequent server, migrate all proxy servers to this array.

Migrating to an Array

You can migrate a single Proxy Server computer to a new array of ISA Server computers. In this case, the configuration information is migrated to the ISA Server array in different ways, depending on the ISA Server array's default enterprise settings.

Unlike Proxy Server, ISA Server can be configured to use an enterprise policy only, an array policy only, or a combination of both. Depending on the enterprise policy settings, Proxy Server rules are migrated differently. Table 2.9 lists the possible enterprise settings and details how the Proxy Server policy is migrated for each setting.

Table 2.9 Settings Migrated from Proxy Server 2.0

Enterprise Policy Settings	Enterprise Administrator Permissions	ISA Server migrates…
Use array policy only	Yes/No	…all the existing Proxy Server rules to the array policy.
Use enterprise policy only	Yes	…all the existing Proxy Server rules. Enterprise policy settings for the new array are configured to use array policy only.
Use enterprise policy only	No	… none of the Proxy Server rules. The new array uses only the enterprise policy.
Use enterprise and array policy	Yes	…all the existing Proxy Server rules. Enterprise policy settings for the new array are configured to use array policy only.
Use enterprise and array policy	No	…only the Proxy Server rules that can be migrated to deny rules (domain filters and not protocols). Enterprise policy settings for the new array are configured to use the enterprise policy, together with the (more restrictive) array policy.

If the enterprise policy allows publishing rules, the Proxy Server publishing settings are migrated to the array policy.

If the enterprise policy does not allow publishing rules, then if you have enterprise administrator permissions, the enterprise policy settings are changed so that publishing rules are allowed. The proxy server publishing settings are then migrated to the array policy.

Migrating Proxy Server 2.0 Configuration

Most Proxy Server rules, network settings, monitoring configuration, and cache configuration will be migrated to ISA Server. This section describes how the configuration information is migrated.

Proxy Chains

Mixed chains of Proxy 2.0 and ISA Servers are supported.

Web Proxy Client Requests

Whereas Proxy 2.0 listens for client HTTP requests on port 80, ISA Server is configured upon installation to listen on port 8080. Therefore, all downstream chain members (or browsers) connecting to this ISA Server must connect to port 8080. Alternatively, you can configure ISA to listen on port 80.

Publishing

Proxy Server 2.0 requires that you configure publishing servers as Winsock Proxy clients. ISA Server allows you to publish internal servers, without requiring any special configuration or software installation on the publishing server. Instead, the ISA Server treats the publishing servers as SecureNAT clients. Web publishing rules and server publishing rules, configured on the ISA Server, make the servers securely accessible to specific external clients. No additional configuration is required on the publishing server.

Cache

The Proxy Server cache configuration is migrated to the ISA Server, including cache drive specifications, size, and all other properties.

Proxy 2.0 cache content will not be migrated due to the vastly different cache storage engine in ISA Server. It will be deleted as part of ISA Server setup and the new storage engine will be instituted based on existing cache and drive settings.

Note Depending on the cache size and content, the deletion process may take some time.

SOCKS

ISA Server includes a SOCKS application filter, which allows client SOCKS applications to communicate with the network, using the applicable array or enterprise policy to determine if the client request is allowed. Migration of Proxy 2.0 SOCKS rules to ISA Server policy is not supported.

Rules and Policies

Table 2.10 lists how Proxy Server rules and other configuration information are migrated on the ISA Server computer:

Table 2.10 Migrating Configuration Information to ISA Server

Proxy Server 2.0	ISA Server
Domain filters	Site and content rules
Winsock permission settings	Protocol rules
Publishing properties	Web publishing rules
Static packet filters	Allow or block IP packet filters
Web Proxy routing rules	Routing rules

Policy elements are created, as necessary, for the new rules. Additional configuration information is also migrated: LAT, automatic dial settings, alerts, log settings, and client configurations.

Lesson Summary

ISA Server extends the functionality of Proxy Server 2.0 by providing more powerful security, caching, management, and extensibility features. If you are already running Proxy Server 2.0 on your system, you can choose to migrate to ISA Server instead of performing a clean installation. A migration will allow you to preserve most of your configuration in the new ISA Server installation, including Proxy Server rules, policy elements, network settings, monitoring configuration, and cache configuration. Cache content, however, will not be migrated.

You can migrate a Proxy Server installation to either a standalone ISA Server computer or to a new array of ISA Server computers. If you want to migrate an array of Proxy Server computers to an ISA Server array, first remove all the members, create an ISA Server array during installation, and then add all subsequent Proxy Server computers to that array. If you migrate a single Proxy Server computer to a new array of ISA Server computers, the configuration information is migrated to the ISA Server array in different ways, depending on the ISA Server array's default enterprise settings. Policy elements are created, as necessary, for the new rules.

Review

The following questions are intended to reinforce key information presented in the chapter. If you are unable to answer a question, review the appropriate lesson and then try the question again. The answers for these questions are located in Appendix A, "Questions and Answers."

1. What hardware recommendations for processor speed, RAM, and hard drive capacity would you make for an ISA Server installation planned to run in Integrated mode and expected to receive 500 to 900 hits per second and to serve up to 2,000 users in your organization?

2. What are the requirements for installing ISA Server as an array?

3. What is the benefit of a perimeter network?

4. What measures must be taken to allow ISA Server to be co-located with a Web server?

5. What is the function of the LAT?

6. What measures must be taken to allow Web browsers of cache server clients to connect to an ISA server after a migration from proxy server?

CHAPTER 3

Configuring Secure Internet Access

Lesson 1 Configuring Local Clients for Secure Internet Access 87

Lesson 2 Configuring ISA Server Dial-up Connections 103

Lesson 3 Configuring Automatic Discovery of ISA Server 112

Lesson 4 Troubleshooting ISA Server Client Connectivity 120

Review 127

About This Chapter

Once you have installed Microsoft Internet Security and Acceleration Server 2000 (ISA Server) as a firewall, all Internet access for your client computers will be blocked by default. This chapter guides you through the steps of configuring secure Internet access for these clients. These steps include assessing your client requirements, determining whether to install Firewall Client software, configuring your network's Web browsers to use the ISA Server as a proxy, and creating a protocol rule allowing Internet traffic to pass through the firewall dynamically, or only as needed. Configuring client access may also entail configuring ISA Server's Automatic Discovery feature, which allows clients to connect automatically to an ISA Server on the network, and configuring a dial-up entry in ISA Server. This chapter also outlines methods and tools for troubleshooting client connectivity.

Before You Begin

To complete the lessons in this chapter, you must have

- Met the requirements as outlined in "About This Book" so that Server1 is configured with an IP address of 192.168.0.1 and Server2 is configured with an IP address of 192.168.0.2. Server1 must also have established a dial-up connection to the Internet.

- Completed the exercise in Chapter 2 so that Server1 has ISA Server installed, in Integrated mode, as an array named MyArray.

Lesson 1 Configuring Local Clients for Secure Internet Access

After you install ISA Server, you can begin to configure Internet access for the client computers. For all client requests, ISA Server processes the request by analyzing access policy rules to determine whether access is allowed. If the client request is allowed, ISA Server dynamically opens and closes the ports required for the communication.

Establishing secure Internet access for local clients requires that you first decide whether to configure your internal clients as secure network address translation (SecureNAT) clients or firewall clients. You can then configure the Web browsers on your client computers to use the ISA Server Web Proxy service. Finally, once your clients are configured, you must create protocol rules in ISA Server that allow Internet protocols to pass through the firewall.

After this lesson, you will be able to

- Describe the differences in features and configuration requirements among SecureNAT, Firewall, and Web Proxy clients
- Configure client computers for secure Internet access through ISA Server
- Configure Microsoft Internet Explorer to use the ISA Server Web Proxy service
- Install Firewall Client software on the client computer

Estimated lesson time: 60 minutes

About ISA Server Clients

ISA Server supports the following three types of clients.

- **Firewall clients** are client computers that have the Firewall Client software installed and enabled.
- **SecureNAT clients** are client computers that do not have the Firewall Client software installed.
- **Web Proxy clients** are client Web applications configured to use ISA Server.

Table 3.1 compares these ISA Server client types.

Table 3.1 Comparison of ISA Server Clients

Feature	SecureNAT client	Firewall client	Web Proxy client
Installation required?	No, but some network configuration changes required	Yes	No, requires Web browser configuration
Operating system support	Any operating system that supports Transmission Control Protocol/Internet Protocol (TCP/IP)	Only Windows platforms	All platforms, but by way of Web application
Protocol support	Requires application filters for multi-connection protocols	All Winsock applications	Hypertext Transfer Protocol (HTTP), Secure HTTP (S-HTTP), File Transfer Protocol (FTP), and Gopher
User-level authentication	No	Yes	Yes
Server applications	No configuration or installation required	Requires configuration file	N/A

Firewall Client computers and SecureNAT client computers may also be Web Proxy clients. This is because all Web Proxy client sessions (in other words, Web requests initiated from any browser configured to use the ISA Server as a proxy) are sent directly to the Web Proxy service. All other network requests, whether Firewall Client sessions or SecureNAT client sessions, are sent directly to the Firewall service on ISA Server.

Assessing Client Requirements

Before you deploy or configure client software, assess the needs of your organization. Determine which applications and services your internal clients require. Decide how you will be publishing servers. Then see how the different client types supported by ISA Server can meet these needs.

Essentially, your choice for each client computer is whether to install Firewall Client software on the computer, or whether simply to configure the client as a SecureNAT client. Table 3.2 displays some of the conditions under which you may favor one or the other client type.

Note Configuring Internet access will not establish Internet access for the ISA Server computer itself. To achieve this, you need to create IP packet filters, which are discussed in Chapter 4.

Table 3.2 Choosing ISA Server Client Type

Network need	Recommended client type	Reason
You want to avoid deploying client software or configuring client computers.	SecureNAT	SecureNAT clients do not require any software or specific configuration. Firewall clients require that you deploy Firewall Client software.
You are using ISA Server only for the forward caching of Web objects.	SecureNAT	If you use SecureNAT clients in this scenario, you will not have to deploy any special software or configure your client computers. Instead, client requests are transparently passed to the ISA Server Firewall service and then on to the Web Proxy service for caching.
You want to create user-based access rules to control non-Web Internet access.	Firewall Client	If you use firewall clients, you can configure user-based access policy rules for non-Web Internet sessions. You can always configure user-based rules for Web Proxy clients on both SecureNAT and Firewall Client computers. However, these rules will be effective only if you configure ISA Server to require Web applications to include authentication information with each session.

(continues)

Table 3.2 Choosing ISA Server Client Type *(continued)*

Network need	Recommended client type	Reason
You are publishing servers that are located on your internal network.	SecureNAT	Internal servers can be published as SecureNAT clients. This eliminates the need for creating special configuration files on the publishing server. Instead, you simply create a server publishing rule on the ISA Server.
Your network supports roaming computers and users.	Firewall Client	SecureNAT clients do not support automatic discovery of ISA Server. When you configure automatic discovery, all Web Proxy and firewall clients automatically discover an appropriate ISA Server computer. In this way, roaming clients can connect to the ISA Server computer as appropriate and when necessary.
Your clients need access (outside of Web browsers) to protocols with secondary connections such as FTP.	Firewall Client	SecureNAT clients do not support protocols with secondary connections.
You want to support dial-on-demand for non-Web sessions from your clients.	Firewall Client	Though Web Proxy sessions support automatic dial-out on both SecureNAT and Firewall client computers, only Firewall Client supports dial-on-demand for non-Web sessions.

Configuring SecureNAT Clients

SecureNAT clients do not require specific software to be deployed on the client computers. However, you must consider your network topology and ensure that the ISA Server computer can service requests from the client computers.

Specifically, the default gateway for the SecureNAT clients must be properly configured. When setting the default gateway property, identify which of the following two types of network topology you are configuring:

- **Simple network.** A simple network topology does not have any routers configured between the SecureNAT client and the ISA Server computer.
- **Complex network.** A complex network topology has one or more routers connecting multiple subnets that are configured between a SecureNAT client and the ISA Server computer.

Configuring SecureNAT Clients on a Simple Network

To configure SecureNAT clients on a simple network, you should set the SecureNAT client's default gateway settings to the IP address of the ISA Server computer's internal network address card. You can set this manually, using the Transmission Control Protocol/Internet Protocol (TCP/IP) settings on the client. (These settings can be configured by clicking the Network icon in Control Panel.) Alternatively, you can configure these settings automatically for the client using the Dynamic Host Configuration Protocol (DHCP) service.

Configuring SecureNAT Clients on a Complex Network

To configure SecureNAT clients on a complex network, you should set the default gateway settings to the last router in the chain between the SecureNAT client and the ISA Server computer. In this case, you do not have to change the default gateway settings for the SecureNAT clients.

Optimally, the router should use a default gateway that routes traffic along the shortest path to the ISA Server computer. Also, the router should not be configured to discard packets destined for addresses outside the corporate network; ISA Server determines how to route the packets.

Additional SecureNAT Configuration for Dial-up Networks

For both simple and complex networks relying upon a dial-up connection to the Internet, SecureNAT clients require additional configuration. To establish Internet access outside of a Web browser from a client computer that does not have Firewall Client installed, you must first create a dial-up entry policy element in ISA Management, and then you need to configure the Network Configuration node properties to use that dial-up entry when routing to upstream servers. This is discussed in more detail in Lesson 2 of this chapter.

Resolving Names for SecureNAT Clients

SecureNAT clients will probably request objects both from computers in the local network and from the Internet. Thus, SecureNAT clients require Domain Name System (DNS) servers that can resolve names both for external and internal computers.

Internet Access Only

If your SecureNAT clients require Internet access only and do not need to resolve DNS names internal to your network, you should configure the TCP/IP settings for these clients to use external (Internet-based) DNS servers. You then need to create a protocol rule allowing the clients to use a DNS Query operation.

Internal Network and Internet Access

If SecureNAT clients will request data both from the Internet and from internal network servers, the clients should use a DNS server located on the internal network. You should configure the DNS server to resolve both internal addresses and Internet addresses. Alternatively, you can configure the clients' TCP/IP properties to recognize an external DNS server as the preferred server and your internal DNS server as an alternate DNS server.

Firewall Clients

A firewall client is a computer with Firewall Client software installed and enabled. The firewall client runs Winsock applications that use ISA Server's Firewall service. When a firewall client uses a Winsock application to request an object from a computer, the client checks its copy of the local address table (LAT) to see whether the specified computer is in the LAT. If the computer is not in the LAT, the request is sent to the ISA Server Firewall service. The firewall service handles the request and forwards it to the appropriate destination as permissions allow. Firewall Client software can send Windows user information, which is required for authentication purposes, to the ISA Server.

After installing the client software, you can modify the server name to which the client connects by specifying a different name either on the ISA Server computer to which the client currently connects or by changing the name in the Firewall Client software. The configuration changes take effect after the firewall configuration is refreshed. To centrally manage the Firewall Client software configuration, modify Firewall Client properties from the Client Configuration node in ISA Management. This node includes centralized configuration control for both the Firewall Client software and the firewall client's Web browser settings.

As shown in Figure 3.1, the ISA Server computer contains a network share named mspclnt to which a client computer can connect over the local network. This share contains the installation program, which you can use to install the Firewall Client software onto your client computer. You can install Firewall Client software on client computers that run Microsoft Windows ME, Windows 95, Windows 98, Windows NT 4.0, or Windows 2000. 16-bit Winsock applications are supported, but only on Windows 2000 and Windows NT 4.0. After you install and enable the Firewall Client software, the computer functions as a firewall client.

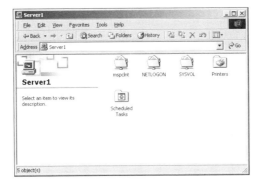

Figure 3.1 The network share mspclnt contains the Firewall Client setup files.

▶ **Follow these steps to install Firewall Client software:**

1. At a command prompt on the client computer, type:

    Path**Setup**

    where *path* is the path to the shared ISA Server client installation files.

    Note The ISA Server client installation files are located in a folder on the ISA Server computer with the share name *ISA_Server_name*\MSPClnt.

2. Follow the on-screen instructions.

    Note Do not install Firewall Client software on the ISA Server computer.

Firewall Client Application Settings

Installing the Firewall Client software does not automatically configure individual Winsock applications. Instead, the client software uses the same Winsock dynamic link library (.dll) that the other applications use. The firewall client then intercepts the application calls and decides whether to route the request to the ISA Server computer.

In processing Winsock requests, the Firewall Client application looks for a Wspcfg.ini file in the directory where the client Winsock application is installed. If this file is found, it looks for a [*WSP_Client_App*] section, where *WSP_Client_App* is the name of the Winsock application without the .exe extension. If this section does not exist, the Firewall Client application next looks for the [Common Configuration] section. If this section also does not exist, it looks for the same sections in the Mspclnt.ini file. The first section, and only that section, found by using this search method is used to apply the application-specific configuration settings.

Advanced Client Configuration

For most Winsock applications, the default Firewall Client configuration works with no need for further modification. However, in some cases, you will need to add client configuration information. You can store the client configuration information in one of the following two locations:

- **Mspclnt.ini.** This is the global client configuration file, which is located in the Firewall Client installation folder. The Mspclnt.ini file is periodically downloaded by the client from the ISA Server computer and overwrites previous versions. Consequently, you can make configuration changes at the ISA Server computer and the settings will automatically be downloaded to the client computers.

    Make configuration changes in ISA Management from the Client Configuration node. In the details pane, access the properties of the firewall client. In the Firewall Client Properties dialog box, click the Application Settings tab, then create, edit or delete application settings. Firewall clients periodically download these settings.

- **Wspcfg.ini.** This file is located in a specific client application folder. The ISA Server computer does not overwrite this file. Consequently, if you can make configuration changes in this file, they will apply only to the specific client.

Sample Wspcfg.ini File

The following is a sample [*WSP_Client_App*] section in a client configuration file for the WSP Client App.exe section:

```
[WSP_Client_App]
Disable=0
NameResolution=R
LocalBindTcpPorts=7777
LocalBindUdpPorts=7000-7022, 7100-7170
RemoteBindTcpPorts=30
RemoteBindUdpPorts=3000-3050
ServerBindTcpPorts=100-300
ProxyBindIp=80:110.52.144.103, 82:110.51.0.0
KillOldSession=1
Persistent=1
ForceProxy=i:172.23.23.23
ForceCredentials=1
NameResolutionForLocalHost=L
```

Table 3.3 describes the entries that can be placed in a configuration file for a Winsock application.

Table 3.3 Firewall Client Configuration Entries for Winsock Applications

Entry	Description
Disable	Possible values: 0 or 1. When the value is set to 1, the Firewall service is disabled for the specific client application.
NameResolution	Possible values: L or R. By default, dotted decimal notation or Internet domain names are redirected to the ISA Server computer for name resolution and all other names are resolved on the local computer. When the value is set to R, all names are redirected to the ISA Server computer for resolution. When the value is set to L, all names are resolved on the local computer.
LocalBindTcpPorts	Specifies a TCP port, list, or range that is bound locally.
LocalBindUdpPorts	Specifies a UDP port, list, or range that is bound locally.
RemoteBindTcpPorts	Specifies a TCP port, list, or range that is bound remotely.
RemoteBindUdpPorts	Specifies a UDP port, list, or range that is bound remotely.
ServerBindTcpPorts	Specifies a TCP port, list, or range for all ports that should accept more than one connection.

(continues)

Table 3.3 Firewall Client Configuration Entries for Winsock Applications *(continued)*

Entry	Description
ProxyBindIp	Specifies an IP address or list that is used when binding with a corresponding port. Use this entry when multiple servers that use the same port need to bind to the same port on different IP addresses on the ISA Server computer. The syntax of the entry is: ProxyBindIp=[*port*]:[*IP address*], [*port*]:[*IP address*] The port numbers apply to both TCP and UDP ports.
KillOldSession	Possible values: 0 or 1. When the value is set to 1, it specifies that, if the ISA Server computer holds a session from an old instance of an application, that session is terminated before the application is granted a new session. This option is useful, for example, if an application crashed or did not close the socket on which it was listening. By closing the old session, ISA Server immediately discovers that the application was terminated and can immediately release the port used by the old session.
Persistent	Possible values: 0 or 1. When the value is set to 1, a specific server state can be maintained on the ISA Server computer if a service is stopped and restarted and if the server is not responding. The client sends a keep-alive message to the server periodically during an active session. If the server is not responding, the client tries to restore the state of the bound and listening sockets upon server restart.
ForceProxy	Used to force a specific ISA Server computer for a specific Winsock application. The syntax of the entry is: ForceProxy=[*Tag*]:[*Entry*] where *Tag* equals i for an IP address or n for a name. *Entry* equals the address or the name. If the n tag is used, the Firewall service only works over IP.
ForceCredentials	Used when running a Windows NT or Windows 2000 service or server application as a Firewall client application. When the value is set to 1, it forces the use of alternate user authentication credentials that are stored locally on the computer that is running the service. The user credentials are stored on the client computer using the Credtool.exe application that is provided with the Firewall Client software. User credentials must reference a user account that can be authenticated by ISA Server, either local to ISA Server or in a domain trusted by ISA Server. The user account is normally set not to expire; otherwise, user credentials need to be renewed each time the account expires.

Entry	Description
NameResolutionForLocalHost	Possible values are L (default), P, or E. Used to specify how the local (client) computer name is resolved, when the gethostbyname API is called.
	The LocalHost computer name is resolved by calling the Winsock API function gethostbyname() using the LocalHost string, an empty string, or a NULL string pointer. Winsock applications call gethostbyname(LocalHost) to find their local IP address and send it to an Internet server. When this option is set to L, gethostbyname() returns the IP addresses of the local host computer. When this option is set to P, gethostbyname() returns the IP addresses of the ISA Server computer. When this option is set to E, gethostbyname() returns only the external IP addresses of the ISA Server computer—those IP addresses that are not in the LAT.
ControlChannel	Possible Values: Wsp.udp (default) or Wsp.tcp. Specifies the type of control-channel used.

Web Proxy Service

The Web Proxy service (w3proxy) is a Windows 2000 service that supports requests from any Web browser. This provides nearly every desktop operating system, including Windows NT, Microsoft Windows 95, Windows 98, Windows 2000, Macintosh, and UNIX with Web access. The Web Proxy service works at the application level on behalf of a client requesting an Internet object that can be retrieved by using one of the protocols supported by the Web Proxy: File Transfer Protocol, Hypertext Transfer Protocol, and Gopher protocol. The Web Proxy service also supports the Secure HTTP (S-HTTP) protocol for secure sessions that use Secure Sockets Layer (SSL) connections.

Web Proxy clients—typically, browsers—must be specifically configured to use the ISA Server computer. When a user requests a Web site, the browser parses the Uniform Resource Locator (URL). If a dot address is used, as in a fully qualified domain name or IP address, the browser considers the destination to be remote and sends the HTTP request to the ISA Server computer for processing.

You can use ISA Management to monitor Web Proxy service status. Similarly, you can use ISA Management to stop or start the Web Proxy service. Monitoring and Service Control is available from the Monitoring node.

When you stop the Web Proxy service, the information in the cache is not deleted. However, when you restart the Web Proxy service, several seconds may pass before the cache is fully enabled and functional. If the Web Proxy service has crashed, ISA Server restores the information in the cache. This takes some time, and performance may not be optimal until the cache is eventually restored.

Configuring Web Proxy Clients

You do not have to install any software to configure Web Proxy clients. However, you must configure the proxy capable applications on the client computers to use the ISA Server computer as the proxy server.

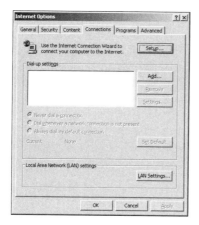

Figure 3.2 Configure LAN settings in Internet Explorer to use the browser with ISA Server.

You can also set an option by which ISA Server automatically downloads a client configuration script located on the ISA Server computer every time a Web browser is opened. The output of this script provides an ordered series of ISA Server computers that the browser uses to retrieve the object that is specified by the URL.

The script is stored at a specific URL on any ISA Server computer in an array. This makes it easy to update all Web browser settings without having to reconfigure each individual Web browser. Internet Explorer version 3.02 and later and Netscape 2.0 and later support this feature.

The default configuration URL is

http://*Computer_name*/array.dll?Get.Routing.Script

where *Computer_name* is the name of the ISA Server computer. This is the URL where the configuration script is located. ISA Server automatically generates this configuration script based on the Direct Access and Backup Route options.

▶ **Follow these steps to manually configure Internet Explorer 5.0 to use the Web Proxy service:**

1. Open Internet Explorer.
2. On the Tools menu, click Internet Options.
3. On the Connections tab, click LAN Settings.
4. Select the Use A Proxy Server check box.
5. In the Address text box, type the name of an ISA Server computer or array, then in the Port text box, type a valid port number (usually 8080).

Direct Access

You can configure computers on the local network to be accessed directly from the client by creating a Web browser exception list. You can also specify that all computers included in the Local Domain Table (LDT) can be accessed directly from the client. Clients use the LDT to determine if a name resolution request should be performed directly or via ISA Server.

Practice 1: Establishing Secure Internet Access for Web Proxy Clients

This practice allows you to take advantage of the secure routing capability of ISA Server and to establish secure Web access from Server2 through Server1. Since ISA Server denies the passage of packets unless they are explicitly allowed, in order to establish secure Web access from Server2, you must create a protocol rule to allow all IP traffic to pass through the ISA Server firewall. This practice demonstrates how to create such a rule. Note that since protocol rules do not open ISA Server up to *incoming* traffic, this practice allows you to configure *secure* Internet access for your clients without using Firewall Client software.

This practice assumes that you have already established Internet connectivity from your ISA Server computer through a dial-up connection, and that you have configured a LAN connection between Server1 and Server2 in the manner described in "About This Book."

Exercise 1: Creating a Protocol Rule

In this exercise, you create a protocol rule that allows secure Internet access.

▶ **To open the New Protocol Rule wizard**

1. Log on to Server1 as Administrator.
2. Click Start, point to Programs, point to Microsoft ISA Server, and then click ISA Management.
3. Click the View menu and verify that Taskpad is selected.
4. In the console tree, expand the Servers and Arrays node, and then expand the MyArray node.

    Configuration nodes for Server1 appear.

5. Expand the Access Policy node and select the Protocol Rules folder.
6. In the details pane, click the Create A Protocol Rule icon.

▶ **To create a new protocol rule with the New Protocol Rule wizard**

1. In the Protocol Rule Name text box, type **AllowIP**.

Note This exercise is intended to provide a simplified means of allowing all internal clients access to all IP traffic. In a real-world deployment scenario, you may want to limit access to specific protocols for specific users, groups, or client sets.

---

2. Click Next.
3. On the Rule Action screen, verify that the Allow radio button is selected, and then click Next.
4. On the Protocols screen, verify that All IP Traffic appears in the Apply This Rule To drop-down list box, and then click Next.
5. On the Schedule screen, verify that Always appears in the Use This Schedule drop-down list box, and then click Next.
6. On the Client Type screen, verify that the Any Request radio button is selected, and then click Next.

7. On the Completing the New Protocol Rule Wizard screen, click Finish.

   The AllowIP rule appears in the details pane.

> **Note** After you create a new protocol rule, you might need to wait a few minutes before it begins to function. Before proceeding to Exercise 2, you may either wait a few minutes or restart the ISA Server services as described in Chapter 3, Lesson 4.

Exercise 2: Configuring Internet Explorer to Use the Web Proxy Service

This exercise enables Internet Explorer to work with the ISA Server Web Proxy service. Use the dial-up connection on Server1 to establish a connection to your ISP.

1. Log on to Domain01 from Server2 as Administrator.
2. Open Internet Explorer.
3. If the Internet Connection Wizard appears, advance through the wizard by configuring a manual (LAN) connection.
4. On the Tools menu, click Internet Options.
5. On the Connections tab, click LAN Settings.
6. Select the Use A Proxy Server check box.
7. In the Address text box, type **192.168.0.1**, then in the Port text box, type **8080**.
8. Click OK to close the Local Area Network (LAN) Settings dialog box.
9. Click OK to close the Internet Options dialog box.

You should now be able to browse Web sites freely with Internet Explorer on Server2.

Practice 2: Installing Firewall Client

In this practice, you install Firewall Client software on the client computer. Without Firewall Client software installed and enabled on the client computer, the Firewall service can only apply access policy rules to IP addresses representing internal clients. When Firewall Client is installed on the client computer, access policy rules can be applied to users and computer names in addition to IP addresses. Firewall clients also improve performance by maintaining a local copy of the LAT and the Local Domain Table (LDT), by providing built-in support for protocols with secondary connections, by allowing for advanced configuration of Winsock applications through its global client configuration file Mspclnt.ini, and by allowing for the automatic discovery of the ISA Server.

Exercise: Installing Firewall Client over the Local Network

Perform this exercise on the Server2 computer.

1. Open My Network Places, and browse the network to find \\server1\mspclnt\.

2. Double-click the SETUP icon in \\server1\mspclnt\.

   The Microsoft Firewall Client – Install wizard appears.

3. Click Next.

4. On the Destination Folder screen, accept the default location, and then click Next.

5. On the Ready To Install The Program screen, click Install.

   The firewall client is installed and then the Install Wizard Completed screen appears.

6. Click Finish.

Lesson Summary

Establishing secure Internet access for local clients requires that you first configure protocol rules in ISA Server that allow Internet protocols to pass through the ISA Server firewall to the client computers. You can then decide whether to configure your internal clients as SecureNAT clients, which requires little configuration, or as firewall clients, which requires you to install the Firewall Client software on the client computers.

Before you deploy or configure client software, assess your organization's needs. If you need to support roaming clients, to apply access policy to authenticated users, to support protocols with secondary connections, or to allow dial-on-demand for non-Web Internet sessions, you should deploy Firewall Client software. If you are using the ISA Server to protect publishing servers, if ISA Server is installed in Cache mode, or if you want to avoid installing software on the client computers, you can configure your client computers as SecureNAT clients.

Both Firewall client computers and SecureNAT client computers may also be Web Proxy clients. The Web Proxy service (w3proxy) is a Windows 2000 service that supports requests from any proxy capable application. You do not have to install any software to configure Web Proxy clients. However, you must configure the Web browser applications on the client computers to use the ISA Server computer as the proxy server.

Lesson 2 Configuring ISA Server Dial-up Connections

ISA Server can provide firewall and caching benefits for your network even when you do not have a dedicated Internet connection. You may use ISA Server to secure a single dial-up connection to your ISP and to share that connection among all computers on your network.

After this lesson, you will be able to

- Create dial-up entries in ISA Server
- Provide complete and secure Internet access to your ISA Server clients through a dial-up connection on your ISA Server computer
- Configure your ISA Server computer for dial-on-demand

Estimated lesson time: 30 minutes

Configuring Dial-up Entries

To configure dial-up entries in ISA Server, you need to create policy elements in ISA Management for dial-up connections. This procedure is not required for Web Proxy and firewall clients to use and share a dial-up connection on your ISA Server computer. However, if through a dial-up connection you want to use non-Web services such as Post Office Protocol (POP3) and Network News Transfer Protocols (NNTP) on clients that do not have Firewall Client installed, you need to configure a dial-up entry and then configure the network to route requests using that dial-up entry.

Besides providing Internet connectivity to SecureNAT clients, creating dial-up entries allows you to apply connection-specific rules and policies to dial-up connections in ISA Server. By creating dial-up entries, you can specify how the ISA Server computer connects to the Internet with those dial-up connections.

Finally, only by configuring dial-up entries can you enable dial-on-demand for Web Proxy and firewall clients.

Each dial-up entry includes the following information:

- The name of the dial-up connection that was previously configured for the remote access server on all the servers in the array
- The user name and password for a user who has permissions to access the Internet Service Provider via the dial-up connection

You can configure dial-up entries only for network dial-up connections that are configured on all the ISA Server computers in an array. See Windows 2000 Help for instructions on creating network dial-up connections.

Although you may create multiple dial-up entries, only one dial-up entry can be active for an array. The active dial-up entry is used whenever ISA Server dials out automatically to the Internet to service a client request.

▶ **Follow these steps to create a dial-up entry:**

1. Open the ISA Management console.
2. Expand the console, expand Servers And Arrays, expand MyArray, and then expand the Policy Elements node.
3. Right-click Dial-up Entries, point to New, then click Dial-Up Entry.

    The New Dial-up Entry dialog box appears.
4. In the Name text box, type the name of the dial-up entry.
5. (Optional) In the Description box, type a description for the dial-up entry.
6. In Use The Following Network Dial-Up Connection text box, type or select the name of an existing Windows 2000 network dial-up connection, and then click Set Account.
7. In the User text box, type the user name supplied by your ISP.
8. In the Password and Confirm Password text boxes, type the user's password.
9. Click OK.

    The New Dial-up Entry dialog box appears.
10. Click OK.

Before you configure dial-up entries in ISA Server, you should also be aware of the following:

- The network dial-up connection to be specified in the dial-up entry must already be configured on each of the array's member servers.
- The dial-up entry that is created becomes the active dial-up entry. This dial-up entry will be used for routing rules and for firewall chaining.
- The user name and password you specify should be the same user name and password that you would type to manually establish a network dial-up connection.

If you have more than one dial-up entry, follow these steps to set an active dial-up entry:

1. Open the ISA Management console.
2. Click the View menu and then click Advanced.
3. Expand the console tree and then expand the Policy Elements node.
4. Click Dial-up Entries.
5. In the details pane, right-click the applicable dial-up entry and then click Set As Active Entry.

Note also the following points about the active dial-up entry:

- You cannot delete the active dial-up entry.
- When you set an active dial-up entry, all existing dial-up connections are disconnected if ISA Server was used to dial those connections.

Dial-on-Demand

You can configure ISA Server to use a dial-up entry to dial out to the Internet for simple routing or for active caching.

- **Routing.** When a client requests an object, if the route for the client request requires establishing a dial-up connection, and if access policy allows the client request, ISA Server will dial out to the Internet using the active dial-up entry.
- **Active caching.** If active caching is enabled, ISA Server dials out to the Internet to retrieve the frequently-accessed files.

In addition, ISA Server dials out to the Internet when ISA Server cannot definitively determine whether access policy allows a client request. This happens, for example, when access policy rules specify a destination by name, while the client specifies the computer by IP address. If a routing rule indicates that a dial-up connection should be established for the request, ISA Server dials out to the Internet either to resolve the name of the computer requested by the client or to do a reverse look-up. ISA Server then checks the access policy rules again to determine if the request is allowed.

Note Only Web Proxy and firewall clients can be configured for dial-on-demand. For SecureNAT clients to connect to the Internet, a dial-up connection must already be established.

Configuring Dial-on-Demand

You can configure ISA Server to dial out to the Internet when necessary, such as when a requested object is not in the ISA Server cache.

▶ **Follow these steps to enable dial-on-demand:**

1. Create a network dial-up connection. See Windows 2000 Help for instructions on creating network dial-up connections.
2. Create a dial-up entry in ISA Management.
3. Enable dialing for the Firewall service (as described below). This step is required only for firewall clients and not Web Proxy clients.
4. Enable automatic dial-out for routing (as described below).
5. Verify that a default gateway is not configured on any of the internal interface cards on the ISA Server computers in the array.

▶ **Follow these steps to enable dialing for the Firewall service:**

1. In the console tree of ISA Management, right-click the Network Configuration node, and then click Properties. (The Network Configuration properties sheet is shown in Figure 3.3.)
2. On the Firewall Chaining tab, click the Use Primary Connection radio button.
3. Click the Use Dial-up Entry check box.

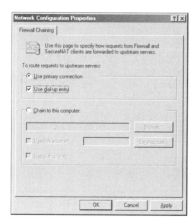

Figure 3.3 Routing via a dial-up entry

Once you have configured the Firewall service to use the dial-up entry to resolve external requests, you can configure the Firewall service to dial out to the Internet automatically through this dial-up entry.

▶ **Follow these steps to enable automatic dial-out for routing:**

1. In the console tree of ISA Management, click Routing.

2. In the details pane, right-click the specific routing rule you want to configure and then click Properties. This properties dialog box is shown in Figure 3.4.

3. On the Action tab, click the Retrieving Them Directly From The Specified Destination radio button.

4. On the Action tab, click the Use Dial-Up Entry For Primary Route check box.

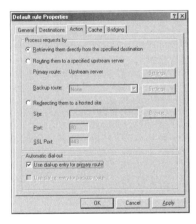

Figure 3.4 Configuring a routing rule for Automatic Dial-out

Limiting ISA Server Dial-out to External Sites

You can restrict ISA Server to dial out to the Internet only when necessary by configuring the LDT so that it includes the names of all internal computers. Clients use the LDT, configured in ISA Management, to determine whether a name resolution request should be performed directly or via ISA Server. This prevents ISA Server from dialing out to an external DNS server, only to determine that the requested computer is actually internal. Firewall clients maintain a local copy of the LDT, which is updated regularly, on their computer. Note that the LDT is checked only for requests from firewall clients.

Closing Dial-up Connections

After ISA Server dials out to the Internet, the connection is maintained until one of the following occurs:

- Another dial-up entry is made active.
- The active dial-up entry is modified so that it specifies a different network dial-up connection.
- The dial-up entry for firewall chaining is disabled.
- The primary route becomes available (if the dial-up connection is designated as the backup route).
- The Firewall service stops.

Practice: Configuring a Dial-up Entry

In this practice, you enable Internet access for SecureNAT clients through a dial-up connection on ISA Server.

This practice assumes the Server1 computer is connected to the Internet via a dial-up connection. The practice also assumes that you have created a protocol rule in ISA Management allowing all IP traffic (as performed in Chapter 3, Lesson 1), and that you have installed and enabled the Firewall Client software on Server2. Finally, Server2's TCP/IP properties should be configured so that the preferred DNS server is set to your external ISP's DNS server, and the alternate DNS server is set to 192.168.0.1.

Exercise 1: Testing Internet Connectivity

In this exercise, you view session status of a firewall client, disable the Firewall Client software, and note the difference in behavior.

▶ **To disable firewall client**

1. Log on to Domain01 from both Server1 and Server2 as Administrator.
2. On Server2, click the Start button and click Run.

   The Run dialog box appears.
3. Type **cmd** and click OK.
4. A command prompt appears.
5. At the command prompt, type **nslookup www.microsoft.com** and press Enter.

   You will receive a response informing you of the IP addresses associated with www.microsoft.com by your preferred DNS server.

6. On Server1, open ISA Management, expand the MyArray node, and then expand the Monitoring node.

7. Click the Sessions folder.

8. Click the View menu and then click Advanced.

9. Right-click the details pane and then click Refresh.

10. Find Server2's current Internet session listed in the details pane.

    Notice that the session type is listed as Firewall Session, the user name as Administrator, and the Client Computer as Server2. When the Firewall Client software is enabled, the user account name and client computer name are provided with the session information.

11. Switch to Server2 and disable the Firewall Client software. (You can disable it by double-clicking the Firewall Client icon in Control Panel, clearing the Enable Firewall Client check box in the Firewall Client Options dialog box, and then clicking OK.)

12. Activate the command prompt window.

13. At the command prompt, type **nslookup www.microsoft.com** and press Enter.

    You will receive a message informing you that the DNS request has timed out. This occurs because the Server2 computer is now a SecureNAT client, and you have not yet configured SecureNAT clients to access the Internet through an ISA Server dial-up connection.

Exercise 2: Creating a New Dial-up Entry

Perform this exercise on Server1. Creating a dial-up entry policy element is the first step in allowing SecureNAT clients to access the Internet through an ISA Server dial-up connection.

▶ **To create a dial-up entry policy element**

1. Open the ISA Management console.

2. Expand the console tree and then expand the Policy Elements node.

3. Right-click the Dial-up Entries node, point to New, and then click Dial-up Entry.

    The New Dial-up Entry dialog box appears.

4. In the Name text box, type **MyDialUp**.

5. Click the Select button.

    The Select Network Dial-up Connection dialog box appears.

6. In the Network Dial-up Connection box, select the available dial-up connection, and then click OK.

7. On the New Dial-up Entry dialog box, click Set Account.

   The Set Account dialog box appears.

8. In the appropriate text boxes, type the user name and password assigned by your ISP.

9. Click OK.

10. On the New Dial-up Entry dialog box, click OK.

    MyDialUp now appears in the details pane of the ISA Management console when the Dial-up Entries folder is selected.

Exercise 3: Configuring ISA Server to Route through the Dial-up Entry

This exercise enables SecureNAT clients to route Internet requests through the active dial-up entry. Perform these steps on Server1.

▶ **To enable SecureNAT clients**

1. In the console tree of ISA Management, locate and right-click the Network Configuration node, and then click Properties.

   The Network Configuration Properties dialog box appears.

2. On the Firewall Chaining tab, verify that the Use Primary Connection radio button is selected.

3. Click the Use Dial-up Entry check box and click OK.

   In the next exercise, you restart the Firewall service so that the new routing configuration takes effect.

Exercise 4: Restarting the Firewall Service

Whenever you make changes to the routing configuration, you need to restart the Firewall and/or Web Proxy services for the changes to take effect. Perform the following steps on Server1.

▶ **To restart the Firewall and/or Web Proxy services**

1. In the console tree of ISA Management, locate and expand the Monitoring node.

2. Click the Services node.

3. In the details pane, right-click the Firewall service and click Stop.

4. When the Firewall service has fully stopped, right-click the Firewall service again and click Start.

   Wait until the Firewall service icon turns green before proceeding to the next exercise.

Exercise 5: Viewing SecureNAT Session Information

In this exercise, you connect to the Internet from a SecureNAT client and then view the session information in ISA Server.

▶ **To connect to the Internet from a SecureNAT client**

1. On Server2, open a command prompt.
2. At the command prompt, type **nslookup www.microsoft.com** and press Enter.

   You will receive a response indicating that your nslookup is successful, even though Server2 is now a SecureNAT client.

3. On Server1, open ISA Management.
4. In the console tree, click the Sessions folder.
5. Right-click the details pane and click Refresh.
6. Find Server2's current Internet session listed in the details pane.

   Notice that the session type is listed as Firewall Session, the user name is blank, and the client computer is noted only by the IP address of 192.168.0.2. SecureNAT clients do not provide user account name and client computer name information with the session information.

7. On Server2, re-enable the Firewall Client software.

Lesson Summary

To ensure complete and secure Internet access for your ISA Server clients through a dial-up connection, you will need to create a dial-up entry policy element and configure the network to route requests to upstream servers using that dial-up entry. Configuring a dial-up entry in ISA Server allows SecureNAT client computers to access the Internet through non-Web connections, and it allows you to apply connection-specific rules to any policies you configure in ISA Server.

Creating dial-up entries also allows you the option of configuring dial-on-demand. This feature allows your ISA Server computer to initiate a dial-up connection to the Internet automatically whenever a Web Proxy or firewall client on the local network requests a remote host.

Lesson 3 Configuring Automatic Discovery of ISA Server

ISA Server's automatic discovery feature allows you to configure clients so that they automatically discover an appropriate ISA Server computer.

After this lesson, you will be able to

- Configure automatic discovery for ISA Server clients
- Troubleshoot automatic discovery on client computers

Estimated lesson time: 30 minutes

Automatic Discovery

It is a simple task to configure the ISA Server computer that connects firewall clients and Web Proxy clients. However, subsequent modifications can be time-consuming, particularly for roaming clients, who may require constant adjustments. When you configure automatic discovery, Web Proxy and firewall clients automatically discover the appropriate ISA Server computers. In this way, roaming clients can connect to an ISA Server computer as appropriate and when necessary.

Configuring automatic discovery requires that you publish automatic discovery on the ISA Server computer; enable automatic discovery on the client computer(s); configure any DHCP servers on your network with a special Web Proxy Autodiscovery Protocol entry; and ensure that your network DNS server has listed both a host (A) record of the ISA Server computer and an alias (CNAME) record named WPAD pointing to the ISA Server computer. For automatic discovery to work on your network, your client computers must have access to an internal DNS server, a DHCP server, or both.

Note Read through the following procedures, but do not complete them if you plan to perform the practice exercise at the end of the lesson.

▶ **Follow these steps to publish automatic discovery:**

1. In the console tree of ISA Management, right-click the applicable array, and select Properties.
2. On the Auto Discovery tab of the *array_name* Properties dialog box, select the Publish Automatic Discovery Information check box.
3. In Use This Port For Automatic Discovery Requests text box, type the appropriate port number (80 by default).

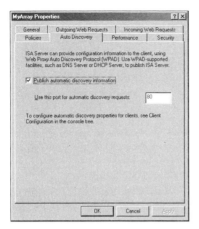

Figure 3.5 Publishing automatic discovery in array properties

▶ **Follow these steps to set automatic discovery for firewall clients:**

1. On the client computer, open Control Panel.

2. Double-click Firewall Client, and select the Automatically Detect ISA Server check box.

When automatic discovery is configured and enabled, the following steps are performed to allow Web Proxy and firewall clients to automatically detect ISA Server:

1. When the client makes a Winsock request, the client connects to the DNS or DHCP server.

   The DNS server or the DHCP server should have a Web Proxy Autodiscovery Protocol (WPAD) entry, which points to a WPAD server that indicates the ISA Server computer.

2. The requests of the client are fulfilled by the ISA Server computer, as identified by the WSPAD entry in the DNS server or DHCP server.

Configuring WPAD and WSPAD on the DNS or DHCP Server

Through automatic discovery, the firewall client or the Web Proxy client requests an object from the ISA Server that is configured to fulfill requests. If the ISA Server does not respond and if automatic discovery is enabled for the client, it starts the automatic discovery process.

ISA Server uses the WPAD entry to determine the appropriate Winsock Proxy Autodetect (WSPAD) entry. You do not have to configure the WSPAD entry explicitly on the DNS server.

Automatic discovery can be configured using DNS for clients running Windows 2000, Windows NT 4.0, Windows 98, and Windows ME.

▶ **Follow these steps to configure DNS Server for automatic discovery of ISA Server:**

1. Click Start, point to Programs, point to Administrative Tools, and then click DNS.

2. In the console tree, right-click the applicable forward lookup zone and click New Host.

3. In the Name text box, type the name of the ISA Server computer or array.

4. Under the IP Address text box, type the internal IP address of the ISA Server computer.

5. Click Add Host.

    If you receive an error message indicating that the host record cannot be created because the record already exists, you may safely click OK to dismiss the message.

6. In the DNS console tree, right-click the applicable forward lookup zone and click New Alias.

7. In the Alias Name text box, type **WPAD**.

8. Click the Browse button and navigate to Host (A) record of the ISA Server computer.

9. Click OK.

Automatic discovery can be configured using DHCP for clients running Windows 2000, Windows 98, and Windows ME.

▶ **Follow these steps to configure DHCP Server for automatic discovery of ISA Server:**

1. Click Start, point to Programs, point to Administrative Tools, and then click DHCP.

2. In the console tree, right-click the applicable DHCP server, and then click Set Predefined Options.

    The Predefined Options and Values dialog box appears.

3. Click Add.

4. In Name field, type **WPAD**.
5. In the Data Type drop-down list box, select String.
6. In the Code field, type **252**.
7. Click OK.

    The Predefined Options and Values dialog box appears with the 252 WPAD entry specified in the Option Name drop-down list box.

8. In the String text box, type **http://*String*/Wpad.dat**, where *String* is specified as follows:

    - WPAD, if DNS is configured to resolve WPAD requests
    - the ISA Server computer name or array name, if DNS is not configured to resolve WPAD requests

9. Click OK.
10. In the DHCP console, right-click Scope options or Server options, and then click Configure Options.
11. Scroll down in the Available Options box and select Option 252 WPAD.
12. Click OK.

Automatic Discovery for Firewall Clients

When you configure Firewall Client in Control Panel on your client computer, you indicate a particular ISA Server computer to which the client should connect. You can also configure the automatic discovery feature so that the firewall client automatically discovers which ISA Server computer it should use. The firewall client can also be centrally configured for automatic discovery from the Client Configuration node of ISA Management.

Verifying Automatic Discovery for Firewall Clients

When you enable automatic discovery in Firewall Client, you should verify afterwards that the automatic discovery feature is functioning. When automatic discovery cannot successfully discover or resolve the ISA Server computer, the firewall client is treated as a SecureNAT client, and the client sessions stop passing user account and client computer name information to ISA Server. To determine whether an internal computer is connecting to ISA Server as a SecureNAT or firewall client, initiate a non-Web Internet session (such as a mail, news, or nslookup session) from the client, and then check session monitoring in ISA Management to see whether user account and client computer names have been passed along with the session. If so, the client is operating as a firewall client, and automatic discovery is working. If not, the client is behaving as a SecureNAT client, and automatic discovery is not working.

Automatic Discovery for Web Proxy Clients

ISA Server provides similar support for Web Proxy clients. You can configure the automatic discovery feature in Internet Explorer LAN Settings so that roaming Web Proxy clients will always connect to the appropriate ISA Server computer when they log on to the Internet. You do not need to have the Firewall Client software installed and enabled for automatic discovery to work with Web Proxy clients.

Automatic discovery is supported for Internet Explorer 5.0 and later.

▶ **Follow these steps to configure Microsoft Internet Explorer 5 for automatic discovery of ISA Server:**

1. Open Microsoft Internet Explorer.
2. On the Tools menu, click Internet Options.
3. On the Connections tab, click LAN Settings.
4. Select the Automatically Detect Settings check box.
5. Verify that the Use A Proxy Server check box is cleared.

Troubleshooting Automatic Discovery

If automatic discovery is not functioning, you should ask the following questions in order to troubleshoot the problem.

1. Do your client and ISA Server have access to a local DNS Server, DHCP server, or both?
2. Is the network connection established among the client computer, the DNS server computer, the DHCP server computer, and the ISA Server computer?
3. Have you published automatic discovery on the ISA Server computer?
4. For firewall automatic discovery, have you installed and enabled the Firewall Client software on the client in question? Have you enabled firewall discovery in the Firewall Client Options dialog box?
5. For Web Proxy automatic discovery, are you using Internet Explorer version 5.0 or later? Have you configured Internet Explorer to automatically detect settings in the Local Area Network (LAN) Settings dialog box?
6. If you are using automatic discovery with a DHCP server, have you ensured that the WPAD entry is correctly configured on the DHCP server? Are you using only Windows 2000, Windows 98, or Windows ME clients? (Automatic discovery through DHCP is not supported for Windows NT and Windows 95 clients.)

7. If you are using automatic discovery with a DNS server, does the DNS server computer have a host (A) record defining the ISA Server computer? Have you added an alias (CNAME) record named WPAD pointing to the ISA Server computer? Have you configured the clients' TCP/IP properties to include this internal DNS server as an alternate DNS server?

Practice: Configuring Automatic Discovery

This practice walks you through the various procedures of configuring automatic discovery on your network. Since DNS will already have listed a host (A) record of the local computer, and since the two-server configuration does not use DHCP, there are only three short procedures you need to perform to configure the automatic discovery feature.

For this practice, you must have the Firewall Client software installed and enabled on Server2. In addition, you must have configured Server2 computer's TCP/IP properties to list your ISP's external DNS server as the preferred DNS server and the Server1 address of 192.168.0.1 as the alternate DNS server. Finally, this practice assumes that you have created a protocol rule in ISA Server that allows all IP traffic.

Exercise 1: Publishing Automatic Discovery

In the following exercise, you configure ISA Server to publish automatic discovery information.

1. Log on to Server1 as Administrator.
2. Open the ISA Management console.
3. Expand the console tree, right-click the MyArray node, and click Properties.

   The MyArray Properties dialog box appears.
4. Click the Auto Discovery tab.
5. Select the Publish Automatic Discovery Information check box.
6. Verify that port 80 is set for automatic discovery requests, and click OK.

   An ISA Server Warning dialog box appears.
7. Click the Save The Changes And Restart The Service(s) radio button.
8. Click OK.

Exercise 2: Creating a WPAD Alias (CNAME) Record in DNS

In order for automatic discovery to work with DNS, you need to create an alias record in DNS named WPAD that points to the ISA Server computer. Perform the following steps on Server1.

1. Click Start, point to Programs, point to Administrative Tools, and then click DNS.

2. In the DNS console tree, right-click the applicable forward lookup zone and click New Alias. This is the domain01 local foward lookup zone if you followed the setup instructions in "About This Book."

3. In the Alias Name text box, type **WPAD**.

4. In the Fully Qualified Name for Target Host text box, type **server1.domain01.local**.

5. Click OK.

Exercise 3: Enabling Automatic Discovery on a Firewall Client

Perform this exercise on the Server2 computer. You must have already installed and enabled the firewall client on Server2 to complete this exercise.

1. Log on to Domain01 from Server2 as Administrator.

2. Open Control Panel.

3. Double-click Firewall Client.

    The Firewall Client Options dialog box appears.

4. Select the Automatically Detect ISA Server check box.

5. Click Update Now.

    A message box appears indicating that the refresh operation was completed successfully.

6. Click OK to dismiss the message box.

7. Click OK to close the Firewall Client Options dialog box.

Exercise 4: Testing Automatic Discovery

After you configure automatic discovery, you should verify that the feature is functioning. Automatic discovery for firewall clients requires that the Firewall Client software be enabled on the client computer. However, when automatic discovery is enabled, firewall clients will only behave as firewall clients if automatic discovery is functioning properly. Otherwise, they become SecureNAT clients.

You can thus determine whether automatic discovery is functioning by checking the client session information in ISA Management. If user and computer names are provided with the session, you know that the feature is working. If the session only provides the IP address of the client session, you know the feature has not been properly configured, and the client computer has not been able to discover ISA Server automatically.

1. While you are logged on to Server2 as Administrator, open a command prompt and type **nslookup www.microsoft.com**.

   You should see output indicating that your computer has successfully connected to an external DNS server.

2. On Server1, expand the console tree in ISA Management and click Sessions.

3. On the View menu, verify that Advanced is checked.

4. Right-click the details pane and click Refresh.

   You should see Server2's Internet session listed among the active sessions. Notice that the user name is listed as Administrator, and the client computer is listed as Server2. Because authentication information is being passed to ISA Server, you know that the client is a firewall client, and automatic discovery is functioning properly.

Lesson Summary

When you configure automatic discovery, all Web Proxy and firewall clients automatically discover an appropriate ISA Server computer. Automatic discovery works with firewall clients to allow them to discover automatically which ISA Server computer they should use. The feature also works with the Web Proxy service so that roaming clients will always connect to an appropriate ISA Server computer when they connect to the Internet. To enable automatic discovery, your network must be configured either for DNS, DHCP, or both. Configuring automatic discovery requires that you publish automatic discovery on the ISA Server computer; enable automatic discovery on the client computer(s); configure any DHCP servers on your network with a special Web Proxy Autodiscovery Protocol entry; and ensure that your network DNS server has both a host (A) record of the ISA Server computer and an alias (CNAME) record named WPAD pointing to the ISA Server computer.

Lesson 4 Troubleshooting ISA Server Client Connectivity

Though establishing secure Internet connectivity through ISA Server is a simple process on a clean installation, any number of factors can complicate your configuration and create connectivity problems. This lesson discusses many of the most common problems leading to client connectivity and dial-up connection problems.

After this lesson, you will be able to

- Troubleshoot problems with ISA Server client connections
- Troubleshoot problems with dial-up connections in ISA Server
- Restart ISA Server services after configuration changes

Estimated lesson time: 20 minutes

Troubleshooting Client Connections

Client connectivity problems range from poor performance to complete lack of Internet access on SecureNAT, Firewall, and Web Proxy clients. To simplify future troubleshooting, it is important to avoid unnecessary complexities in your network configuration and to keep track of all changes made after your initial, successful installation. In general, you will profit from using a systematic approach in your troubleshooting, one that begins with the examination of physical connectivity and works up through the various network layers to the examination of specific access policies configured in ISA Server.

To further assist you in your troubleshooting, you can use Table 3.4 to check for the most common errors in client configurations that hinder Internet connectivity.

Table 3.4 Common Errors in Client Configurations

Problems	Causes	Solutions
Internal connections are slow for firewall clients.	Clients are unable to resolve local names using a external DNS server because the external DNS server may not have the correct records needed. The client must waste time waiting for the queries to the DNS server to time out before trying other methods of name resolution.	An internal DNS server should be configured with the names and addresses of all internal hosts. In addition, if packet filtering is operating, create an IP packet filter that uses DNS Lookup—a predefined filter—to allow the ISA Server computer to send out DNS name queries for Internet names.
SecureNAT clients cannot connect to the Internet.	If SecureNAT clients are not configured properly, the ISA Server will not be able to connect them to the Internet.	Configure the default gateway and configure the DNS server.
Clients cannot connect to external SSL sites.	When a client connects through the Web Proxy service to a secure Web site, ISA Server must open a tunnel for the traffic, since the traffic is encrypted end to end. By default, ISA Server only allows tunnel connections to ports 443 and 563 (Secure-News). If a client attempts to connect to a secure site that is running on a port other the 443 or 563, the connection fails.	To allow tunneling on additional ports, modify the ISA Administration COM object, FPCProxyTunnelPortRange.
SecureNAT connections work when the client specifies IP addresses but not when the client specifies computer names.	If the DNS server used by the client is an internal DNS server, it cannot resolve Internet domain names.	Configure the DNS server to forward the request to an external (Internet) DNS server. As an alternative, configure the clients to use a DNS server that forwards name resolution requests to an external DNS server.

(continues)

Table 3.4 Common Errors in Client Configurations *(continued)*

Problems	Causes	Solutions
SecureNAT clients cannot connect to a specific port because the connection times out, even though a Protocol Rule allows "Any IP traffic."	SecureNAT clients can only connect using protocols that are listed in the Protocol Definitions node of ISA Management. Furthermore, the protocol cannot require a secondary connection, unless an application filter that implements the protocol is available.	If the application only uses a single port, define a protocol in which the specific port is the primary port. If the application uses multiple ports, some of which are determined dynamically, they must be specified and defined by an application filter.
Server cannot bind to or allocate required port.	There is an allocation conflict for a port—more than one service on the ISA Server computer, possibly including ISA Server itself, is requesting to bind with a specific port on the external interface.	In general, Microsoft recommends that you do not run additional services on your primary firewall. If possible, install computers running other services behind the ISA Server computer. Bind the other server to the internal interface, so that only ISA Server listens on the external interface.

Troubleshooting Dial-up Entries

Problems with dial-up connections generally stem from only a few possible causes. Use Table 3.5 below to troubleshoot your dial-up connections.

Table 3.5 Troubleshooting Your Dial-up Connections

Problems	Causes	Solutions
Automatic dial-out to the Internet failed, although manual dial-out works.	The dial-up entry credentials were not specified correctly, although you may have specified credentials for the network dial-up connection correctly.	Reconfigure the dial-up entry credentials.
	The ISA Server computer does not have permissions to use the dial-up connection.	Reconfigure the dial-up connection, allowing everyone to use the connection. See Windows 2000 online Help for more information.
	The client is configured as a SecureNAT client.	Install and enable the Firewall Client software on the client computer.

Problems	Causes	Solutions
Failed to dial out to the Internet, because the connection is already being dialed.	Another service on the computer is connecting with this dial-up connection.	Wait a while—ISA Server will reattempt the connection when a request is subsequently made. If the problem persists, restart the ISA Server services.
The dial-up connection was dropped.	Someone may have inadvertently disconnected the dial-up connection.	Restart the ISA Server services. The services will automatically re-establish the connection.
The dial-up connection never hangs up, even though there is no dialing activity.	Whenever a client request is made, even if for a computer on the local network, ISA Server sends name resolution requests to both the internal DNS server and an external DNS server.	Configure ISA Server to use only internal DNS servers. Note that this solution works only if the internal DNS Server is capable of forwarding name resolution requests externally when necessary.
Cannot connect to the Internet via a dial-up connection.	The client is configured as a SecureNAT client, and a dial-up entry has not been fully configured.	Install the Firewall Client software on the client computer, or create a dial-up entry and configure Network Configuration properties to route upstream through the dial-up entry.

Restarting Services after Configuration Changes

If Internet connectivity suddenly stops on your client computers after having been active, try restarting one of the ISA Server services, such as the Firewall service and/or the Web Proxy service. Some changes to the ISA Server configuration require that you restart one or more of the ISA Server services on all the servers in the array. Without restarting ISA Server services, client connectivity will be lost. In the case of such a configuration change, ISA Management usually, but not always, displays a message box informing you that the service needs to be restarted.

Table 3.6 lists the configuration changes for which services must be restarted.

Table 3.6 Configuration Changes Requiring Service Restart

Configuration change	Service restarted
Installing, removing, enabling, or disabling an application filter	Firewall service
Reducing or increasing cache size, and adding or removing a disk from the cache	Firewall service
Changes to the LAT that affect a network adapter's internal or external state	Firewall service, Web Proxy service
Enabling or disabling packet filtering	Firewall service
Enabling or disabling a network adapter	Firewall service, Web Proxy service
Changing IP address of a network adapter	Firewall service, Web Proxy service
Routing table changes	Firewall service
Installing, enabling, disabling, removing, or changing order of Web filter	Web Proxy service
Changing port numbers for Web Proxy	Web Proxy service
Changing Firewall Client application settings in ISA Management	Firewall service
Updating SSL certificate	Web Proxy service
Adding or removing a server to or from the array	Web Proxy service
Changing H.323 Gatekeeper network interface	H.323 Gatekeeper service
Changing network configuration properties, or configuring firewall chaining	Firewall service

Figure 3.6 shows the Monitor Servers And Services taskpad in ISA Management, on which you can start and stop an ISA Server service.

Chapter 3 Configuring Secure Internet Access 125

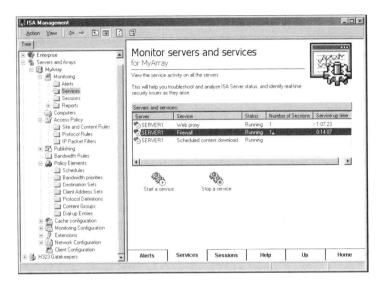

Figure 3.6 Starting and stopping a service in ISA Management in Taskpad view. Service control is also accomplished in Advanced view.

▶ **Follow these steps to start a service:**

1. In the console tree of ISA Management, click Services.
2. On the View menu, click Advanced.
3. In the details pane, right-click the applicable service, and then click Start.

▶ **Follow these steps to stop a service:**

1. In the console tree of ISA Management, click Services.
2. On the View menu, click Advanced.
3. In the details pane, right-click the applicable service, and then click Stop.

Lesson Summary

Connectivity problems are minimized by avoiding unnecessary complexities in your ISA Server configuration and by keeping track of all changes you have made from your base installation. When troubleshooting connectivity, you will profit from a systematic approach and from a review of common problems, causes, and solutions presented in this lesson.

In addition, many breaks in client connectivity result from changes to the ISA Server configuration. Such changes require that one or more of the ISA Server services be restarted on all servers in an array.

Review

The following questions are intended to reinforce key information presented in the chapter. If you are unable to answer a question, review the appropriate lesson and then try the question again. The answers for these questions are located in Appendix A, "Questions and Answers."

1. You are configuring an ISA Server installation for Firewall and Web caching service in each of two company branch offices. You need to assess requirements and make recommendations about how to configure the client computers. In addition to the 20 employees at each branch office, there are 10 field workers who spend time at both offices and who plug their portable computers into any available Ethernet port when they arrive at either office. The office desktop computers are more or less permanently positioned, and you do not anticipate that you will need to set specific access rules configured for any user accounts. To maximize efficiency for installation and maintenance, which (if any) computers do you recommend be configured as SecureNAT clients, and which (if any) as firewall clients?

2. What is the difference between the Mspclnt.ini file and the Wspcfg.ini file on Firewall Client computers?

3. When automatic discovery is configured, what are the steps it takes to fulfill a client request?

4. Does configuring dial-up entries in ISA Server allow you to share a secure Internet dial-up connection among Web Proxy clients?

5. Having recently switched from a dedicated connection to a dial-up connection to the Internet, you disabled your external network adapter and configured a dial-up entry for your existing dial-up connection. However, when your ISA Server dials up to your ISP through this dial-up connection, none of your clients can connect to the Internet any longer. What is the first step you should take to troubleshoot the problem?

CHAPTER 4

Configuring Internet Security Using Access Policies

Lesson 1 Creating an Access Policy with ISA Server 131

Lesson 2 Creating Customized Policy Elements 140

Lesson 3 Configuring Protocol Rules 152

Lesson 4 Configuring Site and Content Rules 165

Lesson 5 Configuring IP Packet Filters 178

Lesson 6 Configuring ISA Server to
          Detect External Attacks and Intrusions 192

Review 199

About This Chapter

Creating an Internet security policy requires that you take into account your particular network configuration and security needs. Your security needs may vary among users, computers, source or destination Internet Protocol (IP) addresses, times, protocols, content types, and requested Web sites. To create an access policy suited to these particulars of your network, you need to understand how Microsoft Internet Security and Acceleration Server 2000 (ISA Server) processes client requests. You will then be able to create policy elements for aspects such as schedules and client sets that are particular to your network. Next, you can begin the process of configuring the three types of rules that comprise an access policy: protocol rules, site and content rules, and IP packet filters. Finally, to prevent unwanted external intrusions into your network, you may choose to enable intrusion detection on your firewall.

Before You Begin

To complete the lessons in this chapter, you must have

- Met the requirements as outlined in "About This Book" so that Server1 is configured as a domain controller with an IP address of 192.168.0.1 and Server2 is configured as a member of the domain with an IP address of 192.168.0.2. Server1 must also have a dial-up connection to the Internet.

- Completed all the exercises in this book through Chapter 3.

Lesson 1 Creating an Access Policy with ISA Server

One of the primary functions of ISA Server is to connect your local network to the Internet while protecting your local network from malicious content originating from external sources. To customize this secure connectivity to suit your network needs, you can use ISA Server to create an access policy that permits internal clients access to specific Internet hosts. The access policy, together with the routing rules, determines how clients access the Internet.

After this lesson, you will be able to
- Describe how ISA Server processes an outgoing request
- Explain the conditions under which ISA Server processes requests from authenticated users from Firewall and Web Proxy clients
- Select ISA Server system security levels

Estimated lesson time: 30 minutes

Controlling Outgoing Requests

When ISA Server processes an outgoing request, it checks routing rules, site and content rules, and protocol rules to determine whether access is allowed. A request is allowed only if both a protocol rule and a site and content rule allow the request and if there is no rule that explicitly denies the request. When ISA Server is installed in Firewall mode or Integrated mode, a predefined site and content rule is enabled, allowing access for all content types and to all sites. However, no protocol rules exist by default.

Protocol rules and site and content rules can be configured to apply either to originating client address sets (IP address ranges) or to specific users or groups requesting an object. ISA Server processes the requests differently depending on the client type (SecureNAT, Firewall, or Web Proxy) and on how ISA Server is configured.

For an outgoing request, rules and packet filters are processed in the following order:

1. Protocol rules
2. Site and content rules
3. IP packet filters
4. Routing rules or Firewall Chaining configuration

Figure 4.1 illustrates the processing flow for an outgoing Web request.

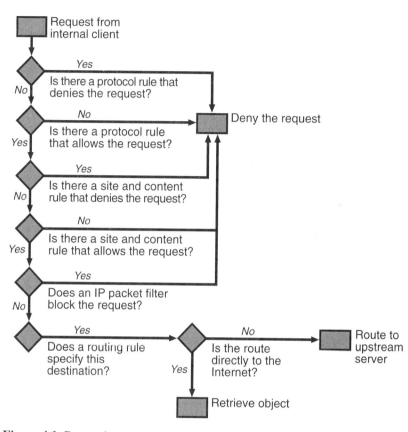

Figure 4.1 Processing access requests

ISA Server first checks the protocol rules before checking other rules or packet filters. ISA Server allows the request only if a protocol rule specifically allows the request and if no protocol rule specifically denies it.

After checking protocol rules, ISA Server checks the site and content rules. ISA Server allows the request only if a site and content rule specifically allows the request and if no site and content rule specifically denies it.

After checking site and content rules, ISA Server checks to determine whether an IP packet filter has been specifically configured to block the request. Note that, unlike protocol rules and site and content rules, IP packet filters do not need to be configured specifically to allow requests from client computers.

Important When it comes to Internet access, the behavior of the ISA Server computer is very different from that of the clients. IP packet filters are necessary to allow full Internet access from the ISA Server computer. In contrast to ISA Server clients, the ISA Server computer will not achieve full Internet access once you configure allow-type protocol rules and site and content rules. However, since IP packet filters are static, unlike rules, which are dynamic, you generally should not plan to use the ISA Server computer for regular Internet access. For this reason this book focuses on configuring secure Internet access for clients located behind ISA Server. (The subject of configuring IP packet filters is discussed in more detail in Lesson 5 of this chapter.)

Finally, ISA Server checks the routing rules (if a Web Proxy client has requested the object) or the Firewall Chaining configuration (if a SecureNAT or Firewall client has requested the object) to determine how the request should be serviced.

For example, assume that you installed ISA Server in Integrated or Firewall mode on a computer with two network cards, one connected to the Internet and the other connected to your local network. Your corporate guidelines allow all users access to all sites. In this case, your policy would consist simply of the following access policy rules:

- **A protocol rule.** This allows all internal clients to use any protocol at all times.

- **A site and content rule.** This allows everyone access to content on all sites at all times. Note that this rule allows internal clients access to the Internet without allowing external clients access to your network.

Configuring Access Policy

Access policies configured in ISA Server consist of site and content rules, protocol rules, and IP packet filters. You create standalone access policies for standalone servers. For an array, you can create an array-level access policy, an enterprise-level access policy, or a combination of rules at both the enterprise and array levels.

Access policy rules apply to all types of clients: Firewall clients, SecureNAT clients, and Web Proxy clients.

Rules and Authentication

Protocol rules and site and content rules can be configured to allow or to deny specific users access to chosen protocols, Internet sites, or content. When such rules are configured and enabled, each client request must be authenticated by ISA Server before the request can be allowed to pass through the ISA Server firewall. ISA Server handles authentication differently for SecureNAT, Firewall, and Web Proxy clients.

Note Unlike policy rules that are applied to specific users and groups, rules that are applied to specific client computers are enforced for all SecureNAT, Firewall, and Web Proxy clients. Rules that are applied to specific client computers are configured for client address sets, which are defined by IP address ranges and not by computer names. Since all client types provide the IP address of the client computer, all client types provide the information necessary for such rules to be successfully enforced.

SecureNAT Clients and Authentication

SecureNAT client requests include all non-Web Internet requests from clients that do not have Firewall Client installed. For example, mail and news requests are treated as SecureNAT sessions when the client computers on which the requests are made do not have the Firewall Client software enabled.

SecureNAT clients do not provide user name or computer name information to ISA Server when making a request. For this reason, all SecureNAT requests are denied passage through ISA Server when an access policy rule requires authentication.

For example, if your access policy consists of both a protocol rule and a site and content rule that allows access to all protocols and all sites at all times for members of the group Domain Users, a mail request from user John will be denied if John is making the request from a SecureNAT client, even if he is a member of the group Domain Users. Because SecureNAT requests cannot be authenticated, and because your access policy rules require authentication, all SecureNAT requests are denied categorically. For John to be granted non-Web Internet access under this access policy, he must have the Firewall Client software installed and enabled on the computer from which he requests access, and he must be a member of the group Domain Users.

Firewall Clients and Authentication

Firewall clients provide user name and computer name information to ISA Server when making a request. Therefore, access policy rules that require authentication can be enforced for Firewall Client sessions, and non-Web requests from Firewall clients are not rejected categorically, as is the case with SecureNAT clients.

For example, if your access policy consists of both a protocol rule and a site and content rule that allows access to all protocols and all sites at all times for members of the group Domain Users, then a mail request from the user John will be allowed to pass through the ISA Server firewall if (and only if) John is a member of the group Domain Users. Similarly, if there is an additional protocol rule denying access to user John, he will be denied access if he makes a non-Web request from a Firewall client.

Web Proxy Clients and Authentication

Web Proxy client requests are anonymous by default, but there are two conditions that force Web Proxy clients to provide user identification. When either of the following conditions is met, rules that are configured for specific users or groups are enforced for Web Proxy client sessions:

- The default ISA Server properties have been modified to require authentication for outgoing Web requests.
- Access policy includes an allow-type rule (whether a protocol rule or a site and content rule) that is configured for specific users or groups.

    Any allow-type rule configured for specific users or groups will prompt Web Proxy clients to generate a user-identified session. When access policy includes a deny-type rule defined for specific users or groups, that rule is ignored for Web Proxy clients unless another allow-type rule exists requiring authentication.

For example, let us assume that you have not modified the default outgoing Web request properties, and that your access policy consists of the following rules:

- A protocol rule allowing access to all protocols for all requests at all times
- A protocol rule denying access to all protocols for user John
- A site and content rule allowing access to all destinations for all requests at all times

Under these conditions, a Web request from the user John will not be denied because no allow-type rule exists that forces user identification from the Web Proxy client. However, if you were to add to this policy an allow-type protocol rule or site and content rule allowing complete access for all members of the group Domain Users, all Web requests would then be denied for user John.

▶ **Follow these steps to require authentication for all Web requests:**

1. In the console tree of ISA Management, right-click the applicable array and then click Properties.
2. On the Incoming Web Requests tab or on the Outgoing Web Requests tab, click the Ask Unauthenticated Users For Identification check box.

Note This change will not take effect until Web Proxy is restarted.

ISA Server System Security (System Hardening)

ISA Server includes the ISA Server Security Configuration wizard which you can use to apply the full range of system security settings to all the servers in an array. The ISA Server Security Configuration wizard allows you to select any of the following security levels:

- **Dedicated.** This setting is appropriate when ISA Server is functioning as a fully dedicated firewall, with no other interactive applications.

- **Limited Services.** This setting is appropriate when ISA Server is functioning as a combined firewall and cache server. It may be protected by an additional firewall.

- **Secure.** This setting is appropriate when the ISA Server computer has other servers installed on it, such as an Internet Information Services (IIS) server, database servers, or Simple Mail Transfer Protocol (SMTP) servers.

You can launch the ISA Server Security Configuration Wizard by selecting the Computers folder in ISA Management, right-clicking the server icon of the server you want to configure in the details pane, and selecting Secure from the shortcut menu. This process is shown in Figure 4.2.

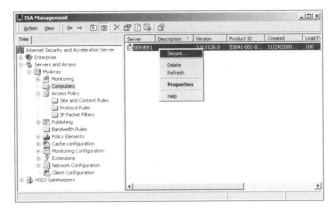

Figure 4.2 Launching the ISA Server Security Configuration wizard

▶ **Follow these steps to set system security:**

1. In the console tree of ISA Management, click Computers.

2. In the details pane, right-click the applicable computer, and then click Secure.

3. In the ISA Server Security Configuration Wizard screen, follow the on-screen instructions.

Getting Started Wizard

ISA Server includes a Getting Started wizard, shown in Figure 4.3, which walks you through the steps of creating an access policy customized for your network. After you finish using the tool, you will have configured a secure network connection to the Internet through ISA Server.

The Getting Started wizard helps you perform the following tasks:

- Configure enterprise policy settings (for array installation only)
- Create enterprise-level policy elements (for array installation only)
- Create enterprise-level protocol rules (for array installation only)
- Create enterprise-level site and content rules (for array installation only)
- Create array-level policy elements
- Create array-level protocol rules
- Create array-level site and content rules

- Set system security level
- Configure packet filtering
- Configuring routing and chaining
- Create cache policy

You can also invoke the Getting Started wizard at any time after setup.

▶ **Follow these steps to begin the Getting Started wizard:**

1. In ISA Management, select Taskpad from the View menu.
2. On the console tree, select the Internet Security And Acceleration Server node.
3. On the details pane, click the Getting Started Wizard icon.
4. Follow the direction appearing in the details pane.

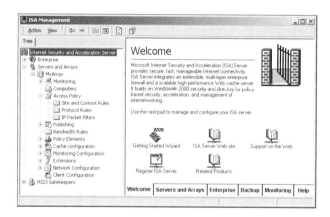

Figure 4.3 Launching the Getting Started wizard

Lesson Summary

You can use ISA Server to configure an access policy, which consists of site and content rules, protocol rules, and IP packet filters. A request is allowed only if both a protocol rule and a site and content rule allow the request and if there is no rule that explicitly denies the request.

SecureNAT clients do not provide user identification, and when rules require authentication, SecureNAT client requests are categorically denied. For Firewall clients, which do provide user identification, group membership and user rights may affect outbound access. When a Web Proxy client requests content, authentication information is not passed to the ISA Server unless ISA Server requires identification, or unless an allow-type policy rule exists requiring authentication.

To enhance system security, ISA Server includes the ISA Server Security Configuration wizard, which you can use to apply a full range of system security settings to all the servers in an array. Finally, to facilitate security and access policy configuration, the Getting Started wizard walks you through the steps of defining access policy rules customized for your network.

Lesson 2 Creating Customized Policy Elements

Access policies configured in ISA Server allow you to determine what kind of traffic will be allowed to pass through the firewall at what times, from what sources, and to what destinations. In any access policy, each specified parameter such as content type, schedule, client set, and destination is called a *policy element*. These policy elements are the building blocks of policy rules. Because ISA Server allows you to define your own policy elements, you can customize rule parameters to suit your particular network needs.

After this lesson, you will be able to
- Create and configure customized policy elements in ISA Server

Estimated lesson time: 45 minutes

Policy Elements

Policy elements are the parameters or building blocks of policy rules. For example, when you deny a set of clients access to certain Web content at certain times, the client set, the Web content, and the specified times all represent policy elements. ISA Server allows you to create policy elements that you can later use in any rules you define. Policy elements can be created at the enterprise level or array level, and they include:

- Schedules
- Bandwidth priorities
- Destination sets
- Client address sets
- Protocol definitions
- Content groups
- Dial-up entries

Array-Level and Enterprise-Level Policy Elements

If you are using ISA Server Enterprise Edition, and if you need to define an enterprise-wide access policy, you can define enterprise-level policy elements. These enterprise-level policy elements can then be used when you create enterprise-level rules.

When array-level policies and enterprise-level policies are used together, you can also apply array-level rules to enterprise-level policy elements.

For standalone servers, you can only create array-level policy elements.

Configuring Schedules

When you create rules, you can apply a schedule to the rule to determine when it goes into effect.

ISA Server comes preconfigured with the following two schedules:

- Weekends, which permits access all day on Saturday and Sunday
- Work Hours, which permits access between 9 A.M. and 5 P.M. on Mondays through Fridays

ISA Server also allows you to define customized schedule policy elements, such as the one shown in Figure 4.4.

The following rules can specify schedules:

- Site and content rules
- Protocol rules
- Bandwidth rules

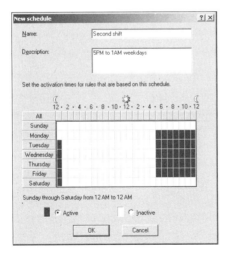

Figure 4.4 Configuring a schedule policy element

▶ **Follow these steps to create a schedule:**

1. In the console tree of ISA Management, right-click Schedules, point to New, and then click Schedule.

2. In the Name field, type the name of the schedule.

3. (Optional) In the Description field, type a description for the schedule.

4. Use the schedule table to set the schedule.

   - Click a cell to select the specific hour on a specific day.
   - Click a day in the left column to select the entire day.
   - Click an hour in the top row to select the same hour on all days.

5. Click the Active radio button to enable the rule during the selected times, or click the Inactive radio button to disable it during the selected times.

   In the schedule table, a dark cell means the rule is in effect (active) during that hour on that day; a white cell means the rule is not in effect (inactive).

Configuring Destination Sets

A *destination set* is a computer name, IP address, domain name, or IP range, and each of these destination sets can include a path. Destination sets include one or more computers or folders on specific computers. Rules can be applied to all destination sets, to all computers except for specified destination sets, or to one specific destination set. When defining a destination set, you can specify a given destination by domain name or by IP address range. Wildcards can be used to specify all host names in the chosen domain. For example, to specify all computers in the microsoft.com domain, you type the destination as ***.microsoft.com**. Note that the wildcard (*) can appear only at the start of the domain name, and can be specified only once in the name. An example of a destination set definition is shown in Figure 4.5. You can also indicate a specific path in a destination set to allow or prevent clients from accessing that path. The path may also include a wildcard.

Use the following formats when you specify your destinations. The computer name, path, and file name are not case sensitive. To include all the files in a folder: */Path/Folder_Name/**. To select a specific file in a folder: */Path/Folder_Name/Filename*. Rules can be applied to internal destination sets or external destination sets. Internal destination sets are groups of computers within your local network. External destination sets include computers outside the local network.

The following rules can specify destination sets:

- Site and content rules
- Bandwidth rules
- Web publishing rules
- Routing rules

For site and content rules and bandwidth rules, destination sets usually include computers that are not on your internal network. For Web publishing rules, destination sets usually include computers on your internal network. For routing rules, destination sets include external computers (on the Internet) for rules that route outgoing Web requests. Routing rules that route incoming Web requests include internal computers.

Figure 4.5 Configuring a destination set policy element

▶ **Follow these steps to create a destination set:**

1. In the console tree of ISA Management, right-click Destination Sets, point to New, and then click Set.

2. In the Name field, type a name for the destination set.

3. (Optional) In the Description field, type a description for the destination set.

4. Click Add and do the following: Click the Destination radio button, and type a computer name or fully qualified domain name in the text box next to the radio button.

5. (Optional) Click IP addresses. Then, in the From and To text boxes, type the appropriate IP addresses.

6. In Path, type the specific path on the specified computers.

Client Address Sets

Client address sets include one or more computers. You can apply rules to one or more client address sets or to all addresses except the specified client address sets.

The following rules can specify client address sets:

- Site and content rules
- Protocol rules
- Bandwidth rules
- Server publishing rules
- Web publishing rules

▶ **Follow these steps to create a client address set:**

1. In the console tree of ISA Management, right-click Client Address Sets, point to New, and then click Set.
2. In the Name field, type a name for the set.
3. (Optional) In the Description field, type a description for the set.
4. Click Add.
5. In the From text box, type an IP address for the lowest IP address in the set.
6. In the To text box, type an IP address for the highest IP address in the set. A sample client address set definition is shown in Figure 4.6.

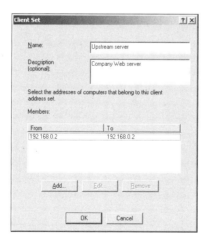

Figure 4.6 Configuring a single computer as a client address set

Client Users and Groups

Users and groups defined in Microsoft Windows 2000 are treated as a client type in ISA Server. When you create rules, you can specify to which internal clients the rule is applied. Clients can be specified either by Windows 2000 users and groups or by client address sets, which define clients by IP address.

When you configure a rule that applies to SecureNAT clients, you must specify clients by client address set and not by users and groups. Otherwise, the rule cannot be enforced, and the SecureNAT client request will be denied. When you configure a rule that applies to Firewall clients, you can specify clients by client address set or by users and groups. Windows 2000 users and groups are configured in the Windows 2000 Computer Management console and the Active Directory Users And Computers console.

Configuring Protocol Definitions

ISA Server includes a wide variety of preconfigured protocol definitions, which you can use when you create protocol rules or server publishing rules. Server publishing rules use protocol definitions whose direction is inbound. Application filters may also include protocol definitions. They can be included when you install ISA Server, or you can install them later. You can further expand the set of protocol definitions by using ISA Management to create your own.

User-defined protocol definitions can be edited or deleted. Protocol definitions installed with application filters cannot be modified, although they can be deleted. Protocol definitions included with ISA Server cannot be modified or deleted. When you create a protocol definition, you specify the following:

- **Port number.** This is a port number between 1 and 65535 that is used for the initial connection.
- **Low-level protocol.** This is either Transmission Control Protocol (TCP) or User Datagram Protocol (UDP).
- **Direction.** These are Send only, Receive only, Send receive, and Receive send.
- **Secondary connections.** (Optional) This is the range of port numbers, protocol, and direction used for additional connections or packets that follow the initial connection. You can configure one or more secondary connections.

Direction

You can configure the direction of the traffic flow when you create a protocol definition. The way you specify the direction of the traffic determines how packets will be communicated. For TCP, the direction determines the direction of the initial communication. For UDP, the direction determines the flow of traffic. For example, you can configure a protocol rule that allows internal clients to initiate TCP communication on port 80 by specifying the direction as Send. The server with which the client is communicating can respond to the client request but cannot initiate communication.

▶ **Follow these steps to create a protocol definition:**

1. In the console tree of ISA Management, right-click Protocol Definitions, point to New, and then click Definition.

2. In the New Protocol Definition wizard, type the name of the protocol definition, and then click Next.

3. On the Primary Connection Information page, specify the port number, protocol type, and direction for the primary connection. Click Next.

    The Primary Connection Information page is shown in Figure 4.7.

4. On the Secondary Connections page, specify if the protocol definition includes a secondary connection. Then, specify the port range, protocol type, and direction for the secondary connection if you choose to configure one.

5. Click Next, and then click Finish to complete the wizard.

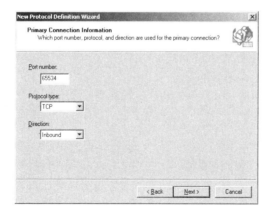

Figure 4.7 Configuring a protocol definition

Configuring Content Groups

Content groups specify Multipurpose Internet Mail Extensions (MIME) types and file name extensions. When you create a site and content rule or a bandwidth rule, you can limit the rule application to specific content groups. This allows you to be more specific when you configure security policy, as you can limit access not only to a particular destination, but also to specific content.

Content groups apply only to Hypertext Transfer Protocol (HTTP) and tunneled File Transfer Protocol (FTP) traffic, which passes through the Web Proxy service.

When a client requests FTP content, ISA Server checks the file name extension of the requested object. ISA Server determines if a rule applies to a content group that includes the requested file name extension and processes the rule accordingly.

When a client requests HTTP content, ISA Server sends the request to the Web server. When the Web server returns the object, ISA Server checks the object's MIME type or its file name extension, depending on the header information returned by the Web server. ISA Server determines if a rule applies to a content group that includes the requested file name extension, and processes the rule accordingly.

Content groups do not apply to Secure Hypertext Transfer Protocol-Secure (S-HTTP or HTTPS) content.

When you create content groups, it is recommended that you specify the content's MIME type and file name extension. For example, to include all Director files in a content group, select the following file name extensions and MIME types:

- .dir
- .dxr
- .dcr
- application/x-director

ISA Server comes preconfigured with the following content groups: Application, Application Data Files, Audio, Compressed Files, Documents, HTML Documents, Images, Macro Documents, Text, Video, and VRML.

▶ **Follow these steps to create a content group:**

1. In the console tree of ISA Management, right-click Content Groups, point to New, and then click Content Group.
2. In the Name field, type the name of the content group.
3. (Optional) In the Description field, type a description for the content group.
4. In the Available Types drop down list box, do one of the following:
    - To select an existing content type, click a file extension or MIME type.
    - To add a new content type, type a new file extension or a MIME type.
5. Click Add.

Note When you create content groups, specify the content's MIME type and file extension.

A sample content group definition is shown in Figure 4.8.

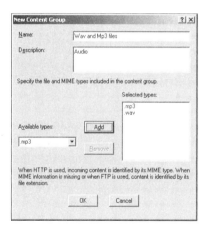

Figure 4.8 Configuring a content group

Practice: Creating Policy Elements

In this practice, you create three policy elements—an after-hours work schedule, a Web site destination, and a content type—that can later be referenced in any access policy rules you define.

Perform this entire practice on the Server1 computer.

Exercise 1: Creating a Schedule

In this exercise, you create a Non–Work Hours schedule that includes 7 P.M.–7 A.M. weekdays and all day weekends.

▶ **To create an expanded work hours schedule**

1. Open the ISA Management console.
2. In the console tree, navigate to Servers and Arrays, MyArray, Policy Elements.
3. Expand Policy Elements, right-click Schedules, point to New, and then click Schedule.

   The New Schedule dialog box appears.

4. In the Name text box, type **Expanded Work Hours**.
5. In the Description text box, type **6 AM - 8 PM Monday-Friday**.
6. Click Sunday to highlight the entire row and select the Inactive radio button.

   The rectangular area appears as a white box.

7. Click Saturday to highlight the entire row and select the Inactive radio button.
8. Highlight a rectangle covering the hours from 12 A.M. to 6 A.M. Monday through Friday, and select the Inactive radio button.
9. Highlight a rectangle covering the hours from 8 P.M. to 12 A.M. Monday through Friday, and select the Inactive radio button.
10. Click OK.
11. Click the Schedules node.

    The Expanded Non–Work Hours schedule appears in the details pane. Notice that there are predefined Weekends and Work Hours schedules in the details pane.

Exercise 2: Creating a Destination Set

In the following exercise, you create a destination set consisting of a particular Web site.

▶ **To create a destination set policy element**

1. In the console tree of ISA Management, navigate to Servers and Arrays, MyArray, Policy Elements.

2. Expand Policy Elements, right-click Destination Sets, point to New, and then click Set.

    The New Destination Set dialog box appears.

3. In the Name text box, type **Microsoft Online Seminars**.

4. In the Description text box, type **Multimedia training at microsoft.com**.

5. Click Add.

    The Add/Edit Destination dialog box appears.

6. Verify that the Destination radio button is selected, and type **www.microsoft.com/seminar** in the Destination text box.

7. Click OK.

    The New Destination Set dialog box reappears.

8. Click OK.

9. Select the Destination Sets node.

    The Microsoft Online Seminars destination set appears in the details pane of ISA Management.

Lesson Summary

Creating customized policy elements enables you to apply policy rules to particular aspects of your network. Policy element types include schedules, bandwidth priorities, destination sets, client address sets, protocol definitions, content groups, and dial-up entries. You can configure these policy element types in ISA Management and later refer to them in any access policy rules, routing rules, publishing rules, or bandwidth rules you define.

You can create a schedule type if you need to apply rules at times that do not match either of ISA Server's preconfigured schedules, which are Work Hours and Weekends. Destination sets help you specify combinations of IP addresses, IP ranges, DNS names, or file pathways. Client address sets can group your client computers by IP addresses. When you create a protocol definition, you specify the protocol's port number, underlying transport protocol, direction, and any secondary connections. Content groups specify MIME types and file name extensions.

Lesson 3 Configuring Protocol Rules

You need to configure protocol rules if you want to allow clients on your internal network to access the Internet. Together with site and content rules and IP packet filters, protocol rules define your access policy. Protocol rules specify which particular protocols are allowed to pass through ISA Server from which clients and at what times.

After this lesson, you will be able to

- Describe the function of protocol rules
- Give several examples of protocol definitions preconfigured in ISA Server
- Create and configure protocol rules in ISA Server

Estimated lesson time: 40 minutes

Protocol Rules

Protocol rules determine which protocols clients can use to access the Internet. You can define protocol rules that allow or deny use of one or more protocol definitions. You can configure protocol rules to apply to all IP traffic or to a specific set of protocols definitions.

For SecureNAT clients, you can apply protocol rules to all computers or to a set of computers specified by IP addresses. For Firewall clients, you can apply protocol rules to all computers, to a set of computers specified by IP addresses, or to specific users and groups defined in Windows 2000.

▶ **Follow these steps to create a protocol rule:**

1. In the console tree of ISA Management, right-click Protocol Rules, point to New, and then click Rule.
2. In the New Protocol Rule Wizard screen, type the name of the protocol rule, and then click Next.
3. On the Rule Action page, specify whether the rule allows or denies the request, and then click Next.
4. On the Protocols page, specify the protocols to which the rule applies, and then click Next.
5. On the Schedule page, specify when the rule is applied, and then click Next.

6. On the Client Type page, specify to which clients the rule applies, and then click Next.

   Note If an enterprise policy is applied to this array, only deny-type rules can be created.

You can also modify protocol rules you have previously created at any time. To do this, simply access the protocol rule's properties dialog box in ISA Management.

▶ **Follow these steps to modify a protocol rule:**

   1. In the console tree of ISA Management, click Protocol Rules.
   2. On the View menu, select Advanced.
   3. In the details pane, right-click the applicable protocol rule, and then click Properties.
   4. On the Protocol tab, do one of the following:
      - If the rule applies to all protocols, even those not explicitly defined by ISA Server, click All IP Traffic.
      - If you want the rule to apply to protocols that you select, click Selected Protocols.
      - If the rule applies to all IP traffic except those protocols you select, click All IP Traffic Except Selected.
   5. If you chose Selected Protocols or All IP Traffic Excepted Selected, in Protocols, select one or more protocol definitions.

   Note If the protocol definition that you want to specify does not exist, you can click New to create it, and then select it in the list.

Protocol Rule Configuration Scenario

Suppose you want to prohibit a group of users in your organization from using MSN Messenger during work hours. If the Firewall Client software has been installed and enabled on all your client computers, you can create a protocol rule to enforce this policy by configuring the following parameters:

- Set Action to Deny The Request.
- Choose Selected Protocols.
- Select the MSN Messenger protocol.

- Select the Work Hours schedule.
- Select the Specific Users And Groups radio button, as shown in Figure 4.9.
- Select the appropriate user group.

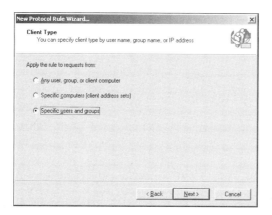

Figure 4.9 Applying a protocol rule to specific users

Protocol Availability

ISA Server includes a list of 86 preconfigured, well-known protocol definitions, including the most widely used Internet protocols. You can also add or modify additional protocols. Note that if ISA Server is installed in Cache mode, protocol rules can be applied only to HTTP, HTTPS, Gopher, and FTP protocols.

When a client requests an object by using a specific protocol, ISA Server checks the protocol rules. If a protocol rule specifically denies use of the protocol, the request is denied. Furthermore, the request is processed only if a protocol rule specifically allows the client to use the specific protocol *and* if a site and content rule specifically allows access to the requested object. In other words, you must perform the following procedure to allow access:

1. Create a protocol rule, indicating which protocols can be used to access the specific destinations.
2. Create a site and content rule, indicating which clients are allowed access to specific destination sets. When you install ISA Server in Integrated mode or Firewall mode, a site and content rule is already enabled by default that allows access to all sites and content types.

Application Filters and Protocol Availability

ISA Management provides information about all 86 preconfigured protocols, along with any new protocols you define, in the Protocol Definitions folder of the Policy Elements node. When you look at the list of protocol definitions on the details pane in ISA Management, you will see that some of these protocols are defined by ISA Server, and others are defined by application filters.

The list of protocol definitions is shown in Figure 4.10.

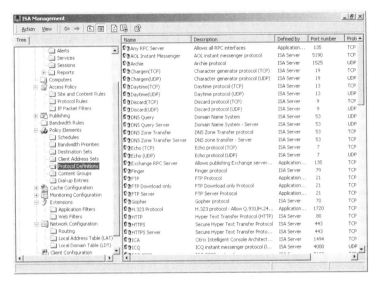

Figure 4.10 Protocols may be defined by ISA Server or by application filters.

For the protocols created and installed by application filters, when the source application filter is disabled, all corresponding protocol definitions are also disabled. That is, traffic that uses this protocol definition is blocked. For example, if you disable the streaming media filter, all traffic that uses the Windows Media and Real Networks protocol definitions is blocked.

Note that some application filters work with protocols that are defined by ISA Server and not by the application filter itself. When these application filters are disabled, the corresponding protocol definitions are not disabled. For example, even if you disable the SMTP filter, SMTP packets may still be allowed to pass because the SMTP protocol is defined by ISA Server and not by the SMTP filter.

Processing Order

Unlike routing rules, protocol rules are not given order of priority, but deny-type protocol rules take priority over rules that allow access. For example, if you create two rules, one that allows use of all protocols and one that denies use of the SMTP protocol, the SMTP protocol will not be allowed.

Array-Level and Enterprise-Level Protocol Rules

Protocol rules can be created at both the array level and at the enterprise level. When an array policy is permitted in addition to an enterprise policy, the array policy's protocol rules can only further restrict enterprise-level protocol rules. In other words, the array-level protocol rules can only deny use of specific protocols when an enterprise policy is applied.

Web Protocols

When you select Protocol Rules on the scope pane in ISA Management, you can use the taskpad in the details pane to create a protocol rule that allows users to access the Internet by using only specific Web protocols. You can achieve this by clicking the icon named Allow Web Protocols. Table 4.1 lists these Web protocol definitions, all of which are preconfigured when you install ISA Server, either by ISA Server or by an application filter installed with ISA Server.

Table 4.1 Protocols Configured by Allow Web Protocols

Name	Port number	Protocol type	Defined by	Description
FTP client	21	TCP	FTP access filter	FTP, used for copying files between hosts
FTP download only	21	TCP	FTP access filter	FTP, used for copying files between hosts
Gopher	70	TCP	ISA Server	Menu-driven front end to other Internet services, including Archie and Wide Area Information Server (WAIS)

Name	Port number	Protocol type	Defined by	Description
HTTP	80	TCP	ISA Server	HTTP, used to implement the World Wide Web
S-HTTP (HTTPS)	443	TCP	ISA Server	Version of HTTP that uses Secure Sockets Layer (SSL) for encryption

Protocol Definitions that are Installed with ISA Server

Table 4.2 lists the protocol definitions that are included with ISA Server.

Table 4.2 Predefined Protocols in ISA Server

Protocol name	Description
Any RPC Server	Allows all RPC interfaces
AOL Instant Messenger	
Archie	
Chargen (TCP)	Character generator (TCP)
Chargen (UDP)	Character generator (UDP)
Daytime (TCP)	
Daytime (UDP)	
Discard (TCP)	
Discard (UDP)	
DNS Query	Domain Name System
DNS Query Server	Domain Name System – Server
DNS Zone Transfer	
DNS Zone Transfer Server	
Echo (TCP)	
Echo (UDP)	
Exchange RPC Server	Allows publishing Exchange server for RPC access from external network

(continues)

Table 4.2 Predefined Protocols in ISA Server *(continued)*

Protocol name	Description
Finger	
FTP	File Transfer Protocol
FTP Download only	File Transfer Protocol – Read only
FTP Server	File Transfer Protocol – Server
Gopher	
H.323	H.323 video conferencing
HTTP	Hyper Text Transfer Protocol
HTTPS	Secure Hyper Text Transfer Protocol
HTTPS Server	Secure Hyper Text Transfer Protocol – Server
ICA	Citrix Intelligent Console Architecture
ICQ	ICQ instant messenger protocol (legacy)
ICQ 2000	
Ident	
IKE	Internet Key Exchange
IMAP4	Interactive Mail Access Protocol
IMAP4 Server	
IMAPS	Secure Interactive Mail Access Protocol
IMAPS Server	
IRC	Internet Relay Chat
Kerberos-Adm (TCP)	Kerberos administration (TCP)
Kerberos-Adm (UDP)	Kerberos administration (UDP)
Kerberos-IV	Kerberos IV authentication
Kerberos-Sec (TCP)	Kerberos V authentication (TCP)
Kerberos-Sec (UDP)	Kerberos V authentication (UDP)
LDAP	Lightweight Directory Access Protocol
LDAP GC (Global Catalog)	
LDAPS	Secure Lightweight Directory Access Protocol
LDAPS GC (Global Catalog)	
Microsoft SQL Server	

Protocol name	Description
MMS – Windows Media	
MMS – Windows Media Server	
MSN	MSN Internet Access
MSN Messenger	
Net2Phone	
Net2Phone Registration	
NetBIOS Datagram	
NetBIOS Name Service	
NetBIOS Session	
NNTP	Network News Transfer Protocol
NNTP Server	
NNTPS	Secure Network News Transfer Protocol
NNTPS Server	Secure Network News Transfer Protocol
NTP (UDP)	Network Time Protocol (UDP)
PNM (Real Networks) protocol Client	Real Networks Streaming Media Protocol – Client
PNM (Real Networks) protocol Server	Real Networks Streaming Media Protocol – Server
POP2	Post Office Protocol v.2
POP3	Post Office Protocol v.3
POP3 Server	
POP3S	Secure Post Office Protocol v.3
POP3S Server	
Quote (TCP)	Quote of the day (TCP)
Quote (UDP)	Quote of the day (UDP)
RADIUS	Remote Authentication Dial-In User Service
RADIUS Accounting	
RDP (Terminal Services)	Remote Desktop Protocol (Terminal Services)
RIP	Routing Information Protocol
Rlogin	Remote login

(continues)

Table 4.2 Predefined Protocols in ISA Server *(continued)*

Protocol name	Description
RTSP	Real Time Streaming Protocol – Client
RTSP Server	Real Time Streaming Protocol – Server
SMTP	Simple Mail Transfer Protocol
SMTP Server	
SMTPS	Secure Simple Mail Transfer Protocol
SMTPS Server	
SNMP	Simple Network Management Protocol
SNMP Trap	Simple Network Management Protocol – Trap
SSH	Secure Shell
Telnet	
Telnet Server	
TFTP	Trivial File Transfer Protocol
Time (TCP)	
Time (UDP)	
Whois	Nickname/Whois protocol

Practice: Assigning Protocol Rules to User Accounts

To prepare for this practice, you should create a domain user account named user1. Do not give this account any additional permissions. This practice also assumes that you have created a protocol rule named AllowIP (as performed in Chapter 3, Lesson 1) that allows all IP traffic to all clients at all times. Verify that proxy settings are correctly configured in Internet Explorer on Server2 for all users.

In this practice, you observe that Web sessions are handled anonymously by default; that is, when the default array properties have not been modified to require user identification and when no allow-type rule has been configured that requires authentication. Under these conditions, users connecting to the Internet through Web browsers are not affected by deny-type policy rules applied to Windows 2000 user accounts. After configuring ISA Server to pass account information along with all client Web sessions, you will create a protocol rule that denies Internet access for a specific user. Finally, you log on as that user to observe the effects of this new protocol rule.

Exercise 1: Monitoring Sessions in ISA Management

In this exercise, you review client session information in ISA Management that is generated by a Web Proxy client.

▶ **To monitor a client Web session in ISA Management**

1. On Server1, open the ISA Management console.

2. Click the View menu and then click Advanced.

3. In the console tree, expand the Monitoring node and then select the Sessions folder.

4. If any sessions are listed in the details pane, close them by right-clicking them and selecting Abort Session.

5. On Server2, log on to Domain01 as user1, open Internet Explorer, and browse to http://www.msn.com.

6. While the MSN Web site is downloading, switch to Server1.

7. On Server1, with the Sessions folder still open in the ISA Management console, right-click the details pane and click Refresh.

    You should see a new Web Session session type with the user Anonymous, with no client computer name, and with an IP address of 192.168.0.2 (the address of Server2).

    Web sessions are anonymous by default. When Web sessions are anonymous, they will not be affected by any deny-type rules you define for specific users. You can force user identification with Web sessions if you create an allow-type rule that requires authentication or if you modify the array properties to require user identification with outgoing Web requests.

Exercise 2: Requiring Authentication for Web Sessions

In this exercise, you disable anonymous Web access and require users accessing the Internet through Web browsers to authenticate themselves. This allows access policy rules configured for specific Windows 2000 users and groups to affect all client Web sessions.

▶ **To provide account information with Web sessions**

1. On Server1, open the ISA Management console and navigate to MyArray in the console tree.

2. Right-click the MyArray node and select Properties.

    The MyArray Properties dialog box appears.

3. Select the Outgoing Web Requests tab.

4. In the Connections area, select the Ask Unauthenticated Users For Identification check box.

5. Verify that the Resolve Requests Within Array Before Routing check box is selected.

6. Click OK.

   An ISA Server Warning dialog box appears.

7. Select the Save The Changes But Don't Restart The Service(s) radio button and click OK.

8. Stop and restart the Firewall and Web Proxy services in ISA Management.

9. On the Server2 computer, while you are logged on as user1, open a Web browser and browse to http://www.msn.com.

10. While this page is still downloading, switch to Server1, select the Sessions folder in the ISA Management console tree, right-click the details pane, and select Refresh.

    A new Web session is listed in the details pane with a user name DomainName\user1 and client address 192.168.0.2.

    Now that you have configured account information to be passed through Web browsers, you can apply ISA Server rules to Windows 2000 users accessing the Internet through Web browsers.

Exercise 3: Assigning a Protocol Rule to a Windows 2000 User

In this exercise, you configure an ISA Server rule to block Internet access for a particular Windows 2000 user.

▶ **To assign a protocol rule to a Windows 2000 user**

1. On Server1, open the ISA Management console and navigate to MyArray, Access Policy, Protocol Rules.

2. Right-click the Protocol Rules folder, point to New and then click Rule.

   The New Protocol Rule Wizard appears.

3. In the Protocol Rule Name text box, type **DenyUser1**.

4. Click Next.

5. On the Rule Action screen, select Deny, and then click Next.
6. On the Protocols screen, leave All IP Traffic as the default, and then click Next.
7. On the Schedule screen, leave Always as the default, and then click Next.
8. On the Client Type screen, select the Specific Users And Groups radio button, and then click Next.
9. On the Users And Groups screen, click Add.

   The Select Users Or Groups window appears.
10. In the top pane, select user1, click Add, and then click OK.

    The Users And Groups screen appears and DOMAIN01\user1 is listed in the Account box.
11. Click Next.

    The Completing The New Protocol Rule Wizard screen appears.
12. Click Finish.

    The ISA Management console appears.

    DenyUser1 is listed as a protocol rule in the details pane of the Protocol Rules folder.
13. In the console tree, select the Services folder of the Monitoring node, and then restart the Web Proxy and Firewall services.
14. Switch to Server2. While you are logged on as user1, open Internet Explorer. If you already have an open browser, refresh your browser window.

    The Enter Network Password dialog box appears. The user1 account name associated with the Web session has been blocked because of the DenyUser1 protocol rule. If you want to browse the Web while logged on as user1, you must provide the user name and password of another Windows 2000 account that has not been blocked by an ISA Server rule.
15. Click Cancel.

Lesson Summary

By creating protocol rules, you allow or refuse to allow clients to pass through ISA Server based on particular protocols or a sets of protocols. Protocol rules, along with site and content rules and IP packet filters, comprise an ISA Server's access policy.

Whenever a client requests an object beyond the firewall, ISA Server checks the protocol rules first. If a protocol rule does not exist allowing the client to communicate using the specific protocol of the request, or if a protocol rule specifically denies use of the protocol, the request is denied.

The protocols you can reference in protocol rules include a list of preconfigured definitions in ISA Server of the most commonly used protocols for networking and Internet services. You can also configure your own additional protocols for use in protocol rules.

Lesson 4 Configuring Site and Content Rules

Site and content rules allow you to specify Internet access policy according to the destination and type of content associated with a client request. Whereas protocol rules allow or block the transmission of specific protocols, site and content rules allow or block sets of Web sites, file-name extensions, or entire content groups such as audio or video. As with protocol rules, you can apply site and content rules to any combination of specific computers, users, IP addresses, and schedules.

After this lesson, you will be able to
- Describe the function of ISA Server site and content rules
- Configure site and content rules for Internet access in ISA Server

Estimated lesson time: 40 minutes

Site and Content Rules

By creating site and content rules, you can allow or deny Internet access according to the destination or content type of a given request. Site and content rules determine if and when users or client address sets can access specific content on specific destination sets.

When a client requests an object, ISA Server checks the site and content rules. If a site and content rule specifically denies the request, access to that object is denied. Furthermore, the request is fulfilled only if a site and content rule specifically allows the client or user to access the content, and a protocol rule allows the client or user to use the specific protocol to communicate. In other words, to allow access to the Internet, you must perform the following steps:

1. Create a site and content rule indicating which clients are allowed access to specific destination sets.
2. Create a protocol rule indicating which protocols can be used to access the specific destinations.

Processing Order

Unlike routing rules, site and content rules are not given order of priority, but deny-type site and content rules take priority over rules that allow access. For example, if you create two rules, one of which allows access to any request and one of which denies access to all users in the Sales department, the Sales department cannot gain access to the Internet.

Allow and Deny Actions

Site and content rules can either allow or deny access to specific sites. If access is denied, for HTTP objects, the request can be redirected to an alternate Uniform Resource Locator (URL)—typically a page on an internal server—explaining why access is denied.

Then, when access is denied, ISA Server sends the alternate URL to the Web browser client. The client Web browser then tries to access the object from the destination to which ISA Server has redirected it.

For example, suppose a site and content rule denies access to http://example.microsoft.com/ and redirects requests for this site to http://internal.acme.com/. When a client requests the Web page http://example.microsoft.com/welcome.htm, ISA Server denies the request, and returns http://internal.acme.com/ to the browser. The browser then requests http://internal.acme.com/welcome.htm.

Important If you choose to redirect the request, the URL that you specify must be accessible to the browser. In other words, either the URL must be on an internal computer or some rule must explicitly allow access to the URL.

Destination Sets and Path Processing

When you create a site and content rule, you specify which destinations are accessible. Destination sets can include IP addresses of specific computers or computer host names. In either case, you can specify a particular path on the computer to include in the destination set.

ISA Server processes site and content rules in different ways, depending on the type of client requesting the object and on the type of content requested. For example, for certain clients and protocols, ISA Server will ignore any path specified in the destination set. Table 4.3 details whether ISA Server processes the path specified for the computers in the destination set.

Table 4.3 Path Processing for ISA Server Clients

	Web Proxy client	SecureNAT client	Firewall client
FTP content	Yes	No	No
HTTP content	Yes	Yes	Yes
S-HTTP content	No	No	No

When enforcing a rule for a given request, and when path processing is not supported for the content associated with the request, ISA Server ignores any destination in the rule that specifies a path. If a rule contains more than one destination set, only the destinations containing the unsupported paths will be ignored; the rule will be enforced for all other destinations. For example, if you have one rule that denies access to two destinations, widgets.microsoft.com and //example.microsoft.com/example, a request to access Network News Transfer Protocol (NNTP) content from example.microsoft.com will not be denied. This is because the destination set contains a path, and since ISA Server does not support path processing for NNTP content, ISA Server will not enforce the deny rule for that destination. However, a request to access NNTP content from widgets.microsoft.com will be denied; the deny rule will be enforced for the second destination set because the destination set does not contain a path.

For S-HTTP requests, if a rule denies requests to a destination that specifies a path, ISA Server denies all content on the computer, not just that limited to the path. For example, if a rule is configured to deny S-HTTP access to example.microsoft.com/example, ISA Server will deny access to all content at example.microsoft.com.

Array-Level and Enterprise-Level Site and Content Rules

Site and content rules can be created at both the array level and at the enterprise level. When an array policy is allowed, its site and content rules can only further restrict enterprise-level site and content rules. The array-level site and content rules can only deny access to specific sites or content.

▶ **Follow these steps to create a site and content rule:**

1. In the console tree of ISA Management, right-click Site and Content Rules, point to New, and then click Rule.

2. In the New Site and Content Rule wizard, type the name of the rule, and then click Next.

3. On the Rule Action page, specify whether the rule allows or denies the request and then click Next.

4. On the Rule Configuration page, select whether the rule applies to specific sites, a specific schedule, specific clients, or all of the above. Then click Next.

5. On the subsequent pages, specify how the rule is applied.

Note If an enterprise policy is applied to this array, only deny-type rules can be created.

Sample Site and Content Rule

If you want to deny access to all images in http://example.microsoft.com/stuff, create a site and content rule with the following properties:

- Set Rule Action to Deny.
- Set Rule Configuration to Custom.
- Set Destination Set to a set that includes the following path: example.microsoft.com/stuff/*.
- Set Schedule to Always.
- Set Client Type to Any Requests.
- Set Content Group to the Images content group.

▶ **Follow these steps to assign a destination set to a site and content rule:**

1. In the console tree of ISA Management, click Site And Content Rules.
2. On the View menu, select Advanced.
3. In the details pane, right-click the applicable rule and then click Properties.
4. On the Destinations tab, select one of the following:
   - All Destinations
   - All External Destinations
   - All Internal Destinations
   - Selected Destination Set
   - All Destinations Except Selected Set
5. If you chose Selected Destination Set or All Destinations Except Selected Set, in the Name field, select a Destination Set.

Content Groups

ISA Server comes preconfigured with the following content groups: Application, Application Data Files, Audio, Compressed Files, Documents, HTML Documents, Images, Macro Documents, Text, Video, and VRML.

When creating a site and content rule, you can apply the rule to any of these content groups, as shown in Figure 4.11.

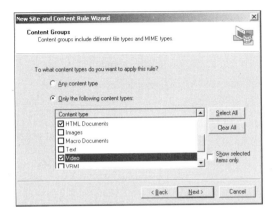

Figure 4.11 Specifying content types in a site and content rule

Depending on the Web server, different MIME types are associated with different file name extensions. Table 4.4 lists the IIS default associations.

Table 4.4 Preconfigured Content Types in ISA Server

File name extension	MIME type
.hta	application/hta
.isp	application/x-internet-signup
.crd	application/x-mscardfile
.pmc	application/x-perfmon
.spc	application/x-pkcs7-certificates
.sv4crc	application/x-sv4crc
.bin	application/octet-stream
.clp	application/x-msclip
.mny	application/x-msmoney
.p7r	application/x-pkcs7-certreqresp
.evy	application/envoy
.p7s	application/pkcs7-signature
.eps	application/postscript
.setreg	application/set-registration-initiation
.xlm	application/vnd.ms-excel

(continues)

Table 4.4 Preconfigured Content Types in ISA Server *(continued)*

File name extension	MIME type
.cpio	application/x-cpio
.dvi	application/x-dvi
.p7b	application/x-pkcs7-certificates
.doc	application/msword
.dot	application/msword
.p7c	application/pkcs7-mime
.ps	application/postscript
.wps	application/vnd.ms-works
.csh	application/x-csh
.iii	application/x-iphone
.pmw	application/x-perfmon
.man	application/x-troff-man
.hdf	application/x-hdf
.mvb	application/x-msmediaview
.texi	application/x-texinfo
.setpay	application/set-payment-initiation
.stl	application/vndms-pkistl
.mdb	application/x-msaccess
.oda	application/oda
.hlp	application/winhlp
.nc	application/x-netcdf
.sh	application/x-sh
.shar	application/x-shar
.tcl	application/x-tcl
.ms	application/x-troff-ms
.ods	application/oleobject
.axs	application/olescript
.xla	application/vnd.ms-excel
.mpp	application/vnd.ms-project

File name extension	MIME type
.dir	application/x-director
.sit	application/x-stuffit
.*	application/octet-stream
.crl	application/pkix-crl
.ai	application/postscript
.xls	application/vnd.ms-excel
.wks	application/vnd.ms-works
.ins	application/x-internet-signup
.pub	application/x-mspublisher
.wri	application/x-mswrite
.spl	application/futuresplash
.hqx	application/mac-binhex40
.p10	application/pkcs10
.xlc	application/vnd.ms-excel
.xlt	application/vnd.ms-excel
.dxr	application/x-director
.js	application/x-javascript
.m13	application/x-msmediaview
.trm	application/x-msterminal
.pml	application/x-perfmon
.me	application/x-troff-me
.wcm	application/vnd.ms-works
.latex	application/x-latex
.m14	application/x-msmediaview
.wmf	application/x-msmetafile
.cer	application/x-x509-ca-cert
.zip	application/x-zip-compressed
.p12	application/x-pkcs12
.pfx	application/x-pkcs12

(continues)

Table 4.4 Preconfigured Content Types in ISA Server *(continued)*

File name extension	MIME type
.der	application/x-x509-ca-cert
.pdf	application/pdf
.xlw	application/vnd.ms-excel
.texinfo	application/x-texinfo
.p7m	application/pkcs7-mime
.pps	application/vnd.ms-powerpoint
.dcr	application/x-director
.gtar	application/x-gtar
.sct	text/scriptlet
.fif	application/fractals
.exe	application/octet-stream
.ppt	application/vnd.ms-powerpoint
.sst	application/vndms-pkicertstore
.pko	application/vndms-pkipko
.scd	application/x-msschedule
.tar	application/x-tar
.roff	application/x-troff
.t	application/x-troff
.prf	application/pics-rules
.rtf	application/rtf
.pot	application/vnd.ms-powerpoint
.wdb	application/vnd.ms-works
.bcpio	application/x-bcpio
.dll	application/x-msdownload
.pma	application/x-perfmon
.pmr	application/x-perfmon
.tr	application/x-troff
.src	application/x-wais-source
.acx	application/internet-property-stream

File name extension	MIME type
.cat	application/vndms-pkiseccat
.cdf	application/x-cdf
.tgz	application/x-compressed
.sv4cpio	application/x-sv4cpio
.tex	application/x-tex
.ustar	application/x-ustar
.crt	application/x-x509-ca-cert
.ra	audio/x-pn-realaudio
.mid	audio/mid
.au	audio/basic
.snd	audio/basic
.wav	audio/wav
.aifc	audio/aiff
.m3u	audio/x-mpegurl
.ram	audio/x-pn-realaudio
.aiff	audio/aiff
.rmi	audio/mid
.aif	audio/x-aiff
.mp3	audio/mpeg
.gz	application/x-gzip
.z	application/x-compress
.tsv	text/tab-separated-values
.xml	text/xml
.323	text/h323
.htt	text/webviewhtml
.stm	text/html
.html	text/html
.xsl	text/xml
.htm	text/html

(continues)

Table 4.4 Preconfigured Content Types in ISA Server *(continued)*

File name extension	MIME type
.cod	image/cis-cod
.ief	image/ief
.pbm	image/x-portable-bitmap
.tiff	image/tiff
.ppm	image/x-portable-pixmap
.rgb	image/x-rgb
.dib	image/bmp
.jpeg	image/jpeg
.cmx	image/x-cmx
.pnm	image/x-portable-anymap
.jpe	image/jpeg
.jfif	image/pjpeg
.tif	image/tiff
.jpg	image/jpeg
.xbm	image/x-xbitmap
.ras	image/x-cmu-raster
.gif	image/gif

Practice: Creating New Site and Content Rules

In this practice, you create a new site and content rule that blocks access to all audio and video content for a certain user. You will then sign on as two different users to observe the effects of the new rule.

This practice assumes that you have created a Domain User account named user1 (as performed in Chapter 4, Lesson 3) and that no additional priveleges have been assigned to this account. The practice also requires you to create a new Domain User account named user2 to which no additional privileges are assigned. It also assumes that you have created a protocol rule in ISA Server that allows all IP traffic to any request at all times (as performed in Chapter 3, Lesson 1). Finally, it assumes that you have modified the outgoing Web request properties to provide identification, as explained in Chapter 4, Lesson 3. Verify that proxy settings are correctly configured in Internet Explorer for all users on Server2.

If you have defined a DenyUser1 protocol rule (as performed in Chapter 4, Lesson 3), you should disable that rule and restart the ISA Server services before beginning this exercise.

Exercise 1: Denying User1 Access to Audio and Video Content

In this exercise, which is performed on Server1, you create a site and content rule that denies all audio and video content to user1.

▶ **To deny user1 access to audio and video content**

1. Log on to Server1 as Administrator.
2. Open ISA Management.
3. Expand the Access Policy node. Right-click the Site And Content Rules folder, point to New and then click Rule.

   The New Site And Content Rule wizard appears.

4. In the Site And Content Rule Name text box, type **DenyUser1AudioVideo**, and then click Next.
5. On the Rule Action screen, leave the Deny radio button selected, and then click Next.
6. On the Rule Configuration screen, select the Custom radio button, and then click Next.
7. On the Destination Sets screen, leave All Destinations as the default, and then click Next.
8. On the Schedule screen, leave Always as the default, and then click Next.
9. On the Client Type screen, select Specific Users And Groups, and then click Next.
10. On the Users And Groups screen, click Add.

    The Select Users Or Groups window appears.

11. In the top pane, select user1, and then click Add.
12. Click OK.

    The Users And Groups screen appears.

13. Verify that Domain01\user1 appears in the Accounts box, and then click Next.
14. On the Content Groups screen, select the Only The Following Content Types radio button.

15. In the Content Type box, select the Audio and Video check boxes.

    Audio and video content will be denied to user1 at all times.

16. Click Next.

    The Completing The New Site And Content Rule Wizard screen appears.

17. Click Finish.

    The details pane of the Site And Content Rules folder lists the DenyUser1AudioVideo content rule. Notice that the preconfigured Allow Rule is also listed in the details pane.

Stop and restart the Web Proxy and Firewall services in ISA Management before proceeding to Exercise 2.

Exercise 2: Testing the Configuration

In this exercise, you log on to Server2 as user2 and attempt to connect to audio content. You then log on to Server2 as user1, attempt to connect to audio content, and observe the difference in behavior.

▶ **To test the new site and content rule**

1. Log on to Domain01 from Server2 as user2.
2. Open Internet Explorer.
3. In the Address text box, enter **http://www.microsoft.com/seminar**.

    You will be directed to the Microsoft SeminarOnline Web site.

4. Click any link to a featured online seminar.

    A Web page will open that includes an audio component.

5. After waiting for the Web page to download completely, click the forward arrow to begin playing the audio.

    You will hear the beginning of an audio lecture.

6. In Internet Explorer, click the Stop icon to stop the audio lecture.
7. Close Internet Explorer.
8. On Server2, log off Domain01 as user2 and log on again as user1.
9. Repeat steps 1 through 4 above.

    When the online seminar page finishes downloading, you will find that the audio content cannot be played. Audio content has been successfully blocked for user1.

Lesson Summary

Site and content rules determine if and when users or client address sets can access specific content on specific destination sets. As with protocol rules, transmission for given packets across ISA Server can only occur if a site and content rule exists indicating that the requesting client is allowed access to the requested content type and destination. Site and content rules can either allow or deny access to specific sites and content types.

When you create a site and content rule, you specify which destinations are accessible. Destination sets can include IP addresses of specific computers, computer names, path names, or Web addresses.

ISA Server comes preconfigured with the following content groups: Application, Application Data Files, Audio, Compressed Files, Documents, HTML Documents, Images, Macro Documents, Text, Video, and VRML. In addition, these content groups are broken down into over 100 file name extensions and MIME types, each of which can be specified in a site and content rule.

Lesson 5 Configuring IP Packet Filters

IP packet filters allow or block packets from passing through specified ports. In a simple network scenario, you do not normally need to create IP packet filters to provide secure Internet access for your client computers. However, in special circumstances, IP packet filters must be used either to allow specific traffic to pass or to block specific traffic from passing from the external to the internal interface on a local network server.

After this lesson, you will be able to

- Describe three network scenarios that require IP packet filters
- Create and configure IP packet filters for your network
- Describe the options that can be configured for packet filtering

Estimated lesson time: 45 minutes

When to Use IP Packet Filters

IP packet filters open or close ports statically; that is, they leave ports open or closed as long as the filters remain enabled. In most cases, however, it is preferable to open and close ports dynamically—only as needed, as protocol rules and site and content rules allow. Therefore, it is usually recommended that you create access policy rules to allow internal clients access to the Internet, or create publishing rules to allow external clients access to internal servers. For example, suppose you want to grant all internal users access to HTTP sites. You should not create an IP packet filter that opens port 80. Rather, you should create the necessary site and content rule and protocol rule that allow this access.

However, in some scenarios, you must use IP packet filters. Configure IP packet filters when:

- You publish servers that are located on a *perimeter network* (also known as a *DMZ, demilitarized zone*, and *screened subnet*).
- You run applications or other services on the ISA Server computer that need to access the Internet.
- You want to allow access to protocols that are not based on UDP or TCP.

You can configure IP packet filters only if you install ISA Server in Firewall mode or Integrated mode.

Creating IP Packet Filters

With IP packet filters, you can intercept and either allow or block packets destined for specific computers on your corporate network. You can configure two types of static IP packet filters: *allow filters* and *block filters*.

Allow filters are exception filters; all packet types are blocked except for those you specify. If you do not have a packet filter activated for a specific port, the service cannot listen on that port unless the port is opened dynamically. Block filters close the specified ports. You can create and configure block filters to further define the traffic allowed through the ISA Server computer.

These two filter types can be used together. For example, you can create an allow filter, as shown in Figure 4.12, that allows TCP traffic on port 25 between all internal and external hosts, which enables SMTP communication. You can then limit access, creating a block filter that blocks a range of external IP addresses—potential intruders—from sending TCP packets to port 25 on your ISA Server computer.

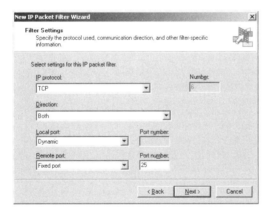

Figure 4.12 Creating an IP packet filter to enable SMTP communication

IP packet filters are defined by the following parameters:

- **Servers.** The filter allows or blocks communication on the specified server.
- **Protocol, port, and direction.** The filter allows or blocks traffic at the specified port, using the specified protocol in the specified direction.
- **Local host.** This is the name of the computer in the internal network for which communication is open or blocked. You can specify a range or a single IP address on the ISA Server computer.
- **Remote host.** This is the name of the computer on the Internet for which communication is allowed or blocked.

> **Note** In order to create IP packet filters, packet filtering must be enabled. Packet filtering is enabled in a default ISA Server installation. It can be manually enabled on the IP Packet Filters Properties dialog box.

▶ **Follow these steps to create an IP packet filter:**

1. In the console tree of ISA Management, right-click IP Packet Filters, point to New, and then click Filter.

2. In the New IP Packet Filter wizard, type the name of the protocol definition, and then click Next.

3. On the Servers page, specify whether you want the IP packet filter to apply to the whole ISA Server array, or to a single server in the array.

4. On the Filter Mode page, specify whether the IP packet filter allows packets or blocks packets from passing.

5. On the Filter Type page, select a predefined filter, or select Custom to create a new filter type.

6. If you select Custom, on the Filter Settings page, specify the IP protocol, direction, and local and remote ports for the IP packet filter.

7. On the Local Computer page, specify a computer on the local network to which the IP packet filter is applied.

8. On the Remote Computers page, select the remote computers to which the IP packet filter is applied.

> **Note** After you create or configure an IP packet filter, you must restart the ISA Server services before the changes will take effect.

▶ **Follow these steps to configure a protocol for an IP packet filter:**

1. On the View menu, select Advanced.

2. In the console tree of ISA Management, click IP Packet Filters.

3. In the details pane, right-click the IP packet filter you want to modify, and then click Properties.

4. Click the Filter Type tab.

5. Do one of the following:
    - Click Predefined, and then click a filter from the list.
    - Click Custom, and then in the IP Protocol drop-down list box, click one of the following: Any, ICMP, TCP, UDP, or Custom Protocol.

6. If you click Custom and the ICMP protocol, do the following:
   - In the Direction drop-down list box, click Inbound, Outbound, or Both.
   - In the Type drop-down list box, click All Types or Fixed Type. If you click Fixed Type, enter the type number in the associated text box.
   - In the Code drop-down list box, click All Codes or Fixed Code. If you click Fixed Code, type the code number in the associated text box.

7. If you click the Custom radio button and then select Any IP Protocol, specify the direction: Inbound, Outbound, or Both.

8. If you click the Custom radio button and then select the UDP protocol, do the following:
   - In Direction, click Receive Only, Send Only, Both, Receive Send, or Send Receive.
   - In Local Port, click All Ports, Fixed Port, or Dynamic. If you click Fixed Port, in Port Number, type the port number.
   - In Remote Port, click All Ports or Fixed Port. If you click Fixed Port, in Port Number, type the port number.

9. If you select Custom and the TCP protocol, do the following:
   - In Direction, click Inbound, Outbound, or Both.
   - In Local Port, click All Ports, Fixed Port, or Dynamic. If you click Fixed Port, in Port Number, type the port number.
   - In Remote Port, click All Ports or Fixed Port. If you click Fixed Port, in Port Number, type the port number.

▶ **Follow these steps to apply an IP packet filter to a server:**

1. If you are in Taskpad view, on the View menu, select Advanced.
2. In the console tree of ISA Management, click IP Packet Filters.
3. In the details pane, right-click the IP packet filter you want to modify, and then click Properties.
4. On the General tab in the Servers That Use This Filter section, do one of the following:
   - Click the All Servers In The Array radio button.
   - Click the Only This Server radio button, and then click the server to which the filter applies.

▶ **Follow these steps to configure an IP packet filter for a local computer:**

1. On the View menu, select Advanced.
2. In the console tree of ISA Management, click IP Packet Filters.
3. In the details pane, right-click the IP packet filter you want to modify, and then click Properties.
4. On the Local Computer tab:
    - To specify that the IP packet filter be applied to the default IP address of each external interface of the local ISA Server computer, click the Default IP Address(es) On The External Interface(s) radio button.
    - To specify that the IP packet filter be applied to a specific IP address of the local ISA Server computer, click the This ISA Server's External IP Address radio button, and type the desired IP address of the ISA Server computer.
    - To select a specific computer on a perimeter network, click the This Computer (On The Perimeter Network) radio button, and type an IP address that is not on the ISA Server computer.
    - To specify a range of IP addresses on the perimeter network, click the These Computers (On The Perimeter Network) radio button, and then type the appropriate information in Subnet and Mask fields.

▶ **Follow these steps to configure an IP packet filter for a remote computer:**

1. On the View menu, select Advanced.
2. In the console tree of ISA Management, click IP Packet Filters.
3. In the details pane, right-click the IP packet filter you want to modify and then click Properties.
4. On the Remote Computer tab, specify the computer to which the IP packet filter should apply by clicking one of the following options:
    - If the filter applies to all external computers, click the All Remote Computers radio button.
    - If the filter applies to one computer, click the This Remote Computer radio button, and then type the IP address of the external computer to which the filter applies.
    - If the filter applies to a range of computers, click the This Range Of Computers radio button, and then type the appropriate information in the Subnet and Mask fields.

Configuring Packet Filter Options

By right-clicking the IP Packet Filters folder in ISA Management, selecting Properties, and selecting the Packet Filters tab, you can configure the following packet filtering features:

- IP fragment filtering
- IP option filtering
- Log packet from "Allow" filters

Figure 4.13 shows the options available on the Packet Filters tab.

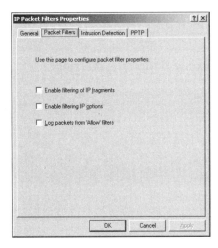

Figure 4.13 Packet filter options can be set on the Packet Filters tab of the IP Packet Filters Properties dialog box.

IP Fragment Filtering

When you check the Enable Filtering Of IP Fragments check box, you allow the Web Proxy service and Firewall service to filter packet fragments. By filtering packet fragments, all fragmented IP packets are dropped. A well-known attack involves sending fragmented packets and then reassembling them in such a way that may cause harm to the receiving system.

Do not enable IP fragment filtering if you want to allow video streams or quality audio streams to pass through ISA Server.

▶ **Follow these steps to enable IP fragment filtering:**

1. In the console tree of ISA Management, right-click IP Packet Filters, and then click Properties.

2. On the General tab, select the Enable Packet Filtering check box if it is not already selected.

3. On the Packet Filters tab, select the Enable Filtering of IP Fragments check box.

IP Options Filtering

By enabling IP options filtering, you can configure ISA Server to refuse all packets that have the words "IP Options" in the header.

▶ **Follow these steps to enable IP options filtering:**

1. In the console tree of ISA Management, right-click IP Packet Filters, and then click Properties.

2. On the General tab, select the Enable Packet Filtering check box if it is not already selected.

3. On the Packet Filters tab, select the Enable Filtering IP Options check box.

Logging Packets

All packets that pass through ISA Server can be logged to the packet filter log. You can configure exactly which packets are logged by following these guidelines:

- By default, when you install ISA Server, all dropped packets are logged to the packet filter log. When you disable packet filtering, logging is turned off altogether.

- You can configure ISA Server to disable logging for packets that are dropped due to any specific block-mode IP packet filter. This is configured on the properties dialog box of the particular block-mode IP packet filter.

- You can configure ISA Server to log all packets—allowed and dropped—that are communicated by way of ISA Server. When you enable logging of allowed packets, all packets that pass through ISA Server are logged in the packet filter log.

Logging allowed packets and blocked packets causes a considerable load on the server.

▶ **Follow these steps to log allowed packets:**

1. In the console tree of ISA Management, right-click IP Packet Filters, and then click Properties.
2. On the Packet Filters tab, select the Log Packets From 'Allow' Filters check box.

Practice: Running Internet Services on the ISA Server Computer

If you need mail, news, and Web access from your ISA Server computer, you can configure five IP packet filters that will allow your system access to the ports used for POP3 (incoming mail), SMTP (outgoing mail), NNTP (news) services, DNS query (Web requests), and HTTP (Web content), respectively. Though you should normally avoid statically opening ports by creating IP packet filters on your firewall server, you can offset the risk of allow-type IP packet filters by creating block filters to block access to IP address ranges outside of those to which you require access (such as the addresses of your POP3, SMTP, and NNTP servers). In addition, you can manually enable and disable IP packet filters to restrict the use of the open ports as needed. Remember to restart ISA Server services whenever you enable or disable an IP packet filter.

Perform the following five exercises on Server1.

Note If your ISA Server computer is connected to the Internet via a dedicated line through a network adapter (and not via a dial-up line through a modem), you do not need to create IP packet filters to establish Web access on the ISA Server computer. You merely need to configure the computer's Web browser to use the IP address of the server's internal network adapter as a proxy server. To use Internet services other than the Web, such as mail and news services, you will still need to create IP packet filters.

Exercise 1: Creating an IP Packet Filter for Incoming (POP3) Mail

In this exercise, you create a packet filter that allows traffic to pass through TCP port 110. This allows your ISA Server computer to receive POP3 mail.

▶ **To create an IP packet filter to allow the POP3 service**

1. Open ISA Management.
2. Navigate to Servers and Arrays, MyArray, Access Policy, IP Packet Filters.

3. Right-click the IP Packet Filters folder, point to New and click Filter.

   The New IP Packet Filter wizard appears.

4. In the IP Packet Filter Name text box, type **POP3 Filter**, and then click Next.

5. On the Servers screen, leave All ISA Server Computers In The Array as the default, and then click Next.

6. On the Filter Mode screen, leave Allow Packet Transmission as the default, and then click Next.

7. On the Filter Type screen, select the Custom radio button, and then click Next.

   The Filter Settings screen appears.

8. Click the IP Protocol drop-down list box and select TCP.

9. Click the Local Port drop-down list box and select Dynamic.

10. Click the Remote Port drop-down list box and select Fixed Port.

    The Port Number text box to the right of the Remote Port drop-down list box becomes available.

11. In the Port Number text box, type **110**.

12. Click Next.

13. On the Local Computer screen, leave Default IP Address(es)... as the default, and then click Next.

14. On the Remote Computers screen, leave All Remote Computers as the default, and then click Next.

    The Completing the New IP Packet Filter Wizard screen appears.

15. Click Finish.

    The POP3 Filter packet filter appears in the list of IP packet filters.

Exercise 2: Creating an IP Packet Filter for Outgoing (SMTP) Mail

In this exercise, you create a packet filter that allows traffic to pass through TCP port 25. This allows your ISA Server computer to send SMTP mail.

▶ **To create an IP packet filter to allow the SMTP service**

1. In ISA Management, navigate to Servers and Arrays, MyArray, Access Policy, IP Packet Filters.
2. Right-click the IP Packet Filters folder, point to New, and click Filter.

    The New IP Packet Filter Wizard appears.

3. In the IP Packet Filter Name text box, type **SMTP Filter**, and then click Next.
4. On the Servers screen, leave All ISA Server Computers In The Array as the default, and then click Next.
5. On the Filter Mode screen, leave Allow Packet Transmission as the default, and then click Next.
6. On the Filter Type screen, select the Custom radio button, and then click Next.

    The Filter Settings screen appears.

7. Click the IP Protocol drop-down list box and select TCP.
8. Click the Local Port drop-down list box and select Dynamic.
9. Click the Remote Port drop-down list box and select Fixed Port.

    The Port Number text box to the right of the Remote Port drop-down list box becomes available.

10. In the Port Number text box, type **25**.
11. Click Next.
12. On the Local Computer screen, leave Default IP Address(es)… as the default, and then click Next.
13. On the Remote Computers screen, leave All Remote Computers as the default, and then click Next.

    The Completing the New IP Packet Filter wizard appears.

14. Click Finish.

    The SMTP Filter appears in the list of IP packet filters in ISA Management.

Exercise 3: Creating an IP Packet Filter for NNTP

In this exercise, you create a packet filter that allows traffic to pass through TCP port 119. This allows your ISA Server computer to connect to NNTP servers and to post and read NNTP messages.

▶ **To create an IP packet filter to allow the NNTP service**

1. In ISA Management, navigate to Servers and Arrays, MyArray, Access Policy, IP Packet Filters.
2. Right-click the IP Packet Filters folder, point to New and click Filter.

    The New IP Packet Filter wizard appears.

3. In the IP Packet Filter Name text box, type **NNTP Filter**, and then click Next.
4. On the Servers screen, leave All ISA Server Computers In The Array as the default, and then click Next.
5. On the Filter Mode screen, leave Allow Packet Transmission as the default, and then click Next.
6. On the Filter Type screen, select the Custom radio button, and then click Next.

    The Filter Settings screen appears.

7. Click the IP Protocol drop-down list box and select TCP.
8. Click the Local Port drop-down list box and select Dynamic.
9. Click the Remote Port drop-down list box and select Fixed Port.

    The Port Number text box to the right of the Remote Port drop-down list box becomes available.

10. In the Port Number text box, type **119**.
11. Click Next.
12. On the Local Computer screen, leave Default IP Address(es)... as the default, and then click Next.
13. On the Remote Computers screen, leave All Remote Computers as the default, and then click Next.

    The Completing the New IP Packet Filter Wizard screen appears.

14. Click Finish.

    The NNTP Filter appears in the list of IP packet filters in ISA Management.

Exercise 4: Creating an IP Packet Filter to Allow Outgoing Web Requests (DNS Queries)

In this exercise, you create a packet filter that allows traffic to pass through UDP port 53. This allows your ISA Server computer to make successful DNS queries.

▶ **To create an IP packet filter to allow DNS queries**

1. Open the ISA Management console.
2. Navigate to Servers and Arrays, MyArray, Access Policy, IP Packet Filters.
3. Right-click the IP Packet Filters folder, point to New and click Filter.

    The New IP Packet Filter wizard appears.

4. In the IP Packet Filter Name text box, type **DNS Query**, and then click Next.
5. On the Servers screen, leave All ISA Server Computers In The Array as the default, and then click Next.
6. On the Filter Mode screen, leave Allow Packet Transmission as the default, and then click Next.
7. On the Filter Type screen, select the Custom radio button, and then click Next.

    The Filter Settings screen appears.

8. Click the IP Protocol drop-down list box and select UDP.
9. Click the Local Port drop-down list box and select Dynamic.
10. Click the Remote Port drop-down list box and select Fixed Port.

    The Port Number text box to the right of the Remote Port drop-down list box becomes available.

11. In the Port Number text box, type **53**.
12. Click Next.
13. On the Local Computer screen, leave Default IP Address(es)... as the default, and then click Next.
14. On the Remote Computers screen, leave All Remote Computers as the default, and then click Next.

    The Completing the New IP Packet Filter Wizard screen appears.

15. Click Finish.

    The DNS query packet filter now appears in the list of IP packet filters in ISA Management.

Exercise 5: Creating an IP Packet Filter for Web Content (HTTP)

In this exercise, you create a packet filter that allows traffic to pass through TCP port 80. This allows your ISA Server computer to receive Web content.

▶ **To create an IP packet filter to allow Web content**

1. Open ISA Management.
2. Navigate to Servers and Arrays, MyArray, Access Policy, IP Packet Filters.
3. Right-click the IP Packet Filters folder, point to New and click Filter.

   The New IP Packet Filter wizard appears.
4. In the IP Packet Filter Name text box, type **HTTP Client**, and then click Next.
5. On the Servers screen, leave All ISA Server Computers In The Array as the default, and then click Next.
6. On the Filter Mode screen, leave Allow Packet Transmission as the default, and then click Next.
7. On the Filter Type screen, select the Custom radio button, and then click Next.

   The Filter Settings screen appears.
8. Click the IP Protocol drop-down list box and select TCP.
9. Click the Local Port drop-down list box and select Dynamic.
10. Click the Remote Port drop-down list box and select Fixed Port.

    The Port Number text box to the right of the Remote Port drop-down list box becomes available.
11. In the Port Number text box, type **80**.
12. Click Next.
13. On the Local Computer screen, leave Default IP Address(es)... as the default, and then click Next.

14. On the Remote Computers screen, leave All Remote Computers as the default, and then click Next.

    The Completing the New IP Packet Filter Wizard screen appears.

15. Click Finish.

    The HTTP Client packet filter now appears in the list of IP packet filters in ISA Management.

    Note that this packet filter only allows HTTP content and not S-HTTP content. To allow the ISA Server to browse secure Web sites, you would need to create an additional allow packet filter set to TCP port 443.

Lesson Summary

Though access policy rules and publishing rules are the preferred means of allowing access to and from your network, you must, in some scenarios, use IP packet filters to control access instead. For example, you will need to use IP packet filters if you publish servers that are located on a perimeter network, or if, on your ISA Server computer, you run applications and services that need to listen to the Internet. A third scenario that calls for IP packet filters is when you want to allow access to protocols that are not based on UDP or TCP. IP packet filters can function as either allow filters or block filters.

You can configure three types of options for IP packet filters: IP fragment filtering, IP option filtering, and "Allow" filter logging. By filtering packet fragments, all fragmented IP packets are dropped, which prevents a well-known type of network attack but also prevents video and audio streams from passing through ISA Server. With IP Options filtering, you can configure ISA Server either to filter or to refuse all packets that have the words IP Options in the header. Finally, through "Allow" filter logging, you can configure ISA Server to log all packets—allowed and dropped—that are communicated by way of ISA Server. (Dropped packets are logged by default.)

Lesson 6 Configuring ISA Server to Detect External Attacks and Intrusions

You can configure ISA Server to detect common types of network attacks. By default, when you enable intrusion detection, ISA Server writes a message to the Windows 2000 Event Log whenever an attack is detected. You can also configure ISA Server to respond to detected intrusions by sending an e-mail, starting a specified program, and starting or stopping selected ISA Server services.

After this lesson, you will be able to

- Describe the types of network attacks that can be detected by ISA Server
- Configure ISA Server to detect external network attacks and intrusions

Estimated lesson time: 25 minutes

Intrusion Types and Alerts

ISA Server features intrusion detection, which identifies when an attack is attempted against your network. When an attack (see Figure 4.14) is detected by ISA Server, ISA Server performs a set of configured actions (or *alerts*). The following events are considered intrusions:

- Port scan attack
- IP half scan attack
- Land attack
- Ping of death attack
- UDP bomb attack
- Windows out-of-band attack

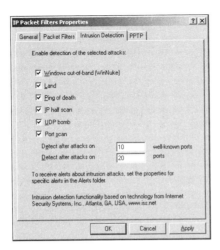

Figure 4.14 Types of attacks detected by ISA Server intrusion detection

Port Scan Attack

Two types of port scan attacks trigger an alert in ISA Server: All Ports Scan Attacks and Enumerated Port Scan Attacks.

All Ports Scan Attack

This alert notifies you that an attempt was made to access more than the preconfigured number of ports. You can specify a threshold, which indicates the number of ports that can be accessed.

Enumerated Port Scan Attack

This alert notifies you that an attempt was made to count the services running on a computer by probing each port for a response.

If this alert occurs, you should identify the source of the port scan. Compare this with the services that are running on the target computer. Also, identify the source and intent of the scan. Check the access logs for indications of unauthorized access. If you do detect indications of unauthorized access, you should consider the system compromised and take appropriate action.

IP Half Scan Attack

This alert notifies that repeated attempts to a destination computer were made, and no corresponding ACK (acknowledge) packets were communicated.

A standard TCP connection is established by sending a SYN (synchronize/start) packet to the destination computer. If the destination is waiting for a connection on the specified port, it responds with a SYN/ACK (synchronize acknowledge) packet. The initial sender replies with an ACK packet, and the connection is established. If the destination computer is not waiting for a connection on the specified port, it responds with an RST (reset) packet.

Most system logs do not log completed connections until the final ACK packet is received from the source. Sending an RST packet instead of the final ACK results in the connection never actually being established, and therefore the connection is not logged. Because the source can identify whether the destination sent a SYN/ACK or RST packet, an attacker can determine exactly which ports are open for connections without the destination being aware of the probing.

If this alert occurs, log the address from which the scan occurs. If appropriate, configure the ISA Server policy rules or IP packet filters to block traffic from the source of the scans.

Land Attack

This alert notifies you that a TCP SYN packet was sent with a spoofed source IP address and port number that matches that of the destination IP address and port. If the attack is successfully mounted, it can cause some TCP implementation to go into a loop that crashes the computer.

If this alert occurs, configure the ISA Server policy rules or IP packet filters to inhibit traffic from the source of the scans.

Ping of Death Attack

This alert notifies you that a large amount of information was appended to an Internet Control Message Protocol (ICMP) echo request (ping) packet. If the attack is successfully mounted, a kernel buffer overflows when the computer attempts to respond, which crashes the computer.

If this alert occurs, create a protocol rule that specifically denies incoming ICMP echo request packets from the Internet.

UDP Bomb Attack

This alert notifies you that there is an attempt to send an illegal UDP packet. A UDP packet that is constructed with illegal values in certain fields will cause some older operating systems to crash when the packet is received. If the target machine does crash, it is often difficult to determine the cause.

Windows Out-of-Band Attack (WinNuke)

This alert notifies you that there was an out-of-band denial-of-service attack attempted against a computer protected by ISA Server. If mounted successfully, this attack causes the computer to crash or causes a loss of network connectivity on vulnerable computers.

Note Intrusion detection functionality is based on technology from Internet Security Systems, Inc., Atlanta, Georgia.

Configuring Intrusion Detection

To detect unwanted intruders, ISA Server compares network traffic and log entries to well-known attack methods. Suspicious activities trigger a set of configured actions, or alerts. Actions include connection termination, service termination, e-mail alerts, logging, and running a program of your choice.

To enable this feature, select the Enable Intrusion Detection check box on the IP Packet Filters Properties dialog box, as shown in Figure 4.15.

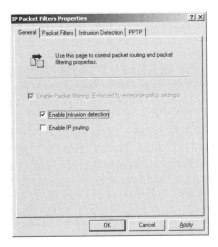

Figure 4.15 Enabling intrusion detection

ISA Server includes an alert preconfigured for intrusion detection named Intrusion Detected, which is shown in Figure 4.16. By default, when intrusion detection is enabled, this alert writes a message to the Windows 2000 Event Log whenever any intrusion type is detected. You can modify the Intrusion Detected alert to carry out additional responses whenever any intrusion is detected. You can also create a new alert to perform any available alert response when a specific intrusion type is detected. In addition, when configuring port scan alerts, you can configure how many port attacks trigger an alert.

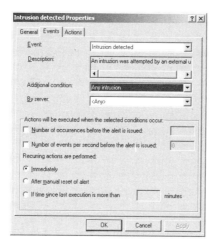

Figure 4.16 The preconfigured alert: Intrusion Detected

▶ **Follow these steps to configure intrusion detection:**

1. In the console tree of ISA Management, right-click IP Packet Filters and then click Properties.

2. On the General tab, select the Enable Packet Filtering check box if it is not already selected, and select the Enable Intrusion Detection check box.

3. On the Intrusion Detection tab, click the types of attacks that should generate events:
    - Windows Out-Of-Band (WinNuke)
    - Land
    - Ping Of Death
    - IP Half Scan
    - UDP Bomb
    - Port Scan

4. If you select Port Scan, do the following:

    - In the Well-Known Ports text box, type the maximum number of well-known ports that can be scanned before generating an event.

    - In the Ports text box, type the total number of ports that can be scanned before generating an alert.

Note A well-known port is any port in the range of 0 to 1023.

Practice: Configuring Intrusion Detection on ISA Server

In this exercise, you enable intrusion detection on ISA Server, which enables ISA Server to write an alert to the event log whenever intrusion is detected.

Exercise: Enabling Intrusion Detection

In this exercise, you enable ISA Server to detect all six intrusion types.

▶ **To enable intrusion detection for all intrusion types**

1. In ISA Management, navigate to Servers And Arrays, MyArray, Access Policy, IP Packet Filters.

2. Right-click the IP Packet Filters folder, and click Properties.

    The IP Packet Filters Properties dialog box appears.

3. On the General tab, click the Enable Intrusion Detection check box.

4. Click the Intrusion Detection tab.

5. Click the Windows Out-Of-Band (WinNuke), Land, Ping Of Death, IP Half Scan, UDP Bomb, and Port Scan check boxes.

    The two Detect After Attacks On text boxes become available.

6. Leave the default settings in these text boxes and click OK.

Lesson Summary

When you enable intrusion detection on the IP Packet Filters properties dialog box in ISA Management, you can configure ISA Server to detect any of six common network attacks. These attacks include a port scan attack, an IP half scan attack, a land attack, a ping of death attack, a UDP bomb attack, and a Windows-out-of-band (WinNuke) attack. By default, when you enable intrusion detection, ISA Server writes a message to the Windows 2000 Event Log that appears as an alert in Event Viewer whenever one of these six attacks is detected. You can also configure ISA Server to respond to attacks by sending an e-mail to an administrator, by starting a specified program, or by starting or stopping selected ISA Server services.

Review

The following questions are intended to reinforce key information presented in the chapter. If you are unable to answer a question, review the appropriate lesson and then try the question again. The answers for these questions are located in Appendix A, "Questions and Answers."

1. Under which of the following conditions will John be able to access the Internet through Internet Security and Acceleration Server 2000 (ISA Server)? Assume that the default Allow site and content rule is in place, and that no other rules or filters have been configured.

    a) You configure a protocol rule to allow access to all IP traffic for any request. You then configure a second protocol rule denying access to all IP traffic for user John. You have not modified the default array properties for outgoing Web requests. Will John be able to access the Internet through a Web browser on a secure network address translation (SecureNAT) client?

    b) You configure a protocol rule to allow access to all IP traffic for all members of the Domain Users group. John is a member of the group Domain Guests (and not Domain Users), and the default array properties for outgoing Web requests have not been changed. Will John be able to access the Internet through a Web browser on a secure network address translation (SecureNAT) client?

    c) You configure a protocol rule to allow access to all IP traffic for any request. You then configure a second protocol rule denying access to all IP traffic for Domain Guests. John is a member (only) of the group Domain Guests, and the default array properties for outgoing Web requests have been changed to require identification for unauthenticated users. Will he be able to access the Internet through a Web browser on a Firewall client?

d) You configure a protocol rule to allow access to all IP traffic for all members of the group Domain Users. John is a member of the group Domain Users. Will he be able to establish an FTP connection across the Internet from a command prompt on a computer not configured with a Firewall client?

2. What protective measure can you take if you detect an IP half scan attack originating from a certain network ID?

3. What are three conditions under which you need to create IP packet filters instead of protocol rule or site and content rules to allow Internet connectivity?

4. You have configured a site and content rule that denies access to two destinations: ftp://movies.acme.com/clips and ftp://radio.acme.com. Assuming that your users have permissions to download files from the FTP site, will your users be able to download content through FTP clients on ftp://movies.acme.com? Will they be able to download content from ftp://radio.acme.com/songs?

5. If you wanted to block a group of Windows 2000 users from downloading all audio content during 10 A.M. and 4 P.M. weekdays, how many policy elements would you need to create?

CHAPTER 5

Configuring Internet Acceleration through the ISA Server Cache

Lesson 1 Creating a Basic Cache Policy in ISA Server 202

Lesson 2 Configuring Cache Properties in ISA Server 214

Lesson 3 Scheduling Cache Content Downloads 226

Review 232

About This Chapter

Microsoft Internet Security and Acceleration Server 2000 (ISA Server) allows you to accelerate your Internet connectivity by enabling the Web Proxy service to retrieve requested Web objects locally from a cache rather than from across the Internet. This cache can also be used to store information published on your network's internal servers. To configure this feature to suit your needs, you need to create a cache policy by configuring routing rules and cache properties (such as time-to-live [TTL] parameters). To augment your cache policy, you can also create scheduled download jobs for Web content.

Before You Begin

To complete the lessons in this chapter, you must have

- Completed all the exercises in this book through Chapter 4

Lesson 1 Creating a Basic Cache Policy with Routing Rules

In its function as a cache server, ISA Server improves network performance by maintaining a cache of frequently requested Web objects. Creating a cache policy entails configuring routing rules, cache configuration properties, and optionally, access policy and publishing rules. This lesson presents an overview of how to configure a cache policy and focuses on the most basic aspect of this process—creating routing rules.

After this lesson, you will be able to

- Describe how ISA Server determines whether to retrieve a requested object from the cache or from its specified location
- Create a routing rule that determines how ISA Server should handle client requests for Web objects

Estimated lesson time: 40 minutes

How Caching Works

ISA Server maintains a cache of frequently requested Hypertext Transfer Protocol (HTTP) and File Transfer Protocol (FTP) objects. Whenever ISA Server receives a request for Web or FTP content, ISA Server attempts to fulfill the client request from the cache. If the request cannot be fulfilled from the cache, the ISA Server computer initiates a new request on behalf of the client. Depending on how you set up routing rules, you can configure ISA Server to cache external content for outgoing requests (forward caching), internal content for incoming requests (reverse caching), or both. Once the destination Web or FTP server responds to the ISA Server computer, the ISA Server computer caches the response to the original client request and sends a response to the client.

ISA Server includes an HTTP redirector filter, which allows both firewall and SecureNAT clients to benefit from the caching features. When the HTTP redirector is enabled, Web requests from Firewall and SecureNAT clients can both be cached.

If ISA Server is installed in Firewall mode, it does not maintain a cache.

Processing Caching Rules

ISA Server consults both cache configuration properties and routing rules to determine whether to retrieve a requested object from its cache or to retrieve it from another server.

Cache Configuration Properties

Cache configuration properties refer to the set of configurable options available on the Cache Configuration Properties dialog box. These options include setting the expiration policy (TTL parameters for objects in the cache), the active caching policy, the maximum size of objects in the cache, the maximum size of Uniform Resource Locators (URLs) cached in memory, and the percentage of available memory to use for caching.

As shown in Figure 5.1, you can access the Cache Configuration Properties dialog box either by right-clicking the Cache Configuration node and selecting Properties, or by selecting the Cache Configuration node and clicking the Configure Cache Policy icon in Taskpad view.

Cache configuration properties are discussed in detail in Lesson 2 of this chapter.

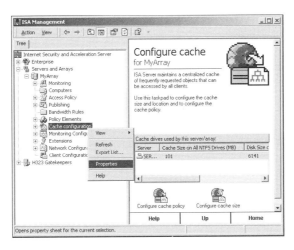

Figure 5.1 Accessing cache configuration properties

Routing Rules

The most basic aspect of creating a cache policy is to configure routing rules that specify when ISA Server should cache content and when ISA Server should retrieve content from the cache. Routing rules can be configured in ISA Management through the Network Configuration node.

When to Cache Content

Routing rules are responsible for storing retrieved objects in the cache. When you create a new routing rule, you can specify whether to store all retrieved objects (including dynamic content) in the cache, to store retrieved objects only when the source and request headers indicate to cache, or never to store retrieved objects in the cache. ISA Server's default routing rule caches content only when the source and request headers indicate to cache, and the cache properties for this rule cannot be modified. To enable ISA Server to store all content in the cache, you must create a new routing rule.

When to Retrieve Objects from the Cache

By using routing rules, you can specify when ISA Server should answer a Web request by consulting the cache and when to forward the request to an upstream server. When defining a new routing rule, you may configure ISA Server to retrieve the requested object from the cache only when a non-expired version of the object exists in the cache, and to route the request upstream when none exists; to retrieve any version of the requested object, and to route the request upstream when none exists; or to retrieve any version of the object and never to route the request.

The default routing rule specifies that ISA Server should route the request unless ISA Server can retrieve a valid version of the requested object from the cache. Since you cannot modify the caching properties of the default routing rule, you must create a new rule if you want to change how and when ISA Server retrieves content from the cache.

Applying Routing Rules to Particular Destinations

A routing rule will apply to a given request when the destination of the request matches the specified destination of a routing rule. You can configure a routing rule for all destinations, for all internal destinations, for all external destinations, for a specific destination set, or for all destinations except a specific destination set. This flexibility allows you to configure separate caching behavior for forward and reverse caching, or to configure caching behavior specific to any particular destination.

Note Reverse caching is configured by routing rules that specify internal destinations.

▶ **Follow these steps to create a routing rule:**

1. In the console tree of ISA Management, right-click the Routing folder, point to New, and then click Rule.

2. In the New Routing Rule wizard, type the name of the routing rule, and then click Next.

3. On the Destination Sets screen, select the type of destination or the destination set to which the rule should apply, and then click Next.

4. On the Request Action screen, select how ISA Server should route client requests: directly from the specified destination, from an upstream server, or from a hosted site. You can also specify if a dial-up entry should be used.

5. On the Cache Retrieval Configuration screen, specify whether ISA Server should look in its cache for the requested object.

6. On the Cache Content Configuration screen, specify when objects should be cached.

Once you create a new routing rule, you can later reconfigure the cache properties for that rule, as shown in Figure 5.2.

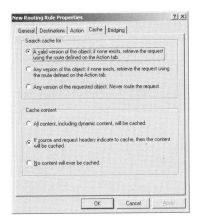

Figure 5.2 Routing rule properties for caching

▶ **Follow these steps to modify caching properties for an existing routing rule:**

1. In the console tree of ISA Management, click the Routing folder.

2. In the details pane, right-click the applicable routing rule, and then click Properties. (You must select a rule other than the default rule.)

3. On the Cache tab, select one of the following options contained in the Search Cache For section:

    - If the object should be retrieved from the cache only if the object is available and has not expired, click the A Valid Version Of The Object; If None Exists, Retrieve The Request Using The Route Defined On The Action Tab radio button. This option will route the request upstream when no valid (non-expired) version of the object exists in the cache.

- If the object should be retrieved from the cache whenever any version of the object is available, click the Any Version Of The Object; If None Exists, Retrieve The Request Using The Route Defined On The Action Tab radio button. This option will route the request upstream when no version of the object (valid or not) exists in the cache.

- If the object should be retrieved only if it is in the cache, click the Any Version Of The Requested Object In The Cache, Never Route The Request radio button. This option will never route requests upstream.

4. On the Cache tab, select one of the following options contained in the Cache Content section:

    - If you want all content to be cached, select the All Content, Including Dynamic Content, Will Be Cached radio button.

    - If you want content to be cached only if source and request headers indicate to cache, select the If Source And Request Headers Indicate To Cache, Then The Content Will Be Cached radio button.

    - If retrieved objects should not be cached, select the No Content Will Ever Be Cached radio button.

▶ **Follow these steps to configure how routing rules retrieve requests:**

1. In the console tree of ISA Management, click the Routing folder.

2. In the details pane, right-click the applicable routing rule, and then click Properties.

3. On the Action tab, select one of the following options:

    - To retrieve the requested object directly from the Internet, click the Retrieving Them Directly From The Specified Destination radio button.

    - If an upstream server should service the request, click the Routing Them to A Specified Upstream Server radio button and configure the primary and backup route.

    - If the request should be redirected to a different computer, click the Redirecting Them to A Hosted Site radio button and configure the site, port, and Secure Sockets Layer (SSL) port.

4. (Optional) If you route the request directly to the specified destination or to an upstream server, and if you want to use a dial-up connection as the primary route for the request, click the Use Dial-up Entry For Primary Route check box.

   Choosing this option will enable auto-dial capability from Web Proxy clients.

5. (Optional) If you select to route the request directly to an upstream server, and you want to specify a dial-up connection as a backup route, click the Use Dial-up Entry For Backup Route check box.

Routing rules also determine whether the results from a request will be cached, and whether to cache dynamic content as well as non–dynamic content. In ISA Server, an object with dynamic content is one that contains a question mark (?) in its address.

Routing rules can be applied either to all request destinations, to all internal destinations, to all external destinations, to a specified destination set, or to all destinations except a specified destination set.

▶ **Follow these steps to specify the destination for a routing rule:**

1. In the console tree of ISA Management, click the Routing folder.
2. In the details pane, right-click the applicable routing rule, and then click Properties.
3. On the Destinations tab, click one of the following destinations to which the routing rule applies.
   - All Destinations
   - All External Destinations
   - All Internal Destinations
   - Selected Destination Set
   - All Destinations Except Selected Set
4. If you chose Selected Destination Set or All Destinations Except Selected Set, in the Name drop-down list box, select a destination set.

Note If the destination set that you want to specify does not exist, you can click New to create it, and then later select it from the list in the Name field.

You can see all of the ISA Server routing rules by selecting the Routing folder under the Network Configuration node in ISA Management and viewing the details pane.

Rule Order

Routing rules are ordered, with the default routing rule processed last. For each new connection, the ISA Server computer processes the routing rules in order from first to last. If the request matches the conditions specified by the rule, the request is routed, redirected, and cached accordingly. Otherwise, the next rule is processed. This continues until the last rule (the default rule) is processed and applied to the request.

▶ **Follow these steps to change the order of a routing rule:**

1. In the console tree of ISA Management, click the Routing folder.

2. In the details pane, right-click the rule whose order you want to change, and then click Move Up or Move Down.

   Two rules plus the default rule must be present for the Move Up and Move Down options to appear.

3. Repeat as necessary to arrange the rules in the desired order.

Note You cannot change the position of the default rule.

Default Routing Rule

When you install ISA Server, it configures a default routing rule. The default rule is initially configured so that a non-expired, cached version of a requested object is retrieved if one exists. If a valid object is not in the cache, the default rule specifies that the object should be retrieved directly from the Internet. It is important to note that the default routing rule specifies that dynamic content should not be cached.

The default routing rule is processed last. You can modify the properties on the Action tab of the Default Rule Properties dialog box, and you can modify how the rule redirects outgoing Web requests (Bridging tab), but you cannot delete the default routing rule.

Processing Flow for Caching

Figure 5.3 illustrates the processing flow for caching objects. The figure illustrates how ISA Server analyzes routing rules, cache configuration, and existing cache content to determine whether an object should be retrieved from the cache.

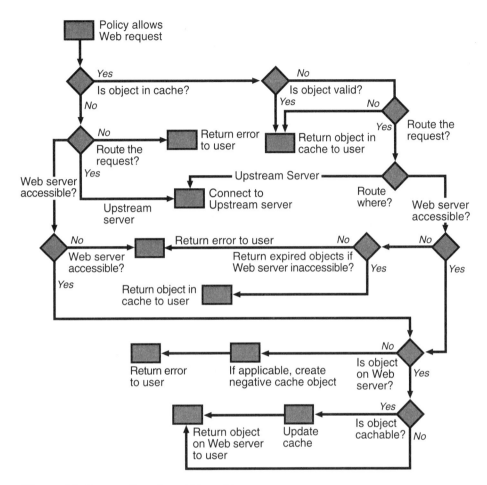

Figure 5.3 Process flow for caching objects

If the user request is allowed, ISA Server checks to determine if the object exists in its cache. If the request is made to an array of ISA Server computers, the Cache Array Routing Protocol (CARP) algorithm is used to determine which server's cache should be checked. If the object is not in the cache, ISA Server checks the routing rule's action to determine how to route the request. If the object is in the cache, ISA Server performs the following steps:

1. ISA Server checks if the object is valid. The object is considered invalid if one of the following conditions is true:

    - The TTL specified in the source has expired.
    - The TTL that you configured in a scheduled cache content download job has expired.
    - The TTL that you configured for the object in the Cache Configuration Properties dialog box has expired.

    If the object is valid, ISA Server retrieves the object from the cache and returns it to the user.

2. If the object is invalid, ISA Server checks the applicable routing rule. If you configured the routing rule cache properties to return any version of the object, ISA Server retrieves the invalid object from the cache.

3. If the routing rule is configured to route the request, ISA Server determines whether to route the request to the upstream server or to the requested Web server.

4. If the routing rule is configured to route the request to the Web server, ISA Server checks to determine if the Web server is accessible.

5. If the Web server is not accessible, ISA Server checks if you configured the server to return expired objects from the cache. If you elected to return the expired object, the object is returned from the cache to the user.

6. If the Web server is available, ISA Server determines if the object is cacheable. If so, and if you configured the routing rule's cache properties to cache the response, ISA Server caches the object and returns the object to the user.

Cache Filtering

By applying different routing rules to different destinations, you can configure ISA Server to cache content only from the destinations you choose. This effectively lets you filter which content will be cached.

For example, you might not want to cache objects from a particular Internet server, called example.microsoft.com. You can configure a routing rule with the following properties:

- A destination set that includes example.microsoft.com.
- A request action set to the applicable routing method.
- The cache configured so that it never caches responses to the request. This ensures that content always comes straight from the source and is never outdated.

Additional Cache Policy

Some cache behavior may be determined by site and content rules and publishing rules.

When you install ISA Server in Cache mode, site and content rules add an access policy mechanism and security features to a cache-only scenario. The site and content rules limit which sites and Multipurpose Internet Mail Extensions (MIME) content can be accessed by specific Internet users and client computers.

Web publishing rules map requests from Internet clients to the appropriate Web server on the corporate network. Web publishing rules affect reverse caching behavior by determining which client address sets can access the cache and which servers can upload data to the cache.

Practice: Caching Dynamic Content

In ISA Server a Web object with dynamic content has a question mark (?) in its address. Caching dynamic content is an option configured in routing rules, and since the default routing rule caches content only if the content is non-dynamic, you need to create a new routing rule specifying that content always be cached if you wish to cache dynamic content.

Exercise: Creating a Routing Rule Caching Both Non-Dynamic and Dynamic Content

The cache properties of the default routing rule are not configurable, so to change the type of content that ISA Server caches, you need to create a new routing rule that always caches content. When this routing rule is applied to a request, it caches the results of the request regardless of whether the content is dynamic or non-dynamic.

▶ **To create a routing rule that always caches content**

1. In ISA Management, navigate to Servers and Arrays, MyArray, Network Configuration, Routing.

2. Right-click the Routing folder, point to New, and then click Rule.

   The New Routing Rule wizard appears.

3. In the Routing Rule Name text box, type **Cache Dynamic Content**.

4. Click Next.

   The Destination Sets screen appears.

5. Leave the default as All Destinations, and then click Next.

   The Request Action screen appears.

6. Leave the default action as Retrieve Them Directly From Specified Destination, and then click Next.

   The Cache Retrieval Configuration screen appears.

7. Leave the default as A Valid Version Of The Object; If None Exists, Retrieve The Request Using The Specified Requested Action, and then click Next.

   The Cache Content Configuration screen appears.

8. Select the All Content, Including Dynamic Content, Will Be Cached radio button and then click Next.

   The Completing The New Routing Rule Wizard screen appears.

9. Click Finish.

   The Cache Dynamic Content routing rule appears in the details pane.

Lesson Summary

Though your complete cache policy in ISA Server includes cache configuration properties and, potentially, access policy and publishing rules, the routing rules you configure will determine what should be cached and when a request should be retrieved from the cache. This is the most fundamental aspect of your cache policy.

Routing rules, which are configured through the Network Configuration node in ISA Management, determine whether ISA Server will handle a request. Routing rules do one of the following:

- Route the request upstream unless ISA Server can return a valid (non-expired) version of the requested object from the cache;
- Route the request upstream unless ISA Server can return any version of the requested object (valid or not) from the cache; or
- Route any version of the requested object from the cache and never routing the request.

Routing rules also determine when to cache content after a request is fulfilled: always, never, or only when both source and request headers indicate to cache.

Any routing rule you create can be applied to all destinations, to all internal destinations, to all external destinations, to a specific destination set, or to all destinations except a specific destination set. By applying different routing rules to different destinations, you can configure ISA Server to cache content only from the destinations you choose.

Routing rules are ordered, and the default routing rule is processed last. If a request matches the conditions specified by a rule, the request is routed, redirected, and cached according to that rule. Otherwise, the next rule is processed. The default routing rule is initially configured to handle Web requests so that requests are routed upstream unless a non-expired version of the requested object exists in the cache. In addition, the default routing rule only stores retrieved objects in the ISA Server cache when both source and request headers indicate to cache. Because these properties of the default routing rule cannot be changed, you must create new routing rules if you want to configure a customized cache policy.

Lesson 2 Configuring Cache Properties in ISA Server

Cache properties are settings that can be configured for cache size, cache location, RAM caching, TTL parameters, active caching, negative caching, cache object restrictions, and caching behavior. These settings can be configured in the Properties dialog box of the Cache Configuration node and in the Properties dialog box of each Server located in the Drives folder in ISA Management.

After this lesson, you will be able to

- Configure cache drive size and location in ISA Management
- Restrict the size of objects that can be stored in the cache
- Adjust the available percentage of RAM used for caching
- Determine whether ISA Server should cache dynamic content
- Set expiration policies for HTTP and FTP objects in the cache
- Determine whether and when ISA Server should return expired objects
- Enable active caching
- Configure negative caching

Estimated lesson time: 45 minutes

Configuring Cache Drives

If you install ISA Server in Cache mode or Integrated mode, then, as part of the setup process, you will be prompted to select cache drives. ISA Server sets aside space to store cached data on the selected drive.

You can change your cache drive configuration at any point by selecting the Drives folder under the Cache Configuration node in ISA Management. In the details pane, double-click the server entry whose drives you want to configure.

Cache Requirements and Recommendations

You must use an NT File System (NTFS) partition for caching, and the drive must be a local drive. Typically, the best performance is obtained if you use a drive different from that on which the ISA Server application files and the Microsoft Windows 2000 operating system are installed. If you are dedicating a drive to caching, you should re-format the drive before assigning it as a cache drive.

If you want to use the ISA Server caching feature, you must install ISA Server on a computer that has at least one partition formatted as an NTFS volume. If your current server disk volume uses file allocation table (FAT) partitions, you can convert these partitions to NTFS by using Convert.exe, which is included with Microsoft Windows 2000 Server. Convert.exe does not overwrite the data on the disk. For more information on using Convert.exe, type **convert /?** at a command prompt.

You can select the disk drives that are available for caching during ISA Server installation. If you plan to use your ISA Server computer for caching, you should reserve as much space as possible for caching. If necessary, cache size can be increased later by adding more disk volumes.

By default, Setup searches for the largest NTFS partition and sets a default cache size of 100 megabytes (MB) if there are at least 150 MB available. When configuring the cache drives, you must allocate at least one drive and 5 MB for caching. However, it is recommended that you allocate at least 100 MB and add 0.5 MB for each Web Proxy client, rounded up to the nearest full megabyte.

You might also want to change the default for the ISA Server cache to your fastest hard disk drive, preferably a small computer system interface (SCSI) drive that has adequate free space.

Windows 2000 allows you to format a drive without assigning a letter. However, ISA Server caching does not recognize these drives.

Configuring Size and Location

For each server, you can configure the size and location of the cache used by the Web Proxy service. It is recommended that you allocate a large cache, since objects are dropped from the cache when it reaches its capacity.

▶ **Follow these steps to configure cache size on a server:**

1. In the console tree of ISA Management, expand the Cache Configuration node and then click Drives.

2. In the details pane, right-click the applicable server, and then click Properties.

3. Click the desired NTFS drive.

4. In the Maximum Cache Size (MB) text box, type the size of the cache, and then click Set.

5. Click OK.

You can also configure the percentage of total memory to use for caching.

▶ **Follow these steps to configure percentage of available memory to use for caching:**

1. In the console tree of ISA Management, right-click the Cache Configuration node, and then click Properties.

2. On the Advanced tab, in the Percentage Of Free Memory To Use For Caching text box, type a number between 1 and 100 that specifies the maximum percentage of memory that should be allocated for caching.

3. Click OK.

When you modify cache properties, the Web Proxy service is stopped and restarted.

Cache Content Files

When you configure a drive for caching (Figure 5.4), ISA Server creates a cache content file on that drive with a .cdat extension. This file is created in the Urlcache folder.

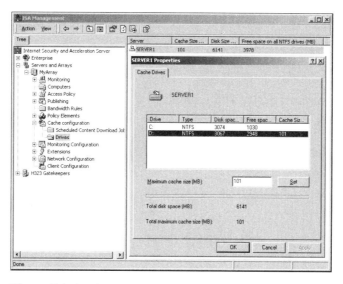

Figure 5.4 Configuring a cache drive and content file

There is a cache content file for each 10 GB of allocated cache space on a disk. For example, if you allocate 12 GB of disk space on a particular drive, ISA Server creates two cache content files. The first file will be 10 GB and the second file will be 2 GB.

As objects are cached, ISA Server appends them to the cache content file. If the cache content file is too full to hold a new object, ISA Server removes older objects from the cache, using a formula that evaluates age, how often the object is accessed, and size.

Warning Do not modify or delete the cache content files.

Configuring How ISA Server Caches Objects

Though routing rules allow you to specify which content should be cached according to destination and according to content type (dynamic versus static), the Cache Configuration Properties dialog box allows you to specify with more precision which objects should be cached, and when.

Configuring Which Content to Cache

You can configure whether ISA Server should cache the following types of HTTP objects:

- Objects larger than a specified size
- Objects whose last modification date is not specified
- Objects that do not have a 200 (normal) response
- Objects with question marks in their URL

▶ **Follow these steps to configure which content to cache:**

1. In the console tree of ISA Management, right-click the Cache Configuration node, and then click Properties.

2. On the Advanced tab, do one or more of the following:

    - To limit size of cached objects, select the Do Not Cache Objects Larger Than check box and type the size and select the unit (KB, MB, GB).
    - To cache objects for which a last modification time is not specified, select the Cache Objects That Have An Unspecified Last Modification Time check box.
    - To cache dynamic content, select the Cache Dynamic Content (Objects With Question Marks In The URL) check box.

3. Click OK.

Note To limit maximum size of URLs cached in memory, in the Maximum Size Of URL Cached In Memory (Bytes) text box, type the maximum number of bytes that can be cached.

In an SSL bridging scenario, ISA Server can cache HTTP and SSL objects. You can use the FPCWebRequestConfiguration COM object to configure whether SSL objects should be cached. For more information, see the ISA Server Software Development Kit.

RAM Caching

ISA Server caches objects to RAM and to the disk. Objects cached to memory can be retrieved faster than objects cached to the disk. By default, objects smaller than 12,800 bytes are stored in RAM and on the disk. By default, all larger objects are cached only to the disk.

You can modify the maximum size of objects that can be stored in memory from the Advanced tab of the Cache Configuration Properties dialog box.

Response Headers

ISA Server does not cache responses to requests that contain the following HTTP response headers:

- cache-control: no-cache
- cache-control: private
- pragma: no-cache
- www-authenticate
- set-cookie

Request Headers

In addition, the ISA Server computer does not cache responses to requests that contain the following HTTP request headers:

- authorization, unless the origin server explicitly allowed this by including 'cache-control: public' header in the response
- cache-control: no-store

Configuring Expiration Policy

ISA Server features highly configurable expiration policies. For HTTP and FTP objects, you can choose whether or not to activate caching, and you can configure the expiration policy. You can also configure whether to return expired objects, under specific circumstances.

HTTP Object Caching

ISA Server can keep and use expired objects in the cache for a specified amount of time if the source Internet site for an object becomes unavailable. An expired object is an object whose TTL period has run out. Expiration policy balances your organization's need for fresh, current data against network performance. Depending on your particular organization's need, you can specify one of the following expiration policies for HTTP objects, as shown in Figure 5.5:

- **Frequently.** This means that objects in the cache will be more current, although there may be a degradation in network performance because objects are retrieved more regularly from the Internet.

- **Less frequently.** This means that objects in the cache will be less current, but network performance will not suffer.

- **Normally.** This balanced approach is the default. Objects are updated somewhat frequently, but network performance is not ignored.

- **Custom settings.** You can set TTL to zero or to a specified percentage of the content's age. The higher the percentage, the less frequently the cache is updated.

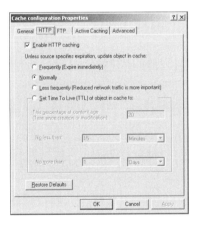

Figure 5.5 Caching properties for HTTP

▶ **Follow these steps to configure HTTP caching:**

1. In the console tree of ISA Management, right-click the Cache Configuration node, and then click Properties.

2. On the HTTP tab, select the Enable HTTP Caching check box.

3. Click one of the following options:
    - If it is more important to make current information available, click the Frequently (Expire Immediately) radio button. This option sets the TTL period to 0.
    - To balance between current information and system load, click the Normally radio button.
    - If it is more important to lessen the system load, click the Less Frequently (Reduced Network Traffic Is More Important) radio button. This option also sets the TTL period to a longer duration.
    - To customize the HTTP cache expiration policy, click the Set Time To Live (TTL) Of Object In Cache To radio button.
4. If you selected the Set Time To Live (TTL) Of Object In Cache To radio button, configure the following options:
    - To require objects to expire after a percentage of their age has elapsed, enter a percentage in the This Percentage Of Content Age (Time Since Creation Or Modification) text box.
    - To specify the minimum and maximum length of time that HTTP objects should remain in the cache:
        - In the No Less Than text box and adjacent drop-down list box, type in a number and specify a unit of time.
        - In the No More Than text box and adjacent drop-down list box, type in a number and specify a unit of time.
5. Click OK.

Note To reset HTTP expiration policy to equal importance, click Restore Defaults.

FTP Object Caching

You can configure how FTP objects are maintained in the ISA Server cache. As shown in Figure 5.6, for FTP objects you can choose whether or not to activate caching, and you can configure the TTL period for all objects.

By default, the TTL for all FTP objects is set to one day (1440 minutes).

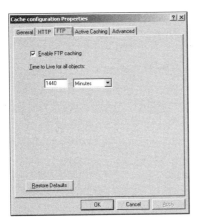

Figure 5.6 Caching properties for FTP

▶ **Follow these steps to configure FTP caching:**

1. In the console tree of ISA Management, right-click the Cache Configuration node, and then click Properties.

2. On the FTP tab, select the Enable FTP Caching check box.

3. In the Time To Live For All Objects text box, type the TTL for all FTP objects.

4. In the drop-down list box, select a unit of time: Seconds, Minutes, Hours, Days, or Weeks.

5. Click OK.

Note To reset FTP caching policy to the default settings, click Restore Defaults.

Returning Expired Objects

Objects stored in the cache are marked with a TTL. When an object's TTL passes, the object has expired. When a client requests an object, ISA Server checks to see whether a valid version of the object is in its cache. If so, the object is returned. Otherwise, depending on the cache policy, ISA Server requests the object from the specified Web server.

If the Web server is accessible, ISA Server retrieves the object and returns it to the client. If the Web server is not accessible, you can configure ISA Server to return an expired version of the object from the ISA Server cache.

You can configure ISA Server to return expired objects on the Advanced tab of the Cache Configuration Properties dialog box, as shown in Figure 5.7.

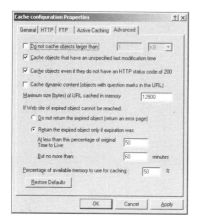

Figure 5.7 Advanced caching properties

▶ **Follow these steps to configure whether to return expired objects from the cache:**

1. In the console tree of ISA Management, right-click the Cache Configuration node, and then click Properties.

2. On the Advanced tab, select one of the following options:

    - **The Do Not Return The Expired Object (Return An Error Page) radio button.** If you select this option, an error page will be returned.

    - **The Return The Expired Object Only If Expiration Was radio button.** This option returns an expired version of the object from the ISA Server cache.

3. If you chose to return the expired object, specify the TTL limits for the object.

    - In the At Less Than This Percentage Of Original Time To Live text box, specify the maximum percentage of the TTL. If the expiration time exceeds this, the object is not returned.

    - In the But No More Than (Minutes) text box, specify the maximum number of minutes that passed since the object expired. If the expiration time exceeds this, the object is not returned.

4. Click OK.

Configuring Active Caching

With active caching enabled, ISA Server analyzes objects that are in the cache to determine which are most frequently accessed. When popular objects in the cache are about to expire, ISA Server automatically refreshes the content in the cache.

When active caching is enabled, if you are using a dial-up connection to the Internet, the computer will dial out to the Internet Service Provider (ISP) when retrieving this content.

You can configure the active caching policy. Select one of the following:

- **Frequently.** In this case, frequently requested objects are downloaded to the cache regularly, as they are about to expire. This helps ensure that an object requested by a client will be in the cache.

- **Normally.** This balanced approach is the default. Objects are updated somewhat frequently, but network performance is not ignored.

- **Less Frequently.** Some frequently requested objects will be downloaded to the cache. Although there is less likelihood that the object will be fresh and in the cache, network performance may be improved, since active caching is at a minimum.

▶ **Follow these steps to configure active caching:**

1. In the console tree of ISA Management, right-click the Cache Configuration node, and then click Properties.

2. On the Active Caching tab, select the Enable Active Caching check box.

3. Do one of the following:

    - If the ISA Server should refresh and revalidate previously cached objects before they expire, click the Frequently radio button.

    - If the ISA Server should balance between fast response and network load, click the Normally radio button.

    - If you do not want to add to the network load, click the Less Frequently radio button.

4. Click OK.

Configuring Negative Caching

When ISA Server cannot retrieve an object from a specific Web server, the response may be cached. This is referred to as *negative caching*. You can configure negative caching, specifying that error responses to client requests should be cached.

When you configure negative caching, you specify that HTTP objects with the following status code should be cached: 203, 300, 301, and 410.

▶ **Follow these steps to configure negative caching:**

1. In the console tree of ISA Management, right-click the Cache Configuration node, and then click Properties.
2. On the Advanced tab, select the Cache Objects Even If They Do Not Have An HTTP Status Code Of 200 check box.
3. Click OK.

Practice 1: Enabling Active Caching

Active caching is a feature in which ISA Server automatically initiates new requests to update the most frequently accessed file objects in the cache. With active caching enabled, ISA Server analyzes objects that are in the cache to determine which are most frequently accessed.

Exercise: Enabling Active Caching

This exercise allows you to enable active caching with default parameters.

▶ **To enable active caching**

1. In ISA Management, navigate to Servers and Arrays, MyArray, Cache Configuration.
2. Right-click on the Cache Configuration node and click Properties.

    The Cache Configuration Properties dialog box appears.
3. Click the Active Caching tab.
4. Click the Enable Active Caching check box.

    The radio buttons under Retrieve Files appear and the Normally radio button is selected.
5. Click OK.

Practice 2: Adjusting the Amount of RAM Used for Caching

ISA Server allows you to designate a certain percentage of the available physical memory to be used for caching. Cache files that are kept in physical memory are accessed more quickly than cache files stored on a hard drive.

Exercise: Adjusting the Percentage of Available Memory Used for Caching

This exercise allows you to change the percentage of available RAM used for caching from the default of 50 percent to 65 percent.

▶ **To adjust the percentage of available memory used for caching**

1. In ISA Management, navigate to Servers And Arrays, MyArray, Cache Configuration.
2. Right-click the Cache Configuration node and click Properties.

    The Cache Configuration Properties dialog box appears.
3. Click the Advanced tab.
4. In the Percentage Of Free Memory To Use For Caching text box, replace the default of 50 by typing **65**.
5. Click OK.

    The ISA Server Warning dialog box appears.
6. Click the Save The Changes And Restart The Service(s) radio button, and then click OK.

Lesson Summary

Cache properties can be configured in the properties dialog box of the Cache Configuration node and in the properties dialog box of each server in the Drives folder in ISA Management.

You can configure the size and location of the cache from the Properties dialog box of each cache server.

In the Cache Configuration Properties dialog box, you can configure FTP caching, configure HTTP caching, set expiration policies, determine when to return cached objects, restrict the size of objects to be cached, configure the percentage of available RAM to be used for caching, enable active caching, and configure negative caching.

Lesson 3 Scheduling Cache Content Downloads

The scheduled cache content download service of ISA Server enables you to schedule Web content downloads from the Internet directly to the ISA Server cache. To support this feature, a background process downloads the content according to a predefined schedule.

After this lesson, you will be able to

- Create and configure scheduled content download jobs in ISA Server

Estimated lesson time: 25 minutes

Scheduled Cache Content Downloads

Scheduled cache content downloads allow you to update the ISA Server cache with HTTP content that may be requested by Web Proxy clients sometime in the near future. When used wisely, scheduled cache content downloads save valuable network bandwidth and improve the overall cache performance without affecting throughput.

Figure 5.8 shows how you can create a new scheduled content download job in ISA Management.

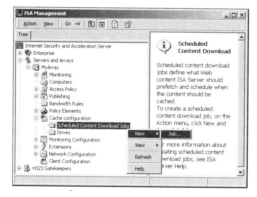

Figure 5.8 Creating a content download job

Updating Cache Content Automatically

By monitoring and analyzing Internet access, you can determine which HTTP content is needed and when. You can then use the scheduled cache content download feature to download the HTTP content directly to the ISA Server cache, upon request or as scheduled. This enables you to update the ISA Server cache with HTTP content that you anticipate will be requested by clients in your organization. This content will be available for access directly from the ISA Server cache, rather than from the Internet.

You can download a single URL, multiple URLs, or an entire Web site. When you create a scheduled cache content download job, you can limit which content should be downloaded. For example, you can limit the download to a single domain. Similarly, you can limit how many links should be followed.

Scheduled content download jobs are created through the New Scheduled Content Download Job wizard. This wizard is shown in Figure 5.9.

Figure 5.9 The New Scheduled Content Download Job wizard

▶ **Follow these steps to create a scheduled cache content download job:**

1. In the console tree of ISA Management, right-click the Scheduled Content Download Jobs folder.
2. Point to New, and then click Job.
3. Follow the on-screen instructions.

Configuring Properties for Existing Download Jobs

You can also configure properties for existing scheduled download jobs. To do this, select the Scheduled Content Download Jobs folder under the Cache Configuration node in ISA Management, right-click a scheduled download job in the details pane, and then click Properties. This procedure is illustrated in Figure 5.10.

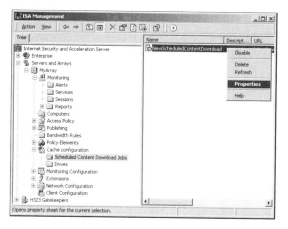

Figure 5.10 Accessing the properties of a scheduled download job

▶ **Follow these steps to configure a location from which to download cache content:**

1. In the console tree of ISA Management, click the Scheduled Content Download Jobs folder.

2. In the details pane, right-click the applicable scheduled content download job, and then click Properties.

3. On the Parameters tab, in the Begin Downloading From URL text box, type the URL from which to download the content.

4. To download only content from the domain specified in the Begin Downloading From URL text box, click the Keep Download Process Inside URL Domain Only check box.

5. To limit the number of links to follow from a single page when downloading content, click the Cache Up To Maximum Links Depth Of check box, and type the number of links.

6. To limit the total number of objects to cache, in the Maximum Number Of Cached Objects text box, type the number of objects.

7. Click OK.

▶ **Follow these steps to configure TTL for downloaded cache content:**

1. In the console tree of ISA Management, click the Scheduled Content Download Jobs folder.

2. In the details pane, right-click the applicable scheduled content download job, click Properties and click the Parameters tab.

3. To override the TTL for an object, click the Always Override Object's TTL check box.

4. To override the TTL for an object, if the TTL is not defined, click the Override TTL If Not Defined check box.

5. To configure a specific TTL for the downloaded objects, type a TTL in Mark Downloaded Objects With A New TTL Of <number> Minutes text box.

6. Click OK.

Note If you click Always Override Object's TTL, the TTL is determined either by the TTL specified here or by the TTL specified in cache configuration properties.

Downloading Dynamic Content

When you schedule a cache content download, you can configure dynamic content to be cached by configuring the ISA Server cache to store the objects, even if the HTTP cache control headers indicate that they are not necessarily cacheable.

Warning If the Web server from which the object is being downloaded requires client authentication, the scheduled content download job will fail.

▶ **Follow these steps to cache dynamic content for scheduled cache content download jobs:**

1. In the console tree of ISA Management, click the Scheduled Content Download Jobs folder.

2. In the details pane, right-click the applicable scheduled content download job, and then click Properties.

3. On the Parameters tab, select the Cache Dynamic Content check box.

4. Click OK.

Configuring the Schedule for Content Download Jobs

The download occurs according to a preconfigured schedule. (You can also specify whether the schedule should recur periodically.) Scheduled content download jobs can be configured for outgoing Web requests and for incoming Web requests.

For outgoing Web requests, you determine which objects on the Internet are most often requested by users. You can then schedule jobs that retrieve the objects from the Internet and load them into the cache.

For incoming Web requests, you can schedule jobs that retrieve content from your internal Web servers.

▶ **Follow these steps to configure a cache content download job schedule:**

1. In the console tree of ISA Management, click the Scheduled Content Download Jobs folder.

2. In the details pane, right-click the applicable scheduled cache content download job, and then click Properties.

3. On the Frequency tab, in the Date calendar box and Time spin box, select the date and time when the content should be downloaded from the Internet.

4. In the Frequency section, do one of the following:

    - To download the content only once at the specified time, click the Once radio button.

    - To download the content every day at the specified time, click the Daily radio button.

    - To download the content on a specified day at a specified time, click the Weekly On radio button and select the check boxes for the days on which to download content.

5. Click OK.

Practice: Creating a Scheduled Content Download Job

In this practice, you schedule a content download job to take place every Sunday at 11:59 P.M. Download jobs that take place weekly are best suited for content that does not normally change from day to day.

Exercise: Scheduling a Content Download for Microsoft Online Seminars

In this exercise, you schedule a content download for training materials at the Microsoft Web site. The scheduled content download includes dynamic content and a maximum of 5,000 objects.

▶ **To schedule a content download**

1. In ISA Management, navigate to Servers And Arrays, MyArray, Cache Configuration.

2. Expand the Cache Configuration node.

3. Right-click the Scheduled Content Download Jobs folder, point to New and then click Job.

   The New Scheduled Content Download Job wizard appears.

4. In the Job Name text box, type Microsoft Online Seminars, and then click Next.

   The Start Time screen appears.

5. Leave the default date as it appears, and change the time to 11:59:59 P.M.

6. Click Next.

   The Frequency screen appears.

7. Click the Weekly On radio button, and then click the Sunday check box.

8. Click Next.

   The Content screen appears.

9. In the Download Content From This URL text box, type **http://www.microsoft.com/seminar/1033/**.

10. Click the Cache Dynamic Content check box.

11. Click Next.

    The Links And Downloaded Objects screen appears.

12. In the Maximum Number Of Cached Objects text box, type **5000** and then click Next.

    The Completing The Scheduled Content Download Job Wizard screen appears.

13. Click Finish.

14. Click on the Scheduled Content Download Jobs folder.

    The Microsoft Online Seminars job appears in the details pane.

Lesson Summary

Scheduled cache content downloads allow you to update the ISA Server cache with content that may soon be requested by Web Proxy clients. By monitoring and analyzing Internet access, you can determine which Web content is needed and when. You can then use the New Scheduled Content Download Job wizard to configure Web content downloads directly to the ISA Server cache. Content download jobs can be configured to occur either once or as scheduled. When you create a download job, you can configure a download for a single URL, multiple URLs, or an entire Web site.

Review

The following questions are intended to reinforce key information presented in the chapter. If you are unable to answer a question, review the appropriate lesson and then try the question again. The answers for these questions are located in Appendix A, "Questions and Answers."

1. A Web Proxy client requests a Web object, and ISA Server consults the cache to see whether a valid version of the object exists. It then finds that the cached version of the object has expired. Following the applicable routing rule, ISA Server then contacts the remote source over the Internet to retrieve the object, but it finds that the remote source cannot be contacted. What does ISA Server do next?

2. How does ISA Server determine whether to cache a Web object that has been retrieved from its original location?

3. Under what conditions will ISA Server cache dynamic content?

4. What is negative caching, and how do you enable it?

5. How does ISA Server handle a scheduled content download when the Web server from which the object is being downloaded requires client authentication?

CHAPTER 6

Secure Server Publishing

Lesson 1 Publishing Servers Securely 234

Lesson 2 Publishing Web Servers Securely 244

Lesson 3 Publishing Mail Servers 256

Review 264

About This Chapter

If your network contains servers that publish to the Internet, such as Web servers, File Transfer Protocol (FTP) servers, or database servers, you need to allow external clients access to those servers without compromising the security of your network. With Microsoft Internet Security and Acceleration Server (ISA Server), you can publish such servers securely because external requests are handled by ISA Server on behalf of internal network servers. ISA Server can then forward the requests securely to the network servers as appropriate. Requests to internal servers that are not explicitly allowed by ISA Server are dropped by default.

Before You Begin

To complete the lessons in this chapter, you must have

- Completed all the exercises in the book through Chapter 5, "Configuring Internet Acceleration through the ISA Server Cache"

Lesson 1 Publishing Servers Securely

ISA Server uses *server publishing* to process incoming requests to internal servers. Requests are forwarded downstream to an internal server that is located behind the ISA Server computer.

Server publishing is configured through server publishing rules. You create a server publishing rule by using the New Server Publishing Rule wizard in the ISA Management console. You modify an existing server publishing rule from the properties dialog box of the rule created in the console.

After this lesson, you will be able to

- Publish an internal network server behind ISA Server
- Publish a server securely on the ISA Server computer
- Publish a server securely on a perimeter network

Estimated lesson time: 35 minutes

Publishing Policy Rules

You can use ISA Server to configure a publishing policy, which consists of server publishing rules and Web publishing rules. Server publishing rules filter all incoming requests and then map these requests to the appropriate servers that are protected by the ISA Server services. Web publishing rules map incoming requests to the appropriate Web servers behind the ISA Server.

When you install ISA Server, you specify the installation mode: Firewall, Cache, or Integrated. The installation mode you choose affects which publishing policy rule types are available, as shown in Table 6.1.

Table 6.1 Publishing Rule Availability

Rule type	Firewall	Cache	Integrated
Web publishing rules	No	Yes	Yes
Server publishing rules	Yes	No	Yes

Server Publishing Rules

Server publishing allows computers on your internal network to securely publish services to the Internet. Security is not compromised because all incoming requests and outgoing responses pass through ISA Server. When a server is published by an ISA Server computer, the Internet Protocol (IP) address that is published is the external IP address of the ISA Server computer. A remote user requesting published services, files or objects communicates directly with the ISA Server computer—whose name or IP address is specified by the requester. After this, the ISA Server computer makes the request on behalf of the user to the appropriate publishing server on your internal network. External users thus communicate with protected publishing servers indirectly through ISA Server.

Server publishing rules essentially filter all requests through the ISA Server computer and then map those requests to the appropriate servers behind the ISA Server computer. These rules grant access dynamically (only as needed) from Internet users to the appropriate publishing server.

The publishing server is a secure network address translation (SecureNAT) client: it does not need to have Firewall Client installed and enabled. Because the publishing server is treated as a SecureNAT client, no special configuration of the publishing server is required after the server publishing rule is created on the ISA Server computer. Note that the IP address assigned to the ISA Server's internal network interface card (NIC) must be configured as the default gateway on the publishing server.

How Server Publishing Works

ISA Server takes these steps to fulfill requests for internal servers:

1. A client computer on the Internet requests an object from an IP address known as that of the publishing server. This IP address, however, is actually associated with the ISA Server computer—it is the IP address of the external interface card belonging to the ISA Server computer.

2. The ISA Server computer processes the request, mapping the IP address to an internal IP address of an internal server. It then makes the request to the internal server on behalf of the external client.

3. The internal server returns the object to the ISA Server computer, which passes it on to the requesting client.

▶ **Follow these steps to create a server publishing rule:**

1. In the console tree of ISA Management, expand the Publishing node, right-click the Server Publishing Rules folder, point to New, and then click Rule.

2. In the New Server Publishing Rule wizard, type the name of the server publishing rule, and then click Next.

3. On the Address Mapping screen (shown in Figure 6.1), type the IP address of the internal server that is being published. Also, type the external IP address of the ISA Server.

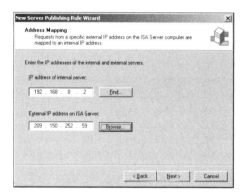

Figure 6.1 Address mapping for server publishing

4. On the Protocol Settings screen (shown in Figure 6.2), select the server protocol to which the rule applies.

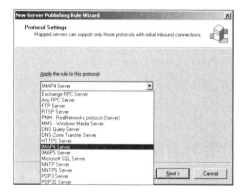

Figure 6.2 Selecting a protocol for server publishing

5. On the Client Type screen, specify whether the rule applies to all clients or to a specific client address set.

Note For array members, if enterprise policy settings are configured so that publishing is not allowed, you will not be able to create a server publishing rule.

Server Publishing Rule Actions

A rule action refers to the action applied to a request by a given rule. You can configure the rule action of a new server publishing rule in the Address Mapping and Protocol Setting screens of the New Server Publishing Rule wizard. You can modify the rule action of an existing rule on the Action tab of the rule's properties, which you can access in ISA Management. In either case, when you configure the action of a server publishing rule, you specify the following:

- **IP address of the ISA Server.** This is the address made available to external clients. When external clients communicate with the publishing server, they actually are communicating with this IP address.

- **IP address of the publishing server.** All requests arriving to the IP address specified on the ISA Server are forwarded to this IP address.

- **Mapped server protocol.** The data passed to the internal server depends on which protocol you specify here. You can select from all protocol definitions configured on the ISA Server with, at minimum, an Inbound direction. Protocol definitions are listed and configured in the Protocol Definitions folder of the Policy Elements node.

Sample Rule Action

Suppose you want to allow external clients access to an SMTP server, whose IP address is 111.111.111.111, and which listens on port 25. You create a server publishing rule with the following parameters:

- Internal server IP address set to 111.111.111.111
- External address on ISA Server set to an IP address on the external interface card belonging to the ISA Server computer
- Mapped server protocol set to SMTP Server

▶ **Follow these steps to modify the action for an existing server publishing rule:**

1. In the console tree of ISA Management, open the Publishing node and click the Server Publishing Rules folder.

2. On the View menu, click Advanced.

3. In the details pane, right-click the appropriate server publishing rule, and then click Properties.

4. On the Action tab, in the IP Address Of Internal Server text box, type the address of the internal server that you want to make available to external users.

5. In the External IP Address On ISA Server text box, type an IP address on one of the ISA Server computer's external interface cards that will be accessed by external clients.

Note In the Mapped Server Protocol drop-down list box, click a protocol definition that can be used by external clients to access the computer.

Client Address Sets

When you configure a server publishing rule to apply to a client address set, you limit the action of the server publishing rule to apply only to the set of requesting computers you specify. These sets are not defined in the server publishing rule itself but in the Policy Elements node in ISA Management.

▶ **Follow these steps to configure clients for an existing server publishing rule:**

1. In the console tree of ISA Management, expand the Publishing node and click the Server Publishing Rules folder.

2. On the View menu, click Advanced.

3. In the details pane, right-click the applicable rule, and then click Properties.

4. To specify clients for the rule, on the Applies To tab, do one of the following:

    - Click the Any Request radio button.
    - Click the Client Address Sets Specified Below radio button.

5. If you clicked the Client Address Sets Specified Below radio button, do the following:

   - To add clients to the Applies To Requests Coming From area, click the accompanying Add button.

   - To add clients to the Exceptions area, click the accompanying Add button.

Note For server publishing rules, client address sets typically include addresses of computers on the Internet.

Server Publishing Rules and IP Packet Filters

Server publishing rules and IP packet filters both open specific ports for communication between the local network and the Internet. In most situations, you use server publishing rules to make internal servers accessible to external clients.

However, in some cases, such as the following, you must use IP packet filters instead of publishing rules:

- When you are publishing servers that are located on a *perimeter network,* to make the servers accessible to external clients

- When you are publishing services that are located on the ISA Server computer itself

Publishing Servers on a Perimeter Network

You configure server publishing rules to allow external clients access to servers situated on the local network. For example, you might want to publish an internal FTP server. In this case, you would simply create a server publishing rule with the following configuration:

- IP address of the internal server set to the IP address of the FTP server

- External IP address on ISA Server set to an IP address on the external interface card belonging to the ISA Server computer

- The FTP Server protocol selected

- Client type set to Any User, Group, Or Client Computer to allow all external clients access to the FTP server

Suppose, however, that the server you want to publish is located on a perimeter network, rather than on the local network. In this case, you must use IP packet filters to open a port on the server. For example, suppose you want to publish an FTP server located on the perimeter network. Create an IP packet filter from the New IP Packet Filter wizard with the following configuration:

- On the Servers screen, set the filter for all ISA Server computers in the array
- On the Filter Mode screen, select to create the filter to allow packet transmission
- On the Filter Type screen, select a custom filter
- On the Filter Settings screen, configure the following settings:
    - IP Protocol to TCP
    - Direction to Both
    - Local Port Fixed to 21
    - Remote Port to All Ports
- On the Local Computer screen, select the option to specify a computer on the perimeter network and then type the IP address of the FTP server
- On the Remote Computers screen, select the option that specifies all remote computers

Server on the Same Computer as ISA Server

Another case that requires an IP packet filter instead of a publishing rule to publish a server is when the publishing server is located on the same computer as ISA Server. If you want to allow communication through to the specific port used by the publishing server, you must create an IP packet filter and not server publishing rules. For example, ISA Server includes a preconfigured IP packet filter, named DNS Filter, which allows DNS queries on the ISA Server computer itself.

Practice: Publishing an Internal Server

In this practice, you publish the FTP service on Server2. To enable users external to your network to connect to the FTP service on Server2, you need to create a publishing rule in ISA Server to allow requests to be passed to the FTP server.

> **Important** This practice requires that you establish a dial-up connection to the Internet and that you perform all three of the following exercises in one dial-up session. Establish a dial-up connection before beginning the exercises by double-clicking the dial-up connection appearing in the Network And Dial-up Connections window.

Also, before proceeding with this exercise, you should stop the FTP Service on Server1. You can stop the FTP Service on Server1 by right-clicking the Default FTP Site icon in Internet Services Manager and clicking Stop.

Exercise 1: Creating a Publishing Rule on Server1

In this exercise, you create a publishing rule that allows all FTP requests to be forwarded through ISA Server to Server2. Complete this exercise on Server1.

1. Verify that Server1 is connected to the Internet through the dial-up connection. If it isn't connected, establish a connection to the Internet now.

2. Open the ISA Management console.

3. In the console tree, expand MyArray, and then navigate to the Publishing node.

4. Expand the Publishing node.

5. Right-click the Server Publishing Rules folder, point to New, and then click Rule.

   The New Server Publishing Rule wizard appears.

6. In the Server Publishing Rule Name text box, type **FTP Server**, and then click Next.

   The Address Mapping screen appears.

7. In the IP Address Of Internal Server text box, type **192.168.0.2**.

8. Click the Browse button.

   A message box appears, displaying the external address of your ISA Server computer.

9. Verify that the external IP address is selected, and then click OK.

   The computer's external IP address appears in the External IP Address On ISA Server text box. Note that this rule is valid only for the current Internet session since your IP address might change every time you dial into your Internet Service Provider (ISP).

10. Enter the external IP address here:

11. Click Next.

    The Protocol Settings screen appears.

12. In the Apply The Rule To This Protocol drop-down list box, select FTP Server, and then click Next.

    The Client Type screen appears.

13. Leave the default set to Any Request, and then click Next.

    The Complete The New Server Publishing Rule Wizard screen appears.

14. Click Finish.

15. Restart the ISA Server services in ISA Management before proceeding to Exercise 2.

Exercise 2: Verifying the FTP Server Connection

In this exercise, you establish an FTP connection to the external IP address of your ISA Server computer. Though your published FTP server is configured on an internal server (Server2) and not on the ISA Server computer itself, the new server publishing rule created in Exercise 1 allows the FTP server to appear as if it is hosted on Server1.

1. Log on to Server1 as Administrator.

2. Point to Start and then Run.

   The Run dialog box appears.

3. In the Open box, type **cmd** and click OK to open a command prompt.

   A command prompt appears.

4. At the command prompt, type **ftp** *<external IP address>*, where *<external IP address>* is the external IP address of the ISA Server computer assigned to you by your ISP and upon which your publishing rule was based in Exercise 1. You recorded this number in step 10 of Exercise 1.

5. Press Enter.

   On the console screen, you will receive a message indicating that you are connected to the FTP Server and prompting you to enter your user name. This message shows that the new publishing rule has allowed you to connect from the Internet to the FTP service configured on Server2.

6. Type **anonymous**.

   You will receive a message indicating that anonymous access is allowed and prompting you for a password.

7. Enter an empty password by pressing the Enter key.

   The FTP prompt appears.

8. At the FTP prompt, type **quit**.

   You will return to the command prompt.

9. Close the command prompt window.

Lesson Summary

Through the use of server publishing rules, ISA Server processes incoming requests to internal servers, such as SMTP servers, FTP servers, and database servers. Server publishing allows virtually any computer on your internal network to publish to the Internet. Security is not compromised because all incoming requests and outgoing responses pass through ISA Server. Like site and content rules and protocol rules, server publishing rules open TCP ports for service requests dynamically, or only as needed.

When a server is published by ISA Server, the IP address of the published server that is visible to the outside world is actually the IP address or addresses of the ISA Server computer. Server publishing rules then map incoming requests from the ISA Server computer to the appropriate server on the local network. ISA Server makes the request to this local server on behalf of the external client, and then responds to the external client on behalf of the local server. To create a server publishing rule, you use the New Server Publishing Rule wizard. You modify an existing server publishing rule from the rule's Properties dialog box in ISA Management.

If you want to publish a server on a perimeter network, or if you want to publish a server on the ISA Server computer itself, you must configure IP packet filters in ISA Server instead of publishing rules.

Lesson 2 Publishing Web Servers Securely

By publishing a Web server behind ISA Server, the ISA Server receives requests on behalf of the internal Web server. When a client on the Internet requests an object from a publishing Web server, the request is actually sent to an external address on the ISA Server computer. Web publishing rules configured on the ISA Server computer then forward the requests to the internal Web server. The publishing Web server requires no special configuration.

To create a new publishing rule, use the New Web Publishing Rule wizard. This wizard is started from the Web Publishing Rules folder located below the Publishing node. You modify an existing Web publishing rule from the rule's Properties dialog box in ISA Management.

After this lesson, you will be able to

- Publish an internal network Web server behind ISA Server
- Publish a Web server securely on the ISA Server computer

Estimated lesson time: 45 minutes

Web Publishing Rules

ISA Server uses Web publishing rules to alleviate concerns about publishing Web content to the Internet and, as a result, compromising internal network security. Web publishing rules determine how ISA Server should intercept incoming Hypertext Transfer Protocol (HTTP) requests on an internal Web server and how ISA Server should respond on behalf of the Web server. When a rule determines that a request be forwarded instead of dropped, the request is sent downstream to an internal Web server located behind the ISA Server computer. If possible, the request is serviced from the ISA Server cache.

Important To enhance security, do not enable directory browsing on the publishing Web server. Likewise, do not configure the Web server for digest or basic authentication. These authentication methods can expose the Web server's internal name or IP address to the external user.

Destination Sets and Client Sets

When configuring Web publishing rules, such as by using the New Web Publishing Rule wizard (shown in Figure 6.3), you are given the option to specify a destination set for the Web publishing rule. For Web publishing rules, destination sets usually include a domain name whose IP address maps to your ISA Server computer. A path may also be included in a destination set if you want your publishing rule to apply directory-specific or file-specific actions to Web requests. (For example, you may want to direct a Web requests for *http://www.microsoft.com/example* to one particular server and a Web request for *http://www.microsoft.com/marketing* to another internal server.) Client address sets usually include addresses of clients located on the Internet, as opposed to clients located on your internal corporate network. Client address sets ease administration by allowing you to group clients that are granted or denied access to a Web publishing server.

Destination sets and client address sets are created and administered from folders below the Policy Elements node.

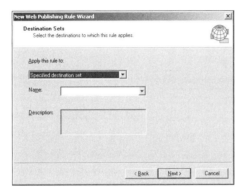

Figure 6.3 Publishing the hosted destination set

▶ **Follow these steps to create a Web publishing rule:**

1. In the console tree of ISA Management, right-click Web Publishing Rules, point to New, and then click Rule.

2. In the New Web Publishing Rule wizard, type the name of the rule, and then click Next.

3. On the Destination Sets screen, select a destination set that includes the IP address of the server that you are publishing, then click Next.

4. On the Client Type screen, select whether the rule applies to all users or to specific client address sets or users, then click Next.

5. On the Rule Action screen, specify how client requests should be directed.

Note For array members, if enterprise policy settings are configured so that publishing is not allowed, you will not be able to create a Web publishing rule.

Web Publishing Rule Actions

As shown in Figure 6.4, Web publishing rule actions are configured on the Rule Action screen of the New Web Publishing Rule wizard. Rule actions for Web publishing rules either discard HTTP requests targeted for specific destination sets or redirect those requests to an alternate site, usually to a Web server on your corporate network.

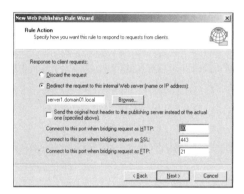

Figure 6.4 Redirecting Web requests to an internal server

▶ **Follow these steps to configure an action for an existing Web publishing rule:**

1. In the console tree of ISA Management, click Web Publishing Rules.

2. On the View menu, click Advanced.

3. In the details pane, right-click the applicable Web publishing rule, and then click Properties.

4. On the Action tab, do one of the following:

    - To refuse requests, click the Discard The Request radio button.

    - To forward requests to the server or servers used for Internet publishing, click Redirect The Request To This Internal Web Server (Name Or IP Address) radio button.

5. If you clicked the Redirect The Requests To This Internal Web Server (Name Or IP Address) radio button, do the following:

    - Type an IP address or a domain name to which requests should be redirected.

    - In Connect To This Port When Bridging Request As HTTP, type the port to use for HTTP requests. By default, the HTTP port is configured to 80.

- In Connect To This Port When Bridging Request As SSL, type the port to use for Secure Hypertext Transfer Protocol (S-HTTP) requests. By default, the S-HTTP port is configured to 443.
- In Connect To This Port When Bridging Request As FTP, type the port to use for Transmission Control Protocol (TCP) requests. By default, the FTP port is configured to 21.

SSL and HTTP Bridging

By accessing the Bridging tab of a Web publishing rule's properties, as shown in Figure 6.5, you can configure how incoming HTTP requests should be redirected—whether as HTTP requests, as Secure Sockets Layer (SSL) requests, or as FTP requests. If the request is redirected as an SSL request, the packets are encrypted.

You can also bridge SSL communication. That is, if the initial communication uses SSL, after ISA Server passes the request to the internal Web server, the communication can be redirected using HTTP, SSL, or FTP. If requests are redirected as SSL requests, ISA Server re-encrypts the packets before passing them on to the Web server. That is, a new secure channel is established for the communication with the SSL Web server.

When you configure HTTP or SSL requests to be passed on as an FTP request to the Web server, ISA Server redirects the requests to the internal Web server using FTP. If you configure bridging in this way, you can specify which port should be used when bridging FTP requests.

Finally, if the internal Web server requires a client certificate, you can configure ISA Server to authenticate with a specific client-side certificate.

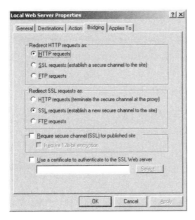

Figure 6.5 Configuring bridging properties for a Web publishing rule

Rule Order

For each incoming Web request, Web publishing rules are processed in order. When a rule matches a request, the request is routed and cached accordingly. If no rule matches the request, ISA Server processes the default rule, which discards the request. If you have created two or more Web publishing rules in addition to the default rule, you may change the order of those rules at any time.

Default Web Publishing Rule

When you install ISA Server, it configures a default Web publishing rule. The default rule is configured so that all requests are discarded. The default Web publishing rule is last in the order. You cannot modify or delete the default Web publishing rule.

▶ **Follow these steps to change the order of a Web publishing rule:**

1. In the console tree of ISA Management, click Web Publishing Rules.
2. On the View menu, click Advanced.
3. In the details pane, right-click the rule whose order you want to change, and then click Move Up or Move Down.
4. Repeat as necessary to arrange the rules in the desired order.

Note You cannot change the position of the default rule.

Sample Web Publishing Rule

Suppose you want to publish two internal Web servers in the domain example.microsoft.com, one called Dev and the other called Mktg. Though the IP address of the example.microsoft.com domain corresponds to the external interface of the ISA Server computer, you would like the internal server Mktg to respond when a client requests example.microsoft.com/Marketing, and the internal server Dev to respond when a client requests example.microsoft.com/Development.

To achieve this goal, you first create two destination sets. The first destination set, called Marketing, should include the computer example.microsoft.com and the path /Marketing/*. The second destination set, called Development, should include the computer example.microsoft.com and the path /Development/*.

Next, create two Web publishing rules that redirect requests to the appropriate internal Web servers. Configure the first Web publishing rule with the following parameters:

- Destination Set configured to the Marketing destination set
- Applies To set to Any User, Group, Or Client Computer
- For the rule action, Redirect To A Hosted Site and Mktg specified as the host

When a client requests an object on example.microsoft.com/Marketing, ISA Server retrieves the request from Mktg/Marketing.

Configure the second Web publishing rule with the following parameters:

- Destination Set configured to the Development destination set
- Applies To set to Any User, Group, Or Client Computer
- For the rule action, Redirect To A Hosted Site and Dev specified as the host

When a client requests an object on example.microsoft.com/Development, ISA Server retrieves the request from Dev/Development.

Publishing a Web Server on the Local Network

▶ **Follow these steps to publish an internal Web server behind the ISA Server firewall:**

1. Verify that the DNS server maps the fully qualified domain name to the external IP address of the ISA Server computer. Internet clients use the domain name to request content.

2. Configure the ISA Server incoming Web request properties. The IP address should include the IP address of the external interface.

3. Create a destination set called Marketing, which should include the computer example.microsoft.com and the path \Marketing*.

4. Create a destination set called Development, which should include the computer example.microsoft.com and the path \Development*.

5. Configure a Web publishing rule with the following parameters:

    - Destination Set configured to the Marketing destination set
    - Applies To set to Any User, Group, Or Client Computer
    - For rule action, Redirect To A Hosted Site selected, and Mktg specified as the host

6. Configure the second Web publishing rule with the following parameters:
   - Destination Set configured to the Development destination set
   - Applies To set to Any User, Group, Or Client Computer
   - For rule action, Redirect To A Hosted Site selected, and Dev specified as the host

Publishing a Web Server Hosted on the ISA Server Computer

By default, Web servers like ISA Server listen on port 80 for incoming requests. This means that hosting a Web server on the ISA Server computer will lead to a conflict if the default HTTP port settings are not changed. To avoid such a conflict, configure the Web server so that it listens on a port other than 80. Then, modify the ISA Server Web publishing rule so that ISA Server forwards the requests to the appropriate port on the Web server.

For example, you can configure the Web server to listen on port 9999. Then, create a Web publishing rule with the following parameters:

- Destination Set configured to a destination set that includes the IP address of the ISA Server computer
- For rule action, Route Requests To An Alternate Site selected
- Site configured to the host name of the Web server
- Port set to **9999**

Using Packet Filters to Publish a Web Server on the ISA Server Computer

Another way to publish a Web server located on the ISA Server computer is by configuring packet filters. In this way, ISA Server allows the Web server to listen on port 80 for the incoming Web requests.

There is no conflict for outgoing Web requests, as ISA Server listens on port 8080 and the Web server listens for requests from internal clients on port 80. However, be sure that the automatic discovery feature of ISA Server is not configured to listen on port 80 when you publish a Web server on the ISA Server computer; this will lead to a conflict from Web requests from internal clients. Also, since port 80 is used by Internet Information Service (IIS), do not create Web publishing rules when using the method described here to publish the Web server located on the ISA Server computer.

▶ **Follow these steps to publish a Web server on the ISA Server computer by using an IP packet filter:**

1. Enable packet filtering if it is not already enabled.

2. Create an IP packet filter with the following parameters specified in the New IP Packet Filter wizard:

    - On the Servers screen, select Only This Server and select the local computer.
    - On the Filter Mode screen, select Allow Packet Transmission.
    - On the Filter Type screen, select Custom.
    - For the IP Protocol setting, select TCP.
    - For the Direction setting, select Inbound.
    - For the Local Port setting, select Fixed port, and then type **80**.
    - For the Remote Port setting, select Any Port.
    - On the Local Computer screen, select This ISA Server's External IP Address.
    - On the Remote Computers screen, select All Remote Computers.

3. Disable automatic discovery if it is enabled, or reconfigure automatic discovery to listen on a port other than 80. This setting can be configured on the Auto Discovery tab of the array's properties.

Practice: Publishing a Web Server on the ISA Server Computer

In this practice, you configure a Web server on the computer running ISA Server. This practice requires that you connect Server1 to your ISP through a dial-up connection and that you perform all of these exercises during a single dial-up session.

Exercise 1: Configuring Incoming Web Request Properties

In this exercise, you enable the ISA Server to listen for incoming Web requests on port 80.

1. Log on to Server1 as Administrator.

2. Establish a dial-up connection with your ISP by double-clicking the Internet Connection you have assigned to the ISA Server computer. Complete this step from the Network And Dial-up Connections window.

3. Open ISA Management.
4. Right-click the MyArray node, and then click Properties.

   The MyArray Properties dialog box appears.
5. Click the Incoming Web Requests tab.
6. In the Identification area, select the Use The Same Listener Configuration For All IP Addresses radio button.
7. Verify that the TCP Port text box is set to 80, and then click OK.

   An ISA Server Warning message box appears.
8. Verify that the Save The Changes But Don't Restart The Service(s) radio button is selected, and then click OK.

Exercise 2: Creating a Destination Set for the Web Server

In the following exercise, you create a destination set corresponding to the external IP address assigned to Server1. Complete this exercise on Server1.

1. In ISA Management, expand the Policy Elements node.
2. Right-click the Destination Sets folder, point to New and then click Set.

   The New Destination Set dialog box appears.
3. In the Name text box, type **External Interface**.
4. Click Add.

   The Add/Edit Destination dialog box appears.
5. Click the IP Addresses radio button.
6. In the From text box, type the IP address currently assigned by your ISP to the external interface on Server1. If you don't know the current IP address, open a command prompt and type **ipconfig** to determine the address of the external interface. Note that this destination set is valid only for the current dial-up session.
7. Click OK.

   The destination IP address appears in the Include These Destinations box of the New Destination Set dialog box.
8. Click OK.

Exercise 3: Preparing the Web Site

In this exercise, you create a Web site on the ISA Server computer and configure the Web server to listen for Web requests on port 9999.

1. While you are still logged on to Server1 as Administrator, copy the file \Exercises\Chapter6\default.htm from the Supplemental Course Materials CD-ROM accompanying this book to the C:\Inetpub\wwwroot folder on Server1.

2. Click the Start menu, point to Programs, point to Administrative Tools, and then click Internet Services Manager.

   The Internet Information Services console appears.

3. In the Internet Information Services console tree, right-click the Default Web Site node and click Stop. (If the Default Web Site is stopped already, you may skip this step.)

   The Default Web Site is stopped.

4. Right-click the Default Web Site node, and click Properties.

   The Default Web Site (Stopped) Properties dialog box appears.

5. In the IP Address text box, type **192.168.0.1**.

6. In the TCP Port text box, highlight 80 and type **9999**.

7. Click OK.

8. Right-click the Default Web Site folder and click Start.

Exercise 4: Creating a Web Publishing Rule

In this exercise, you create a Web Publishing Rule to direct Web requests destined for the external interface on the ISA Server computer toward the internal Web server hosted on the same computer.

1. While you are still logged on to Server1 as Administrator, open ISA Management.

2. In the console tree, expand the Publishing node.

3. Right-click the Web Publishing Rules folder, point to New, and then click Rule.

   The New Web Publishing Rule wizard appears.

4. In the Web Publishing Rule Name text box, type **Local Web Server**, and then click Next.

   The Destination Sets screen appears.

5. In the Apply This Rule To drop-down list box, select Specified Destination Set.

   The Name drop-down list box appears.

6. In the Name drop-down list box, select External Interface, and then click Next.

   The Client Type screen appears.

7. Click Next.

   The Rule Action screen appears.

8. Select the Redirect The Request To This Internal Web Server (Name Or IP Address) radio button.

9. In the text box associated with this option, type **192.168.0.1**.

10. In the Connect To This Port When Bridging Request As HTTP text box, select and replace the default of 80 by typing **9999**.

11. Click Next.

    The Completing The New Web Publishing Rule Wizard screen appears.

12. Click Finish.

13. Stop and restart the Web Proxy and Firewall services in ISA Management before proceeding to the next exercise.

Exercise 5: Testing the Configuration

In this exercise, you test the Web publishing configuration from Server2 by connecting to the external IP address of Server1 in a Web browser.

1. Log on to Server2 as Administrator.

2. Open Internet Explorer.

3. In the Address text box, type the external IP address assigned by your ISP to Server1, and press Enter.

You see a sample Web page and a welcome message. Because you have connected to the internal Web server through an external IP address and from behind the ISA Server firewall, you know that you have securely published the Default Web Site to the Internet.

Lesson Summary

Through Web publishing rules, ISA Server responds to client requests on behalf of publishing Web servers. When an Internet client makes a Web request to an external IP address on the ISA Server computer, the request is forwarded to the Web publishing server specified in the Web publishing rule matching the request. Web publishing rules thus determine how ISA Server should intercept incoming Web requests.

For Web publishing rules, destination sets usually include a domain name (whose IP address maps to your ISA Server computer) and a path. Client address sets usually include IP addresses of clients located on the Internet. Rule actions for Web publishing rules either discard HTTP requests targeted for specific destination sets or redirect those requests to an alternate site, usually to a Web server on your corporate network. When you create a Web publishing rule, you can also configure how incoming HTTP and SSL requests should be redirected—whether as HTTP, SSL, or FTP requests. This process is known as bridging.

To publish a Web server hosted on the ISA Server computer, configure the Web server so that it listens on a port other than 80. Then, modify the ISA Server Web publishing rule so that ISA Server forwards the requests to the appropriate port on the Web server.

Lesson 3 Publishing Mail Servers

Mail servers may provide various services through several different protocols, and as a result, publishing a mail server behind a firewall normally requires you to allow each protocol access through the firewall. In ISA Server, the Mail Server Security wizard simplifies this process of publishing mail servers. By running the wizard, you simply specify the services you want to run, the location of your mail server, and the external address of the ISA Server computer. All the necessary rules and/or IP packet filters will be created for you.

After this lesson, you will be able to

- Use the Mail Server Security wizard to publish a mail server on an internal network computer
- Use the Mail Server Security wizard to publish a mail server on the ISA Server computer

Estimated lesson time: 30 minutes

Mail Server Security Wizard

ISA Server includes the Mail Server Security wizard, which you can use to host a mail server securely behind ISA Server. The wizard configures ISA Server rules to securely publish internal mail services to your external users.

To run the Mail Server Security wizard, right-click the Server Publishing Rules folder in ISA Management and select Secure Mail Server. You can modify an existing mail server publishing rule from the rule's Properties dialog box in the Server Publishing Rules folder in ISA Management.

▶ **Follow these steps to run the Mail Server Security wizard:**

1. In the console tree of ISA Management, right-click the Server Publishing Rules folder and then click Secure Mail Server.
2. Follow the on-screen instructions.

Mail Wizard Settings

By using the Mail Server Security wizard, you can configure the following parameters:

- The protocol for the selected mail service
- The published IP address of the mail server, which is the external IP address of the ISA Server
- The internal IP address of the mail server

The Mail Server Security wizard also creates a protocol rule that allows outgoing mail traffic. The protocol rule has the following parameters:

- The protocol is SMTP (client).
- The client set includes the internal IP address of the mail server computer.

Depending on which settings you select when running the wizard, different rules are created. ISA Server marks rules created by the wizard with a name beginning with "Mail Wizard Rule." For example, if you run the wizard, and configure it to publish outgoing SMTP mail, ISA Server creates a protocol rule named Mail Wizard Rule—SMTP (client). Internal IP: *IP_Address*, where *IP_Address* is the internal IP address that you specified when running the wizard. You can view these rule names in the details pane of the Server Publishing Rules folder.

If the mail server is located on the same computer as the ISA Server, the Mail Server Security wizard creates an IP packet filter rather than a protocol rule to allow the SMTP protocol.

Content Filtering

If the SMTP filter is installed and enabled, you can apply content filtering for all incoming mail by selecting the Apply Content Filtering check box in the wizard. The content will be filtered in accordance with the SMTP filter configuration.

Note that if the SMTP filter is already enabled, you cannot use the Mail Server Security wizard to disable it.

Configuring Exchange Server on the Local Network

By using ISA Server Mail Server Security wizard, you can configure an internal Microsoft Exchange Server so that it is available to external clients through one or more of the following protocols:

- Messaging Application Programming Interface (MAPI)
- Post Office Protocol 3 (POP3)
- Internet Messaging Access Protocol 4 (IMAP4)
- Network News Transfer Protocol (NNTP)
- Secure NNTP

The wizard creates one or more server publishing rules corresponding to each mail service that ISA Server protects. The server publishing rules created by the wizard have the following parameters:

- The mail server's internal address
- The external address exposed by the ISA Server
- The protocol for the selected mail service

The new rules created by the wizard are all named with the prefix "Mail Wizard Rule."

Exchange Server on the ISA Server Computer

You can use the Mail Server Security Wizard to publish an Exchange server on the ISA Server computer. In this scenario, the Mail Server Security wizard creates an IP packet filter. IP packet filters are created for each mail service that you select. For example, suppose you run the Mail Server Security wizard and configure ISA Server to allow outgoing SMTP mail and POP3 client requests. In this scenario, Microsoft Outlook clients will still not be able to access the Exchange server from outside the local network. To allow qualified clients inside and outside the network to use the SMTP server, you would need to create the following four IP packet filters:

- An IP packet filter allowing Inbound TCP connections on local port 25 from any remote port (to allow incoming SMTP packets)
- An IP packet filter allowing Outbound TCP connections on all local ports from remote port 25 (to allow outgoing SMTP packets)
- An IP packet filter allowing Inbound TCP connections on local port 110 from any remote port (to allow incoming POP3 packets)
- An IP packet filter allowing Outbound TCP connections on all local ports from remote port 110 (to allow outgoing POP3 packets)

Practice: Publishing the SMTP Service

In this practice, you configure the SMTP service on Server2 and then use the Mail Server Security wizard in ISA Server to publish the SMTP service to the Internet. You then test your configuration by sending an e-mail message using the published address of the internal SMTP server.

This practice requires you to have connected to the Internet through a dial-up connection and complete all four exercises during a single dial-up session. Therefore, establish a dial-up connection before beginning the exercises by double-clicking the dial-up connection appearing in the Network And Dial-up Connections window.

Also, before proceeding with this exercise, you should stop the SMTP Service on Server1. You can stop the SMTP Service on Server1 by right-clicking the Default SMTP Virtual Server icon in the Internet Services Manager and clicking Stop.

This practice also requires you to have created and enabled an IP packet filter allowing the SMTP protocol, as described in Chapter 4, Lesson 5.

Exercise 1: Configuring the SMTP Service

In this exercise, you configure the SMTP service on Server2. The function of the SMTP service is to send mail, and SMTP relies on other services, such as the POP3 service, to deliver mail to individual mailboxes. Though Windows 2000 does not include a built-in POP3 service, the SMTP service can still be used without POP3 to store all successfully sent mail in the local mail domain's Drop directory. From the Drop directory, messages can be opened and read manually, or they can be further processed and routed through the use of scripts.

1. Log on to Domain01 from Server2 as Administrator.
2. Click the Start menu, point to Programs, point to Administrative Tools, and click Internet Services Manager.

    The Internet Information Services console appears.

3. In the Internet Information Services console tree, expand the * server2 node.
4. Right-click the Default SMTP Virtual Server node, and then click Properties.

    The Default SMTP Virtual Server Properties dialog box appears.

5. In the IP Address drop-down list box, select 192.168.0.2.
6. Click OK.

Exercise 2: Creating a Mail Wizard Rule

In this exercise, you use the Mail Server Security wizard to create a rule mapping the external IP address of the ISA Server computer to the internal mail server on Server2.

1. Log on to Server1 as Administrator.
2. Open ISA Management.
3. Expand the Publishing node.
4. Right-click the Server Publishing Rules folder and click Secure Mail Server.

   The Mail Server Security wizard appears.
5. Click Next.

   The Mail Services Selection screen appears.
6. In the Default Authentication column, select the Incoming SMTP and Outgoing SMTP check boxes.
7. Click Next.

   The ISA Server's External IP Address screen appears.
8. Click Browse.

   The Browse For External IP Addresses dialog box appears and the external IP address assigned by your ISP to Server1 appears.
9. Click OK.

   The external IP address appears in the External IP Address text box.
10. Click Next.

    The Internal Mail Server screen appears.
11. Select the At This IP Address radio button, and type **192.168.0.2** in the text box.
12. Click Next.

    The Completing The Mail Server Security Wizard screen appears.
13. Click Finish.
14. Restart the Web Proxy and Firewall services in ISA Management before proceeding to the next exercise.

Exercise 3: Configuring Outlook Express

In this exercise, you configure Outlook Express to send mail using the SMTP server hosted on Server2. For the SMTP server's IP address, you specify its published address—the address corresponding to the external IP address of Server1.

1. Log on to Server1 as Administrator.
2. Click the Start menu, point to Programs, and click Outlook Express.

   Outlook Express opens and the Internet Connection wizard appears.

   The Your Name screen appears.

3. In the Display Name text box, type **Test User**.
4. Click Next.

   The Internet E-mail Address screen appears.

5. In the E-mail Address text box, type **testuser**.
6. Click Next.

   A message appears warning that the e-mail address does not appear to be valid.

7. Click Yes to dismiss this warning.

   The E-mail Server Names screen appears.

8. In the Incoming Mail (POP3, IMAP, or HTTP) Server text box, type **example.microsoft.com**. (This name is used merely as a placeholder and does not represent a real server. Alternatively, you may enter the name of any valid POP3 server you use for e-mail.)
9. In the Outgoing Mail (SMTP) Server text box, type the external IP address assigned to Server1 by your ISP. This must be the same IP address that you used for the Mail Wizard rule in Exercise 2.
10. Click Next.

    The Internet Mail Logon screen appears.

11. Click Next.

    The Congratulations screen appears.

12. Click Finish.

    Outlook Express appears.

13. Click the Tools menu, and then click Accounts.

    The Internet Accounts dialog box appears.

14. Click the Mail tab, verify that the example.microsoft.com account is selected, and then click Properties.

    The Example.microsoft.com Properties dialog box appears.

15. Click the Servers tab.

16. In the Outgoing Mail Server section, click the My Server Requires Authentication check box.

17. Click the Settings button.

    The Outgoing Mail Server dialog box appears.

18. Click the Log On Using radio button.

19. In the Account Name text box, type **Administrator**.

20. In Password text box, type the password you have assigned the Administrator account on Server2.

21. Click OK.

    The Example.microsoft.com Properties dialog box appears.

22. Click OK.

23. On the Internet Accounts dialog box, click Close.

Exercise 4: Testing the Configuration

In this exercise, you test the configuration first by sending an e-mail by using the published SMTP server and then by verifying that the SMTP server has successfully sent the message to the Drop folder on Server2.

1. While you are still logged on to Server1 and with Outlook Express still open, click the New Mail icon on the toolbar.

   A New Message e-mail dialog box appears.

2. In the To text box, type *Your_Name***@server2.domain01.local**, where *Your_Name* corresponds to your first name. Note that this name need not be a valid user account.

3. In the Subject text box, type **SMTP test mail**.

4. In the body of the message, type a short message such as **This is a test**.

5. Click the Send icon on the toolbar.

6. From Server2, log on as Administrator to Domain01. Then, browse to the C:\Inetpub\mailroot\Drop folder.

7. Click the Tools menu and then click Folder Options.

8. Click the View tab.
9. Clear the Hide File Extensions For Known File Types check box.
10. Click OK.

    The folder now contains an Outlook Express Mail Message file (.eml) with a long alphanumeric name.

11. Right-click the file, and then click Open.

    The Internet Connection wizard appears.

12. Click Cancel.

    A warning message appears stating that you have not created a mail account on this computer.

13. Click Yes to dismiss the warning message.

    Another warning message appears, stating that there is no default mail client.

14. Click OK to dismiss the warning message.

    You should see the message you just sent from Server1. Because the mail client has specified an external IP address for the SMTP server, this confirms that the SMTP server is securely published to the Internet from behind ISA Server.

15. Close the SMTP Test Mail dialog box.

Lesson Summary

The Mail Server Security wizard simplifies the process of publishing mail servers on your network. When you publish a mail server by using the Mail Server Security wizard, you create server publishing rules specifying the published IP address of the mail server (which corresponds to the external IP address of the ISA Server computer) and the internal IP address of the mail server computer. The new server publishing rules created by the wizard are all named with the prefix "Mail Wizard Rule." The Mail Server Security wizard also creates a protocol rule allowing outgoing mail traffic. If the mail server is located on the same computer as the ISA Server, the Mail Server Security wizard creates an IP packet filter rather than a protocol rule to allow the SMTP protocol.

To run the Mail Server Security wizard, right-click the Server Publishing Rules folder in the console tree of ISA Management and select Secure Mail Server.

Review

The following questions are intended to reinforce key information presented in the chapter. If you are unable to answer a question, review the appropriate lesson and then try the question again. The answers for these questions are located in Appendix A, "Questions and Answers."

1. Which types of publishing rules are available in Firewall mode? In Cache mode?

2. Using ISA Server, how would you publish an Simple Mail Transfer Protocol (SMTP) server that is located on a perimeter network?

3. When ISA Server receives a Hypertext Transfer Protocol (HTTP) request, which protocols can ISA Server use to bridge the request to the internal destination server?

4. What port does Internet Information Service (IIS) Web server use to listen to requests, by default? What port does the automatic discovery feature use to listen to requests? What port does ISA Server use to listen to internal and external requests by default?

5. If you have a mail server hosted on the ISA Server computer, what four IP packet filters would you need to create to allow both internal and external clients access to SMTP and Post Office Protocol 3 (POP3) services?

CHAPTER 7

Securing Enterprise Networks with ISA Server

Lesson 1 Applying Enterprise Policies 266

Lesson 2 Configuring ISA Server Arrays 279

Lesson 3 Securing Virtual Private Networks with ISA Server 294

Review 305

About This Chapter

Large enterprise networks often require Internet security solutions that are multitiered, robust, and flexible. Through the use of enterprise policies and settings, Microsoft Internet Security and Acceleration Server 2000 (ISA Server) allows multitiered policy enforcement by providing the capability for both enterprise-level and array-level Internet security that can be used together or separately. Through the use of multiserver arrays, ISA Server provides security that is robust enough for large organizations. Finally, ISA Server provides flexible Internet security for networks that span multiple locations and include roaming users.

Before You Begin

To complete the lessons in this chapter, you must have

- Completed the setup procedures described in "About This Book"
- Completed all the exercises in this book through Chapter 4

Lesson 1 Applying Enterprise Policies

Enterprise policies in ISA Server are configured at the headquarters level of an organization and may apply to any or all arrays. Array policies are configured at the branch level and may inherit an enterprise policy. For any given array, ISA Server allows you to apply enterprise policies, array policies, or both.

After this lesson, you will be able to

- Configure an enterprise policy in ISA Server
- Apply an enterprise policy to an array
- Create a default enterprise policy that is inherited by arrays

Estimated lesson time: 40 minutes

Enterprise Policies and Arrays

Enterprise policies are configured and applied to ISA Server arrays by enterprise administrators. For any given ISA Server array, enterprise policy settings determine whether array policies are included and, if so, what kinds of rules are included in the array policy.

How Enterprise Policies are Applied

Whenever you install ISA Server after the enterprise has been initialized, you are given the option to install ISA Server as an array member. If you are joining an existing array, the enterprise policies of the existing array are inherited. If you are creating a new array, ISA Server Setup searches for any enterprise policies on the network to apply to the new array. If you are logged on as a member of the Enterprise Admins group, you may select whether your new array will use default enterprise policy settings, inherit the settings of an existing enterprise policy, inherit the settings of a new enterprise policy, or ignore enterprise policies and use an array policy only. If you are not a member of the Enterprise Admins group, your new ISA Server installation will automatically inherit the default enterprise policy settings that an enterprise administrator has configured for your network.

Note If an existing array has already been configured to use an array policy only (no enterprise policy), you cannot modify the array's policy settings to use an enterprise policy. Likewise, if an existing array uses an enterprise policy, you cannot change the array's policy settings to ignore enterprise settings and use an array policy only.

Creating an Enterprise Policy

Enterprise policy includes site and content rules and protocol rules. This enterprise policy can be applied to any available array and can be further restricted (if permitted) by the array's own policy. You can also create policy elements at the enterprise level. These policy elements are used by enterprise-level rules or by array-level rules.

Though by default only users who are members of the Enterprise Admins group have permissions to configure enterprise policies, the properties of each enterprise policy can be modified to allow other users privileges to change the policy. In other words, as an enterprise administrator, you can give any user or group permissions to modify any particular enterprise policy.

▶ **Follow these steps to create an enterprise policy:**

1. In the console tree of ISA Management, expand the Enterprise node.

2. Right-click the Policies node, point to New, and then click Policy.

3. In the New Enterprise Policy wizard, follow the on-screen instructions.

▶ **Follow these steps to configure the enterprise policy of an array:**

1. In the console tree of ISA Management, right-click the applicable array, and then click Properties.

2. On the Policies tab, click the Use Custom Enterprise Policy Settings radio button.

3. Click the Use This Enterprise Policy Radio button, and then click an enterprise policy to apply to the array.

Before you create or configure an enterprise policy, you should be aware of the following:

- To create an enterprise policy, you must be logged on as a user who is a member of the Enterprise Admins group.

- You can create a new enterprise policy only if you installed ISA Server as an array member or if you are managing an enterprise.

Configuring the Policy Settings for an Enterprise

Enterprise policy settings refer to the inheritance properties that affect how an enterprise policy is applied at the array level. An enterprise administrator can modify these settings by right-clicking the Enterprise node in ISA Management and selecting Set Defaults. They can also be configured when an enterprise administrator installs an array or modifies an array's properties.

Figure 7.1 shows the enterprise policy settings available on the Set Defaults dialog box. This dialog box is opened from the Enterprise node in ISA Management. The default enterprise policy settings configured in this dialog box apply to all arrays unless a particular array's properties are configured by an enterprise administrator.

Figure 7.1 Default enterprise policy settings

Figure 7.2 shows the enterprise policy settings available by selecting the properties of an array and clicking the Policies tab. When you select the Use Default Enterprise Policy Settings radio button, the settings configured in the Set Defaults dialog box are applied to the array. When you select the Use Custom Enterprise Policy Settings radio button, the newly configured settings override the default enterprise policy settings. You can only modify the enterprise policy settings for an array if you have enterprise administrator privileges. If you install ISA Server or create an array without enterprise administrator privileges, the default enterprise policy settings are applied to the new array.

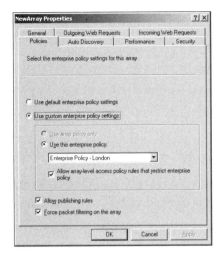

Figure 7.2 Enterprise policy settings for an array

Enterprise policy settings include:

- **Enterprise policy only.** This setting is configured by selecting the Use This Enterprise Policy radio button and by selecting a particular policy. In this case, the administrator at the enterprise level dictates that only the selected enterprise policy applies. No new protocol rules or site and content rules can be added at the array level.

- **Combined enterprise and array policy.** This setting is configured by selecting the Allow Array-Level Access Policy Rules That Restrict Enterprise Policy check box along with the Use This Enterprise Policy radio button. By configuring this setting, array-level site and content rules and protocol rules are allowed. However, these array-level rules can only include deny-type rules. That is, the protocol rules and site and content rules configured for the array can only impose additional limitations on enterprise-level rules.

- **Array policy only.** This setting is configured by selecting the Use Array Policy Only radio button. In this case, no enterprise policy is applied to the array. The array administrator is able to create any rule to allow or deny access. When an array has been configured in this way, the array cannot be configured later to use an enterprise policy.

Note The Use Array Policy Only radio button is unavailable in Figure 7.2.

- **Allow publishing rules.** This setting, which is configured by selecting the Allow Publishing Rules check box, controls whether publishing rules may be created on an array. Note that publishing rules themselves cannot be created at the enterprise level.

- **Force packet filtering on the array.** This setting, which is configured by selecting the Force Packet Filtering On The Array check box, determines whether packet filtering for an array should be mandatory or made available according to the decision of array-level administrators. Note that IP packet filters themselves can neither be created at the enterprise level nor forbidden by enterprise policy settings.

You can change the default enterprise settings, but only if no array in the enterprise is currently using them. If an array is currently using the default settings, a member of the Enterprise Admins group can change the enterprise settings that are active for the array by selecting the Use Custom Enterprise Policy Settings radio button in the array properties Policy tab. This allows an enterprise administrator to determine whether a given array will ignore all enterprise policy settings, inherit a specific enterprise policy, or inherit an enterprise policy that is further restricted at the array level.

▶ **Follow these steps to configure default enterprise policy settings:**

1. In the console tree of ISA Management, right-click the Enterprise node.
2. Click Set Defaults.
3. In the Set Defaults dialog box, click one of the following:
   - Use Array Policy Only radio button (if only the array policy should be applied to the array)
   - Use This Enterprise Policy radio button (if the enterprise policy should be applied to the array)
4. If you select the Use This Enterprise Policy radio button, do one or both of the following:
   - From the drop-down list box, select the enterprise policy to apply to the array.
   - (Optional) To allow array-level policy rules to restrict the chosen enterprise policy, click the Allow Array-level Access Policy Rules That Restrict Enterprise Policy check box.

Before you configure default enterprise policy settings, you should also be aware of the following:

- You can only apply enterprise policies when administering ISA Server on a computer that belongs to an array.
- If you configure enterprise settings to use array policy only, you cannot subsequently modify the settings to use enterprise policy.

Caution When an enterprise policy is applied to an array, all previously defined array-level site and content rules and protocol rules are deleted.

Backing Up and Restoring an Enterprise Configuration

All enterprise configuration parameters can be backed up and stored locally in a file. You can save your configuration to any directory and file name you choose. The backup process saves all enterprise-specific information, including all enterprise policies and enterprise policy elements. The backup process also saves information about which arrays use which enterprise policies, but it does not save array-specific configuration information.

You can fully restore the enterprise configuration if that configuration has been backed up and saved to a file. The restore operation rolls back all changes in the parameters that pertain to the enterprise to the configuration that existed when the backup was run.

Caution Restoring an enterprise configuration may impact policies for arrays that use enterprise policies, so after you back up the enterprise configuration, back up all the arrays in the enterprise. After you restore the enterprise configuration, restore all the array configurations.

▶ **Follow these steps to back up an enterprise configuration:**

1. In the console tree of ISA Management, right-click the Enterprise node, and then click Back Up.

    The Backup Enterprise Configuration dialog box appears.

2. In the Store Backup Information In This Location text box, type the file name and path in which the backup should be stored.

    The backup file is given the .bef extension by default.

3. (Optional) In the Comment box, type any information which you find helpful.

4. Click OK.

   After a few moments, a Backup Enterprise Configuration message box appears, stating that the backup was successful.

▶ **Follow these steps to restore an enterprise configuration:**

1. In the console tree of ISA Management, right-click the Enterprise node and then click Restore.

   An ISA Server message box appears, stating that the existing configuration will be replaced.

2. If you are sure you want to overwrite the existing enterprise configuration with the backed up configuration, click Yes.

3. The Restore Enterprise Configuration dialog box appears.

4. In the Restore Configuration From The Following Backup (.BEF) File text box, type the path to the backup folder and the name of the backup file.

5. Click OK.

   The Restore Enterprise Configuration dialog box appears.

6. Click OK.

   After a few moments, a Restore Enterprise Configuration message box appears, stating that the restore was successful.

Practice: Creating and Applying an Enterprise Policy

In this practice, you create an enterprise policy. You then install ISA Server on Server2, apply the enterprise policy you have configured, and observe the results.

Exercise 1: Creating an Enterprise Policy

In this exercise, you configure settings for an enterprise policy on Server1.

▶ **To create an enterprise policy on Server1**

1. Log on to Server1 as Administrator.

2. In the console tree of ISA Management, expand the Enterprise node, and then expand the Policies node.

3. Right-click the Enterprise Policy 1 node and click Properties.

   The Enterprise Policy 1 Properties dialog box appears.

4. Rename Enterprise Policy 1 by typing **Test Enterprise Policy** in the Name text box.

5. Click OK.

6. Expand the Test Enterprise Policy node.

7. Right-click the Protocol Rules folder, point to New and click Rule.

   The New Protocol Rule wizard appears.

8. In the Protocol Rule Name text box, type **Deny Archie Protocol**, and then click Next.

   The Rule Action screen appears.

9. Click the Deny radio button, and then click Next.

   The Protocols screen appears.

10. On the Apply This Rule To drop-down list box, select Selected Protocols.

    The Protocols (Enterprise Level) list box appears.

11. Click the Archie check box and then click Next.

    The Schedule screen appears, and Always is highlighted in the Use This Schedule drop-down list box.

12. Click Next.

    The Client Type screen appears and the Any Request radio button is selected.

13. Click Next.

    The Completing the New Protocol Rule Wizard screen appears.

14. Click Finish.

15. In the console tree, right-click the Enterprise node and click Set Defaults.

    The Set Defaults dialog box appears.

16. Verify that the Use This Enterprise Policy radio button is selected.

    The Test Enterprise Policy is selected in the drop-down list box.

17. Verify that the Allow Array-Level Access Policy Rules That Restrict Enterprise Policy check box is selected.

18. Click OK.

    You have now configured an enterprise policy that blocks the use of the Archie protocol to all requests. Because the array MyArray has been configured to use array policy only, the newly configured enterprise policy cannot be applied to MyArray. You can, however, create a new array and apply Test Enterprise Policy to this new array. You will complete this procedure in Exercise 2.

Exercise 2: Creating a New Array that Inherits the Default Enterprise Policy

In this exercise, you install ISA Server on Server2 as a new array member. You will perform this exercise while you are logged on as a user who is a member of the Domain Admins group but not a member of the Enterprise Admins group. Because you have configured Test Enterprise Policy as the default enterprise policy, and because you do not have privileges granted to the Enterprise Admins group, the new array you create will automatically inherit the Test Enterprise Policy settings. After you install the new array, you will not have the necessary permissions to choose whether to apply an enterprise policy or to determine which enterprise policy to apply to the new array. Instead, the default enterprise policy will be applied automatically.

▶ **To create an array that inherits the enterprise policy**

1. Create a new user in Domain01 named ArrayAdmin. Make ArrayAdmin a member of the Domain Admins group only. You may leave ArrayAdmin as a member of the Domain Users group.

2. Log on to the Domain01 domain from Server2 as ArrayAdmin.

3. Install ISA Server, as described in the Installing ISA Server Enterprise Edition practice.

    This practice is located in Chapter 2 at the end of Lesson 2.

    You do not have to perform an ISA Server Enterprise Initialization, as outlined in the Installing ISA Server Enterprise Edition practice, because this step was completed when you installed ISA Server on Server1.

4. When prompted, choose to perform a full installation and to install the server as an array member.

    Early in the installation process, a Microsoft ISA Server Setup dialog box appears, allowing you to choose either to join the array MyArray or to create a new array.

5. Click New to create a new array.

   The New Array dialog box appears.

6. In the Array Name text box, replace the default name of Server2 by typing **NewArray**.

7. Click OK.

   The Microsoft ISA Server Setup dialog box appears and the Integrated Mode radio button is selected.

8. Click Continue.

9. Finish the ISA Server installation by accepting the default settings for the ISA Server cache and by constructing the Local Address Table (LAT) based on the internal Internet Protocol (IP) address range of 192.168.0.0 to 192.168.0.255.

Exercise 3: Testing the Configuration

In this exercise, you see how the Test Enterprise Policy settings affect array-level policy for the array NewArray.

▶ **To test the configuration**

1. Log on to Domain01 from Server2 as ArrayAdmin.

2. Open the ISA Management console.

3. In the console tree, expand the Enterprise node, and then expand the Policies node.

   The Test Enterprise Policy node appears under the Policies node.

4. Open the Test Enterprise Policy node and select the Protocol Rules folder.

   The Deny Archie Protocol is listed in the details pane.

5. In the console tree, expand the Servers And Arrays node, and then expand the NewArray node.

6. Expand the Access Policy node, and then select the Protocol Rules folder.

   The Deny Archie Protocol is listed in the details pane. The NewArray access policy has inherited the Test Enterprise Policy settings. Because you installed ISA Server while you were logged on as a member of Domain Admins but not as a member of Enterprise Admins, your new array has inherited the default enterprise policy settings.

7. On the View menu, click Advanced.

8. In the details pane, right-click the Deny Archie Protocol protocol rule and then click Delete.

   The Confirm Delete dialog box appears.

9. Click Yes to confirm that you want to delete the rule.

   An ISA Error message box appears, informing you that you do not have the necessary permissions to perform the action.

   To ensure that an enterprise policy is enforced, an organization should plan not to allow branch-level array administrators to become members of the group Enterprise Admins. However, branch-level array administrators must be granted Domain Admins privileges.

10. Click Continue.

11. If the message appears again, click Continue again to dismiss the message.

12. In the console tree, right-click the Protocol Rules folder appearing below the Access Policy node, point to New and then click Rule.

    The New Protocol Rule wizard appears.

13. In the Protocol Rule Name text box, type **Array-Level Protocol Rule**, and then click Next.

    The Rule Action screen appears. Notice that the Allow radio button is unavailable, indicating that you can only create Deny rules at the array level when an enterprise-level policy is being enforced. The same is true for site and content rules.

14. Click Cancel to exit the New Protocol Rule wizard.

15. In the console tree of ISA Management, right-click the IP Packet Filters folder, point to New and then click Filter.

    The New IP Packet Filter wizard appears.

16. In the IP Packet Filter Name text box, type **OpenAll**, and then click Next.

    The Servers screen appears.

17. Click Next.

    The Filter Mode screen appears.

18. Click Next.

    The Filter Type screen appears.

19. Click the Custom radio button, and then click Next.

    The Filter Settings screen appears. Notice that the IP protocol is set to Any and the Direction is set to Both.

20. Click Next.

    The Local Computer screen appears.

21. Click Next.

    The Remote Computers screen appears.

22. Click Next.

    The Completing The New IP Packet Filter Wizard screen appears.

23. Click Finish.

24. In the console tree, click the IP Packet Filters folder.

    The OpenAll packet filter is listed in the details pane. Enterprise policy does not restrict the use of IP packet filters.

25. Log off of Server2 as ArrayAdmin, and then log on again as Administrator.

26. Run ISA Server Setup again and remove all ISA Server components. When a dialog box appears asking you whether to remove all logs and configuration backup files, click Yes.

Lesson Summary

If you are a member of the group Enterprise Admins, you may create any number of enterprise policies, each of which may be applied to groups of ISA Server arrays. Enterprise policies include site and content rules and protocol rules. Enterprise policies also include policy elements, which are used both by enterprise-level and array-level rules.

You must also be a member of the group Enterprise Admins to configure the group of settings known as enterprise policy settings. Enterprise policy settings include the default enterprise settings for all arrays and the enterprise-level settings associated with any particular array. For any given array, these settings determine whether enterprise policy only, a combined enterprise and array policy, or an array policy only is allowed; whether publishing rules are allowed; and whether packet filtering on the array level should be forced. When a combined enterprise and array policy is allowed on an array, the array policies may only further restrict the rules defined at the enterprise level. If an array is configured to use an array policy only, it cannot later be configured to inherit an enterprise policy. Similarly, if an existing array uses an enterprise policy, you cannot change the array's policy settings to ignore enterprise settings and use an array policy only.

Whenever an array is created by a user who lacks enterprise administrator privileges, the default enterprise policy and policy settings are applied to the new array.

All enterprise configuration parameters can be backed up and stored locally in a file. The backup process saves all enterprise-specific information, including all enterprise policies and enterprise policy elements. These enterprise configuration parameters can then be restored from the backup file at any time.

Lesson 2 Configuring ISA Server Arrays

ISA Server computers are grouped together in arrays. Arrays allow a group of ISA Server computers to be treated and managed as a single, logical entity. Arrays also allow client requests to be distributed among several ISA Server computers. This improves server performance and reliability by decreasing server response time and providing fault-tolerance.

After this lesson, you will be able to

- Create multiserver arrays of ISA Server computers
- Promote standalone servers to arrays
- Remove a server from an array
- Back up and restore an array configuration

Estimated lesson time: 50 minutes

Creating ISA Server Arrays

When you install ISA Server, you can choose to install the new server as an array member or as a standalone server, as shown in Figure 7.3. In both cases, ISA Management shows the server as belonging to an array.

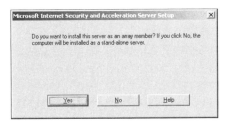

Figure 7.3 Installing ISA Server as an array member or standalone server

Note Before you can set up ISA Server as an array member, the ISA Server schema updates must be applied to the Active Directory directory services schema. This process is known as initializing the enterprise. You must be an administrator on the local computer and a member of the Enterprise Admins group to initialize the enterprise.

To create the first array on your network, install ISA Server as an array member. When no existing arrays are found, a new array will be created. With each subsequent ISA Server installation, if you choose to install ISA Server as an array member, ISA Server Setup presents a list of existing arrays that the server can join, as shown in Figure 7.4. When you add a server to an existing array, that server inherits all the policy settings of the array. For this reason, all the servers within an array share a common configuration.

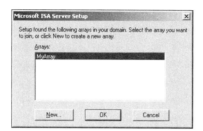

Figure 7.4 Joining an existing array

Array Requirements

All array members must be in the same domain and in the same site. A site is a set of computers in a well-connected TCP/IP subnet. A domain is a collection of computers, defined by the administrator, that share a common directory database.

Arrays and Standalone Servers

If you choose not to install ISA Server as an array member, you can install ISA Server as a standalone server. Standalone server installations do not require that the computer belong to a Microsoft Windows 2000 domain. For standalone servers, as part of the installation process, the ISA Server is given the same name as the ISA Server computer.

Table 7.1 compares features of array members and standalone servers.

Table 7.1 Comparison of Arrays and Standalone Servers

Characteristic	Array member	Standalone server
Scalability	Can have one or more member servers.	Limited to only one member.
Active Directory directory services required?	Yes. Can be installed only in Windows 2000 domains with Active Directory directory services installed.	No. Configuration information is stored in the registry of the ISA Server computer. Can also be installed in Windows NT 4.0 domains.
Enterprise policy	Yes. A single policy can be applied to all arrays in the enterprise.	Not applicable.

Promoting Standalone Servers

An ISA Server installation configured as a standalone server cannot join an array. However, standalone servers can be promoted to become array members. When the standalone server is promoted, a new array is created. The ISA Server computer is made a member of the new array.

Whenever you promote a standalone server when you are not logged on with enterprise administrator privileges, the new array adopts the default enterprise policy settings. In this case, all enterprise policy rules apply to the array. If the enterprise policy allows publishing, any publishing rules defined for the array are retained.

Note that, depending upon which default enterprise policy settings have been configured, some existing array policy rules may be deleted. For example, if the default enterprise policy settings do not allow an array policy, all array policy rules are deleted. If the default enterprise policy settings enforce an enterprise policy but allow array policies to further restrict the enterprise policy, all deny-type array policy rules will be allowed, and all allow-type array policy rules will be deleted.

As a member of the Enterprise Admins group, you can configure the enterprise policy settings. When configuring enterprise policy settings for a given array, you can choose to use the default enterprise policy settings or configure custom enterprise policy settings.

▶ **Follow these steps to promote a standalone server:**

1. Click the View menu, and then click Advanced.

2. In the console tree of ISA Management, right-click the applicable array, and then click Promote.

   An ISA Server message box appears, stating that you are about to promote the server to become an array.

3. Click Yes.

   The Enterprise Policy Settings dialog box appears.

4. Click one of the following radio buttons:
   - Use Default Enterprise Policy Settings
   - Use Custom Enterprise Policy Settings

5. If you selected the Use Custom Enterprise Policy Settings radio button, click one of the following radio buttons:
   - Use Array Policy Only
   - Use This Enterprise Policy

6. If you clicked the Use This Enterprise Policy radio button, then select one or both of the following:
   - Select an enterprise policy appearing in the drop-down list box to apply to the array.
   - (Optional) Click the Also Allow Array Policy check box.

7. (Optional) If you select the Use Custom Enterprise Policy Settings radio button, select one or both of the following check boxes:
   - Allow Publishing Rules To Be Created On The Array
   - Force Packet Filtering On The Array

8. Click OK.

   A Promoting Server message box appears as the server is promoted.

You should also be aware of the following when promoting standalone servers:

- You can only promote standalone servers that belong to a Windows 2000 domain.
- You must initialize the enterprise before you can promote an ISA Server computer.

Array Member Settings

The following list describes how features and settings are configured for array members.

- **Installation Modes.** When you install an ISA Server computer as a member of an existing array, ISA Server Setup automatically installs ISA Server in the same mode as the other array members: Cache, Firewall, or Integrated. For example, if all the servers in the array were installed in Firewall mode, this server will also be installed in Firewall mode.

- **Policy Configuration.** The array policy of ISA Server—access policy, publishing, and bandwidth rules—is defined once at the array level and applied to all the servers. Similarly, the cache is centrally configured at the array level; the policy and scheduled content download jobs are identical for all servers.

- **Extensions.** Extensions include Web filters and applications filters. When you install an extension on one server in an array, it is not automatically installed on all the servers in the array. You must install the extension on each server in the array.

- **Alert Configuration.** Alerts can be configured for each server in the array or for all the servers in the array.

- **Reports.** Reports display information about the activity on all the ISA Server computers in the array. The report data is stored in a database on a computer and in a directory that you specify—by default, the ISA Server computer on which you configure the report jobs.

- **Cache.** Space for the ISA Server cache is allocated on each server according to the amount you specify when you install ISA Server or reconfigure the cache. All cache configuration properties, however, are common for all the servers in an array. This includes Hypertext Transfer Protocol (HTTP) caching properties, File Transfer Protocol (FTP) caching properties, and Cache Array Routing Protocol (CARP) properties. Scheduled cache content download jobs are common for all servers in an array.

Storing an Array Configuration

Though configuration information for standalone servers is stored in the registry, configuration information for arrays is stored in the Active Directory store. When you promote a standalone server to an array, its configuration information is installed in the Active Directory store.

When you change the properties of any array member, the changes are applied to all array members. Each member has the same information as all the others, thereby ensuring that the system is fault tolerant.

Some configuration data is specific to the server. For example, IP packet filters, Web filters, and application filters are applied at the server level. Cache content and activity logs are stored on the local computer. Reports are generated for all the servers in the array, but are stored on a specific server. Server-specific configuration information is not saved when you back up the array configuration.

Because every member of the array has current information about every other array member, a client needs to query only a single array member. This provides additional fault tolerance and transparency for the client.

Controlling Array Membership

ISA Server computers that belong to arrays can join, leave, or be removed from an array. To remove an ISA Server computer from an array, uninstall ISA Server from that computer by re-running the ISA Server Setup program and choosing to remove all ISA Server components. To move a computer to another array, uninstall and then reinstall ISA Server. When reinstalling ISA Server, specify the name of the new array that the server should join. Although anyone can query the array members, only members of the domain group Administrators (which includes the Administrator account as well as all members of Domain Admins and Enterprise Admins) can change array membership.

When you change an enterprise configuration by adding or removing a server from an array, the configuration information is updated in the Active Directory directory services store. The changes are applied to a Windows 2000 domain controller on the network to which the enterprise is connected. Active Directory directory services then replicate the updated information to the other domain controllers.

Make sure to back up the array configuration whenever you change array membership in any way. When you restore an array configuration, ISA Server uses the membership list specified in the backup file.

Backing Up and Restoring an Array Configuration

ISA Server includes a backup and restore feature that enables you to save and restore most array configuration information. The array configuration parameters can be backed up and stored locally in a file. You can save your configuration to any directory and file name on the local computer. For maximum security, save the backup files to an NT file system (NTFS) disk partition.

If ISA Server is set up as an array member, its configuration information is stored in the Active Directory directory services store. If ISA Server is installed as a standalone server, the configuration settings are stored in the server's local registry.

Backing Up the Configuration

ISA Server backs up all of the array's general configuration information. This includes access policy rules, publishing rules, policy elements, alert configuration, cache configuration, and array properties.

Some server-specific configuration information is not backed up. This includes cache content, activity logs, reports, and effective enterprise policy.

Back up the array configuration after any major modification to the array, including:

- Changing the enterprise policy settings
- Changing the array's installation mode
- Adding, removing, or renaming a member server
- Changing cache size or location
- Adding or removing Web filters

It is recommended that you also periodically back up the server-specific configuration. You can use Windows Backup (Ntbackup) to back up ISA Server information, including passwords, local registry parameters, cache store configuration information, H.323 Gatekeeper configuration, reports, local settings for application filters, performance-tuning parameters, cache contents, and log files. Although Windows Backup can be used to back up server-specific information, it cannot back up array configuration information unless the ISA Server computer is also a domain controller. This is because array information is stored in Active Directory directory services store, which is located only on domain controllers. It is therefore recommended that you back up the array configuration before using Windows Backup. It is also recommended that you restore the array configuration immediately after using the Restore facility included with Windows Backup.

▶ **Follow these steps to back up an array configuration:**

1. In the console tree of ISA Management, right-click the applicable array, and then click Back Up.

   The Backup Array dialog box appears.

2. In the Store Backup Configuration In This Location text box, type the path in which the backup file should be stored, and then type the name of the backup file.

   The backup file is given a .bif extension by default.

3. (Optional) In the Comment text box, type a comment for the backup file.

4. Click OK.

   After a few moments, a Backup Array message box appears, stating that the backup was successful.

5. Click OK.

Note The backup file can be saved to any drive on the local computer or on the network by specifying a UNC or a mapped network drive path.

Backing Up a Standalone Server Configuration

You can back up a standalone server configuration. The configuration can be restored to the same standalone server.

Restoring the Configuration

The restore process reconstructs most configuration parameters that pertain to the array.

▶ **Follow these steps to restore an array configuration:**

1. In the console tree of ISA Management, right-click the appropriate array, and then click Restore.

   An ISA Server message box appears, stating that the existing configuration information will be replaced when the restore operation runs.

2. If you are sure that you want to replace the existing configuration with the configuration in the backup file, click Yes.

3. In the Restore Array Configuration From The Following Backup (.BIF) File text box, type the name of the path of the configuration backup file.

4. Click OK.

   The Restore Array dialog box appears.

5. Click OK.

   After a few moments, a Restore Array message box appears, stating that the restore was successful.

You should also be aware of the following when restoring an array configuration:

- You cannot back up an array configuration and subsequently restore the configuration to another array or standalone server.
- You cannot restore an enterprise configuration (.bef file) to an array.
- You cannot restore an array configuration if the array to which the configuration is being restored does not use the same enterprise policy settings as when the backup took place.

Using Arrays to Provide Fault Tolerance

Fault tolerance is an important feature of an ISA Server cache array scenario, in which the CARP algorithm is used to ensure that client requests are serviced by the appropriate ISA Server. The array configuration ensures that even if one array member fails, the other array members can continue to service client requests.

Fault tolerance for the ISA Server Firewall service, however, varies among client and installation types. For example, ISA Server alone cannot ensure fault tolerance and load balancing in the following cases:

- For SecureNAT clients, which cannot identify the ISA Server by array name.
- For standalone servers, which cannot be grouped in arrays.

In these scenarios, ISA Server is used together with other operating system services to create a fault-tolerant, balanced network. The following sections describe how to configure DNS Server and how to configure Microsoft Windows 2000 Advanced Server Network Load Balancing to accomplish this goal.

Fault Tolerance for Firewall Clients

For Firewall clients, fault tolerance can be achieved when two or more ISA Server computers are used with a DNS server.

When this is the case, all the ISA Server computers are assigned the same DNS name. This way, when a client requests an object from the ISA Server computer, specifying the DNS name of the ISA Server computer, the DNS server resolves the name using round robin distribution to any one of the ISA Server computers.

Note Round robin distribution is a mechanism used by DNS servers to share and distribute loads for network resources. When DNS responds to resolve a name query, it returns an IP address matching one of the ISA Server's IP addresses. For more information on DNS and round robin distribution, consult Windows 2000 Server Help and the Windows 2000 Server Resource Kit.

▶ **Follow these steps to configure the DNS server for an ISA Server array:**

1. Click Start, point to Programs, point to Administrative Tools, and then click DNS.
2. In the console tree, expand the Forward Lookup Zones node.
3. Right-click the domain containing the ISA Server array, and then click New Host.

   The New Host dialog box appears.
4. In the Name text box, type the DNS computer name for the ISA Server computer or array.
5. In the IP Address text box, type the IP address for the new host.
6. Click Add Host to add the new host record to the zone.

   Repeat steps 3 to 5 for each ISA Server computer. Make sure to give each computer the same name.

Fault Tolerance for SecureNAT Clients

For SecureNAT clients, fault tolerance can be achieved for the firewall service when two or more ISA Server computers are used together with Windows 2000 Advanced Server Network Load Balancing. Network Load Balancing is one form of clustering in Windows 2000. By combining the resources of two or more computers running Windows 2000 Advanced Server into a single cluster, Network Load Balancing delivers the reliability and performance that Web servers and other mission-critical servers need.

Network Load Balancing clusters together several computers running server programs that use the TCP/IP networking protocol. Network Load Balancing allows all of the computers in the cluster to be addressed by a single IP address (while each maintains a unique and dedicated IP address internally). Network Load Balancing distributes incoming client requests in the form of TCP/IP traffic across the hosts in a cluster.

Important Network Load Balancing is only available with Windows 2000 Advanced Server and Windows 2000 Datacenter Server.

Network Load Balancing requires that each ISA Server computer have a unique IP address on its internal network adapter. In addition, the Network Load Balancing cluster must have an IP address, which will be used by both ISA Server computers. For more information on Network Load Balancing and clusters, see Network Load Balancing in Windows 2000 Advanced Server Help.

▶ **Follow these steps to configure the ISA Server computers for Network Load Balancing:**

1. Verify that the ISA Server computers are installed in the same mode.

2. For the internal network adapter on each ISA Server computer, modify the Network Load Balancing properties as follows:

   - Set the Primary IP address to the IP address of the Network Load Balancing cluster. This address is a cluster IP address and must be set identically for all hosts in the cluster. This IP address is used to address the cluster as a whole and it should be the IP address for the full Internet name that you specify for the cluster.

   - Assign a unique priority to each machine in the NLB cluster.

   - Set the Dedicated IP address to the IP address of the ISA Server computer's internal network adapter. This IP address is used to individually address each host in the cluster, so it should be unique for each host. In general, it is the original IP address assigned to the host prior to selecting an IP address for cluster operations.

For a single network adapter, the TCP/IP stack must be configured with both dedicated and cluster address, with the dedicated address ordered first. For a computer with two network adapters, the network adapter with the dedicated address must have a lower metric value (that is, higher priority) than that of the network adapter with the cluster address.

The default gateway for SecureNAT clients should be configured to the cluster's (dedicated) IP address. In other words, the cluster's virtual address should be used as the gateway address. This way, all requests will be handled by Network Load Balancing.

Cache Array Routing Protocol

ISA Server uses the CARP to determine the best path through an array to resolve a Web request. The request resolution path determines either exactly where in the array the requested information is cached or whether ISA Server must route the request to the Internet to retrieve the requested information.

How CARP Works

The CARP process provides efficient routing for requests. This process is summarized in the following steps:

1. All servers are tracked through an array membership list, which is maintained in the Active Directory directory services store. Array members are notified when servers are added or removed from the array.

2. Periodically, the Web Proxy client or a downstream server polls and, if necessary, updates the array membership list. As part of this process, Web Proxy clients send a array.dll?get.routing.script request to the array member. Downstream servers send a array.dll?get.info.v1 request to the array member.

3. When requesting an object, the client or downstream server uses the membership list, together with the hash function it computes for the name of each requested URL, to determine which server should service the request.

4. The hash value of the URL is combined with the hash value for each ISA Server. The URL+ISA Server hash that comes up with the highest value becomes "owner" of the information cache.

5. The server checks whether it should handle the request. If not, then it sends the request to another member server, specifying its intra-array IP address.

This process determines the location for all cached information, allowing Web browsers or downstream servers to know exactly where a requested URL is stored locally (or will be stored after caching). Because the hash functions used to assign values are so numerous, the load is statistically distributed and balanced across the array. Also, because CARP provides an efficient request resolution path algorithm, there is no need to maintain massive location tables for cached information. The browser simply runs the same math function across an object to determine where the cached information is stored.

ISA Server computers in an array may have different hardware, and because some members may be more powerful than others, you may want to divide the cache load unequally. To achieve this, you configure the CARP functions, specifying the load factor for any given server in the array.

Furthermore, you can configure CARP differently for incoming and outgoing Web requests. For example, CARP can be enabled for all outgoing Web requests (requests destined for a Web server on the Internet), and disabled for all incoming Web requests (requests originating from the Internet destined for an internal Web server).

Configuring CARP

By default, CARP is enabled for outgoing Web requests and disabled for incoming Web requests. That is, by default, ISA Server uses CARP to cache objects from outgoing Web requests on any server in the array, but when reverse caching is enabled for server publishing, objects from incoming Web requests are cached on one specific server.

▶ **Follow these steps to Enable Cache Array Routing Protocol:**

1. In the console tree of ISA Management, right-click the applicable array and then click Properties.

    The *array_name* Properties dialog box appears.

2. On the Incoming Web Requests tab or on the Outgoing Web Requests tab, select the Resolve Requests Within Array Before Routing check box.

When an array member determines that the requested object is not in its cache, it sends the request to another array member by using the destination server's intra-array IP address. Typically, this is the same IP address that downstream clients and ISA Server computers use to communicate with this ISA Server computer. Because this value must be replicated to all ISA Server computers in the array, it is recommended that you do not change this value.

▶ **Follow these steps to configure intra-array communication:**

1. In the console tree of ISA Management, click Computers.

2. In the details pane, right-click the applicable server and then click Properties.

    The *computer_name* Properties dialog box appears.

3. On the Array Membership tab, type the intra-array IP address in the text box.

4. Click OK.

> **Note** In order for CARP to function for incoming Web requests, be sure that the IP address that is used for intra-array communication—by default, an internal IP address—listens for requests on the same port as the IP address configured to listen for incoming Web requests. (The default port is 80.) To do this, configure the array's incoming Web request properties to use the same listener configuration for all IP addresses. This option is found on the Incoming Web Requests tab of the *array_name* Properties dialog box. You can also add the IP address used for intra-array communication to the list of incoming Web request listeners.

Configuring the Load Factor

You can configure the member servers so that different servers have different loads. For example, if one server in the array has a disk four times as large as all the other member servers, you can configure that server to receive a proportionate amount of the cache load by configuring its load factor. The load factor determines how to divide the load among members of an array. Changing this value increases or decreases the load on an ISA Server computer.

▶ **Follow these steps to configure the load factor:**

1. In the console tree of ISA Management, click the Computers folder.

2. In the details pane, right-click the applicable computer and then click Properties.

   The *computer_name* Properties dialog box appears.

3. On the Array Membership tab, in the Load Factor text box, type the load factor.

4. Click OK.

CARP and Scheduled Content Download

ISA Server checks the outgoing Web request settings for CARP when retrieving objects for a scheduled content download job. This is true for download jobs that apply to outgoing Web requests and to jobs that apply to incoming Web requests. For this reason, consider disabling CARP for outgoing Web requests if you want the scheduled content download job to cache objects to all the servers in the array.

Lesson Summary

ISA Server is installed as either an array or as a standalone server. Standalone servers do not need to be members of Windows 2000 domains and are not affected by enterprise policies. Arrays join together many ISA Server computers and inherit enterprise policies when configured to do so. To create a multiserver array of ISA Server computers, install the first ISA Server computer as an array, and then join each subsequent ISA Server computer to that array. You must initialize the enterprise before you can create an array. Initializing the enterprise updates the Active Directory directory services schema with ISA Server schema information. Once the enterprise is initialized, you can also promote standalone servers to become array members.

Arrays provide a number of benefits, including improved reliability and performance. For Firewall clients, fault tolerance is achieved when two or more ISA Server computers are used together with a DNS server. In this scenario, all the ISA Server computers are assigned the same DNS name, and DNS provides round robin distribution to resolve requests to one of the ISA Server computers. For SecureNAT clients, fault tolerance is achieved when two or more ISA Server computers are used together with Network Load Balancing. Network Load Balancing is available in Windows 2000 Advanced Server or Datacenter Server.

Arrays also improve cache performance. The Cache Array Routing Protocol (CARP) optimizes Web caching and routes Web requests. By default, ISA Server uses CARP to cache objects from outgoing Web requests on any server in the array, but objects cached from incoming Web requests are stored on a single server.

ISA Server includes a backup and restore feature that enables you to save and restore array configuration information. This includes access policy rules, publishing rules, policy elements, alerts configuration, cache configuration, and array properties.

Lesson 3 Securing Virtual Private Networks with ISA Server

ISA Server can be used to secure a virtual private network (VPN) connection for roaming users and other workers connecting across branch offices. Configuring VPN connections in this way is simplified through the use of ISA Server's VPN wizards, which are accessed through the Network Configuration node of ISA Management.

After this lesson, you will be able to

- Configure ISA Server to provide secure access to roaming users connecting to an ISA Server network through the Internet
- Configure ISA Server to provide secure VPN connectivity across branch offices

Estimated lesson time: 35 minutes

Integrating Virtual Private Networks with ISA Server

When a computer on the local network communicates with a computer on the remote network through an ISA Server computer, data is encapsulated and sent through a VPN tunnel. The computer uses either Point-to-Point Tunneling Protocol (PPTP) or Layer 2 Tunneling Protocol (L2TP) to manage tunnels and encapsulate private data. Data that is tunneled must also be encrypted to use a VPN connection.

Figure 7.5 illustrates a VPN between two networks, both running ISA Server.

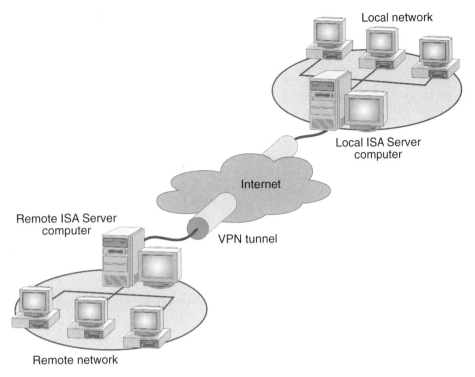

Figure 7.5 VPN integration with ISA Server

Configuring the Network for VPN Connectivity

When used with a VPN, ISA Server is installed in Integrated mode. A network connection is configured on the ISA Server computer to connect to the Internet Service Provider (ISP). The ISA Server computer also has a network adapter connected to the internal network.

Through the use of wizards, the ISA Server is then configured as a VPN server to allow communication from specific remote clients to network resources. Clients that connect via VPN to the ISA Server must be able to access corporate network resources, such as DNS and Windows Internet Naming Service (WINS).

Clients establish a VPN connection to a remote ISA Server network either as roaming users connecting through an ISP or as branch office users connecting behind another ISA Server.

For roaming users, the client computers must already have a connection configured (typically, a dial-up connection is configured in the Network and Dial-up Connections window) to connect to a local ISP. Then, a VPN connection must be configured on the client computer. To create a VPN connection, run the Network Connection wizard in Windows 2000 and select the Connect To A Private Network Through The Internet radio button. Configure the VPN connection's destination address as the IP address of the ISA Server computer.

For users connecting to an ISA Server network from a branch office behind another ISA Server computer, the connection is configured by running both the local and remote ISA Server VPN configuration wizards on each ISA Server computer.

Using the ISA Server VPN Configuration Wizards

ISA Server includes wizards that help you set up and secure a VPN. You can use the wizards to configure various VPN situations, including a mobile user connecting to the local network, and one branch office connecting to another.

ISA Server includes the following three wizards that you can use to create ISA VPN connections. These wizards are accessed by right-clicking the Network Configuration node in ISA Management:

- **Local ISA Server VPN Configuration wizard.** Use this wizard to set up the local ISA Server computer that receives connections. The local ISA VPN Server can also be set up to initiate connections.

- **Remote ISA Server VPN Configuration wizard.** Use this wizard to set up the remote ISA Server computer that initiates and receives connections.

- **ISA Virtual Private Network Configuration wizard.** Use this wizard to allow roaming users to connect to the VPN.

Local ISA Server VPN Configuration Wizard

The Local ISA Server VPN Configuration wizard sets up a local ISA VPN server that receives connections from a remote ISA VPN server. The wizard creates any dial-on-demand interfaces required to receive connections from remote VPN servers. It also configures the IP packet filters that are required to protect the connection and that are specific to the protocol(s) you select when running the VPN wizard. It also sets the static routes to forward traffic from the local network to hosts on the remote network via the tunnel.

As part of the process, the wizard also creates a VPN configuration settings (.vpc) file, which will be used when setting up the remote ISA VPN server.

▶ **Follow these steps to set up a local ISA Server VPN:**

1. In the console tree of ISA Management, right-click the Network Configuration node.
2. Click the Set Up Local ISA VPN Server menu option.

   The Local ISA Server VPN Configuration wizard appears.
3. Follow the directions in the Local ISA Server VPN Configuration wizard.

Before you run the Local ISA Server VPN Configuration wizard, you should be aware of the following:

- As part of the Local ISA Server VPN Configuration wizard configuration procedure, you will be prompted to type the domain or computer name of the remote server on which the user account for the VPN connection is to be created. If the computer is a domain controller, type its domain name. Otherwise, type the computer's NetBIOS name.
- You cannot set up a VPN if you install ISA Server in Cache mode.

Remote ISA Server VPN Configuration Wizard

The Remote ISA Server VPN Configuration wizard sets up a remote ISA VPN server that initiates connections to a local ISA VPN server. The wizard uses the .vpc file that the Local ISA Server VPN Connection wizard creates to configure any dial-on-demand interfaces that are required to initiate connections to a specific local VPN server. It also configures the IP packet filters required to protect the connection and sets the static routes to forward traffic from the local network to hosts on the remote network via the tunnel.

The specific IP packet filters that are created depend on the protocol(s) selected when the .vpc file is created by the Local ISA Server VPN Configuration wizard.

▶ **Follow these steps to set up a remote ISA Server VPN:**

1. In the console tree of ISA Management, right-click the Network Configuration node.
2. Click the Set up Remote ISA VPN Server menu option.

   The Remote ISA Server VPN Configuration wizard appears.
3. In the Remote ISA Server VPN Configuration wizard, follow the on-screen instructions.

ISA Virtual Private Network Configuration Wizard

The ISA Virtual Private Network Configuration wizard sets up a VPN server on the ISA Server computer that supports roaming clients. The VPN server supports both Point-to-Point Tunneling Protocol (PPTP) and IP Security/Layer Two Tunneling Protocol (IPSec/L2TP) tunnels and opens the appropriate ports on the ISA Server computer to allow clients to connect to the VPN service.

▶ **Follow these steps to set up ISA Server to accept client-side VPN requests:**

1. In the console tree of ISA Management, right-click the Network Configuration node.
2. Click the Allow VPN Client Connections menu option.

   The ISA Virtual Private Network Configuration wizard appears.

3. In the ISA Virtual Private Network Configuration wizard, follow the on-screen instructions.

Reconfiguring the VPN

After you set up the ISA VPN servers, you may want to add support for other protocols as well. For example, when you initially configure the servers, you may choose to use the PPTP protocol. Later, you may want to use the L2TP protocol.

▶ **Follow these steps to configure the ISA Server to allow the use of additional protocols:**

1. Use the Routing and Remote Access console to locate the appropriate network interface.
2. Access the properties of the interface and then, on the Networking tab, select the relevant protocol.
3. To add PPTP support, use ISA Management to create an IP packet filter allowing the PPTP protocol.

   The IP packet filter should be configured with the following parameters:

   - Both predefined filters, PPTP Call and PPTP Receive, are used.
   - The Local Computer setting is configured as the external IP address of the local ISA VPN server.
   - The Remote Computer setting is configured as the IP address of the remote ISA VPN server.

4. To add L2TP support, you must create two IP packet filters. Configure one IP packet filter with the following parameters:
   - The filter applies only to the local server.
   - The filter mode is Allow.
   - The filter type is Custom, using the User Datagram Protocol (UDP) on port 500.
   - The Local Computer setting is configured as the external IP address of the local ISA VPN server.
   - The Remote Computer setting is configured as the IP address of the remote ISA VPN server.

   Configure a second IP packet filter with the following parameters:
   - The filter applies only to the local server.
   - The filter mode is Allow.
   - The filter type is Custom, using UDP on port 1701.
   - The Local Computer setting is configured as the external IP address of the local ISA VPN server.
   - The Remote Computer setting is configured as the IP address of the remote ISA VPN server.

ISA Server and IPSec

When ISA Server is configured as an IPSec/L2TP VPN server, the IPSec driver is enabled on the ISA Server computer.

When IPSec is enabled, Authentication Header (AH) and Encapsulating Security Payload (ESP) (IP protocols 50 and 51) are controlled by the IPSec driver and not by the ISA Server's packet filter driver. In this case, the IPSec driver allows control over the tunneled traffic. The IPSec driver ensures that only valid AH and ESP protected traffic is admitted into the network.

When IPSec is not enabled on the ISA Server computer, the ISA Server policy controls which packets are allowed and which are blocked. The policy also logs all traffic that passes through the ISA Server, including IPSec AH and ESP protocols.

If ISA Server is configured to block IP fragments, all IP fragments will be blocked, including AH and ESP fragments, even if IPSec is enabled.

Large Network Scenario with VPN and Routing

ISA Server can be deployed in a large network that is geographically dispersed. To accommodate user needs, arrays of ISA Server computers can be deployed in the main office and at branch offices as necessary. This allows corporate network administrators to centralize the security and caching policy for the entire corporation. It also alleviates performance concerns in the branch office, as an ISA Server computer can service user requests for Internet objects from the local cache.

Large Network VPN Description

This section presents a scenario in which a large corporation requires ISA Server to be used with a virtual private network. The corporation used in this scenario has a headquarters in the United States and two branch offices, one in Canada and one in the United Kingdom. The corporation needs secure Internet access and has the following requirements:

- Internet access guidelines, determined at the headquarters in the United States, should be applied consistently throughout the corporation. All employees are allowed access to all sites using common Web protocols: HTTP, Secure Hypertext Transfer Protocol (HTTPS), and FTP.

- There should be extra firewall security in the United Kingdom branch office.

- There should be low costs for connecting the United Kingdom branch office to the United States headquarters.

- The ISA Server computers in the United Kingdom branch office should cache local content from Web servers located in the United Kingdom.

- The cache server must be in place in the Canada branch office, so that content is closer to the employees in that office and Internet traffic is reduced.

Meeting Network Requirements

Because the corporation requires a common enterprise policy for all the branch offices, the ISA Server computers must be installed as array members at all the branches, even though there will be only one computer at each branch.

ISA Server Array at the United States Headquarters

Each member of the array at the headquarters is configured with two network adapters: one network adapter to connect to the internal network and one network adapter to connect to the Internet. You can assume that there is direct connectivity to the ISP through a router and a T1/E1 line.

ISA Server Array at the Canada Branch Office

The ISA Server computers at the Canada branch office are used to reduce network traffic by caching Web content. This reduces some of the work performed by the central office ISA Server computers. The ISA Server computer in the Canada office is installed in Cache mode and is chained to the ISA Server computer at the headquarters. The ISA Server computer has two network adapters, one connected to a local router and the other connected to a router at the headquarters.

ISA Server Array at the United Kingdom Branch Office

The ISA Server computers at the United Kingdom branch are set up with two adapters: one network adapter to connect to the local network at the branch office and a modem or Integrated Services Digital Network (ISDN) adapter to connect to the Internet. User requests for local content from Web servers located in the United Kingdom are routed directly to an ISP. All other requests are routed to the headquarters.

The ISA Server array in the United Kingdom is set up in Integrated mode, serving as the branch firewall and cache server. The ISA Server computer is connected via a VPN to the array at the headquarters.

Figure 7.6 illustrates this network configuration.

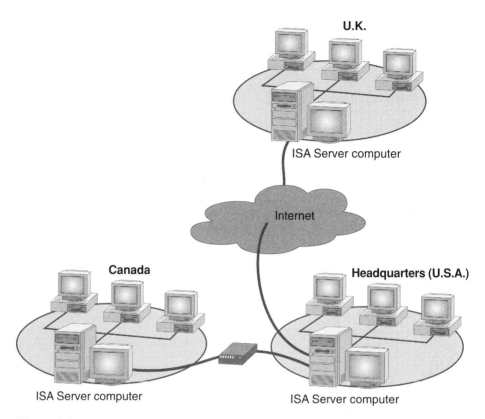

Figure 7.6 A VPN scenario

Enterprise Policy at Headquarters

After setting up the ISA Server computers at Headquarters, the administrator uses ISA Management to implement the enterprise policy. The enterprise policy is configured at Headquarters and is applied to all the arrays in the enterprise—the Canada branch office, the United Kingdom branch office, and Headquarters in the United States.

To configure the network and apply enterprise policy, the enterprise administrator performs the following tasks at Headquarters:

1. Creates an enterprise policy, called Corporate Policy, with the following rules:

    - A site and content rule that always allows everyone access to all sites
    - A protocol rule that allows everyone to use the following protocols: FTP, HTTP, and HTTPS

2. Sets Corporate Policy as the default enterprise policy to be inherited by all branch offices.

3. Configures the United Kingdom branch office to connect to the ISA Server array at Headquarters via a VPN. At least one of the ISA Server computers in the United States must be configured as a VPN server.

4. Configures the LAT on the ISA Server in the United States, adding the address ranges of the network in the United Kingdom.

5. Uses the Local ISA Server VPN Configuration wizard to set up ISA Server for VPN connections. The wizard creates IP packet filters, depending on which protocol is selected: L2TP or PPTP. It also sets the static routes to forward traffic from the local network to hosts on the remote network via the tunnel. Finally, the wizard also creates a .vpc file, which is used by the remote VPN server (in the United Kingdom) when configuring ISA Server.

ISA Server Policy at the Canada Branch Office

Since the ISA Server computer in the Canada branch office is on the Headquarters network, it requires an external network adapter (as opposed to a modem) to connect to the Headquarters ISA Server computer.

Since the enterprise policy Corporate Policy has been set as the default, it is applied to the ISA Server computer in the Canada branch automatically. As a result, no specific access policy rules need to be configured for the Canada branch office.

Scheduled content download jobs are configured to pre-cache specific content from the Headquarters. This further improves perceived network performance.

The network administrator for the Canada branch office performs these steps to configure the local ISA Server computer:

1. Configures a routing rule that redirects requests from Web Proxy clients to the upstream ISA Server computer at Headquarters.

2. Creates scheduled content download jobs to download frequently accessed objects to the local cache. If the objects are already in the cache at Headquarters, they will be downloaded from there. Otherwise, the ISA Server computers at Headquarters will forward the requests to the Internet.

ISA Server Policy at the United Kingdom Branch Office

The branch office in the United Kingdom is connected over the Internet, by way of a VPN, to the headquarters in the United States.

The network administrator at the United Kingdom branch office performs the following steps to configure the ISA Server computer as a VPN server:

1. Sets up a DNS server on the local network that is secondary to the corporate network domains typically accessed. The DNS server should use a DNS server on the Internet as a forwarder to help resolve all other name queries.

2. Configures the LAT on the local ISA Server, adding the address range of the corporate network (in the United States). Any external (Internet) IP addresses must be excluded.

3. Uses the Remote ISA Server VPN Configuration wizard to set up the network's ISA Server for VPN connections by using the .vpc file created by the enterprise administrator at Headquarters.

   The Remote ISA Server VPN Configuration wizard sets up an ISA VPN server that can initiate connections to a remote ISA VPN server.

4. Creates a routing rule that routes all requests for Internet objects in the United Kingdom (with a .uk suffix in the domain name) directly to the Internet. He or she then creates a routing rule that routes all other requests to the upstream ISA Server array at Headquarters.

Lesson Summary

When a computer on a local network communicates across the Internet with a computer on a remote network through an ISA Server computer, the computer uses either Point-to-Point Tunneling Protocol (PPTP) or Layer Two Tunneling Protocol (L2TP) to manage tunnels and encapsulate private data. This is known as a virtual private network (VPN).

ISA Server includes wizards that help you set up and secure a VPN. You can use the wizards to connect mobile users to the local network or to connect one branch office to another.

The Local ISA Server VPN Configuration wizard allows you to set up the local ISA Server computer to initiate and receive connections. The Remote ISA Server VPN Configuration wizard allows you to configure the remote ISA Server computer to initiate and receive connections. The ISA Virtual Private Network Configuration wizard allows roaming users to connect to the VPN.

Review

The following questions are intended to reinforce key information presented in the chapter. If you are unable to answer a question, review the appropriate lesson and then try the question again. The answers for these questions are located in Appendix A, "Questions and Answers."

1. You have created an enterprise policy and now you want to apply that policy to the array Branch1. How can you apply the enterprise policy to the array? Under what circumstances will array-level policies be deleted? Under what circumstances will you be unable to apply the policy to the array?

2. How can you modify your default enterprise policy when the defaults are being used by existing arrays?

3. How can you allow a computer within an array to handle more than its proportional share of network requests?

4. Do standalone ISA Servers need to be installed in a domain? Can you apply an enterprise policy to a standalone ISA Server installation?

5. ISA Server includes three wizards to simplify VPN configuration. What is the purpose of each of these three wizards?

CHAPTER 8

Secure Videoconferencing with H.323 Gatekeeper

Lesson 1 Configuring Clients to Use H.323 Gatekeeper 309

Lesson 2 Routing Conference Calls with H.323 Gatekeeper 322

Review 336

About This Chapter

The H.323 standard is a collection of protocols designed to allow real-time, interactive videoconferencing over simple and complex networks. Normally, it is difficult to provide H.323 service to clients behind a firewall because of the complexity and dynamic nature of H.323 connections. However, Microsoft H.323 Gatekeeper interacts with the Microsoft Internet Security and Acceleration Server 2000 (ISA Server) firewall and the H.323 Filter application filter to facilitate secure videoconferencing in your network. Once your clients register with H.323 Gatekeeper, you can apply routing rules and other forms of control over videoconferencing just as you can with any network traffic.

Before You Begin

To complete the lessons in this chapter, you must have

- Completed the setup procedures explained in "About This Book"
- Completed all exercises through Chapter 4

Lesson 1 Configuring Clients to Use H.323 Gatekeeper

H.323 Gatekeeper facilitates conference calling on your network and allows you to conduct real-time sessions through the ISA Server firewall. You need to register H.323 clients, such as Microsoft NetMeeting 3.0, with H.323 Gatekeeper in order to take advantage of its services.

After this lesson, you will be able to

- Describe the various functions of H.323 Gatekeeper in videoconferencing
- Register a client with H.323 Gatekeeper

Estimated lesson time: 40 minutes

H.323 Protocol

The H.323 standard is a set of protocols developed by the International Telecommunications Union (ITU) to meet videoconferencing needs for a wide range of networking environments. H.323 makes real-time multimedia possible over networks that do not provide quality of service (QoS). It can also bridge audio and video sessions from packet-switched networks, such as an intranet or the Internet, to circuit-switched and cell-switched networks such as Integrated Services Digital Network (ISDN) networks, Asynchronous Transfer Mode (ATM) networks, and the Public Switched Telephone Network (PSTN). For example, it is possible to make a call from an H.323 client to a regular telephone on the PSTN. The H.323 standards also provide for communications between a standard PSTN telephone and a computer-based client.

H.323 defines four major components for a network-based conferencing system: terminals, gateways, gatekeepers, and multipoint control units (MCUs). Terminals are the client endpoints on the local area network (LAN) running an H.323-compliant application such as NetMeeting 3.0. An H.323 gateway provides connectivity between an H.323 network and a non–H.323 network, such as the PSTN. A gatekeeper acts as the central point for conference calls and provides control services and call routing to registered endpoints. The MCU supports conferences between three or more endpoints.

Overview of H.323 Gatekeeper

As the focal point of the H.323 network, ISA Server's H.323 Gatekeeper works with the H.323 protocol filter to provide registered clients with address resolution, call authentication, and call routing. Clients registered with H.323 Gatekeeper can use its services to participate in video, audio, and data conferences—in local area networks, in wide area networks, across multiple firewalls, and over the Internet. The H.323 Gatekeeper can also be used to route calls intelligently, in a way that is based on the called party's address.

H.323 Gatekeeper Snap-in

The management tool for H.323 Gatekeeper is the H.323 Gatekeeper snap-in. This tool appears as a node in ISA Management when H.323 Gatekeeper is installed. Whenever you perform a full installation of ISA Server, the H.323 Gatekeeper node appears in the console tree of ISA Management, but you must still add a gatekeeper before you can begin using the service. You can add a gatekeeper by right-clicking the H.323 Gatekeeper node in ISA Management and selecting Add Gatekeeper.

Once you add a gatekeeper, you can use the H.323 Gatekeeper snap-in to configure routing rules for calls specified by phone number, user alias, or Internet Protocol (IP) address. You can also use the H.323 Gatekeeper snap-in to register static users and to define destinations for routing rules you later configure.

H.323 Gatekeeper Usage Scenarios

The following scenarios illustrate various situations and contexts in which H.323 Gatekeeper can be used to enable real-time, point-to-point, and multipoint communications in your network.

Intra-Enterprise Conference Call Scenario

In this scenario, numerous users within a single organization use applications, such as NetMeeting 3.0 or later, that are H.323-compliant. ISA Server and H.323 Gatekeeper are installed and running. Users register themselves with H.323 Gatekeeper using a well-known alias (for example, an e-mail address) and a phone number. All users are able to call each other using the called party's well-known alias or phone number. Users are able to use audio, video, and T.120 (multipoint) data and application sharing.

An intra-enterprise conference call scenario with H.323 Gatekeeper is illustrated in Figure 8.1.

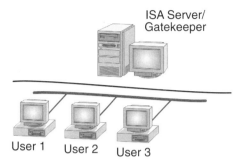

Figure 8.1 Intra-enterprise conferencing

Inter-Enterprise Conference Call Scenario

In this scenario, numerous users within the organization use applications that are compliant with H.323 Gatekeeper, such as NetMeeting 3.0 or later. ISA Server, H.323 Gatekeeper, and the H.323 protocol filter are installed and running on the firewalls of both organizations. Users register themselves with their respective H.323 Gatekeeper using a well-known alias. All users in each organization are able to call all users in the other organization using the called party's alias. Users are then able to use audio, video, and T.120 data and application sharing. For example, User1 can communicate with User4 by typing **User4@organizationB.microsoft.com** in the NetMeeting 3.0 Place A Call dialog box and then clicking the Call button. The call reaches User4, regardless of his or her location within organization B. User4's IP address is concealed from User1 and all other callers from organization A.

This inter-enterprise conference call scenario with H.323 Gatekeeper is illustrated in Figure 8.2.

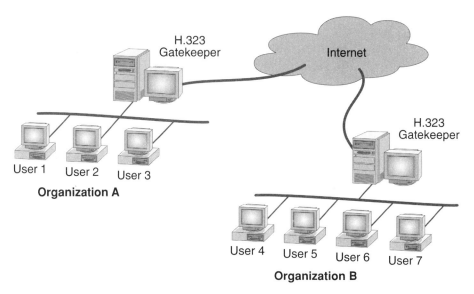

Figure 8.2 Inter-enterprise conferencing

PSTN Call Scenario

The Public Switched Telephone Network (PSTN) is a circuit-switched network that is optimized for real-time voice communication. When you place a call, you close a switch by dialing, which establishes a direct circuit with the other party. The PSTN guarantees QoS by dedicating the circuit to your call until you disconnect. Whether you and your connected party are talking or silent, you continue to use the same circuit until you disconnect.

In this scenario, numerous users within the organization use applications such as NetMeeting 3.0 that are H.323-compliant. H.323 Gatekeeper is installed and running on the network. Users register themselves with H.323 Gatekeeper using a well-known alias (such as an e-mail address) and a phone number. An H.323 gateway is also installed and running on the network. It is configured to enable H.323 Gatekeeper to direct calls between the IP and PSTN networks. All users are able to make calls to PSTN numbers by using NetMeeting to dial the number from their desktops. Users are also able to receive calls from the PSTN network through NetMeeting 3.0 or later.

A conferencing scenario in which H.323 clients connect to the PSTN is illustrated in Figure 8.3.

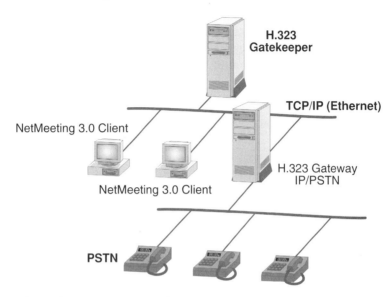

Figure 8.3 IP-to-PSTN conferencing

Registering Clients with H.323 Gatekeeper

Every H.323 transaction has two endpoints, an origination endpoint and a destination endpoint. An endpoint can be an H.323 client (for example, a terminal running NetMeeting), a proxy server (such as an ISA Server computer running the Web Proxy service), or a gateway. Endpoints typically register automatically with H.323 Gatekeeper by using the H.323 Registration, Admission, and Status (H.323 RAS) protocol. You can also use the H.323 Gatekeeper snap-in to add a static registration to endpoints that do not support H.323 RAS registration.

Note Statically registered clients cannot accept inbound calls.

H.323 Gatekeeper supports the following three types of H.323 RAS addressing:

- **E164 phone number addressing**, which uses characters 0-9.
- **H.323 ID addressing**, which uses anything similar to e-mail addresses or Domain Name System (DNS) strings, including account names and machine names. No syntax is defined.
- **Email-ID type addressing.**

Endpoint Attributes

When an endpoint is registered through H.323 RAS, the following attributes are specified:

- **The Q931 address for the endpoint.** For H.323 calls, this address consists of a combination of the IP address of the endpoint and the port used for H.323 communications (by default, 1720). For example, 192.168.0.2:1720 and 10.0.0.5:1720 both constitute possible Q931 addresses.

  Note The Q.931 protocol is a connection-control protocol for establishing connections and framing data. Roughly comparable to Transmission Control Protocol (TCP), the Q.931 protocol is used to manage connection setup and breakdown for H.323 calls.

- **The RAS address for the endpoint.** This address consists of an IP address and a distinct port number used for RAS communications. A unique RAS ID number is also assigned to each registered terminal.

- **List of aliases.**

Aliases

An alias consists of two fields, a type and a name, where the type would be E164, H323-ID, or Email-ID.

For example, when you register a NetMeeting client with H.323 Gatekeeper, as shown in Figure 8.4, the account name text box is registered in H.323 Gatekeeper as an H323-ID alias, and the phone number as an E164 alias.

Figure 8.4 NetMeeting fields used by H.323 Gatekeeper

When you select the Active Terminals node in the ISA Management console tree, the H323-ID (or Email-ID) and E164 aliases are displayed in the Account and Phone columns, respectively, in the details pane. You can right-click the terminal in the list and select Properties to display all registered aliases. Figure 8.5 displays the properties dialog box for the terminal registered by the NetMeeting client shown in Figure 8.4.

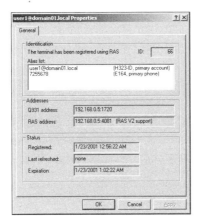

Figure 8.5 E164 and H.323-ID aliases for a NetMeeting client

Note H.323 Gatekeeper enforces unique Q931 addresses, but it does not enforce unique aliases. Allowing multiple instances of an alias registration with a unique Q931 address enables the client to register at multiple terminals. Only the most recent registration for an alias is active for resolving alias requests.

Client Address Translation

Any client who wants to be available through a well-known alias must register with H.323 Gatekeeper. (A well-known alias can be an e-mail address, such as *someone@microsoft.com*.) In addition, clients must register with H.323 Gatekeeper if they use translation services when placing outbound calls—for example, if they use NetMeeting 3.0 or later to place a call to a PSTN device.

Note Outbound calls that do not require translation services may be placed without H.323 Gatekeeper.

Suppose you are in your company office and want to contact a person over the Internet. His name is *Someone*, and he works at Microsoft. The person is registered at Microsoft with H.323 Gatekeeper as *someone@microsoft.com*. Because he is registered with H.323 Gatekeeper, you can contact him using his well-known alias—*someone@microsoft.com*—even if there is no real e-mail address corresponding to that alias. If you placed a call to *someone@microsoft.com* using NetMeeting 3.0, the following events would take place.

From within Your Company

1. NetMeeting 3.0 connects with your in-house H.323 Gatekeeper.

2. The H.323 Gatekeeper does not recognize microsoft.com as an internal address and forwards the call to the ISA Server computer within your company.

3. ISA Server looks up the address for microsoft.com and makes the query over the Internet to microsoft.com.

At the Destination

1. When the ISA Server computer at microsoft.com receives the query for *someone@microsoft.com*, it contacts the internal H.323 Gatekeeper at microsoft.com to obtain the correct in-house address.

2. The H.323 Gatekeeper at microsoft.com translates the alias into a network address for ISA Server.

3. The ISA Server at microsoft.com sends a confirmation back to ISA Server at your company and establishes the connection.

4. From this point through the end of the communication, the ISA Server holds open the link established by H.323 Gatekeeper.

5. *Someone* is not required to have a valid, externally routable IP address, and the address will remain hidden from other endpoints by the ISA Server. This is because the H.323 Gatekeeper performs address translation for the internal client.

You can set restrictions within the ISA Server H.323 Filter application filter to permit or deny video, audio, T.120 data, and application sharing. You can also set time restrictions to limit the hours available for H.323-compliant communications.

Installing H.323 Gatekeeper

H.323 Gatekeeper installation is performed automatically when the Full Installation option is selected during ISA Server installation. However, H.323 Gatekeeper can be installed at any time.

▶ **Follow these steps to install H.323 Gatekeeper:**

1. Click the Start button, point to Settings, click Control Panel, and then double-click Add/Remove Programs.

2. In the Currently Installed Programs area, click Microsoft Internet Security And Acceleration Server, and then click the Change button.

3. In ISA Server Setup, click the Add/Remove button.

4. In the Installation dialog box, click Add-in services and then click the Change Option button.

5. Click the Install H.323 Gatekeeper Service and then click OK.

6. Click the Continue button to complete the installation.

Before you install or configure H.323 Gatekeeper, you should also consider the following:

- H.323 Gatekeeper does not provide any security.

- If you are managing ISA Server or H.323 Gatekeeper remotely on a computer running Microsoft Windows 2000 Professional, you cannot access all of the tools and Help topics unless you have installed the ISA Server and H.323 Gatekeeper Administration Tools.

- H.323 Gatekeeper does not enforce uniqueness of aliases for registration. However, each Q931 address must be unique. The H.323 Gatekeeper uses only the most recently registered active terminal for any one alias. This allows a user to register under one alias from multiple locations.

- The H.323 Filter application filter does not support H.225 signaling across ISA Server. For example, a NetMeeting 3.0 user who is located on an internal network cannot register with a gatekeeper that is located on the Internet. Also, an H.323 Gatekeeper that is running on the internal network cannot exchange location messages with a gatekeeper running on the Internet.

- ISA Server provides support for fast Kernel-mode data pumping of Real-Time Transport Protocol (RTP) audio and video media while making calls across ISA Server using NetMeeting 3.0 or later.

Practice: Configuring a Client to use H.323 Gatekeeper

To enable H.323 clients to call each other by specifying an alias instead of an IP address, you must register each client with an H.323 Gatekeeper. In this practice, you add a gatekeeper to your ISA Server installation and configure NetMeeting on a client to make calls through the gatekeeper. You then verify that your new client's alias is registered with H.323 Gatekeeper.

To prepare for this practice, you must have performed a full installation of ISA Server. You must also have created a protocol rule allowing all IP traffic. Finally, you must have created a domain user named User1. You created this user account at the beginning of the "Assigning Protocol Rules to User Accounts" practice in Chapter 4.

Exercise 1: Adding a Gatekeeper

When you perform a full installation of ISA Server, the H.323 Gatekeeper node appears in ISA Management. However, you still need to add a gatekeeper if you want to take advantage of H.323 Gatekeeper services.

▶ **To add a gatekeeper**

1. Log on to Server1 as Administrator.
2. In ISA Management, right-click the H.323 Gatekeepers node and click Add Gatekeeper.

   The Add Gatekeeper dialog box appears.
3. Leave the This Computer radio button selected as the default, and click OK.
4. The Server1 icon appears beneath the H.323 Gatekeeper node in the console tree.

Exercise 2: Configuring NetMeeting to Use H.323 Gatekeeper

The H.323 RAS protocol makes possible automatic registration of H.323 terminals (clients) with an H.323 Gatekeeper. To initiate this registration using NetMeeting, you simply need to configure the client to place calls with the gatekeeper. In this exercise, you configure NetMeeting first and then register the client with your network's H.323 Gatekeeper.

▶ **To register NetMeeting with H.323 Gatekeeper**

1. Log on to domain01 from Server2 as User1.

2. Click the Start menu, point to Programs, point to Accessories, point to Communications, and click NetMeeting.

   A NetMeeting page appears describing the features of NetMeeting.

3. Click Next.

   A new page appears asking you to supply information about yourself.

4. In the First Name text box, type **Test**.

5. In the Last Name text box, type **User**.

6. In the Email Address text box, type **testuser@domain01.local**.

7. Click Next.

   A new page appears prompting you for information about a directory server.

8. Clear the Log On To A Directory Server When NetMeeting Starts check box.

9. Click Next.

   A new page appears asking you to specify the speed of your connection.

10. Select the Local Area Network radio button.

11. Click Next.

    A new page appears allowing you to put shortcuts on your desktop and on the Quick Launch portion of your taskbar.

12. Click Next.

    The Audio Tuning Wizard page appears.

13. Click Next through all of the remaining pages, leaving all of the default settings. You can safely ignore any warning messages you receive about the quality of your sound card, microphone, or audio.

14. Click Finish to exit the Audio Tuning wizard.

    The NetMeeting – Not In A Call console appears on your desktop.

15. In the NetMeeting – Not In A Call console, click the Tools menu and then click Options.

    The Options dialog box appears.

16. Click the Advanced Calling button.

    The Advanced Calling Options dialog box appears.

17. Select the Use A Gatekeeper To Place Calls check box.

18. In the Gatekeeper text box, type **server1**.

19. Click the Log On Using My Account Name check box.

20. In the Account Name text box, type **MyName**.

21. Click OK.

22. In the Options dialog box, click OK.

Exercise 3: Testing the Configuration

In this exercise, you check the list of active H.323 terminals in ISA Management to verify that your NetMeeting client has been recognized by the gatekeeper.

▶ **To test the configuration**

1. On Server1, open ISA Management.

2. In the console tree, expand the H.323 Gatekeeper node, and then expand the Server1 node.

3. In the console tree, click the Active Terminals icon.

   MyName is listed in the details pane. The user MyName is now ready to send and receive calls through H.323 Gatekeeper.

Lesson Summary

H.323 is a standard developed by the ITU to provide real-time, interactive videoconferencing for a wide range of network environments. As the focal point of the H.323 network, ISA Server's H.323 Gatekeeper provides registered clients with address resolution, call authentication, and call routing. H.323 Gatekeeper also allows H.323-compatible clients to conference across the Internet and through the ISA Server firewall. An example of an H.323-compatible client is NetMeeting 3.0 or later.

Any client user who wants to be available through an alias instead of an IP address must register with H.323 Gatekeeper. Clients typically register automatically with H.323 Gatekeeper by using the H.323 Registration, Admission, and Status (H.323 RAS) protocol. You can also use the H.323

Gatekeeper snap-in to add a static registration to endpoints that do not support H.323 RAS registration. H.323 Gatekeeper supports three types of aliases: E164 addressing (phone number), H.323-ID addressing (open syntax allowing e-mail addresses, DNS strings, account names, and machine names), and Email-ID addressing.

The management tool for H.323 Gatekeeper is the H.323 Gatekeeper snap-in. This tool appears as a node in ISA Management when H.323 Gatekeeper is installed. H.323 Gatekeeper installation is performed automatically when the Full Installation option is selected during ISA Server installation. However, H.323 Gatekeeper can be installed at any time.

Lesson 2 Routing Conference Calls with H.323 Gatekeeper

H.323 clients such as NetMeeting 3.0 register with H.323 Gatekeeper by using an alias such as a user name or e-mail address that is easier to remember than an IP address. The purpose of call routing rules is to assist H.323 Gatekeeper in resolving these aliases and to determine whether and where to route conference calls.

After this lesson, you will be able to

- Describe the purpose of call routing rules
- Explain how H.323 Gatekeeper processes call routing rules
- Configure call routing rules to forward conference calls in H.323 Gatekeeper

Estimated lesson time: 45 minutes

Call Routing Rules

To enable real-time conferencing between endpoints, H.323 Gatekeeper needs to know how to route calls that are destined for alias names. H.323 call routing rules specify a destination and parameters to match part or all of a requested alias. When a unique Q931 address is not included in a call request, H.323 Gatekeeper tries to match each H.323 routing rule that has been configured with the requested alias.

Figure 8.6 shows the routing rule types and parameters that you can configure through the H.323 Gatekeeper snap-in. The default call routing rules that H.323 Gatekeeper includes resolve all requested destinations within the local registration database or on the local network. This means that you do not need to configure any additional routing rules if you only want to enable videoconferencing on your local network.

Chapter 8   Secure Videoconferencing with H.323 Gatekeeper

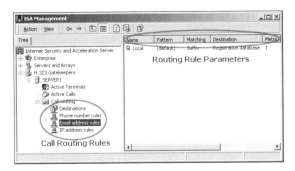

Figure 8.6 Call routing rules and rule parameters

▶ **Follow these steps to create a call routing rule:**

1. In the console tree of ISA Management, expand the Call Routing folder.

2. Do one of the following:

   - To create a phone number rule, right-click the Phone Number Rules icon, and then click Add Routing Rule and follow the on-screen instructions.

   - To create an e-mail address rule, right-click the Email Address Rules icon, and then click Add Routing Rule and follow the on-screen instructions.

   - To create an IP address rule, right-click the IP Address Rules icon, and then click Add Routing Rule and follow the on-screen instructions.

The following section describes how H.323 Gatekeeper searches for the alias of a registered active terminal according to routing rules.

Phone Number Rules

Phone number (E164) rules specify the parameters shown in Table 8.1. The item names in parentheses are those given to parameters in the New Routing Rule wizard when those parameter names differ from the corresponding column names in the details pane of ISA Management.

Table 8.1 Phone Number Rule Parameters

Item	Description
Name	Descriptive name for the rule.
Description	Descriptive text for this rule.
Pattern (Prefix or Phone Number)	Specifies the pattern of numbers you are trying to match.
Matching (Route All Phone Numbers Using This Prefix)	Specifies whether the pattern type must be a string at the beginning of the phone number (also called a prefix type), or an exact match for the entire phone number (also called an exact type), for the rule to take effect. A prefix type is configured when you leave the Route All Phone Numbers Using This Prefix check box selected. When you clear the check box, the pattern is configured as an exact type.
Destination type	Specifies the server to which the call request is routed if this rule takes effect.
Discard digits	Specifies how many digits are removed from the phone number before it is routed to the destination. This feature is only supported for phone numbers (E164) and gateway destinations.
Add prefix	Specifies a prefix that will be added to the destination. This feature is only supported for phone numbers (E164) and gateway destinations.
Metric	Specifies how this rule is ranked compared to other rules. The lower the metric number, the more precedence this rule is given.
Status	Specifies whether this rule is enabled or disabled.

H.323 Gatekeeper determines which rules match the alias in the call request. A phone number alias can use the numbers 0 through 9 and the number sign (#), asterisk (*), and comma (,).

Example of a Phone Number Rule

Suppose that a caller requests translation for the phone number 95551234#3344.

H.323 Gatekeeper attempts to match the digits up to the first special character or the end of the string, if there is no special character. In the phone number 95551234#3344, the alias used for rule matching is 95551234.

Tables 8.2 and 8.3 contain example phone number rule patterns and matching parameter types (prefix or exact).

As specified in Table 8.1, when you configure the matching parameter as a prefix type, this designates that the pattern specified in the routing rule will be declared a match if it matches the first numbers of a phone number alias. A matching parameter configured as exact designates that the pattern will be declared a match only if the pattern specified matches the complete phone number alias. Note that a null or blank pattern will always match when the matching parameter is prefix.

Note A prefix type is configured in a phone number rule when you leave the Route All Phone Numbers Using This Prefix check box selected. When you clear the check box, the pattern is configured as an exact type.

The examples listed in Table 8.2 will successfully match the 95551234#3344 phone number. In the first example, the pattern 9 is configured as a prefix type, which matches the phone number's prefix. In the second example, the pattern 9555 is also specified as a prefix type, and these four digits match the first four digits of the phone number alias. In the third example, the pattern 95551234 is specified as an exact type. This is the only exact type pattern that will correctly match the given phone number alias. Finally, in the last example, an empty pattern is configured as a prefix type. Such a rule will match every phone alias. The default phone number rule is configured with an empty pattern of the prefix type.

Table 8.2 Phone Number Rule Pattern Examples – Matching

Pattern	Matching Parameter Value
9	Prefix
9555	Prefix
95551234	Exact
[empty]	Prefix

The examples in Table 8.3 would not match the 95551234#3344 number. In the first rule, the pattern 8 is specified as a prefix type. This does not match the phone number, which begins with the number 9. The second rule specifies the pattern 9555 as an exact type. This rule will not match because the exact phone alias is 95551234, not 9555.

Table 8.3 Phone Number Rule Pattern Examples – Not Matching

Pattern	Matching Parameter Value
8	Prefix
9555	Exact

IP Address Rules

IP address rules apply only to requests for translation of IP address strings that take the form of a.b.c.d., for example, 192.168.154.13.

IP address rules specify the parameters shown in Table 8.4.

Table 8.4 IP Address Rule Parameters

Item	Description
Name	Descriptive name for the rule.
Description	Descriptive text for this rule.
Pattern	Specifies the pattern of the IP address you are trying to match, with the subnet mask included.
Destination	Specifies the destination to which the call request is routed if this rule takes effect.
Metric	Specifies how this rule is ranked compared to other rules. The lower the metric number, the more precedence this rule is given.
Status	Specifies whether this rule is enabled or disabled.

When a specified pattern matches and the IP address rule affects a given call, the call is routed to the destination specified in the IP address rule. The destination types for IP address rules you can select are the following:

- **None (no destination).** The call is disconnected.
- **Gateway/proxy.** The call is forwarded to the selected H.323 Gateway, Proxy server or Internet firewall.
- **Gatekeeper.** The call is forwarded to a gatekeeper residing in a different zone.
- **Multicast gatekeeper.** The call is forwarded to a group of multicast gatekeepers.
- **Local network.** The called party resides in the same network as the caller. The call is returned to the callee to resolve.

IP Address Rule Resolution Example

Suppose that a caller requests translation for an IP address string in the form of a.b.c.d. After attempting to match the digits of the string with the patterns configured in various IP address rules, H.323 Gatekeeper finds three matching rules for a.b.c.d.

Once H.323 Gatekeeper has established which routing rules match, the routing rules are sorted for additional processing according to the following requirements.

- Rules with the highest number of bits in the subnet mask have precedence over rules with fewer bits in the subnet mask. For example, an IP address string of 192.168.154.13, with a subnet mask of 255.255.255.192, would have a higher number of bits then an IP address string of 192.168.154.13 with a subnet mask of 255.255.255.0.

- If two rules contain the same pattern, a rule with matching type exact has precedence over a rule with matching type prefix.

- If two rules contain the same pattern and the same matching type, a rule with a lower metric number assigned to it has precedence over a rule with a higher metric number.

E-mail Address Rules

E-mail address rules specify the parameters shown in Table 8.5. The item names in parentheses are those given to parameters in the New Routing Rule wizard when those parameter names differ from the corresponding column names in the details pane of ISA Management.

Table 8.5   E-mail Address Rule Parameters

Item	Description
Name	Descriptive name for the rule.
Description	Descriptive text for this rule.
Pattern (Domain Name Suffix)	Specifies the text pattern you are trying to match.

(continues)

Table 8.5   E-mail Address Rule Parameters *(continued)*

Item	Description
Matching	Specifies whether the pattern must be a suffix (a string at the end of the e-mail address) or exact (an exact match for the entire e-mail address) for the rule to take effect. A suffix type is configured when you leave the Route All E-mail Addresses That Include This General DNS Domain Name check box selected. When you clear this check box, the pattern is configured as an exact type.
Destination	Specifies to which server the call request is routed if this rule takes effect.
Metric	Specifies how this rule is ranked compared to other rules. The lower the metric number, the more precedence this rule is given.
Status	Specifies whether this rule is enabled or disabled.

H.323 Gatekeeper attempts to match the domain portion of the e-mail alias with the rules. Table 8.6 describes how the domain portion is obtained from an alias.

Table 8.6   Domain Portions of User Aliases

Alias example	Domain portion
Someone@microsoft.com	microsoft.com
accounting1.microsoft.com	accounting1.microsoft.com
accounting1	N/A

Note   The alias accounting1 is an example of what is known as a dotless alias, which is not a standard alias format.

If a call request contains the e-mail address *someone@microsoft.com*, the domain portion is *microsoft.com*.

Table 8.7 presents examples of parameter specifications in four e-mail address rules. The following pattern and matching parameter specifications would match the alias *someone@microsoft.com* correctly. In the first example, the pattern "com" is specified as a suffix type. This matches the alias *someone@microsoft.com* because the alias does end in the letters "com." In the second example, the pattern "microsoft.com" is specified as a suffix type. This pattern matches the alias *someone@microsoft.com* because this alias includes the string "microsoft.com" as its suffix. The third example shows that the pattern "microsoft.com" will match the alias "someone@microsoft.com" when this pattern is specified as an exact type. This is because what is being matched in email address rules is not the entire user alias but only the domain portion of the user alias. This is in fact the only pattern of type exact that will match the alias "someone@microsoft.com." Finally, the fourth example shows that a blank pattern of suffix type will match the given alias; in fact, it will match every email alias. The default e-mail address rule uses a blank pattern of suffix type.

Table 8.7 Sample Pattern Matches for an E-mail Address Rule

Pattern	Matching Parameter Value
com	Suffix
microsoft.com	Suffix
microsoft.com	Exact
[empty]	Suffix

The rules whose parameters are specified in Table 8.8 would not match the alias *someone@microsoft.com* correctly. In the first example, the pattern "com" is configured as an exact type. This does not match the exact string of the domain portion of the email alias. In the second example, a blank pattern is configured as an exact type. This pattern will only match an email alias with no domain specified.

Table 8.8 Sample Non-Matching Patterns for an E-mail Address Rule

Pattern	Matching Parameter Value
Com	Exact
[empty]	Exact

If a call request alias contains *someone* and the domain portion is an empty string, the only rules that match this domain portion are those shown in Table 8.9.

Table 8.9 Dotless Alias Matches for an E-mail Address Rule

Pattern	Matching Parameter Value
[empty]	Exact
[empty]	Suffix

After H.323 Gatekeeper has established which routing rules match, the routing rules are sorted for additional processing according to the following conditions:

- Rules with patterns containing more domain elements have precedence over rules with patterns containing fewer domain elements. For example, accounting1.accounting.microsoft.com has precedence over microsoft.com.

- If two rules contain the same pattern, a rule with the matching type exact has precedence over a rule with the matching type suffix.

- If two rules contain the same pattern and the same matching type, a rule with a lower metric number has precedence over a rule with a higher metric number.

Rule Processing and Destinations

After H.323 Gatekeeper creates the sorted list of rules that match an alias specified in a call, it processes each rule in order. How the rules are processed depends on the type of destination specified by the rule.

The function of a call routing rule is to specify a destination. Each rule can specify one of the nine destination types described below. If you want to make a particular gateway/proxy, Internet Locator Service (ILS) server, gatekeeper, or multicast group available for selection in a routing rule, you must first run the Add Destination wizard. You can run the Add Destination wizard by right-clicking the Destinations node in the H.323 Gatekeeper snap-in and clicking Add Destination.

None

This destination stops rule processing. Even if there are other matching rules having lower metric values (higher numeric value) following the None rule, H.323 Gatekeeper rejects the request and returns the message "Cannot be resolved."

Registration Database

This destination finds the alias in the local registration database. If the alias is of type E164, H.323 Gatekeeper looks for the phone number string up to, but not including, any special characters. For example, if the original string is 95551212#3344, Gatekeeper uses only 95551212. The registration database can then match the string to an IP address.

If the alias is of Email-ID or H323-ID type, the lookup is done using the complete alias, not only the domain portion. Because the two types are interchangeable, a user registered with an Email-ID of *someone@microsoft.com* is successfully resolved when querying for the H323-ID of *someone@microsoft.com*, and vice versa. If an entry is found, its address is returned in the confirmation to the client and the processing stops. Otherwise the processing continues with the next rule.

This destination cannot be used for IP aliases.

Gateway/Proxy

This destination specifies a particular H.323 proxy, or gateway, and lists an IP, DNS, or NetBIOS address. H.323 gateways are required if you want to route your call through the PSTN. (ISA Server does not include an H.323 gateway.)

In networks with multiple proxies or gateways, if name resolution is required, H.323 Gatekeeper randomly chooses one of the returned IP addresses. The process of random IP address selection balances the network load by allowing H.323 Gatekeeper to choose from multiple proxies or gateways. The resulting address is returned to the client. The client is responsible for proceeding with the call to connect to the supplied address. If an entry is found, the address is returned in the confirmation to the client and the processing stops. Otherwise, the processing continues with the next rule.

Internet Locator Service (ILS)

This destination specifies a Microsoft Site Server computer running Internet Locator Service (ILS) for name resolution. It works only for the e-mail address namespace queries. It is an uncommon format that is used to support backward compatibility.

First, the H.323 Gatekeeper conducts name resolution for the IP address of the server running Site Server ILS. If necessary, it then queries the server.

The H.323 Gatekeeper performs at least one query with the complete alias. If the query fails and the alias has the standard e-mail address format, such as *someone@microsoft.com*, the H.323 Gatekeeper extracts the user name and queries again the ILS for entries beginning with someone. This provides the client that tries to find *someone@microsoft.co*m with the opportunity to find an ILS entry such as *someone@accounting5.accounting.microsoft.com*. If neither query returns an entry, H.323 Gatekeeper moves to the next rule.

Gatekeeper

This destination specifies the IP, DNS, or NetBIOS address of another H.323 Gatekeeper. The local H.323 Gatekeeper conducts name resolution to determine the IP address of the destination H.323 Gatekeeper. After that, the local gatekeeper queries the remote gatekeeper with a special location request. When H.323 Gatekeeper receives a location request, it attempts to resolve the alias by using its local registration database, regardless of what the rules specify. If the distant H.323 Gatekeeper returns a Q931 address, it is returned to the client. Otherwise, rule processing continues.

Multicast Gatekeeper

The destination type specifies that the destination is a multicast group. The H.323 Gatekeeper sends a location request message using the multicast protocol. H.323 Gatekeeper listens and processes incoming location requests only on the 224.0.1.41 multicast group, even though other multicast groups may exist. If any entry is found, the address is returned in the confirmation to the client and the processing stops. Otherwise, processing continues with the next rule.

DNS

This destination type can only be used for e-mail address queries. The H.323 Gatekeeper resolves the domain of the alias using DNS, regardless of the user portion of the alias. In *someone@microsoft.com*, the domain of the alias is microsoft.com. If any entry is found, the address is returned in the confirmation to the client and the processing stops. Otherwise, rule processing continues.

Active Directory Directory Services

Active Directory can be specified as a rule destination for e-mail address rules. When Active Directory is configured as the destination, the Active Directory store is queried for the ipPhone attribute of the matching user object, and the call is routed to this IP phone number.

Local Network

This destination type is valid only for IP aliases. H.323 Gatekeeper returns the address represented by the alias. Because a resolution or translation is not required and the destination is directly reachable, the IP address that is represented by the requested alias can be used as the query address.

Applying Rules to Calls

The following section provides examples of how call routing rules are applied to inbound and outbound calls.

Inbound Calls

When H.323 Gatekeeper receives an inbound query, it identifies the type of alias request—whether it is an E164, H.323-ID, or Email-ID. H.323 Gatekeeper then compares this alias to the list of configured rules, compiles the matching rules, and sorts them by placing those rules with the lowest metric value highest on the list. Next, the gatekeeper goes through the list of rules, in order, until either the requested address of the alias is resolved, or the search fails. Finally, H.323 Gatekeeper sends a confirmation or rejection to the originating client, depending upon whether the address is found.

For example, an e-mail namespace request would be processed in this manner. Suppose you are working at Microsoft and want to use NetMeeting 3.0 to call a person who also works at Microsoft and uses the e-mail alias *someone@microsoft.com*.

An admission request is sent to H.323 Gatekeeper for *someone@microsoft.com*. H.323 Gatekeeper searches the rules list, which could consist of the rules listed in Table 8.10.

Table 8.10   Main List of Rules (Example)

Domain	Matching	Rule name	Weighted metric value
microsoft.com	Suffix	Registration database	1
microsoft.com	Suffix	Gatekeeper "otherzone"	2
microsoft.com	Suffix	ILS Server named "Bogus"	3
microsoft.com	Suffix	Active Directory	4
microsoft.com	Suffix	None (cannot be resolved)	6
(empty)	Suffix	Gateway/Proxy named "Bogus2"	10
(empty)	Exact	Registration database	2
(empty)	Exact	None (cannot be resolved)	10

The H.323 Gatekeeper rule engine sorts the matching rules for the domain part microsoft.com and creates the filtered rules list shown in Table 8.11.

Table 8.11 Example Rule Matches

Domain	Matching	Rule name	Weighted metric value
microsoft.com	Suffix	Registration database	1
microsoft.com	Suffix	Gatekeeper "otherzone"	2
microsoft.com	Suffix	ILS Server named "Bogus"	3
microsoft.com	Suffix	Active Directory	4
microsoft.com	Suffix	None (cannot be resolved)	6
(empty)	Suffix	Gateway/Proxy named "Bogus2"	10

H.323 Gatekeeper uses the first rule to try to find *someone@microsoft.com* in the local registration database. If the registration exists, H.323 Gatekeeper returns a confirmation along with the address to the origination client. If no address is returned, H.323 Gatekeeper continues looking, going to the second rule, Gatekeeper "otherzone," for resolving the request. H.323 Gatekeeper works its way down the rules list until an address is returned or until it gets to the *None rule*. When the None rule is encountered, the query fails and a "Cannot be resolved" message is sent. Once the None rule has been reached, no other rules are processed, regardless of their weighted metric value.

Outbound Calls

When a registered client places an outbound call, an admission request is sent to the H.323 Gatekeeper. In the request, the H.323 client specifies the destination alias. If H.323 Gatekeeper finds the address for the destination alias, it returns an admission confirm, and the requested destination address is sent to the originating client. If the destination address is not found, it continues to process the rules list to resolve the request.

An outbound request to another domain will be forwarded to the remote ISA Server and resolved. This process is explained in following example.

A NetMeeting 3.0 client at the Acme company calls *someone@microsoft.com*. If the domain name is external or unknown, the following rule listed in Table 8.12 may be the first to match.

Table 8.12 Sorted List of Rules (Example)

Domain	Matching	Rule Name	Weighted Metric Value
(empty)	Suffix	Gateway/Proxy named "Outbound"	10

In this case, H.323 Gatekeeper informs the ISA Server computer that the address is external to the network. The ISA Server computer then initiates the DNS lookup sequence. If the query returns a fully qualified DNS computer name, H.323 Gatekeeper then performs an additional DNS query to find the destination IP address.

Lesson Summary

Call routing rules allow H.323 Gatekeeper to resolve alias names and to determine whether and where to route videoconference calls. When a unique IP address is not included in a call request, H.323 Gatekeeper tries to match each H.323 routing rule you have configured with the requested alias.

Call routing rules include phone number rules, e-mail address rules, and IP address rules. Phone number rules designate patterns of numbers to match phone number aliases. E-mail address rules configure domain name suffixes to match H.323-ID aliases. IP address rules configure IP address patterns to forward to specified locations. Once H.323 Gatekeeper has established which routing rules match, the routing rules are sorted for additional processing.

When H.323 Gatekeeper receives an inbound query, it identifies the type of alias request—whether it is an E164, H.323-ID, or Email-ID. H.323 Gatekeeper then compares this alias to the list of configured rules. It then compiles the matching rules and sorts them by placing those rules with the lowest metric value highest on the list. Next, the gatekeeper goes through the list of rules, in order, until either the requested address of the alias is resolved, or the search fails. Finally, H.323 Gatekeeper sends a confirmation or rejection to the originating client, depending upon whether the address is found.

When a registered client places an outbound call, an admission request is sent to the H.323 Gatekeeper. In the request, the H.323 client specifies the destination alias. If H.323 Gatekeeper finds the address for the destination alias, it returns an admission confirm, and the requested destination address to the originating client. If the destination address is not found, it continues to process the rule list to resolve the request.

Review

The following questions are intended to reinforce key information presented in the chapter. If you are unable to answer a question, review the appropriate lesson and then try the question again. The answers for these questions are located in Appendix A, "Questions and Answers."

1. What four major components does the H.323 standard define for real-time, network-based, interactive videoconferencing?

2. What functions does H.323 Gatekeeper provide for H.323 videoconferencing clients?

3. Describe the process by which an H.323 client registered with H.323 Gatekeeper on one network calls the e-mail alias of an H.323 client registered with H.323 Gatekeeper on another network.

4. An H.323 client attempts to call another client by specifying the client's alias, *someone@microsoft.com*. Two e-mail address rules match the requested alias. The first rule specifies the suffix pattern *microsoft.com* and has a metric of 4. The second specifies the exact pattern *microsoft.com* and has a metric of 5. Which rule will be applied to the call?

5. What is the benefit of a call routing rule configured to route to a gateway destination?

CHAPTER 9

Monitoring and Optimizing ISA Server Performance

Lesson 1 Configuring Alerts 339

Lesson 2 Logging ISA Server Activity 350

Lesson 3 Creating ISA Server Reports 374

Lesson 4 Controlling Bandwidth 386

Lesson 5 Additional Tuning and Monitoring Tools 397

Review 422

About This Chapter

Microsoft Internet Security and Acceleration Server 2000 (ISA Server) includes many tools for monitoring, optimizing, and tuning performance. Alerts, logs, and reports can all be configured through the Monitoring Configuration node in ISA Management. In addition, bandwidth rules allow you to control and optimize the performance of connections passing through ISA Server by assigning priorities for specific traffic based on any criteria you specify. ISA Server performance can also be tuned according to the number of expected daily connections, and the cache performance can be optimized by adjusting the amount of RAM used to store Web content. Finally, ISA Server includes many performance objects and counters that you may use to monitor very specific activity either in real time or through the use of reports, logs, and alerts in the Windows 2000 Performance console.

Before You Begin

To complete the lessons in this chapter, you must have

- Completed the setup procedures described in "About This Book"
- Completed all exercises through Chapter 8

Lesson 1 Configuring Alerts

The ISA Server alert service is responsible for capturing events, checking whether certain conditions are met, and taking appropriate action. You can use ISA Management to view the full list of events supplied with ISA Server and to configure which actions should be triggered when any of these events occur.

After this lesson, you will be able to

- View ISA Server events in Event Viewer
- View ISA Server alerts in ISA Management
- Configure an alert condition, location, threshold, and action

Estimated lesson time: 35 minutes

Preconfigured Alerts

By default, ISA Server includes 45 alerts, 39 of which are enabled. You can view this list of alerts in ISA Management by selecting the Alerts folder in the Monitoring Configuration node, as shown in Figure 9.1.

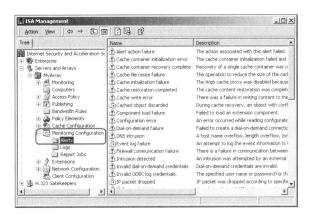

Figure 9.1 Preconfigured alerts in ISA Server

▶ **Follow these steps to enable an alert:**

1. In the console tree of ISA Management, expand the Monitoring Configuration node and click the Alerts folder.

2. In the details pane, right-click the appropriate alert, and then click Enable.

Each alert specifies an event. Every enabled alert is configured by default to report the specified event to the Windows 2000 Event Log. These events can be seen in Event Viewer's Application Log. Figure 9.2 shows sample ISA Server events visible in the Windows 2000 Event Log.

Note You can also view ISA Server events in the Alert folder of the Monitoring node in ISA Management. However, ISA Management only shows the first occurrence of an event since the previous shutdown. For complete information about ISA Server events, use Event Viewer.

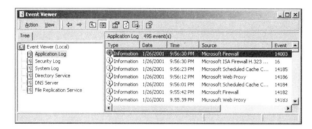

Figure 9.2 ISA Server alerts in Event Viewer

You can create a new alert or modify any of the pre-existing alerts. New alerts are created by using the New Alert wizard.

▶ **Follow these steps to create an alert:**

1. In the console tree of ISA Management, expand the Monitoring Configuration node.

2. Right-click the Alerts folder, point to New, and then click Alert.

3. When the New Alert wizard opens, follow the on-screen instructions.

Alert Conditions

New alerts are based on existing alerts, but they normally include an additional, more specific condition that must be met. For example, the Domain Name System (DNS) Intrusion alert normally has the Any DNS Intrusion condition specified as the additional condition. However, you can create an alert called Hostname Overflow based on the DNS Intrusion alert. To create this alert, you select DNS Intrusion as the alert event and select Hostname Overflow as the additional condition, as shown in Figure 9.3.

You can also modify the alert condition of any preconfigured alert.

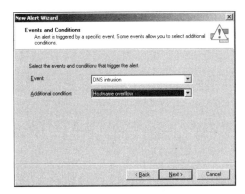

Figure 9.3 Creating a Host Overflow alert

▶ **Follow these steps to modify an alert condition:**

1. In the console tree of ISA Management, expand the Monitoring Configuration node and click the Alerts folder.

2. In the details pane, right-click the applicable alert and then click Properties.

3. On the Events tab,

    - In the Event drop-down list box, click the event that triggers the alert.

    - If the event needs an additional key, in the Additional Condition drop-down list box, click the condition.

    - In the By Server drop-down list box, click the server in the array for which the alert should be triggered or leave it at the default of <Any> if it should apply to all array members.

Event Location

You can also configure a new alert that includes the same event and additional condition as one of the pre-existing alerts, but that limits the detection of the event to a particular server in the array. The computer on which an event is detected is known as the event location. All pre-existing alerts by default specify the event location as any server on the array. However, you can always re-configure the event location of an alert as one particular server, so that the alert will trigger only when the event occurs on the server you choose.

Event Thresholds

Once an alert is configured, you can modify the alert by specifying the following thresholds, which determine when the alert action should be performed:

- How many times per second the event should occur before issuing an alert (also called the *event frequency threshold*)
- How many events should occur before the alert is issued
- How long to wait before issuing the alert again

You can modify the threshold on the Events tab of an alert's Properties dialog box, as shown in Figure 9.4.

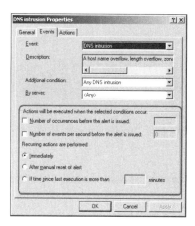

Figure 9.4 Modifying thresholds

▶ **Follow these steps to configure an alert threshold:**

1. In the console tree of ISA Management, expand the Monitoring Configuration node and click the Alerts folder.
2. In the details pane, right-click the applicable alert, and then click Properties.
3. On the Events tab, select the Number Of Occurrences Before The Alert Is Issued check box, and type the number of events that should occur before the alert is issued.
4. Select the Number Of Events Per Second Before The Alert Is Issued check box, and type how many events should occur per second before the alert is issued.
5. Select one of the following options:
   - If the alert should be reissued immediately if the event recurs, click the Immediately radio button.
   - If the alert should be reissued only after the alert is reset, click After Manual Reset Of Alert radio button.
   - If the alert should be reissued after a specified amount of time, click If Time Since Last Execution Is More Than <*number*> Minutes radio button, and then type the number of minutes that should elapse before the action should be performed.

Alert Action

You can set one or more of the following actions to be performed when an alert condition is met:

- Send an e-mail message
- Run a specific program
- Log the event in the Windows 2000 Event Log
- Stop or start any ISA Server service: Firewall service, Web Proxy service, or Scheduled Content Download service

When you configure an alert to run a specific program, you can specify which credentials should be used when an application is executed. Be sure that the specified user has Logon As A Batch Job privileges. Use the Local Security Policy to configure user privileges. When the alert action is to run a program, the path specified for the command action must exist on all servers in the array. Use environment variables (such as %SystemDrive%) within the path name so if the application path is different from one array member to the next, the environment variable will be able to locate the program.

You can set an alert action either when you run the New Alert wizard or when you modify the settings on the Actions tab of the alert's Properties dialog box, as shown in Figure 9.5.

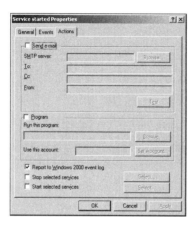

Figure 9.5 Configuring an alert action

▶ **Follow these steps to modify an alert action:**

1. In the console tree of ISA Management, expand the Monitoring Configuration node and click the Alerts folder.

2. In the details pane, right-click the applicable alert, and then click Properties.

3. On the Actions tab,

- To send an e-mail when the alert condition occurs, click the Send E-mail check box, and then type the name of the Simple Mail Transfer Protocol (SMTP) server, recipient, and sender.

- To run an application when the alert condition occurs, click the Program check box, and then type the command to run at a command prompt and the account from which to run the program.

- To log the event, click the Report To Windows 2000 Event Log check box.

- To stop ISA Server, click the Stop Selected Services check box, and then click the Select button to select which ISA Server services to stop when the alert condition occurs.

- To start ISA Server, click the Start Selected Services check box, and then click the Select button to select which services to start when the alert condition occurs.

Note If you configure an e-mail action to use an external SMTP server, you must create a static packet filter that allows the SMTP protocol.

ISA Server Events

Table 9.1 lists the events and, where relevant, additional keys that are defined by ISA Server. When you create an alert, you specify one of the following events that triggers the alert.

Table 9.1 ISA Server Events

Preconfigured Alert	Description
Alert action failure	The action associated with this alert failed.
Asymmetric installation	A component that was configured for the array is missing on this server. <%user friendly component identification%>
Cache container initialization error	The cache container initialization failed and the container was ignored.
Cache container recovery complete	The recovery of a single container was completed.
Cache file resize failure	There was a failure to reduce the cache file size.
Cache initialization failure	The Web cache proxy was disabled because of global failure.
Cache recovery completed	The cache content recovery was completed.
Cache write error	There was a failure to write cached content to the cache.
Cached object ignored	During cache recovery, an object with conflicting information was detected. The object was ignored.

(continues)

Table 9.1 ISA Server Events *(continued)*

Preconfigured Alert	Description
Client/server communication failure	Communication between the Firewall client and the Firewall service of ISA Server failed.
Component load failure	There was a failure to load an extension component. <%module name%>
Configuration error	The ISA Server configuration is invalid <%storage path%>.
Dial on demand failure	There was a failure to create a dial-on-demand connection, because there is no answer or the line is busy.
DNS Intrusion	A host name overflow, length overflow, zone high port, or zone transfer attack occurred.
Event logging failure	There was a failure to log the event information to the system event log.
Failed to retrieve object	The object <URL> could not be loaded. <error>
Intra-array credentials	The intra-array credentials were incorrect.
Intrusion detected	An external user attempted an intrusion attack.
Invalid dial-on-demand credentials	Invalid dial-on-demand credentials were detected.
Invalid ODBC log credentials	The specified user name or password for this Open Database Connectivity (ODBC) database is invalid.
IP packet dropped	An Internet Protocol (IP) packet that is not allowed by the policy was dropped.
IP Protocol violation	A packet with invalid IP options was detected and dropped.
IP Spoofing	The IP packet source address is not valid.
Log failure	<service name> log failed.
Network configuration changed	A network configuration change that affects ISA Server was detected.
OS component conflict	There is a conflict with one of the operating system components: NAT editor, ICS, or Routing and Remote Access.

Preconfigured Alert	Description
Oversize UDP packet	ISA Server dropped a User Datagram Protocol (UDP) packet because it exceeded maximum size, as specified in the registry key.
POP Intrusion	ISA Server detected a Post Office Protocol (POP) buffer overflow.
Report Summary Generation Failure	ISA Server received an error while generating a report summary from log files.
Resource allocation failure	There was a resource allocation failure, for example, the system ran out of memory.
RPC filter - server connectivity changed	The connectivity to the publishing RPC service <server name> changed. <additional key>
Server Publishing Failure	The server publishing rule cannot be applied.
Service Initialization failure	There was a service initialization failure.
Service not responding	An ISA Server service terminated or stopped functioning unexpectedly.
Service shutdown	A service stopped properly. <%service name%>
Service started	A service started properly. <%service name%>
SMTP Filter Event	A SMTP filter event occurred.
SOCKS configuration failure	The port specified in SOCKS properties is in use by another protocol.
SOCKS request was refused	A SOCKS request was refused due to policy violation.
The server is out of array's site	All members of the array must be in the same site, but this server is in a different site.
Unregistered event	An unregistered event was raised. The event internal ID is %1.
Upstream chaining credentials	The upstream chaining credentials are incorrect.
Web Proxy routing failure	The Web Proxy service of ISA Server failed to route the request to an upstream proxy server.

(continues)

Table 9.1 ISA Server Events *(continued)*

Preconfigured Alert	Description
Web Proxy routing recovery	Web Proxy resumed routing to an upstream proxy server.
WMT live stream splitting failure	The streaming application filter encountered an error during Windows Media Technology (WMT) live stream splitting.

Practice: Configuring an Alert to Send an E-mail Message

In this practice, you configure an alert to send an e-mail message to an administrator whenever an intrusion is detected. By default, alerts only send a message to the Windows 2000 Event Log. To ensure that an alert is seen by ISA administrators, you should plan to modify the alert to send an e-mail message to the appropriate personnel.

Exercise: Configuring the Intrusion Detected Alert to Send You an E-mail Message

In this exercise, you modify the Intrusion Detected alert to send you an e-mail message whenever an external intrusion of your network is detected by ISA Server. You complete most of this exercise on Server1, but Server2 must be available and configured to run the SMTP service.

▶ **To configure the Intrusion Detected alert to send you an e-mail message**

1. Log on to Server1 as Administrator.
2. Open ISA Management, and expand the Monitoring Configuration node.
3. Select the Alerts folder.
4. In the details pane, right-click the Intrusion Detected alert and click Properties.

   The Intrusion Detected Properties dialog box appears.
5. Click the Actions tab.
6. Click the Send E-mail check box.
7. In the SMTP Server text box, type **192.168.0.2**.
8. In the To text box, type **testuser@server2.domain01.local**.

9. In the From text box, type **testuser@server2.domain01.local**.

10. Click the Test button.

    You receive a message box indicating that the simulation was completed successfully.

11. Click OK.

12. In the Intrusion Detected Properties dialog box, click OK.

    After a few minutes, you should receive your test e-mail in the C:\Inetpub\mailroot\Drop folder on Server2. This indicates that the service is working properly.

Lesson Summary

By default, ISA Server includes 45 alerts, 39 of which are enabled. Each alert specifies an event and four properties, including the alert condition, the event location, the alert threshold, and the alert actions.

Alert conditions refer to the conditions that trigger an alert. Many predefined alerts, such as the DNS Intrusion alert, are triggered by default when any of a set of listed conditions occurs. However, you can configure a more specific alert that selects just one of these particular conditions as the basis for the alert.

The event location is the server on which the event must be located for the alert to be triggered. By default, all predefined alerts specify that the event can occur on any ISA Server computer for the alert to be triggered. However, you may specify a particular ISA Server computer as the location for the alert event.

The alert actions determine what action will be taken when the alert is triggered. By default, all alerts only report the specified event to the Windows 2000 Event Log. However, you can also configure an alert to send an e-mail, to run a program, and to start or stop ISA Server services.

Alert thresholds determine the number of times the alert condition needs to occur before the alert action should be performed, and they also determine how long ISA Server should wait before performing the action again. By default, alerts specify that the alert condition only needs to occur once for an alert action to take place, and that the alert action should take place immediately.

You can view and modify all defined alerts in the Alerts folder in the Monitoring Configuration node of ISA Management.

Lesson 2 Logging ISA Server Activity

ISA Server features detailed security and access logs that can be generated in standard data formats like World Wide Web Consortium (W3C) and Open Database Connectivity (ODBC). The three logs built into ISA Server monitor activity of the Firewall service, the Web Proxy service, and packet filtering. New logs can be created daily, weekly, monthly, or yearly.

After this lesson, you will be able to

- Locate and view ISA Server logs for the Firewall service, for the Web Proxy service, and for packet filtering
- Modify ISA Server logging properties such as log location, log fields, and log file compression.
- Configure ISA Server to use an ODBC data source for logging.

Estimated lesson time: 75 minutes

Managing ISA Server Logs

ISA Server logs packet filtering activity, Firewall service activity, and Web Proxy service activity. By default, one new log file is generated for each service per day. Each new log file is stored in the ISALogs folder in the ISA Server installation folder. A typical path for this location is %ProgramFiles%\Microsoft ISA Server\ISALogs\.

You can modify many of the default settings for these three service logs. For example, you can modify the logging format. By default, ISA Server logs to a file in W3C format, but you can also choose to log to a file in ISA format. A third option is to log to a database in ODBC format. Another property you can modify is the frequency of log reports. You can configure ISA Server to generate a log report daily, monthly, weekly, or yearly. Other properties you can modify in ISA Server logging include the specific fields to generate in the log report, and the location to store the log file.

Logging properties are modified in ISA Management in the Logs folder of the Monitoring Configuration node. Figure 9.6 shows the three service logs you can configure when the Logs folder is selected.

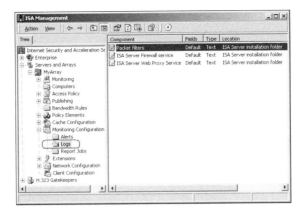

Figure 9.6 Managing logs in ISA Management

Properties for each service log can be configured by double-clicking any one of the service log icons in the details pane. Figure 9.7 shows the Log tab associated with the Properties dialog box of a service log. This tab allows you to configure the log format and storage location.

Figure 9.7 The Log tab of a service log's properties

Figure 9.8 shows the Fields tab associated with the Properties dialog box of a service log. This tab allows you to specify which fields are included in the log report.

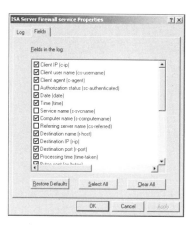

Figure 9.8 The Fields tab of a service log's properties

When a service log is enabled, logs are generated for each server in the array. The ISA Server reporting system then centralizes the logs, collecting data from all the servers and combining them into a single report.

Logging to a File

You can save ISA Server logs to a file in either of the following formats:

- W3C format
- ISA format

Although the logging configuration is array-wide, log files are created on every ISA Server in the array. You can specify the location of a log file in the Options dialog box, as shown in Figure 9.9, which you access by clicking the Options button in the specific service log's Properties dialog box.

Chapter 9 Monitoring and Optimizing ISA Server Performance

Figure 9.9 Specifying a log file location

The default location for the log file is the ISALogs folder. When you leave this option selected, the log file is saved to the same location within the ISA Server installation folder on every ISA Server computer in the array. If you specify another folder, however, the path you specify for the log file must exist on every server in the array.

Important It is recommended that you log to Windows NT file system (NTFS) partitions so that the log files benefit from advanced file system features like NTFS security and data compression.

W3C Format

W3C logs contains both data and directives describing the version, date and logged fields. Because the fields are described in the file, unselected fields are not logged. The tab character is used as delimiter. Date and time are displayed in Greenwich Mean Time (GMT). Figure 9.10 shows part of a Web Proxy log file in W3C format.

Figure 9.10 A Web Proxy log file in W3C log format

ISA Format

ISA format contains only data with no directives. All fields are always logged; unselected fields are logged with a dash to indicate that they are empty. The comma character is used as delimiter. The Date and Time fields display local time. A sample Firewall service log file in ISA format is shown in Figure 9.11.

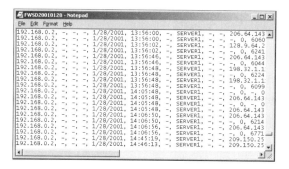

Figure 9.11 A Firewall service log file in ISA format

Log File Names

A log file name is derived from the name of the service being logged, the log file format, and the date of the log.

The first three letters of the service log file name indicate the service being logged. FWS indicates the Firewall service, WEB indicates the Web Proxy service, and IPP indicates IP packet filters. This is followed by the letters EXT if the file is in the W3C extended log file format. (A file in ISA Server file format is designated by the absence of the letters EXT.) Next in the file name is a letter indicating the frequency of the log: the letter D represents a daily log, the letter W indicates a weekly log, the letter M represents monthly, and the letter Y indicates a yearly log. Finally, the date of the log file follows in the form yyyymmdd. The date May 21, 2002 would thus be represented as 20020521, and a daily W3C Web Proxy service log created on that date would be named WEBEXTD20020521.log. A monthly Firewall service log file in ISA format created on the same date would be named FWSM20020521.log.

Log File Options

In order to save the amount of disk space required for the log files, ISA Server allows you to configure the following options:

- Compress log files to reduce the disk space required. Files are compressed only if stored on NTFS partitions.
- Limit the number of log files saved on all the servers in the array.
- Limit the number of fields to log in log files.

▶ **Follow these steps to configure logging to a file:**

1. In the console tree of ISA Management, expand the Monitoring Configuration node and click the Logs folder.
2. In the details pane, right-click the applicable service, and then click Properties.
3. On the Log tab, click the File radio button.
4. In the Format drop-down list box, select the log format.
5. In the Create A New File drop-down list box, click a time period that specifies how often a new log file will be created.
6. To modify the location of the log file, click the Options button and then do one of the following:
    - To save the file to the default folder, click the ISALogs Folder (In The ISA Server Installation Folder) radio button.
    - To save the file to another folder, click the Other Folder radio button and then type a folder name in the text box or click Browse and find a storage location.
7. To set the maximum number of log files, click the Limit Number Of Log Files check box, and in the associated text box, type the maximum number of log files to keep for the array.
8. To compress the log files, click the Compress Log Files check box.

Logging to a Database

You can store ISA Server logs to an ODBC database instead of a file. You configure this option by selecting the Database radio button on the Log tab of a service log's Properties dialog box.

Before configuring ISA Server to log data to a database, you must create a database and tables to support logging. The root folder of the ISA Server CD-ROM includes the following sample scripts that create tables and indexes to support database logging:

- Pf.sql defines the packet filter log table called PacketFilterLog and indexes to support table queries.
- W3PROXY.sql defines the Web Proxy service log table WebProxyLog and indexes to support table queries.
- FWSRV.sql defines the Firewall service log table called FirewallLog and indexes to support table queries.

For example, to create a SQL Server 2000 log database named ISALogs that can grow to a maximum size of 100 MB and a transaction log file that can grow to a maximum size of 50 MB, perform the following steps:

1. Open SQL Query Analyzer and connect to the SQL Server where you will create the log database.
2. In the Editor pane of the Query window, enter the following Transact-SQL code:

   ```
   USE master
   GO
   CREATE DATABASE ISALogs
   ```

   This code creates a database with the name ISALogs.

3. Directly beneath the code that you just entered in the Editor pane, enter the following code:

```
ON PRIMARY
(
   NAME = ISALog_dat,
   FILENAME = 'C:\Program Files\Microsoft SQL Server\MSSQL\Data\ISALog.mdf',
   SIZE = 50,
   MAXSIZE = 100,
   FILEGROWTH = 1
)
```

This code defines the primary file. The logical name of the file is ISALog_dat. The path and file name used by the operating system is C:\Program Files\Microsoft SQL Server\MSSQL\Data\ISALog.mdf. The initial size of the file is 50 MB, and the maximum size that the file can grow is 100 MB. The growth increment of the file is 1 MB.

Note If the path specified in the code is different on your computer, you must specify the correct path in the code, or leave the code as is and create the file path on the C: drive before running this code in step 5.

4. Directly beneath the code that you just entered in the Editor pane, enter the following code:

```
LOG ON
(
   NAME = ISALog_log,
   FILENAME = 'C:\Program Files\Microsoft SQL Server\MSSQL\Data\ISALog.ldf',
   SIZE = 25,
   MAXSIZE = 50,
   FILEGROWTH = 1
)
GO
```

This code defines the log file. The logical name of the file is ISALog_log. The path and file name used by the operating system is C:\Program Files\Microsoft SQL Server\MSSQL\Data\ISALog.ldf. The initial size of the file is 25 MB, and the maximum size that the file can grow is 50 MB. The growth increment of the file is 1 MB.

Note If the path specified in the code is different on your computer, you must specify the correct path in the code, or leave the code as is and create the file path on the C: drive before running this code in step 5.

5. Execute all the code as one batch.

   The Messages tab of the Results pane displays two messages, one saying that 100 MB of disk space has been allocated to the primary file and the other saying that 50 MB of disk space has been allocated to the transaction log file.

6. Verify that the current database is ISALogs, then open and execute each of the .sql files appearing on the root of the ISA Server CD-ROM.

7. The log tables and indexes are created for each service.

After you create the database and the log tables and indexes, you must set up the ISA Server computer to use the data source name. Perform the following steps:

1. On the ISA Server computer, click Start, point to Programs, point to Administrative Tools, and then click Data Sources (ODBC).

2. On the System DSN tab, click the Add button.

3. In the Create New Data Source screen, select the appropriate driver for the database.

   If you are using SQL Server 2000, select SQL Server.

4. Follow the on-screen instructions to create the database.

   The data source name is the one you enter in the ODBC data source (DSN) text box when you configure the log database properties.

   Caution Do not use spaces in the data source name or ISA Server services will stop.

▶ **Follow these steps to configure logging to a database:**

1. In the console tree of ISA Management, expand the Monitoring Configuration node and click the Logs folder.

2. In the details pane, right-click the applicable service, and then click Properties.

3. On the Log tab, click the Database radio button.

4. Confirm or modify the following parameters:
   - ODBC data source (DSN)
   - Table name

     This is the name of each table as specified in the .sql files on the root of the ISA Server CD-ROM. For example, the table name for the Packet Filters log is PacketFilterLog.
   - User account
5. Click the Set Account button, type the user name in the User text box, and type the password in the Password and Confirm Password text boxes. You can use a SQL Server logon ID or a Windows user account, depending on how you configure SQL Server authentication.

Logging Packets

All packets that pass through ISA Server can be logged to the packet filter log. You can configure exactly which packets are logged by following these guidelines:

- By default, when you install ISA Server, all dropped packets are logged to the packet filter log. When you disable packet filtering, logging is turned off altogether.
- You can configure ISA Server to disable logging for packets that are dropped due to any specific block-mode IP packet filter.
- You can configure ISA Server to log all packets—allowed and dropped—that are communicated by way of ISA Server. When you enable logging of allowed packets, all packets that pass through ISA Server are logged in the packet filter log.

Logging allowed packets and blocked packets causes a considerable load on the server.

▶ **Follow these steps to log allowed packets:**

1. In the console tree of ISA Management, expand the Access Policy node, right-click the IP Packet Filters folders, and then click Properties.
2. On the Packet Filters tab, select the Log Packets From 'Allow' Filters check box.

Note You can only log allowed packets if packet filtering is enabled.

▶ **Follow these steps to log blocked packets:**

1. In the console tree of ISA Management, expand the Access Policy node and click the IP Packet Filters folder.

2. On the View menu, confirm that the Advanced option is selected.

3. In the details pane, right-click the block-mode IP packet filter whose packets you want to log and then click Properties.

4. On the General tab, select the Log Any Packets Matching This Filter check box.

Firewall and Web Proxy Log Fields

When you select the Fields tab of a service log's properties, you can select any of the available number of fields to log. By default, the packet filters log reports nine of a possible twelve fields. Also by default, the Firewall service and Web Proxy service logs report 18 of a possible 27 fields. You can change these default selections at any time or restore the defaults by clicking the Restore Defaults button.

▶ **Follow these steps to specify fields to log:**

1. In the console tree of ISA Management, expand the Monitoring Configuration node and click the Logs folder.

2. In the details pane, right-click the applicable service, and then click Properties.

3. Click the Fields tab.

   You complete the following tasks from this tab:

   - To select specific fields for logging, enable the appropriate check box.
   - To clear all the check boxes in the field list, click the Clear All button.
   - To enable all the check boxes in the field list, click the Select All button.
   - To enable a default set of fields in the ISA Server log file, click the Restore Defaults button.

Table 9.2 lists the fields that you can include in each of the ISA Server Firewall and Web Proxy log files. The field name noted in parentheses is relevant when you use the 3C extended log file format. For W3C names, note that the prefix "c" represents client actions, "s" represents server actions, "cs" represents client-to-server actions, "sc" represents server-to-client actions, and "r" represents remote actions.

Some fields are relevant for either Web Proxy Service or Firewall Service, but not both. For each of these fields, the table indicates which service the field applies to. Note that, in ISA Server log format, an empty field appears in the log with a hyphen (-). In W3C log file format, the field does not appear at all if it is not applicable to the service.

Tables 9.2 through 9.6 list possible values for some of these fields. You can view these field names through the Monitoring Configuration node in ISA Management. To do so, click the Logs folder, and then double-click the log files belonging to the ISA Server Firewall Service and the ISA Server Web Proxy Service. Finally, click on the Fields tab to review the fields available for logging.

Table 9.2   Available Logging Fields for Firewall and Web Proxy Services

Field position	Descriptive name (field name)	Description
1	Client IP (c-ip)	The IP address of the requesting client.
2	Client user name (cs-username)	Account of the user making the request. If ISA Server Access Control is not being used, ISA Server uses *anonymous*.
3	Client agent (c-agent)	The client application type sent by the client in the Hypertext Transfer Protocol (HTTP) header. When ISA Server is actively caching, the client agent is *ISA Server*.
		For Firewall service, this field includes information about the client's operating system. See Table 9.3 for possible Client Agent values.
4	Authorization status (sc-authenticated)	Indicates whether or not the client has been authenticated with ISA Server. Possible values are *Y* and *N*.
5	Date (date)	The date that the logged event occurred.
6	Time (time)	The time that the logged event occurred. In W3C format, this is in Greenwich mean time.

(continues)

Table 9.2 Available Logging Fields for Firewall and Web Proxy Services *(continued)*

Field position	Descriptive name (field name)	Description
7	Service name (s-svcname)	The name of the service that is logged. *w3proxy* indicates outgoing Web requests to the Web Proxy service. *fwsrv* indicates Firewall service. *w3reverseproxy* indicates incoming Web requests to the Web Proxy service.
8	Computer name (s-computername)	The name of the computer running ISA Server. This is the computer name that is assigned in Windows 2000.
9	Referring server name (cs-referred)	If ISA Server is used upstream in a chained configuration, this indicates the server name of the downstream server that sent the request.
10	Destination name (r-host)	The domain name for the remote computer that provides service to the current connection. For the Web Proxy service, a hyphen (-) in this field may indicate that an object was retrieved from the Web Proxy server cache and not from the destination.
11	Destination IP (r-ip)	The network IP address for the remote computer that provides service to the current connection. For the Web Proxy service, a hyphen (-) in this field may indicate that an object was sourced from the Web Proxy server cache and not from the destination. One exception is negative caching. In that case, this field indicates a destination IP address for which a negative-cached object was returned.
12	Destination port (r-port)	The reserved port number on the remote computer that provides service to the current connection. This is used by the client application initiating the request.

Field position	Descriptive name (field name)	Description
13	Processing time (time-taken)	This indicates the total time, in milliseconds, that is needed by ISA Server to process the current connection. It measures elapsed server time from the time that the server first received the request to the time when final processing occurred on the server—when results were returned to the client and the connection was closed. For cache requests that were processed through the Web Proxy service, *processing time* measures the elapsed server time needed to fully process a client request and return an object from the server cache to the client.
14	Bytes sent (cs-bytes)	The number of bytes sent from the internal client to the external server during the current connection. A hyphen (-), a zero (0), or a negative number in this field indicates that this information was not provided by the remote computer or that no bytes were sent to the remote computer.
15	Bytes received (sc-bytes)	The number of bytes sent from the external computer and received by the client during the current connection. A hyphen (-), a zero (0), or a negative number in this field indicates that this information was not provided by the remote computer or that no bytes were received from the external computer.
16	Protocol name (cs-protocol)	Specifies the application protocol used for the connection. Common values are HTTP, File Transfer Protocol (FTP), and Secure Hypertext Transfer Protocol (HTTPS). For Firewall service, the port number is also logged.

(continues)

Table 9.2 Available Logging Fields for Firewall and Web Proxy Services *(continued)*

Field position	Descriptive name (field name)	Description
17	Transport (cs-transport)	Specifies the transport protocol used for the connection. Common values are Transmission Control Protocol (TCP) and UDP.
18	Operation (s-operation)	Specifies the application method used. For Web Proxy, common values are GET, PUT, POST, and HEAD. For Firewall service, common values are CONNECT, BIND, SEND, RECEIVE, GHBN (GetHostByName), and GHBA (GetHostByAddress).
19	Object name (cs-uri)	For the Web Proxy service, this field shows the contents of the Uniform Resource Locator (URL) request. This field applies only to the Web Proxy service log.
20	Object MIME (cs-mime-type)	The Multipurpose Internet Mail Extensions (MIME) type for the current object. This field may also contain a hyphen (-) to indicate that this field is not used or that a valid MIME type was not defined or supported by the remote computer. This field applies only to the Web Proxy service log.
21	Object source (s-object-source)	Indicates the source that was used to retrieve the current object. This field applies only to the Web Proxy service log. See Table 9.4 for a list of possible values.
22	Result code (sc-status)	This field can be used to indicate: - For values less than 100, a Windows (Win32) error code - For values between 100 and 1,000, an HTTP status code - For values between 10,000 and 11,004, a Winsock error code See Table 9.5 for a list of possible values.

Field position	Descriptive name (field name)	Description
23	Cache info (s-cache-info)	This number reflects the cache status of the object, which indicates why the object was or was not cached. This field applies only to the Web Proxy service log. See Table 9.6 for a list of possible values.
24	Rule #1 (rule#1)	This reflects the rule that either allowed or denied access to the request, as follows: If an outgoing request is allowed, this field reflects the protocol rule that allowed the request. If an outgoing request is denied by a protocol rule, this field reflects the protocol rule. If an outgoing request is denied by a site and content rule, this field reflects the protocol rule that would have allowed the request. If an incoming request was denied, this field reflects the Web publishing or server publishing rule that denied the request. If no rule specifically allowed the outgoing or incoming request, the request is denied. In this case, the field is empty.
25	Rule #2 (rule#2)	This reflects the second rule that either allowed or denied access to the request. If an outgoing request is allowed, this field reflects the site and content rule that allowed the request. If an outgoing request is denied by a site and content rule, this field reflects the site and content rule that denied the request. If no rule specifically allowed the outgoing or incoming request, the request is denied. In this case, the field is empty.

(continues)

Table 9.2 Available Logging Fields for Firewall and Web Proxy Services *(continued)*

Field position	Descriptive name (field name)	Description
26	Session ID (sessionid)	This identifies a session's connections. For Firewall clients, each process that connects through the Firewall service initiates a session. For SecureNAT clients, a single session is opened for all the connections that originate from the same IP address. This field is not included in the Web Proxy service log. This field applies only to the Firewall service log.
27	Connection ID (connectionid)	This identifies entries that belong to the same socket. Outbound TCP usually has two entries for each connection: when the connection is established and when the connection is terminated. UDP usually has two entries for each remote address. This field is not included in the Web Proxy service log. This field applies only to the Firewall service log.

Table 9.3 presents the possible values for the client agent (c-agent in W3C format) parameter reported by the ISA Server Firewall service log. This expands on the information presented in row 3 of Table 9.2. When all fields are selected to be logged, one of the values listed in Table 9.3 appears in the third field position of the log. This value indicates the operating system used by the client.

Table 9.3 Operating System Values

Value	Description
0:3.95	Windows 95 (16-bit)
2:4.10	Windows 98 (32-bit)
2:4.0	Windows 95 (32-bit)
3:4.0	Windows NT 4.0
3:5.0	Windows 2000

Table 9.4 lists the possible values for the object source (s-object-source in W3C format) parameter reported by the ISA Server Web Proxy service log. This expands on the information presented in row 21 of Table 9.2. When all fields are selected to be logged, one of the values listed in Table 9.4 appears in the 21st field position of the log. This value indicates which source was used to retrieve the current object.

Table 9.4 Object Source Values

Source values	Description
0	No source information is available.
Cache	Source is the cache. Object returned from cache.
Inet	Source is the Internet. Object added to cache.
Member	Returned from another array member.
NotModified	Source is the cache. Client performed an If-Modified-Since request and object had not been modified.
NVCache	Source is the cache. Object could not be verified to source.
Upstream	Object returned from an upstream proxy cache.
Vcache	Source is the cache. Object was verified to source and had not been modified.
VFInet	Source is the Internet. Cached object was verified to source and had been modified.

Table 9.5 lists some of the possible values for the result code (or sc-status in W3C format) parameter reported by the ISA Server Firewall and Web Proxy service logs. This expands on the information presented in row 22 of Table 9.2.

This value is often used to indicate a Windows error code (for values less than 100), an HTTP status code (for values between 100 and 1,000), or a Winsock error code (for values between 10,000 and 11,004). A connection usually has two log entries: the first entry is for when the connection is established; the second entry is for when the connection is terminated. The first entry is logged with a result code of either 0 (Successful Connection) or 13301 (Connection Refused) and a byte count of 0. The second entry is logged with a result code of either 20000 (Normal Connection Termination) or 20001 (Unexpected Connection Termination) and the corresponding byte count.

For additional information about error codes, consult the Microsoft Developers Network online at *http://msdn.microsoft.com*, or Microsoft Technet at *http://www.microsoft.com/technet*.

Table 9.5 Sample Result Code Values

Value	Description
0	Successful connection
200	OK - Successful connection
201	Created
202	Accepted
204	No content
301	Moved permanently
302	Moved temporarily
304	Not modified
400	Bad request
401	Unauthorized
403	Forbidden
404	Not found
500	Internal server error
501	Not implemented
502	Bad gateway
503	Service unavailable
10054	Connection reset by remote side
10060	Connection timed out
10061	Connection refused by destination
10065	Host unreachable
11001	Host not found
13301	Connection rejected (due to filtering or protocol permissions)
20000	Normal connection termination
20001	Unexpected connection termination

Table 9.6 lists the possible values for the cache info (s-cache info in W3C format) parameter reported by the ISA Server Web Proxy service log. This expands on the information presented in row 23 of Table 9.2. This value indicates why the object was or was not cached.

Table 9.6 Cache Info Values

Value	Description
0x00000001	Request should not be served from the cache
0x00000002	Request includes the IF-MODIFIED-SINCE header
0x00000004	Request includes one of these headers: CACHE-CONTROL:NO-CACHE or PRAGMA:NO-CACHE
0x00000008	Request includes the AUTHORIZATION header
0x00000010	Request includes the VIA header
0x00000020	Request includes the IF-MATCH header
0x00000040	Request includes the RANGE header
0x00000080	Request includes the CACHE-CONTROL: NO-STORE header
0x00000100	Request includes the CACHE-CONTROL: MAX-AGE, or CACHE-CONTROL: MAX-STALE or CACHE-CONTROL: MIN-FRESH header
0x00000200	Cache could not be updated.
0x00000400	IF-MODIFIED-SINCE time specified in the request is newer than cached LASTMODIFIED time
0x00000800	Request includes the CACHE-CONTROL: ONLY-IF-CACHED header
0x00001000	Request includes the IF-NONE-MATCH header
0x00002000	Request includes the IF-UNMODIFIED-SINCE header
0x00004000	Request includes the IF-RANGE header
0x00008000	More than one VARY header
0x00010000	Response includes the CACHE-CONTROL: PUBLIC header
0x00020000	Response includes the CACHE-CONTROL: PRIVATE header
0x00040000	Response includes the CACHE-CONTROL: NO-CACHE or PRAGMA: NO-CACHE header
0x00080000	Response includes the CACHE-CONTROL: NO-STORE header
0x00100000	Response includes either the CACHE-CONTROL: MUST-REVALIDATE or CACHE-CONTROL: PROXY-REVALIDATE header

(continues)

Table 9.6 Cache Info Values *(continued)*

Value	Description
0x00200000	Response includes the CACHE-CONTROL: MAX-AGE or S-MAXAGE header
0x00400000	Response includes the VARY header
0x00800000	Response includes the LAST-MODIFIED header
0x01000000	Response includes the EXPIRES header
0x02000000	Response includes the SET-COOKIE header
0x04000000	Response includes the WWW-AUTHENTICATE header
0x08000000	Response includes the VIA header
0x10000000	Response includes the AGE header
0x20000000	Response includes the TRANSFER-ENCODING header
0x40000000	Response should not be cached.

Packet Filter Log Fields

You can use the ISA Server log to monitor and analyze the status of the packet filters. Table 9.7 lists the fields that you can include in each of the Packet Filter log files. You can view these field names through the Monitoring Configuration node in ISA Management. To do so, click the Logs folder, and then double-click the Packet Filters log file. Finally, click the Fields tab to review the fields available for logging.

Table 9.7 Log Fields for Packet Filtering

Field position	Descriptive name (field name)	Description
1	Date (date)	Date the packet was received.
2	Time (time) (service info fields)	The time the packet was received.
3	Source IP (source-ip)	The IP address of the source (remote) computer. The source computer is the computer from which the data packets originated.
4	Destination IP (destination-ip)	The IP address of the destination (local) computer. The destination computer is usually the ISA Server computer.

Field position	Descriptive name (field name)	Description
5	Protocol (protocol)	The particular transport level protocol that is used during the connection, such as TCP, UDP, or Internet Control Message Protocol (ICMP).
6	Source port (or protocol type, if ICMP) (param#1)	For TCP and UDP protocols, the remote port used to create a connection. For ICMP protocol, the type used when creating the connection.
7	Destination port (or protocol code, if ICMP) (param#2)	For TCP and UDP protocols, the local port used to create a connection. For ICMP protocol, the code used when creating the connection.
8	TCP flags (tcp-flags)	For a TCP data packet, represents the TCP flag value in the IP header. The possible values are FIN, SYN, RST, PSH, ACK, and URG.
9	Rule (filter-rule)	Indicates whether the packet was accepted (1) or dropped (0). By default, only dropped packets are logged.
10	Interface IP address (interface)	Interface on which the packet was received; usually only one interface.
11	Header (ip-header)	The entire IP header of the data packet that generated the alert event. The IP header is logged in hexadecimal format.
12	Payload (payload)	A listing of a portion of the data packet (after the IP header). The IP packet is logged in hexadecimal format.

Practice: Reading Web Logs

In this practice, you answer questions about a sample log generated by the Web Proxy service. Note that the column headings don't perfectly align with the column content of the sample file. The appearance of this log file has not been modified from what ISA Server creates. If you are using Notepad to view the file, make sure to disable the Word Wrap feature.

Exercise: Analyzing a Web Log

To prepare for this exercise, open the sample Web Proxy log named WEBEXTD20010129, which can be found in the \Exercises\Chapter9\ folder of the Supplemental Course Materials CD-ROM accompanying this book. The log file is in W3C format. Once you have opened the file, use the tables and information in this chapter to answer the following questions. Be sure to provide the specific code value or values that are essential to answer each question.

1. For the first Web connection in the log (initiated at 02:31:35), was the traffic heavier from the client to the server, or vice versa? Hint: Use Table 9.2 to help you determine the W3C field names for Bytes Sent and Bytes Received. Then find the Bytes Sent and Bytes Received values in the first entry in the log.

2. For this same connection, was the Web request fulfilled from the cache or from the Internet? Hint: Use Table 9.2 to help you determine the W3C field name for Object Source. Then use Table 9.4 to help you understand the Object Source value you find in the first entry in the log.

3. At what time was a connection reset by the remote side? Hint: Use Table 9.5 to help you determine the result code value corresponding to this event. Then scan the log for this result code, highlight the appropriate log entry, and note the time of the connection.

4. Was the object requested at 02:31:45 found in the cache? Had the object been modified? What source was ultimately used to fulfill the request? Hint: Locate and highlight the log entry in the log file corresponding to the time given. Use Table 9.2 to help you determine the W3C field name for Result Code. Then use Table 9.5 to help you understand the Result Code value you find in the highlighted log entry.

5. Which Web operation was conducted at 04:55:14? Was the destination found? Hint: Locate and highlight the log entry in the log file corresponding to the time given. Use Table 9.2 to help you determine the W3C field name for Operation. Then find the Operation value in the highlighted log entry. Next, use Table 9.5 to help you understand the Result Code value in the same log entry.

Lesson Summary

Three logs are built into ISA Server that monitor the activity of ISA Server packet filters, the Firewall service, and the Web Proxy service. By default, one new log file is generated for each service per day. Also by default, each new log file is stored in the ISALogs folder below the ISA Server installation folder. Logging properties are modified in ISA Management in the Logs folder of the Monitoring Configuration node.

You can save ISA Server logs either to a file or to an ODBC database. When you save to a file, you can specify either the W3C format or the ISA format. To conserve disk space required for the log files, ISA Server allows you to compress log files and to limit the number of log files saved on all the servers in the array.

ISA Server allows you to specify which fields to report to the service logs. You should consult ISA Server Help to determine which fields are available for each service and what each field value represents.

Lesson 3 Creating ISA Server Reports

ISA Server can automatically generate graphical reports from information stored in the logs. You can schedule these reports, which display patterns in Internet usage and connectivity, to be generated once, daily, monthly, or on selected days of the week.

After this lesson, you will be able to

- Configure ISA Server to generate reports according to a specific schedule
- View reports in ISA Server to analyze patterns in Internet usage

Estimated lesson time: 45 minutes

Configuring Reports

You can use the reporting feature of ISA Server to create reports about the Internet usage patterns of your client users and computers. These reports are generated when you configure report jobs in the Monitoring Configuration node of ISA Management, as shown in Figure 9.12. Report jobs can create reports once or according to a specific schedule, and they summarize log information over any period of time you specify.

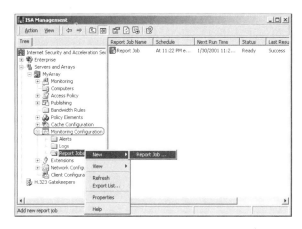

Figure 9.12 Creating a new report job

Viewing Reports

Each report job actually creates a set of five reports, each of which can be viewed in a separate folder in the Monitoring node of ISA Management, as shown in Figure 9.13. The five folders, named Summary, Web Usage, Application Usage, Traffic & Utilization, and Security, contain reports corresponding to each folder name. Each report is viewed as a Web page and itself contains a number of smaller reports.

Figure 9.13 Viewing report folders in the Monitoring node

Summary Reports

Summary reports include a set of reports that illustrate network traffic usage, sorted by application. These reports are most relevant to the network administrator or the person managing or planning a company's Internet connectivity.

The Summary reports combine data from the Web Proxy service and Firewall service logs. A sample report found in the Summary folder is shown in Figure 9.14.

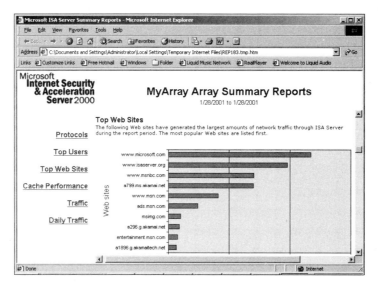

Figure 9.14 Sample summary report

Web Usage Reports

Web Usage reports include a set of reports that display top Web users, common responses, and browsers. These reports are most relevant to the network administrator or the person managing or planning a company's Internet connectivity. It shows how the Web is being used in a company.

Web Usage reports are based on the Web Proxy service logs.

Application Usage Reports

Application Usage reports illustrate Internet application usage in a company, including incoming and outgoing traffic, top users, client applications, and destinations. These reports can help determine network saturation and are therefore useful to network administrators managing or planning a company's Internet connectivity.

Application Usage reports are based on the Firewall service logs.

Traffic & Utilization Reports

Traffic & Utilization reports illustrate total Internet usage by application, protocol, and direction; average traffic and peak simultaneous connections; cache hit ratio; errors; and other statistics. These reports can help you plan and monitor network capacity.

Traffic & Utilization reports combine data from the Web Proxy and Firewall service logs.

Security Reports

Security reports list attempts to breach network security. Security reports can help identify attacks or security violations after such violations have occurred.

Security reports are based on the Web Proxy service, Firewall service, and Packet Filter logs.

▶ **Follow these steps to view a report:**

1. In the console tree of ISA Management, expand the Monitoring node, expand the Reports folder, and then click the applicable report type: Summary, Web Usage, Application Usage, Traffic & Utilization, or Security.

2. In the details pane, right-click the applicable report and then click Open.

▶ **Follow these steps to sort report data:**

1. In the console tree of ISA Management, expand the Monitoring node, expand the Reports folder, right-click a report type, and then click Properties.

2. Click a tab (if more than one tab is present) and then, in the Sort Order area, click the option that should be used to sort the data in the report.

Note The report will be sorted the next time you view it.

Configuring Report Jobs

The ISA Server reporting mechanism enables you to schedule reports based on the data collected from the log files. You can schedule reports to be generated on a recurring basis: daily, on specified days of the week, or monthly. The report can include daily, weekly, monthly, or yearly data; or it can include data collected over any specific period of time you define.

To configure report generation, create a report job. For each report job you create, you can specify a period of time over which the information in the logs will be collected, and the schedule by which a report based on that period will be generated.

▶ **Follow these steps to create a report job:**

1. In the console tree of ISA Management, expand the Monitoring Configuration node, right-click the Report Jobs folder, point to New, and then click Report Job.

2. On the General tab, in the Name text box, type the name of the report job.

3. (Optional) In the Description text box, type a description of the report job.

   On the Period, Schedule, and Credentials tabs, specify the following:

   - Period of activity that the report should cover
   - When and how often the report should be generated
   - User name of a user authorized to create the report

▶ **Follow these steps to configure the period for an existing report job:**

1. In the console tree of ISA Management, expand the Monitoring Configuration node and click the Report Jobs folder.

2. In the details pane, right-click the applicable report job, and then click Properties.

3. On the Period tab,

   - To generate reports that show the previous day's activity, click the Daily radio button.
   - To generate reports that show the previous week's activity, click the Weekly radio button.
   - To generate reports that show the previous month's activity, click the Monthly radio button.
   - To generate reports that show the previous year's activity, click the Yearly radio button.
   - To generate reports that show activity for a specified period, click the Custom radio button and then type the appropriate dates in the From and To text boxes.

▶ **Follow these steps to configure the schedule for an existing report job:**

1. In the console tree of ISA Management, expand the Monitoring Configuration node and click the Report Jobs folder.

2. In the details pane, right-click the applicable report job, and then click Properties.

3. On the Schedule tab,

    - To generate the report immediately, click the Immediately radio button.

    - To generate the report at the specified time, click the At radio button, and then type a date and a time.

4. In the Recurrence Pattern area,

    - To generate a report once, click the Generate Once radio button.

    - To generate reports every day, click the Generate Every Day radio button.

    - To generate reports on specific days, click the Generate On The Following Days radio button and select the appropriate check boxes.

    - To generate reports once a month, click the Generate Once A Month radio button and type the day of the month on which to generate the reports.

Report Job Credentials

For each report job you must configure, whether locally or remotely, a user name and password with appropriate credentials to generate the reports on every server in the array. To begin with, all members of the Domain Admins group can generate reports. In addition, users that meet the following criteria can generate reports:

- The user must have local administrator privileges on every ISA Server computer in the array.

- The user must be able to access and launch DCOM objects on every ISA Server in the array.

▶ **Follow these steps to specify user credentials for an existing report job:**

1. In the console tree of ISA Management, expand the Monitoring Configuration node and click the Report Jobs folder.

2. In the details pane, right-click the applicable report job, and then click Properties.

3. On the Credentials tab, in the Username text box, type the name of a user with permissions to generate the report.

4. In the Domain text box, type the user's domain.

5. In the Password text box, type the user's password.

Configuring Report Log Summaries

Reports are generated from a database that includes data collected from the ISA Server logs. This data is saved in daily and monthly summaries.

When you enable the summary process, the daily summary process runs every day at 12:30 A.M., regardless of whether you have scheduled reports. The process collates all the logs available on all the servers in the array.

The monthly summary process combines all the daily databases into a single monthly summary. If a daily summary is missing, the monthly summary process checks the logs to see if the information is available from the logs. If the information is not available, the monthly summary process generates an error.

Scheduled reports may be created even if daily and monthly summaries are disabled. If the daily and monthly processes are disabled, the report generator gets the data from the logs. However, the data in the report may not be complete and current since it will not include the latest log information.

▶ **Follow these steps to enable and configure the log summary:**

1. In the console tree of ISA Management, expand the Monitoring Configuration node, right-click the Report Jobs folder, and then click Properties.

2. On the Log Summaries tab, select the Enable Daily And Monthly Summaries check box.

3. In Number Of Summaries Saved area, in the Daily Summaries text box, type the number of daily summaries to save.

4. In the Monthly Summaries text box, type the number of monthly summaries to save.

> **Note** You may specify between 35 and 999 daily summaries and between 13 and 999 monthly summaries to save. These minimums ensure that enough summaries will be saved to generate monthly and yearly reports.

Report Database

The ISA Server reporting mechanism combines the summary logs from all the ISA Server computers in a given array into a database on each ISA server. When a report is created, all relevant summary databases are combined into a single report database. The new report database resides in the location specified when the report job was created, as shown in Figure 9.15. By default, that location is the ISAReports folder of the ISA installation folder. A typical path is %ProgramFiles%\Microsoft ISA Server\ISAReports.

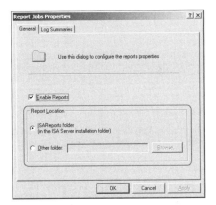

Figure 9.15 Configuring report database location

The reports can then be viewed on the ISA Server computer on which the report database is located. You cannot view the reports if you run ISA Management from another ISA Server computer in the same array.

▶ **Follow these steps to configure the location of reports:**

1. In the console tree of ISA Management, expand the Monitoring Configuration node, right-click the Report Jobs folder, and then click Properties.

2. On the General tab, confirm that the Enable Reports check box is selected.

3. Do one of the following:
   - To save the reports in the ISAReports subfolder of the ISA Server installation folder, click the ISAReports Folder (In The ISA Server Installation Folder) radio button.
   - To save the reports in another folder, click the Other Folder radio button, type a path or click the Browse button, and then select the folder in which to save the reports.

▶ **Follow these steps to configure the location of the daily summary database:**

1. In the console tree of ISA Management, expand the Monitoring Configuration node, right-click the Report Jobs folder, and then click Properties.
2. On the Log Summaries tab, select the Enable Daily And Monthly Summaries check box.
3. Do one of the following:
   - To save the reports in the ISASummaries subfolder on this computer, click the ISASummaries Folder (In The ISA Server Installation Folder) radio button.
   - To save the reports in another folder, click the Other Folder radio button, type a path or click the Browse button, and then select the folder in which to save the daily summaries.

Practice: Creating and Viewing Reports

In this practice, you configure a report job to create a report based on past network activity. You then review the reports generated by this report job.

Exercise 1: Creating a Report Job

In this exercise, you configure a report job to generate a set of reports based on the past month of network activity.

▶ **To create a report job**

1. Log on to Server1 as Administrator.
2. Open ISA Management, and then expand the Monitoring Configuration node.
3. Click the Report Jobs folder once.

4. Right-click the Report Jobs folder, point to New, and then click Report Job.

   The Report Job Properties dialog box appears.

5. On the General tab, in the Name text box, type **Last Month's Activity**.

6. Click the Period tab.

7. Select the Custom radio button.

   The From and To date boxes appear with the current date indicated.

8. Click the down arrow next to the From drop-down list box.

   A month window appears beneath the From drop-down list box, displaying the present month in calendar format.

9. Click the left arrow in the month window to move the calendar one month earlier.

   The month window now displays the previous month in calendar format. The day corresponding to one month before the present day of the month is highlighted with a blue oval.

10. Click the highlighted day.

    The From date box now displays the day one month before the present date.

11. Click the Schedule tab. Note that in the Start Report Generation area, the Immediately radio button is selected. Also note that in the Recurrence Pattern area, the Generate Once radio button is selected.

12. Click the Credentials tab.

13. In the User Name text box, type **Administrator**.

14. In the Domain text box, type **domain01**.

15. In the Password text box, type the password you have assigned to the domain01\Administrator account.

16. Click OK.

    You will see the Last Month's Activity report job listed in the details pane in ISA Management. Note that the current status is listed as Running.

17. Right-click the Report Jobs folder in ISA Management and click Refresh.

    Notice that the report job's status is now listed as Running.

18. After another minute, again right-click the Report Jobs folder in ISA Management and click Refresh. If the status of Last Month's Activity has changed to Ready, proceed to Exercise 2. Otherwise, wait another minute and repeat this step until the status changes to Ready.

Exercise 2: Viewing Reports

In this exercise, you view all five sets of reports generated by the report job that has just completed.

▶ **To view reports in ISA Server**

1. In ISA Management, expand the Monitoring node, and then expand the Reports folder.
2. Last Month's Activity report appears in the Details pane.
3. Click the Summary folder.
4. In the details pane, right-click the Last Month's Activity icon and click Open.

    ISA Server opens a Web page displaying the MyArray Array Summary reports.

5. Review the six Summary reports contained on the Web page by clicking each report link in the left frame of the page.
6. Close the Summary Reports Web page containing the Summary reports.
7. In ISA Management, select the Web Usage folder.
8. In the details panc, right-click the Last Month's Activity icon and click Open.

    ISA Server opens a Web page displaying the MyArray Array Web Usage reports.

9. Review the eight Web Usage reports contained on the Web page by clicking on each report link in the left frame of the page.
10. Close the Web Usage Reports Web page.
11. In ISA Management, select the Application Usage folder.
12. In the details pane, right-click the Last Month's Activity icon and click Open.

    ISA Server opens a Web page displaying the MyArray Array Applications Usage reports.

13. Review the five Applications Usage reports contained on the Web page by clicking on each report link in the left frame of the page.
14. Close the Applications Usage Reports Web page.
15. In ISA Management, select the Traffic & Utilization folder.

16. In the details pane, right-click the Last Month's Activity icon and click Open.

    ISA Server opens a Web page displaying the MyArray Array Traffic and Utilization reports.

17. Review the seven Traffic and Utilization reports contained on the Web page by clicking each report link in the left frame of the page.

18. Close the Traffic and Utilization Reports Web page.

19. In ISA Management, select the Security folder.

20. In the details pane, right-click the Last Month's Activity icon and click Open.

    ISA Server opens a Web page displaying the MyArray Array Security reports.

21. Review the two Security reports contained on the Web page by clicking on each report link in the left frame of the page.

22. Close the Security Reports Web page.

Lesson Summary

The ISA Server reporting mechanism enables you to create graphical summaries of Internet usage. These reports are based on data collected from the log files and are generated by report jobs you configure in the Monitoring Configuration node of ISA Management.

Every report job generates a set of five reports, each of which appears as a Web page. These reports can be viewed in five specific folders in the Monitoring node of ISA Management. These five folders are named Summary, Web Usage, Application Usage, Traffic & Utilization, and Security.

You can schedule reports to be generated once, daily, on specified days of the week, or monthly on a specified day. The report can include daily, weekly, monthly, or yearly data; or data collected over any specific period of time you define. For each report job you configure, you must specify a user name and password with credentials to generate reports on every server in the ISA Server array.

Reports are generated from a database of log summaries, which include data collected from the ISA Server logs. The ISA Server reporting mechanism combines the summary logs from all the ISA Server computers in a given array into a database on each ISA server. When a report is created, all relevant summary databases are combined into a single report database. You can only view reports on the ISA Server computer on which this report database is located.

Lesson 4 Controlling Bandwidth

As communication within your network and with the Internet becomes more congested, network performance may deteriorate. Once you determine the source of network congestion through ISA Server reports, you can allocate different priorities to traffic through the use of bandwidth priorities and bandwidth rules. Bandwidth priorities are policy elements that designate priority values between 1 and 200 for incoming and outgoing bandwidth. These bandwidth priorities can then be applied to specific connections through the use of bandwidth rules.

After this lesson, you will be able to

- Configure the effective bandwidth of a connection
- Create bandwidth priorities
- Create bandwidth rules

Estimated lesson time: 40 minutes

Determining Effective Bandwidth

Effective bandwidth is the actual data transfer rate available to your network clients through a particular Internet connection (for example, a dial-up connection or dedicated Internet connection). Before you create bandwidth rules, you need to specify the effective bandwidth of your Internet connection in ISA Management so that ISA Server can properly enforce bandwidth priorities.

Effective Bandwidth for Dial-up Connections

The first step in configuring effective bandwidth is to determine the maximum effective bandwidth of the connections on the ISA Server computer or array. For a modem, the bandwidth depends on the modem speed, compression, and other factors. When you configure a dial-up connection's properties to display its icon on the task bar when the connection is active, you can view the effective bandwidth by holding your mouse over that icon in the status area of the task bar.

You can specify the effective bandwidth for a dial-up connection by modifying the dial-up entry associated with that connection in ISA Management, as shown in Figure 9.16. To configure effective bandwidth for a dial-up entry in ISA Management, modify the settings on the Bandwidth tab of the dial-up entry's Properties dialog box.

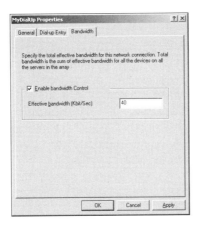

Figure 9.16 Configuring effective bandwidth for a dial-up connection

▶ **Follow these steps to set effective bandwidth for an existing dial-up entry:**

1. In the console tree of ISA Management, expand the node of the array containing the dial-up entry you want to modify, and then expand the Policy Elements node.

2. Click the Dial-up Entries folder.

3. In the details pane, right-click the applicable dial-up entry and then click Properties.

   The *Dial-up_entry_name* Properties dialog box appears.

4. On the Bandwidth tab, click the Enable Bandwidth Control check box.

5. In the Effective Bandwidth (Kbit/Sec) text box, type the effective bandwidth for all the devices in the array.

6. Click OK.

Effective Bandwidth for Dedicated Network Connections

For frame relay networks (E1/T1 or E3/T3), the maximum effective bandwidth is determined by your wide area network (WAN) provider. When you configure a dedicated network connection's properties to display its icon on the task bar when the connection is active, you can view the effective bandwidth by holding your mouse over that icon in the task bar status area.

You can configure effective bandwidth for a dedicated network connection by modifying bandwidth rules properties in ISA Management, as shown in Figure 9.17.

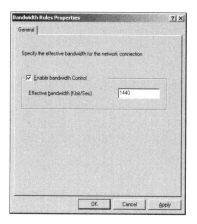

Figure 9.17 Configuring effective bandwidth for a dedicated connection

▶ **Follow these steps to set effective bandwidth for a network card:**

1. In the console tree of ISA Management, right-click the Bandwidth Rules folder and click Properties.

    The Bandwidth Rules Properties dialog box appears.

2. On the General tab, click the Enable Bandwidth Control check box.

3. In the Effective Bandwidth (Kbit/Sec) text box, type the effective bandwidth for the network connection.

4. Click OK.

After you have determined the maximum bandwidth, study reports generated for peak-hour activity. Analyze how much bandwidth is actually allocated for all the requests, on both the internal card and the external card.

Configure the effective bandwidth to the lowest maximum bandwidth available for the devices on the ISA Server computer. For example, if a device used for internal communication has 100 KB effective bandwidth and the external device has 56 KB, you should configure the effective bandwidth at 56 KB.

Calculate bandwidth requirements for internal communication by considering the following types of internal communication:

- Communication between computers on the local network
- Cached content returned from the ISA Server computer to a computer on the local network
- Communication between array members, unless you have an additional card configured for intra-array communication

Bandwidth rules are not applied when ISA Server returns cached content to an internal computer or to intra-array communication.

Configuring Bandwidth Priorities

Bandwidth priorities are policy elements that define the priority level applied to connections passing through the ISA Server computer. These policy elements are then assigned to bandwidth rules to prioritize specific connections or traffic types. Network connections without an assigned bandwidth priority have lower priority than connections with assigned priorities, and network connections with lower priorities have less of a chance to pass through ISA Server than a connection with a higher bandwidth priority.

Bandwidth priorities are specified according to the following directions:

- **Outbound bandwidth.** This is the bandwidth priority allocated for requests from internal clients for objects on the Internet.
- **Inbound bandwidth.** This is the bandwidth priority allocated for requests from external clients for objects on the local network.

The bandwidth priority can be assigned any number between 1 and 200.

ISA Server includes a built-in bandwidth priority named Default Bandwidth Priority. The Default Bandwidth Priority assigns a value of 100 to both outbound and inbound bandwidth.

You use a bandwidth priority when you create and configure bandwidth rules, which determine how much scheduling priority is allocated for specific network connections. For example, you can create a bandwidth priority called Best Access with outbound and inbound bandwidth priority set to 150. You can also create a bandwidth priority called Good Access, with outbound and inbound bandwidth set to 80. You can later use these bandwidth priorities when you configure bandwidth rules.

New bandwidth priorities are created in ISA Management by right-clicking the Bandwidth Priorities folder, pointing to New, and then clicking Bandwidth Priority, as shown in Figure 9.18. This procedure opens the New Bandwidth Priority dialog box, as shown in Figure 9.19.

Note When the new bandwidth priorities you create are applied to a connection, more processing is required than when the default bandwidth priority is applied.

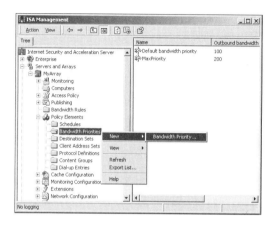

Figure 9.18 Creating a new bandwidth priority

Figure 9.19 The New Bandwidth Priority dialog box

▶ **Follow these steps to create a bandwidth priority:**

1. In the console tree of ISA Management, expand the node corresponding to the array for which you want to create a bandwidth priority, and then expand the Policy Elements node.

2. Right-click the Bandwidth Priorities folder, point to New, and then click Bandwidth Priority.

   The New Bandwidth Priority dialog box appears.

3. In the Name text box, type the name of the bandwidth priority.

4. In the Description (Optional) text box, type a description for the bandwidth priority.

5. In the Outbound Bandwidth (1-200) text box, type a number between 1 and 200.

6. In the Inbound Bandwidth (1-200) text box, type a number between 1 and 200.

7. Click OK.

Configuring Bandwidth Rules

Bandwidth rules apply predefined bandwidth priorities to traffic passing through ISA Server. When you create a bandwidth rule, you can specify a traffic type by any combination of the following parameters:

- Protocol definition
- Requesting user or source IP addresses
- Request destination
- Schedule
- Content type

The default bandwidth rule applies the default bandwidth priority (100) to all inbound and outbound traffic. As a result, all traffic passing through ISA Server is assigned a priority of 100 unless otherwise specified.

To create a new bandwidth rule, launch the New Bandwidth Rule wizard in ISA Management by right-clicking the Bandwidth Rules folder, pointing to New, and then clicking Rule, as shown in Figure 9.20.

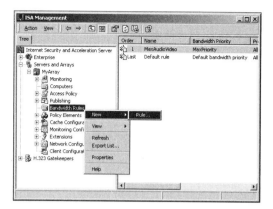

Figure 9.20 Creating a new bandwidth rule

▶ **Follow these steps to create a bandwidth rule:**

1. In the console tree of ISA Management, right-click the Bandwidth Rules folder, point to New, and then click Rule.

    The New Bandwidth Rule wizard opens.

2. In the New Bandwidth Rule wizard, follow the on-screen instructions.

Note Before you use the New Bandwidth Rule wizard to create a rule, be sure to create policy elements for the new rule. Depending on how you configure the rule, you may require the following policy elements: protocol definitions, schedules, client address sets, destination sets, content groups, and bandwidth priorities.

▶ **Follow these steps to configure bandwidth priority for an existing bandwidth rule:**

1. In the console tree of ISA Management, click the Bandwidth Rules folder.

2. In the details pane, right-click the applicable bandwidth rule, and then click Properties.

    The *Bandwidth_rule_name* Properties dialog box appears.

3. On the Bandwidth tab,
   - To use the Windows 2000 default scheduling, click the Default Scheduling Priority radio button.
   - To specify a priority, click the Specified Priority radio button and then in the Name drop-down list box, select a bandwidth priority to apply to the rule and type an outbound bandwidth and inbound bandwidth.

You can set the bandwidth priority either to the default scheduling priority or to a bandwidth priority you have configured. If you select the default setting, the specified communication is guaranteed a minimum network bandwidth.

Note that connections that have specific bandwidth priorities will require some additional overhead while establishing the connection.

Rule Order

Like routing rules, bandwidth rules are ordered. Each rule is assigned a specific number, with the default bandwidth rule always processed last. You can change the order of all bandwidth rules other than the default bandwidth rule.

For each bandwidth rule, ISA Server compares the parameters defined in the rule to the details of the connection. The rule numbered 1 is processed first. If the connection matches the conditions specified by the rule, the bandwidth priority of that rule is applied to the request. Otherwise, the next rule is processed. This continues until the last default rule is processed and applied to the request. For example, if the first bandwidth rule applies to UserX and has assigned an inbound and outbound bandwidth priority of 150, and the second bandwidth rule applies to all audio content and has an inbound and outbound bandwidth priority of 200, a connection in which UserX sends audio content is assigned a bandwidth priority of 150 by ISA Server. The first bandwidth rule is applied because it is the first to match the connection.

▶ **Follow these steps to change the order of a bandwidth rule:**

1. In the console tree of ISA Management, click the Bandwidth Rule folder.
2. In the details pane, right-click the rule whose order you want to change, and then click Move Up or Move Down.

   Move Up and Move Down are available only after there are at least three bandwidth rules listed.

3. Repeat as necessary to arrange the rules in the desired order.

Default Bandwidth Rule

When you install ISA Server, it configures a default bandwidth rule. The default rule assures that communication without an assigned bandwidth rule will be allocated the default scheduling priority assured by the Windows 2000 quality of service (QoS) packet scheduling service.

The default bandwidth rule is always last in the ordered list. It cannot be modified or deleted.

Practice: Creating a Bandwidth Rule

In this practice, you create a bandwidth priority and then use this policy element in a new bandwidth rule.

Exercise 1: Creating a New Bandwidth Priority Policy Element

In this exercise, you create a new bandwidth priority that assigns a maximum value of 200 to both incoming and outgoing traffic.

▶ **To create a new bandwidth priority**

1. Log on to Server1 as Administrator.
2. In ISA Management, expand the MyArray node, and then expand the Policy Elements node.
3. Right-click the Bandwidth Priorities folder, point to New, and then click Bandwidth Priority.

   The New Bandwidth Priority dialog box appears.
4. In the Name text box, type **MaxPriority**.
5. In the Outbound Bandwidth (1-200) text box, type **200**.
6. In the Inbound Bandwidth (1-200) text box, type **200**.
7. Click OK.

Exercise 2: Creating a New Bandwidth Rule

In this exercise, you apply the new policy element MaxPriority to all audio and video content.

▶ **To create a new bandwidth rule**

1. While you are still logged on to Server1 as Administrator and ISA Management is open, right-click the Bandwidth Rules folder in the console tree, point to New, and then click Rule.

    The New Bandwidth Rule wizard appears.

2. In the Bandwidth Rule Name text box, type **MaxAudioVideo**.
3. Click Next.

    The Protocols screen appears.

4. Leave All IP Traffic selected as the default, and then click Next.

    The Schedule screen appears.

5. Leave Always as the default, and then click Next.

    The Client Type screen appears.

6. Leave Any Request selected as the default, and then click Next.

    The Destination Sets screen appears.

7. Leave All Destinations selected as the default, and then click Next.

    The Content Groups screen appears.

8. Click the Selected Content Groups radio button.
9. In the list box, select the Audio check box, and then select the Video check box.
10. Click Next.

    The Bandwidth Priority screen appears.

11. Click the Custom radio button.
12. In the Name drop-down list box, select MaxPriority.
13. Click Next.

    The Completing the New Bandwidth Rule Wizard screen appears.

14. Click Finish.

You can now view the MaxAudioVideo bandwidth rule in the details pane by selecting the Bandwidth Rules folder in the console tree of ISA Management.

Lesson Summary

ISA Server allows you to allocate more bandwidth to specific types of network traffic through bandwidth priorities and bandwidth rules.

Bandwidth priorities are policy elements that are assigned a value between 1 and 200 for incoming and outgoing bandwidth, with higher values representing higher priorities. Bandwidth priorities are based upon the effective bandwidth of a network connection, a figure which you must specify manually in ISA Server. Bandwidth priorities themselves are configured in ISA Management through the Policy Elements node. ISA Server includes a default bandwidth priority policy element named Default Bandwidth Priority, which assigns a value of 100 to both incoming and outgoing bandwidth.

Bandwidth rules, which are configured through the Bandwidth Rules folder in ISA Management, apply these bandwidth priorities to connection types. Connection types may be specified by associated protocol, schedule, client source, request destination, and/or content type. Bandwidth rules are ordered like routing rules, with the default rule (which assigns the default bandwidth priority to all network traffic) always processed last.

Lesson 5 Additional Tuning and Monitoring Tools

ISA Server includes additional tools that you may use to optimize and monitor ISA Server performance. For example, you can tune performance in ISA Server by adjusting the server's configuration to the number of expected daily connections, and you can tune performance of the cache by adjusting the amount of physical RAM used for storing Web content.

In addition to the alerting, logging, and reporting features available in ISA Management, ISA Server includes many performance counters that can be used to gather performance-related data. These data can be viewed in the Windows 2000 Performance console or in ISA Server's built-in console, ISA Server Performance Monitor.

After this lesson, you will be able to

- Tune ISA Server performance by adjusting to the number of expected daily connections
- Tune ISA Server cache performance by adjusting the amount of RAM used for caching.
- Describe the features and advantages of ISA Server Performance Monitor
- Use ISA Server performance counters to monitor server performance

Estimated lesson time: 50 minutes

Tuning ISA Server Performance

You can tune ISA Server performance settings by adjusting to the number of daily connections you anticipate for your site. ISA Server tunes performance for all of the servers in the array, depending on your settings. Figure 9.21 shows the Performance tab of the array's Properties dialog box, on which you can adjust these settings.

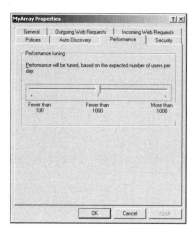

Figure 9.21 Tuning ISA Server performance

▶ **Follow these steps to tune performance for an array:**

1. In the console tree of ISA Management, right-click the appropriate array, and then click Properties.

    The *Array_name* Properties dialog box appears.

2. On the Performance tab,

    - If you expect fewer than 100 users per day, move the slider to Fewer Than 100.

    - If you expect fewer than 1,000 users per day, move the slider to Fewer Than 1000.

    - If you expect more than 1,000 users per day, move the slider to More Than 1000.

Tuning Cache Performance

When storing Web content in the cache, ISA Server uses a percentage of available RAM for cache space. By adjusting this percentage, you can tune the performance of the cache. Designating a higher percentage improves cache response time by allocating more Web content to be stored in faster physical memory than on disk. However, if you set this percentage too high, performance decreases because you decrease the memory available for other tasks performed by ISA Server, by other applications, and by the operating system.

You can adjust the amount of space available for RAM caching on the Advanced tab of the Cache Configuration Properties dialog box, as shown in Figure 9.22.

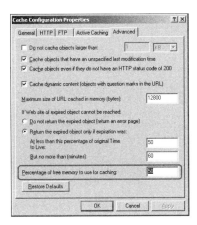

Figure 9.22 Configuring RAM caching

▶ **Follow these steps to configure percentage of available memory to use for caching:**

1. In the console tree of ISA Management, right-click the Cache Configuration node and then click Properties.

   The Cache Configuration Properties dialog box appears.

2. On the Advanced tab, in the Percentage Of Free Memory To Use For Caching text box, type a number between 1 and 100 that specifies the maximum percentage of available memory that should be allocated for caching.

ISA Server Performance Objects and Counters

Data gathered through performance counters are an important resource for analyzing server function. Using this information, you can measure your server workload and its corresponding impact on resources; track trends and changes in performance, allowing you to tune configurations and plan future changes; test configuration changes and track the effects of these changes; and generally diagnose any problems in performance that might arise.

When you install ISA Server, seven additional performance objects are installed for monitoring in the Windows 2000 Performance console:

- ISA Server Firewall Service object
- ISA Server Cache object
- ISA Server Web Proxy Service object
- ISA Server Packet Filter object
- ISA Server Bandwidth Control object
- H.323 Filter object
- SOCKS Filter object

Each of these performance objects contains several counters that you can use to monitor ISA Server, either in real time by using the System Monitor node, or through counter logs, trace logs, and alerts by using the Performance Logs and Alerts node.

ISA Server Performance Monitor

ISA Server includes a preconfigured Windows 2000 Performance console, called ISA Server Performance Monitor. You can access ISA Server Performance Monitor from the Start menu, as shown in Figure 9.23.

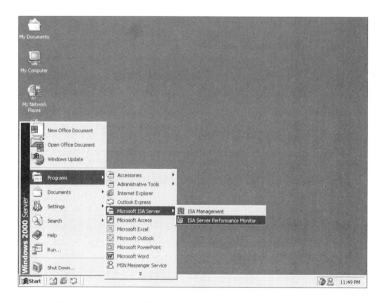

Figure 9.23 Accessing ISA Server Performance Monitor

The ISA Server Performance Monitor contains the System Monitor node and a Performance Logs and Alerts node. This pre-configured performance monitor specifically monitors ISA Server performance characteristics. It contains 21 ISA Server performance counters preloaded for real-time monitoring in the System Monitor node. These counters belong to the ISA Server Cache (of which there are 6 counters), ISA Server Firewall service (8 counters), ISA Server Packet Filter (1 counter), and ISA Server Web Proxy service performance objects (6 counters). These preloaded counters are shown in histogram view in Figure 9.24.

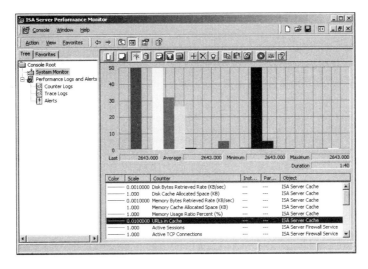

Figure 9.24 Real-time monitoring with System Monitor

Using ISA Server Performance Monitor, you can view performance data in a report or in various graph and log formats. Reports display data gathered from counters textually; graphs display the data visually. A performance log can be useful in monitoring counters over an extended period of time. In addition, performance alerts can be configured to create an event when any counter you select reaches a designated value. Such events may include a log entry, sending a network message, or running a program. For more information about the functions and features available in Windows 2000 performance monitoring, consult Windows 2000 Server Help.

Note The performance monitoring capability is not available in a remote administration installation.

Performance Objects and Counters Included in ISA Server

The following section provides an overview of ISA Server's seven performance objects and their respective performance counters. It also reveals which counters are preloaded into the System Monitor snap-in of ISA Server Performance Monitor.

Table 9.8 describes the counters available for the ISA Server Bandwidth Control performance object.

Table 9.8   ISA Server Bandwidth Control Performance Object Counters

Performance counter	Preloaded in System Monitor?	Description
Actual Inbound Bandwidth	No	Measures the actual inbound bandwidth.
Actual Outbound Bandwidth	No	Measures the actual outbound bandwidth.
Assigned Connections	No	Tracks the number of connections with an assigned bandwidth priority. Connections with assigned bandwidth priorities have higher precedence than those without assigned priorities.
Assigned Inbound Bandwidth	No	Tracks the assigned inbound bandwidth
Assigned Outbound Bandwidth	No	Tracks the assigned outbound bandwidth.

Table 9.9 describes the counters available for the ISA Server Cache performance object.

Table 9.9 ISA Server Cache Performance Object Counters

Performance counter	Preloaded in System Monitor?	Description
Active Refresh Bytes Rate (KB/Sec)	No	Measures the rate at which bytes of data are retrieved from the Internet to actively refresh popular URLs in the cache. This relates to the configuration set for active caching.
Active URL Refresh Rate (URL/Sec)	No	Measures the rate at which popular cached URLs are actively refreshed from the Internet. This relates to the configuration set for active caching.
Disk Bytes Retrieved Rate (KB/sec)	Yes	Measures that rate at which "bytes of data" are retrieved from the disk cache. This counter is similar to Disk URL Retrieve Rate but monitors bytes rather than URLs.
Disk Cache Allocated Space (KB)	Yes	Measures how much space is being used by the disk cache. It will be equal to or less than the amount configured for the disk cache.
Disk Content Write Rate (Writes/Sec)	No	Measures the number of writes per second to the disk cache for the purpose of writing URL content to the cache disk.
Disk Failure Rate (Fail/Sec)	No	Measures the number of input/output (I/O) failures per second. An I/O failure occurs when ISA Server fails to read from or write to the disk cache. This counter, together with Total Disk Failures, provides a clear indication of disk cache problems.

(continues)

Table 9.9 ISA Server Cache Performance Object Counters *(continued)*

Performance counter	Preloaded in System Monitor?	Description
Disk URL Retrieve Rate (URL/Sec)	No	Measures how many URLs are sent to clients from the disk cache in one second. This is a useful counter to measure at peak and offpeak times to check how the disk cache is performing. It can be compared with Memory URL Retrieve Rate to see how cache disk and memory are being utilized.
Max URLs Cached	No	Measures the maximum number of URLs that have been stored in the cache.
Memory Bytes Retrieved Rate (KB/Sec)	Yes	Measures the rate at which bytes of data are retrieved from the memory cache. This counter is similar to Memory URL Retrieve Rate but monitors bytes rather than URLs.
Memory Cache Allocated Space (KB)	Yes	Measures how much space is being used by the memory cache. It should be equal to or less than the amount configured for the memory cache.
Memory URL Retrieve Rate (URL/Sec)	No	Measures how many URLs are sent to clients from the memory cache in one second. This is a useful counter to measure at peak and offpeak times, to check how the memory cache is performing and whether available memory allocated for caching purposes is being used efficiently.
Memory Usage Ratio Percent (%)	Yes	Shows the ratio between the amount of cache fetches from the memory cache in a percentage and the amount of cache fetches in total. A high percentage may indicate that it is worthwhile allocating more available memory resources to the cache. A low counter may indicate that memory resources may be better used elsewhere.

Performance counter	Preloaded in System Monitor?	Description
Total Actively Refreshed URLs	No	Displays the cumulative number of popular URLs in the cache that have been actively refreshed from the Internet. This counter provides an indication of active caching performance.
Total Bytes Actively Refreshed (KB)	No	Displays the total number of bytes that have been retrieved from the Internet to actively refresh popular URLs in the cache. This counter provides an indication of active caching performance.
Total Disk Bytes Retrieved (KB)	No	Measures the cumulative number of disk bytes that have been retrieved from the disk cache. This counter, added to Total Memory Bytes Retrieved (KB), indicates the total number of bytes retrieved from the cache.
Total Disk Failures	No	Measures the number of times that the Web Proxy service failed to read from or write to the disk cache due to an I/O failure. A low counter indicates that a disk is performing properly. A high counter indicates a cache disk that is too small, too slow, or corrupted.
Total Disk URLs Retrieved	No	Measures the cumulative number of URLs that have been retrieved from the disk cache. This counter, added to Total Memory URLs Retrieved, indicates the total number of URLs retrieved from the cache.
Total Memory Bytes Retrieved (KB)	No	Measures the cumulative number of memory bytes that have been retrieved from the memory cache in response to client requests to the cache. A low number might indicate that memory resources dedicated to the cache are not being used efficiently. A high number might indicate that more memory resources should be allocated to the cache.

(continues)

Table 9.9 ISA Server Cache Performance Object Counters *(continued)*

Performance counter	Preloaded in System Monitor?	Description
Total Memory URLs Retrieved	No	Measures the cumulative number of URLs that have been retrieved from the memory cache in response to client requests to the cache. A low number might indicate that memory resources dedicated to the cache are not being used efficiently. A high number might indicate that more memory resources should be allocated to the cache.
Total URLs Cached	No	Measures the cumulative number of URLs that have been stored in the cache. If this counter and URLs in Cache is low, it may indicate a problem with the cache. The cache may not be configured for optimal use or the cache size may be too small.
URL Commit Rate (URL/Sec)	No	Indicates the speed at which URLs are being written to the cache. If rate of this counter is comparable to the rate of Disk Failure Rate(Fail/Sec), it indicates that a high proportion of attempts to write to the cache are failing. This could indicate a problem with cache configuration, a cache disk that is too slow, or a cache size that is too small.
URLs in Cache	Yes	Measures the current number of URLs in the cache.

Table 9.10 describes the counters available for the ISA Server Firewall Service performance object.

Table 9.10 ISA Server Firewall Service Performance Object Counters

Counter	Preloaded in System Monitor?	Description
Accepting TCP Connections	No	Number of connection objects that wait for a TCP connection from Firewall clients.
Active Sessions	Yes	The number of active sessions for the Firewall service.
Active TCP Connections	Yes	The total number of active TCP connections currently passing data. Connections pending or not yet established are counted elsewhere.
Active UDP Connections	Yes	Total number of active UDP connections.
Available Worker Threads	Yes	The number of Firewall worker threads that are available or waiting in the completion port queue.
Back-connecting TCP Connections	No	Total number of TCP connections awaiting an inbound connect call to complete. These are connections placed by the Firewall service to a client after the Firewall service accepts a connection from the Internet on a listening socket.
Bytes Read/sec	Yes	Number of bytes read by the data-pump per second.
Bytes Written/sec	No	Number of bytes written by the data-pump per second.
Connecting TCP Connections	No	Total number of TCP connections pending. These are connections awaiting completion between the Firewall service and remote computers.
DNS Cache Entries	No	The current number of DNS domain name entries cached as a result of Firewall service activity.
DNS Cache Flushes	No	The total number of times that the DNS domain name cache has been flushed or cleared by the Firewall service.

(continues)

Table 9.10 ISA Server Firewall Service Performance Object Counters *(continued)*

Counter	Preloaded in System Monitor?	Description
DNS Cache Hits	No	The total number of times a DNS domain name was found within the DNS cache by the Firewall service.
DNS Cache Hits %	No	The percentage of DNS domain names serviced by the DNS cache, from the total of all DNS entries that have been retrieved by the Firewall service.
DNS Retrievals	No	The total number of DNS domain names that have been retrieved by the Firewall service.
Failed DNS Resolutions	No	Number of gethostbyname and gethostbyaddr application programming interface (API) calls that have failed. These are calls used to resolve host DNS domain names and IP addresses for Firewall service connections.
Kernel Mode Data Pumps	Yes	The number of Kernel mode data pumps created by the Firewall service.
Listening TCP Connections	No	Number of connection objects that wait for TCP connections from remote Internet computers.
Non-connected UDP mappings	No	The number of mappings available for UDP connections.
Pending DNS Resolutions	No	Number of gethostbyname and gethostbyaddr API calls pending resolution. These are calls used to resolve host DNS domain names and IP addresses for Firewall service connections.
SecureNAT Mappings	Yes	The number of mappings created by SecureNAT.
Successful DNS Resolutions	No	Number of gethostbyname and gethostbyaddr API calls successfully returned. These are calls used to resolve host DNS domain names and IP addresses for Firewall service connections.

Counter	Preloaded in System Monitor?	Description
TCP Bytes Transferred/sec by Kernel Mode Data Pump	No	The number of TCP bytes transferred by the Kernel mode data-pump per second.
UDP Bytes Transferred/sec by Kernel mode Data Pump	No	The number of UDP bytes transferred by the Kernel mode data-pump per second.
Worker Threads	Yes	The number of Firewall worker threads that are currently active.

Table 9.11 describes the counters available for the ISA Server Packet Filter performance object.

Table 9.11 ISA Server Packet Filter Performance Object Counters

Counter	Preloaded in System Monitor?	Description
Packets Dropped Due to Filter Denial	No	This counter tracks the total number of packets dropped because dynamic packet filtering rejected the data. Dropped packets counted here are any packets which are not covered by Packets Dropped Due to Protocol Violations. In other words, this counter represents packets dropped because of the default "deny-all" policy in ISA Server. The only exceptions are where exception filters have been set, explicitly allowing these packets through.
Packets Dropped Due to Protocol Violations	No	This counter represents the total number of packets dropped as a result of a protocol anomaly. These are packets dropped due to reasons other than the default filtering rules. For example, if you have chosen to implement packet filtering of IP fragments, or you have enabled intrusion detection, packets dropped because of these configuration choices will increment this counter.

(continues)

Table 9.11 ISA Server Packet Filter Performance Object Counters *(continued)*

Counter	Preloaded in System Monitor?	Description
Total Dropped Packets	Yes	This counter represents the total number of dropped or filtered packets, regardless of why they have been dropped or filtered.
Total incoming connections	No	The total number of connections made through the filtered interfaces.
Total Lost Logging Packets	No	The total number of dropped packets that cannot be logged.

Table 9.12 describes the counters available for the ISA Server Web Proxy Service performance object.

Table 9.12 ISA Server Web Proxy Service Performance Object Counters

Counter	Preloaded in System Monitor?	Description
Array Bytes Received/Sec (Enterprise)	No	Tracks the rate at which data bytes are received from other ISA Server computers within the same array.
Array Bytes Sent/Sec (Enterprise)	No	Tracks the rate at which data bytes are sent to other ISA Server computers within the same array.
Array Bytes Total/Sec (Enterprise)	No	Represents the sum of Array Bytes Sent/Sec and Array Bytes Received/Sec. This is the total rate for all data bytes transferred between the ISA Server computer and other members of the same array.

Counter	Preloaded in System Monitor?	Description
Cache Hit Ratio %	Yes	Determines how many Web Proxy client requests have been served using cached data (Total Cache Fetches), as a percentage of the total number of successful Web Proxy client requests to the ISA Server computer (Total Successful Requests). Its value gives a good indication of the effectiveness of the cache. A high counter indicates that a high level of requests are being serviced from the cache, meaning faster response times. A zero counter indicates that caching is not enabled. A low counter may indicate a configuration problem. The cache size may be too small, or requests may not be cacheable.
Cache Running Hit Ratio (%)	Yes	Measures the amount of requests served from the cache as a percentage of total successful requests serviced. This ratio is the same as that measured by Cache Hit Ratio (%). The difference between these two counters is that Cache Running Hit Ratio measures this ratio for the last 10,000 requests serviced, and Cache Hit Ratio measures this ratio since the last time that the Web Proxy service was started. This means that Cache Running Hit Ratio gives a more dynamic evaluation of cache effectiveness.
Client Bytes Received/sec	No	Indicates the rate at which data bytes are received from Web Proxy clients. The value will change according to the volume of Web Proxy client requests, but a consistently slow rate may indicate a delay in servicing requests.

(continues)

Table 9.12 ISA Server Web Proxy Service Performance Object Counters *(continued)*

Counter	Preloaded in System Monitor?	Description
Client Bytes Sent/Sec	No	Measures the rate at which data bytes are sent to Web Proxy clients. The value will change according to the volume of Web Proxy client requests, but a consistently slow rate may indicate a delay in servicing requests.
Client Bytes Total/Sec	Yes	Represents the sum of Client Bytes Sent/Sec and Client Bytes Received/Sec. This is the total rate for all bytes transferred between the ISA Server computer and Web Proxy clients.
Current Array Fetches Average (Milliseconds/ Request)	No	Gives the mean number of milliseconds required to service a Web Proxy client request that is fetched through another array member. This does not include requests for services by the Secure Sockets Layer (SSL) tunnel.
Current Average (Milliseconds/ Request)	Yes	Represents the mean number of milliseconds required to service a Web Proxy client request, not including requests serviced by the SSL tunnel. This counter can be monitored at peak and off-peak times to get a comprehensive picture of how fast client requests are being serviced. A counter that is too high might indicate that the ISA Server is having difficulty in handling all requests and that requests are being delayed.
Current Cache Fetches Average (Milliseconds/ Request)	No	The mean number of milliseconds required to service a Web Proxy client request from cache. This does not include requests for services by the SSL tunnel.
Current Direct Fetches Average (Milliseconds/ Request)	No	The mean number of milliseconds required to service a Web Proxy client request directly to the Web server or upstream proxy. This does not include requests for services by the SSL tunnel.

Counter	Preloaded in System Monitor?	Description
Current Users	Yes	Indicates how many clients are currently running the Web Proxy service. Monitoring this counter at both peak and off-peak times provides a good indication of server usage. The configuration setting for maximum Web request connections influences this value. This counter may also be useful if you need to temporarily stop ISA Server services.
DNS Cache Entries	No	Details the current number of DNS domain name entries cached by the Web Proxy service. A high counter suggests a beneficial impact on performance, since a DNS cache entry eliminates the need for a DNS lookup, saving system resources.
DNS Cache Flushes	No	Details the total number of times that the DNS domain name cache has been flushed or cleared by the Web Proxy service. When there is no room left for more data in the DNS cache, the DNS cache is flushed to allow new entries to be made.
DNS Cache Hits	No	Tracks the total number of times a DNS domain name was found within the DNS cache by the Web Proxy service. This counter can be compared with previous DNS counters to find out if DNS caching is working efficiently. A low number of DNS cache hits impacts performance, as every DNS lookup slows performance down, particularly if a problem arises in the lookup process.

(continues)

Table 9.12 ISA Server Web Proxy Service Performance Object Counters *(continued)*

Counter	Preloaded in System Monitor?	Description
DNS Cache Hits %	No	Determines how many DNS entries have been resolved using cached data (DNS cache hits), as a percentage of the total number of DNS domain names retrieved by the Web Proxy service (DNS retrievals). A high counter means better performance as the DNS data is served from the cache, rather than incurring the overhead of resolving DNS lookups.
DNS Retrievals	No	Represents the total number of DNS domain names that have been retrieved by the Web Proxy service.
Failing Requests/Sec	No	Monitors the rate per second that Web Proxy client requests that have completed with some type of error. This counter can be compared with Requests/Sec to give an indication of how well ISA Server is servicing incoming Web requests. A high failure rate, in comparison to the rate of incoming requests, suggests that ISA Server is having difficulty in coping with all incoming requests. Connection settings for incoming Web requests may be incorrectly configured, or connection bandwidth may be insufficient.
FTP Requests	No	Tracks the number of FTP requests that have been made to the Web Proxy service. A consistently low counter may influence the caching policy for FTP objects.
Gopher Requests	No	Tracks the number of Gopher requests that have been made to the Web Proxy service.
HTTP Requests	No	Tracks the number of HTTP requests that have been made to the Web Proxy service.

Counter	Preloaded in System Monitor?	Description
HTTPS Sessions	No	Represents the total number of HTTPS secured sessions serviced by the SSL tunnel.
Maximum Users	No	Tracks the maximum number of users that have connected to the Web Proxy service simultaneously. This counter can be useful for determining load usage and license requirements.
Requests/Sec	Yes	Monitors the rate of incoming requests that have been made to the Web Proxy service. A higher value means that more ISA Server resources will be required to service incoming requests.
Reverse Bytes Received/sec	No	Monitors the rate at which data bytes are received by the Web Proxy service from Web publishing servers in response to incoming requests. This rate can be monitored at peak and off-peak times as an indication of how ISA Server is performing in servicing incoming Web requests.
Reverse Bytes Sent/sec	No	Monitors the rate at which data bytes are sent by the Web Proxy service to Web publishing servers in response to incoming requests. This rate can be monitored at peak and off-peak times as an indication of how ISA Server is performing in servicing incoming Web requests.
Reverse Bytes Total/sec	No	Represents the total sum of Reverse Bytes Sent/Sec and Reverse Bytes Received/Sec. This is the total rate for all bytes transferred between the Web Proxy service and Web publishing servers in response to incoming requests.

(continues)

Table 9.12 ISA Server Web Proxy Service Performance Object Counters *(continued)*

Counter	Preloaded in System Monitor?	Description
Site Access Denied	No	Tracks the total number of Internet sites to which the Web Proxy service has denied access. An excessively high number might indicate an access policy that is too restrictive.
Site Access Granted	No	Tracks the total number of Internet sites to which the Web Proxy service has granted access. This can be compared with Site Access Denied to give a numeric summary of the results of access policy configuration.
SNEWS Sessions	No	Represents the total number of SNEWS sessions serviced by the SSL tunnel.
SSL Client Bytes Received/Sec	No	Measures the rate at which SSL data bytes are received by the Web Proxy service from secured Web Proxy clients. Similar to Client Bytes Recieved/Sec, but counts only SSL requests.
SSL Client Bytes Sent/Sec	No	Measures the rate at which SSL data bytes are sent by the Web Proxy service to secured Web Proxy clients. Similar to Client Bytes "Sent"/Sec, but counts only SSL requests.
SSL Client Bytes Total/Sec	No	Represents the sum of SSL Client Bytes Sent/Sec and SSL Client Bytes Received/Sec. This is the total rate for all bytes transferred between the Web Proxy service and SSL clients.
Thread Pool Active Sessions	No	Represents the number of sessions being actively serviced by thread pool threads.
Thread Pool Failures	No	Represents the number of requests rejected because the thread pool was full.
Thread Pool Size	No	Represents the number of threads in the thread pool. This thread pool represents the resources available to service client requests.

Counter	Preloaded in System Monitor?	Description
Total Array Fetches (Enterprise)	No	Totals the number of Web Proxy client requests that have been served by requesting the data from another ISA Server within this array. These requests are the result of the Cache Array Routing Protocol (CARP) algorithm, which randomly stores objects in any one of the member servers cache. This counter is influenced by the cache size for each ISA Server in the array, since a server with a larger cache holds more cache items. The load factor for each server can also be configured, to determine how workload is divided amongst array members.
Total Cache Fetches	No	Monitors the total number of Web Proxy client requests that have been served by using cached data. A high number indicates a cache being fully exploited.
Total Failed Requests	No	Represents the total number of requests that have failed to be processed by the Web Proxy service due to errors. Errors can be the result of the Web Proxy service failing to locate a requested server URL on the Internet or because the client did not have authorized access to the requested URL. This counter should be far lower than Total Successful Requests. If it is not, it is an indication that ISA Server is failing to service requests effectively. This could be a configuration problem, or a connection that is too slow. It could also indicate an access policy that is too restrictive.
Total Pending Connects	No	The total number of pending connections to the Web Proxy service.

(continues)

Table 9.12 ISA Server Web Proxy Service Performance Object Counters *(continued)*

Counter	Preloaded in System Monitor?	Description
Total Requests	No	Represents the total number of requests that have been made to the Web Proxy service. It is the total of two other counters, Total Successful Requests and Total Failed Requests.
Total Reverse Fetches	No	Represents the total number of incoming requests that have been served by requesting the data from Web publishing servers.
Total SSL Sessions	No	Represents the total number of SSL sessions serviced by the SSL tunnel.
Total Successful Requests	No	Represents the total number of requests that have been successfully processed by the Web Proxy service. This counter can be compared with Total Requests and Total Failed Requests to indicate the effectiveness of ISA Server in servicing requests.
Total Upstream Fetches	No	Tracks the total number of requests that have been served by using data from the Internet or from a chained proxy computer. This counter can be compared to Total Cache Fetches to see what proportion of requests are being serviced from remote servers on the Internet or upstream proxies, compared with those being serviced from the cache.
Total Users	No	Represents the total number of users that have ever connected to the Web Proxy service. It represents a history of past server usage.
Unknown SSL Sessions	No	Represents the total number of unknown SSL sessions serviced by the SSL tunnel.

Counter	Preloaded in System Monitor?	Description
Upstream Bytes Received/Sec	No	Indicates the rate at which data bytes are received by the Web Proxy service from remote servers on the Internet or from a chained proxy computer in response to requests from the Web Proxy service. The value of this counter depends to some extent on the connection bandwidth. If the counter value is consistently low, it may indicate a bottleneck caused by a slow connection. Changing the bandwidth priority configuration may help in this situation, or a faster connection may be required.
Upstream Bytes Sent/Sec	No	Indicates the rate at which data bytes are sent by the Web Proxy service to remote servers on the Internet or to a chained proxy computer. The value of this counter depends to some extent on the connection bandwidth. If the counter value is consistently low, it may indicate a bottleneck caused by a slow connection. Changing the bandwidth priority configuration may help in this situation, or a faster connection may be required.
Upstream Bytes Total/Sec	No	The sum of Upstream Bytes Sent/Sec and Upstream Bytes Received/Sec. It represents the total rate for all bytes transferred between the Web Proxy service and remote servers on the Internet or a chained proxy server.

The H.323 filter object contains counters for the number of H.323 calls handled by the ISA Server H.323 Filter. Table 9.13 describes the two counters available for the H.323 Filter performance object.

Table 9.13 H.323 Filter Performance Object Counters

Counter	Preloaded in System Monitor?	Description
Active H.323 Calls	No	The number of H.323 calls that are currently active.
Total H.323 Calls	No	The total number of H.323 calls handled by the H.323 filter since the ISA Server computer was started.

SOCKS is a networking protocol that allows applications to communicate through a proxy server. The SOCKS filter provided with ISA Server forwards requests from SOCKS applications to the Firewall service. Table 9.14 describes the counters available for the SOCKS Filter performance object.

Table 9.14 SOCKS Filter Performance Object Counters

Counter	Preloaded in System Monitor?	Description
Active Connections	No	The total number of active connections currently passing data. Connections pending or not yet established are counted elsewhere.
Active Sessions	No	The number of active SOCKS sessions.
Bytes Read/sec	No	Number of bytes read on all SOCKS connections per second.
Bytes Written/sec	No	Number of bytes written on all SOCKS connections per second.
Connecting Connections	No	The number of SOCKS connections waiting for a remote computer to connect to.
Listening Connections	No	Number of connection objects that wait for remote computers to connect to.
Pending DNS Resolutions	No	Number of pending name resolution requests. These requests resolve host DNS names and IP addresses for SOCKS connections.
Successful DNS Resolutions	No	Number of name resolution requests resolved each second. These requests resolve host DNS names and IP addresses for SOCKS connections.

Lesson Summary

By adjusting the settings on the Performance tab of an array's properties, you can tune the array's performance to adjust to the number of daily connections you anticipate for your site. You can also tune the performance of the ISA Server cache by adjusting the amount of physical RAM used to store Web content. This setting is configured on the Advanced tab of the Cache Configuration Properties dialog box.

In addition to the alerting, logging, and reporting features, ISA Server includes seven performance objects, each containing multiple counters that you can use to gather information related to ISA Server performance. You can use these counters in the Windows 2000 Performance console or in the preconfigured ISA Server Performance Monitor console. ISA Server Performance Monitor allows you to monitor ISA Server performance separately from other Windows 2000 functions, and it has 21 counters preloaded into the System Monitor snap-in, the real-time monitoring tool.

Review

The following questions are intended to reinforce key information presented in the chapter. If you are unable to answer a question, review the appropriate lesson and then try the question again. The answers for these questions are located in Appendix A, "Questions and Answers."

1. What four actions can be configured for an alert? Which of these actions is enabled by default whenever an alert is enabled?

2. What would the name be for a Firewall service log file in ISA format created on October 23, 2002?

3. What credentials must a user have to configure a report job?

4. What is one disadvantage of applying a bandwidth priority other than the default bandwidth priority to a connection?

5. What is the advantage of using ISA Server Performance Monitor to view data gathered by ISA Server performance counters?

CHAPTER 10

Troubleshooting ISA Server

Lesson 1 Troubleshooting Tools in ISA Server 424

Lesson 2 Troubleshooting Strategies in ISA Server 436

Review 446

About This Chapter

Effective troubleshooting in a complex network requires a knowledge of the tools available for troubleshooting and of the proper strategies for determining the precise cause of network problems. This chapter presents a brief overview of the tools and strategies you can use to resolve problems in your Microsoft Internet Security and Acceleration Server 2000 (ISA Server) environment.

Before You Begin

To complete the lessons in this chapter, you must have

- Completed the setup procedures discussed in "About This Book"
- Completed all exercises through Chapter 9

Lesson 1 Troubleshooting Tools in ISA Server

To determine the causes of connectivity, security, and service errors in ISA Server, you need to become familiar with the full range of tools available for network troubleshooting. These troubleshooting tools include features specific to ISA Server as well as common Transmission Control Protocol/Internet Protocol (TCP/IP) commands and Microsoft Windows 2000 utilities. This lesson introduces many of these tools and discusses how you use them to diagnose and repair errors in ISA Server installations.

After this lesson, you will be able to

- Use several tools to troubleshoot ISA Server errors
- Verify and modify routing tables
- Verify port status using Netstat and Telnet

Estimated lesson time: 45 minutes

Troubleshooting Tools

When unexpected problems arise in your ISA Server installation, you can take advantage of a range of troubleshooting tools to determine the cause. Depending on the type of problem you need to troubleshoot, you can consult any combination of the following tools:

- ISA Server Reports
- Event Viewer
- Performance Monitor
- Netstat
- Telnet
- Network Monitor
- The Routing Table

ISA Server Reports

ISA Server reports are useful as a first stop in troubleshooting. These reports can be viewed individually or together to pinpoint the cause of a performance problem. For example, if your users are complaining about sluggish Web performance, you can first review the Cache Performance report in the Traffic and Utilization reports file, as shown in Figure 10.1. However, even if the report indicates a low cache hit ratio, you should review other reports to determine whether the slow Web response is a result of the cache being underused. If active caching is disabled, and if no download jobs are scheduled, ISA Server will not be able to retrieve Hypertext Transfer Protocol (HTTP) requests frequently from the cache, and the end user will experience slow Web performance. However, if reports reveal that the cache is being used frequently, slow response can result from high network saturation, which can be caused by (among other things) too-frequent download jobs or too-short time-to-live (TTL) parameter settings.

Note Poor performance resulting from a low cache hit ratio can be remedied by configuring more frequent or extensive download jobs after hours, or by lengthening the TTL parameters in the Cache Configuration Properties dialog box.

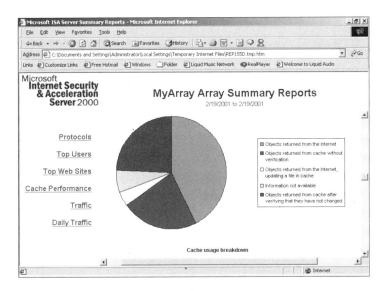

Figure 10.1 A sample cache performance report

Event Viewer

When you are troubleshooting an error related to the function of an ISA Server service, you should consult the Microsoft Windows 2000 Event Viewer. Windows 2000 Event Viewer displays all event messages generated by the ISA Server services. These messages may be warnings or error notifications, or they may simply be informational. When you find a particular event message reported by the service you are troubleshooting, always double-click the event message and note its Event ID. Using the Event ID, you can search ISA Server Help or Appendix C of this book to learn recommended ways to remedy the problem associated with the event message.

Performance Monitor

The ISA Server Performance Monitor can help you resolve problems related to network usage, hardware, and configuration. For example, when attempting to determine the cause of slow cache performance, you might find % Disk Time to be high. If, in addition, the Disk Bytes/sec counter indicates a slow rate of data transfer to and from a disk, you might determine that slow cache performance will be improved by adding a new disk. If, on the other hand, the Disk Bytes/sec reading does not appear unusually low but the Pages/sec counter indicates a high rate of page faults, you might determine that slow cache performance will be improved by increasing the amount of physical RAM in your system, or by increasing the percentage of physical memory used for caching.

Troubleshooting successfully with ISA Server Performance Monitor requires you to establish baselines of counters before problems occur. This way, when you perceive that a given counter has diverged significantly from its baseline, you will be able to determine that a problem is occurring with a particular system element.

Netstat

Netstat is a command-line tool that is useful for troubleshooting security and connectivity problems. By typing **netstat** at the command line, you can check your ISA Server computer's port configuration and see every connection being made to and from your computer.

Note Ports are used in Transmission Control Protocol (TCP) and User Datagram Protocol (UDP) to name the ends of logical connections. Port numbers may range from 0 to 65535, and are divided into the following three ranges: well-known ports, registered ports, and dynamic and/or private ports. Well-known ports are those whose numbers range from 0 through 1023. Registered ports' numbers range from 1024 through 49151. Dynamic and/or private ports have numbers spanning 49152 through 65535. For more information on ports, consult the port numbers Web site at *http://www.isi.edu/in-notes/iana/assignments/port-numbers*.

By using the –a switch with the Netstat command, you will receive an output of all listening ports in addition to all active connections. When you use the –n switch, addresses and port numbers are not converted to names. This enables you to differentiate between connections to the external and internal

Internet Protocol (IP) addresses of your ISA Server computer and to determine which ports are open at any given moment on a particular interface. You can learn which services are active on which particular ports by comparing the output of netstat –an to that of netstat –a.

You can limit the output of the Netstat –an command by specifying a particular protocol with the –p TCP or –p UDP switch. For example, the Netstat –an –p TCP command will print an output of all active TCP connections and listening ports, and the Netstat –an –p UDP command will print an output of the port status for UDP only.

Knowing your port configuration allows you to check for connectivity problems, port conflicts, and security holes. For example, if you are unable to connect to a remote server, the netstat output may confirm that the problem is not local, and indicate that it is the remote computer that is rejecting your connection attempt. You can also verify that you are receiving TCP resets or ICMP Port Unreachable packets each time you attempt to connect.

Finally, Netstat can be used to diagnose attacks on your system. For example, a SYN attack is used to create a large number of half-open TCP connections and render a server inoperative. The foreign address in this case is typically a spoofed address with incrementally increasing port numbers. The distinctive nature of SYN attacks make them recognizable from the following netstat output:

```
C:\> netstat -a

C:\>netstat -n -p tcp

Active Connections

    Proto   Local Address        Foreign Address       State
    TCP     127.0.0.1:1030       127.0.0.1:1032        ESTABLISHED
    TCP     127.0.0.1:1032       127.0.0.1:1030        ESTABLISHED
    TCP     10.1.1.5:21          192.168.0.1:1025      SYN_RECEIVED
    TCP     10.1.1.5:21          192.168.0.1:1026      SYN_RECEIVED
    TCP     10.1.1.5:21          192.168.0.1:1027      SYN_RECEIVED
    TCP     10.1.1.5:21          192.168.0.1:1028      SYN_RECEIVED
    TCP     10.1.1.5:21          192.168.0.1:1029      SYN_RECEIVED
    TCP     10.1.1.5:21          192.168.0.1:1030      SYN_RECEIVED
    TCP     10.1.1.5:21          192.168.0.1:1031      SYN_RECEIVED
    TCP     10.1.1.5:21          192.168.0.1:1032      SYN_RECEIVED
    TCP     10.1.1.5:21          192.168.0.1:1033      SYN_RECEIVED
    TCP     10.1.1.5:21          192.168.0.1:1034      SYN_RECEIVED
    TCP     10.1.1.5:21          192.168.0.1:1035      SYN_RECEIVED
```

> **Note** For more information on SYN attacks and on how to configure Microsoft Windows 2000 to defend against them, see *Windows 2000 TCP/IP Protocols and Services Technical Reference,* by Thomas Lee and Joseph Davies (Seattle: Microsoft Press, 2000).

Telnet

By specifying a port number after the Telnet command, you can test whether a server is accepting commands through that port. For example, after running the Netstat –an –p TCP command, you may find that port 3149 is listening for incoming requests. You can then determine whether ISA Server will allow users to telnet to that port by typing **telnet** *external_ip_address* **3149** at the command prompt, where *external_ip_address* is the public IP address assigned to your ISA Server computer. If you receive a blank screen, or any response output other than one indicating a connection failure, an external user may theoretically communicate with the service located at the port by typing service commands directly. Note that this status does not normally indicate a security hole, but if there are security weaknesses associated with a given service, a hacker will often use Telnet to exploit them.

You may also use Telnet to determine whether a given service is active on your computer. For example, if you are able to Telnet to port 25 of your ISA Server computer, this indicates that your Simple Mail Transfer Protocol (SMTP) service is running and accessible to external users. If you would like to prevent external users from accessing the SMTP service on your ISA Server computer, you can choose to remedy the situation by shutting down the service, by verifying that packet filtering is enabled on ISA Server, and/or by ensuring that no IP packet filters are enabled in ISA Server allowing inbound traffic to pass through port 25. If, on the other hand, you are publishing a server and want to test external access, you may want to Telnet to the service's port to see if it is accepting connections. For example, if you are publishing a Web server on port 9999 of your ISA Server computer, you can type **telnet** *external_ip_address* **9999** to ensure that you are able to connect to that port.

Network Monitor

Network Monitor, or Netmon, is a tool used to capture and display the contents of frames that a Windows 2000 computer receives from the local area network (LAN). To ease analysis of network traffic, Network Monitor breaks down and organizes 40 of the most common network protocols. This means that for most network traffic, Network Monitor displays virtually all information associated with network sessions, including source and destination ports and addresses, server responses, and traffic payloads.

The following is an example frame taken from a Network Monitor trace, or capture.

```
Network Monitor trace  Wed 03/07/2001 08:55:17 AM  Captur
1.txt

+ Frame: Base frame properties
+ ETHERNET: ETYPE = 0x0800 : Protocol = IP:  DOD Internet
Protocol
+ IP: ID = 0xAD6; Proto = TCP; Len: 327
+ TCP: .AP..., len:   287, seq:3184161250-3184161537,
ack:4040781620,
win:17520, src: 1225  dst:    80
+ HTTP: GET Request (from client using port 1225)
```

For each frame displayed, the encapsulated protocols it contains are listed in order from the outside of the frame in, or from a networking perspective, from the lowest layer up. By clicking on the + sign at the start of any line, you can reveal more information contained in the given protocol. The first line, named Frame, is added by Network Monitor to introduce the frame captured. The next line presents the data-link layer protocol by which the frame is put on the network (in this case, Ethernet). Such a protocol represents the lowest layer protocol in the frame, corresponding to layer 2 in the Open Systems Interconnect (OSI) model. This is followed by the network layer protocol, or layer 3, which in this case is the IP protocol. Next is the transport layer protocol, or layer 4, which in the given frame is TCP. Finally, in this example, HTTP is the highest protocol layer in the frame.

Each protocol layer contains information relating to the present connection or transmission. For example, on the TCP line, the src and dst parameters refer to the source port and destination port of the TCP connection associated with the frame or packet. In this packet, the source was TCP port 1225 on the client side and TCP port 80 on the destination side. By looking at the TCP or UDP line within a captured frame in Network Monitor, you can always find the source and destination of traffic on the network. This is an essential tool for configuring and monitoring firewalls.

In addition, by creating traces of network activity, you can analyze traffic and determine the source of a network problem. For example, suppose your users are complaining about logon delays through a virtual private network (VPN) connection. When you run a Network Monitor capture, the trace may reveal the presence of both Layer Two Tunneling Protocol (L2TP) and Point-to-Point Tunneling Protocol (PPTP) traffic during logons. This would indicate that you have configured the Local ISA VPN wizard to connect to the remote network by using L2TP by default, but to use PPTP when L2TP is unavailable. If L2TP is unavailable on the remote VPN server, your users will experience a delay while attempting to connect through both protocols. Network Monitor thus allows you to find out when the L2TP connection is not working. This allows you to remedy the logon delays by configuring ISA Server to connect to the remote VPN server through PPTP only.

Even if you don't require a VPN in your network environment, a Network Monitor capture may reveal that your network is slowed by protocols your network does not need for communication. For example, the tunneling protocol PPTP is not needed for private LAN connections.

The Routing Table

Every computer using TCP/IP as a network protocol has a routing table. The route that an IP packet takes from one computer to another is determined by the routing table of the computer that sent the network packet.

You can view and modify the routing table by using the Route command-line utility. Type **route print** at the command prompt to display the local routing table, as shown in Figure 10.2.

Figure 10.2 A sample routing rable

The Route Determination Process

To determine a single route to use to forward an IP packet, the IP protocol uses the routing table in the following way:

1. For each route in the routing table, IP performs a bit-wise logical AND operation between the Destination IP address and the subnet (the netmask column in Figure 10.2) to determine if the network is local or remote. IP compares the result with the network destination for a match. If there is a match, IP marks the route as one that matches the Destination IP address.

2. From the list of matching routes, IP determines the route that has the most bits in the netmask. This is the route that matched the most bits to the Destination IP address and is therefore the most specific route for the IP packet. This is known as finding the longest or closest matching route.

3. If multiple closest matching routes are found, IP uses the route with the lowest metric.

4. If multiple closest matching routes with the lowest metric are found, IP randomly chooses the route to use.

The end result of the route determination process is the choice of a single route in the routing table. If the route determination process fails to find a route, IP declares a routing error.

Troubleshooting Routing Tables

By using IP utilities such as Ping and Tracert, you will be able to determine when certain network segments are inaccessible to the rest of the network. When you are installing ISA Server on a complex network, you can use the Route command to modify the routing tables and configure viable routes for all network segments. For example, if your ISA Server does not have an interface on a given (remote) subnet, you will need to add a static route to allow traffic to be forwarded to that subnet. (Static routes are those that do not appear automatically in routing tables.)

To add a static route, you can use the Route utility as follows:

```
route add 172.16.41.0 mask 255.255.255.0 172.16.40.1 metric 2
```

In this example, the Route add command states that to reach the 172.16.41.0 subnet with a mask of 255.255.255.0, gateway 172.16.40.1 should be used. Note also that in this case the metric is set to 2 because the subnet is two hops away. (The metric is usually set to the number of hops, or routers crossed, to the network destination.) In this case, you may also need to add static routes on downstream routers telling packets there how to get back to the 172.16.40.0/24 subnet.

Since your computer's routing table is automatically rebuilt each time you restart your computer, you will need to add persistent entries to the routing table if you want static routes to remain in the routing table. Persistent entries are automatically reinserted in your route table each time your computer's route table is rebuilt. Persistent entries are added using the Route add -p command.

Static routes can also be added by using the Routing and Remote Access console in Windows 2000. All static routes are treated as persistent routes when they are added by using the Routing and Remote Access console.

▶ **Follow these steps to add a static route in Routing and Remote Access:**

1. Click Start, point to Programs, point to Administrative Tools, and click Routing And Remote Access.

2. Double-click IP Routing to expand that object.

3. Right-click Static Routes and click New Static Route.

   The Static Route dialog box appears.

4. Complete the fields of the static route as necessary.

Practice: Testing Port Status

In this practice, you use the Netstat and Telnet commands to determine the status of ports on the ISA Server computer. This technique can be used to verify security, or it can be used to determine whether a service running on the ISA Server computer is available to external sites.

Exercise: Testing ISA Server ports

In this exercise, you run the Netstat utility at a command prompt and note the various ports that are open on the external interface of the ISA Server computer. You then try to telnet to these open ports.

▶ **To test the status of ports on the ISA Server computer**

1. Log on to Server1 as Administrator.

2. Click the Start menu, and then click Run.

   The Run dialog box appears.

3. In the Open text box, type **cmd** and click OK.

   A command prompt appears.

4. At the command prompt, type **netstat –an –p tcp**.

   An output of all active TCP ports on the ISA Server computer appears. On the output screen, the left column of IP addresses with port numbers represents the local address of each active connection, and the right column of IP addresses with port numbers represents the foreign address of each active connection. Most of the local addresses in the output refer to the internal interface, 192.168.0.1. However, at the end of the list, there may be a few connections whose local address is the external IP address of the ISA Server computer.

5. In the Local Address column, how many connections are currently active for the external interface of the ISA Server computer? Look at the foreign address for each of those connections. Are the addresses listed as foreign truly remote, or do they merely represent another port of the same local address? Which ports are being used in these foreign addresses to send information to the local external address of your ISA Server computer?

   Write your answers in the space below:

6. On the ISA Server computer, open Microsoft Internet Explorer and connect to an external Web site such as *www.microsoft.com*.

7. While the Web page is still downloading in Internet Explorer, switch to the command prompt window and type **netstat –an –p tcp** again.

   An output of all active TCP ports on the ISA Server computer appears.

8. Look at the end of the output list. In the Local Address column, how many more connections are active for the external interface of the ISA Server computer than you recorded in Step 5? Do you see any active ports on foreign addresses that you did not list before? After you view this data, which foreign port can you determine is used to send Web data to the local external IP address?

9. To which local ports on the external interface of ISA Server computer is this Web data sent? These are dynamic ports that vary from connection to connection. Write the number corresponding to these ports in the space below.

Suppose that you find evidence of an intrusion in your network, and you want to troubleshoot security by testing the status of external ports through which a hacker may try to gain access. You can attempt to telnet to external ports to see whether a service located at that port responds to your connection request. (Ordinarily you would want to perform this from an external computer.)

10. Attempt to telnet to one of the external ports that you wrote down in Step 9 as follows: At the command prompt, type **telnet** [*external_ip_address*] [*port_number*], where [*external_ip_address*] is the external IP address currently assigned to your ISA Server computer and [*port_number*] is one of the local ports you have noted in Step 9 (for example, **telnet 64.43.113.110 10123**).

    A message appears, indicating that the connection to the port has failed. The port is not a listening port. When a port is accepting external connections, you will either get a blank screen or a message output from the service communicating at that port.

11. In the command prompt window, attempt to telnet to each the ports listed in the left column of the table below. Do this by specifying the external IP address currently assigned to your computer. For example, if your IP address is 64.43.113.110, you can telnet to port 25 by typing **telnet 64.43.113.110 25** at the command prompt. Write the status of each of these ports as either Open or Closed in the corresponding column to the right.

Port Number	Port Status
25	
7	
389	
443	
21	
8080	
1030	

An open port status does not normally indicate a security weakness, but there are some ports that, for security reasons, you may not want to leave open statically, such as port 15 (Netstat), 21 (FTP), 23 (Telnet), 25 (SMTP), 79 (Finger), and 80 (HTTP).

12. Close the command prompt window.

Lesson Summary

Many tools are available to help you troubleshoot problems in ISA Server. As a starting point, ISA Server reports can help you determine the cause of a performance problem. Event Viewer is useful in that it displays all event messages generated by the ISA Server services. The ISA Server Performance Monitor can help resolve problems related to network usage, hardware, and configuration. Netstat is a command-line tool that shows all active TCP and/or UDP connections, which is useful for troubleshooting security and connectivity problems. You can also use the Telnet utility to test whether a server is accepting commands through given ports. Network Monitor is used to capture and display the contents of frames that a Windows 2000 server receives from the LAN. Finally, the Route command is useful for verifying and modifying the routing tables to make sure all network segments can be accessed through viable routes.

Lesson 2 Troubleshooting Strategies in ISA Server

Successful troubleshooting requires a systematic approach. When you experience unexpected behavior in ISA Server, you can begin troubleshooting by determining whether the error is user-based or packet-based. The following lesson offers strategies for troubleshooting both types of connection problems.

After this lesson, you will be able to

- Troubleshoot user-based access problems
- Troubleshoot packet-based access problems
- Troubleshoot VPN connections in ISA Server

Estimated lesson time: 30 minutes

Troubleshooting User Access

When user account access is intermittent or unavailable, the problem could be caused by overly restrictive user security, improperly configured rules, or inadequate authentication methods. Tools such as Ping and Tracert may function properly even in these conditions.

To troubleshoot user-based access problems, first check access policy rules. Make sure that users unable to establish a network connection have been granted proper permissions to connect to the site(s), content group(s), and protocol(s) in question through configured access policy rules.

If you have configured rules that are not being successfully applied to user sessions, verify that your array properties are configured to ask unauthenticated users for identification. Note also that if you create an allow-type access policy rule that is applied to specific users and groups, user sessions will be forced to authenticate with the ISA Server. On the other hand, if access is being denied to Web sessions when you want all Web sessions to remain anonymous, make sure that the array properties do not force anonymous users to authenticate themselves. In addition, delete any allow-type site and content rules or protocol rules that are applied to specific Windows 2000 users or groups.

Authentication

Your choice of authentication method for an ISA Server array can affect the users' ability to connect. Each authentication method is designed to accommodate specific network environments. If an incompatible authentication method is chosen for a network configuration, or if an authentication method is improperly configured, users will be denied access to the ISA Server computer and the network.

For example, the default authentication mode on an array is Integrated Windows authentication, but this authentication method cannot authenticate clients not running Windows operating systems. If you need to provide authenticated access for such clients in ISA Server, you must configure the array properties to use another authentication method. Similarly, Integrated Windows authentication is incompatible with Netscape browsers because Netscape cannot pass user credentials in NTLM format. Another limitation of Integrated Windows authentication in Windows 2000 is that it can rely either on the Kerberos V5 authentication protocol or its own challenge/response authentication protocol. However, in a pass-through authentication scenario, as shown in Figure 10.3, ISA Server does not support Kerberos V5 authentication because Kerberos V5–based authentication requires that the client be able to identify the authenticating server.

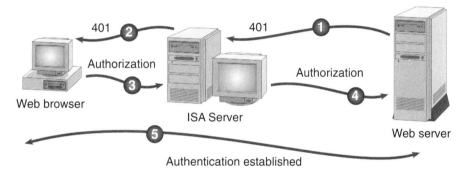

Figure 10.3 Pass-through authentication is not compatible with Kerberos V5–based authentication

The alternative authentication methods available in ISA Server include Basic, Digest, and Client Certificate. Basic authentication is compatible with all client types. However, because Basic authentication sends user names and passwords over the network in clear, unencrypted format, it is not a sufficient method of security by itself. Digest authentication can be used only in Windows 2000 domains. With this method, passwords are sent in clear but encrypted text. Client Certificate authentication uses an Secure Sockets Layer (SSL) channel for authentication and requires that the client certificate be installed in the Microsoft Web Proxy Service certificate store on the ISA Server computer and that the certificate be mapped to the appropriate user account. ISA Server can present client certificates only in SSL bridging configurations.

Troubleshooting Packet-Based Access Problems

Access problems are likely packet-based when network access fails for all users, or when IP-based utilities such as Ping or Tracert fail.

To troubleshoot packet-based access problems in ISA Server, begin by simplifying the network configuration as much as possible to create a testing environment.

▶ **Follow these steps to set up a network troubleshooting configuration:**

1. With packet filtering enabled, create a custom packet filter to allow any IP protocol to transmit in both directions.

2. Create a protocol rule to allow all IP traffic for any request, and ensure that you have a site and content rule allowing access to all sites and content groups.

3. Return all application filters and routing rules to default settings.

4. Verify that you have defined the local address table (LAT) as the range of internal ISA Server clients.

5. Enable IP Routing in the IP Packet Filters Properties dialog box.

   Note The IP Routing option provides routing capabilities to protocols with secondary connections. This setting is especially important for perimeter network configurations. You can enable the IP Routing option either in the IP Packet Filters Properties dialog box in ISA Management or in the Routing and Remote Access console.

6. On the ISA Server computer, make sure that no default gateway is defined for the internal interface. However, make sure that a proper default gateway is specified on the external interface.

7. On the client computers for which you are trying to establish access, disable the Firewall Client software and assign the ISA Server computer as the default gateway.

Once you have configured ISA Server in this simplified way, restart the ISA Server services. If you still cannot gain access, reboot the ISA Server computer. If this does not fix the problem, the network problem may not be related to your ISA Server configuration. In this case, you should perform network troubleshooting as you would with any network, performing Network Monitor traces and reviewing Domain Name System (DNS), routing tables, alerts, reports, and logs as appropriate.

If you can establish Internet access with the simplified testing configuration, you can then reintroduce network elements one by one to determine the cause of the problem. For example, if you can establish Internet access from a given client computer, you can attempt to use specific Internet applications from that computer. If you encounter problems, you can assume that either the application has been improperly configured to use ISA Server as a proxy or that the application is not designed to use a proxy server. For applications that are not able to use a proxy server, you must configure the client for SecureNAT or run the Firewall Client software. After reconfiguring the client, note any changes in behavior. If you use the Firewall Client software and access fails when you enable automatic discovery, you can assume that automatic discovery is improperly configured. Proceed incrementally, fixing problems as they arise, until you have added all the network components required for your particular configuration.

VPN Network Considerations

In VPN Networks, begin troubleshooting by creating the simplified network configuration as outlined above. If you have already run the VPN wizards, you should verify first that the Routing and Remote Access service has been started. Next, make sure that you have configured the client as a secure network address translation (SecureNAT) client and not a Firewall client.

You should also verify that the Local ISA Server VPN Configuration wizard has created the appropriate demand-dial interfaces in Routing and Remote Access. This can be checked in the Routing Interfaces node, as shown in Figure 10.4.

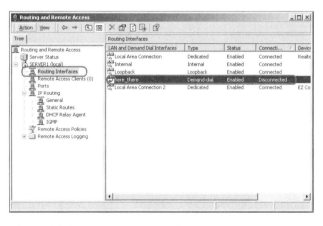

Figure 10.4 Demand-dial interfaces in Routing and Remote Access

After this, verify that two IP packet filters have been created for each authentication protocol you have chosen for your VPN connection. For example, if you have configured your VPN to use either L2TP or PPTP, the Local ISA Server VPN Configuration wizard should have created and enabled four IP packet filters. (For L2TP, the wizard creates custom filters for ports 500 and 1701, and for PPTP, the wizard creates predefined filters for PPTP Call and PPTP Receive.)

If the appropriate interfaces and IP packet filters have been created, and if rebooting the computer does not help, it is recommended that you delete the IP packet filters created by the VPN wizards, disable Routing and Remote Access, and run the wizards again.

Additional Troubleshooting Notes

When you are troubleshooting errors in ISA Server, you can begin by consulting the following tables. The following tables summarize common problems and solutions relating to various aspects and functions of ISA Server.

Table 10.1 Troubleshooting Access Policy

Problem	Possible Cause(s)	Possible Solution(s)
Clients cannot browse external Web sites.	Initially, ISA Server does not allow any communication to or from the Internet. You can create rules that will allow communication in a manner consistent with your corporate security policy.	Create protocol rules to allow specific users to use the protocols. Then create site and content rules that allow users access to particular sites, using the protocols specified by the protocol rules.
		Check the browser settings of the client to ensure that the proxy port is specified correctly. The default port for ISA Server is 8080.
Clients receive a 502 error every time they try to browse the Web.	Initially, ISA Server does not allow any communication to or from the Internet. You can create IP packet filters or rules that will allow communication in a manner consistent with corporate security policy.	Create protocol rules to allow specific users to use the protocols. Then create site and content rules that allow users access to particular sites, using the protocols specified by the protocol rules.
	Some access policy rules require authentication, but no authentication methods were configured for the listener.	Select an authentication method for the listener. Clients will be allowed access, in accordance with configured rules, if they authenticate using the specified method.

Problem	Possible Cause(s)	Possible Solution(s)
Clients cannot use a specific protocol, such as HTTP, RealAudio, or others.	Initially, ISA Server does not allow any communication to and from the Internet. You can configure IP packet filters or rules that will allow use of particular protocols.	Create protocol rules to allow users to communicate using the specified protocols. Also check to see whether a particular protocol is not blocked by a disabled application filter.
After disabling a protocol rule, clients can still use the specified protocol that is allowed by the rule.	Existing client sessions are not terminated when you disable a protocol rule, although new sessions will not be opened. For example, if a client is using a RealAudio protocol, in accordance with configured rules, the session will continue even after you disable the protocol rule allowing the access.	Disconnect the client sessions.
Clients cannot use a specific protocol definition, although a protocol rule has been configured to allow access.	If you disable an application filter, all traffic that uses the protocol definition is blocked, even if protocol rules seem to allow the traffic.	Enable the application filter.

Table 10.2 Troubleshooting Authentication

Problem	Possible Cause(s)	Possible Solution(s)
ISA Server failed to authenticate a Netscape user.	ISA Server may have been configured only to accept Windows integrated authentication. Netscape browsers cannot pass user credentials in Windows NT LAN Manager (NTLM) format.	You can configure ISA Server to require other authentication methods, including Basic or Digest.

Table 10.3 Troubleshooting Caching

Problem	Possible Cause(s)	Possible Solution(s)
Not all traffic is saved to the ISA Server cache.	ISA Server caches only items that meet the caching criteria.	To broaden cache criteria, you can adjust cache properties and routing rules to enable active caching, cache dynamic content, lengthen the TTL parameters of cached objects, and allow the cache to return some or all expired objects.
The Web Proxy service will not start.	The cache contents file is corrupted.	If the cache contents file becomes corrupted for whatever reason, the Web Proxy service will not be able to start. To overcome this problem, reconfigure the drives allocated for caching.

Table 10.4 Troubleshooting Logging

Problem	Possible Cause(s)	Possible Solution(s)
The client authentication (user names) information cannot be found in the log file.	ISA Server does not always require that clients authenticate themselves. If clients are not authenticated, they are granted anonymous access and their authentication information is not logged.	Configure ISA Server to always require that Web Proxy clients authenticate themselves, by configuring the incoming and outgoing Web request properties.

Table 10.5 Troubleshooting Publishing

Problem	Possible Cause(s)	Possible Solution(s)
Clients receive a 403 error every time they try to access the published Web server.	Some access policy rule requires authentication, but no authentication methods were configured for the listener.	Select an authentication method for the listener. Clients will be allowed access, in accordance with configured rules, if they can authenticate using the particular method chosen.

Problem	Possible Cause(s)	Possible Solution(s)
External clients cannot send mail via the computer running Microsoft Exchange Server that is set up as a Firewall client behind the ISA Server computer.	There is a port conflict between a server publishing rule and a Firewall client configuration file.	If you published a mail server in a Microsoft Proxy Server 2.0 environment, you had to configure the mail server as a Winsock Proxy client. In this case, you created a Wspclnt.ini file on the mail server. With ISA Server, publishing servers do not require special configuration, since they are published as SecureNAT clients. Remove the Wspclnt.ini file from the publishing server. Then, in ISA Management, run the Mail Server Security wizard.
	The Microsoft Exchange Server may be unable to bind to the SMTP port on the ISA Server computer.	Be sure that there is no other local service or application running on the ISA Server computer that is binding to port 25 before the Exchange Server.
	The Exchange Server loses its connection to the ISA Server computer.	If the connection between the ISA Server computer and the Exchange Server was temporarily disrupted, you must restart the Exchange services so that it will bind to the necessary ports on the ISA Server computer.
External clients cannot send mail via the Exchange Server, which is set up as a SecureNAT client, behind the ISA Server computer.	The server publishing rules may not be configured correctly.	Check that the server publishing rules are configured so that the external interface passes all traffic on port 25 for SMTP traffic and port 110 for Post Office Protocol 3 traffic to the correct IP address and port on the internal Exchange Server.

Table 10.6   Troubleshooting Services

Problem	Possible Cause(s)	Possible Solution(s)
Services did not start after installation completed successfully.	If the LAT was configured incorrectly and does not include the internal network adapter that communicates with Active Directory directory services, the ISA Server services cannot start.	Perform the following steps to add the appropriate entries to the LAT: 1. Stop ISA Server services and packet filtering. To do this, at a command prompt, type **net stop mspfltext**. 2. Reconfigure the LAT. Since you cannot run ISA Management, you will have to configure the LAT using the ISA Server Administration COM objects. For more information on how to do this, see "Constructing the Local Address Table" in the *ISA Server Software Development Kit*. 3. Reboot the computer.

Lesson Summary

A good way to begin troubleshooting an access problem in ISA Server is to determine whether the problem is user-based or packet-based. Access problems can be distinguished as user-based when connectivity varies among users, or when network resources are accessible from IP utilities such as Ping or Tracert but not through all user accounts. Access problems can be distinguished as packet-based when network access does not vary among users, or when you are unable to connect to a network resource using an IP utility.

To troubleshoot user-based access problems, you should check access policy rules to make sure that the proper users have been granted access to the proper sites, content groups, and protocols. In addition, if you want access policy rules configured for specific users and groups to apply to Web sessions, you should verify that your array properties have been configured to require authentication for outgoing Web requests. Finally, you should make sure that an authentication method has been properly configured for your array.

To troubleshoot packet-based access problems in ISA Server, begin by simplifying the network configuration as much as possible and then performing the access test. If you are still experiencing a network problem in a simplified test environment, the network problem might not be related to your ISA Server configuration. If it is unrelated to ISA Server, proceed to troubleshoot the configuration as you would with any network access problem. If you can establish Internet access with the simplified testing configuration, you can then reintroduce the elements of your network one by one until you can determine the cause of the problem. Additional troubleshooting considerations for VPN connections include verifying that VPN clients are configured as SecureNAT clients, that Routing and Remote Access is started, that the proper demand-dial interfaces are created for the VPN, and that two IP packet filters are enabled for each authentication protocol selected for the VPN.

Review

The following questions are intended to reinforce key information presented in the chapter. If you are unable to answer a question, review the appropriate lesson and then try the question again. The answers for these questions are located in Appendix A, "Questions and Answers."

1. Your network configuration consists of an ISA Server installed on a DMZ. The address space behind the ISA Server consists of the 192.168.0.0/24 subnet, and the DMZ in front of the ISA Server computer has been configured with the 192.168.1.0/24 subnet. The ISA Server computer has an internal address of 192.168.0.1 and an external address of 192.168.1.99. The external gateway has an address of 192.168.1.1.

   You are unable to access the Internet from any client computer behind ISA Server. On the ISA Server computer, you run the Route print command at the C:> prompt and receive the output shown in Figure 10.5.

   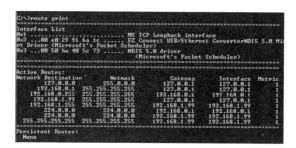

   Figure 10.5 Routing table – Question 1

   What is the error in the routing table? How can you fix the problem by using the Route command?

2. After you reboot the server specified in Question 1, you find that the problem returns. How can you avoid reconfiguring the routing table every time the computer reboots?

3. With what tool could you spot a SYN attack in progress? What is the telltale sign of a SYN attack?

4. What is the purpose of attempting to telnet to a specific TCP or UDP port?

5. If you run the Local ISA Server VPN Configuration wizard and specify L2TP as the authentication protocol, how many IP packet filters will be created? Which ports will be opened statically by these IP packet filters?

APPENDIX A

Questions and Answers

Chapter 1

Review

1. What protocol enables Web browsers to connect automatically to an ISA Server computer?

    Web Proxy Autodiscovery Protocol (WPAD).

2. What is the function of the HTTP redirector filter?

    The HTTP Redirector Filter forwards HTTP requests from the Firewall and SecureNAT clients to the Web Proxy service. This creates transparent caching for clients that do not have their browser configured to direct to the Web Proxy service.

3. How and when is Active Directory directory services used in ISA Server configurations?

    All users, rules, and configuration information can be centrally stored and managed in the Active Directory directory services. In ISA Server Enterprise Edition, the Active Directory directory services allows organizations to share schema, implement caching arrays, and automatically adopt enterprise settings, access policies, publishing policies and monitoring configurations.

4. What advantages does CARP provide over ICP?

   First, ICP arrays have "negative scalability" in that the more servers added to the array, the more querying required between servers to determine location. This is avoided in CARP arrays because CARP provides a deterministic request resolution path that eliminates the need for query messaging between servers. Second, in an ICP network, an array can evolve into essentially duplicate caches of the most frequently requested URLs. The hash-based routing of CARP keeps this from happening, allowing all proxy servers to exist as a single logical cache.

5. What is the purpose of using a multitier policy approach with ISA Server Enterprise Edition?

   By allowing both enterprise and array policies, you ensure that a corporate policy is implemented throughout the organization. At the same time, you are able to allow nuances at the department or branch level, enabling departmental managers to create additional rules as necessary.

6. What feature in Windows 2000 Advanced Server or Windows 2000 Datacenter Server benefits array performance in ISA Server Enterprise Edition?

   ISA Server Enterprise Edition uses the Windows Network Load Balancing (NLB) Services of Microsoft Windows 2000 Advanced Server to provide fault tolerance, high availability, efficiency, and enhanced performance through the clustering of multiple ISA Server machines.

Chapter 2

Review

1. What hardware recommendations for processor speed, RAM, and hard drive capacity would you make for an ISA Server installation planned to run in Integrated mode and expected to receive 500 to 900 hits per second and to serve up to 2,000 users in your organization?

   550 MHz Pentium III, 256 MB RAM, 10 GB free space on hard drive.

2. What are the requirements for installing ISA Server as an array?

   The ISA Server computer must be a member of a Windows 2000 domain, and you must initialize the enterprise before installation.

3. What is the benefit of a perimeter network?

   It allows external client access to your publishing servers without allowing them access to your internal network.

4. What measures must be taken to allow ISA Server to be co-located with a Web server?

   ISA Server, like a Web server, listens on port 80 for incoming requests. To avoid this conflict, you can configure the Web server so that it listens on a port other than 80. Then, you can modify the ISA Server Web publishing rule so that ISA Server forwards the requests to the appropriate port on the Web server. Alternatively, you can configure the Internet Information Services (IIS) server to listen on a different IP address. You could set the IIS Server to listen on 127.0.0.1, thereby allowing it to accept requests only from the ISA Server computer.

5. What is the function of the LAT?

   The LAT allows the ISA Server to determine which network adapter to use in order to access the internal network.

6. What measures must be taken to allow Web browsers of cache server clients to connect to an ISA server after a migration from proxy server?

   You must either configure all downstream chain members (or browsers) connecting to the ISA Server to connect to port 8080, or you can configure the ISA Server to listen on port 80. This is necessary since, whereas Proxy 2.0 listened for client HTTP requests on port 80, ISA Server is configured upon installation to listen on port 8080.

Chapter 3

Review

1. You are configuring an ISA Server installation for Firewall and Web caching service in each of two company branch offices. You need to assess requirements and make recommendations about how to configure the client computers. In addition to the 20 employees at each branch office, there are 10 field workers who spend time at both offices and who plug their portable computers into any available Ethernet port when they arrive at either office. The office desktop computers are more or less permanently positioned, and you do not anticipate that you will need to set specific access rules configured for any user accounts. To maximize efficiency for installation and maintenance, which (if any) computers do you recommend be configured as SecureNAT clients, and which (if any) as Firewall clients?

   Since desktop computers do not roam, and since you do not anticipate that access rules will be configured for specific user accounts, these computers should be configured as secure network address translation (SecureNAT) clients to simplify installation and maintenance (which will be minimal). The portable computers, on the other hand, should be configured as Firewall clients since they will profit from the use of automatic discovery, which only works with Firewall clients.

2. What is the difference between the Mspclnt.ini file and the Wspcfg.ini file on Firewall client computers?

   Both files apply configuration settings for Winsock clients, but in processing Winsock requests, the Firewall Client software gives precedence to the Wspcfg.ini file over the Mspclnt.ini file. The Wspcfg.ini file is found in the specific directory of the Winsock application and therefore applies settings specific to a given client. If the Wspcfg.ini file cannot be found, or if no settings exist on the file, the Firewall Client application looks for settings in the Mspclnt.ini file, which is located in the Firewall Client installation folder. This file applies general Winsock settings that are not specific to any particular application.

3. When automatic discovery is configured, what are the steps it takes to fulfill a client request?

   First the client connects to a Domain Name System (DNS) or Dynamic Host Configuration Protocol (DHCP) server. The DNS server or the DHCP server should have a WPAD entry which points to a Web Proxy Autodiscovery (WPAD) server that indicates the ISA Server computer. Next, the requests of the client will be fulfilled by the ISA Server computer, as identified by the WSPAD entry in the DNS server or DHCP server.

4. Does configuring dial-up entries in ISA Server allow you to share a secure Internet dial-up connection among Web Proxy clients?

   No. Web Proxy clients can share a secure dial-up connection without having a dial-up entry configured in ISA Server. Configuring a dial-up entry allows SecureNAT clients to share a secure dial-up connection.

5. Having recently switched from a dedicated connection to a dial-up connection to the Internet, you disabled your external network adapter and configured a dial-up entry for your existing dial-up connection. However, when your ISA Server dials up to your ISP through this dial-up connection, none of your clients can connect to the Internet any longer. What is the first step you should take to troubleshoot the problem?

   Whenever you enable or disable a network adapter, you will need to restart the Firewall and Web Proxy services before you can re-establish connectivity to your ISA Server clients.

Chapter 4

Review

1. Under which of the following conditions will John be able to access the Internet through Internet Security and Acceleration Server 2000 (ISA Server)? Assume that the default Allow site and content rule is in place, and that no other rules or filters have been configured.

   a) You configure a protocol rule to allow access to all IP traffic for any request. You then configure a second protocol rule denying access to all IP traffic for user John. You have not modified the default array properties for outgoing Web requests. Will John be able to access the Internet through a Web browser on a secure network address translation (SecureNAT) client?

John will be able to access the Internet through the Web browser. Because the default array properties for outgoing Web requests have not been modified to require user identification, and because you have not configured an allow-type rule that requires authentication, John's Web session will remain anonymous, and the deny rule will not affect him.

b) You configure a protocol rule to allow access to all IP traffic for all domain users. John is a member of the group Domain Guests (and not Domain Users), and the default array properties for outgoing Web requests have not been changed. Will John be able to access the Internet through a Web browser on a secure network address translation (SecureNAT) client?

John will not be able to access the Internet through the Web browser. Because you have configured an allow-type protocol rule for Domain Users, this rule will force all Web Proxy clients to authenticate themselves. Once authenticated, John will not be able to access the Web because he is not a member of the group Domain Users.

c) You configure a protocol rule to allow access to all IP traffic for any request. You then configure a second protocol rule denying access to all IP traffic for Domain Guests. John is a member (only) of the group Domain Guests, and the default array properties for outgoing Web requests have been changed to require identification for unauthenticated users. Will he be able to access the Internet through a Web browser on a Firewall client?

John will not be able to access the Internet because anonymous access has been disabled. His session is now subject to authentication by the Web Proxy service, and since he is a member of the group Domain Guests, his request will be denied.

d) You configure a protocol rule to allow access to all IP traffic for all members of the group Domain Users. John is a member of the group Domain Users. Will he be able to establish an FTP connection across the Internet from a command prompt on a computer not configured with a Firewall client?

John will not be able to access the Internet through an FTP client because his computer is not configured as a Firewall client. For non-Web requests, only firewall clients can send account information to ISA Server. Since John remains cannot be authenticated, his request will be denied.

2. What protective measure can you take if you detect an IP half scan attack originating from a certain network ID?

   You can create a site and content rule or IP packet filter to block all traffic from the range of IP addresses for the network ID.

3. What are three conditions under which you need to create IP packet filters instead of protocol rule or site and content rules to allow Internet connectivity?

   You need to create IP packet filters when you publish servers that are located on a perimeter network, or DMZ, when you run applications or other services on the ISA Server computer that need to listen to the Internet, and when you want to allow access to protocols that are not based on User Datagram Protocol (UDP) or Transmission Control Protocol (TCP).

4. You have configured a site and content rule that denies access to two destinations: ftp://movies.acme.com/clips and ftp://radio.acme.com. Assuming that your users have permissions to download files from the FTP site, will your users be able to download content through FTP clients on ftp://movies.acme.com? Will they be able to download content from ftp://radio.acme.com/songs?

   They will be able to access ftp://movies.acme.com because the rule denies access only to the subfolder. They will not be able to access ftp://radio.acme.com/songs because this subfolder is implicitly denied by the rule denying access to //radio.acme.com.

5. If you wanted to block a group of Windows 2000 users from downloading all audio content during 10 A.M. and 4 P.M. weekdays, how many policy elements would you need to create?

   You would only need to create one policy element, a schedule for the hours between 10 A.M. and 4 P.M. Audio content is a preconfigured content group policy element, and Windows 2000 users and groups are configured outside of ISA Server. Once you have created this schedule, you can create a site and content rule to deny the group access to the audio content group at all destinations during the scheduled hours.

Chapter 5

Review

1. A Web Proxy client requests a Web object, and ISA Server consults the cache to see whether a valid version of the object exists. It then finds that the cached version of the object has expired. Following the applicable routing rule, ISA Server then contacts the remote source over the Internet to retrieve the object, but it finds that the remote source cannot be contacted. What does ISA Server do next?

   ISA Server checks to see whether you have configured the server to return expired objects from the cache. This setting is configured on the Advanced tab of the Cache Configuration Properties sheet. If you selected the Return The Expired Object Only If Expiration Was radio button, so long as the specific expiration time did not pass, the object is returned from the cache to the user.

2. How does ISA Server determine whether to cache a Web object that has been retrieved from its original location?

   ISA Server determines whether the object is cacheable by checking its properties against the parameters set in the Cache Configuration Properties sheet. For example, it checks to see whether its size surpasses the maximum size set on the Advanced tab, and if the object's address contains a question mark (?), it checks to see whether dynamic content is configured to be cached. If the object meets these conditions, and if you configured the routing rule's cache properties to cache the response, ISA Server caches the object and returns the object to the user.

3. Under what conditions will ISA Server cache dynamic content?

   ISA Server caches dynamic content if you have enabled dynamic content caching (on the Advanced tab on the Cache Configuration Properties sheet) and if the routing rule applied to the request specifies that content should always be cached (on the Cache tab of the Routing Rule's Properties sheet). For scheduled content downloads, you need to configure ISA Server to cache dynamic content in the download job's properties.

4. What is negative caching, and how do you enable it?

Negative caching is the caching of error response messages returned to ISA Server when a requested Web object is not available from a remote location. To enable negative caching, select the Advanced tab on the Cache Configuration Properties sheet, and then click the Cache Objects Even If They Do Not Have An HTTP Status Code Of 200 check box.

5. How does ISA Server handle a scheduled content download when the Web server from which the object is being downloaded requires client authentication?

In such an instance, the scheduled content download will fail.

Chapter 6

Review

1. Which types of publishing rules are available in Firewall mode? In Cache mode?

In Firewall mode, only server publishing rules are available. In Cache mode, only Web publishing rules are available.

2. Using ISA Server, how would you publish an Simple Mail Transfer Protocol (SMTP) server that is located on a perimeter network?

Create an Internet Protocol (IP) packet filter allowing packet transmission of the protocol Transmission Control Protocol (TCP) in both directions, with the local port set to 25 and the remote port set to Any. Set the local computer as the IP address of the SMTP server.

3. When ISA Server receives a Hypertext Transfer Protocol (HTTP) request, which protocols can ISA Server use to bridge the request to the internal destination server?

Requests can be bridged as HTTP, Secure Sockets Layer (SSL), or File Transfer Protocol (FTP).

4. What port does Internet Information Service (IIS) Web server use to listen to requests, by default? What port does the automatic discovery feature use to listen to requests? What port does ISA Server use to listen to internal and external requests by default?

   IIS listens for requests on port 80 by default. Automatic discovery also listens for requests on port 80 by default. ISA Server listens for internal requests on port 8080 and for external requests on port 80 by default.

5. If you have a mail server hosted on the ISA Server computer, what four IP packet filters would you need to create to allow both internal and external clients access to SMTP and Post Office Protocol 3 (POP3) services?

   For SMTP, you would need one IP packet filter allowing inbound TCP connections on local port 25 from any remote port and another IP packet filter allowing outbound TCP connections on all local ports from remote port 25. For POP3, you would need one IP packet filter allowing Inbound TCP connections on local port 110 from any remote port, and another IP packet filter allowing outbound TCP connections on all local ports from remote port 110.

Chapter 7

Review

1. You have created an enterprise policy and now you want to apply that policy to the array Branch1. How can you apply the enterprise policy to the array? Under what circumstances will array-level policies be deleted? Under what circumstances will you be unable to apply the policy to the array?

   You can apply the enterprise policy to the array by accessing the enterprise policy's properties and selecting the array to which you want the policy applied. Array-level protocol rules and site and content rules are deleted when they are incompatible with the enterprise policy you are applying. You will be unable to apply the policy to the array when the array has been configured to use an array policy only.

2. How can you modify your default enterprise policy when the defaults are being used by existing arrays?

   To change your default enterprise policy when the policy is being used, you must modify each array to use custom enterprise settings.

3. How can you allow a computer within an array to handle more than its proportional share of network requests?

   To allow an array member to accept a greater share of the network requests than are configured by default, you can modify the load factor for that particular computer. You can access this setting through the Computers folder in ISA Management. Access the server's properties dialog box and select the Array Membership tab.

4. Do standalone ISA Servers need to be installed in a domain? Can you apply an enterprise policy to a standalone ISA Server installation?

   Standalone servers need to be installed in a domain, but it does not have to be a Windows 2000 domain. This is because standalone server configuration information is stored in the registry, not in the Active Directory store. You cannot apply an enterprise policy to a standalone ISA Server installation.

5. ISA Server includes three wizards to simplify VPN configuration. What is the purpose of each of these three wizards?

   The Local ISA Server VPN Configuration wizard allows you to set up the local ISA Server computer to initiate and receive connections. The Remote ISA Server VPN Configuration wizard allows you to configure the remote ISA Server computer to initiate and receive connections. The ISA Virtual Private Network Configuration wizard allows roaming users to connect to the VPN.

Chapter 8

Review

1. What four major components does the H.323 standard define for real-time, network-based, interactive videoconferencing?

   H.323 defines terminals, gateways, gatekeepers, and multipoint control units (MCUs).

2. What functions does H.323 Gatekeeper provide for H.323 videoconferencing clients?

   H.323 Gatekeeper provides address translation that allows H.323 clients to call each other by specifying aliases instead of IP addresses. H.323 Gatekeeper also provides automatic client registration through the RAS protocol. Next, it allows you to apply call control rules and routing rules that specify where to forward calls. Finally, a gatekeeper is also necessary if you want to videoconference through firewalls or use an H.323 gateway to route client calls through the PSTN.

3. Describe the process by which an H.323 client registered with H.323 Gatekeeper on one network calls the e-mail alias of an H.323 client registered with H.323 Gatekeeper on another network.

   The H.323 client connects with your local H.323 Gatekeeper. When H.323 Gatekeeper does not recognize the domain specified in the e-mail alias as an internal address, it forwards the call to the ISA Server computer within your company. ISA Server looks up the address for the domain and makes the query over the Internet to resolve the domain name's associated IP address. When the ISA Server at the remote organization receives the query for the H.323 client alias, it contacts its internal H.323 Gatekeeper to obtain the correct in-house address. The H.323 Gatekeeper at the remote site then translates the alias into a network address for its ISA Server. The remote ISA Server then sends a confirmation back to the ISA Server at your company and establishes the connection. From this point through the end of the communication, both ISA Servers hold open the link established by the H.323 Gatekeepers.

4. An H.323 client attempts to call another client by specifying the client's alias, *someone@microsoft.com*. Two e-mail address rules match the requested alias. The first rule specifies the suffix pattern *microsoft.com* and has a metric of 4. The second specifies the exact pattern *microsoft.com* and has a metric of 5. Which rule will be applied to the call?

   The second rule will be applied because an exact pattern type always takes precedence over a suffix pattern type.

5. What is the benefit of a call routing rule configured to route to a gateway destination?

   When a call gets forwarded to an H.323 gateway, the gateway can allow the call to traverse to the PSTN.

Chapter 9

▶ Page 372

1. For the first Web connection in the log (initiated at 02:31:35), was the traffic heavier from the client to the server, or vice versa?

   The traffic was heavier from the server to the client. The cs-bytes value is 259, and the sc-bytes value is 2200.

2. For this same connection, was the Web request fulfilled from the cache or from the Internet?

   The request was fulfilled from the cache, as evidenced by the s-object-source value of Cache.

3. At what time was a connection reset by the remote side?

   02:34:47. This is the time that the Web Proxy service received an sc-status code value of 10054.

4. Was the object requested at 02:31:45 found in the cache? Had the object been modified? What source was ultimately used to fulfill the request?

   The object was found in the cache, but the object had been modified. The Internet was the ultimate source of the request. This is known because the s-object-source value for the request is VFInet.

5. Which Web operation was conducted at 04:55:14? Was the destination found?

   A POST operation was made, and the destination was not found. This is because the s-operation value is POST and the sc-status value is 404.

Review

1. What four actions can be configured for an alert? Which of these actions is enabled by default whenever an alert is enabled?

   You may configure an alert to send an e-mail message, run a specific program, log the event in the Windows Event Log, stop or start any ISA Server service. By default, alerts are configured to log the event to the Windows 2000 Event Log.

2. What would the name be for a Firewall service log file in ISA format created on October 23, 2002?

   The log file would be named FWSD20021023.

3. What credentials must a user have to configure a report job?

   The user must have local administrator privileges on every ISA Server computer in the array, and the user must be able to access and launch DCOM objects on every ISA Server in the array.

4. What is one disadvantage of applying a bandwidth priority other than the default bandwidth priority to a connection?

   New bandwidth priorities require more processing power than the default bandwidth priority does.

5. What is the advantage of using ISA Server Performance Monitor to view data gathered by ISA Server performance counters?

   ISA Server Performance Monitor allows you to monitor ISA Server data separately from other system data, and it includes 21 ISA Server performance counters that are preloaded into System Monitor, the real-time monitoring tool.

Chapter 10

▶ Page 433

5. In the Local Address column, how many connections are currently active for the external interface of the ISA Server computer? Look at the foreign address for each of those connections. Are the addresses listed as foreign truly remote, or do they merely represent another port of the same local address? Which ports are being used in these foreign addresses to send information to the local external address of your ISA Server computer?

   Write your answers in the space below:

   Answers will vary.

6. On the ISA Server computer, open Microsoft Internet Explorer and connect to an external Web site such as *www.microsoft.com*.

7. While the Web page is still downloading in Internet Explorer, switch to the command prompt window and type **netstat –an –p tcp** again.

   An output of all active TCP ports on the ISA Server computer appears.

▶ Page 434

8. Look at the end of the output list. In the Local Address column, how many more connections are active for the external interface of the ISA Server computer than you recorded in Step 5? Do you see any active ports on foreign addresses that you did not list before? After you view this data, which foreign port can you determine is used to send Web data to the local external IP address?

   Port 80 is used to send Web data to the local computer.

9. To which local ports on the external interface of ISA Server computer is this Web data sent? These are dynamic ports that vary from connection to connection. Write the number corresponding to these ports in the space below.

   Answers will vary. Several dynamic ports are active on the external interface.

Review

1. Your network configuration consists of an ISA Server installed on a DMZ. The address space behind the ISA Server consists of the 192.168.0.0/24 subnet, and the DMZ in front of the ISA Server computer has been configured with the 192.168.1.0/24 subnet. The ISA Server computer has an internal address of 192.168.0.1 and an external address of 192.168.1.99. The external gateway has an address of 192.168.1.1.

   You are unable to access the Internet from any client computer behind ISA Server. On the ISA Server computer, you run the Route print command at the C:> prompt and receive the output shown in Figure 10.5.

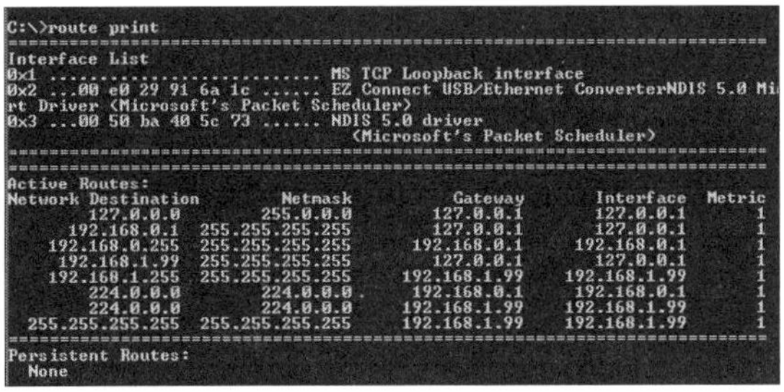

```
C:\>route print
===========================================================================
Interface List
0x1 ........................... MS TCP Loopback interface
0x2 ...00 e0 29 91 6a 1c ...... EZ Connect USB/Ethernet ConverterNDIS 5.0 Mi
rt Driver (Microsoft's Packet Scheduler)
0x3 ...00 50 ba 40 5c 73 ...... NDIS 5.0 driver
                                 (Microsoft's Packet Scheduler)
===========================================================================
===========================================================================
Active Routes:
Network Destination        Netmask          Gateway       Interface  Metric
        127.0.0.0        255.0.0.0        127.0.0.1       127.0.0.1       1
      192.168.0.1  255.255.255.255        127.0.0.1       127.0.0.1       1
    192.168.0.255  255.255.255.255      192.168.0.1     192.168.0.1       1
     192.168.1.99  255.255.255.255        127.0.0.1       127.0.0.1       1
    192.168.1.255  255.255.255.255     192.168.1.99    192.168.1.99       1
        224.0.0.0        224.0.0.0.     192.168.0.1     192.168.0.1       1
        224.0.0.0        224.0.0.0     192.168.1.99    192.168.1.99       1
  255.255.255.255  255.255.255.255     192.168.1.99    192.168.1.99       1
===========================================================================
Persistent Routes:
  None
```

Figure 10.5 Routing table – Question 1

   What is the error in the routing table? How can you fix the problem by using the Route command?

   The problem with the routing table is that it has not been configured with a default route pointing to the external gateway. To fix the problem, you can type the following command:

```
route add 0.0.0.0 mask 0.0.0.0 192.168.1.1
```

2. After you reboot the server specified in Question 1, you find that the problem returns. How can you avoid reconfiguring the routing table every time the computer reboots?

   You can avoid the problem by adding a persistent route. You can achieve this either by adding a static route in the Routing and Remote Access console or by using the –p switch with the ROUTE utility, as follows:

   ```
   route add -p 0.0.0.0 mask 0.0.0.0 192.168.1.1
   ```

3. With what tool could you spot a SYN attack in progress? What is the telltale sign of a SYN attack?

   You could spot a SYN attack in progress with the Netstat command. SYN attacks are distinguished by a flood of half-open connections originating from spoofed source addresses with incrementally increasing port numbers.

4. What is the purpose of attempting to telnet to a specific TCP or UDP port?

   When you can successfully Telnet a specific TCP or UDP port, this means that the service located at that port can accept commands from external users. This may be a desirable condition if you want to publish a service on a given port, but it may also be a security hazard if certain exploitable services are left open to attack.

5. If you run the Local ISA Server VPN Configuration wizard and specify L2TP as the authentication protocol, how many IP packet filters will be created? Which ports will be opened statically by these IP packet filters?

   Two IP packet filters will be created to allow the L2TP protocol, at ports 500 and 1701.

Appendix B

Questions

You plan to upgrade the two existing computers in the Seattle office running Windows NT 4.0 Server and Proxy Server 2.0 to ISA server. You also plan to deploy ISA Server at Contoso's two branch offices in Paris and Orlando, as shown in Figure B.1. The Contoso Microsoft Exchange Server computer, published internally in the Proxy Server 2.0 environment, sends and receives Internet mail for internal clients.

Appendix A Questions and Answers 465

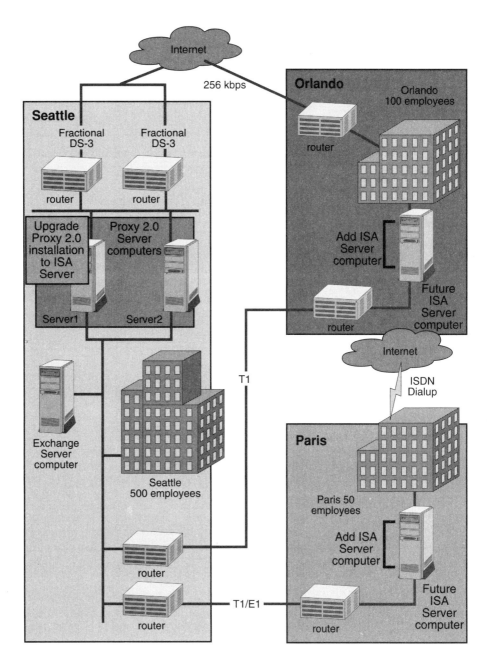

Figure B.1 Established network at Contoso, Ltd. showing the future placement of ISA Server computers

1. What must you do to successfully upgrade your Proxy Server 2.0 installation environment to ISA Server?

   Remove the two Proxy 2.0 members from the array and then upgrade their operating system installations to Windows 2000 Server and Service Pack 1. Windows 2000 Setup will warn you that Proxy Server 2.0 is not compatible, but it will continue with the upgrade. Once the Windows 2000 Server installation is complete, update the Active Directory schema for the domain by running the Initialize The Enterprise routine. Install ISA Server on the first computer and create an array and enterprise policy. Install ISA Server on the other computer and migrate it to this new array. The cache from the Proxy Server 2.0 computer will be deleted and a new cache will be created for ISA Server. Settings from the Proxy Server 2.0 installation will be migrated to the new array depending how the enterprise policy is configured. Refer to the ISA Server Help file topic titled "Microsoft Proxy Server 2.0 array considerations" for a table describing how rules migrate between Proxy Server 2.0 and ISA Server.

2. After the migration to ISA Server, the Seattle Exchange Server computer cannot send and receive e-mail from the Internet. What changes must you make to allow it to do this?

   Publishing an Exchange Server computer in a Proxy Server 2.0 environment requires that the server run the Winsock client with a custom configuration file, WspClnt.ini. This configuration is not supported in ISA Server.

   On the Exchange Server computer rename or delete WspClnt.ini and configure it as a secure network address translation (SecureNAT) client by setting the internal network adapter's default gateway to the Internet Protocol (IP) address of the internal network adapter in the ISA Server computer. Verify the default gateway and other network adapter settings with the command *ipconfig /all*. Do not install the Firewall Client software on the Exchange Server computer. You must publish the e-mail server in ISA Server so that external Simple Mail Transfer Protocol (SMTP) mail will be forwarded to it. Run the Secure Mail Server wizard and ISA Server will walk you through steps to publish SMTP, Post Office Protocol 3 (POP3), and Exchange Server Remote Procedure Call (RPC) ports.

Publishing the SMTP protocol permits the Exchange Server computer to receive mail from the Internet. The POP3 and RPC protocols allow external clients to connect to the Exchange Server computer to receive mail. Alternatively, without the help of the wizard, manually create a server publishing rule for the SMTP Server protocol definition and the others, as required. The Exchange Server computer initiates its own outbound connections independent of any publishing (inbound) Transmission Control Protocol/Internet Protocol (TCP/IP) session and connection. Therefore you must create a protocol rule that permits SMTP (port 25) outbound traffic from the Exchange Server computer to external clients (i.e., the Internet) to send outbound mail.

The Contoso main office and two branch offices are in the same Windows 2000 domain. The branch offices are directly connected to the main office by two 1.54 mbps T1/E1 wide area network (WAN) connections. The Orlando office is connected to the Internet via a 256 kbps circuit and the Paris office is connected over a dial-up 56 kbps Integrated Services Digital Network (ISDN) line. Seattle and Orlando clients use Windows 2000 Professional, and the Paris office uses a mix of Windows 2000 and UNIX clients. You have migrated to two ISA Server computers as a single array in Seattle and wish to deploy ISA Server computers in the two branch offices to increase Internet application performance. You want to provide a redundant connection to the Internet for all offices and log Web activity by user. You also want to centrally manage this solution from Seattle and route all Internet traffic through the main branch array.

3. How would you deploy ISA Server into these branch offices to provide centralized management?

   Install ISA Server at the two branch offices in Integrated mode to provide caching and secure the redundant Internet connections. Configure ISA Server at the branch offices as separate arrays and name them Paris and Orlando, respectively. Add the new Paris and Orlando arrays to the enterprise policy that includes the Seattle array. The enterprise policy enables centralized management of the protocol, site and content rules, and many of the array policy elements.

4. Describe how to improve Web and File Transfer Protocol (FTP) performance for the three offices.

   Configure caching for the three arrays to provide optimum Web and FTP performance. From the properties of the Network Configuration node in ISA Management, chain the Paris and Orlando branch office arrays to the main office Seattle array. For each array, configure all outgoing Web requests to "resolve requests within array before routing." Enable this from the array properties Outgoing Web Requests tab. This creates a hierarchical cache and all outgoing requests will use the Cache Array Routing Protocol (CARP) to efficiently determine what array (if any) contains the cached object before being routed directly to the Internet. For each array, enable the HTTP Redirector Filter application filter to allow SecureNAT and Firewall clients to take advantage of caching. This option appears in the details pane of the Application Filters node. To help relieve Internet traffic congestion during work hours, configure scheduled caching to shift network usage to off-peak times. Enable and configure active caching to refresh popular content in the cache before it expires. Scheduled caching and active caching are configured from the Cache Configuration node in ISA Management.

5. After configuring caching for the arrays, you notice in Performance Monitor that the Cache Hit Ratio is low. What can you do to improve the Cache Hit Ratio?

   The Cache Hit Ratio provides a quick means of determining the effectiveness of your caching configuration. A Cache Hit Ratio of zero means that caching is not functional, and a low cache hit ratio means that most of the requests are being served from the Internet and that the content is not cacheable or the cache size is too small. Increase the size of the cache or increase the time-to-live (TTL) for cached objects.

6. Describe how to route all Internet traffic from the branch offices through the Seattle ISA Server array while providing a backup connection if the primary connection fails.

   Create a destination set that includes the internal computers within each branch office. For each branch office array (Paris and Orlando), create a routing rule to route all requests not in the branch office destination set to a specified upstream server and enter the name of the main branch array (Seattle). In the same routing rule, specify that when the primary route is unavailable retrieve the requests directly from the backup route via the dedicated Internet connection in Orlando or the ISDN dial-up connection in Paris.

7. You review the Web proxy logs and notice that all of the users are anonymous. What changes should you make to log the names of these users?

The Windows 2000 Professional clients running Microsoft Internet Explorer support Web Proxy user authentication. On UNIX platforms, configure the clients with a (Conseil Européen pour la Recherche Nucléaire) CERN–compatible browser that also supports Web Proxy user authentication. From the Properties dialog box on each array, click the Outgoing Web Requests tab and then enable the Ask Unauthenticated Users For Identification check box to provide user level authentication and logging. From this same property dialog box, select integrated authentication (the Integrated check box) or digest authentication (the Digest With This Domain check box) for a secure means of authentication and select basic authentication (Basic With This Domain check box) for Hypertext Transfer Protocol (HTTP) authentication compatibility. This last option allows browser clients that do not support Windows NT Challenge/Response authentication to authenticate using clear-text account information. If the client's browser is not able to transparently pass authentication information to the ISA Server computer, the browser will prompt the user for authentication information. This authentication is valid for the session and independent of Web server site authentication requests.

The users in the Paris office have been denied access to some regional sites because their outgoing source IP address is that of the Seattle office ISA Server computer instead of a Paris IP address.

8. How would you permit all regional traffic (defined as all sites in the .fr top-level domain) originating from the Paris office to route to the Internet through the ISDN dial-up line and continue to route the remaining traffic through the main office?

Create a destination set that includes *.fr domains and a routing rule that retrieves these requests directly. Order the rule appropriately so that it is processed before the other routing rules that route traffic to the main office array.

In Seattle, Contoso Ltd. wants to deploy three Web servers in a Web farm using Network Load Balancing (NLB). The Web farm will be located in a perimeter network and protected by ISA Server. External clients can access this Web farm via HTTP and Secure Hypertext Transfer Protocol (HTTPS) protocols as shown in Figure B.2. These Web servers need to connect to and exchange information across MS SQL Sockets (TCP port 1433) with a Microsoft SQL Server computer that is located in the internal network.

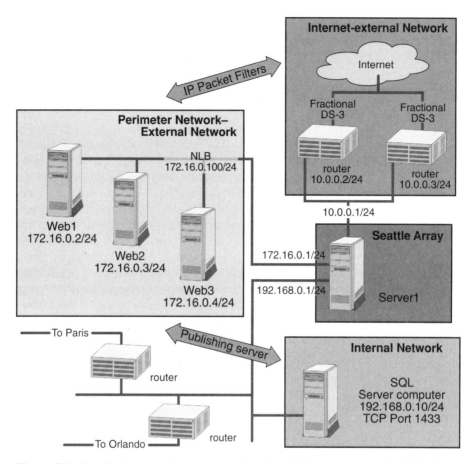

Figure B.2 Configuring a perimeter network and publishing servers using ISA Server

9. How would you configure the perimeter network and publish the three Web servers to allow the required access?

    Configure the ISA Server computer that will connect to the perimeter network with a third network adapter (172.16.0.1/24). The network adapter connecting to the perimeter network must be defined as an external network in ISA server. Verify that the Local Address Table (LAT) of the Seattle array does not include the perimeter network (172.16.0.0/24). Communication between two external networks (such as from the Internet to the perimeter network) across the ISA Server computer is handled by IP Routing and restricted by IP Packet Filters. To permit this enable IP Packet Filters and IP Routing for the Seattle array. Both of these options are configured in the properties of the IP Packet Filters node. This node is located below the Access Policy node in ISA Management.

Configure the Seattle array to allow Internet access to the perimeter network. Create an IP Packet Filter for HTTP (port 80), and HTTPS (port 443) that allows all remote users access to this local perimeter network.

In order for the Web servers to communicate with the SQL Server on the internal network, you must publish the SQL Server computer. The SQL Sockets protocol is not defined in the default installation of ISA Server. Therefore, create a new protocol definition named SQL Sockets and define its properties as inbound direction TCP port 1433. You want your external Web users to access the Web servers that in turn access the SQL Server. You do not want other external users directly accessing the SQL Server. Limit access to only the Web servers using a Client Address Set. Create a Client Address Set that includes the IP address of each of the Web servers (172.16.2–4). Confirm that IP Packet Filtering is enabled. If IP packet filtering is not enabled, the server publishing rule applies to all clients, and the Client Address Set is not reference. Next, publish the server using the protocol and client set you just defined. Configure the publishing rule so that the external interface address is the perimeter network adapter IP address (172.16.0.1) and the internal address is the SQL Server IP address (192.168.0.10). Configure the SQL Server as a SecureNAT client by setting its network adapter's default gateway to the IP address of the internal network adapter in the ISA Server computer (192.168.0.1).

Contoso Ltd. purchased a proprietary server application and installed it on the internal network. You wish to allow remote access to this application for employees only. The employees will access this application by first connecting to the Internet and then running a client application that uses TCP port 2122.

10. Explain how to publish the proprietary server application.

    Web server publishing supports rule restrictions that apply to both client address sets and to user and group. However, server publishing rules only support client address sets (IP address), so you must identify and restrict access based on IP address ranges alone. Create a client address set or sets that include all of your remote users, such as the IP address range of Contoso's Internet Service Provider (ISP).

    Next, create an inbound protocol definition for TCP port 2122. A protocol must be defined as inbound for it to be listed in the available server publishing protocols. Publish the server by specifying the external IP address of the ISA Server computer and the internal IP address of the proprietary server application. Restrict access to the defined client address set.

The Contoso networking group has redesigned the network to create an Information Technology (IT) maintenance subnet and added a Quality Assurance (QA) lab on its own subnet as illustrated in Figure B.3. However, since adding these new subnets and routers, the QA staff members are unable to access the Internet from their lab.

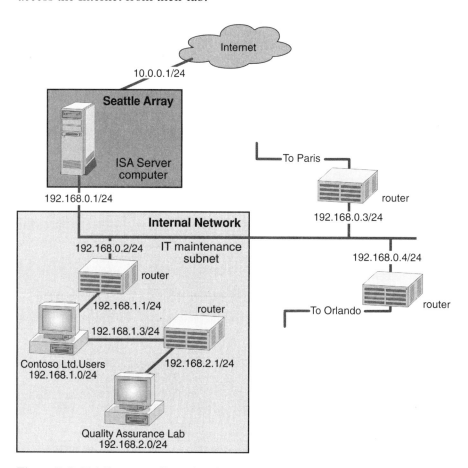

Figure B.3 ISA Server configuration for complex subnets

Appendix A Questions and Answers   473

11. What should you reconfigure on the ISA Server computer and on the clients in these subnets to restore connectivity?

   Check the routing table for the ISA Server computer and add a destination and gateway for the QA lab assigned to the ISA Server computer's internal interface. In this example, the ISA Server computer must be configured to route packets destined for the 192.168.1.0/24 and 192.168.2.0/24 subnets to the gateway 192.168.0.2 via the interface 192.168.0.1. Use the *route* command to verify and troubleshoot the routing problem. Configure the default gateway of the intermediate routers to point to the router upstream, and ultimately to the internal interface of the ISA Server computer.

   Verify that the default gateways for SecureNAT clients are configured for the appropriate intermediate router IP address. For this example, configure the computers in the QA lab with a default gateway of 192.168.2.1. Also, verify that the proxy address for the Firewall clients and Web Proxy clients are configured for the Internal IP address of the ISA Server computer (192.168.0.1). Once the intermediate routers and the clients are configured correctly, TCP/IP routing will ensure client connections.

Executive management is asking you to reduce expenses in your department. You think you can do this by replacing the dedicated T1/E1 WAN connection between the main office and the Paris branch office with a virtual private network (VPN) connection and by upgrading the dial-up ISDN connection connecting the Paris office to the Internet with a higher-capacity circuit. You want the Paris office to access its Internet content directly and to no longer be managed from or through the main office in Seattle. Staff in the Seattle office will initiate the VPN connection. You have also created a separate domain for Paris and located its domain controller in the Paris office. The networking team has successfully upgraded the network and you have removed the dial-up adapter from the Paris ISA Server computer and added the external network adapter to connect the Paris office to the Internet, as shown in Figure B.4.

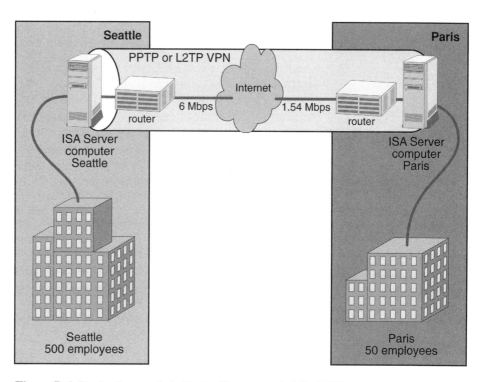

Figure B.4 Revised network in Paris office expanded for VPN

12. What are the steps that you must perform to reconfigure the ISA Server computer to support this new topology?

    Remove the Paris ISA Server array from the enterprise policy and uninstall ISA Server to remove the member computer from the array. Add this computer to the Paris domain and run the ISA Enterprise Initialization tool to update the new Paris domain Active Directory schema for ISA Server. Reinstall ISA Server and create a new ISA Server array in the Paris domain. This will add the computer to this new array. Add protocol and site and content rules to allow Paris staff members Internet access.

    In Seattle, configure a VPN connection to the Paris office by walking through a Local VPN configuration. On the Paris ISA Server computer, use the Configure A Remote Virtual Private Network wizard and the VPN data file created when configuring the Local VPN to set up the Paris office VPN endpoint.

13. You have configured the VPN for the Seattle office but are unable to connect to the Paris office. What configurations should you review to troubleshoot this connection?

    Check the specified protocol. ISA Server supports both Layer Two Tunneling Protocol (L2TP) and Point-to-Point Tunneling Protocol (PPTP). L2TP uses the Internet Protocol Security (IPSec). Also be sure to properly configure the remote endpoint by importing the appropriate *.vpc VPN wizard file. By default the VPN wizard does not permit two-way connection initiation unless specified. Also, run the Routing and Remote Access console to ensure that the static routes are configured and the demand-dial interface appearing in the details pane of the General node is operational.

Contoso Ltd. employs a remote sales force that travels the world and connects to the main office via a toll-free private connection modem service. This direct access is expensive and often busy during times of heavy use. You believe you can save money and provide more people access by configuring a VPN using ISA Server.

14. Explain how to migrate the users from this private dial-up service to VPN across an ISA Server deployment.

    Run the Virtual Private Network Configuration wizard in ISA Management on the Seattle array. Running this wizard starts Routing and Remote Access Server and configures it with VPN ports for PPTP and L2TP tunnels. The wizard also adds four IP Packet Filter rules to permit PPTP and L2TP packets access to the ISA Server computer. For each client, configure a dial-up account to the Internet and a secondary VPN connection. For Windows 2000 clients, use the Network Connection wizard and configure a new connection to a private network through the Internet. Specify the VPN host name as the IP address or fully qualified domain name of the external adapter on the ISA Server computer.

These remote users frequently visit the other two Contoso offices and dock their portable computers into the Local Area Network (LAN). However, whenever they are not connected to their home office LAN, they are unable to access the Internet. These users run the Firewall Client software.

15. Why are the users not able to access the Internet from remote offices? Describe an administratively efficient means for fixing this problem without manually configuring every portable computer.

    The Firewall client or Web Proxy client and the ISA Server computer might not be configured for automatic discovery. From the Control Panel on a client computer, double-click the Firewall Client icon and select the Automatically Detect ISA Server check box. The automatic discovery of a Web Proxy client is done through the client's Web browser. When automatic discovery is disabled clients will be unable to update their connections to other ISA Server computers automatically, such as when visiting other offices.

    ISA Server supports updating clients over the Web Proxy Auto Discovery Protocol (WPAD). From the array properties dialog box, click the Auto Discovery tab. Then, select the Publish Automatic Discovery Information check box and specify the port for automatic discovery requests. By default this is port 80. This port designation is the default port for the Web server. Therefore, if you are running Internet Information Services (IIS) on the ISA Server computer, verify that no Web sites on the server are using port 80, otherwise it will conflict with autodiscovery set to the same port. Use a tool such as *netstat –an* to check for other applications sharing this port. Next, configure either DNS or DHCP to configure the clients with the appropriate WPAD entry. Detailed instructions for how to configure the DNS and DHCP entries are located in this training kit and in the ISA Server Help files.

The Orlando office has reorganized and re-branded with a new company name. To reflect this, the entire office has migrated to a new Active Directory domain. However, the network traffic from Orlando is still configured to route to the Internet via the Seattle office ISA Server computer.

16. After the domain change, you notice that your network traffic to the Internet has increased significantly and your users have slower intranet access. The Orlando staff members run the Firewall Client software. What is the most likely reason for the network delay that users are experiencing?

    Check the logical locations for both the internal and external domain name servers (DNS) and confirm that the clients are not configured to resolve internal computer requests by external name servers. With the Firewall Client software enabled, the client sends name resolution requests to be resolved by the ISA Server computer instead of the client resolving them. Because clients are using the Firewall Client software, configure the Local Domain Table (LDT) with the names of the internal domains. The Firewall Client software will first query the LDT for its destination domain. If the domain is listed then the client will resolve the name locally and not forward the request to the ISA Server computer for name resolution. This is an efficient means for resolving names of internal domains. This LDT query will only work with computers configured as Firewall clients.

APPENDIX B

Deploying and Administering ISA Server in a Complex Network

About This Appendix

This appendix walks you through several hypothetical installations of Microsoft Internet Security and Acceleration Server 2000 (ISA Server) Enterprise Edition to test your understanding of and ability to troubleshoot the product. To create realistic deployment and administration strategies, the situations in this scenario require that you have knowledge of networking and Microsoft Windows 2000. These situations are developed throughout the chapter and explore different aspects of ISA Server. You will be asked several questions after reading a brief background to different situations in the scenario. The answers to these questions are listed in Appendix A.

Before You Begin

To complete the activities and answer questions in this appendix you should have a thorough understanding of the following:

- The contents of this training kit

- Windows 2000 Server fundamentals—including Routing and Remote Access Server, authentication types, domain design, Performance Monitor, and security account management

- Internetworking concepts—including routing across subnets, packet fundamentals (Transmission Control Protocol [TCP], User Datagram Protocol [UDP], source and destination port), Domain Name Resolution (DNS) services, and Dynamic Host Configuration Protocol (DHCP)

- Common Windows 2000 troubleshooting and utility tools—including ipconfig, netstat, route, and ping

Scenario Background

You are responsible for the network and security design for Contoso Ltd., a large multinational company with headquarters in Seattle, Washington. Contoso markets and sells its product through a large field sales team and has branch offices in Orlando, Florida and Paris, France. There are approximately 500 sales, marketing, and development staff members based in Seattle; 100 staff members based in Orlando; and 50 staff members based in Paris. You have been with Contoso for five years and have designed and deployed its existing infrastructure. You are now planning to upgrade your Microsoft Proxy Server 2.0 installations with ISA Server because you want to take advantage of its higher performance caching engine and added security features. This scenario walks you through parts of the installation and administration and asks you questions to test your knowledge of ISA Server.

Questions

You plan to upgrade the two existing computers in the Seattle office running Windows NT 4.0 Server and Proxy Server 2.0 to ISA Server. You also plan to deploy ISA Server at Contoso's two branch offices in Paris and Orlando, as shown in Figure B.1. The Contoso Microsoft Exchange Server computer, published internally in the Proxy Server 2.0 environment, sends and receives Internet mail for internal clients.

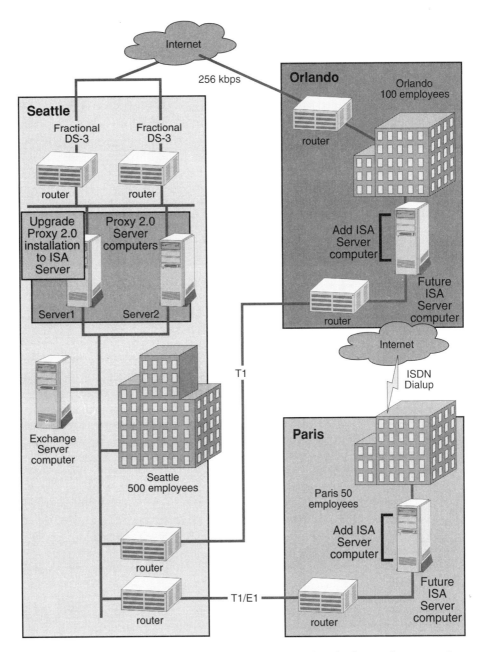

Figure B.1 Established network at Contoso, Ltd. showing the future placement of ISA Server computers

1. What must you do to successfully upgrade your Proxy Server 2.0 installation environment to ISA Server?

2. After the migration to ISA Server, the Seattle Exchange Server computer cannot send and receive e-mail from the Internet. What changes must you make to allow it to do this?

The Contoso main office and two branch offices are in the same Windows 2000 domain. The branch offices are directly connected to the main office by two 1.54 mbps T1/E1 wide area network (WAN) connections. The Orlando office is connected to the Internet via a 256 kbps circuit and the Paris office is connected over a dial-up 56 kbps Integrated Services Digital Network (ISDN) line. Seattle and Orlando clients use Windows 2000 Professional, and the Paris office uses a mix of Windows 2000 and UNIX clients. You have migrated to two ISA Server computers as a single array in Seattle and wish to deploy ISA Server computers in the two branch offices to increase Internet application performance. You want to provide a redundant connection to the Internet for all offices and log Web activity by user. You also want to centrally manage this solution from Seattle and route all Internet traffic through the main branch array.

3. How would you deploy ISA Server into these branch offices to provide centralized management?

4. Describe how to improve Web and File Transfer Protocol (FTP) performance for the three offices.

5. After configuring caching for the arrays, you notice in Performance Monitor that the Cache Hit Ratio is low. What can you do to improve the Cache Hit Ratio?

6. Describe how to route all Internet traffic from the branch offices through the Seattle ISA Server array while providing a backup connection if the primary connection fails.

7. You review the Web proxy logs and notice that all of the users are anonymous. What changes should you make to log the names of these users?

The users in the Paris office have been denied access to some regional sites because their outgoing source IP address is that of the Seattle office ISA Server computer instead of a Paris IP address.

8. How would you permit all regional traffic (defined as all sites in the .fr top-level domain) originating from the Paris office to route to the Internet through the ISDN dial-up line and continue to route the remaining traffic through the main office?

In Seattle, Contoso Ltd. wants to deploy three Web servers in a Web farm using Network Load Balancing (NLB). The Web farm will be located in a perimeter network and protected by ISA Server. External clients can access this Web farm via HTTP and Secure Hypertext Transfer Protocol (HTTPS) protocols as shown in Figure B.2. These Web servers need to connect to and exchange information across MS SQL Sockets (TCP port 1433) with a Microsoft SQL Server computer that is located in the internal network.

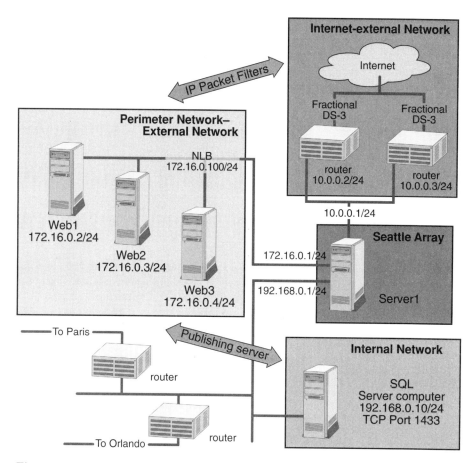

Figure B.2 Configuring a perimeter network and publishing servers using ISA Server

9. How would you configure the perimeter network and publish the three Web servers to allow the required access?

Contoso Ltd. purchased a proprietary server application and installed it on the internal network. You wish to allow remote access to this application for employees only. The employees will access this application by first connecting to the Internet and then running a client application that uses TCP port 2122.

10. Explain how to publish the proprietary server application.

The Contoso networking group has redesigned the network to create an Information Technology (IT) maintenance subnet and added a Quality Assurance (QA) lab on its own subnet as illustrated in Figure B.3. However, since adding these new subnets and routers, the QA staff members are unable to access the Internet from their lab.

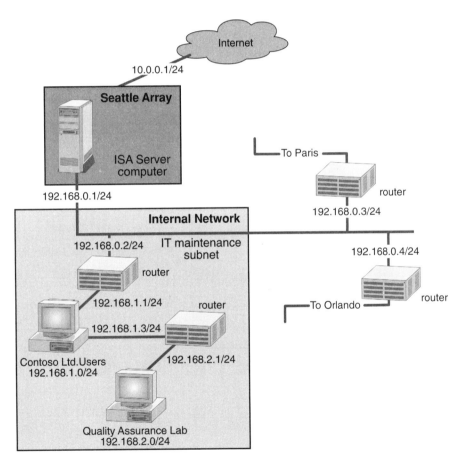

Figure B.3 ISA Server configuration for complex subnets

11. What should you reconfigure on the ISA Server computer and on the clients in these subnets to restore connectivity?

Executive management is asking you to reduce expenses in your department. You think you can do this by replacing the dedicated T1/E1 WAN connection between the main office and the Paris branch office with a virtual private network (VPN) connection and by upgrading the dial-up ISDN connection connecting the Paris office to the Internet with a higher-capacity circuit. You want the Paris office to access its Internet content directly and to no longer be managed from or through the main office in Seattle. Staff in the Seattle office will initiate the VPN connection. You have also created a separate domain for Paris and located its domain controller in the Paris office. The networking team has successfully upgraded the network and you have removed the dial-up adapter from the Paris ISA Server computer and added the external network adapter to connect the Paris office to the Internet, as shown in Figure B.4.

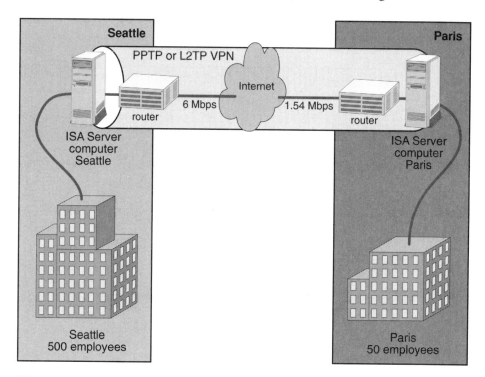

Figure B.4 Revised network in Paris office expanded for VPN

12. What are the steps that you must perform to reconfigure the ISA Server computer to support this new topology?

13. You have configured the VPN for the Seattle office but are unable to connect to the Paris office. What configurations should you review to troubleshoot this connection?

Contoso Ltd. employs a remote sales force that travels the world and connects to the main office via a toll-free private connection modem service. This direct access is expensive and often busy during times of heavy use. You believe you can save money and provide more people access by configuring a VPN using ISA Server.

14. Explain how to migrate the users from this private dial-up service to VPN across an ISA Server deployment.

These remote users frequently visit the other two Contoso offices and dock their portable computers into the Local Area Network (LAN). However, whenever they are not connected to their home office LAN, they are unable to access the Internet. These users run the Firewall Client software.

15. Why are the users not able to access the Internet from remote offices? Describe an administratively efficient means for fixing this problem without manually configuring every portable computer.

The Orlando office has reorganized and re-branded with a new company name. To reflect this, the entire office has migrated to a new Active Directory domain. However, the network traffic from Orlando is still configured to route to the Internet via the Seattle office ISA Server computer.

16. After the domain change, you notice that your network traffic to the Internet has increased significantly and your users have slower intranet access. The Orlando staff members run the Firewall Client software. What is the most likely reason for the network delay that users are experiencing?

APPENDIX C

Event Messages

Microsoft Internet Security and Acceleration (ISA) Server uses Event Viewer to record events that occur during its operation. You can use Event Viewer to monitor and troubleshoot events.

This section provides information about ISA Server events, including:

- **ID number.** This is the number that identifies the event type. The event number helps technical support representatives track events in the system.
- **Event message.** This is a description of the event that also appears on the property page for the event.
- **Explanation.** This is a description of the possible cause of the event.
- **User action.** This is a description of the actions you can take to solve or prevent the problem.

There are four severity levels for individual event messages:

- Success
- Informational
- Warning
- Error

Use Event Viewer to view the severity level or to view more information regarding individual messages. Successful events do not appear in Event Viewer.

In the following sections, event messages are grouped by category.

Alert Event Messages

These messages refer to events related to alerts in ISA Server.

Event ID: 14033
Event Message
Alert service did not start. Alerts are limited to event reporting. There might be a problem in the Microsoft ISA Server Control Service. Restart the service. The Firewall and Web Proxy services are dependent on this service, so you also need to restart them.

Event ID: 14040
Event Message
Mail Alert service stopped responding because Mapi.dll cannot be located.

Event ID: 14045
Event Message
Mail alert for %1 failed.

Event ID: 14050
Event Message
Mail alert %1 stopped because of a configuration error (%2).

Event ID: 14051
Event Message
Mail alert %1 (%2) stopped because it could not log on or connect to the server. The server may be down or incorrectly specified.

Event ID: 14052
Event Message
Mail alert %1 stopped because the mail server refused to accept the message.

Event ID: 14053
Event Message
Mail alert %1 stopped because the sender name is not valid.

Event ID: 14054
Event Message
Mail alert %1 stopped because the recipient name is not valid.

Event ID: 14064
Event Message
Unknown event %1 signaled the alert service. The reported event does not appear in storage. If you recently installed an application filter, it is probably the source of the error. Remove any application filters that have been installed recently. If this does not solve the problem, reinstall ISA Server.

Event ID: 14065
Event Message
Alert service: One or more of the actions associated with alert %1 has failed. The failure is linked to configuration settings. The mail server may be down, or the specified command may not exist. Check the Event Viewer for related errors and fix them accordingly.

Event ID: 14069

Event Message
The alert service found more then one alert with the same event condition, server name, and additional key. The duplicated alert '%1' is ignored. For more information about this event, see ISA Server Help.

Explanation
The alert duplication is the result of one or more configuration settings that are inconsistent or missing in the registry or Active Directory, depending on ISA Server configuration. This could be the result of an error in the configuration, an incomplete administration operation, or other internal errors. The actions in this duplicate alert are specified in the initial alert and are ignored by the service.

User Action
Delete the erroneous alert with ISA Management or a script. To locate the alert, use the name of the alert as it appears in the message.

Event ID: 14072

Event Message
The alert service failed to logon as user %2 to run the command %3 specified for the alert '%1'. The error code in the Data area of the event properties indicates the cause of the failure. For more information about this event, see ISA Server Help.

Explanation
Incorrect credentials can be caused by a misspelled user name, password, or domain name. It is also possible that the Windows 2000 password has changed and the password that is stored in ISA Server is now incorrect or that the domain name changed.

User Action
Verify that all the credentials for this alert are set correctly.

Event ID: 14144

Event Message
The alert service failed to initialize because system call %1 failed. Some information in the response may have already expired in the cache. If an error code is shown in the Data area of the event properties, it indicates the cause of the failure.

Event ID: 14180

Event Message
Alert Service: failed to log event to system log. The following message '%1' could not be logged.

Bandwidth Event Messages

These messages refer to events related to the bandwidth control in ISA Server.

Event ID: 13002

Event Message
Bandwidth control completed successfully.

Event ID: 13103

Event Message
Initialization of bandwidth control failed. The ISA Server that uses the bandwidth controller failed to initialize the client dynamic-link library (DLL). Look at previous event entries to find the reason for the failure.

Event ID: 13104

Event Message

The call to %1 failed. The failure is probably due to insufficient memory. Close some applications and try again. If that does not work, verify that Active Directory is working. For more information about managing memory resources, see Windows 2000 Help.

Event ID: 13105

Event Message

Insufficient memory for %1. The bandwidth control did not have sufficient memory resources. Close some applications and try again. For more information about managing memory resources, see Windows 2000 Help.

Event ID: 13106

Event Message

Cannot match IP to an interface. Flow control for the specified IP address did not take effect. If message was reported during network configuration changes it can be ignored. If you continue to receive this message, you may need to restart ISA services.

Cache Event Messages

These messages refer to events connected to ISA Server cache.

Event ID: 13107

Event Message

The Scheduled Content Download Service has stopped the job %1. %2 pages (objects) visited.

Event ID: 13108

Event Message

The Scheduled Content Download Service found an unauthorized URL and called unauthorized page %2 while executing the job %1.

Event ID: 13109

Event Message

The Scheduled Content Download Service was unable to connect to the Web Proxy Service while executing the job %1. Check that the Web Proxy Service is running using ISA Management. If not, start the service.

Event ID: 14094

Event Message

The Microsoft Scheduled Cache Content Download service cannot start because the ISA Server was installed in Firewall mode. Usually the Scheduled cache content download service is disabled if ISA Server is not installed in Cache or Integrated mode. It is possible that during the first boot after the Cache component was uninstalled, the service was started, and shortly after stopped. To use the service, reinstall ISA Server in Integrated or Cache mode.

Event ID: 14111

Event Message

ISA Server Cache could not start because it was configured incorrectly. Use ISA Management or manually edit the registry to correct the error, and then restart the service. For more information about this event, see ISA Server Help.

Explanation

The cache could not start because of incorrect settings in the cache configuration or conflicts with other configuration settings.

User Action

Stop the Web Proxy Service. In ISA Management, correct cache settings. To do this, in the ISA Management console tree, click Servers And Arrays, click Name, click Cache Configuration, click the HTTP tab, and then select the Restore Defaults check box. Restart the Web Proxy Service. If cache initialization still fails, run Setup and click Reinstall.

Event ID: 14137

Event Message

Some of this information may be out of date because of network problems. An attempt to respond to this request from a remote location was unsuccessful. The response is an expired version of the object found in the cache.

Event ID: 14138

Event Message

Some of this information has not been updated in the past 24 hours.

Event ID: 14140

Event Message

Some of this information may be out of date.

Event ID: 14150

Event Message

The ISA Server cache could not initialize the URL cache on disk. The ISA Server cache files are corrupted.

Event ID: 14151

Event Message

The ISA Server cache could not initialize the URL cache on disk. The ISA Server cache disk is full.

Event ID: 14164

Event Message

Cache drives failed to initialize properly. Caching is disabled. Identify the specific reason for failure from previous event logs. If previous events indicate that the error belongs to a specific drive, then check the drive configuration and then stop and restart the Web Proxy service to enable caching.

Event ID: 14165

Event Message

There is inconsistency in some cache files. While initializing cache, some cache files were detected as being from previous cache configurations. For more information about this event, see ISA Server Help.

Explanation

When changes are made to cache configurations some cache data may remain from old configurations and this can cause inconsistencies in cache data.

User Action

Identify warning events regarding data inconsistencies. To avoid inconsistent data retrieval, consider deleting the cache files that were added recently to the configuration. To apply changes, restart the Web Proxy service.

Event ID: 14166

Event Message

Cache is intentionally disconnected from the rest of the network. Information is now being served from the cache and there is no connection to the Internet at the present time.

Event ID: 14167

Event Message

Recovery of data cache file %1 was completed. If the operation did not complete successfully the error code in the Data area of the Event Viewer indicates the cause of the failure. All cache data is now available. Recovery operation result is: %2%0.

Event ID: 14168

Event Message

Some errors were encountered during the restoration of specific data cache files. For more information about this event, see ISA Server Help.

Explanation

Restoration of cache data file failed, only partial cache data may only be available. If an error code appears in the Data area of the event properties, it will indicate the cause of the failure. If the error code indicates that data is corrupt, then consider deleting the cache file. If error code does not indicate file corruption, stop and then restart the Web Proxy service to retry restoration of the cache file.

User Action

Identify warning events regarding data inconsistencies. To avoid inconsistent data retrieval, consider deleting the cache files that were recently added to the configuration. To apply changes, restart the Web Proxy service.

Event ID: 14169

Event Message

While restoring cache data, %1 objects with conflicting information were detected. These objects were ignored, and were not restored. This may occur when there is conflict between cache data from previous and present cache configurations. You may consider deleting the cache files that were added to the current configuration, in order to avoid inconsistent data retrieval.

Event ID: 14170

Event Message

Restoration of cache data completed. Cache performance will now be at optimal level.

Event ID: 14171

Event Message

Cache data was restored successfully from all data cache files.

Event ID: 14172

Event Message

Cache failed to initialize properly. Caching will be disabled. The error code in the Data area of the event properties indicates the cause of the failure. (internal code %2). Identify the specific reason for failure from previous relevant event logs. Fix the problem and restart the Web Proxy service to enable caching.

Event ID: 14173

Event Message

Path name too long for disk cache %1. Specify a shorter path name.

Event ID: 14174

Event Message

Invalid size specified for disk cache %1. Specify a valid disk cache size and restart the Web Proxy service.

Event ID: 14175

Event Message

Invalid volume specified for disk cache %1. The volume used as cache drive is invalid. The volume must be a NTFS volume with supported sector sizes. Specify a valid volume as a cache drive. You may need to change your hardware if the required sector size is not supported. Restart the Web Proxy service.

Event ID: 14176

Event Message

Disk cache %1 failed to initialize and is disabled. Identify the reason for cache failure by examining previous recorded events, or the error code. Once the problem has been fixed, restart the Web Proxy service to enable the cache. The error code in the Data area of the event properties indicates the cause of the failure (internal code: %2).

Event ID: 14184

Event Message

The Schedule Cache Content Download Service was stopped gracefully.

Event ID: 14185

Event Message

The Scheduled Cache Content Download Service was started successfully.

Common Service Event Messages

These messages refer to events common to ISA Server services.

Event ID: 11000

Event Message

%1 failed to start. The failure occurred during %5 because the configuration property %4 of the key %3 could not be accessed. Use the source location %6 to report the failure. The error code in the Data area of the event properties indicates the cause of the failure. For more information about this event, see ISA Server Help. The error description is: %2.

Explanation

The service failed to start because the data in the storage is corrupt, due to incorrect configuration of either the registry or Active Directory.

User Action

If a backup exists, in ISA Management click Servers And Arrays, then right-click Name, and choose Restore. This restores the configuration, except for server-specific configuration information, such as cache content. If this does not solve the problem, uninstall ISA Server from the Control Panel. When you uninstall, you lose all the configuration parameters and you have to reinstall ISA Server. Reinstalling ISA Server without uninstalling the previous copy does not resolve this problem.

Event ID: 11001

Event Message

%1 failed. The failure occurred during %5 because the configuration property %4 of the key %3 could not be accessed. Use the source location %6 to report the failure. The error code in the Data area of the event properties indicates the cause of the failure. For more information about this event, see ISA Server Help. The error description is: %2.

Explanation

The service failed to start because the data in the storage is corrupt, due to incorrect configuration of either the registry or Active Directory.

User Action

If a backup exists, in ISA Management click Servers And Arrays, then right-click Name, and choose Restore. This will restore the configuration, except for server-specific configuration information, such as cache content. If this does not solve the problem, uninstall ISA Server from the Control Panel. You will lose all the configuration parameters and will have to reinstall. Reinstalling a new copy of ISA Server without uninstalling the previous copy will not solve the problem.

Event ID: 11002

Event Message

%1 failed to start. The failure occurred during %5 because the configuration property %4 of key %3 is not valid. Use the source location %6 to report the failure. The error code in the Data area of the event properties indicates the cause of the failure. For more information about this event, see ISA Server Help. The error description is: %2.

Explanation

Service failed to start because the data in the storage is corrupt, due to incorrect configuration of either the registry or Active Directory.

User Action

If a backup exists, in ISA Management click Servers And Arrays, then right-click Name, and choose Restore. This will restore the configuration, except for server-specific configuration information, such as cache content. If this does not solve the problem, uninstall ISA Server from the Control Panel. You will lose all the configuration parameters and will have to reinstall. Reinstalling a new copy of ISA Server without uninstalling the previous copy will not solve the problem.

Event ID: 11003

Event Message

%1 failed. The failure occurred during %5 because the configuration property %4 of key %3 is not valid. Use the source location %6 to report the failure. For more information about this event, see ISA Server Help. The error code in the Data area of the event properties indicates the cause of the failure. For more information about this event, see ISA Server Help. The error description is: %2.

Explanation

Service failed to start because the data in the storage is corrupt, due to incorrect configuration of either the registry or Active Directory.

User Action

If a backup exists, in ISA Management click Servers And Arrays, then right-click Name, and choose Restore. This will restore the configuration, except for server-specific configuration information, such as cache content. If this does not solve the problem, uninstall ISA Server from the Control Panel. You will lose all the configuration parameters and will have to reinstall. Reinstalling a new copy of ISA Server without uninstalling the previous copy will not solve the problem.

Event ID: 11004

Event Message

%1 failed to start. The failure occurred during %4 because the system call %3 failed. Use the source location %5 to report the failure. The error code in the Data area of the event properties indicates the cause of the failure. For more information about this event, see ISA Server Help. The error description is: %2.

Explanation

The failure is due to a shortage of resources, probably memory.

User Action

Close other applications that are running. Use the Task Manager to check programs and processes that are using large amounts of system resources. Make sure that Active Directory is working. For more information about managing memory resources, see Windows 2000 Help.

Event ID: 11005

Event Message

%1 failed to start. The failure occurred during %4 because the system call %3 failed. Use the source location %5 to report the failure. The error code in the Data area of the event properties indicates the cause of the failure. For more information about this event, see ISA Server Help. The error description is: %2

Explanation

The failure is due to a shortage of resources, probably memory.

User Action

Close other applications that are running. Use the Task Manager to check programs and processes that are using large amounts of system resources. Make sure that Active Directory is working. For more information about managing memory resources, see Windows 2000 Help.

Event ID: 11006

Event Message

%1 failed to start. A shortage of available memory caused the service to fail during %2. Use the source location %3 to report the failure. For more information about this event, see ISA Server Help.

Explanation

Either the service or some processes are utilizing excessive memory resources.

User Action

Close other programs that are running. Use the Task Manager to check programs and processes that are using large amounts of system resources. For more information about managing memory resources, see Windows 2000 Help.

Event ID: 11007

Event Message

A shortage of available memory caused the %1 to fail during %2. Use the source location %3 to report the failure. For more information about this event, see ISA Server Help.

Explanation

Either the service or some processes are using excessive memory.

User Action

Close other programs that are running. Use the Task Manager to check programs and processes that are using large amounts of system resources. For more advice on managing memory resources, see Windows 2000 Help.

Event ID: 11008

Event Message

%1 failed to start. The service failed to register for storage notification on key during %3. Use the source location %4 to report the failure. The error code in the Data area of the event properties indicates the cause of the failure. For more information about this event, see ISA Server Help. The error description is: %2.

Explanation

The failure is probably due to insufficient memory or a problem accessing the storage.

User Action

Close other programs that are running. Use the Task Manager to check programs and processes that are using large amounts of system resources. For more information about managing memory resources, see Windows 2000 Help.

Event ID: 14048

Event Message

Failed to stop the %1 during %2. Use the source location %3 to report the failure. The error code in the Data area of the event properties indicates the cause of the failure. The computer should be restarted.

Event ID: 14077

Event Message

Failed to start the %1 during %2. Use the source location %3 to report the failure. The error code in the Data area of the event properties indicates the cause of the failure. For more information about this event, see ISA Server Help.

Explanation

Service failed to start.

User Action

Restart the service by doing one of the following:

- In the ISA Management console tree, click Servers And Arrays, Name, Monitoring Configuration, click Services and then right-click the service and choose Start).

- Click Start, point to Programs, point to Administrative Tools, and then click Services.

Look at the Event Viewer for errors regarding the failed service.

Event ID: 14079

Event Message

Due to an unexpected error, the service %1 stopped responding to all requests. This occurred %2 time(s) in the past %3 hours. Try to stop the service or kill the corresponding process if it does not respond, and start it again. Check the Event Viewer for related error messages.

Dial-up Connection Events

These messages refer to events related to dial-up connections in Microsoft Internet Security and Acceleration (ISA) Server.

Event ID: 14066

Event Message
Failed to read the dial-up entry configuration. The error code in the Data area of the event properties indicates the cause of the failure. For more information about this event, see ISA Server Help.

Explanation
This event is logged when the specified dial-up configuration or the Firewall service configuration cannot be recognized.

User Action
Check the configuration for dial-up entries in ISA Management and the Firewall service. To view the dial-up entries, in the ISA Management console tree, click Servers And Arrays, click Name, click Policy Elements, and then click Dial-up entries. To view the dial-up entries for the Firewall service, click Start, point to Programs, point to Administrative Tools, and then click Services.

Event ID: 14067

Event Message
Failed to load Rasapi32.dll. The system configuration is incorrect. Check the system configuration for errors. Manually dial an entry to verify that the dial-out works and then restart the failed service. The error code in the Data area of the event properties indicates the cause of the failure.

Event ID: 14136

Event Message
ISA Server dial-out connection failed. The administrator should manually dial the specified phonebook entry to determine if the number can be reached.

Event ID: 14142

Event Message
A dial-out to the Internet failed. The error code shown in the Data area of the event properties is specific to the Routing and Remote Access service (RRAS). For more information about this event, see ISA Server Help.

Explanation
This log entry or event is generated by the dial-up entry component of ISA Server when a dial-up attempt fails. The problem could be related to authentication.

User Action
The ISA Server administrator should verify that the specified phonebook entry in the dial-up entry configuration can be dialed manually. To do this, in the ISA Management console tree, click Servers And Arrays, click Name, click Policy Elements, and then click Dial-Up Entries. In addition, check authentication settings.

Firewall Service Event Messages

These messages refer to events connected with the ISA Server Firewall service.

Event ID: 14001

Event Message
Firewall Service failed to initialize. The internal error code in the Data area of the event properties indicates the cause of the failure. Previous event log entries might help determine the proper action.

Event ID: 14002

Event Message
The Firewall service cannot initialize WinSock. The error code in the Data area of the event properties indicates the cause of the failure. For more information about this event, see ISA Server Help.

Explanation
The Firewall service cannot start. The system is probably out of memory, or the registry might be corrupt.

User Action
Check the Firewall service configuration. To do this, click Start, point to Programs, point to Administrative Tools, and then click Component Services. Try to stop and restart the service. If this does not work, restart the computer.

Event ID: 14003

Event Message
Firewall service started.

Event ID: 14004

Event Message
The Firewall service cannot start due to a shortage of available memory. The error code in the Data area of the event properties indicates the cause of the failure. For more information about this event, see ISA Server Help.

Explanation
Either an application is using too much memory or the page file size is too small.

User Action
Close other programs that are running. Use the Task Manager to check programs and processes that are using large amounts of system resources. For more information about managing memory resources, see Windows 2000 Help.

Event ID: 14006

Event Message
The Firewall service cannot start the performance counters. Restart the Firewall service. The error code in the Data area of the event properties indicates the cause of the failure.

Event ID: 14007

Event Message
A shortage of available memory caused the Firewall service to fail. The Event Viewer Data window displays the number of active connections. For more information about this event, see ISA Server Help.

Explanation
The ISA Server computer cannot support additional connections for the server.

User Action

Check the number of current connections and reduce that number to an acceptable level. Close other programs that are running. Use the Task Manager to check programs and processes using large amounts of system resources. For more information about managing memory resources, see Windows 2000 Help.

Event ID: 14010

Event Message

The Firewall service did not start due to corrupt data in the registry or Active Directory, depending on the ISA Server configuration. The error code in the Data area of the event properties indicates the cause of the failure. For more information about this event, see ISA Server Help.

Explanation

The Firewall service did not start due to corrupted data in the registry or in the Active Directory configuration.

User Action

Wait a few minutes and then restart the service. If this does not work and a backup exists, in ISA Management click Servers And Arrays, then right-click Name, and choose Restore. This restores the configuration, except for server-specific configuration information, such as cache content. If this does not solve the problem, uninstall ISA Server from Control Panel. When you uninstall, you lose all the configuration parameters and you have to reinstall ISA Server. Reinstalling ISA Server without uninstalling the previous copy does not resolve this problem.

Event ID: 14011

Event Message

The Firewall service failed to bind its socket to %1, port %2. This could be caused by another service that is already using the same port or by the network interface that is not functional. The error code in the Data area of the event properties indicates the cause of the failure. For more information about this event, see ISA Server Help.

Explanation

Either the requested service port is already in use or there is a problem with the network interface.

User Action

Click Start, click Run and then type **netstat -a** to display statistics for the current TCP/IP connections. Check for port conflicts or network problems. Close the other application that is using the requested port. For more information about the Netstat command, see Windows 2000 Help.

Event ID: 14012

Event Message

Client from %1 attempted to access ISA Server using control protocol version %2. The server supports version %3. The version of the client software is incompatible with the server version. If the client software is older than the server software, upgrade the client software. If the server software is older, either upgrade the server or direct the client to a different server that uses the newer software.

Event ID: 14013

Event Message
The Firewall service requires Windows 2000 Server with Service Pack 1 or later.

Event ID: 14014

Event Message
The Firewall service requires Windows 2000 Server with Service Pack 1 or later.

Event ID: 14015

Event Message
The Firewall service failed to load a security dynamic-link library (DLL). The required DLL is missing or cannot be found. Make sure that the Security.dll is located in the Windows 2000 system directory (typically, %systemroot%\System32 directory), and then restart the Firewall service.

Event ID: 14016

Event Message
The Firewall service failed to determine the network addresses because either there are improper network connections or there is insufficient memory. Check network connections and restart the service. If this problem occurs again, close some applications, stop the service, and then restart the service.

Event ID: 14017

Event Message
Incorrect network configuration. The server address is not internal and is not in the Local Address Table (LAT). For more information about this event, see ISA Server Help.

Explanation
An Internet Protocol (IP) address configured for the internal network adapter for the server needs to be included within the Local Address Table (LAT) for the server.

User Action
To configure the Local Address Table (LAT), open ISA Management, click Network configuration and then click Local Address Table (LAT). To modify an existing LAT entry, in the ISA Management console tree, click Servers And Arrays, click Name, click Network Configuration, and then click the relevant LAT entry.

Event ID: 14021

Event Message
The Firewall service failed to initialize because the system call %1 failed. If an error code appears in the Data area of the event properties, it indicates the cause of the failure. For more information about this event, see ISA Server Help.

Explanation
The failure is probably due to insufficient memory or a problem accessing the storage.

User Action
Close other programs that are running. Use the Task Manager to check programs and processes that are using large amounts of system resources. Verify that Active Directory is working. For more information about managing memory resources, see Windows 2000 Help.

Event ID: 14028

Event Message

The Firewall service did not initialize the network dial-up entry. Try an alternative manual dial-up entry. If successful, retry the dial-up entry. If the problem still exists, restart the Firewall service. If this does not solve the problem, restart Windows 2000.

Event ID: 14029

Event Message

The Firewall service failed to create a socket. If an error code appears in the Data area of the event properties, it indicates the source of the failure.

Event ID: 14030

Event Message

The Firewall service failed to associate a control socket with a completion port.

Event ID: 14031

Event Message

The Firewall service failed to initialize control or refresh sockets.

Event ID: 14034

Event Message

The Firewall service did not listen on all Transmission Control Protocol (TCP) sockets. The reason for the failure of the service can be determined by examining previous event log entries.

Event ID: 14035

Event Message

The Firewall service failed to listen on the Transmission Control Protocol (TCP) socket bound to %1. The error code in the Data area of the event properties indicates the cause of the failure.

Event ID: 14036

Event Message

The IP address (or DNS name) %1, from configuration file %2, cannot be used to connect to the ISA Server. Use ISA Management to configure the IP address or DNS name to which Firewall clients should connect.

Event ID: 14048

Event Message

Failed to stop the %1 during %2. Use the source location %3 to report the failure. The error code in the Data area of the event properties indicates the cause of the failure. The computer should be restarted.

Event ID: 14055

Event Message

The Firewall service encountered an illegal operation (runtime error R6025), in a pure virtual function. To resolve this error, remove recently installed application filters and restart the service.

Event ID: 14056

Event Message
The application filter (%2, CLSID=%3) performed an illegal operation inside the Firewall service process at method %1. The Firewall service terminated. To resolve this error, remove recently installed application filters and restart the service. If this does not resolve the problem, contact the component vendor.

Event ID: 14057

Event Message
The Firewall service stopped because an application filter module %1 generated an exception code %3 in address %2 when function %4 was called. To resolve this error, remove recently installed application filters and restart the service.

Event ID: 14058

Event Message
The Firewall service cannot connect to another proxy server. Authentication was rejected. Check the credentials for the account that is used for proxy-to-proxy authentication.

Event ID: 14059

Event Message
The Firewall service cannot connect to another proxy server. Authentication failed. A chained proxy server or array member requires proxy-to-proxy authentication. Authentication failed because the credentials that were supplied were incorrect. Check authentication credentials and try again.

Event ID: 14060

Event Message
Cannot load an application filter %1 (%4). %2 failed with code 0x%3. To attempt to activate this application filter again, stop and restart the Firewall service.

Event ID: 14061

Event Message
The Firewall service detected that the upstream proxy server '%1' is not available. If the upstream proxy server %1 becomes available, you may proceed as usual. If it does not become available, check the status of the upstream proxy server.

Event ID: 14062

Event Message
The Firewall service detected that the upstream proxy '%1' is now available.

Event ID: 14063

Event Message
The Firewall service failed to initialize because of a corrupted registry. Error Code %1, Key='%2' Value='%3'. For more information about this event, see ISA Server Help.

Explanation
The Firewall Service failed to initialize because of a corrupted registry.

User Action
If a backup exists, in ISA Management click Servers And Arrays, then right-click Name, and choose Restore. This restores the configuration, except for server-specific

configuration information, such as cache content. If this does not solve the problem, uninstall ISA Server from Control Panel. When you uninstall, you lose all the configuration parameters and you have to reinstall ISA Server. Reinstalling ISA Server without uninstalling the previous copy does not resolve this problem.

Event ID: 14071

Event Message

The Firewall service did not start because the application filter component %1 did not start on time. Reinstall the application filter. Contact the application filter vendor.

Event ID: 14093

Event Message

The Microsoft Firewall Service cannot start because the ISA Server was installed in Cache mode. Usually the Firewall service is disabled if ISA Server is not installed in Integrated or Firewall mode. It is possible that during the first boot after the Firewall component was uninstalled, the service was started, and shortly after stopped. To use the service, reinstall ISA Server in Integrated or Firewall mode.

Event ID: 14152

Event Message

A User Datagram Protocol (UDP) packet was dropped because it was larger than the maximum UDP packet allowed by the Firewall service.

Event ID: 14182

Event Message

The Firewall Service was stopped gracefully.

Winsock Error Code Messages

Event ID: 10000

Event Message

Name entered is too long. The name entered is either incorrect or has too many characters. Check that the name entered is a valid name. Type the name again and check that no added characters were included.

Event ID: 10001

Event Message

System is not ready.

Event ID: 10002

Event Message

Current version is not supported. For more information about this event, see ISA Server Help.

Explanation

The application is using a later version of Windows Sockets that is not supported.

User Action

Check to see if you have the WinSock dynamic-link library (DLL) that supports the version of the WinSock specification required by the application. If so, check if there is an older DLL in a folder in the path ahead of the folder containing the newer DLL. If not, obtain a later version of Windows Sockets.

Event ID: 10003

Event Message
Service cannot send after socket shutdown. For more information about this event, see ISA Server Help.

Explanation
The operation cannot be completed because the connection for this application has been closed.

User Action
Restart the application or place a new connection before retrying the operation.

Event ID: 10004

Event Message
An interrupted system call was received. For more information about this event, see ISA Server Help.

Explanation
The current connection was interrupted, and the socket operation did not complete as expected. The problem might be caused by the current application, or caused by a temporary problem or condition on the network.

User Action
Check the network connection for the computer or try reconnecting. If the problem continues, contact your network administrator.

Event ID: 10005

Event Message
Host was not found. For more information about this event, see ISA Server Help.

Explanation
The name you have used is not an official hostname or alias. Most WinSock implementations use domain name system (DNS) protocol for hostname to address resolution, although a few use Network Information System (NIS). Assuming you have a name server configured instead of or as well as a host table, a hostname resolution request causes a WinSock DLL to send an address query to the configured DNS server. If you have more than one server configured, the hostname query fails only after the WinSock DLL has queried all servers.

User Action
Check that you have a name server and/or host table configured. If you have a name server, use Ping to check that the server host is available. Check that DNS/NIS is running by trying to resolve another hostname you know should work. If you have using a host table exclusively, add the destination hostname and address to the table.

Event ID: 10006

Event Message
Try again. For more information about this event, see ISA Server Help.

Explanation
The server was temporarily unable to process the current request.

User Action
Reenter the request or renew the connection to the server (now or at a later time).

Event ID: 10007

Event Message
Nonrecoverable error encountered. For more information about this event, see ISA Server Help.

Explanation
The Firewall service encountered a fatal error. The name server encountered an error. Most WinSock implementations use domain name system (DNS) protocol for hostname to address resolution, although a few use Network Information System (NIS). Assuming you have a name server configured instead of or as well as a host table, a hostname resolution request causes a WinSock DLL to send an address query to the configured DNS server. If you have more than one server configured, the hostname query fails only after the WinSock DLL has queried all servers.

User Action
Try restarting the Firewall application on the client and initiating a new connection. You can also check that you have a name server and/or host table configured. If you have a name server, use Ping to check that the server host is available. Check that DNS/NIS is running by trying to resolve another hostname you know should work. If you have using a host table exclusively, add the destination hostname and address to the table.

Event ID: 10008

Event Message
No data record is available. For more information about this event, see ISA Server Help.

Explanation
For host resolution, the requested name is valid, but does not have an Internet IP address at the name server. For protocol or service resolution, the name or number was not found in the respective database. Most WinSock implementations use domain name system (DNS) protocol for hostname to address resolution, although a few use Network Information System (NIS).

User Action
Check that you have a name server(s) and/or host table configured. If you have a name server, use Ping to check that the server hosts are available. Check that the name resolution server application is running by trying to resolve another hostname you know should work. If you are using a host table exclusively, add the destination hostname and address to the table.

Event ID: 10009

Event Message
Bad file number encountered. For more information about this event, see ISA Server Help.

Explanation
The specified file number is not a valid file handle value or it does not refer to an open file. An attempt might have been made to write to a file or device opened for read-only access. Or, the socket input parameter is not a valid socket handle: either it never was valid; or it is a file handle (not a socket handle); or, if it was a socket handle, it has been closed.

User Action

If this message was displayed when you tried to open or write to a file, check the permissions on the file or directory that you were trying to open. Otherwise, no user action is required.

Event ID: 10010

Event Message

Operation would block. For more information about this event, see ISA Server Help.

Explanation

The socket is marked as nonblocking (that is, nonblocking operation mode), and the requested operation is not complete at this time. This is a temporary condition. Later calls to the same routine might complete normally.

User Action

Try the operation again later.

Event ID: 10011

Event Message

Operation is in progress. For more information about this event, see ISA Server Help.

Explanation

A blocking operation is outstanding. Only a single blocking operation can be outstanding per task (or thread). Any other function call, to this or any other socket, will fail with this error.

User Action

Handle this as a non-fatal error.

Event ID: 10012

Event Message

Operation is already in progress. For more information about this event, see ISA Server Help.

Explanation

The asynchronous operation you attempted to cancel has already been canceled.

User Action

None.

Event ID: 10013

Event Message

Bad network address encountered. For more information about this event, see ISA Server Help.

Explanation

The system detected an invalid address used as an argument of a call. This error can occur if the length of the buffer is too small. This error can also occur when an application passes an invalid pointer value.

User Action

For developers, check the return value from a memory allocation to be sure it succeeded. Always be sure to allocate enough space.

Event ID: 10014

Event Message

Destination address required. For more information about this event, see ISA Server Help.

Explanation

A required address was omitted from an operation on a socket. In order to connect to or send to a destination address, the address must be provided.

User Action

If a destination hostname was entered the application might have had a problem resolving the name. Check that you have a name server(s) and/or host table configured. If you are using a name server, use Ping to check that the server host(s) are available. Check that the name resolution server application is running by trying to resolve another hostname you know should work. If you are using a host table exclusively, add the destination hostname and address to the table.

Event ID: 10015

Event Message

Message is too long. For more information about this event, see ISA Server Help.

Explanation

A message sent on a socket was larger than the internal message buffer or some other network limit. Since the buffering requirements for sending datagrams are less than for receiving datagrams, it is conceivable that you can send a datagram larger than you can receive.

User Action

None.

Event ID: 10016

Event Message

Protocol family not supported. For more information about this event, see ISA Server Help.

Explanation

The protocol family has not been configured on the system or no implementation for it exists.

User Action

If you are using a third-party Transmission Control Protocol/Internet Protocol (TCP/IP), verify that it is compatible with Wsock32.dll. If you are using Microsoft TCP/IP, remove and reinstall TCP/IP. Or use another protocol that is compatible with Wsock32.dll.

Event ID: 10017

Event Message

Directory is not empty. For more information about this event, see ISA Server Help.

Explanation

The directory cannot be removed. It still contains other files or subdirectories.

User Action

Move or delete the other files or subdirectories and try the operation again.

Event ID: 10018

Event Message

EPROCLIM returned. A software error occurred. Too many processes are running simultaneously. Quit and restart the current application.

Event ID: 10019

Event Message
EUSERS returned. For more information about this event, see ISA Server Help.

Explanation
Inbound and outbound packets that include a Fully Qualified Domain Name longer than 255 characters cannot be processed by Windows 2000 Server. Such packets usually remain in the queue until the queue is flushed. Also, directory paths and file names cannot exceed 255 characters.

User Action
Verify that domain names do not exceed 255 characters. For example, if you are running Gopher, the domain name for e-mail addresses should be less than 255 characters. Also, verify that all directory paths and file names are less than 255 characters.

Event ID: 10020

Event Message
Disk quota exceeded. The operation required additional disk space that is not authorized by the server. Cancel the current disk operation and change file share permissions to allow more space for the current user.

Event ID: 10021

Event Message
ESTALE returned. An unexplained service error occurred in the current environment. Quit the application and restart it.

Event ID: 10022

Event Message
Invalid argument. For more information about this event, see ISA Server Help.

Explanation
An application passed an invalid input parameter in a function call. The error refers to content as well as a value (for example, it might occur when a pointer to a structure is invalid or when a value in a structure field is invalid). In some instances, it also refers to the current state of the socket input parameter.

User Action
Contact the vendor of the application that issued this message. A software patch might be available.

Event ID: 10023

Event Message
Too many open files. For more information about this event, see ISA Server Help.

Explanation
The network system has run out of socket handles. You might have too many WinSock applications running simultaneously, but this is unlikely because most network systems have many socket handles available. This message can also occur if an application opens and closes sockets often without closing them properly (that is, leaving them open as "orphans").

User Action
To recover the orphaned sockets, close and restart the application. You might have to quit all WinSock applications to force the WinSock DLL to unload.

Event ID: 10024
Event Message
Too many levels of symbolic links. A software error occurred. Contact the supplier of the current application.

Event ID: 10025
Event Message
The object is remote.

Event ID: 10026
Event Message
Socket operation was attempted on non-socket. For more information about this event, see ISA Server Help.

Explanation
The socket input parameter is not a valid socket handle. Either it was never valid; or it is a file handle (not a socket handle). If it is a socket handle, it has been closed.

User Action
For developers, use socket state in an application or handle this error as a non-fatal error.

Event ID: 10027
Event Message
Bad or unassigned address. For more information about this event, see ISA Server Help.

Explanation
The network address used for the remote server is invalid for the current network. An attempt was made to create a socket with a remote socket name (protocol, port and address).

User Action
Before retrying, verify that the address is typed correctly and that you can reach the remote network address from the local network.

Event ID: 10028
Event Message
Address is already in use. For more information about this event, see ISA Server Help.

Explanation
The requested address cannot be obtained because it is in use elsewhere on the network. Only one usage of each address is permitted. The "address" refers to the local "socket name," which is comprised of the following three elements: protocol, port-number, and IP address.

User Action
Verify that network address settings for the client are correct for the local network. Do not run two server applications of the same type on the same computer. For instance, this error occurs if you try to run two applications that connect to one FTP server. Check that the network address setting for the client is correct on the local machine and assign a different fixed network address to the client. Contact your network administrator to resolve problems of address duplication.

Event ID: 10029
Event Message
Address family is not supported by protocol family. For more information about this event, see ISA Server Help.

Explanation

An address incompatible with the requested protocol was used. For example, you might not be able to use NS addresses with ARPA Internet protocols.

User Action

Check that the address is in the correct format and has been typed correctly before retrying the operation. If the problem continues, contact the network administrator.

Event ID: 10030

Event Message

Socket type is not supported. For more information about this event, see ISA Server Help.

Explanation

The support for the socket type has not been configured on the system or no implementation for it exists.

User Action

Check that the correct transport protocol (for example, Transmission Control Protocol (TCP), User Datagram Protocol (UDP)) is selected for use with the current application and with the Firewall service. For developers, handle the request as a non-fatal error (if possible), since some WinSock calls can legally fail the request.

Event ID: 10031

Event Message

Protocol is not supported. For more information about this event, see ISA Server Help.

Explanation

The protocol selected for use with the current application is not supported for the Firewall service or has not been defined for this service. An incompatible protocol has been selected for establishing the connection.

User Action

Check that the protocol is defined for use with the Firewall service. Try again, using a different protocol. If you are using a third-party Transmission Control Protocol/Internet Protocol (TCP/IP), verify that it is compatible with Wsock32.dll. If you are using Microsoft TCP/IP, remove and reinstall TCP/IP. Or use another protocol that is compatible with Wsock32.dll. For developers, if you are trying to use an optional feature, handle the request as a non-fatal error (if possible), since some WinSock calls can legally fail the request.

Event ID: 10032

Event Message

No buffer space is supported. The WinSock implementation was unable to allocate additional memory to accommodate the function request. For more information about this event, see ISA Server Help.

Explanation

This error indicates a shortage of resources on your system. It can occur when you try to run too many applications simultaneously on your computer. An operation on a socket or pipe was not performed because the system lacked sufficient buffer space to buffer connection throughput or a queue was full. WinSock was unable to allocate additional memory to accommodate the function request. If this error tends to occur when you run certain applications, it might indicate that the applications do not properly return system resources (for example, memory). It might also indicate that you are not closing the applications correctly.

User Action

Close unnecessary applications. If you continue to get this message, close Windows 2000 and restart your computer. Also, verify that buffer space is adjusted for the server. For the Firewall service, check the server registry entries for User Datagram Protocol (UDP) or Transmission Control Protocol (TCP) buffer size and consider increasing these values.

Event ID: 10033

Event Message

Connection timed out. For more information about this event, see ISA Server Help.

Explanation

A connection cannot be placed between the client and the remote server within the preset time allowed for a response. (The time-out period is dependent on the communication protocol.) No connection was opened.

User Action

Verify that the remote server and the client are present on the network and configured properly. If the current client or application supports adjusted time-out values, you can also adjust the connection time-out interval. Check that the destination address is a valid IP address. If you used a hostname, check that it resolved to the correct address. If the hostname resolution uses a local host table, it is possible you resolved to an obsolete address. Try to ping the hostname. If a router is configured, check that the router is up and running (check by pinging it, and then ping an address on the other side of it). Use the Tracert command at the command prompt to determine the path to the destination address and to check that all the routers are functioning. Check your subnet mask. If you don't have the correct subnet mask, your network system might treat a local address as a remote address (so it forwards addresses on the local subnet to the router, rather than broadcasting an ARP request locally), or vice versa.

Event ID: 10034

Event Message

Socket is already connected. For more information about this event, see ISA Server Help.

Explanation

A connect request was made on an already connected socket.

User Action

Contact the vendor of the application. They might have a software patch to fix the problem.

Event ID: 10035

Event Message

Socket is not connected. For more information about this event, see ISA Server Help.

Explanation

A request to send or receive data was disallowed because the socket is not connected and (when sending on a datagram socket) no address was supplied. An application attempted an input/output network function call before establishing an association with a remote socket (i.e. before calling connect() or accept().)

User Action

Open a connection to the remote source using the current application. If you were previously connected, try reconnecting. Ping the remote host you were connected to. If it does not respond, it might be off-line or there might be a network problem along the way. If it does respond, then this problem might have been a transient one (so you can reconnect now), or the server application you were connected to might have terminated (so you might not be able to connect again). In addition, ping a local host to verify that your local network is still functioning. For a serial connection, ping your local router address. If you are on a serial connection, your local router is the IP address of the host you initially logged on to using SLIP or PPP. In addition, ping a host on the same subnet as the host you were connected to (if you know of one). This will verify that the destination network is functioning. Use the Tracert command at the command prompt to determine the path to the host you were connected to. This will not reveal too much unless you know the router addresses at the remote end, but it might help to identify if the problem is somewhere along the way.

Event ID: 10036

Event Message

Unsupported protocol option used. For more information about this event, see ISA Server Help.

Explanation

The application selected an unsupported protocol for this operation. Check the protocol settings.

User Action

For developers, check the parameters. Are you using an optional level or socket option that might not be supported on all WinSock implementations? If so, treat this as a non-fatal error and ignore it, if possible.

Event ID: 10037

Event Message

Connection reset by peer. For more information about this event, see ISA Server Help.

Explanation

A connection was forcibly closed by a peer. This normally results from a loss of the connection on the remote socket due to a time-out or a reboot. This error is also possible on a datagram socket. For instance, this error could result if your application sends a UDP datagram to a host, which rejects it by responding with an ICMP Port Unreachable.

User Action

You can attempt to reestablish the connection. Report the problem to your network administrator or check the connection logs for other servers on the network for more information. In addition you can ping the remote host you were connected to. If it does not respond, it might be off-line or there might be a network problem along the way. If it does respond, then this problem might have been a transient one (so you can reconnect now), or the server application you were connected to might have terminated (so you might not be able to connect again). You can also ping a local host to verify that your local network is still functioning. For a serial connection, ping your local router address. If you are on a serial connection, your local router is the IP address of the host you initially logged on to using SLIP or PPP. In addition, ping a host on the same subnet as the host you were connected to (if you know of one). This will verify that the destination network is functioning. Use the Tracert command at the command prompt to determine the path to the host you were connected to. This will not reveal too much unless you know the router addresses at the remote end, but it might help to identify if the problem is somewhere along the way.

Event ID: 10038

Event Message

Software caused connection to abort. For more information about this event, see ISA Server Help.

Explanation

This error can occur when the local network system aborts a connection, such as when WinSock closes an established connection after data retransmission fails (receiver never acknowledges data sent on a datastream socket).

User Action

Exit the application, restart and try to reconnect. You can also check the following: 1. Ping the remote host you were connected to. If it does not respond, it might be off-line or there might be a network problem along the way. If it does respond, then this problem might have been a transient one (so you can reconnect now), or the server application you were connected to might have terminated (so you might not be able to connect again). 2. Ping a local host to verify that your local network is still functioning (if on a serial connection, see next step) 3. Ping your local router address. If you are on a serial connection, your local router is the IP address of the host you initially logged on to using SLIP or PPP. 4. Ping a host on the same subnet as the host you were connected to (if you know of one). This will verify that the destination network is functioning. 5. Use the Tracert command at the command prompt to determine the path to the host you were connected to. This won't reveal too much unless you know the router addresses at the remote end, but it might help to identify if the problem is somewhere along the way.

Event ID: 10039

Event Message

Network is down. For more information about this event, see ISA Server Help.

Explanation

There are problems maintaining a connection to the local network. The current connection has failed because a socket operation encountered an unavailable network.

User Action

Check the client network connection or reconnect the client to the network. You can also check your WinSock, protocol stack, network driver, and network adapter configuration. If this message appears when you try to connect from other clients, check for problems in network cabling or termination, and verify that network hardware or software is not offline. Note that this error occurs rarely since a WinSock implementation cannot reliably detect hardware problems.

Event ID: 10040

Event Message
Network was reset. For more information about this event, see ISA Server Help.

Explanation
The host you were connected to crashed and rebooted or the network temporarily went down.

User Action
Check the following: 1. Ping the remote host you were connected to. If it does not respond, it might be off-line or there might be a network problem along the way. If it does respond, then this problem might have been a transient one (so you can reconnect now), or the server application you were connected to might have terminated (so you might not be able to connect again). 2. Ping a local host to verify that your local network is still functioning (if on a serial connection, see next step). 3. Ping your local router address. If you are on a serial connection, your local router is the IP address of the host you initially logged on to using SLIP or PPP. 4. Ping a host on the same subnet as the host you were onnected to (if you know of one). This will verify that the destination network is functioning. 5. Use the Tracert command at the command prompt to determine the path to the host you were connected to. This won't reveal too much unless you know the router addresses at the remote end, but it might help to identify if the problem is somewhere along the way.

Event ID: 10041

Event Message
Connection refused. For more information about this event, see ISA Server Help.

Explanation
No connection could be made because the target computer actively refused it. This usually results from trying to connect to a service that is inactive on the foreign host. You might have gone to the wrong host, or the server application you are trying to contact might not be running. In TCP, an attempt to connect (TCP SYN packet) caused the destination host to respond by returning a reset (TCP RST packet). If an application sends a UDP packet to a host that has no socket listening, the host may send by a ICMP Port Unreachable packet.

User Action
Check the destination address you are using. If you used a hostname, verify that it was resolved to the correct address. If your hostname resolution uses a local host table, it is possible the name was resolved to an obsolete address. It is also possible that the local services file has an incorrect port number (although this is unlikely). You can run **netstat -a** at the command line to check port configuration. You can verify that the remote computer is rejecting your connection attempt by checking the network statistics locally and to verify that you are receiving TCP resets or ICMP Port Unreachable packets each time you attempt to connect.

Event ID: 10042

Event Message
Host is down. For more information about this event, see ISA Server Help.

Explanation
The socket operation failed because the destination host was down.

User Action

Contact your network administrator to confirm the status of the remote host. Check the following: 1. Ping the remote host you were connected to. If it does not respond, it might be off-line or there might be a network problem along the way. If it does respond, then this problem might have been a transient one (so you can reconnect now), or the server application you were connected to might have terminated (so you might not be able to connect again). 2. Ping a local host to verify that your local network is still functioning (if on a serial connection, see next step). 3. Ping your local router address. If you are on a serial connection, your local router is the IP address of the host you initially logged on to using SLIP or PPP. 4. Ping a host on the same subnet as the host you were connected to (if you know of one). This will verify that the destination network is functioning. 5. Use the Tracert command at the command prompt to determine the path to the host you were connected to. This won't reveal too much unless you know the router addresses at the remote end, but it might help to identify if the problem is somewhere along the way.

Event ID: 10043

Event Message

Host is unreachable. For more information about this event, see ISA Server Help.

Explanation

The remote host cannot be reached at this time or has been shut down. A socket operation was attempted on an unreachable target host. The ICMP message means that the router cannot forward the IP datagram to the target host, possibly because it did not get a response to the ARP request (which might mean the destination host is down).

User Action

Try to ping the destination host, to see if you get the same results, which is likely. Check the destination address. Check whether you have a router configured in your network system (your WinSock implementation). Use the Tracert command at the command prompt to try to determine where the failure occurs along the route between your host and the destination host. You can also contact your network administrator to confirm the status of the remote host.

Event ID: 10044

Event Message

Protocol is the wrong type for socket. For more information about this event, see ISA Server Help.

Explanation

The application requires a socket call that is not supported by the current protocol settings for the client application. For example, you cannot use the ARPA Internet UDP protocol with the SOCK_STREAM socket type. This error occurs if you specifically reference a protocol that is not part of the Internet address family you are also referencing. An incompatible protocol has been selected for the socket. The device driver for the protocol stack might not be compatible with Wsock32.dll.

User Action

Check the current configuration for the protocol type in use for the remote connection and check the Transmission Control Protocol (TCP) or User Datagram Protocol

(UDP) configuration for the Firewall service. Also, if you are using a third-party Transmission Control Protocol/Internet Protocol (TCP/IP), verify that it is compatible with Wsock32.dll. If you are using Microsoft TCP/IP, remove and reinstall TCP/IP.

Event ID: 10045

Event Message

Operation is not supported on socket. For more information about this event, see ISA Server Help.

Explanation

The attempted operation was not supported for the type of object referenced. Usually this occurs when a file descriptor refers to a file or socket that cannot support this operation, for example, trying to accept a connection on a datagram socket. Or the device driver for the protocol stack might not be compatible with Wsock32.dll.

User Action

You can contact your network administrator to confirm the status of the remote host. If you are using a third-party Transmission Control Protocol/Internet Protocol (TCP/IP), verify that it is compatible with Wsock32.dll. If you are using Microsoft TCP/IP, remove and reinstall TCP/IP. Or use another protocol that is compatible with Wsock32.dll.

Event ID: 10046

Event Message

Internet Control Message Protocol (ICMP) network is unreachable. For more information about this event, see ISA Server Help.

Explanation

The local network system might generate this error if there is no default route configured. Typically though, WinSock generates this error when it receives a "host unreachable" Internet Control Message Protocol (ICMP) message from a router. Note: This error might also result if you are trying to send a multicast packet and the default gateway does not support multicast (check your interface configuration).

User Action

Investigate routers on local or remote networks to see that they are active and properly configured. Contact your network administrator to confirm the status of the remote host. Try to ping the destination host, to see if you get the same results, which is likely. Check the destination address. Check whether you have a router configured in your network system (your WinSock implementation). Use the Tracert command at the command prompt to try to determine where the failure occurs along the route between your host and the destination host.

Event ID: 10047

Event Message

Too many references used. The requested operation contained additional information that cannot be processed correctly through the remote connection. Retry the request, or contact the supplier for the current application.

Event ID: 10048

Event Message

Not owner. You do not have permission or ownership rights to access this remote shared resource. Ask the network administrator to check permissions.

Event ID: 10049

Event Message

No such file or directory exists. The requested file operation cannot be completed because the file or directory does not exist on the remote server. Check file or directory settings.

Event ID: 10050

Event Message

No such process exists. The requested operation is not recognized by the remote server. The operation might be the result of errors in data or invalid user input. Try the operation again.

Event ID: 10051

Event Message

System call interrupted. For more information about this event, see ISA Server Help.

Explanation

The current connection was interrupted, and the socket operation did not complete as expected. The problem might be with the current application, or a temporary problem or condition on the network.

User Action

Check the network connection for the computer or try to reconnect. If the problem continues, contact the network administrator to confirm the status of the remote host. For developers, be prepared to handle this error on any functions that reference blocking sockets, or any calls to blocking functions, if you allow the user to cancel a blocking call. You can handle it as a fatal error or non-fatal error, depending on the application and the context.

Event ID: 10052

Event Message

Input/Output (I/O) Error encountered. The problem might be caused by instability in the local system environment. Quit the application and restart the computer. Try the operation again.

Event ID: 10053

Event Message

No such device or address exists. For more information about this event, see ISA Server Help.

Explanation

The device or address cannot be located on the network.

User Action

Verify that the device name and address were entered correctly and that the device is operational. Verify that the address can reply to test utilities (for example, Ping) and is active on the network.

Event ID: 10054

Event Message
Argument list too long. The requested operation contained additional information or parameters that cannot be processed correctly through the current connection. Retry the request.

Event ID: 10055

Event Message
Executed format error. A software error has occurred. Retry the operation.

Event ID: 10056

Event Message
Bad file number encountered. For more information about this event, see ISA Server Help.

Explanation
The specified file number might not be a valid file handle value or it does not refer to an open file. An attempt might have been made to write to a file or device opened for read-only access. Or, the socket input parameter is not a valid socket handle: either it never was valid or it is a file handle (that is, not a socket handle). If it is a socket handle, it has been closed.

User Action
If this message was displayed when you tried to open or write to a file, check the permissions on the file or directory that you were trying to open. Otherwise, no user action is required.

Event ID: 10057

Event Message
No children exist for parent object.

Event ID: 10058

Event Message
Operation would block one in progress. For more information about this event, see ISA Server Help.

Explanation
The requested operation would prevent an operation already in progress from completing. WinSock only allows a single blocking operation to be outstanding per task (or thread). It means that there is a blocking operation outstanding. It is also possible that WinSock might return this error after an application calls connect() a second time on a non-blocking socket while the connection is pending.

User Action
Wait for the system to complete the processing of the current operation, or cancel the current operation before retrying. If this does not work, then contact the vendor of the application that issued this message. They might have a software patch to fix this problem. For developers, handle this as a non-fatal error. Any application that uses a blocking socket or calls any blocking functions must handle this error.

Event ID: 10059

Event Message
Not enough memory is available. For more information about this event, see ISA Server Help.

Explanation

There is a shortage of memory resources.

User Action

Close other applications that are not in use before retrying. In Task Manager, identify applications that are consuming memory resources. For more information about managing memory resources, see Windows 2000 Help.

Event ID: 10060

Event Message

Permission denied. The remote server refused access to the requested resource. Contact the administrator for the remote server and report the problem.

Event ID: 10061

Event Message

Bad address encountered. For more information about this event, see ISA Server Help.

Event ID: 10062

Event Message

Mount device or directory is busy. The remote server drive is unavailable or is out of space. Wait and retry the requested operation.

Event ID: 10063

Event Message

File already exists. The attempt to create or save a file on the remote server cannot be completed because a file of the same name already exists. Save the new file under a different name, or rename the old file.

Event ID: 10064

Event Message

A cross-device link exists. A device on the remote server system that is required for this operation cannot be accessed for the current connection. Confirm that the device is available and is not already in use by other connected sessions.

Event ID: 10065

Event Message

No such device exists. The device or address entered cannot be located on the network. Make sure that the device name or address has been entered correctly and that the device is operational and configured properly on the client computer.

Event ID: 10066

Event Message

Is not a directory. A file object has been selected for the current operation where a directory was expected. Select a directory to complete this operation, or cancel the operation.

Event ID: 10067

Event Message

Is a directory. A directory object has been selected for the current operation where a file was expected. Select a file to complete this operation, or cancel the operation.

Event ID: 10068

Event Message
Invalid argument used. For more information about this event, see ISA Server Help.

Explanation
The requested operation contained additional information or parameters that cannot be processed correctly through the current connection. An application passed an invalid input parameter in a function call. The error refers to content as well as a value (e.g. it might occur when a pointer to a structure is invalid or when a value in a structure field is invalid). In some instances, it also refers to the current state of the socket input parameter.

User Action
Retry the request. If this does not solve the problem then contact the vendor of the application that issued this message. The vendor might have a software patch to fix this problem.

Event ID: 10069

Event Message
File table has overflowed. For more information about this event, see ISA Server Help.

Explanation
The current operation has exceeded available disk capacity or other resources on the system.

User Action
Clear the message and verify that sufficient disk space and resources are available on the local system before retrying.

Event ID: 10070

Event Message
Too many files are open. For more information about this event, see ISA Server Help.

Explanation
The system defines the number of file descriptors that any process can open at one time. That number has been reached and no more files can be opened. You might have too many WinSock applications running simultaneously, but this is unlikely because most network systems have many socket handles available. This message can also occur if an application opens and closes sockets often without closing them properly (that is, leaving them open as "orphans").

User Action
To recover the orphaned sockets, close and restart the application. You might have to quit all WinSock applications to force the WinSock DLL to unload.

Event ID: 10071

Event Message
Is not a typewriter. The current configuration does not support the attempted method of input. Check application instructions or contact the supplier of the application and report the problem.

Event ID: 10072

Event Message
File is too large. A disk restriction did not permit the file operation to be completed. A disk quota might be set for the destination folder, or there is a lack of available space on

the targeted drive. Verify that sufficient space is available on the drive and that the folder does not have disk space restrictions.

Event ID: 10073

Event Message

No space is left on device. There is a lack of available space on the destination drive. The file copy operation cannot be completed, possibly because a disk quota has been set for the destination folder path. Make sure that the amount of disk space is sufficient on the destination drive and the folder does not have disk-space restrictions.

Event ID: 10074

Event Message

Illegal seek performed. There is an error in shared file permissions or possible errors in the file table. Verify that permissions are set. If the problem continues, verify the integrity of the disk by using appropriate utilities for the disk operating system that is in use.

Event ID: 10075

Event Message

Read-only file system in use. For more information about this event, see ISA Server Help.

Explanation

The file system that is selected for a file copy or transfer operation does not allow write modification. Permissions might be in effect to prohibit write access, or the drive media might be of a type that does not permit write access.

User Action

Verify that the drive is using a media type that supports write access, and that write permissions are assigned and in effect.

Event ID: 10076

Event Message

Too many links used. You have reached the maximum number of links that can be opened. Close other connections or applications and retry the operation. If the problem continues, report it to the application supplier.

Event ID: 10077

Event Message

Pipe has broken. The current operation was suspended because the data or connection is experiencing a failing network connection or errors on the network. Reconnect to the remote source. If the problem continues, check for further errors on the network or excessive traffic on the network segment.

Event ID: 10078

Event Message

Math argument used. The input for the current operation was of an invalid type or unexpected for the current application, possibly because of an error in the data or software-based restrictions. Enter the data again. If the problem continues, report the problem to the application supplier.

Event ID: 10079
Event Message
Result is too large. The output for the current operation was invalid for the system or application, possibly because of an error in the data or because of software-based restrictions. Enter the data again. If the problem continues, report the problem to the application supplier.

Event ID: 10080
Event Message
A resource deadlock would occur. The requested operation cannot be completed because sufficient resources do not exist or are not available on the local system. Close other applications to free resources or restart the system. If the problem continues, check your computer configuration.

Event ID: 10081
Event Message
No message of desired type exists. A message cannot be located, or the current application does not support messages of this type. Verify that the message exists at the expected source location. If a message exists, report the problem to the application supplier or see the application's documentation.

Event ID: 10082
Event Message
Identifier removed. For more information about this event, see ISA Server Help.

Explanation
Some identifying information for the connecting socket is missing or was parsed in communications transfer or operation. The cause might be a software problem or an intermediate device used to service the connection.

User Action
Retry the operation. If the problem continues, contact the application supplier to report the problem and obtain an updated file or workaround. Also, when troubleshooting the network, check for invalid packet errors. If unusual numbers of errors are occurring, interference on cabling or data lines could be causing the problem.

Event ID: 10083
Event Message
Channel number is out of range. A port or protocol error has occurred in the application or network environment. Check that all service ports are defined correctly for the application and the Firewall service. If the problem continues, contact the application supplier to report the problem and obtain an updated file or workaround.

Event ID: 10084
Event Message
Level 2 is not synchronized. There is a data line problem for the currently connected operation, possibly because of noise or interference on the line. Check for performance problems or further errors on the line. For further assistance in resolving the problem, report the line problem to your appropriate service provider.

Event ID: 10085

Event Message

Level 3 halted. The network has been stopped. The current connection probably failed. Check the client network connection or have the client reconnect to the network. If the message is repeated for other clients, check for problems in network cabling or termination. Or, check that network hardware or software has not been stopped.

Event ID: 10086

Event Message

Level 3 reset. The network has been reset, probably because an intermediate network host servicing the current connection (for example, a router) was reset. The current connection has failed. Reestablish the remote connection. If the problem continues, check for errors or excess traffic on the network.

Event ID: 10087

Event Message

Link number is out of range. The number specified for linking is invalid. The link is broken. Attempt to re-create the link by using the options within the application. If the problem continues, contact the application supplier to report the problem and obtain an updated file or workaround.

Event ID: 10088

Event Message

Protocol driver is not attached. There is no driver for a supported protocol bound to the network adapter on the local computer. Check the network configuration for the local computer. Verify that a supported network protocol for the Firewall service is bound to the network adapter.

Event ID: 10089

Event Message

No CSI structure is available. A required, specialized component is missing. The operation cannot be completed within the active application. For further assistance in resolving the problem, contact the application supplier to report the problem and obtain an updated file or workaround.

Event ID: 10090

Event Message

Level 2 halted. A problem has occurred at the data-link level, or the link connection has been cleared. Check for errors logged for data link or data communications hardware devices. For further assistance in resolving the problem, report the line to the appropriate service provider.

Event ID: 10091

Event Message

An invalid exchange was made. There is an error in the data, or an exchange between the remote server and the client has been attempted that is not allowed within the software. Reenter the data and retry the operation. If the problem continues, contact the supplier of the current application to report the problem and obtain a fix or workaround.

Event ID: 10092

Event Message

Invalid request descriptor used. There is an error in the data, or an exchange between the remote server and the client has been attempted that is not allowed within the software. Reenter the data and retry the operation. If the problem continues, contact the supplier of the current application to report the problem and obtain a fix or workaround for the problem.

Event ID: 10093

Event Message

Exchange is full. There is an error in the data, or an exchange between the remote server and the client has been attempted that cannot be completed. The system might be too busy to process the request at this time. Retry the operation later. If the problem continues, contact the application supplier to report the problem and obtain an updated file or workaround.

Event ID: 10094

Event Message

No anode exists. There is an error in the data or an exchange between the remote server and the client has been attempted that is not allowed within the software. Reenter the data and retry the operation. If the problem continues, contact the application supplier to report the problem and obtain an updated file or workaround.

Event ID: 10095

Event Message

Invalid request code used. For more information about this event, see ISA Server Help.

Explanation

The requested operation is not recognized or supported by protocol services that are in use between the remote server and the client.

User Action

Confirm that the protocol and port types are correctly configured for the Firewall service and for use with the current application. Specifically, verify that any port types (that is, User Datagram Protocol (UDP) or Transmission Control Protocol (TCP)), port initial direction (that is, inbound or outbound), and port numbers in use for the connection. If the problem cannot be traced to port settings or if the problem continues, report the problem to the application supplier.

Event ID: 10096

Event Message

Invalid slot used. A configuration error in hardware settings has been applied by the current operation. Review the settings used for hardware device access or communication within the application to ensure that the settings are correct.

Event ID: 10097

Event Message

Bad font file format used. A font file is of incorrect format or is outdated. To report the problem and obtain an updated file or workaround, contact the application supplier to report the problem and obtain an updated file or workaround.

Event ID: 10098

Event Message

Device is not a stream. There is an error in the data, or an exchange between the remote server and the client has been attempted that is not allowed within the software. Reenter the data and try the operation again. If the problem continues, contact the application supplier to report the problem and obtain an updated file or workaround.

Event ID: 10099

Event Message

No data was found. No data was received to complete the current operation. Enter the data again and retry the operation. If the problem continues, verify that the connection to the network is still active.

Event ID: 10100

Event Message

Timer has expired.

Event ID: 10101

Event Message

System is out of streams resources. Insufficient streams buffers are available, or a buffer overrun has occurred. Increase the buffer count for streaming protocol (that is, Transmission Control Protocol (TCP)) or modify the connection rate.

Event ID: 10102

Event Message

Machine is not on network. The local computer is not connected to the network. Connection to the network must be made before the request can be processed.

Event ID: 10103

Event Message

Package is not installed. The requested application feature is not currently installed. Reinstall the application or upgrade to install the missing application feature. For more information, see the application documentation.

Event ID: 10104

Event Message

The object is remote. For more information about this event, see ISA Server Help.

Explanation

The selected object cannot be used for the current operation because it is not locally sourced. The attempt to operate on the remote object was not completed.

User Action

1. Check that the WinSock DLL (WinSock.dll or Wsock32.dll) is in the current path. 2. Check that the WinSock DLL file is from the same vendor as your underlying protocol stack. (WinSock DLL files must be supplied by the vendor who provided your underlying protocol stack). 3. You cannot use more than one WinSock implementation simultaneously. If you have more than one WinSock DLL file on your system, be sure the first one in the path is appropriate for the network subsystem currently loaded. 4. Check your WinSock implementation documentation to be sure all necessary components are currently installed and configured correctly.

Event ID: 10105

Event Message
The link has been severed. The current connection has been broken. Quit the application and check for other related communications hardware and software failures on the local computer. Restart the application and try to connect again. If the problem continues, check for other failures on the network or verify that the remote server has not been shut down or removed from the network.

Event ID: 10106

Event Message
Advertise error occurred. For more information about this event, see ISA Server Help.

Explanation
A network shared resource cannot advertise service on the local network. Possibly, network or routing problems, or packet filtering is being applied.

User Action
Verify that the network is online. Also, verify that any required routing advertising protocols, such as Routing Information Protocol (RIP) or Service Advertising Protocol (SAP), are implemented properly on the network and that the current application requires these routing services. Use other utilities to verify that the shared resource can be accessed or browsed from the network.

Event ID: 10107

Event Message
Server mount error occurred. The server is advertising on the network, but a resource on the server is not mounted or is otherwise unavailable. Check for hardware failure on the remote server or to verify that the requested server resource is mounted.

Event ID: 10108

Event Message
Communication error in sending. An error occurred in sending information between the remote server and the local client. Retry the requested communication. If the problem continues, check for network errors. If there are no significant errors on the network, contact the application supplier to report the problem.

Event ID: 10109

Event Message
Protocol error encountered. A protocol error has occurred in the application or network environment. Check that all service ports are defined correctly for the application and the Firewall service. If the problem continues, contact the application supplier.

Event ID: 10110

Event Message
Multihop attempted. For more information about this event, see ISA Server Help.

Explanation
The remote connection attempted to cross an excessive number of intermediate routes between devices. If the connection has multiple routers available for forwarding, this might indicate a problem in other network forwarding devices, such as routers or bridges on the network.

User Action

Check that the maximum number of hops allowed for the protocol service with this connection is sufficient. Also, use network monitoring tools to check statistics on bridges or routers to see if excessive hop counts have been obtained.

Event ID: 10111

Event Message

Inode is remote. Input for the current operation cannot be obtained from a remote source. Contact the supplier of the current application to obtain and report the problem.

Event ID: 10112

Event Message

Cross mount point achieved.

Event ID: 10113

Event Message

Trying to read unreadable message. The message input has errors or is of an incorrect type to be processed by this operation. Check the message data for errors or report the problem to the supplier of the current application.

Event ID: 10114

Event Message

Log name used is not unique. For more information about this event, see ISA Server Help.

Explanation

The service is attempting to name a log by using a file name that is already in use at the service logging path.

User Action

Rename or delete the previous log file or select a different name for the new log file.

Event ID: 10115

Event Message

Remote address changed. The network address for the remote server has been changed to a different address. Reconnect to the remote server, or contact the administrator for the remote server to obtain more information about this problem.

Event ID: 10116

Event Message

Can't access a needed shared library. Software components installed or called by the current application are missing or corrupted. Or, there might be disk errors. Reinstall the current application and retry the current operation. If the problem continues, contact the application supplier to obtain an update, fix, or workaround.

Event ID: 10117

Event Message

Accessing a corrupted shared library. There might be disk errors on the remote drive. In some cases, the file system might be of an unrecognized or unsupported type for the current application or platform. Check that the remote disk drive is not corrupted, and review the installation requirements for the current application.

Event ID: 10118

Event Message

Library section in code file corrupted. Software components installed or called by the current application are missing or corrupted, or there might be disk errors. Reinstall the current application and check the system for disk errors by using disk utilities appropriate for the current disk operating system. If the problem continues, contact the application supplier to obtain an update, fix, or workaround.

Event ID: 10119

Event Message

Attempting to link in too many libraries. For more information about this event, see ISA Server Help.

Explanation

The current operation is attempting to link to libraries that are not permitted by the system or application.

User Action

Check that the current platform meets the application manufacturer's requirements for installation and that any special additional software and configuration changes have been implemented. If the problem continues, contact the application supplier to obtain an update, fix, or workaround for the problem.

Event ID: 10120

Event Message

Attempting to execute a shared library. An incorrect file type was specified for execution on the system, possibly because a required shared library is missing. Reinstall the current application to restore missing libraries or components. If the problem continues, contact the application supplier to obtain an update, fix, or workaround.

Event ID: 10121

Event Message

Socket operation attempted on non-socket.

Event ID: 10122

Event Message

Cannot assign requested address. For more information about this event, see ISA Server Help.

Explanation

A request for a server-provided address was not honored. The address might already be in use elsewhere on the network, or there might not be addresses left to assign for the local subnetwork. This error normally results from an attempt to create a socket with an address found on another computer. The "address" it refers to is the remote socket name (protocol, port, and address).

User Action

Check the network address configuration to verify that the client is configured for dynamic addressing or assign a different address for the client. For networks using DHCP dynamic addressing for clients, check that there are addresses available to assign in the available address pool.

Event ID: 10123

Event Message
Address is already in use. For more information about this event, see ISA Server Help.

Explanation
The requested address cannot be obtained because it is in use elsewhere on the network. Only one usage of each address is permitted. The "address" refers to the local "socket name," which is comprised of the following three elements: protocol, port number, and IP address.

User Action
Check that network address settings for the client are correct for the local network. Assign a different fixed network address to the client. Contact your network administrator for further assistance in resolving address duplication on the local network. Do not run two server applications of the same type on the same computer. For instance, this error occurs if you try to run two applications that connect to one FTP server.

Event ID: 10124

Event Message
Address family is not supported by protocol family. For more information about this event, see ISA Server Help.

Explanation
The network address provided is not correct or is not supported for the local network. An address incompatible with the requested protocol was used. For example, you might not be able to use NS addresses with ARPA Internet protocols.

User Action
Make sure that the address is of the correct format and has been typed correctly before retrying the operation. If the problem continues, report the problem to your network administrator or to your technical support team.

Event ID: 10125

Event Message
Socket type is not supported. For more information about this event, see ISA Server Help.

Explanation
The support for the socket type has not been configured on the system or no implementation for it exists. You can expect this error if a WinSock implementation does not support socket type SOCK_RAW, for example, within the Internet address family (AF_INET).

User Action
For developers, handle the request as a non-fatal error (if possible), since some WinSock calls can legally fail the request.

Event ID: 10126

Event Message
Protocol is not supported. For more information about this event, see ISA Server Help.

Explanation
The protocol selected for use with the current application is not supported for the Firewall service, or has not been defined for the service. The support for the socket type has not been configured for the system, or no implementation of it exists.

User Action

Check that the protocol used for the current application has been added, or defined correctly for use with the Firewall service.

Event ID: 10127

Event Message

No buffer space is available. There is no buffer space available to maintain the current streamed connection. Allocate space for streams buffers on the server. For more information about setting Transmission Control Protocol (TCP) or User Datagram Protocol (UDP) buffer size for clients by using the registry on the server, see Windows 2000 Help.

Event ID: 10128

Event Message

Connection timed out. For more information about this event, see ISA Server Help.

Explanation

A connect or send request failed because the connected party did not properly respond after a period of time. (The time-out period is dependent on the communication protocol.)

User Action

Check that the destination address is a valid IP address. If you used a hostname, check that it resolved to the correct address. If the hostname resolution uses a local host table, it is possible you resolved to an obsolete address. Try to ping the hostname. Is a router configured? Check that the router is up and running (check by pinging it, and then ping an address on the other side of it). Use the Tracert command at the command prompt to determine the path to the destination address and to check that all the routers are functioning. Check your subnet mask. If you do not have the correct subnet mask, your network system might treat a local address as a remote address (so it forwards addresses on the local subnet to the router, rather than broadcasting an ARP request locally), or vice versa.

Event ID: 10129

Event Message

Socket is already connected. For more information about this event, see ISA Server Help.

Explanation

The current operation is unnecessary. A connect request was made on an already connected socket.

User Action

Contact the vendor of the application. They might have a software patch to fix the problem. For developers, make your application more portable with datagram sockets that do not use connect() and sendto() on the same datagram socket in an application, and always "disconnect" before calling connect() more than once. With datastream sockets, do not call connect() more than once (use select() or WSAAsyncSelect() to detect connection completion).

Event ID: 10130

Event Message

Socket is not connected. For more information about this event, see ISA Server Help.

Explanation

The current operation cannot be completed because the remote connection has been lost or was not made. A request to send or receive data was disallowed because the socket is not connected and (when sending on a datagram socket) no address was supplied. An application attempted an input/output network function call before establishing an association with a remote socket (i.e. before calling connect() or accept()).

User Action

Check the following: 1. Ping the remote host you were connected to. If it doesn't respond, it might be off-line or there might be a network problem along the way. If it does respond, then this problem might have been a transient one (so you can reconnect now), or the server application you were connected to might have terminated (so you might not be able to connect again). 2. Ping a local host to verify that your local network is still functioning (if on a serial connection, see next step). 3. Ping your local router address. If you are on a serial connection, your local router is the IP address of the host you initially logged on to using SLIP or PPP. 4. Ping a host on the same subnet as the host you were connected to (if you know of one). This will verify that the destination network is functioning. 5. Use the Tracert command at the command prompt to determine the path to the host you were connected to. This will not reveal too much unless you know the router addresses at the remote end, but it might help to identify if the problem is somewhere along the way.

Event ID: 10131

Event Message

Bad protocol option used. For more information about this event, see ISA Server Help.

Explanation

The application has selected an unsupported protocol for use with this operation.

User Action

Check your application for protocol settings, or review the documentation included with the application on how to review or change the current settings. If the problem continues, contact the supplier of the current application. For developers, check the parameters. Are you using an optional level or socket option that might not be supported on all WinSock implementations? If so, treat this as a non-fatal error and ignore it, if possible.

Event ID: 10132

Event Message

Connection reset by peer. For more information about this event, see ISA Server Help.

Explanation

The current connection has been closed by another peer user or peer server process. This normally results from a lost connection on the remote socket due to a time-out or a reboot.

User Action

You can attempt to reestablish the connection. Check the following: 1. Ping the remote host you were connected to. If it does not respond, it might be off-line or there might be a network problem along the way. If it does respond, then this problem might have been a transient one (so you can reconnect now), or the server application you were connected to might have terminated (so you might not be able to connect again). 2. Ping a local host to verify that your local network is still functioning (if on a serial connection, see next step). 3. Ping your local router address. If you are on a serial connection, your local router is the IP address of the host you initially logged on to using SLIP or PPP. 4. Ping a host on the same subnet as the host you were connected to (if you know of one). This will verify that the destination network is functioning. 5. Use the Tracert command at the command prompt to determine the path to the host you were connected to. This will not reveal too much unless you know the router addresses at the remote end, but it might help to identify if the problem is somewhere along the way. Report the problem to your network administrator, or check the connection logs for other servers on the network for more information.

Event ID: 10133

Event Message

Software caused connection to abort. For more information about this event, see ISA Server Help.

Explanation

Another application process has caused the current connection to fail. This error can occur when the local network system aborts a connection, such as when WinSock closes an established connection after data retransmission fails (receiver never acknowledges data sent on a datastream socket).

User Action

Check the following: 1. Ping the remote host you were connected to. If it does not respond, it might be off-line or there might be a network problem along the way. If it does respond, then this problem might have been a transient one (so you can reconnect now), or the server application you were connected to might have terminated (so you might not be able to connect again). 2. Ping a local host to verify that your local network is still functioning (if on a serial connection, see next step). 3. Ping your local router address. If you are on a serial connection, your local router is the IP address of the host you initially logged on to using SLIP or PPP. 4. Ping a host on the same subnet as the host you were connected to (if you know of one). This will verify that the destination network is functioning. 5. Use the Tracert command at the command prompt to determine the path to the host you were connected to. This will not reveal too much unless you know the router addresses at the remote end, but it might help to identify if the problem is somewhere along the way. Exit and restart the application, then reconnect. If the problem continues, report it to the supplier of the current application.

Event ID: 10134

Event Message

Network is down. For more information about this event, see ISA Server Help.

Explanation

There are problems maintaining a connection to the local network. The current connection has failed. A socket operation encountered an unavailable network.

User Action

Check the client network connection or have the client reconnect to the network. If the message is repeated for other clients, check for problems in network cabling or termination, or that network hardware or software has not been taken offline. Check your WinSock, protocol stack, network driver, and network adapter configuration. Note that this error occurs rarely since a WinSock implementation cannot reliably detect hardware problems.

Event ID: 10135

Event Message
Connection refused. For more information about this event, see ISA Server Help.

Explanation
No connection could be made because the target computer actively refused it. This usually results from trying to connect to a service that is inactive on the foreign host. You might have gone to the wrong host, or the server application you are trying to contact might not be running.

User Action
Check the destination address you are using. If you used a hostname, verify that it was resolved to the correct address. If your hostname resolution uses a local host table, it is possible the name was resolved to an obsolete address. It is also possible that the local services file has an incorrect port number (although this is unlikely). You can verify that the remote computer is rejecting your connection attempt by checking the network statistics locally. If your network system has a WinSock utility such as **ping** or **nbtstat** that shows network statistics, use this to verify that you are receiving TCP resets or ICMP Port Unreachable packets each time you attempt to connect. Try again later. If connection is still refused, contact your network administrator.

Event ID: 10136

Event Message
Host is unreachable. For more information about this event, see ISA Server Help.

Explanation
The remote host cannot be reached at this time or has been shut down. A socket operation was attempted to an unreachable target host. The ICMP message means that the router cannot forward the IP datagram to the target host, possibly because it did not get a response to the ARP request (which might mean the destination host is down).

User Action
Try again later.

Event ID: 10137

Event Message
Protocol is wrong type for socket. For more information about this event, see ISA Server Help.

Explanation
The application requires a socket call that is not supported by the current protocol settings for the client application. A protocol was specified that does not support the semantics of the socket type requested. For example, you cannot use the ARPA Internet UDP protocol with the SOCK_STREAM socket type. This error occurs if you specifically reference a protocol that is not part of the Internet address family you are also referencing.

User Action
Check the current application settings for the protocol type in use for the remote connection. Also check to see if TCP or UDP protocol support is used for the application and configure accordingly. If you are using a third-party Transmission Control Protocol/Internet Protocol (TCP/IP), verify that it is compatible with Wsock32.dll. If you are using Microsoft TCP/IP, remove and reinstall TCP/IP.

Event ID: 10138

Event Message
Operation not supported on socket. For more information about this event, see ISA Server Help.

Explanation
The current operation is not supported for Windows Sockets with the current application. Usually this occurs when a file descriptor refers to a file or socket that cannot support this operation, for example, trying to accept a connection on a datagram socket. Or the device driver for the protocol stack might not be compatible with Wsock32.dll.

User Action
Check your application settings or contact the supplier for the current application and report the problem. If you are using a third-party Transmission Control Protocol/Internet Protocol (TCP/IP), verify that it is compatible with Wsock32.dll. If you are using Microsoft TCP/IP, remove and reinstall TCP/IP. Or use another protocol that is compatible with Wsock32.dll. For developers, if you close a socket inadvertently in one part of an application without keeping another part notified, use socket state in an application and/or handle this error gracefully as a non-fatal error.

Event ID: 10139

Event Message
IP Subnet table is full. The address table for routing hosts on the network indicates that all addresses on this subnetwork are in use. Rebuild routing tables for affected hosts, or assign the host to a new subnetwork with available address space.

Event ID: 10140

Event Message
Subnet module not linked. A required software component is missing or is not configured. Check network configuration settings for the client and try to reinstall the application. If the problem continues, report the problem to the application supplier.

Event ID: 10141

Event Message
Unknown input/output (I/O) control call used. A software error occurred. Report the problem to the application supplier.

Event ID: 10142

Event Message
Failure in streams buffer allocation. There is insufficient buffer space available to maintain the currently streamed connection. Increase the allocated space for streams buffers on the server. For more information about setting Transmission Control Protocol (TCP) or User Datagram Protocol (UDP) buffer size for clients by using the registry on the server, see Windows 2000 Help.

Event ID: 10143

Event Message
Internet Control Message Protocol (ICMP) protocol is unreachable. The remote server is not responding. You might be unable to reach the remote server because hardware has failed or because a nonexistent address was specified. Verify that the address entered for the connection is correct and retry the operation. If the problem reoccurs, contact the network administrator for the remote server.

Event ID: 10144

Event Message

Internet Control Message Protocol (ICMP) port is unreachable. The remote server port is not responding. You might be unable to reach the remote server because hardware has failed or because a nonexistent address was specified. Verify that the address entered for the connection is correct and retry the operation. If the problem reoccurs, contact the network administrator for the remote server.

Event ID: 10145

Event Message

Internet Control Message Protocol (ICMP) network is unreachable. A routing failure has occurred. The local network system might generate this error if there is no default route configured. Typically, WinSock generates this error when it receives a "host unreachable" Internet Control Message Protocol (ICMP) message from a router. Investigate routers on local or remote networks to see that they are active and properly configured. Contact your network administrator to confirm the status of the remote host.

Event ID: 10146

Event Message

Invalid Ethernet packet in use. For more information about this event, see ISA Server Help.

Explanation

A routing failure has occurred. The local network system might generate this error if there is no default route configured. Typically, though, WinSock generates this error when it receives a "host unreachable" ICMP message from the router. The ICMP message means that a router cannot forward the IP datagram, possibly because it did not get a response to the ARP request (which might mean the destination host is down). Note: This error might also result if you are trying to send a multicast packet and the default gateway does not support multicast (check your interface configuration).

User Action

Check the client network configuration to confirm that the selected frame type matches the frame type used by servers on the local network. If the problem continues, review the local router configuration for packet-length settings, or use a packet analysis tool to further investigate packet framing that is currently in effect on the network. You can also try to ping the destination host, to see if you get the same results (chances are, you will). Check the destination address. Check whether you have a router configured in your network system (your WinSock implementation). Use the Tracert command at the command prompt to try to determine where the failure occurs along the route between your host and the destination host. Investigate routers on local or remote networks to see that they are active and properly configured.

Event ID: 10147

Event Message

An error in type registration occurred. A software error occurred. Report the problem to the application supplier.

Event ID: 10148

Event Message
Sockets library is not initialized. For more information about this event, see ISA Server Help.

Explanation
Linked libraries for Windows Sockets are not initialized properly for client configuration. The Hypertext Transfer Protocol (HTTP) failed to initialize the sockets library. This problem occurs if there is some incorrect TCP/IP configuration.

User Action
- Check the bindings, and verify that TCP/IP is bound at the top of the protocol stack. If you continue to receive this message, reinstall TCP/IP.
- Check that the WinSock DLL (WinSock.dll or Wsock32.dll) is in the current path.
- Check that the WinSock DLL file is from the same vendor as your underlying protocol stack. (WinSock DLL files must be supplied by the vendor who provided your underlying protocol stack.)
- You cannot use more than one WinSock implementation simultaneously. If you have more than one WinSock DLL file on your system, be sure the first one in the path is appropriate for the network subsystem currently loaded.
- Check your WinSock implementation documentation to be sure all necessary components are currently installed and configured correctly.

Event ID: 10149

Event Message
Unknown error number encountered. A software error occurred. Report the problem to the application supplier.

Intrusion Detection Event Messages

These messages refer to events connected to intrusion detection in Microsoft Internet Security and Acceleration (ISA) Server.

Event ID: 15001

Event Message
ISA Server detected a windows out-of-band attack. For more information about this event, see ISA Server Help.

Explanation
A windows out-of-band denial-of-service attack was attempted against a computer protected by ISA Server. If successful, this attack crashes the computer.

User Action
If logging for dropped packets has been set you can view details of this attack in the packet filter log in the ISALogs folder, which is located under the ISA Server installation folder. You can use this log to monitor any further intruder activity. Steps against intruder activity might include setting up a packet filter or policy rules to inhibit traffic from the source of the intrusion.

Event ID: 15002

Event Message
ISA Server detected an Internet Protocol (IP) half scan attack. For more information about this event, see ISA Server Help.

Explanation
An Internet Protocol (IP) half scan attack was attempted against a computer protected by ISA Server. This alert occurs when an unexpected Transmission Control Protocol (TCP) packet with a particular flag (for example, Fin, Ack, All, None) is detected.

User Action
If logging for dropped packets has been set, you can view details of this attack in the packet filter log in the ISALogs folder, which is located under the ISA Server installation folder. You can use this log to monitor intruder activity. Steps against intruder activity include setting up a packet filter or policy rules to inhibit traffic from the source of the intrusion.

Event ID: 15003

Event Message
ISA Server detected a land attack. For more information about this event, see ISA Server Help.

Explanation
A land attack was attempted against a computer protected by ISA Server. This alert occurs when a Transmission Control Protocol (TCP) SYN packet or User Datagram Protocol (UDP) packet is sent with a spoofed source Internet Protocol (IP) address and port number that is identical to that of the destination IP address and port. The effect of this makes it appear that the host computer has sent a packet to itself. If this attack is successful, then a loop is created and the computer crashes.

User Action
If logging for dropped packets has been set, you can view details of this attack in the packet filter log in the ISALogs folder, which is located under the ISA Server installation folder. You can use this log to monitor intruder activity. Steps against intruder activity include setting up a packet filter or policy rules to inhibit traffic from the source of the intrusion.

Event ID: 15004

Event Message
ISA Server detected a well-known port scan attack. A well-known port is any port in the range of 0-1023. For more information about this event, see ISA Server Help.

Explanation
A well-known port scan attack was attempted against a computer protected by ISA Server. This alert occurs when an attempt is made to scan well-known ports on a computer to detect services running on these ports.

User Action
If logging for dropped packets has been set, you can view details of this attack in the packet filter log in the ISALogs folder, which is located under the ISA Server installation folder. You can use this log to monitor intruder activity. Steps against intruder activity include setting up a packet filter or policy rules to inhibit traffic from the source of the intrusion.

Event ID: 15005

Event Message
ISA Server detected an all port scan attack. For more information about this event, see ISA Server Help.

Explanation
An all port scan attack was attempted against a computer protected by ISA Server. This alert occurs when an attempt is made to scan ports on a computer to detect services running on these ports.

User Action
If logging for dropped packets has been set, you can view details of this attack in the packet filter log in the ISALogs folder, which is located under the ISA Server installation folder. You can use this log to monitor intruder activity. Steps against intruder activity include setting up a packet filter or policy rules to inhibit traffic from the source of the intrusion.

Event ID: 15006

Event Message
ISA Server detected a User Datagram Protocol (UDP) bomb attack. For more information about this event, see ISA Server Help.

Explanation
A User Datagram Protocol (UDP) bomb attack was attempted against a computer protected by ISA Server. This alert occurs when there is an attempt to send an illegal UDP packet.

User Action
If logging for dropped packets has been set, you can view details of this attack in the packet filter log in the ISALogs folder, which is located under the ISA Server installation folder. You can use this log to monitor intruder activity. Steps against intruder activity include setting up a packet filter or policy rules to inhibit traffic from the source of the intrusion.

Event ID: 15007

Event Message
ISA Server detected a ping of death attack. For more information about this event, see ISA Server Help.

Explanation
A ping of death attack was attempted against a computer protected by ISA Server. This alert occurs when a large amount of information is appended to an Internet Control Message Protocol (ICMP) echo request (ping) packet. If this attack is successful, the computer crashes.

User Action
If logging for dropped packets has been set, you can view details of this attack in the packet filter log in the ISALogs folder, which is located under the ISA Server installation folder. You can use this log to monitor intruder activity. Steps against intruder activity include setting up a static packet filter to block incoming ICMP packets or enabling the filtering of IP fragments by using ISA Management. To enable filtering, in the ISA Management console tree, click Servers And Arrays, click Name, click Access Policy, click IP Packet Filters properties, and then click the Packet Filters tab.

Event ID: 15101

Event Message
ISA Server detected a windows out-of-band attack from Internet Protocol (IP) address %1. For more information about this event, see ISA Server Help.

Explanation
A windows out-of-band denial-of-service attack was attempted against a computer protected by ISA Server. If successful, this attack crashes the computer.

User Action
If logging for dropped packets has been set, you can view details of this attack in the packet filter log in the ISALogs folder, which is located under the ISA Server installation folder. You can use this log to monitor intruder activity. Steps against intruder activity include setting up a packet filter or policy rules to inhibit traffic from the source of the intrusion.

Event ID: 15102

Event Message
ISA Server detected an Internet Protocol (IP) half-scan attack from IP address %1. For more information about this event, see ISA Server Help.

Explanation
An Internet Protocol (IP) half-scan attack was attempted against a computer protected by ISA Server. This alert occurs when an unexpected Transmission Control Protocol (TCP) packet with a particular flag (for example, Fin, Ack, All, None) is detected.

User Action
If logging for dropped packets has been set, you can view details of this attack in the packet filter log in the ISALogs folder, which is located under the ISA Server installation folder. You can use this log to monitor intruder activity. Steps against intruder activity include setting up a packet filter or policy rules to inhibit traffic from the source of the intrusion.

Event ID: 15103

Event Message
ISA Server detected a land attack on Internet Protocol (IP) address %1. For more information about this event, see ISA Server Help.

Explanation
A land attack was attempted against a computer protected by ISA Server. This alert occurs when a Transmission Control Protocol (TCP) SYN packet or User Datagram Protocol (UDP) packet is sent with a spoofed source Internet Protocol (IP) address and port number that is identical to that of the destination IP address and port. The effect of this makes it appear that the host computer has sent a packet to itself. If this attack is successful, a loop is created and the computer crashes.

User Action
If logging for dropped packets has been set, you can view details of this attack in the packet filter log in the ISALogs folder, which is located under the ISA Server installation folder. You can use this log to monitor intruder activity. Steps against intruder activity include setting up a packet filter or policy rules to inhibit traffic from the source of the intrusion.

Event ID: 15104

Event Message
ISA Server detected a well-known port scan attack from Internet Protocol (IP) address %1. A well-known port is any port in the range of 0-1023. For more information about this event, see ISA Server Help.

Explanation
A well-known port scan attack was attempted against a computer protected by ISA Server. This alert occurs when an attempt is made to scan ports on this computer to detect the services running on these ports.

User Action
If logging for dropped packets has been set, you can view details of this attack in the packet filter log in the ISALogs folder, which is located under the ISA Server installation folder. You can use this log to monitor intruder activity. Steps against intruder activity include setting up a packet filter or policy rules to inhibit traffic from the source of the intrusion.

Event ID: 15105

Event Message
ISA Server detected an all port scan attack from Internet Protocol (IP) address %1. For more information about this event, see ISA Server Help.

Explanation
An all port scan attack was attempted against a computer protected by ISA Server. This alert occurs when an attempt is made to scan ports on this computer to detect the services running on it.

User Action
If logging for dropped packets has been set, you can view details of this attack in the packet filter log in the ISALogs folder, which is located under the ISA Server installation folder. You can use this log to monitor intruder activity. Steps against intruder activity include setting up a packet filter or policy rules to inhibit traffic from the source of the intrusion.

Event ID: 15106

Event Message
ISA Server detected a User Datagram Protocol (UDP) bomb attack from Internet Protocol (IP) address %1. For more information about this event, see ISA Server Help.

Explanation
A User Datagram Protocol (UDP) bomb attack was attempted against a computer protected by ISA Server. This alert occurs when there is an attempt to send an illegal UDP packet.

User Action
If logging for dropped packets has been set, you can view details of this attack in the packet filter log in the ISALogs folder, which is located under the ISA Server installation folder. You can use this log to monitor intruder activity. Steps against intruder activity include setting up a packet filter or policy rules to inhibit traffic from the source of the intrusion.

Event ID: 15107

Event Message
ISA Server detected a ping-of-death attack from Internet Protocol (IP) address %1. For more information about this event, see ISA Server Help.

Explanation
A ping-of-death attack was attempted against a computer protected by ISA Server. This alert occurs when a large amount of information is appended to an Internet Control Message Protocol (ICMP) echo request (ping) packet. If this attack is successful, the computer crashes.

User Action
If logging for dropped packets has been set, you can view details of this attack in the packet filter log in the ISALogs folder, which is located under the ISA Server installation folder. You can use this log to monitor intruder activity. Steps against intruder activity include identifying the source of the intrusion, setting up a static packet filter to block incoming ICMP packets, creating a protocol rule that specifically denies incoming ICMP echo request packets from the Internet, or enabling the filtering of IP fragments by using ISA Management. To enable filtering, in the ISA Management console tree, click Servers And Arrays, click Name, click Access Policy, click IP Packet Filters properties, and then click the Packet Filters tab.

Log Event Messages

These messages refer to events related to logging in Microsoft Internet Security and Acceleration (ISA) Server.

Event ID: 1

Event Message
The %1 was unable to load Odbc32.dll for SQL logging due to the following error: %2. The data is the error code. For more information about this event, see ISA Server Help.

Explanation
Open Database Connectivity (ODBC) allows applications to access data in a DBMS (database management system). Odbc32.dll (dynamic-link library file) is required for this process and it could not be located in the current system path.

User Action
Verify the existence of Odbc32.dll in the Windows system directory. The system directory is typically %systemroot%\system32. If the file does not exist, then reinstall ODBC.

Event ID: 2

Event Message
The %1 was unable to open ODBC Data Source %2, Table: %3, under User Name %4. The ODBC Error is: %5. For more information about this event, see ISA Server Help.

Explanation
Open Database Connectivity (ODBC) allows applications to access data in a database management system (DBMS). It uses a data

source to maintain connection information for the database. The ODBC-specified data source could not be opened because it does not exist or because the table and user name information is incorrect.

User Action

Open ISA Management and check the log properties to verify that the ODBC Data Source, Table name, User Name, and Password are correct in the corresponding logging service. To do this, in the ISA Management console tree, click Servers And Arrays, click Name, click Monitoring Configuration, and then click Logs. Check the property sheet where logging is enabled for this service.

Event ID: 3

Event Message

The %1 was unable to create the log file directory %2. For more information about this event, see ISA Server Help.

Explanation

The log file folder specifies where log files should be saved. This information may be missing or incorrect.

User Action

Open ISA Management and check the log properties to verify that the ODBC Data Source, Table name, User Name, and Password are correct in the corresponding logging service. To do this, in the ISA Management console tree, click Servers And Arrays, click Name, click Monitoring Configuration, and then click Logs. Check the property sheet where logging is enabled for this service.

Event ID: 4

Event Message

The %1 failed to log information. The log object was never created, possibly due to wrong configuration. For more information about this event, see ISA Server Help.

Explanation

The server failed to find correct logging information. This information may be missing or incorrect.

User Action

Open ISA Management and check the log properties to verify that the ODBC Data Source, Table name, User Name, and Password are correct in the corresponding logging service. To do this, in the ISA Management console tree, click Servers And Arrays, click Name, click Monitoring Configuration, and then click Logs. Check the property sheet where logging is enabled for this service.

Event ID: 5

Event Message

The %1 failed to log information to file %2 in path %3. The data is the error code. For more information about this event, see ISA Server Help.

Explanation

The server failed to find the correct location for logging information. This information may be missing or incorrect.

User Action

Open ISA Management and check the log properties to verify that file information is correct in the corresponding logging service. To do this, in the ISA Management console tree, click Servers And Arrays, click Name, click Monitoring Configuration, and then click Logs. Check the property sheet where logging is enabled for this service.

Event ID: 6

Event Message
The %1 failed to log information to ODBC Data Source %2, Table: %3, under User Name %4. The ODBC Error is: %5. For more information about this event, see ISA Server Help. The data is the error code.

Explanation
Open Database Connectivity (ODBC) allows applications to access data in a database management system (DBMS). It uses a data source to maintain connection information for the database. Information connected with the data source is either missing or incorrect.

User Action
Open ISA Management and check the log properties to verify that the ODBC Data Source, Table name, User Name, and Password are correct in the corresponding logging service. To do this, in the ISA Management console tree, click Servers And Arrays, click Name, click Monitoring Configuration, and then click Logs. Check the property sheet where logging is enabled for this service.

Event ID: 7

Event Message
The %1 created the log file directory %2 due to logging configuration changes.

Event ID: 14102

Event Message
The server was unable to load Odbc32.dll for SQL logging because of the following error: %1. The specified dynamic-link library (DLL) could not be located in the current system path. Verify the existence of the specified DLL in the Windows system directory. The system directory is typically %systemroot\Winnt\System32%. The error code in the Data area of the event properties indicates the cause of the failure.

Event ID: 14103

Event Message
The server was unable to open Open Database Connectivity (ODBC Data Source %1, Table: %2, under User Name %3. The ODBC Error is: %4. The error code in the Data area of the event properties indicates the cause of the failure. For more information about this event, see ISA Server Help.

Explanation
The Open Database Connectivity (ODBC) data source could not be opened because it does not exist or because the table and user name information is incorrect.

User Action
Open ISA Management and check the log properties to verify that the ODBC Data Source, Table name, User Name, and Password are correct in the corresponding logging service. To do this, in the ISA Management console tree, click Servers And Arrays, click Name, click Monitoring Configuration, and then click Logs.

Event ID: 14104
Event Message
The logging parameters specified are too long. Field: %1; Data Given: %2. The database table used for service logging requires an adjustment. Either the field is not long enough to contain the data or the field type is incorrectly set in the database design. Check configuration of table fields and data types for each field.

Event ID: 14107
Event Message
The server could not log information. The log object was never created. For more information about this event, see ISA Server Help.

Explanation
Information for configuring service logging might be missing or incorrect.

User Action
In ISA Management, verify that logging information is configured correctly for the service. To do this, in the ISA Management console tree, click Servers And Arrays, click Name, click Monitoring Configuration, and then click Logs.

Event ID: 14108
Event Message
The server was unable to find the log file directory %1. The error code in the Data area of the event properties indicates the cause of the failure. For more information about this event, see ISA Server Help.

Explanation
The log file folder is either missing or has been set incorrectly.

User Action
In ISA Management, verify that logging information is configured correctly for the service. To do this, in the ISA Management console tree, click Servers And Arrays, click Name, click Monitoring Configuration, and then click Logs. For a specified log file location, verify that the specified folder location exists. Create the folder again, if necessary.

Event ID: 14047
Event Message
Failed to write to %1 log file in directory %2. There is no space on the disk drive. Delete unnecessary files.

Event ID: 14049
Event Message
%1 was stopped because of a logging failure. For more information about this event, see ISA Server Help.

Explanation
A service stops when an activity log stops responding. If you log to a file on your local file system, it is most likely that a logging failure was caused by insufficient disk space. If you log to a database, the failure is probably related to an error in configuration, insufficient disk space, or connectivity problems.

User Action
If the failure is the result of insufficient disk space, move old files to another media or

delete them manually and configure the system to delete old files in the future. To edit logging configuration, in the ISA Management console tree, click Servers And Arrays, click Name, click Monitoring Configuration, and then click Logs. If you log to a database, check the database configuration. To reconfigure disk space, select a shorter period for logging (for example, weekly or daily), click Location and then select the option to compress log files.

Control Service Event Messages

These messages refer to events connected to the ISA Server Control Service.

Event ID: 14022

Event Message

Microsoft ISA Server Control Service failed to initialize because the system call %1 failed. The error occurred during %2. Use the source location %3 to report the failure. If an error code appears in the Data area of the event properties, it indicates the cause of the failure. For more information about this event, see ISA Server Help.

Explanation

The failure is probably due to insufficient memory or a problem accessing the storage.

User Action

Restart the service. If that does not resolve the problem, close other programs that are running. Use the Task Manager to check programs and processes that are using large amounts of system resources. For more information about managing memory resources, see Windows 2000 Help.

Event ID: 14024

Event Message

Microsoft ISA Server Control Service requires Windows 2000 Server with Service Pack 1 or later.

Event ID: 14025

Event Message

Microsoft ISA Server Control Service requires Windows 2000 Server with Service Pack 1 or later.

Event ID: 14026

Event Message

The Microsoft ISA Server Control Service failed to initialize. The internal error code in the Data area of the event properties indicates the cause of the failure. Restart the service.

Event ID: 14027

Event Message

The Microsoft ISA Server Control Service started.

Event ID: 14076

Event Message

Microsoft ISA Server Control Service failed to execute the security editing application. For more information about this event, see ISA Server Help. Error code: %1.

Explanation

The Secedit system application, which is used for security configuration and analysis, might fail due to an incorrect configuration specified in the security template files.

User Action

Use the Securwiz.log file in the ISA Server installation directory to identify the error. The file contains text in UNICODE (use Notepad to edit it). Search for the keywords "Warning" and "Error."

Event ID: 14078

Event Message

Microsoft ISA Server Control Service failed to delete Web Proxy cache file %1 during %2. Use the source location %3 to report the failure. Try to delete the folder manually.

Event ID: 14080

Event Message

Microsoft ISA Server Control Service failed because an application filter component (%2) performed an illegal operation at method %1 GUID=%3. Try removing recently installed application filters and restart the service. Otherwise, contact the component vendor.

Event ID: 14081

Event Message

ISA Server Control Service discovered a missing application filter component (%1) GUID %2. The application filter cannot be found on this server. Check that the specified filter was installed. The error code in the Data area of the event properties indicates the cause of the failure.

Event ID: 14082

Event Message

ISA Server Control Service cannot load the application filter component (%1) GUID %2, because it does not support necessary interfaces. This indicates a version mismatch, and the filter can no longer be used. Check the filter was installed correctly, or contact the component vendor. The error code in the Data area of the event properties indicates the cause of the failure.

Event ID: 14083

Event Message

ISA Server Control Service cannot load the application filter component (%1) GUID %2. Check that the application filter is installed properly. The error code in the Data area of the event properties indicates the cause of the failure.

Event ID: 14084

Event Message

ISA Server Control Service failed to start. All array members must be in the same site (%2). However, this server is in site %1. The server may have been moved to a different site that its containing array. Move the server to an array in its new site.

Event ID: 14085

Event Message

ISA Server Control Service failed to start. All array members must be in the same domain (%2). However, this server is in domain %1. The server was apparently moved to a different domain than its containing array. The server should be added to an array in its new domain.

Event ID: 14181

Event Message
The ISA Server Control Service was stopped gracefully.

Packet Filter Event Messages

These messages refer to events connected to packet filtering in Microsoft Internet Security and Acceleration (ISA) Server.

Event ID: 14038

Event Message
ISA Server packet filter log service cannot allocate memory. The packet filter log component of ISA Server logs this event when it fails to allocate memory where memory resources are low. The packet filter log component cannot operate until the low memory situation is resolved. The ISA Server administrator can stop and restart the ISA Server services to resolve the low memory situation if logging of packet filter data is mandatory.

Event ID: 14039

Event Message
ISA Server packet filter logging component cannot obtain the log contents. Restarting the service might solve the problem.

Event ID: 14043

Event Message
The system-wide packet filter log event cannot be created.

Event ID: 14044

Event Message
The packet filter is dropping Internet Protocol (IP) packets. For more information about this event, see ISA Server Help.

Explanation
The IP packet drop rate of the ISA Server exceeds the specified level. The Internet Protocol (IP) packet drop rate is configured in ISA Management. To configure the drop rate, in the ISA Management console tree, click Servers And Arrays, click Name, click Monitoring Configuration, click Alerts, and then click Dropped Packets Alert Properties.

User Action
An administrator can examine the packet filter logs to detect the nature of the drop rate and take further action.

Event ID: 14046

Event Message
Packet filter protocol violation. For more information about this event, see ISA Server Help.

Explanation
The dropped packet rate of some special kinds of packets (for example, spoofed packets or fragments) exceeds the rate specified in the configuration for dropped packets. To configure the drop rate, in the ISA Management console tree, click Servers And Arrays, click Name, click Monitoring Configuration, click Alerts, and then click Dropped Packets Alert Properties.

User Action
Examine the packet filter logs to detect the nature of the drop rate and take further action.

Event ID: 14086

Event Message
Insecure configuration detected. Internet Protocol (IP) routing is enabled while packet filtering is disabled. All packets will be routed, regardless of access policy. It is recommended that you enable IP routing only when you also enable packet filtering.

Event ID: 14119

Event Message
An external interface could not be found for packet filtering. For more information about this event, see ISA Server Help.

Explanation
This event can occur if the Local Address Table (LAT) includes all the addresses associated with the external interfaces. The event might also occur if another application is controlling the packet filter driver. Since only one application can control the packet filter driver at a time, the Firewall service cannot filter packets.

User Action
Verify that the LAT is configured properly and no other applications are configured to use packet filtering on the external network interfaces of the ISA Server. To do this, in the ISA Management console tree, click Servers And Arrays, click Name, click Network Configuration, and then click Local Address Table.

Event ID: 14120

Event Message
The ISA Server services cannot create a packet filter %1. This event occurs when there is a conflict between the Local Address Table (LAT) configuration and the Windows 2000 routing table. Check the routing table and the LAT to find the source of the conflict.

Event ID: 14121

Event Message
The packet filter dial-out interface cannot be rebound. For more information about this event, see ISA Server Help.

Explanation
This alert is generated when the ISA Server services are not able to bind a network interface with the packet filter driver. ISA Server typically rebinds interfaces and packet filters for the dial-out connections when they are dialed and disconnected. The alert also logs the error code that the underlying layers return.

User Action
This alert should not occur on a properly configured system. Check the configuration, including the LAT table. To do this, in the ISA Management console tree, click Servers And Arrays, click Name, click Network Configuration, and then click Local Address Table. Confirm that configuration of the specified phonebook entry in the dial-up entries configuration is correct. To do this, in the ISA Management console tree, click Servers And Arrays, click Name, click Policy Elements, and then click Dial-Up Entries.

Event ID: 14122

Event Message
A packet filter interface could not be bound. For more information about this event, see ISA Server Help.

Explanation

Packet filtering cannot be enabled on a specific interface. The configuration of the interface might have changed, been enabled or disabled, or a dial-out connection might have been dropped immediately after being connected.

User Action

Restart the Firewall and Web Proxy services. In ISA Management, check the system configuration to make sure it is consistent with packet filtering configuration, including the internal network addresses in the Local Address Table (LAT), or run Ipconfig at the command line to check current TCP/IP configuration values. To check the system configuration, in the ISA Management console tree, click Servers And Arrays, click Name, click Network configuration, and then click Local Address Table.

Event ID: 14123

Event Message

Failed to create the Internet Protocol (IP) packet filter. For more information about this event, see ISA Server Help.

Explanation

A static packet filter could not be created. System configuration might be incorrect, and the service might have attempted to create the filter for an external remote host on an ISA Server internal interface, due to incorrect configuration for default routing. Otherwise, memory resources might be low.

User Action

For system configuration problems, check the Local Address Table (LAT) configuration, run ipconfig/all to check TCP/IP configuration, and run Route -Print to obtain a list of registered, persistent routes. To check the LAT, in the ISA Management console tree, click Servers And Arrays, click Name, click Network Configuration, and then click Local Address Table. For low memory resources, close other applications or stop and restart the services.

Event ID: 14124

Event Message

Filtering disabled as requested.

Server Event Messages

These messages are connected to server and server publishing events in Microsoft Internet Security and Acceleration (ISA) Server.

Event ID: 12260

Event Message

Fatal error occurred when attempting to access '%1' certificate private key. For more information about this event, see ISA Server Help. The error code in the Data area of the event properties indicates the cause of the failure.

Explanation

The server cannot access certificate private key because the certificate and its private key are not installed in the same store.

User Action

Check configuration of certificates.

Event ID: 14087

Event Message

Insecure configuration detected. ISA Server uses its own Network Address Translation (NAT) editor to fully secure your system. However, ISA Server found one or more different NAT editors, which might have been installed by the following drivers: %1. It is recommended that you uninstall the drivers listed. For more information about this event, see ISA Server Help.

Explanation

Non-system Network Address Translation (NAT) editors are considered insecure by default. Such editors enable Internet Protocol (IP) traffic to pass through without applying policies.

User Action

It is not recommended to allow any third party to install NAT editors. Uninstall the driver that installed the insecure NAT editor.

Event ID: 14088

Event Message

Server publishing rule [%1] that maps %2 %3 to %4 for protocol [%5] violates %6 rule [%7]. For more information about this event, see ISA Server Help.

Explanation

There is a conflict between the configuration of the server publishing rule and the configuration of an access policy rule.

User Action

Change the rule configurations to resolve the conflict. To view server publishing rules in ISA Management, click Servers And Arrays, click Name, click Publishing, and then click Server Publishing Rules. To view access policy rules in ISA Management, click Servers And Arrays, click Name, click Access Policy, and then click the appropriate rule.

Event ID: 14089

Event Message

Server publishing rule [%1] failed. Cannot create session for the server %2. Location %3. For more information about this event, see ISA Server Help.

Explanation

The server publishing rule cannot be applied. The Firewall service failed to obtain a session with the server. The internal server address might not be included in the Local Address Table (LAT).

User Action

Check that the internal server address is included in the LAT. To do this, in the ISA Management console tree, click Servers And Arrays, click Name, click Network Configuration, click Local Address Table (LAT) and review the existing LAT entries. If the internal server address in not included, construct a new LAT entry by right-clicking Local Address Table (LAT).

Event ID: 14090

Event Message

Server publishing rule [%1] that maps %2 %3 to %4 for protocol [%5] failed to bind to external interface. The server publishing rule cannot be applied. The Firewall service failed to bind a socket for the server. The error code in the Data area of the event properties indicates the cause of the failure.

Event ID: 14091

Event Message
Server publishing rule [%1] failed. The protocol specified cannot be used for publishing. Location %2. The server publishing rule cannot be applied. The protocol must be inbound. Check with the application filter vendor.

Event ID: 14092

Event Message
Server publishing rule [%1] failed. The protocol specified cannot be used for publishing. Location %2. For more information about this event, see ISA Server Help.

Explanation
The server publishing rule cannot be applied. The protocol definition used for this rule is not inbound and is not valid.

User Action
Define a protocol that has an inbound primary connection for use with server mapping rules. To do this, in the ISA Management console tree, click Servers And Arrays, click Name, click Policy Elements, and then click Protocol Definitions.

Event ID: 14095

Event Message
Failed to initialize server publishing. Location %1. Internal error. Storage might be corrupted.

Event ID: 14096

Event Message
Failed to read server publishing rules. Location %1. Internal error. Storage might be corrupted.

Event ID: 14097

Event Message
Failed to read one or more server publishing rules. Location %1. Internal error. Storage might be corrupted.

Event ID: 14098

Event Message
Failed to read parameters of the publishing rule [%1]. The rule is discarded. Location %2. The storage might be corrupted. Delete this rule and create a new one.

Event ID: 14099

Event Message
Publishing rule [%1] could not be applied to this array member because IP %2 is not available. A server publishing rule can only be applied to one server from the array. All other servers will report this event. Note that an Internet Protocol (IP) address might be temporarily unavailable (for example, dial-up connection is disconnected).

Event ID: 14100

Event Message
The server was unable to log on the Windows 2000 account '%1' due to the following error: %2. The account name that was entered is not an account recognized by

Windows 2000. Confirm that you entered the correct user name. The error code in the Data area of the event properties indicates the cause of the failure.

Event ID: 14101

Event Message

The server could not add the virtual root '%1' for the directory '%2' due to the following error: %3. The directory name is not recognized for the server volume that is specified in the virtual root mapping. Check that the directory name entered for drive mapping is correct. The error code in the Data area of the event properties indicates the cause of the failure.

Event ID: 14105

Event Message

ISA Management might not be able to recognize this server, because the server was unable to register on the network. Check for a server name conflict on the Internet. The error code in the Data area of the event properties indicates the cause of the failure.

Event ID: 14143

Event Message

ISA Server is too busy to handle this request. Reenter the request or renew the connection to the server (now or at a later time).

Event ID: 14145

Event Message

ISA Server failed to initialize due to a corrupted registry. Restart the service. If this does not resolve the problem, reinstall the server to replace any missing files. If the condition persists, restore the registry. Error Code %1, Key='%2', Value='%3'.

Event ID: 14146

Event Message

ISA Server failed to load ISAPI Filter DLL %1. The error code shown in the Data area of the event properties indicates the cause of the failure.

Event ID: 14159

Event Message

Failed to read reference to the protocol from the server publishing rule [%1]. Location %2. Storage may be corrupted. Delete this rule and create a new rule.

Event ID: 14160

Event Message

Server publishing rule [%1] that maps %2 %3 to %4 for protocol [%5] is not applied since enterprise policy does not allow publishing. The enterprise policy can be changed to allow publishing.

Event ID: 14161

Event Message

Server publishing rule [%1] that maps %2 %3 to %4 for protocol [%5] was applied successfully. This rule previously failed, but now completed successfully.

Event ID: 14162

Event Message

Server publishing rule [%1] will not be applied since the filter that supports the protocol is not enabled. Enable the filter and then apply the rule.

Event ID: 14163

Event Message

Server publishing rule [%1] that maps %2 %3 to %4 for protocol [%5] failed because the port on the external interface is being used by another application. The Firewall service failed to bind socket for the server on the firewall since another process is using the same port. Check for any other process using the same port and terminate if necessary.

Web Proxy Service Event Messages

These messages refer to events connected to the ISA Server Web Proxy service.

Event ID: 14125

Event Message

The Web Proxy service received %1 requests from the Internet port during the past %2 seconds while Web publishing was disabled. When ISA Server publishing is disabled, this event message displays the number of requests from the Internet during the specified time, in seconds.

Event ID: 14126

Event Message

The Web Proxy service configuration has been modified %1 times during the past %2 seconds.

Event ID: 14127

Event Message

The Web Proxy service could not initialize (error code %1). The internal error code in the Data area of the event properties indicates the cause of the failure.

Event ID: 14128

Event Message

The Web Proxy service is paused.

Event ID: 14129

Event Message

The Web Proxy service was resumed. No further action necessary.

Event ID: 14130

Event Message

The Web Proxy service detected that the upstream proxy '%1' is not available. For more information about this event, see ISA Server Help.

Explanation

The upstream proxy is offline.

User Action

Verify the reason and predicted time frame for the continuation of the problem. If necessary, configure a backup route. To do this, in the ISA Management console tree, click Servers And Arrays, click Name, click Network Configuration, and then click Routing. Open the rule and then click the Action tab. Or, you can route the request to an alternate destination.

Event ID: 14131

Event Message

The Web Proxy service detected that the upstream proxy '%1' is now available. If you were able to work around the upstream proxy server, no further action is necessary. If you changed the configuration of the primary route to the upstream ISA Server, you might want to change it back.

Event ID: 14132

Event Message

The Web Proxy service detected that the array member '%1' is down. Check the array member intra-array address or the network to find out why this array member is not available.

Event ID: 14133

Event Message

The Web Proxy service detected that the array member '%1' is available.

Event ID: 14141

Event Message

ISA Server detected a proxy chain loop. There is a problem with the configuration of the ISA Server routing policy. In ISA Management, check the routing configuration on all chained proxies. To do this, in the ISA Management console tree, click Servers And Arrays, click Name, click Network Configuration, and then click Routing.

Event ID: 14148

Event Message

Web Proxy service failed to bind its socket to %1 port %2. This could be caused by another service that is already using the same port or by a network interface card that is not functional. The error code specified in the Data area of the event properties indicates the cause of the failure. For more information about this event, see ISA Server Help.

Explanation

The requested service port is already in use, or data loss may have resulted from a large number of packet collisions on the local network segment. It is also possible that there is a problem with the network interface card (NIC).

User Action

Check the NIC. Monitor the service that failed for the server and the client, or monitor traffic on your local network.

Event ID: 14149

Event Message
Web Proxy service failed to listen to %1 port %2. The network interface card might not be functional. The error code specified in the Data area of the event properties indicates the cause of the failure. For more information about this event, see ISA Server Help.

Explanation
The Web Proxy service is unable to register itself to listen on the port specified. Some other application might be using the port.

User Action
Use **netstat -a** to check which ports are in use. Check the port details for each protocol defined for ISA Server. To do this, in the ISA Management console tree, click Servers And Arrays, click Name, click Policy Elements, and then click Protocol Definitions.

Event ID: 14153

Event Message
The Web Proxy service is not listening on the defined *IntraArrayAddress* although resolving requests within an array is enabled. For more information about this event, see ISA Server Help.

Explanation
If Cache Array Routing Protocol (CARP) is enabled, the Web Proxy service on each ISA Server in the array must listen on its *Intra-array address*.

User Action
Verify that there is a listener set for the *Intra-array address* on the server for all the directions on which CARP is enabled.

Event ID: 14154

Event Message
The Scheduled Content Download Service started the job %1.

Event ID: 14155

Event Message
The Scheduled Content Download Service finished the job %1. %2 pages.

Event ID: 14156

Event Message
The Web Proxy Service switched from primary route %1 to backup route %2. The Web Proxy Service is configured to switch to the backup route if there is some problem with the primary route.

Event ID: 14157

Event Message
The Web Proxy Service switched from backup route %1 to primary route %2. Following a problem with the primary route, the Web Proxy service switches to the configured backup route. While using the backup route, the service moves back to the primary route when it is available.

Event ID: 14158

Event Message
The *Intra-array address* defined on this server is not in the Local Address Table (LAT). For more information about this event, see ISA Server Help.

Explanation

The *Intra-array address* defined in the storage for this server is not in the Local Address Table (LAT).

User Action

Set an Internet Protocol (IP) that is in the LAT as the value of the *Intra-array address* property. To do this, in the ISA Management console tree, click Servers And Arrays, click Name, click Computer, click the computer name and then click the Array membership tab.

Event ID: 14177

Event Message

Some certificates cannot be initialized (error code %1). The Web Proxy service could not initialize. Check that all certificates used by the Web Proxy servce are valid. The internal error code in the Data area of the event properties indicates the cause of the failure.

Event ID: 14178

Event Message

The Web Proxy service identified that the address %1 was removed from the interface table and stopped listening on port %2.

Event ID: 14179

Event Message

The Web Proxy Service identified that the address %1 was added to the interface table and start listening on port %2.

Event ID: 14183

Event Message

The Web Proxy Service was stopped gracefully.

HTTP Messages

Event ID: 12150

Event Message

The requested header was not found. Reload the document using the Refresh function of your Web browser.

Event ID: 12151

Event Message

The server does not support the requested protocol level. Verify that the protocol you typed is a supported protocol (such as FTP, Gopher, HTTP) for the Web Proxy service.

Event ID: 12152

Event Message

The server returned an invalid or unrecognized response. The HTTP request cannot be fully or correctly interpreted by the server. The request might have been corrupted by transmission errors. Try reloading the document in your Web browser to correct the problem.

Event ID: 12153

Event Message

The supplied HTTP header is invalid and not recognized by the remote server. Check that your browser is supported.

Event ID: 12154

Event Message

The request for a HTTP header is invalid. A header contained within the Uniform Resource Locator (URL) request is not recognized by the remote server. Check that your browser is supported.

Event ID: 12155

Event Message

The HTTP header already exists. Contact your ISA Server administrator.

Event ID: 12201

Event Message

A chained proxy server or array member requires proxy-to-proxy authentication. Please contact your server administrator.

Event ID: 12202

Event Message

The ISA Server denies the specified Uniform Resource Locator (URL).

Event ID: 12204

Event Message

The specified Secure Sockets Layer (SSL) port is not allowed. ISA Server is not configured to allow SSL requests from this port. Most Web browsers use port 443 for SSL requests. Check the configuration for outgoing Web requests. Contact your ISA Server administrator.

Event ID: 12206

Event Message

The ISA Server detected a proxy chain loop. There is a problem with the configuration of the ISA Server routing policy. Please contact your server administrator.

Event ID: 12209

Event Message

The ISA Server requires authorization to fulfill the request. Access to the Web Proxy service is denied. The configuration for outgoing Web requests should be checked. Contact your ISA Server administrator.

Event ID: 12210

Event Message

An Internet Server API (ISAPI) filter caused an error or terminated with an error.

Event ID: 12211

Event Message

The ISA Server requires a secure channel connection to fulfill the request. ISA Server is configured to respond to outgoing secure (that is, Secure Sockets Layer (SSL)) channel requests. The configuration for outgoing Web requests need to be checked. Contact your ISA Server administrator.

Event ID: 12212

Event Message

The ISA Server requires a high-security connection to fulfill the request. An Secure Sockets Layer (SSL) Web server requires 128-bit encryption, an enhanced security mechanism, for access to published sites. Use a browser that supports this enhanced encryption.

Event ID: 12213

Event Message

The ISA Server requires a client certificate to fulfill the request. An Secure Sockets Layer (SSL) Web server, during the authentication process, requires a client certificate. The configuration for outgoing Web requests should be checked. Contact your ISA Server administrator.

Event ID: 12214

Event Message

An Internet Server API (ISAPI) filter caused an error or terminated with an error.

Event ID: 12221

Event Message

A chained server requires authentication. Contact the server administrator.

Event ID: 12227

Event Message

The dial-out connection failed. The dial-out connection failed with the specified phonebook entry. The administrator should manually dial the specified phonebook entry to confirm that the problem is not the Windows 2000 auto-dial facility.

Event ID: 12228

Event Message

The server is too busy to handle this request. Reenter request or try again later.

Event ID: 12229

Event Message

The server requires authorization to fulfill the request. Access to the Web server is denied. Contact the server administrator.

Event ID: 12230

Event Message

An Internet Server API (ISAPI) filter has finished handling the request. Contact the server administrator.

Event ID: 12231

Event Message

The page must be viewed over a secure (that is, Secure Sockets Layer (SSL)) channel. Contact the server administrator.

Event ID: 12232

Event Message

The page requires 128-bit encryption, an enhanced security mechanism. To view the page contents, use a browser that supports this enhanced encryption.

Event ID: 12233
Event Message
The page requires a client certificate as part of the authentication process. Contact the server administrator.

Event ID: 12234
Event Message
An Internet Server API (ISAPI) filter caused an error or terminated with an error.

HTML Messages

Event ID: 14201
Event Message
HTTP proxy report message.

Event ID: 14202
Event Message
HTTP proxy reports.

Event ID: 14203
Event Message
The ISA Server encountered an error.

Event ID: 14204
Event Message
Server error message.

Event ID: 14205
Event Message
ISA Server: extended error message.

Event ID: 14206
Event Message
Directory is empty.

Event ID: 14207
Event Message
Root directory.

Event ID: 14208
Event Message
Gopher root at %%s.

Event ID: 14209
Event Message
FTP root at %%s.

Event ID: 14210
Event Message
Gopher directory at %%s.

Event ID: 14211
Event Message
FTP directory %%s at %%s.

Event ID: 14212
Event Message
Web Proxy Cache initialization failed due to thread initialization failure.

Gopher Messages

Event ID: 12130

Event Message

A Gopher protocol error occurred. In some cases, protocol errors can occur between a server that supports only standard Gopher and a client that uses Gopher Plus. Verify that the server supports the same version of Gopher protocol used by the client.

Event ID: 12131

Event Message

The Uniform Resource Locator (URL) must be for a file. The URL that was entered describes a directory location and not a file. Type a Gopher URL that contains a file name. Browse through the directory listing to locate the file.

Event ID: 12132

Event Message

An error was detected while parsing the data. There may be a problem with the Gopher server that you are trying to connect to. In some cases, protocol errors can occur between a server that supports only standard Gopher and a client that uses Gopher Plus. Try again later and in addition, verify that the server supports the same version of Gopher protocol that is used by the client.

Event ID: 12133

Event Message

There is no more data. No more data exists beyond the last block of data returned from the server. Stop the request for additional data by canceling the operation in progress.

Event ID: 12134

Event Message

The Uniform Resource Locator (URL) is not valid for the remote Gopher server. Browse through the directory to verify that you used the correct path to locate the requested file.

Event ID: 12135

Event Message

The Uniform Resource Locator (URL) type is incorrect for this operation. A file name or directory name might be applied incorrectly. Verify that the name that specifies the location is a file or directory name and matches the operation.

Event ID: 12136

Event Message

The request must be for a Gopher Plus item. The server and client do not support the same version of Gopher protocols. Modify or upgrade the client to use Gopher Plus.

Event ID: 12137

Event Message

The requested attribute is supported for Gopher Plus servers and was not found on the server. Reconfigure the client to use standard Gopher protocol and resend the request.

Event ID: 12138

Event Message

The Uniform Resource Locator (URL) type is not recognized. An incorrect Gopher type was used, or the Gopher type is not supported. Verify that the name that specifies the location is a file or directory name and is correctly matched for the operation.

FTP Messages

Event ID: 12110

Event Message

There is already an File Transfer Protocol (FTP) request in progress during this session. For more information about this event, see ISA Server Help.

Explanation

You can make only one File Transfer Protocol (FTP) request per session.

User Action

Wait for the current request to finish. You can also disconnect from the FTP server and then reconnect to check for server availability. No further action is required.

Event ID: 12111

Event Message

The File Transfer Protocol (FTP) session was terminated. The connection was closed because of either a possible attempted security violation or a time out on the remote server. Reconnect to the server or check for server availability. No further action is required.

Internet Messages

Event ID: 12001

Event Message

No more Internet handles can be allocated. The Web server does not have enough available resources to support the request for service at this time. Try again later.

Event ID: 12002

Event Message

The operation timed out. The remote server did not respond within the set time allowed. The server might be unavailable at this time. Try again later or contact the server administrator.

Event ID: 12003

Event Message

The server returned extended information. This is typically a string or buffer containing a verbose error message. For more information, review the request output.

Event ID: 12004

Event Message

A software error occurred for a Windows Internet extension application that is required for the current operation.

Event ID: 12005

Event Message

The Uniform Resource Locator (URL) is invalid. The request was not entered correctly. Enter the correct URL and try again.

Event ID: 12006

Event Message

The Uniform Resource Locator (URL) does not use a recognized protocol. Either the protocol is not supported or the request was not typed correctly. Confirm that a valid protocol is in use (for example, HTTP for a Web request).

Event ID: 12007

Event Message

The server name or address could not be resolved. This message might indicate an error in client or server configuration settings for DNS, WINS, or DHCP services that are actively in use. Review the TCP/IP properties for these services.

Event ID: 12008

Event Message

A protocol with the required capabilities was not found. ISA Server does not support the request protocol. Enter the request again. Verify that the protocol is a supported type (for example, HTTP, FTP, or Gopher).

Event ID: 12009

Event Message

The option is invalid. The requested option is not available with your current configuration. Clear the message and select a different option, or check configuration.

Event ID: 12010

Event Message

The length is incorrect for the option type. Reselect the current option and type the data again. Verify that you did not type extra characters and that the value you typed in is within the permitted length.

Event ID: 12011

Event Message

The option value cannot be set. The server does not support this value, or the value was typed incorrectly. Retry the operation. If you still get this message, ask your network administrator to check the status of the remote computer.

Event ID: 12012

Event Message

Windows Internet Extension support has been shut down. Open the required Internet Extension application and reselect the command option.

Event ID: 12013

Event Message

The user name was not allowed. Try a different name, or retry the same name after verifying that it is typed correctly.

Event ID: 12014

Event Message

The password was not allowed. The password might have been changed or typed incorrectly. Try typing the password again. If the problem continues, contact the administrator for the remote server and report the problem.

Appendix C   Event Messages

Event ID: 12015

Event Message

The login request was denied. The logon account might have been disabled or logon information might have changed. Log on again to verify that the information was typed correctly. If the problem continues, report the problem to the administrator of the Internet server you are requesting.

Event ID: 12016

Event Message

The requested operation is invalid. The operation entered in the Uniform Resource Locator (URL) is not allowed or is not recognized by the remote Internet server. Type the URL again or select a different operation.

Event ID: 12017

Event Message

The operation has been cancelled. Try the operation again.

Event ID: 12018

Event Message

The supplied handle is the wrong type for the requested operation.

Event ID: 12019

Event Message

The handle is in the wrong state for the requested operation.

Event ID: 12020

Event Message

The request cannot be made on an ISA Server session.

Event ID: 12021

Event Message

The registry value could not be found.

Event ID: 12022

Event Message

The registry parameter is incorrect.

Event ID: 12023

Event Message

Direct Internet access is not available.

Event ID: 12024

Event Message

No context value was supplied. An asynchronous request could not be made because a zero context value was supplied.

Event ID: 12025

Event Message

No status callback was supplied.

Event ID: 12026

Event Message

There are outstanding requests. The required operation could not be completed because one or more requests are pending.

Event ID: 12027
Event Message
The information format is incorrect.

Event ID: 12028
Event Message
The requested item could not be located.

Event ID: 12029
Event Message
A connection with the server cannot be established.

Event ID: 12030
Event Message
The connection with the server was terminated abnormally.

Event ID: 12031
Event Message
The connection with the server was reset.

APPENDIX D

Glossary

abuse of privilege   When a user performs an action that he or she should not have, according to organizational policy or law.

access control list (ACL)   A level of Windows 2000 permission that can be set on a file or a directory allowing specified users access within an NTFS directory. An access control entry (ACE) is an entry in the list. For details, see the Windows 2000 documentation.

access policy   A set of protocol rules and site and content rules that determines the behavior of an enterprise or array.

active caching   An ISA Server feature that automatically initiates new requests to update cached file objects without user intervention. Requests can be activated based on the length of time an object has been cached or since it was last retrieved from the object's source location. This type of caching can be used to assure the validity of specified data in the cache.

Active Directory directory services
The directory service included with Windows 2000 Server.

address resolution   The mapping of an IP address to a hardware address.

Address Resolution Protocol (ARP)
A protocol in the TCP/IP suite that provides IP address-to-MAC address resolution for IP packets.

alerting   A feature that warns administrators about suspicious network events, such as rejected packets and protocol violations. Alerting is made available when packet filtering is turned on and is recorded in the packet filtering log. A message generated as the result of an alert can be sent to a user account by e-mail.

anonymous logon   A feature that allows a user remote access to a computer on the Internet without having to supply a user name or password, but only with the guest permissions assigned to that account. Commonly used in HTTP and FTP requests.

application filter   Software that can perform protocol-specific or system-specific tasks, such as authentication. An application filter provides an extra layer of security for the Firewall service.

application-layer firewall A firewall system in which service is provided by processes that maintain complete TCP connection state and sequencing. Application-level firewalls often re-address traffic so that outgoing traffic appears to have originated from the firewall, rather than from the internal host.

array A group of ISA Server computers grouped together to provide distributed caching, load balancing, and fault tolerance. Arrays allow a group of ISA Server computers to be treated and managed as a single, logical enterprise.

array member An ISA Server computer that is part of an array.

authentication Validation of a user's logon information to determine permission to access a resource or perform an operation, or the process of determining the identity of a user who is attempting to access a system.

authentication token A portable device or hashing algorithm used for authenticating a user. Authentication tokens operate by challenge/response, time-based code sequences, or other techniques. A portable device, can be as simple as a paper-based lists of one-time passwords.

authorization The process of determining what types of activities are permitted. Usually, authorization is in the context of authentication: once you have authenticated a user, he or she can be authorized for different types of access or activity.

automatic discovery A feature that allows Firewall clients to be configured so that they automatically find the appropriate ISA Server computer.

bandwidth control An ISA Server mechanism that informs the Windows 2000 QoS packet scheduling service how to prioritize connections that pass through ISA Server.

bandwidth priority A priority level set with bandwidth rules to define priority for connections passing through ISA Server.

bandwidth rules A mechanism used to determine which connection gets priority over another.

basic authentication A method of authentication that encodes the user name and password. Basic authentication is called *plaintext* because the encoding (base-64) can be decoded by anyone with a common decoding utility. Note that encoding is not the same as encryption.

bastion host A system that has been hardened to resist attack, and which is installed on a network in such a way that it is expected to come under attack. Bastion hosts are often components of firewalls, or may be "outside" Web servers or public access systems. Generally, a bastion host runs some form of general purpose operating system (e.g., UNIX, VMS, WNT, etc.) rather than a ROM-based or firmware operating system.

broadcasting The delivery of data packets to all computers on a network segment.

cache A store of frequently retrieved objects and URLs located on the cache drive of an ISA Server computer. Instead of retrieving an object directly from an Internet Web server, the object is stored and retrieved from the cache. Caches improve network performance by reducing the number of times objects need to be retrieved from the Internet. This means faster client access to popular objects and less bandwidth overhead.

Cache Array Routing Protocol (CARP) A routing algorithm used to provide efficiency and prevent duplication of cache contents when multiple ISA Server computers are arrayed as a single logical cache.

cache drive The amount of space reserved on a selected server disk drive for use in storing cached files.

cache filtering The ability either to cache or not cache objects retrieved from World Wide Web, FTP, or Gopher sites.

Cache mode One of the selections available during the setup process to define features available for ISA Server. If Cache mode is chosen, caching features are available but no firewall features will be.

cache policy A set of rules and configuration parameters that determine the behavior of the ISA Server cache.

CARP *See* Cache Routing Array Protocol.

.cdat The file created when a cache drive is configured. The size of the .cdat file will be the size of the cache drive specified.

chained authentication The authentication that an ISA Server computer provides when routing requests to an upstream server.

chaining A method of linking multiple ISA Server computers together. Individual ISA Server and proxy computers and arrays or any combination can be chained. Communication between ISA Server computers occur in an upstream, hierarchical order.

challenge/response An authentication technique whereby a server sends an unpredictable challenge to the user, who computes a response using some form of authentication token.

client certificate Used when the SSL protocol provides authentication by checking the contents of an encrypted digital identification submitted by the client's Web browser during the logon process. This certificate contains information about the client and about the entity, usually an organization, that issued the certificate.

client set A group of one or more local client computers, joined together for the purpose of applying rules and policies to the set.

cryptographic checksum A one-way function applied to a file to produce a unique "fingerprint" of the file for later reference. Checksum systems are a primary means of detecting file system tampering on UNIX.

data-driven attack A form of attack in which the attack is encoded in innocuous-seeming data that is executed by a user or other software to implement an attack. In the case of firewalls, a data-driven attack is a concern since it may get through the firewall in data form and launch an attack against a system behind the firewall.

database logging A feature that logs events that are generated by ISA Server services to a database instead of a text file.

datagram *See* packet.

default gateway In TCP/IP, the intermediate network device on the local network that has knowledge of the network IDs of the other networks in the Internet, so it can forward the packets to other gateways until they are delivered to the one connected to the specified destination.

defense in depth   The security approach whereby each system on the network is secured to the greatest possible degree. May be used in conjunction with firewalls.

destination set   A group of one or more computers or folders on specific computers, grouped together for the purpose of applying rules and policies.

DHCP   *See* Dynamic Host Configuration Protocol.

dial-up connection   A connection that uses a telephone device, such as a modem.

digest authentication   A means of passing credentials securely through a hashing function that encrypts credentials so that they cannot be deciphered by an unauthorized person. This security feature is designed for use in Windows 2000 domains.

distributed caching   A means by which the cache is distributed across an array of ISA Server computers and set up as a single, logical entity, preventing duplication and increasing efficiency.

domain controller   A computer that manages user access to a network, including logging on, authentication, and access to shared resources.

DMZ   *See* perimeter network.

DNS   *See* Domain Name System.

DNS server   The server containing information for name resolution involved in mapping computer IP addresses to their domain name.

DNS spoofing   Assuming the DNS name of another system by either corrupting the name service cache of a victim system, or by compromising a valid DNS.

domain name   The computer name that substitutes for a network IP address. For example, you may use *http://www.microsoft.com* instead of the IP address 157.45.60.81.

Domain Name System (DNS)   A protocol and computer-naming hierarchy used throughout the Internet to map computer IP addresses to their domain name.

dual-homed gateway   A dual-homed gateway is a system that has two or more network interfaces, each of which is connected to a different network. In firewall configurations, a dual-homed gateway usually acts to block or filter some or all of the traffic trying to pass between the networks.

dynamic filtering   A method of controlling the flow of IP packets to and from ISA Server, by means of access policy or publishing rules. Through dynamic filtering, dynamic packet filters are applied and removed only as needed when rule conditions are met.

Dynamic Host Configuration Protocol (DHCP)   A protocol that offers dynamic assignment of IP addresses and related information for network clients. DHCP provides safe, reliable, and simple TCP/IP network configuration; prevents address conflicts; and helps conserve the use of IP addresses through centralized management of address allocation.

encrypting router   *See* tunneling router and virtual network perimeter.

encryption   The process of making information indecipherable to protect it from unauthorized viewing or use, especially during network transmission or when it is stored on a transportable magnetic medium.

endpoint   The originating or destination location of a call request. Each computer participating in a conference call is an endpoint.

enterprise   A collection of one or more ISA Server arrays that share common enterprise policy settings.

enterprise policy   A configuration that enables centralized management of arrays in a corporate network, allowing common rules to be applied to arrays within the enterprise.

event message   A text message generated during the operation of Microsoft ISA Server. Event messages appear in the Event Viewer, which can be used to monitor and troubleshoot events.

File Transfer Protocol (FTP)   The Internet standard protocol for transferring files between computers. The server requires a client to supply a logon user name and password before honoring requests.

firewall   A system or combination of systems that enforces a boundary between two or more networks and keeps intruders out of internal networks. Firewalls serve as barriers for packets passing from one network to another.

firewall chaining   Configures how requests from Firewall clients should be routed, either directly to the Internet, or to an upstream proxy server.

Firewall client   A computer with Firewall client software installed and enabled.

Firewall mode   One of the selections available during the setup process to define features available for ISA Server. If Firewall mode is chosen, features are available that will secure network communication between the corporate network and the Internet.

Firewall service (fwsrv)   A Windows 2000 service that supports requests from Firewall and SecureNAT clients.

forward caching   Caching that is implemented for clients on the internal network accessing servers on the Internet.

FTP   *See* File Transfer Protocol.

gatekeeper   A program that supplies call control services for registration, address translation and bandwidth management. Gatekeepers are not required in an H.323 network, but if a gatekeeper is present, endpoints must use the gatekeeper service.

gateway   A device that connects networks that use different communication protocols. A gateway translates different transmission formats and protocols so that information can be passed from one network to another.

Gopher   A hierarchical system for finding and retrieving information from the Internet or an intranet. An enhanced version, Gopher Plus, returns more information about an item, such as file size, last date of modification, and the administrator's name.

H.323 client   A client who has registered with H.323 Gatekeeper and who uses computer applications that support H.225 Registration, Admission, and Status (RAS) protocol.

H.323 Gatekeeper H.323 is a communications standard for audio, video, and data communication across IP-based networks, including the Internet. In ISA Server, H.323 Gatekeeper works together with the H.323 protocol filter to provide full communications capabilities to H.323 registered clients using applications that are compliant with II.323 Gatekeeper.

H.323 gateway A gateway translates different transmission formats and protocols so that information can be passed from one network to another. Gateways commonly provide translation for communications between H.323 terminals and public switched telephone devices. H.323 gateways provide H.323 clients with services so that they are able to communicate with endpoints that are not H.323 compliant.

header In data packet communications, a specified number of bytes that precedes the actual data being transmitted. The header identifies control information used to deliver, route, and process the data contents of a packet.

hierarchical caching The forwarding of a client HTTP request from an ISA Server computer to another proxy computer upstream. The downstream (source) proxy computer forwards client requests that it cannot service from its own cache.

hit rate The percentage of client requests fulfilled through previously cached data, in contrast to the total number of client requests that have been processed by the caching service.

host-based security The technique of securing an individual system from attack. Host-based security is operating system and version dependent.

host name The name of a device on a network. For a device on a Windows NT 4.0 or Windows 2000 network, this can be the same as the computer name, but it does not have to be.

HTTPS *See* Secure HTTP.

ICMP *See* Internet Control Message Protocol.

inbound bandwidth Bandwidth allocated for requests from external clients for objects on the local network.

insider attack An attack originating from inside a protected network.

integrated authentication A secure form of authentication, where user name and password are not sent across the network.

Integrated mode One of the selections available during the setup process to define features available for Microsoft ISA Server. If Integrated mode is chosen, both caching and firewall features are available.

Internet Control Message Protocol (ICMP) An extension to the Internet Protocol (IP) that supports packets containing error control and informational messages. For example, the Ping utility uses ICMP to test an Internet connection.

Internet Protocol (IP) Protocol that specifies the format of data in packets, also known as datagrams, and the addressing scheme for these packets. Most networks combine IP with a higher-level protocol, TCP, to establish a virtual connection between a destination and a source.

Internet Service Provider (ISP) A company that provides customers with access to the Internet and other Internet-related services.

intra-array addressing The address used when sending a request to another server in the same array. This address must be in the Local Address Table (LAT).

intrusion detection A mechanism used to detect when an attack is attempted against a network protected by ISA Server.

IP *See* Internet Protocol.

IP address An identifier for a computer or device on a TCP/IP network.

IP fragment A single IP datagram can be broken up into multiple datagrams of a smaller size, known as IP fragments. These fragments can be filtered by the ISA Server, since one method of intrusion is to send fragmented packets and then reassemble them to cause harm to the system.

IP splicing/hijacking An attack whereby an active, established session is intercepted and co-opted by the attacker. IP splicing attacks may occur after an authentication has been made, permitting the attacker to assume the role of an authorized user. Primary protections against IP splicing rely on encryption at the session or network layer.

IP spoofing An attack whereby a system attempts to illicitly impersonate another system by using its IP network address.

ISA Management The Microsoft Management Console (MMC) snap-in used to manage ISA Server enterprise, arrays and standalone servers.

ISA Server schema The extension to the Active Directory directory services schema that allows ISA Server to operate in an array configuration.

ISA Server Control service A Windows 2000 service that is responsible for various services and functions within ISA Server.

ISP *See* Internet Service Provider.

Kerberos A network authentication protocol supporting authentication services. Windows 2000 implements Kerberos V5 in its security schema.

L2DP *See* Layer Two Tunneling Protocol.

LAT *See* Local Address Table.

Layer Two Tunneling Protocol (L2DP) An extension to the PPP protocol that enables ISPs to operate VPNs.

LDT *See* Local Domain Table.

least privilege The most restrictive security configuration that still allows for the completion of a task. This reduces the authorization level at which various actions are performed and decreases the chance that a process or user with high privileges may be caused to perform unauthorized activity resulting in a security breach.

load factor A number which determines the proportionate amount of the cache load on each member server in an array. Different member servers can be configured to have different load factors.

Local Address Table (LAT) A table of all internal IP address ranges used by the local network behind the ISA Server computer.

Local Domain Table (LDT)   A table of all the domain names or computer names in the local network served by the ISA Server computer.

logging   The process of storing information about events that occurred on the firewall or network.

log retention   The length of time that audit logs are retained and maintained.

MCU   *See* multiple control unit.

MIME   *See* Multipurpose Internet Mail Extensions.

multiple control unit (MCU)   The central connection or hub that provides support for conferencing between three or more terminals. An MCU may also manage the media stream and audio-video negotiations between endpoints. Sometimes called Multipoint Conferencing Server (MCS) or multipoint control unit (MCU).

Multipurpose Internet Mail Extensions (MIME)   A feature that enables browsers to view files that are in multiple formats. MIME makes available the exchanging of objects, different character sets, and multimedia in e-mail on different computer systems.

NAT   *See* Network Address Translation.

NAT editor   NAT provides translation of the IP, TCP, UDP headers. A NAT editor is used to make modifications to the IP packet beyond the translation of these headers.

negative caching   The caching of HTTP error conditions associated with accessing a particular URL. If the URL is unavailable, the error response message can be cached and returned to subsequent clients that request the same URL.

Network Address Translation (NAT)   An Internet standard that enables a local network to use one set of IP addresses for internal traffic and a second set for external traffic. In effect it hides internal IP addresses and enables a company to use more internal IP addresses, which, since they are only used internally, will not conflict with IP addresses used by other organizations. Typically, private IP addresses are used on the internal network. NAT translates requests from the private addresses used internally to public IP addresses used on the Internet.

network interface card   An adapter card that plugs into the system bus of a computer and allows the computer to send and receive signals on a network. A network interface card (NIC) is also known as a network adaptor card or simply a network card.

network-layer firewall   A firewall in which traffic is examined at the network protocol packet level.

Network News Transfer Protocol (NNTP)   The Internet standard protocol for posting, distributing, and reading network news messages posted among news groups on the Internet. Messages are posted to NNTP servers and are accessed by NNTP clients (newsreaders).

NIC   *See* network interface card.

NNTP   *See* Network News Transfer Protocol.

NTFS   Short for New Technology file system; an advanced file system designed for use specifically within the Windows NT and Windows 2000 operating system.

outbound bandwidth   Bandwidth allocated for requests from internal clients for objects on the Internet.

packet A piece of a message transmitted as a fixed number of bytes over a packet-switching network, which is a network using a protocol that divides messages into packets before sending them. Each packet is transmitted individually, perhaps through different routes, and the original message is reassembled at the destination. A packet contains the destination address as well as the data. In an IP network, these packets are often known as datagrams.

packet filtering A method of controlling the flow of IP packets to and from ISA Server. When packet filtering is enabled, all packets are dropped unless explicitly allowed by a packet filter.

pass-through authentication A feature of ISA Server that allows a client's authentication information to be passed on to a destination server for both incoming and outgoing Web requests.

performance counter A tool that tracks ISA Server activity to monitor array performance and usage.

perimeter-based security The technique of securing a network by controlling access to all entry and exit points of the network.

perimeter network (DMZ) A network set up separately from an organization's private network and the Internet. The advantage of a perimeter network is that it allows external users access to specific servers located in the perimeter network, while preventing access to the internal corporate network.

Ping A TCP/IP utility that verifies connections to one or more remote computers by sending ICMP packets and listening for reply packets.

Point-to-Point Tunneling Protocol (PPTP) A networking protocol that enables remote users to access corporate networks securely across the Internet by dialing into an ISP or by connecting directly to the Internet. PPTP supports multiprotocol VPNs. Because PPTP allows multiprotocol encapsulation, users can send any packet type over an IP network.

policy Organization-level rules governing acceptable use of computing resources, security practices, and operational procedures.

policy element A group of properties defined for a rule.

POP *See* Post Office Protocol.

port In TCP/IP networks, an endpoint to a logical connection. Certain services and protocols often use default port numbers, identifying a certain Internet application with a specific connection.

Post Office Protocol (POP) A network protocol that permits a client computer to access e-mail on a server. Usually this means that a POP3 server is used to allow a client computer to retrieve mail that an SMTP server is holding for it.

PPTP *See* Point-to-Point Tunneling Protocol.

protocol Software that allows computers to communicate over a network. The protocol used for the Internet is TCP/IP.

proxy A software agent that acts on behalf of a user. Typical proxies accept a connection from a user, make a decision as to whether or not the user or client IP address is permitted to use the proxy, perhaps does additional authentication, and then completes a connection on behalf of the user to a remote destination.

publishing rule   A feature used by ISA Server to control the handling of incoming requests for internal network resources. Web publishing rules are configured to decide how incoming requests to internal Web servers are handled, while server publishing rules are used to deal with incoming requests to servers (such as SMTP and FTP) on the internal network.

Q931 address   The combination of the IP address and the port address used for H.323 calls. Each registered endpoint has a unique Q931 address. Q931 was originally developed as a network-layer protocol for out-of-band call control in ISDN and is now used in the H.323 standard for client call signaling.

QoS   *See* Quality of Service.

QoS Admission Control   A Windows 2000 Server feature that controls how, by whom, and when shared network resources are used.

QoS Packet Scheduling service   A Windows 2000 Server feature used by ISA Server in setting bandwidth priorities. ISA Server bandwidth control does not limit the amount of bandwidth used. It informs the Windows 2000 QoS Packet Scheduling service how to prioritize network connections. If there is no bandwidth rule for a connection, a default priority will apply.

Quality of Service (QoS)   A Windows 2000 Server set of service requirements that the network must meet to assure an adequate service level for data transmission. Implementing QoS has enabled real-time programs to make the most efficient use of network bandwidth.

remote administration   The practice of administering a computer from another computer connected across the network.

reverse caching   Caching implemented for incoming requests to local Web servers from the Internet.

routing   In the context of ISA Server, the process of directing client requests for one ISA Server to a specified upstream server.

scheduled cache   A cache feature that can be customized to download HTTP content directly to the ISA Server cache, upon request or by configuring a schedule. This means that cache content can be updated in anticipation of client requests.

screened host   A host on a network behind a screening router. The degree to which a screened host may be accessed depends on the screening rules in the router.

screened subnet   A subnet behind a screening router. The degree to which the subnet may be accessed depends on the screening rules in the router.

screening router   A router configured to permit or deny traffic based on a set of permission rules installed by the administrator.

secondary connection   A range of port numbers, protocol, and direction used for additional connections or packets that follow the initial connection. One or more secondary connections can be configured.

Secure HTTP (HTTPS)   A proposed extension to HTTP that supports various encryption and authentication measures to keep all transactions secure from end to end.

SecureNAT   *See* Secure Network Address Translation clients.

Secure Network Address Translation clients (SecureNAT clients) Client computers that do not have Firewall client software installed but are configured to make requests through ISA Server. Requests from SecureNAT clients are essentially handled by the Firewall service and derive the benefits provided by this service.

Secure Sockets Layer (SSL) A protocol that supplies secure data communication through data encryption and decryption. SSL enables communications privacy over networks.

security template A snap-in provided with ISA Server that provides a view of the configuration seen with the ISA Server Security wizard, which is used to apply a full range of predefined system security settings to all the servers in the array.

server certificate A means of identifying information about the server. When a client requests an SSL object from a server, it requests that the server authenticate itself to the client. A server certificate does this.

server publishing rule A rule that is configured to specify how incoming requests to internal servers on the local network should be handled.

Session Stealing *See* IP splicing.

Simple Mail Transport Protocol (SMTP) An Internet standard protocol used for exchanging e-mail between SMTP servers on the Internet.

Simple Network Management Protocol (SNMP) A standard protocol used for network monitoring and systems management.

SMTP *See* Simple Mail Transport Protocol.

SNMP *See* Simple Network Management Protocol.

social engineering An attack based on deceiving users or administrators at the target site. Social engineering attacks are typically carried out by someone telephoning users or operators and pretending to be an authorized user, to attempt to gain illicit access to systems.

socket A logical communications channel used by TCP/IP applications. Sockets are data structures created by using a combination of device IP addresses and reserved TCP/UDP port numbers to indicate connection and delivery service information. Winsock is a Windows-based implementation of sockets.

SOCKS filter The SOCKS filter provided with ISA Server forwards requests from SOCKS applications to the Firewall service.

SSL *See* Secure Sockets Layer.

SSL bridging The ability of ISA Server to encrypt or decrypt client requests and pass on the request to a destination Web server.

SSL tunneling The ability of ISA Server to allow a client to establish a tunnel through the ISA Server directly to the Web server with the requested HTTPS object. Whenever a client browser requests an HTTPS object through the ISA Server, SSL tunneling is used.

standalone server In the context of ISA Server, an ISA Server computer that is not installed as an array member. Standalone server computers do not have to belong to a Windows 2000 domain, do not require Active Directory directory services, and have no enterprise policy.

static IP filtering A type of IP filter that involves configuration of a static, ever-present IP packer filter. In most cases, dynamic IP filtering is preferred, meaning that the creation of access policy rules results in an IP packet filter, which is dynamically applied as policy rule conditions are met.

subnet mask A TCP/IP configuration parameter that extracts network and host configuration from an IP address. This 32-bit value enables the recipient of IP packets to distinguish the network ID portion (domain name) of the IP address from the host ID (host name).

TCP *See* Transmission Control Protocol.

TCP/IP *See* Transmission Control Protocol/Internet Protocol.

terminals In the context of multi-media computing technology, equipment that provides real-time communications. Terminals must support audio communications, but support for video or data communications is optional. A computer running Microsoft NetMeeting 3.0 or higher is an example of an H.323 terminal.

time-to-live (TTL) A custom setting that can be set to 0 or to a specified percentage of the age of an HTTP object. This setting determines the expiration policy of HTTP objects held in the ISA Server cache.

Transmission Control Protocol (TCP) The Internet standard transport protocol that provides the reliable, two-way connected service, allowing an application to send a stream of data end-to-end between two computers across a network.

Transmission Control Protocol/Internet Protocol (TCP/IP) A family of networking protocols that allows computers with diverse hardware architectures and various operating systems to communicate across interconnected networks and the Internet. TCP/IP includes standards for how computers communicate and conventions for connecting networks and routing traffic. Every computer on the Internet supports TCP/IP.

trojan horse A software entity that appears to do something normal but which, in fact, contains a trapdoor or attack program.

TTL *See* time-to-live.

tunneling router A router or system capable of routing traffic by encrypting it and encapsulating it for transmission across an untrusted network, for eventual de-encapsulation and decryption.

UDP *See* User Datagram Protocol.

User Datagram Protocol (UDP) A standard transport protocol in TCP/IP networking that provides connectionless service for unacknowledged delivery of packets. UDP adds port addresses to the service provided by IP.

verbose logging An option that supplies additional or supplemental information for a network event in a log file.

virtual network perimeter A network that appears to be a single protected network behind firewalls, which actually encompasses encrypted virtual links over untrusted networks.

virtual private network (VPN) A network that is constructed using public systems such as the Internet but uses security mechanisms to ensure privacy and that only authorized users are allowed to access.

virus A self-replicating code segment. Viruses may or may not contain attack programs or trapdoors.

.vpc file A file generated by ISA Server that includes information about a remote ISA VPN server.

VPN *See* virtual private network.

Web Proxy client A client computer that has a Web browser application, which complies with HTTP 1.1, and is configured to use the Web Proxy service of ISA Server.

Web Proxy service (w3Proxy) A Windows 2000 service that supports requests from any Web browser. It works at the application level on behalf of a client requesting an Internet object that can be retrieved by one of the Web Proxy supported protocols: FTP, HTTP, HTTPS, and Gopher.

Web publishing rule A rule that is configured to specify how incoming requests to internal Web servers should be handled.

well-known alias An alternative name used to direct calls or connection requests to a person at a terminal. An alias can be a phone number, an account name, a computer name, an e-mail address, or some other similar name.

well-known port A well-known port is any port in the range of 1 to 2048.

Windows NT challenge/response authentication A method of authentication in which a server uses Windows NT security to allow access to its resources.

Winsock Also called WinSock; a Windows implementation of the widely used UC Berkeley Sockets application programming interface (API). Windows Sockets is a networking API used to create TCP/IP-based sockets applications. Windows Sockets provides interfaces between applications and the transport protocol and works as a bi-directional connection for incoming and outgoing data.

Index

A

access control policies, 14, 19. *See also*
    policy elements
  arrays, 133
  configuration, 133
  content rules, 39
  creating, 131, 137–138
  default settings, 71
  destination sets, 154
  enterprise, 133
  external clients, 30, 38–39
  Firewall service, 90, 133, 135
  Integrated mode, 133
  internal clients, 28–29, 38
  Internet, 133
  ISA Server Enterprise Edition, 3
  log files, 15
  modes, 53
  protocols, 39
  requests, 131–133
  secondary connections, 90
  site and content rules, 39, 166, 168, 174–176
  standalone servers, 133
  troubleshooting, 438–441
  Web Proxy service, 99, 135–136
accounts. *See* user accounts
actions
  alerts, 343–345
  server publishing rules, 237–238
  Web publishing rules, 246–247
active caching, 223
  dial-on-demand connections, 105
  enabling, 31–32
Active Directory, 54
  arrays, 68
  directory services, 2, 7, 332
  integration, 14
  permissions, 67
  schemas, 67
adapters, 64–65
Add Destination wizard, 330
add-in services, 68
adding
  array membership, 284
  gatekeepers, 318
  protocols to VPNs, 298–299
  servers to arrays, 280
  static routes, 431
addressing
  client translation, 315–316
  H.323 RAS, 313

addressing, *continued*
    LANs, 6
    NetMeeting 3.0 client translation, 316
    server publishing, 238–239
administration
    COM object, 8
    enterprise policy privileges, 268
    integration, 38
    remote installation, 48
    tools, 69
Alert action failure event, 345
alerts. *See also* events
    actions, 343–345
    array membership, 283
    conditions, 341
    configuration, 348–349
    creating, 340
    default settings, 72
    editing, 342–343
    enabling, 340
    events, 340, 342–343
    log files, 15
    modes, 53
    port scan attacks, 193
    preconfigured, 339–340
    Windows 2000 Event Log, 8
aliases, 314–315, 318, 328
All Ports Scan Attack alert, 24, 193
allocation, ports, 122
allowing/denying
    log files, 359
    packet filters, 18, 179
    site and content rules, 168, 174–176
    Web site access, 166
AOL Instant Messenger, 157

Application content group, 168
Application Data Files content group, 168
Application Usage reports, 376
applications
    filtering, 11, 19–22, 53
    Firewall service, 88
    protocol definitions, 155
    SecureNAT service, 88
    Web Proxy service, 88
Archie, 157
architecture, ISA Server, 10–11
arrays
    alerts, 283
    backups, 285–287
    bandwidth, 9
    caching, 283
    configuration, 267, 281, 283
    creating, 279–280
    default settings, 266, 274–275, 282
    domains, 280
    enterprise policies, 41, 266–267, 271
    extensions, 283
    fault tolerance, 9, 287–288
    installation, 50–51, 68, 281, 283
    load balancing, 9
    membership, 284
    packet filtering, 270
    policies, 40, 48, 133, 140–141, 283
    protocol rules, 156
    Proxy Server 2.0, 80–81
    reports, 283
    requirements, 280
    restoring, 285–287
    security, 301–302
    site and content rules, 51, 167–168

Index   583

arrays, *continued*
    standalone servers, 51–52, 281–282
    storing, 283–284
assigning protocol rules, Windows 2000, 162–163
Asymmetric installation event, 345
attacks. *See* intrusions
Audio content group, 168
authentication, users
    Basic, 7
    digital certificates, 7
    dual-hop SSL, 13
    Firewall service, 88, 135
    Integrated Windows, 437
    Kerberos, 7
    NT LAN Manager (NTLM), 7
    protocol rules, 134, 161–162
    SecureNAT service, 88, 134
    site and content rules, 134
    strong, 12
    troubleshooting, 441
    user accounts, 436–437
    Web Proxy service, 88, 135–136
Authentication Header (AH), 299
autodiscovery protocol, 8
automatic configuration, SecureNAT, 91
automatic dial-out connections, 107, 122
automatic discovery
    DHCP Server, 114–115
    DNS Server, 114
    Firewall service, 115, 118
    Internet Explorer 5.0, 116
    publishing, 112–113, 117
    testing, 118–119
    troubleshooting, 116–117
    Web Proxy service, 116
    WPAD, 118
automating cache content updates, 226–227

B

back-to-back perimeter networks, 61–62
BackOffice Server 4.0, 80
backups
    arrays, 285–287
    enterprise policies, 271–272
bandwidth, 402
    arrays, 9
    dedicated network connections, 387–389
    dial-up connections, 386–387
    filtering rules, 22
    frame relay networks, 387
    inbound, 389
    management, 14
    objects, 400
    outbound, 389
    policy elements, 140, 142
    priorities, 389–392
    QoS, 8
    rules, 143–144, 391–395
Basic authentication, 7, 437
binding ports, 122
Block packet filters, 18, 179, 360
bridging, 247
broad application support, 22
buffers, overflow, 25

C

c-agent field, 366
c-ip field, 366
c-username field, 366
Cache Array Routing Protocol. *See* CARP
Cache mode, 52–53, 69
    installation, 4
    packet filtering, 71
    publishing, 234

caching
  active, 31–32, 105, 223
  arrays, 283
  configuration, 69, 203
  content files, 216–217
  default settings, 72
  distributed, 13
  downloads, 226–231
  drives, 214–216
  dynamic content, 31, 211–213, 229
  events, 345
  expiration policies, 218
  filtering, 210–211
  Firewall service, 368–370
  forward, 5, 49–50, 202
  FTP, 202, 220–221
  hierarchy, 33–34
  HTTP, 31, 202, 219–220
  installation, 50
  location, 215–216
  modes, 53
  negative, 224
  non-dynamic content, 211–213
  objects, 28–29, 208–210, 217–218, 222
  performance, 398–399, 401, 403–406
  Proxy Server 2.0, 82
  publishing, 211
  RAM, 218, 225, 399
  requests, 202
  response headers, 218
  reverse, 5, 30, 50, 202
  routing rules, 203–208
  scheduling, 31–32
  site and content rules, 211
  size, 215–216
  troubleshooting, 425, 442
  updating, 31, 226–227

caching, *continued*
  URLs, 406
  Web Proxy service, 13, 97
call routing rules, 322–323, 333–334
CARP (Cache Array Routing Protocol),
    33–34, 210
  configuration, 290–291
  content download, 292
  deterministic request resolution path,
    32–33
  enabling, 291
  intra-array communication, 291–292
  load balancing, 292
  performance, 32
  requests, 290
certificates, 7
chained caching, 33–34, 82
Chargen, 157
check boxes, 360
circuit-level filtering, 18–19
clearing check boxes, 360
Client/server communication failure
    event, 346
clients. *See also* Firewall service;
    SecureNAT service; Web Proxy service
  access control, 89
  address sets, 140, 144–145, 238–239
  agents, 366
  certificate authentication, 437
  comparing, 89–90
  configuration, 72
  connections, 120–122
  external, 30, 38
  firewalls, 10
  H.323 Gatekeeper, 313, 315–316
  internal, 28–29, 38
  NetMeeting 3.0, 316

clients, *continued*
    rules, 134
    SecureNAT, 10
    sessions, 161
    VPNs, 298
    Web publishing, 244–245
    Web Proxy, 8, 10
closing
    dial-up connections, 108
    ports, 178
CNAME record, 118
COM (Component Object Model), 8
comparing
    arrays with standalone servers, 52
    clients, 89–90
complex networks, 91
Component load failure event, 346
Component Object Model (COM), 8
Compressed Files content group, 168
compression, log files, 355
computers. *See* local networks; remote networks
conditions, alerts, 341
conference calls
    inbound calls, 333–334
    inter-enterprise, 311–312
    intra-enterprise, 310–311
    outbound calls, 334–335
    PSTN, 312–313
    routing, 322–326
configuration
    alerts, 343–349
    arrays, 267, 281, 283
    bandwidth, 389–393
    caching, 69
        drives, 214–216
        location, 215–216

configuration, caching, *continued*
        objects, 217–218
        properties, 203
        size, 215–216
    CARP, 290–291
    clients, 72
    default gateways, 64–65
    dial-on-demand connections, 106–107
    dial-up connections, 65, 91–92, 103–105
    DSN, 358, 359
    enterprise policies, 56–57, 268–271, 275–276
    Firewall service, 123–125
    FTP, 156, 221
    Gopher, 156
    H.323 Gatekeeper, 124–125, 318–319
    HTTP, 157
    installation, 64
    intrusion detection, 196–197
    IP packet filters, 178, 180–182
    ISDN adapters, 65
    LATs, 66, 70–71
    log files, 355
    Mail Server Security wizard, 257
    Microsoft Exchange Server, 258
    modems, 65
    Mspclnt.ini file, 94
    Outlook Express, 261–262
    performance, 397–399
    policy element schedules, 141–142
        access, 141–142
        client address sets, 144–145
        content groups, 147–148
        destination sets, 142–143, 150
        protocol definitions, 145–146
        schedules, 149
    protocol rules, 152–153

configuration, *continued*
   reports, 374, 377–381
   S-HTTP, 157
   SecureNAT, 89, 91
   server publishing, 234
   SMTP service, 259–260
   standalone servers, 286
   Web Proxy service, 98–99, 101, 123–125
   wizards, 14
   WPAD, 113–114
   WSPAD, 113–114
   Wspcfg.ini file, 94–95
Configuration error event, 346
connections. *See also* dial-up connections
   clients, 120–122
   dial-on-demand, 105–107
   inspecting, 11
   installation requirements, 49
   ISPs, 53
   network adapters, 64
   secondary, 90
   troubleshooting, 426
   VPNs, 295, 296
content groups
   access control, 39
   files, 169–174, 216–217
   filtering, 257
   installation, 168–174
   policy elements, 140, 147–148
   server publishing, 40
counters
   Bandwidth Control, 402
   cache, 401, 403–406
   Firewall service, 401, 407–409
   H.323 filter, 420
   packet filtering, 401, 409–410

counters, *continued*
   performance, 399–400
   remote administration, 401
   SOCKS filter, 420
   Web Proxy service, 410–419
creating. *See also* configuration
   alerts, 340
   arrays, 279–280
   bandwidth rules, 394–395
   dial-up connections, 109–110
   enterprise policies, 267, 272–274
   extensions, 9
   IP packet filters, 179–182
   Mail Server Security wizard rules, 260
   policies, 131–138, 149
   reports, 382–383
   routing rules, 204–205
   scripts, 9
   server publishing rules, 236–237
   Web publishing rules, 245
   WPAD alias, 118
cs-bytes field, 363
cs-mime type field, 364
cs-protocol field, 363
cs-referred field, 362
cs-transport field, 364
cs-uri field, 364

D

data source name (DSN), 358–359
databases
   location, 382
   log files, 356–359
   reports, 381–382
date field, 361

dedicated network connections, 136–137, 387–389
Default Bandwidth Priority, 389
default gateways
    configuration, 64–65
    SecureNAT, 91
default settings
    access control, 71
    alerts, 72
    bandwidth rules, 394
    caching, 72
    clients, 72
    enterprise policies, 71, 268
        arrays, 266, 274–275, 282
        editing, 270–271
        overriding, 268
    LATs, 70–71
    log files, 350, 353
    packet filtering, 71
    publishing, 72
    routing, 72, 204, 208
    Web publishing rules, 248
deinstallation, ICS, 55
destination endpoints, 313
destination sets
    computer names, 18
    bandwidth rules, 143
    H.323 Gatekeeper, 330–332
    policy element, 140–143, 150
    protocol rules, 154
    routing rules, 143, 204–207
    site and content rules, 143, 154, 166–167
    Web publishing rules, 143, 244–245, 252
    wildcards, 142
detection, intrusions, 195–197
    DNS, 25
    filtering, 21

detection, intrusions, *continued*
    integration, 24–25
    POP, 25
deterministic request resolution path, 32–33
DHCP Server, 64–65, 113–115
dial-on-demand connections, 90, 105–107, 346
dial-up connections, 11, 107, 120–121. *See also* connections
    bandwidth, 386–387
    closing, 108
    configuration, 65, 103–105
    creating, 109–110
    Firewall service, 108–109
    NNTP, 103
    policy elements, 140
    POP3, 103
    requests, 110
    SecureNAT, 91–92, 122
    troubleshooting, 122–123, 426
digital certificates authentication, 7, 437
Digital Subscriber Line (DSL), 53
direct connections, 64
direction, protocol definitions, 145–146
Discard protocol, 157
disk allocation, 49
distributed caching. *See* CARP
DMZ (perimeter networks), 60–62
DNS (Domain Name System), 92, 97
    arrays, 280
    automatic discovery, 114
    destination, 332
    hostname overflow, 25
    intrusion detection, 21, 25, 346
    IP addresses, 25
    queries, 157, 189
    registration, 53–54

DNS (Domain Name System), *continued*
  round robin distribution, 288
  wildcards, 142
  WPAD, 113–114, 118
  WSPAD, 113–114
  zone transfers, 25, 157
Documents content group, 168
Domain Admins, 274
Domain Name System. *See* DNS
downloads
  cache content, 226–231
  CARP, 292
  content schedules, 303
  dynamic content, 229
  Time To Live (TTL), 228–229
  URLs, 31, 227
drives, cache, 214–216
DSL (Digital Subscriber Line), 53
DSN (data source name), 358–359
dual-hop SSL authentication, 13
duplication, proxy servers, 32
dynamic content, caching, 31, 211–213, 229
dynamic filtering, 19
dynamic host configuration protocol (DHCP), 64–65, 113–115

E

E-mail
  address aliases, 328
  H.323 Gatekeeper rules, 327–330
  sending, 343–344, 348–349
  SMTP, 345
E1/T1 networks, 387
E164 phone number addressing, 313, 323
E3/T3 networks, 387

Echo protocol, 157
editing
  actions, rules, 238
  alerts, 341–345
  content files, 217
  enterprise policies, 270–271
  log files, 350
  protocol rules, 153
  RAM caching, 225
  routing rules, 205–206
Email-ID type addressing, 313
enabling/disabling
  active caching, 31–32, 223–224
  alerts, 340
  automatic discovery, 118
  caching, 425
  CARP, 291
  check boxes, 360
  dial-up connections, 108–109
  intrusion detection, 195–197
  IP fragment filtering, 184
  IPSec, 299
  NNTP, 188
  option filtering, 184
  packet filtering, 10, 180
  POP3 mail service, 185–186
  Proxy Server 2.0 services, 79
  service log files, 352
  SMTP mail, 187
  SMTP service, 259
  Web content, 190–191
  Web requests, 189
Encapsulating Security Payload (ESP), 299
encryption, 23
endpoints, 313–314

Enterprise Admins
  initialization, 279
  policies, 267, 270
Enterprise Edition, 3–4
  Active Directory Storage, 7
  arrays, 9
  policy elements, 140
enterprise policies, 41
  arrays, 266–267, 274–275, 282
  backups, 271–272
  configuration, 268–271, 275–276
  creating, 267, 272–274
  default settings, 71, 268–271
  firewalls, 4
  initialization, 67, 73–74, 279
  installation, 48, 67
  modes, 53
  networks, 56–57
  policy elements, 133, 150–151
  privileges, 268
  protocol rules, 156, 267
  Proxy Server 2.0, 81
  publishing, 270
  restoring, 271–272
  site and content rules, 167–168, 267
  tiered management, 7
  VPNs, 56, 302–303
Enumerated Port Scan attack, 24, 193
error messages, 346–348
Event logging failure event, 346
events
  Alert action failure, 345
  Asymmetric installation, 345
  Cache, 345
  Client/server communication failure, 346
  Component load failure, 346
  Configuration error, 346

events, *continued*
  Dial on demand failure, 346
  DNS Intrusion, 346
  error messages, 348–349
  Event logging failure, 346
  Failed to retrieve object, 346
  Intra-array credentials, 346
  Intrusion detected, 346
  Invalid ODBC log credentials, 346
  IP packet dropped, 346
  IP Protocol violation, 346
  IP Spoofing, 346
  location, 342
  Log failure event, 346
  log files, 343–344
  messages, 347–348
  Network configuration changed, 346
  OS component conflict, 346
  thresholds, 342–343
  viewing, 340, 425–426
Exchange Server. *See* Microsoft Exchange Server
executing
  alerts, 343–345
  programs, 343–344
expiration policies
  caching, 218
  FTP, 218
  HTTP, 218, 220
  objects, 221–222
extensions
  arrays, 283
  content group files, 169–174
  creating, 9
  protocols, 15
  SDK, 15

external networks
  access control, 38
  clients, 30
  dial-out connections, 107
  Exchange Server, 258
  name resolution, 92
  Ping utility, 65
  publishing, 54
  troubleshooting, 440

F

Failed to retrieve object event, 346
fault tolerance
  arrays, 9, 287–288
  chaining, 33
  Firewall service, 288
  ISA Server Enterprise Edition, 3
  SecureNAT service, 288–289
fields
  check boxes, 360
  Firewall services, 360–367
  log files, 360–361
  packet filtering, 370–371
  Web Proxy services, 360–367
File Transfer Protocol. *See* FTP
files, content groups, 169–174
filtering. *See also* IP packet filters; packet filtering
  applications, 11, 19–22
  bandwidth rules, 22
  caching, 210–211
  circuit-level (protocol), 18–19
  dynamic, 19
  FTP access, 20
  H.323 Gatekeeper, 20–21
  HTTP Redirector, 20

filtering, *continued*
  intrusion detection, 24–25
  packets, 17–18
  ports, 19
  protocols, 19, 22
  RPC, 20
  sessions, 18
  SMTP, 20
  SOCKS, 20
  streaming media, 21
  Web, 8
Finger protocol, 158
Firewall mode, 52–53, 69
  access control, 133
  packet filtering, 71
  publishing, 234
Firewall service
  access control, 89–90
  applications, 88
  authentication, 12–13, 88, 135
  automatic discovery, 112–115, 118
  cache, 368–370
  chaining, 133
  clients, 10
  connections, 90, 106, 108–109
  fault tolerance, 288
  fields, 360–367
  installation, 4, 48–49, 88, 92–93, 101–102
  internal networks, 121
  instrusion detection, 12
  LATs, 71
  log files, 350, 356, 366
  media, 12
  Mspclnt.ini file, 94
  name resolution, 97
  object source, 367

Firewall service, *continued*
  operating systems, 88, 93
  performance counters, 401, 407–409
  protocols, 88, 152
  requests, 92
  restarting, 110, 123–125
  result code, 367–368
  roaming computers, 90
  secure server publishing, 12
  security, 4–5
  transparency, 12
  troubleshooting, 121
  VPN, 12
  Web cache integration, 5
  Winsock applications, 94–97
  Wspcfg.ini file, 94–95
502 error message, 440
forward caching, 5, 28–29, 49–50, 202
403 error message, 442
FQDN (fully qualified domain name), 53
fragment filtering, 183–184
frame relay networks, 387
FTP (File Transfer Protocol), 8, 158
  Access Filter, 20
  caching, 202
  clients, 156
  expiration policies, 218
  objects, 220–221
  server connections, 242–243
fully qualified domain name (FQDN), 53

G

gatekeepers, 309, 318
gateway, 309, 331
Getting Started wizard, 137–138
GMT (Greenwich Mean Time), 353

Gopher, 156, 158
graphical reports. *See* reports
graphical taskpads, 14
Greenwich Mean Time (GMT), 353
groups, 2, 145

H

H.323 Gatekeeper, 20–21, 158
  addressing, 313
  clients, 313, 315–319
  conference calls, 310–312, 322–326
  destinations, 330–332
  E-mail address rules, 327–330
  endpoints, 313–314
  filters, 400
  gateways, 309
  inbound calls, 333–334
  installation, 317
  IP address rules, 326–327
  MCUs, 309
  outbound calls, 334–335
  performance counters, 420
  phone number rules, 323–326
  PSTN, 312–313
  restarting, 124–125
  snap-in, 310
  standards, 309
hardware, 4, 48–49
hierarchy, caching, 13, 33–34
high ports, 25
hostnames, overflow, 25
HTML Documents content group, 168
HTTP (Hypertext Transfer Protocol), 8, 147
  caching, 31, 202
  configuration, 157
  expiration policies, 218, 220

HTTP (Hypertext Transfer Protocol), *continued*
  HTTPS, 158
  objects, 10, 219–220
  Redirector Filter, 20
  response headers, 218

I

I/O (input/output) failures, 403
IANA (Internet Assigned Numbers Authority), 70
ICA (Intelligent Console Architecture), 158
ICANN (Internet Corporation for Assigned Names and Numbers), 53
ICMP (Internet Control Message Protocol), 24
ICQ protocol, 158
ICS (Internet Connection Sharing), 55
Ident protocol, 158
IETF (Internet Engineering Task Force), 6
IIS (Internet Information Services), 58
IKE protocol, 158
Images content group, 168
IMAP4 (Internet Messaging Access Protocol 4), 158, 258
inbound bandwidth, 389
incoming mail. *See* mail; POP3 mail
inheritance, enterprise policies, 274–275
initialization, enterprise, 67, 73–74, 279
input/output (I/O) failures, 403
installation
  Active Directory, 54
  add-in services, 68
  administration tools, 69
  arrays, 50–51, 68, 281, 283

installation, *continued*
  caching, 4, 49–50, 69
  connection requirements, 49
  content groups, 168–174
  disk allocation, 49
  enterprise, 67, 73–74
  Firewall service, 4, 48–49, 88, 92–93, 101–102
  H.323 Gatekeeper, 317
  hardware requirements, 48–49
  integrated mode, 4
  ISA Server, 4, 68, 69–77
  ISPs, 53
  LATs, 70–71
  memory, 49
  modes, 52, 69
  networks, 47, 64
  operating systems, 48
  protocol definitions, 157–160
  publishing, 50
  RAM, 49
  remote administration, 48
  schemas, 67
  SecureNAT service, 88
  Setup screen, 66–67
  standalone servers, 279–281
  Web Proxy service, 88
  Windows NT 4.0, 54
Integrated mode, 4, 52, 69
  access control, 133
  packet filtering, 71
  server publishing, 234
  Web publishing, 234
Integrated Services Digital Network (ISDN), 48, 65

Integrated Windows, 437
integration
    Active Directory, 14
    administration, 38
    firewall and Web cache server, 5
    intrusion detection, 24–25
    vendor support, 15
    VPNs, 7, 12, 22–23, 294–295
Intelligent Console Architecture (ICA), 158
inter-enterprise conference calls, 311–312
Interactive Mail Access Protocol (IMAP),
    158, 258
internal networks
    clients, 28–29, 38
    Firewall, 121
    LATs, 70
    memory, 49
    name resolution, 92
    Ping utility, 65
    protocol rules, 133
    publishing, 54, 90, 240–242
    SecureNAT, 90
    site and content rules, 133
Internet
    access control, 133
    connections, 108–109
    firewalls, 5
    IANA, 70
    ICS, 55
    ICMP, 24
    ICANN, 53
    IIS, 58
    IKE, 158
    ILS, 331
    IMAP4, 158, 258

Internet, *continued*
    IRC, 158
    ISAPI, 8
    ISPs, 53
    RFC, 6
Internet Explorer 5.0
    automatic discovery, 116
    Web Proxy service, 99, 101
intra-array communication, 291–292, 346
intra-enterprise conference calls, 310, 311
Intrusion Detected event, 346, 348–349
intrusions 12,
    detection, 21, 24–25, 195–197
    IP half scan attacks, 192–194
    land attacks, 192–194
    ping of death attacks, 192–194
    port scan attacks, 24, 192–193
    troubleshooting, 427–428
    UDP bomb attacks, 192, 195
    Windows out-of-band attacks, 192
Invalid dial-on-demand credentials event, 346
Invalid ODBC log credentials event, 346
IP addresses
    H.323 Gatekeeper, 326–327
    LATs, 70
    length overflow, 25
    network adapters, 65
    private, 70
    rules, 134
    SecureNAT, 121
    server publishing, 26
IP half scan attack, 24, 192, 194
IP packet filters, 17–18, 178
    allow filters, 179
    block filters, 179

IP packet filters, *continued*
   creating, 179–182
   dropped event, 346
   Exchange Server, 258
   fragment filtering, 183–184
   local computers, 182
   log files, 183–185
   NNTP, 188
   option filtering, 183–184
   parameters, 179–180
   POP3 mail service, 185–186
   ports, 178
   protocols, 180–181
   publishing, 239–240
   remote computers, 182
   servers, 181
   SMTP mail, 187
   Web content, 190–191
   Web requests, 189
IP Protocol violation event, 346
IP Spoofing event, 346
IPSec, 299
IPX protocol, 80
IRC (Internet Relay Chat), 158
ISA Management, 7, 8, 37–41
   client sessions, 161
   remote adminstration, 48
   Web Proxy service, 97
ISA Server
   Enterprise Edition, 3, 4, 7–9, 40–41, 140
   Exchange Server, 258
   Firewall service, 400
   installation, 4, 72–77
   objects, 400
   packet filters, 400
   procedures, 68–70
   log files, 352, 354

ISA Server, *continued*
   Reports tool, 424–425
   Security Configuration wizard, 136–137
   Standard Edition, 4
   starting/stopping, 345
   Web Proxy service, 400
   Web publishing server, 249–250
   Windows 2000, 68
ISA Services, 68
ISA Virtual Private Network Configuration wizard, 296, 298
ISAPI (Internet server application programming interface), 8
ISDN (Integrated Services Digital Network), 48, 65
ISPs (Internet Service Providers), 53

K-L

Kerberos-Adm protocol, 7, 158

L2TP (Layer 2 Tunneling Protocol), 7, 294
Land attacks, 24, 192, 194
LANs, addresses, 6
large networks, VPNs, 300
LATs (local address tables), configuration, 66, 70–71
Layer 2 Tunneling Protocol (L2TP), 7, 294
LDAP protocol, 158
LDTs (Local Domain Tables), 107
Lightweight Directory Access Protocol (LDAP), 158
limited services security, 136–137
load balancing, 9, 288–289, 292
local address tables (LATs), 66
Local Domain Tables (LDTs), 107

Local ISA Server VPN Configuration
    wizard, 296–297, 439
local networks. *See also* Firewall service;
    SecureNAT service; Web Proxy service
  Exchange Server, 60
  Firewall Client software, 101–102
  H.323 Gatekeeper, 332
  IP packet filters, 182
  Microsoft Exchange Server, 258
  subnet masks, 65
  VPNs, 23
  Web Proxy service, 99
  Web publishing, 59, 249–250
location
  caching, 215–216, 228
  databases, 382
  events, 342
  log files, 355
  reports, 381–382
lock down, 7, 12
Log failure event, 346
log files
  access, 15
  alerts, 15
  compression, 355
  configuration, 355
  databases, 356–359
  default settings, 350, 353
  events, 343–344
  fields, 360–361
  Firewall services, 350, 356, 366
  IP packet filters, 183–185
  location, 355
  naming, 354
  NTFS, 353

log files, *continued*
  packet filtering, 350, 356, 359–360,
    370–371
  paths, 357
  properties, 351
  reporting, 15
  saving, 352–354
  security, 15
  services, 351–352
  troubleshooting, 442
  W3C, 356
  Web Proxy service, 350, 372
Logs folder, 351–352
low-level protocols, 145

M
MAC addresses, 65
Macro Documents content group, 168
mail
  POP3, 185
  server publishing, 256–257
  troubleshooting, 443
Mail Server Security wizard, 256
  configuration, 257
  Exchange Server, 258
  rules, 260
  running, 256
management
  bandwidth, 14
  ISA Management, 7
  policies, 14
  remote, 14
  unified, 38
  user-level, 15

manual configuration, 91
MAPI (Messaging Application Programming Interface), 258
MCUs (multipoint control units), 309
media, splitting, 12
membership, arrays, 284–287
memory
    caching, 225
    internal networks, 49
Messaging Application Programming Interface (MAPI), 258
Microsoft Active Directory, 2, 54
    arrays, 68
    directory service, 2, 7, 332
    integration, 14
    permissions, 67
    schemas, 67
Microsoft Exchange Server, 26, 157
    configuration, 258
    local networks, 60, 258
    publishing, 59, 60
Microsoft Management Console (MMC), 2, 7–8, 37–41
Microsoft Proxy Server 2.0, 78
Microsoft SQL Server, 158
Microsoft Terminal Server, 48
migration
    Microsoft Proxy Server 2.0, 78
    Proxy Server 2.0, 81, 83
MIME (Multipurpose Internet Mail Extensions), 147
MMC (Microsoft Management Console), 7–8, 37–41
modems
    bandwidth, 386
    configuration, 65
    installation requirements, 48

modes. *See also* Cache mode; Firewall mode; Integrated mode
    access policies, 53
    alerts, 53
    application filters, 53
    enterprise policies, 53
    installation, 52, 69
    packet filtering, 53
    publishing, 53
    reports, 53
monitoring
    firewall security, 5
    ISA Management, 161
    real-time, 53
MSN Messenger, 159
Mspclnt.ini file, 94
Multicast Gatekeeper destination (H.323 Gatekeeper), 332
multilevel management, 14
multipoint control units (MCUs), 309
multiprocessing, 8–9
Multipurpose Internet Mail Extensions (MIME), 147

N

name resolution, 92, 97
naming log files, 354
NAT (Network Address Translation), 6
Netstat, 426–428
negative caching, 224
Net2Phone, 159
NetBIOS, 159
NetMeeting 3.0. *See also* H.323 Gatekeeper
    client address translation, 316
    conference calls, 310–311
    registration, 318–320
    verification, 320

network adapters, 64–65
    DHCP, 64–65
    installation requirements, 48
    IP addresses, 65
    MAC addresses, 65
    Ping utility, 65
    subnet masks, 65
    TCP/IP properties, 64
Network Address Translation (NAT), 6
Network configuration changed event, 346
Network Connection wizard, 296
Network News Transfer Protocol (NNTP),
        103, 159, 188, 258
Network Time Protocol (NTP), 159
networks. *See also* complex networks; local
        networks; simple networks, 91
    installation, 47
    instrusion detection, 12
    load balancing, 9, 23, 288–289
    monitoring, 429–430
    topologies, 55–56, 58–59
    VPNs, 300
New Alert wizard, 340
New Bandwidth Rule wizard, 391–392
New Protocol Rule wizard, 100
New Routing Rule wizard, 323
New Server Publishing Rule wizard, 234
New Site and Content Rule wizard, 167
New Web Publishing Rule wizard, 244
non-dynamic content caching, 211–213
None destination (H.323 Gatekeeper), 330
NT file system (NTFS), 353
NT LAN Manager (NTLM) authentication, 7
NTFS (NT file system), 353
NTP (Network Time Protocol), 159

O

objects
    caching, 28–29
        configuration, 217–218
        process flow, 208–210
        retrieving, 204
    expiration policies, 221–222
    FTP, 220–221
    HTTP, 219–220
    performance, 400
    refreshing, 32–33
    sources, 367
    storing, 33, 203–204
ODBC (Open Database Connectivity), 346,
        356, 358–359
opening
    Getting Started wizard, 138
    Performance Monitor, 400–401
    ports, 178
operating systems
    client agents, 366
    Firewall service, 88, 93
    installation requirements, 48
    lock down, 7, 12
    Proxy Server 2.0, 78
    SecureNAT service, 88
    Web Proxy service, 88
option filtering, 183–184
order. *See* priority
origination endpoints, 313
OS component conflict event, 346
outbound bandwidth, 389
outbound calls, 335
outgoing mail. *See* mail; SMTP

outgoing requests, 131–133
    protocol rules, 132
Outlook Express, 261–262
overriding
    enterprise policies, 268
    TTL, 229
Oversize UDP packet event, 347

P

packet filters, 17–18. *See also* IP packet
    filters
    arrays, 270
    blocking, 18
    Cache mode, 71
    default settings, 71
    destination computer names, 18
    enabling/disabling, 10, 180
    Firewall mode, 71
    Integrated mode, 71
    intrusion detection, 24–25
    log files, 350, 356, 359–360, 370–371
    modes, 53
    outgoing requests, 133
    performance counters, 401, 409–410
    port numbers, 18
    server publishing, 239–240
    service types, 18
    source computer names, 18
    troubleshooting, 438–439
    Web server publishing, 250–251
parameters
    IP packet filters, 179–180
    protocol rules, 153–154
path processing
    log files, 357
    site and content rules, 166–167

pattern matching, 329–330
performance
    Bandwidth Control, 402
    cache, 13, 398–401
    counters, 403–406
    CARP, 32
    counters, 399–400
    Firewall service, 407–409
    H.323 filter, 420
    objects, 400
    packet filtering, 401, 409–410
    remote administration, 401
    settings, 397–398
    SOCKS filter, 420
    Web Proxy service, 410–419
Performance Monitor, 426
    opening, 400–401
    Performance Logs and Alerts node, 401
    System Monitor node, 401
perimeter networks (DMZ), 60–62, 239–240
permissions, Active Directory, 67
phone number rules, H.323 Gatekeeper,
    323–326
Ping of Death attacks, 24, 192, 194
Ping utility, 65
PNA (Progressive Networks Audio), 21
Point-to-Point Tunneling Protocol (PPTP),
    7, 294
policies
    access control, 14, 19, 38–40
        creating, 131, 137–138
        enterprise, 133
        requests, 131–133
        standalone servers, 133
    arrays, 40, 48, 51, 133, 283
    enterprise, 41, 48, 53, 56–57, 71, 81

policies, *continued*
　management, 14
　modes, 53
　server publishing, 234
　tiered-management, 7
　Web publishing, 234
　wizards, 14
policy elements
　array-level, 140–141
　bandwidth, 140–142
　client addresses, 140, 144–145
　content groups, 140, 147–148
　creating, 149
　destination sets, 140, 142–143, 150
　dial-up connections, 140
　enterprise-level, 140–141
　protocol definitions, 140, 145–146
　schedules, 140–142
　site and content, 142
POP3 (Post Office Protocol 3), 159, 258
　buffer overflow, 25
　dial-up connections, 103
　intrusion detection, 21, 25, 347
　IP packet filters, 185–186
ports
　alerts, 192–193
　allocation, 122
　binding, 122
　closing, 178
　connections, 122
　filtering, 19
　high, 25
　intrusion detection, 24
　IP packet filters, 178
　numbers, 18, 145
　opening, 178

ports, *continued*
　privileged, 25
　testing, 432–435
　troubleshooting, 426–427
　Web server publishing, 250
Post Office Protocol 3. *See* POP3
PPTP (Point-to-Point Tunneling Protocol), 7, 294
preconfigured alerts, 339–341
priority
　bandwidth rules, 389–391, 393
　protocol rules, 155–156
　routing rules, 208
　site and content rules, 165–166
　Web publishing rules, 248
private IP addresses, 70
privileges
　administration, 268
　ports, 25
procedures, ISA Server installation, 68–70
processing
　objects, 208–210
　outgoing requests, 131–133
　paths, 166–167
　protocol rules, 155–156
programs, executing, 343–344
Progressive Networks Audio (PNA), 21
promoting standalone servers, 281–282
properties
　caching, 203
　log files, 351
protocols
　access control, 39
　application filters, 155
　arrays, 156
　authentication, 134

protocols, *continued*
  client address sets, 144
  configuration, 152
  destination sets, 154
  direction, 145–146
  editing, 153
  enterprise policies, 156, 267
  extensions, 15
  filtering, 18–19, 22
  Firewall service, 88, 152
  FTP, 8
  HTTP, 8
  internal networks, 133
  installation, 157–160
  IP packet filters, 180–181
  ISAPI, 8
  low-level, 145
  parameters, 153–154
  policy elements, 140, 142, 145–146
  port numbers, 145
  PPTP, 7
  priority, 155–156
  requests, 131, 154–155
  secondary connections, 145
  SecureNAT service, 88, 152
  troubleshooting, 441
  user accounts, 160–162
  VPNs, 298–299
  Web Proxy service, 8, 88, 99–100, 156
  Windows 2000, 162–163
proxy servers. *See also* servers
  duplication, 32
  requests, 32
  versions, 78–83
  Web Proxy routing rules, 34–35

PSTN (Public Switched Telephone Network), 312–313
publishing. *See also* server publishing; Web publishing
  automatic discovery, 112–113, 117
  caching, 211
  default settings, 72
  enterprise policies, 270
  external networks, 54
  installation requirements, 50
  internal networks, 54, 90
  mail servers, 256–257
  Microsoft Exchange Server, 59–60
  modes, 53
  Proxy Server 2.0, 82
  rules, 19
  servers, 25–26, 40
  services, 5
  SMTP service, 259
  troubleshooting, 442–443

Q-R

Q.931 protocol, 314
Quality of Service (QoS), 2, 8
Quote protocol, 159

r-host field, 362
r-ip field, 362
r-port field, 362
RADIUS (Remote Authentication Dial-In User Service), 159
RAM, 49, 218, 225, 399
RAS (Remote Access Server), 55
RDP (Remote Desktop Protocol), 159

reading Web Proxy service log files, 372
real-time conferencing, 53, 322–326
Real-Time Streaming Protocol (RTSP), 21, 160
RealNetworks, 21
recommendations, caching, 214–215
refreshing
    objects, 32–33
    URLs, 403–405
registration
    domain names, 53–54
    H.323 Gatekeeper, 313
    NetMeeting 3.0, 318–320
Registration Database destination (H.323 Gatekeeper), 330–331
Remote Access Server (RAS), 55
Remote Authentication Dial-In User Service (RADIUS), 159
Remote Desktop Protocol (RDP), 159
Remote ISA Server VPN Configuration wizard, 296–297
remote networks
    installation, 48
    IP packet filters, 182
    login, 159
    management, 14
    performance counters, 401
    server publishing, 235
    VPNs, 23, 296–297
removing array membership, 284
Report Summary Generation Failure event, 347
reports
    Application Usage, 376
    array membership, 283

reports, *continued*
    configuration, 374
    creating, 382–383
    databases, 381–382
    location, 381–382
    log files, 15
    modes, 53
    scheduling, 377–379
    Security, 377
    summaries, 380–381
    Summary, 375–376
    Traffic & Utilization, 377
    user credentials, 379–380
    viewing, 375–385
    Web Usage, 376
Request for Comments (RFC), 6
request headers, 218
requests
    caching, 28–29, 202
    CARP, 290
    Firewall service, 92, 94, 133
    HTTP objects, 10
    packet filters, 133
    policies, 131–133
    protocol rules, 131–132, 154–155
    Proxy Server 2.0, 82
    proxy servers, 32
    publishing servers, 26
    routing rules, 206–207
    schedule content download, 31
    SecureNAT service, 110
    server publishing, 235
    site and content rules, 131–132
    Web caching server, 28–29
    Web Proxy service, 34–35, 58, 97

requirements
  arrays, 280
  caching, 214–215
Resource allocation failure event, 347
response headers, 218
restarting services, 110, 123–125
restoring
  array backups, 285–287
  enterprise policies, 271–272
result code, 367–368
retrieving
  caching, 204
  routing rules, 206–207
returning expiration policy objects, 221–222
reverse caching, 202
  installation requirements, 50
  routing rules, 204
  Web caching servers, 5, 30
RFC (Request for Comments), 6
RIP (Routing Information Protocol), 159
Rlogin (rcmotc login), 159
roaming clients, 90, 298
round robin distribution, 288
Route command-line utility, 430
routing rules
  automatic dial-out connections, 107
  caching, 203, 211–213
  conference calls, 322–326
  creating, 204–205
  default settings, 72, 208
  destination sets, 143, 204–207
  dial-on-demand connections, 105
  editing, 205–206
  Firewall Chaining configuration, 133
  orders, 208

routing rules, *continued*
  RIP, 159
  RAS, 432
  requests, 206–207
  SecureNAT service, 110
  Web Proxy, 34–35
routing tables
  route determination process, 431
  static routes, 431–432
  troubleshooting, 430–432
  Windows 2000, 66, 71
RPC filter, 20, 157, 347
RTSP (Real Time Streaming Protocol), 21, 160
rules
  clients, 134
  configuration, 391–393
  creating, 394–395
  default settings, 394
  IP addresses, 134
  mail servers, 257, 260
  order, 248, 393
  priorities, 392
  Proxy Server 2.0, 83
  server publishing, 235–237, 241–242, 253
running Mail Server Security wizard, 256

S

s-cache, 365, 368–370
s-computername field, 362
S-HTTP/HTTPS (Secure Hypertext Transfer Protocol-Secure), 147, 157
s-objects, 364, 367
s-operation field, 364

s-svcname field, 362
saving log files, 352–354
sc-authenticated field, 361
sc-bytes field, 363
sc-status field, 364, 367–368
schedules
    bandwidth, 142
    caching, 31, 32, 229–231
    CARP, 292
    client address sets, 144–145
    content groups, 147–148
    creating, 149
    destination sets, 142–143, 150
    downloads, 31, 226–228, 303
    policy elements, 140–141
    protocols, 142, 145–146
    site and content rules, 142
    reports, 377–379
    Web caching server, 13
schemas, 67
scripts, 9
SDK (software development kit), 9, 15
secondary connections
    access control, 90
    protocol definitions, 145
Secure Hypertext Transfer Protocol-Secure
    (S-HTTP/HTTPS), 147, 157
Secure network address translation. *See*
    SecureNAT service
Secure NNTP, 258
secure server publishing, 12
Secure Shell (SSH), 160
Secure Socket Layer (SSL) sites, 121
SecureNAT service (Secure network address
    translation), 6, 10, 71, 87
    applications, 88
    authentication, 88, 134

SecureNAT service (Secure network address
    translation), *continued*
    clients, 134
    complex networks, 91
    computer names, 121
    configuration, 89
    default gateway, 91
    DNS/name resolution, 92
    fault tolerance, 288–289
    hardware requirements, 49
    HTTP objects, 10
    installation, 88
    internal networks, 90
    IP addresses, 121
    LATs, 71
    name resolution, 92
    operating systems, 88
    ports, 122
    protocols, 88, 152
    requests, 110
    session information, 111
    simple networks, 91
    troubleshooting, 121
security
    arrays, 301–302
    dedicated, 136–137
    limited services, 136–137
    log files, 15
    reports, 377
    secure, 136–137
    troubleshooting, 426
    VPNs, 300
    Web publishing, 244
sending e-mail, 343–344, 348–349
server publishing, 25–26
    actions, 237–238
    Cache mode, 234

server publishing, *continued*
   client address sets, 238–239
   configuration, 234
   Firewall mode, 234
   Integrated mode, 234
   internal networks, 240–242
   perimeter networks, 239–240
   policy rules, 234
   remote networks, 235
   requests, 235
   rules, 40, 144, 235–237, 241–242
   secure, 12
Server Publishing Failure event, 347
servers. *See also* proxy servers
   adding to arrays, 280
   clustering, 3
   Exchange, 26
   IP packet filters, 181
   management, 3
   security, 136–137
   standalone, 40, 52
Service Initializaiton failure event, 347
service log files, 351–352
Service not responding event, 347
Service Pack 1 (Windows 2000), 68
Service shutdown event, 347
Service started event, 347
services
   add-in, 68
   ISA, 68
   packet filtering, 18
   Proxy Server 2.0, 79
   publishing, 5
   starting/stopping, 343
   troubleshooting, 444

session information
   filtering, 18
   identification, 366
   protocols, 19
   SecureNAT service, 111
settings. *See* configuration; default settings
Setup screen, 66–67
Simple Mail Transfer Protocol (SMTP),
   11, 160
simple networks, 91
single servers, 51
site and content rules
   access control, 39, 166–168, 174–176
   arrays, 51, 167–168
   authentication, 134
   caching, 211
   client address sets, 144
   destination sets, 143, 154, 166–167
   enterprise policies, 167–168, 267
   internal networks, 133
   path processing, 166–167
   policy element schedules, 142
   priority, 165–166
   requests, 131
   testing, 176
sizing, caching, 215–216
small offices, network topologies, 55–56, 80
smart caching, 13
SMTP (Simple Mail Transfer Protocol),
   11, 20, 160, 187, 259–260, 345, 347
snap-ins, H.323 Gatekeeper, 310
SNMP (Simple Network Management
   Protocol), 160

SOCKS, 20
    events, 347
    filters, 400
    performance counters, 420
    Proxy Server 2.0, 82
software development kit (SDK), 9, 15
source computer names, 18
spaces, DSN, 358
splitting media, 12
SQL Server, 158
SSH (Secure Shell), 160
SSL (Secure Sockets Layer), 218, 247
standalone servers
    arrays, 40, 51–52
    configuration, 286
    installation, 279–281
    policies, 133
    promoting, 281–282
    Proxy Server 2.0, 80
Standard Edition (ISA Server), 4
standards, H.323 Gamekeeper, 309
starting/stopping
    ISA Server, 345
    services, 343
static routes, 431–432
storing
    array membership, 283–284
    caching, 203–204
    objects, 33
streaming media filter, 21
strong user authentication, 12
subnet masks, 65
summaries, reports, 375–376, 380–381
symmetric multiprocessing (SMP), 8–9
SYN attacks, 427–428
system hardening, 12
System Monitor node, 401

T

taskpads, graphical, 14
TCP/IP, 24, 64
Telnet, 160, 428
Terminal Server, 48
terminals, H.323 Gamekeeper, 309
testing
    automatic discovery, 118–119
    enterprise policies, 275–276
    Internet, 108, 109
    Outlook Express, 262
    ports, 432–435
    site and content rules, 176
Text content group, 168
TFTP (Trivial File Transfer Protocol), 160
three-homed perimeter networks, 62
thresholds, events, 342–343
tiered management, 7
time field, 361
Time protocol, 160
Time To Live (TTL), 220, 228–229
time-taken field, 363
tools
    administration, 69
    Event Viewer, 425–426
    ISA Server reports, 424–425
    Netstat, 426–428
    Network Monitor, 429–430
    Performance Monitor, 426
    Telnet, 428
traffic, direction, 146
Traffic & Utilization reports, 377
transparency, firewalls, 12
Trivial File Transfer Protocol (TFTP), 160
troubleshooting
    access control, 438–441
    authentication, 441

troubleshooting, *continued*
   automatic dial-out, 122
   automatic discovery, 116–117
   caching, 442
   clients, 120–122
   connections, 122–123, 426
   error messages, 440, 442
   Event Viewer, 425–426
   external networks, 440
   Firewall service, 121
   intrusions, 427
   ISA Server, 72, 424–425
   log files, 442
   mail, 443
   Netstat, 426–428
   Network Monitor, 429–430
   Performance Monitor, 426
   ports, 122, 426–427
   protocol definitions, 441
   publishing, 442–443
   routing tables, 430–432
   Secure Socket Layer (SSL) sites, 121
   SecureNAT, 121–122
   security, 426
   services, 444
   SYN attacks, 427–428
   Telnet, 428
   user accounts, 436–437
   VPN Networks, 439–440
   Web Proxy service, 442
TTL (Time To Live), 220, 228–229
tuning performance settings, 397–398
tunnels, VPNs, 23, 294–295

U

UDP Bomb attacks, 24, 192, 195
Unified Management, 38
Unregistered event, 347
updating cache content, 31, 226–227
Upstream chaining credentials event, 347
URLs
   caching, 217, 406
   downloading, 31, 227
   refresh rates, 403–405
user accounts, 12
   authentication, 134–136, 436–437
   client address sets, 145
   management, 15
   protocol rules, 160–162
   reports, 379–380

V

vendors, support integration, 15
verification
   Firewall service, 115
   FTP server connections, 242–243
   NetMeeting 3.0, 320
Video content group, 168
videoconferencing. *See* conference calls;
   H.323 Gatekeeper
viewing
   events, 340
   reports, 384–385
      Application Usage, 376
      Security, 377
      Summary, 375–376

viewing, reports, *continued*
    Traffic & Utilization, 377
    Web Usage, 376
  SecureNAT service, 111
  integration, 12
VPNs (virtual private networks), 7
  connections, 295–296
  encryption, 23
  enterprise policies, 56, 302–303
  integration, 7, 12, 22–23, 294–295
  L2TP, 294
  large networks, 300
  protocols, 298–299
  remote connections, 296–297
  roaming clients, 298
  security, 300
  troubleshooting, 439–440
  tunneling, 23, 294–295
VRML content group, 168

W

W3C format. *See* Web Proxy service
Web caching servers
  firewall integration, 5
  forward, 5, 28–29
  hierarchy, 13
  ISA Server Standard Edition, 4
  objects, 28–29
  performance, 13
  reverse, 5, 30
  smart caching, 13
Web Proxy service, 10, 87, 97
  access control, 99
  applications, 88

Web Proxy service, *continued*
  authentication, 88, 135–136
  automatic discovery, 112–113, 116
  c-agent, 366
  caching, 97
  configuration, 98
  content, 190–191
  fields, 360–367
  installation, 88
  Internet Explorer 5.0, 99, 101
  ISA Management, 97
  log files, 350, 352–353, 356, 372
  operating systems, 88
  performance counters, 410–419
  protocols, 88, 99–100, 156
  routing events, 34–35, 347–348
  requests, 97
  restarting, 110, 123–125
  s-cache, 368–370
  s-objects, 367
  sc-status, 367–368
  troubleshooting, 442
  WPAD, 8, 113
Web publishing. *See also* publishing; server publishing
  actions, 246–247
  bridging, 247
  client address sets, 144
  destination sets, 143
  filters, 8
  installation, 58–59
  local networks, 59, 249–250
  modes, 53
  order of rules, 248
  policies, 234

Web publishing, *continued*
　requests, 58, 82, 189, 253
　rules, 244–245, 253
　security, 244
　SSL, 247
Web Usage reports, 376
Whois protocol, 160
wildcards, 142
Windows 2000
　alerts, 8
　ISA Server, 68
　network adapters, 65
　Network Address Translation (NAT), 6
　protocol rules, 162–163
　Proxy Server 2.0, 78–79
　routing tables, 66, 71
Windows Network Load Balancing (NLB)
　　Services, 9
Windows NT 4.0, 54, 79–80
Windows Out of Band attack, 24, 192, 195
Winsock applications, 94–97
Winsock Proxy Autodetect (WSPAD),
　　113–114
wizards
　Add Destination, 330
　configuration, 14
　Getting Started, 137–138
　ISA Server Security Configuration,
　　136–137

wizards, *continued*
　ISA Virtual Private Network Configuration,
　　296, 298
　Local ISA Server VPN Configuration,
　　296–297, 439
　Mail Server Security, 256
　Network Connection, 296
　New Alert, 340
　New Protocol Rule, 100
　New Routing Rule, 323
　New Server Publishing Rule, 234
　New Site and Content Rule, 167
　New Web Publishing Rule, 244
　policies, 14
　Remote ISA Server VPN Configuration,
　　296–297
WMT live stream splitting failure event, 348
WPAD (Web Proxy Autodiscovery
　　Protocol), 8, 113–114, 118
writing URLs to cache, 406
WSPAD (Winsock Proxy Autodetect),
　　113–114
Wspcfg.ini file, 94–95

X-Z

zone transfers, 25

MICROSOFT LICENSE AGREEMENT
Book Companion CD

IMPORTANT—READ CAREFULLY: This Microsoft End-User License Agreement ("EULA") is a legal agreement between you (either an individual or an entity) and Microsoft Corporation for the Microsoft product identified above, which includes computer software and may include associated media, printed materials, and "on-line" or electronic documentation ("SOFTWARE PRODUCT"). Any component included within the SOFTWARE PRODUCT that is accompanied by a separate End-User License Agreement shall be governed by such agreement and not the terms set forth below. By installing, copying, or otherwise using the SOFTWARE PRODUCT, you agree to be bound by the terms of this EULA. If you do not agree to the terms of this EULA, you are not authorized to install, copy, or otherwise use the SOFTWARE PRODUCT; you may, however, return the SOFTWARE PRODUCT, along with all printed materials and other items that form a part of the Microsoft product that includes the SOFTWARE PRODUCT, to the place you obtained them for a full refund.

SOFTWARE PRODUCT LICENSE

The SOFTWARE PRODUCT is protected by United States copyright laws and international copyright treaties, as well as other intellectual property laws and treaties. The SOFTWARE PRODUCT is licensed, not sold.

1. **GRANT OF LICENSE.** This EULA grants you the following rights:
    a. **Software Product.** You may install and use one copy of the SOFTWARE PRODUCT on a single computer. The primary user of the computer on which the SOFTWARE PRODUCT is installed may make a second copy for his or her exclusive use on a portable computer.
    b. **Storage/Network Use.** You may also store or install a copy of the SOFTWARE PRODUCT on a storage device, such as a network server, used only to install or run the SOFTWARE PRODUCT on your other computers over an internal network; however, you must acquire and dedicate a license for each separate computer on which the SOFTWARE PRODUCT is installed or run from the storage device. A license for the SOFTWARE PRODUCT may not be shared or used concurrently on different computers.
    c. **License Pak.** If you have acquired this EULA in a Microsoft License Pak, you may make the number of additional copies of the computer software portion of the SOFTWARE PRODUCT authorized on the printed copy of this EULA, and you may use each copy in the manner specified above. You are also entitled to make a corresponding number of secondary copies for portable computer use as specified above.
    d. **Sample Code.** Solely with respect to portions, if any, of the SOFTWARE PRODUCT that are identified within the SOFTWARE PRODUCT as sample code (the "SAMPLE CODE"):
        i. **Use and Modification.** Microsoft grants you the right to use and modify the source code version of the SAMPLE CODE, *provided* you comply with subsection (d)(iii) below. You may not distribute the SAMPLE CODE, or any modified version of the SAMPLE CODE, in source code form.
        ii. **Redistributable Files.** Provided you comply with subsection (d)(iii) below, Microsoft grants you a nonexclusive, royalty-free right to reproduce and distribute the object code version of the SAMPLE CODE and of any modified SAMPLE CODE, other than SAMPLE CODE (or any modified version thereof) designated as not redistributable in the Readme file that forms a part of the SOFTWARE PRODUCT (the "Non-Redistributable Sample Code"). All SAMPLE CODE other than the Non-Redistributable Sample Code is collectively referred to as the "REDISTRIBUTABLES."
        iii. **Redistribution Requirements.** If you redistribute the REDISTRIBUTABLES, you agree to: (i) distribute the REDISTRIBUTABLES in object code form only in conjunction with and as a part of your software application product; (ii) not use Microsoft's name, logo, or trademarks to market your software application product; (iii) include a valid copyright notice on your software application product; (iv) indemnify, hold harmless, and defend Microsoft from and against any claims or lawsuits, including attorney's fees, that arise or result from the use or distribution of your software application product; and (v) not permit further distribution of the REDISTRIBUTABLES by your end user. Contact Microsoft for the applicable royalties due and other licensing terms for all other uses and/or distribution of the REDISTRIBUTABLES.
2. **DESCRIPTION OF OTHER RIGHTS AND LIMITATIONS.**
    - **Limitations on Reverse Engineering, Decompilation, and Disassembly.** You may not reverse engineer, decompile, or disassemble the SOFTWARE PRODUCT, except and only to the extent that such activity is expressly permitted by applicable law notwithstanding this limitation.
    - **Separation of Components.** The SOFTWARE PRODUCT is licensed as a single product. Its component parts may not be separated for use on more than one computer.
    - **Rental.** You may not rent, lease, or lend the SOFTWARE PRODUCT.
    - **Support Services.** Microsoft may, but is not obligated to, provide you with support services related to the SOFTWARE PRODUCT ("Support Services"). Use of Support Services is governed by the Microsoft policies and programs described in the user manual, in "on-line" documentation, and/or in other Microsoft-provided materials. Any supplemental software code provided to you as part of the Support Services shall be considered part of the SOFTWARE PRODUCT and subject to the terms and conditions of this EULA. With respect to technical information you provide to Microsoft as part of the Support Services, Microsoft may use such information for its business purposes, including for product support and development. Microsoft will not utilize such technical information in a form that personally identifies you.
    - **Software Transfer.** You may permanently transfer all of your rights under this EULA, provided you retain no copies, you transfer all of the SOFTWARE PRODUCT (including all component parts, the media and printed materials, any upgrades, this EULA, and, if applicable, the Certificate of Authenticity), **and** the recipient agrees to the terms of this EULA.

- **Termination.** Without prejudice to any other rights, Microsoft may terminate this EULA if you fail to comply with the terms and conditions of this EULA. In such event, you must destroy all copies of the SOFTWARE PRODUCT and all of its component parts.

3. **COPYRIGHT.** All title and copyrights in and to the SOFTWARE PRODUCT (including but not limited to any images, photographs, animations, video, audio, music, text, SAMPLE CODE, REDISTRIBUTABLES, and "applets" incorporated into the SOFTWARE PRODUCT) and any copies of the SOFTWARE PRODUCT are owned by Microsoft or its suppliers. The SOFTWARE PRODUCT is protected by copyright laws and international treaty provisions. Therefore, you must treat the SOFTWARE PRODUCT like any other copyrighted material **except** that you may install the SOFTWARE PRODUCT on a single computer provided you keep the original solely for backup or archival purposes. You may not copy the printed materials accompanying the SOFTWARE PRODUCT.

4. **U.S. GOVERNMENT RESTRICTED RIGHTS.** The SOFTWARE PRODUCT and documentation are provided with RESTRICTED RIGHTS. Use, duplication, or disclosure by the Government is subject to restrictions as set forth in subparagraph (c)(1)(ii) of the Rights in Technical Data and Computer Software clause at DFARS 252.227-7013 or subparagraphs (c)(1) and (2) of the Commercial Computer Software—Restricted Rights at 48 CFR 52.227-19, as applicable. Manufacturer is Microsoft Corporation/One Microsoft Way/Redmond, WA 98052-6399.

5. **EXPORT RESTRICTIONS.** You agree that you will not export or re-export the SOFTWARE PRODUCT, any part thereof, or any process or service that is the direct product of the SOFTWARE PRODUCT (the foregoing collectively referred to as the "Restricted Components"), to any country, person, entity, or end user subject to U.S. export restrictions. You specifically agree not to export or re-export any of the Restricted Components (i) to any country to which the U.S. has embargoed or restricted the export of goods or services, which currently include, but are not necessarily limited to, Cuba, Iran, Iraq, Libya, North Korea, Sudan, and Syria, or to any national of any such country, wherever located, who intends to transmit or transport the Restricted Components back to such country; (ii) to any end user who you know or have reason to know will utilize the Restricted Components in the design, development, or production of nuclear, chemical, or biological weapons; or (iii) to any end user who has been prohibited from participating in U.S. export transactions by any federal agency of the U.S. government. You warrant and represent that neither the BXA nor any other U.S. federal agency has suspended, revoked, or denied your export privileges.

6. **NOTE ON JAVA SUPPORT.** THE SOFTWARE PRODUCT MAY CONTAIN SUPPORT FOR PROGRAMS WRITTEN IN JAVA. JAVA TECHNOLOGY IS NOT FAULT TOLERANT AND IS NOT DESIGNED, MANUFACTURED, OR INTENDED FOR USE OR RESALE AS ON-LINE CONTROL EQUIPMENT IN HAZARDOUS ENVIRONMENTS REQUIRING FAIL-SAFE PERFORMANCE, SUCH AS IN THE OPERATION OF NUCLEAR FACILITIES, AIRCRAFT NAVIGATION OR COMMUNICATION SYSTEMS, AIR TRAFFIC CONTROL, DIRECT LIFE SUPPORT MACHINES, OR WEAPONS SYSTEMS, IN WHICH THE FAILURE OF JAVA TECHNOLOGY COULD LEAD DIRECTLY TO DEATH, PERSONAL INJURY, OR SEVERE PHYSICAL OR ENVIRONMENTAL DAMAGE. SUN MICROSYSTEMS, INC. HAS CONTRACTUALLY OBLIGATED MICROSOFT TO MAKE THIS DISCLAIMER.

DISCLAIMER OF WARRANTY

NO WARRANTIES OR CONDITIONS. MICROSOFT EXPRESSLY DISCLAIMS ANY WARRANTY OR CONDITION FOR THE SOFTWARE PRODUCT. THE SOFTWARE PRODUCT AND ANY RELATED DOCUMENTATION ARE PROVIDED "AS IS" WITHOUT WARRANTY OR CONDITION OF ANY KIND, EITHER EXPRESS OR IMPLIED, INCLUDING, WITHOUT LIMITATION, THE IMPLIED WARRANTIES OF MERCHANTABILITY, FITNESS FOR A PARTICULAR PURPOSE, OR NONINFRINGEMENT. THE ENTIRE RISK ARISING OUT OF USE OR PERFORMANCE OF THE SOFTWARE PRODUCT REMAINS WITH YOU.

LIMITATION OF LIABILITY. TO THE MAXIMUM EXTENT PERMITTED BY APPLICABLE LAW, IN NO EVENT SHALL MICROSOFT OR ITS SUPPLIERS BE LIABLE FOR ANY SPECIAL, INCIDENTAL, INDIRECT, OR CONSEQUENTIAL DAMAGES WHATSOEVER (INCLUDING, WITHOUT LIMITATION, DAMAGES FOR LOSS OF BUSINESS PROFITS, BUSINESS INTERRUPTION, LOSS OF BUSINESS INFORMATION, OR ANY OTHER PECUNIARY LOSS) ARISING OUT OF THE USE OF OR INABILITY TO USE THE SOFTWARE PRODUCT OR THE PROVISION OF OR FAILURE TO PROVIDE SUPPORT SERVICES, EVEN IF MICROSOFT HAS BEEN ADVISED OF THE POSSIBILITY OF SUCH DAMAGES. IN ANY CASE, MICROSOFT'S ENTIRE LIABILITY UNDER ANY PROVISION OF THIS EULA SHALL BE LIMITED TO THE GREATER OF THE AMOUNT ACTUALLY PAID BY YOU FOR THE SOFTWARE PRODUCT OR US$5.00; PROVIDED, HOWEVER, IF YOU HAVE ENTERED INTO A MICROSOFT SUPPORT SERVICES AGREEMENT, MICROSOFT'S ENTIRE LIABILITY REGARDING SUPPORT SERVICES SHALL BE GOVERNED BY THE TERMS OF THAT AGREEMENT. BECAUSE SOME STATES AND JURISDICTIONS DO NOT ALLOW THE EXCLUSION OR LIMITATION OF LIABILITY, THE ABOVE LIMITATION MAY NOT APPLY TO YOU.

MISCELLANEOUS

This EULA is governed by the laws of the State of Washington USA, except and only to the extent that applicable law mandates governing law of a different jurisdiction.

Should you have any questions concerning this EULA, or if you desire to contact Microsoft for any reason, please contact the Microsoft subsidiary serving your country, or write: Microsoft Sales Information Center/One Microsoft Way/Redmond, WA 98052-6399.

Get a **Free**
e-mail newsletter, updates,
special offers, links to related books,
and more when you
register on line!

Register your Microsoft Press® title on our Web site and you'll get a FREE subscription to our e-mail newsletter, *Microsoft Press Book Connections.* You'll find out about newly released and upcoming books and learning tools, online events, software downloads, special offers and coupons for Microsoft Press customers, and information about major Microsoft® product releases. You can also read useful additional information about all the titles we publish, such as detailed book descriptions, tables of contents and indexes, sample chapters, links to related books and book series, author biographies, and reviews by other customers.

Registration is easy. Just visit this Web page and fill in your information:

http://mspress.microsoft.com/register

Microsoft®

Proof of Purchase

Use this page as proof of purchase if participating in a promotion or rebate offer on this title. Proof of purchase must be used in conjunction with other proof(s) of payment such as your dated sales receipt—see offer details.

MCSE Training Kit: Microsoft® Internet Security and Acceleration Server 2000
0-7356-1347-8

CUSTOMER NAME

Microsoft Press, PO Box 97017, Redmond, WA 98073-9830

System Requirements

To get the most out of the *MCSE Training Kit: Internet Security and Acceleration Server 2000*, and the Supplemental Course Materials CD-ROM, which includes exercise files, the electronic version of this training kit, and the Evaluation Edition of the Microsoft Windows 2000 ISA Server, Enterprise Edition, you will need a computer equipped with the minimum configuration listed below. To complete some of the procedures, you must have two networked computers. Both computers must be capable of running Windows 2000 Server and Service Pack 1 must be installed on each computer.

- 300-MHz or higher Pentium II-compatible CPU

- Microsoft Windows 2000 Server or Advanced Server with Service Pack 1 or later, or Windows 2000 Datacenter Server operating system

- 256 MB of RAM

- Hard drive of at least 2 GB formatted as a single NTFS partition

- 200 MB hard-disk space after the operating system is installed

- Network adapter for communicating with the internal network

- Modem for communicating with the Internet

- 24x CD-ROM drive

- Sound card and audio output

- Microsoft mouse or compatible pointing device

- Display system capable of 800 x 600 resolution or better

For the best viewing experience of the *MCSE Training Kit: Internet Security and Acceleration Server 2000* eBook, the following system configuration is recommended:

- Microsoft Windows 95, Windows 98, Microsoft Windows NT, Windows 2000 (Professional or Server), or Windows Me

- Pentium II (or similar) with 266-MHz or higher processor

- 64 MB RAM

- 8x CD-ROM drive or faster

- Display system capable of 800 x 600 resolution or better